Praise for *An African Introduction to the New Testament*

An African Introduction to the New Testament is a monumental achievement in biblical scholarship, showing that God has new light to shine on his word when it is viewed through the eyes of African believers and explained in their own voices. The issues faced by the churches in Africa are different to those in the Global North, and this is reflected in the application sections of each chapter. The editors have assembled an amazing cast of contributors to showcase the views, vision, and values of African biblical interpretation today. An ideal way to experience the wisdom and excellence of contemporary African scholarship!

—**Rev. Dr. Michael F. Bird**, deputy principal at Ridley College, Melbourne, Australia

It is exciting to see African biblical scholarship come into its own! *An African Introduction to the New Testament* represents a major milestone in both biblical scholarship and the African enterprise of New Testament interpretation, as a crop of African scholars have contributed a seminal work that engages each New Testament writing through an African lens. This will serve as an invaluable resource not only for biblical scholars but also for anyone (student, pastor, teacher, layperson) interested in grasping some of the distinctive African contributions to biblical studies. The diversity of contributors' ecclesial affiliations also reflects the nonsectarian nature of African biblical scholarship, projecting a less fractured African religious landscape.

—**Andrew M. Mbuvi**, NEH Chair in Humanities and associate professor in religion, Albright College, Reading, Pennsylvania, USA

An African Introduction to the New Testament is a wonderful gift from the church in Africa to the church in Africa and the rest of the world, especially the West/Global North. At once traditional and innovative, academic and pastoral, contextual and global, it is a treasure chest of diverse voices that bears witness to the holistic gospel of Jesus Christ. This is the most interesting—and perhaps the best—type of New Testament introduction; may it do well and do good.

—**Michael J. Gorman**, Raymond E. Brown Professor of Biblical and Theological Studies, St. Mary's Seminary & University, Baltimore, Maryland, USA

Most introductions to the Bible or to one testament wax eloquent on debates about author, date, place of writing, audience, and purpose. Sometimes they add brief comments on the theology of a given book or section, though not always. Readers often long for the opposite proportions—heavy on theological emphases. If they could have some contemporary application, so much the better. This new introduction does precisely that, with incisive application to key African cultural issues. But what does that have to do with other parts of the world? Read the applications and you'll quickly see how universal many of them are! A wonderful gift to the church worldwide.

—**Craig L. Blomberg**, distinguished professor emeritus of New Testament, Denver Seminary, Littleton, Colorado, USA

Bible teachers, students, and pastors will appreciate the skillful juxtaposition of classic historical and theological material with relevant issues facing African Christians today. This is an insightful and edifying must-have and must-read for African Christians aiming to grow in understanding God's word—at the seminary, Bible college, local church, or small-group setting.

—**Daniel K. Darko**, global scholar in residence and professor of biblical studies and leadership, Taylor University, Upland, Indiana, USA

This volume is both distinctive and vital. It brings together New Testament scholarship and illumination of African contexts, integrating the two with insight and clarity. This is a must-read for biblical scholars who want to listen to the global conversation on the New Testament.

—**Jeannine K. Brown**, Bethel Seminary, Saint Paul, Minnesota, USA

An African Introduction to the New Testament builds on the classic Eurocentric template and distinguishes itself by making the New Testament books relatable and relevant for Africans across ecclesial, cultural, and geographical lines. Readers will find the essays on African cultural issues, religious phenomena, and hermeneutical approaches instructive in the way Africans encounter God's word in the New Testament.

An African Introduction to the New Testament is an organic voice of experienced and emerging African biblical scholarship. It's truly African! This voluminous work presents how the New Testament stories and texts resonate with the African context. It responds to the long-standing cry for an African voice in the field. The various chapters combine to create one of the best textbooks for African New Testament courses available, focusing on issues facing African Christianity today. Beyond Africans, the volume can serve the wider audience interested in biblical studies. More importantly, it can serve as a model work in biblical scholarship, where academic rigor is only a means, not an end in itself. In this volume, African spirituality is in conversation with the message of the New Testament; it's a goodbye to secularism!

—**Rev. Bruk A. Asale**, former president of Mekane Yesus Seminary, Addis Ababa, Ethiopia

An African Introduction to the New Testament breaks new ground and creates a much needed and long-awaited space for African voices in the study of the New Testament. By placing New Testament texts and figures in conversation with disparate African socio-religious traditions, contributors offer fresh and powerful insights that have deep implications for African realities. I hope this compendium will stimulate wider conversations about non-Western scholars in New Testament studies.

—**Johnson Thomaskutty**, professor of New Testament, The United Theological College, Bengaluru, India; editor of *An Asian Introduction to the New Testament* (Fortress Press, 2022).

An African Introduction to the New Testament offers a groundbreaking and contextually rich perspective on the study of the New Testament. Although tailored specifically for African theological students, pastors, and church leaders, it serves as a complement to other introductory studies written from different geographical locations around the world. In contrast to Eurocentric textbooks that often overlook the pressing questions of African realities, this volume engages the New Testament through the lens of Africa's diverse cultural, social, and political landscapes.

With contributions from scholars across different Christian faith traditions and a wide geographical spread across the continent, the book affirms that faithful biblical interpretation must resonate with the lived experiences of African peoples.

Emphasizing a dialogical relationship between Scripture and context, the book equips readers to encounter the Triune God meaningfully within their everyday lives. Ultimately, this work is more than just another textbook—it is a prophetic call for contextual theological reflection that empowers African Christians to embody the gospel in both word and deed, leading to personal, communal, and societal transformation.

—**J. Ayodeji Adewuya**, professor of New Testament, Pentecostal Theological Seminary, Austin, Texas, USA

An African Introduction to the New Testament is an important and timely work from a uniquely African perspective. Written by eminent African New Testament scholars, it examines the authorship, historical context, literary features, and theological themes of the various New Testament writings in view of the pressing challenges facing African communities today. Corruption, tribalism, traditional beliefs, and spiritual warfare are some of the challenges discussed. For anyone seeking to understand how the New Testament can be authentically embraced within diverse African contexts, this resource provides invaluable insights that honor both textual integrity and cultural relevance.

—**Marius J. Nel**, professor in New Testament, Stellenbosch University, South Africa

Reflecting the pluralist, vibrant, faithfully committed, and academically focused spectrum of New Testament scholarship among scholars from Africa, this volume brings fresh, learned, and Africa-focused introductory perspectives to students of the New Testament and makes these insights accessible to a wide audience. This book will provide theology students in

Africa with the skills they need to understand and tackle both biblical and local issues they will face in ministry or academic settings, and can serve also as a conversation starter to make the New Testament texts more readily available to Christians on the continent and beyond.

—**Jeremy Punt**, professor of New Testament, Stellenbosch University, South Africa; author of *Postcolonial Biblical Interpretation: Reframing Paul* (Brill, 2015).

It repeatedly strikes me that the Ethiopian culture is much closer to that of the New Testament than American and European cultures are. With *An African Introduction to the New Testament*, we have the perfect opportunity to read the New Testament with the enhanced vision of African scholars. To offer only one of many possible examples, consider how Western scholars tend to treat biblical accounts of the demonic world mostly with embarrassment. In contrast, the contributors to this volume intuitively understand these accounts and are able to show how they form an integrated part of the New Testament message of Christ's victory over evil. While not everyone will agree with everything they read in this work, every serious reader will be enriched by new insights into the transformative message of the New Testament.

—**Sigurd Grindheim**, professor of New Testament, Mekane Yesus Seminary, Addis Ababa, Ethiopia; missionary, Norwegian Mission Society

Until recently, African theological teachers and students had little choice—virtually all theological textbooks were written in the Western world, and they asked and answered Western questions. Recently, African scholars have contributed essays and monographs that focus attention on the African reader of the biblical text. This volume continues that trend but fills an important gap. Now African students and scholars have a resource that addresses traditional "questions of introduction" but also includes profound reflection on how each book of the New Testament relates to contemporary Africa. The church and the academy will both benefit from this magnificent achievement.

—**Grant LeMarquand,** emeritus professor of biblical studies, Trinity Anglican Seminary, Ambridge, Pennsylvania, USA; retired Anglican bishop for the Horn of Africa

An African Introduction to the New Testament

An African Introduction to the New Testament

Abeneazer G. Urga,
Elizabeth W. Mburu,
Ferdinand I. Okorie
editors

FORTRESS PRESS
Minneapolis

AN AFRICAN INTRODUCTION TO THE NEW TESTAMENT

31 30 29 28 27 26 25 1 2 3 4 5 6 7 8 9

Library of Congress Control Number: 2025942416 (print)

Cover image: Ethiopian Religious Painting/Wikimedia Commons
Cover design: Laurie Ingram Art + Design.com

Print ISBN: 979-8-8898-3651-3
eBook ISBN: 979-8-8898-3652-0

CONTENTS

TABLES

CONTRIBUTORS

Sofanit T. Abebe holds a PhD from the University of Edinburgh and is a tutor in theology and lead tutor for potential theological educators at Trinity College, Bristol, UK, having previously taught at the Ethiopian Graduate School of Theology. She is the author of *Apocalyptic Spatiality in 1 Peter and Selected 1 Enoch Literature: A Comparative Analysis* (Mohr Siebeck, 2024), "Comparing Apples and Oranges? Eschatological Perspectives from 1 Enoch and 1 Peter," in *Beyond Canon: Early Christianity and the Ethiopic Textual Tradition* (ed. M. T. Gebreananaye, L. Williams, and Francis Watson; T&T Clark, 2020), and "Suffering, Liminality and *ʿĂnāwîm* Identity in 1 Enoch 108: Towards a Theology of Persecution," in *The Blessing of Enoch: 1 Enoch and Contemporary Theology* (ed. Philip F. Esler; Wipf & Stock, 2017), and coedited *Reading Hebrews and 1 Peter from Majority World Perspectives* (T&T Clark, 2024). She is currently engaged in writing a commentary on 1 Peter for the Hippo Exegetical Bible Commentary Series.

Daniel Nii Aboagye Aryeh holds a PhD in New Testament from Trinity Theological Seminary, Ghana. He is a senior lecturer and acting rector of Perez University College and adjunct faculty at Trinity Theological Seminary, Legon, Ghana. He is a member of the Society of Biblical Literature (SBL), Ghana Association of Biblical Exegetes (GABES), Missiological Society of Ghana (MSG), and West Africa Association of Theological Institutions (WAATI). He has published numerous articles, book chapters, and books, including *Biblical, Traditional, and Theological Framework for Understanding Christian Prophetism in Ghana Today* (Resource Publications, 2019).

Bekele Deboch Anshiso earned his PhD in New Testament from Stellenbosch University, South Africa. He is the academic dean and lecturer in New Testament studies at the Ethiopian Graduate School of Theology, Addis Ababa, Ethiopia. He is the author of *Jesus's Identification with the Marginalized and the Liminal: The Messianic Identity in Mark* (Langham Academic, 2018).

Devison Telen Banda received his PhD in New Testament interpretation from The University of the Free State, South Africa. He teaches at Justo Mwale University in Zambia. He is a former principal and deputy vice chancellor of Justo Mwale University. Currently he is an oral Bible translation consultant at The Word for the World, Zambia. He is the author of several articles and a book entitled *New Testament Interpretation and African Culture: Selections from 1 Corinthians as a Test Case* (Lambert Academic, 2019).

Elkanah K. Cheboi holds a PhD in New Testament from Africa International University, Nairobi, Kenya. Currently, he is a lecturer in theology and biblical studies at Kabarak University, Kenya. He is also the founder and director of ShahidiHub Africa, a Christian organization that deals with news perspectives, Christian research, and publications. He is the author of *Crucified and Cursed Christ: An Analysis of Galatians 3:1–14 in the Context of Curses in Biblical Times and Its Relevance to Marakwet Culture* (Langham Academic, 2023).

Cornelia van Deventer obtained her PhD in New Testament from Stellenbosch University. She is the vice principal for the South African Theological Seminary. Until recently, she was the editor of *Conspectus* journal. She is the author of numerous articles. Her dissertation explored "Embracing Vulnerability: A Drama Analysis of the Johannine Prologue and Crucifixion Scenes."

Mphumezi Hombana received his PhD in New Testament from Stellenbosch University, South Africa. Until recently, he was a lecturer in New Testament studies at the Department of New Testament and Related Literature, Faculty of Theology and Religion, University of Pretoria, South Africa. He has just begun his lectureship at the University of South Africa. He is the author of several articles and his dissertation was on "The Crucifixion and Death of Jesus in Mark 15:21–41, from the Perspective of Its Redaction History in the New Testament Gospels."

Julius Kithinji is a senior lecturer and dean of the School of Theology at St. Paul's University in Limuru, Kenya. He earned his doctorate from Kenyatta University, Kenya, and is an expert in biblical studies, specializing in the New Testament. He is a council member at the Presbyterian University of East Africa where he chairs the Academics and Statutes committee. His interest is in interpreting the Bible from a postcolonial perspective. He is the author of *Absolute Authority in Mark's Gospel: A Postcolonial Power Analysis of Power Abuse in Kenya* (Borderless Press, 2021) and numerous articles.

Jean-Claude Loba Mkole holds a PhD in theology (Leuven, Belgium) and works as a global translation advisor with the United Bible Societies. He has held the positions of extraordinary professor at the University of Pretoria and visiting professor at Hekima University College, Nairobi, Université de l'Alliance Chrétienne, Abidjan, and St Paul's University Limuru, Kenya, and has been a research associate at the University of the Free State, Bloemfontein, South Africa. He is also the chairman of the Society of New Testament Studies Africa Liaison Committee. He has published numerous articles and books, including, among others, *Le fils de l'homme neotestamentaire: Etude interculturelle* (Éditions Universitaires Européennes, 2014).

Dogara Ishaya Manomi holds a PhD in New Testament from Johannes Gutenberg Universität, Mainz, Germany. He holds the Alexander von Humboldt Postdoctoral Research

Fellowship at Goethe University, Frankfurt, Germany. He has served as head of the Biblical Studies Department, Theological College of Northern Nigeria, and has authored several articles and coedited numerous books. His publications include *Virtue Ethics in the Letter to Titus: An Interdisciplinary Study* (Mohr Siebeck, 2021).

Elizabeth W. Mburu is the regional coordinator of Langham Literature in Anglophone Africa and an associate professor of New Testament and Greek at Africa International University, Kenya. She pursued her doctoral studies at Southeastern Baptist Theological Seminary, Wake Forest, North Carolina, USA. She is actively involved in research and publishing in the areas of New Testament, intercultural hermeneutics, contextual theology, and worldview studies. She is the author of *Qumran and the Origins of Johannine Language and Symbolism* (T&T Clark, 2010) and *African Hermeneutics* (Langham HippoBooks, 2019), and coedited *Reading Hebrews and 1 Peter from Majority World Perspectives* (Bloomsbury T&T Clark, 2024) and *Prophet, Priest, and King: Christology in Global Perspective* (Zondervan Academic, 2025).

Endale Sebsebe Mekonnen holds a PhD in New Testament from Stellenbosch University, South Africa, and a PhD in development studies from the University of the Western Cape, South Africa. He is the president of Shiloh International Theological Seminary in Hawassa, Ethiopia. His dissertation was on "The Torah and Community Formation: A Comparative Study of Romans 13:8–14 and Matthew 22:34–40."

Gift Mtukwa is a lecturer and chair of the department in the School of Religion and Christian Ministry at Africa Nazarene University, Nairobi, Kenya. He was born and raised in Harare, Zimbabwe, and currently lives in Nairobi, Kenya. He is an ordained minister with the Church of the Nazarene and he teaches New Testament and Greek. He earned a PhD from the University of Manchester in England, UK. Mtukwa is the author of *Work and Community in the Thessalonian Correspondence* (Langham Monographs, 2021).

François Batuafe Ngole received his PhD in biblical theology from the Pontifical Gregorian University in Rome. He teaches biblical exegesis at the Catholic University of Congo, Kinshasa, where he holds the position of academic secretary of the Faculty of Theology. He is a member of several international academic associations. His published works include *L'accomplissement de toute Justice* (Peter Lang, 2017) and *Évangiles synoptiques: Introduction à la lecture scientifique* (L'Harmattan, 2023).

Caroline Nkoberanyi (PhD, The Catholic University of Eastern Africa) is a Ugandan lecturing at the Apostles of Jesus Theologicum and Chemchemi ya Uzima Institute of Pastoral Ministry, Nairobi. She is also the secretary of the Catholic Biblical Conferences of Africa and Madagascar (BICAM) in Nairobi. She is the author of *A Narrative Approach of Acts 18: 24–28 in the New Evangelization in Catholic-Founded Universities in East Africa* (CUEA Press, 2022).

Alice Matilda Nsiah is senior lecturer and head of the Department of Religion and Human Values at the Faculty of Arts, College of Humanities and Legal Studies, University of Cape Coast, Ghana, from which she received her PhD. Her area of specialization is Greek and New Testament studies. Her research interests include the role of women in Christianity and controversial biblical passages on women. Her recent publications include "Religious Spaces as Tourist Sites in Ghana," in *The Oxford Handbook of Religious Space* (ed. Jeanne Halgren Kilde; Oxford University Press, 2022) and, as coauthor with Gifty A. K. Dei Dawson, "Rahab Reimagined: A Ghanaian Perspective on Hebrews 11.31 and Its Resonance with Female Sex Workers," in *Reading Hebrews and 1 Peter from Majority World Perspectives* (T&T Clark, 2024).

Ferdinand I. Okorie earned a PhD in New Testament and Early Christianity from Loyola University, Chicago. He is the vice president and academic dean at Catholic Theological Union in Chicago, and also an associate professor of New Testament Studies. He is the editor-in-chief of *U.S. Catholic* magazine and the author of *Favor and Gratitude: Reading Galatians in Its Greco-Roman Context* (Lexington Books and Fortress Academic, 2020), and coedited *Bible, Interpretation and Context: Reading Meaning from an African Perspective* (Lexington Books and Fortress Academic, 2023).

Axolile N. M. Qina earned his PhD in New Testament and Christian Origins from the School of Divinity, New College, University of Edinburgh. His doctoral research is entitled "The Dilemma of Jesus' Sacrifice: Towards a Xhosa Christian Hermeneutic for Animal Sacrifice." His recent publications include "Jesus' Sacrifice in Hebrews: A Xhosa Christian Reading of Hebrews 10:1–18," in *Reading Hebrews and 1 Peter from Majority World Perspectives* (T&T Clark, 2024).

Bitrus A. Sarma is provost of ECWA Theological Seminary, Kagoro, Nigeria, where he is also professor of biblical studies (NT). He has a PhD in New Testament from ECWA Theological Seminary, Jos, Nigeria, and has been involved in theological education for almost three decades. He has conducted postgraduate research at Stellenbosch University, South Africa, and as a research scholar at Fuller Theological Seminary's Global Research Institute, California, USA. He is the author of many books, including *Hermeneutics of Mission in Matthew: Israel and the Nations in the Interpretative Framework of Matthew's Gospel* (Langham Academic, 2015) and *Drums of Redemption: A New Testament Theology for Africa* (Langham Hippo Books, 2023).

Tibebu Teklu Senbetu holds a PhD in New Testament from Concordia Seminary (CSL), St. Louis, Missouri. He is the director of the Gudina Tumsa Research Center and a lecturer in the Department of Bible Studies and Historical Theology at Mekane Yesus Seminary in Addis Ababa, Ethiopia. His dissertation on "Worthy Admission to the Eucharist: The Ethiopian Orthodox *Tewahedo* Church and 1 Cor. 11:27–29" is being published by Peter Lang.

Vuyani S. Sindo received his PhD in New Testament from Stellenbosch University in South Africa. He is the vice principal of development, head of biblical studies, and senior lecturer at George Whitefield College. He is the author of *Paul as a Prototype and Entrepreneur of Christian Identity: An Investigation into Leadership and Identity in 1 Corinthians 1–4* (Langham Academic, 2024).

Abeneazer G. Urga received his PhD from Columbia International University and has served as the department head for the MA in biblical studies, lectures in biblical studies at the Evangelical Theological College in Addis Ababa, Ethiopia, and is an adjunct professor at Columbia International University and the Ethiopian Graduate School of Theology. He is a member of Equip International, SIL Ethiopia/International, and associate member of Studiorum Novi Testamenti Societas (SNTS). He is the author of *Intercession of Jesus in Hebrews* (Mohr Siebeck, 2023) and coedited *Reading Hebrews Missiologically* (William Carey Publishing 2023), *Reading 1 Peter Missiologically* (William Carey Publishing, 2024), *Reading Hebrews and 1 Peter from Majority World Perspectives* (Bloomsbury T&T Clark, 2024), and *Reading James Missiologically* (William Carey Publishing, 2025).

Geraldine Chimbuoyim Uzodimma received her Doctor of Sacred Theology in New Testament from Boston College School of Theology and Ministry. Her dissertation, "Reading Romans 5:12–21 in Light of Roman Imperial Domination: Understanding Paul's Apocalyptic Response" is being considered for publication in the Catholic Biblical Quarterly Monograph Series.

Gesila Nneka Uzukwu (PhD, Katholieke Universiteit Leuven, Belgium) is a member of the Daughters of Mary Mother of Mercy. She is also a senior lecturer and head of the Department of Philosophy and Religious Studies at Nasarawa State University, Keffi, Nigeria. She is the author of *The Unity of Male and Female in Jesus Christ: An Exegetical Study of Galatians 3.28c in Light of Paul's Theology of Promise* (T&T Clark, 2018).

Michael F. Wandusim is a lecturer in the Department of Religious Studies, KNUST, Kumasi, Ghana. He completed his doctoral studies in New Testament at the Theological Faculty of the University of Göttingen, Germany in 2020. He has held adjunct positions at the University of Rostock, the University of Applied Sciences for Intercultural Theology Hermannsburg, and the Theological Faculty of the University of Göttingen. He is the author of *The Lord's Prayer in the Ghanaian Context: A Reception-Historical Study* (De Gruyter, 2021).

PREFACE

An African Introduction to the New Testament is designed for African students in theological institutions and Bible colleges. In most instances, students in Africa use introductory texts that have a Eurocentric orientation. These are ultimately unable to ask and answer questions that are relevant in the African context. This volume seeks to address this gap. Pastors, ministers, and any church leadership—perhaps those who lead Bible study groups—will also benefit from this book as they seek to find meaning in the biblical texts from their African contexts. Therefore, this volume offers Christian Africans a helpful introduction to the New Testament with the right hermeneutical tools as they encounter God the Father, Jesus Christ, and the Holy Spirit, who are present to humankind in the biblical texts in a contextual milieu. So then, in this encounter in search of meaning, the revelation of God and Jesus Christ within the context of the original recipients of divine presence in human history interact with the contemporary everydayness of the African peoples.

This volume aims to address introductory issues in the books of the New Testament through a contextual framework that seeks to promote the role of context in reading Scripture. The dialogue between text and context forms an essential component of this book as it allows for interaction with the worlds behind, of, and in front of the text. It follows a biblical-theological approach that allows themes in the books of the New Testament to resonate with African contextual realities. Ultimately, the biblical text holds epistemological authority. The authority of the African epistemological framework is based on the understanding that the meaning of biblical texts does not necessarily reside in the text alone, but at the same time the importance of the text in and to a given social location is acknowledged. Readers of this volume will come to an appreciation of how the authors of this volume's chapters have engaged themes in each book of the New Testament and highlighted the African interpretative contextual experience. By so doing, the theological, christological, pneumatological, and ecclesial dimensions of the Christian faith in the African context are broadly identified as readers are invited to deepen their appreciation of these themes in their various contexts and experiences of encounter with God.

Readers of this volume, for instance, will notice the two chapters that address themes that are significant to the African interpretative contexts. The chapter by Bitrus Sarma invites Christian Africans to consider the important place their cultural contexts occupy in their interaction with the Triune God through the biblical narrative. The explanation he provides challenges the African contexts and invites Christians to engage these sociocultural, economic, and political challenges prevalent in their contexts in their interaction with the biblical material. Similarly, the chapter by Elizabeth Mburu on African hermeneutics introduces readers to effective tools of interpretation that aid Christian Africans' interaction with the biblical texts. Readers will notice that the authors of this volume engage the books of the New Testament by appealing to various approaches of biblical interpretation including that described by Mburu.

In light of this, the purpose of this volume is to equip theological students in the African context with the tools necessary to understand and address both biblical and contextual issues in ministry and/or academia. It is not meant to replace Eurocentric introductory books, but rather to complement them by offering an African lens.

This volume recognizes that the African context is not monolithic. This is because Africa is a vast continent and its topography stretches from the desert land in the north into the Sahel and Sahara regions in the west, which make way for the tropical rainforest and vegetation in the eastern, central, and southern regions. In fact, the diversity of the topography and the climatic conditions of Africa correspond to the continent's diverse cultural heritage. Africa's vast landscape reveals the diversity of its peoples and the richness of the continent's material and immaterial cultures. Therefore, this anthology includes the perspectives of authors from different countries, ecclesiastical traditions, and sociocultural contexts. It is impossible to select authors from each one of the cultures of African peoples to contribute to this anthology; however, the representative voices from the continent in this volume offer readers an invitation to delve deeper into a contextual interaction with the biblical texts from their own peculiar and unique cultural world. One's modes of expression and interactions with the world are critical features of one's relationship with God, who is present to humankind through the biblical texts. In order to attain a deeper appreciation of their encounters with God, the peoples of Africa must be intentional in their application of the modes of their cultural expressions in their encounter with the divine.

In addition to contextual interaction with the writings of the New Testament, each chapter in this anthology addresses traditional introductory matters such as authorship, recipients, date, and provenance. As an introductory textbook, therefore, this volume invites readers to engage with the overview of the authorial and contextual realities of the original Christian communities in their telling and writing of their experiences of God in the early centuries of the Greco-Roman world. The editors of this volume discerned that this was necessary because of the epistemological value of knowing the contexts of the communities that chronicled their experiences of God, the gospel of Jesus Christ, and the works of the Holy Spirit. This supports the invitation of this volume to Christian Africans to also engage with their contexts in their interaction with God the Father, Son, and Holy Spirit. Additionally, engagement with the original Greek language in which the New Testament is written is also a critical feature of this volume. This is because language is the medium with which every people and culture communicates their reality with each other and with the world outside their context. The intelligibility of their world and the meaning of their context are communicated and shared through language. It is for this reason that, just as the Greek language was the mode of expression and meaning-making for the early Christians in their encounter with God, likewise the peoples of Africa in their various cultural worlds must also prioritize the use of their native languages in their expressions and appreciation of the presence of God and Jesus Christ in their contexts. To this end, in this volume, one will notice the various ways authors draw from the languages of their various cultural expressions in Africa to invite readers to engage their own languages in their understanding and appreciation of God's presence in their world through the interpretation of the New Testament.

We hope that this volume, which attempts to read the New Testament as authoritative but also relevant, will assist African students, scholars, and clergy members to take the New Testament and their contextual realities seriously so that they can experience the transforming power of the Scriptures.

Abeneazer G. Urga, Addis Ababa, Ethiopia
Elizabeth W. Mburu, Nairobi, Kenya
Ferdinand I. Okorie, Chicago, Illinois
March 2025

ACKNOWLEDGMENTS

We are delighted that *An African Introduction to the New Testament* is finally in the flesh. From its conception to its publication, many have assisted us with prayers, technical support, and verbal encouragement. At times, we were excited about the project. At other times, we felt it was an impossible task to fulfill.

We would like to acknowledge Rev. Dr. Johnson Thomaskutty, the editor of *An Asian Introduction to the New Testament* (Fortress Press, 2022) for his time and invaluable advice on practical issues related to the project and for sharing his experience of editing his volume.

We would like to thank Mulubirhan Gezahegn, Dr. Jessica A. Udall, the Wednesday morning prayer team in Addis Ababa, the librarians at the Ethiopian Graduate School of Theology, Prof. Sigurd Grindheim, and Bishop Grant LeMarquand for their encouragement and technical support.

We also would like to express our gratitude to Bethany Dickerson and her team at Fortress Press for their warm welcome of the project and Langham Partnership for their willingness to partner with Fortress Press to make this book available for African theological institutions.

Finally, we are grateful to God who has spoken to us by his Son through the New Testament and helped us to relish the transforming power of the gospel in our contexts in Africa.

CHAPTER ONE

The New Testament and the Sociocultural and Religious Realities of the African Contexts

Bitrus A. Sarma
ECWA Theological Seminary Kagoro
Nigeria

Introduction

THE NEW TESTAMENT is a narrative of the kingdom of God manifest on earth through Jesus Christ. This kingdom began with the proclamation of good news, authenticated by miraculous signs and wonders. The beauty of the gospel's transformative power could be illustrated by Jesus's response to John the Baptist through his (John's) disciples: "Go back and report to John the Baptist what you hear and see. The blind receive sight, the lame walk, those who have leprosy are cleansed, the deaf hear, the dead are raised, and the good news is proclaimed to the poor" (Matt 11:4–5, NIV). This is a defeat of the kingdom of darkness. Likewise, the New Testament records the inclusion into the kingdom of heaven of people who were regarded as sinners (Matt 9:11, 13; 11:19; Mark 2:15–17) and the marginalized in society (1 Cor 1:26–31). Moreover, implied in Jesus's designation of his followers as the salt and light of the world is the potential power of the gospel to transform the sociocultural and religious realities of all those who embrace the gospel of the kingdom of heaven. Jesus came so that the world may have life in abundance (John 10:10) and that the will of God may be done on earth as it is in heaven (Matt 6:10). And as history testifies, wherever the gospel is preached and embraced holistically, the sociocultural and religious landscape of the people is also transformed significantly.

A random sampling of media headlines about some parts of Africa resonate with New Testament portraits of the sociocultural and religious realities of first-century Palestine. Similarities include social insecurity, the quest for miraculous powers, abject poverty, diseases, the marginalization of women, hopes for deliverers (human messiah figures) heightened by political domination, prophets and prophetic declarations, power encounters, exorcism, religious fanaticism and hypocritical worship, religious and social unrest, protests, bandits and banditry, rebel groups, and much more. It is not surprising, then, that when Jesus began his ministry, it fulfilled the prophecy of Isaiah:

> *Land of Zebulun, land of Naphtali,*
> *on the road by the sea, across the Jordan, Galilee of the Gentiles—*

the people who sat in darkness
have seen a great light,
and for those who sat in the region and shadow of death
light has dawned. (Matt 4:14–16; cf. Isa 9:1, 2)

Graphic metaphors in the text include "the people who sat in darkness" and "the region and shadow of death." Both describe the miserable condition of people afflicted by sin and its multifaceted effects on their sociocultural, political, and religious milieu. The "great light" that "dawned" on them is the good news encapsulated in Jesus's mission statement:

The Spirit of the Lord is upon me,
because he has anointed me
to bring good news to the poor.
He has sent me to proclaim release to the captives
and recovery of sight to the blind,
to let the oppressed go free,
to proclaim the year of the Lord's favor. (Luke 4:18, 19)

From the passages above, Jesus is "the true light, which enlightens everyone" (John 1:9). His holistic ministry includes bringing good news to the poor, proclaiming release to the captives and recovery of sight to the blind, letting the oppressed go free, and proclaiming the year of the Lord's favor. This transforming power of the gospel began in Galilee of the gentiles but spread "like a mustard seed, which, when sown upon the ground, is the smallest of all the seeds on earth; yet when it is sown it grows up and becomes the greatest of all shrubs, and puts forth large branches, so that the birds of the air can make nests in its shade" (Mark 4:31–32). The fulfillment of this parable is that the transforming power of the gospel has spread to alter the narrative of the entire human race.

In this chapter, our primary focus is on some of the adverse sociocultural and religious realities of the African context. What are these realities? How do they affect and influence lives in Africa? Are they surmountable or not? How does the gospel of Christ address these realities? To explore the subject, we will attempt to: provide an overview of the sociocultural and religious realities of first-century Palestine; describe the sociocultural and religious realities of the continent of Africa; evaluate, from a retrospective and prospective standpoint, the gospel's impact on these realities in Africa; and propose biblical remedies for the sociocultural and religious challenges in Africa before drawing conclusions.

An Overview of the Sociocultural and Religious Realities of First-Century Palestine

This section is an overview, describing the sociocultural and religious realities of first-century Palestine. What were the basic sociocultural and religious factors that characterized the lives of the Jews in Palestine of Second Temple Judaism? These factors are varied and include elements such as language, demography, family, religious beliefs, values, social interaction and behaviors, work habits, trades and professions, peasant farming, food, dress, social organizations, government and political structures, wealth distribution, hospitality, education, demographics, social classes, and sexuality.[1] From the myriad sociocultural and religious challenges of first-century Palestine, we shall limit ourselves to a few areas below.

Palestine Under the Yoke of Colonial Powers[2]

Sociocultural and sociopolitical factors are interwoven. They dictate such things as security of the people, income generation, wealth distribution, equality and inequality, social integration, and political instability or conflicts. The sociocultural, religious, and sociopolitical undercurrents of the Jews were largely affected by Rome. This explains the general sense of discontent among the people and the constant longing and clamor for political emancipation.

Jewish servitude had a long history. Even after her return from Babylonian captivity, Israel never fully recovered from her overlords. First, the returnees in Palestine lived under the governor of Syria in the Persian Empire (400–344 BCE). The Jews in Palestine were led by the high priests but were accountable to the governor (satrap) of Syria.[3] Second was the Alexandrian period (334–324 BCE). The favorable disposition of the regime enticed some Jews to embrace the Hellenization agenda of Alexander the Great in terms of "Greek ways, customs, and speech" to the detriment of the "exclusive spirit of Hebrew tradition and ancestry."[4] Third is the Egyptian period (324–204 BCE), which might be considered to have been favorable for the Jews except that Palestine now became a battleground between Egypt and Syria. The Syrian period (204–165 BCE) is the fourth period, when Israel "entered through the valley of the shadow of death."[5] This period is characterized by the martyrdom of Jews who chose to remain faithful to their faith and practices. In the fifth period, under the Maccabees (165–63 BCE), the Jews gained brief political and religious independence. Religious worship was restored and the Temple, which had been desecrated under the Syrian overlords, was rededicated. Sixth, the Roman period (63 BCE–135 CE) saw Palestine under Roman government. The Roman government was tolerant toward the Jews, but they had to pay taxes to Rome and "were subject to the rulers appointed over them by Rome"[6] (cf. Matt 22:15–17; Mark 12:13–14; Luke 20:20–22; 23:2).

Speaking about Palestine in Jesus's day, Bruce L. Shelley notes, "Its two million or more people, ruled by Rome, were divided by region, religion, and politics. In a day's journey a man could travel from rural villages, where farmers tilled their fields with primitive plows,

1. See also Ralph Gower, *The New Manners and Customs of Bible Times* (Moody Publishers, 2005).

2. What is said here and following does not mean that the coming of Jesus brought an end to all of these social evils. This is a mere depiction of the situation as the Gospels portray it.

3. Irving L. Jensen, *Jensen's Survey of the New Testament* (Moody Press, 1981), 47.

4. Jensen, *Jensen's Survey of the New Testament*, 48.

5. Jensen, *Jensen's Survey of the New Testament*, 48.

6. Jensen, *Jensen's Survey of the New Testament*, 49.

to bustling cities where men enjoyed the comforts of Roman civilization. In the Holy City of Jerusalem, Jewish priests offered sacrifices to the Lord of Israel, while at Sebaste, only thirty miles away, pagan priests held rites in honor of the Roman god Jupiter."[7] The Jews, comprising half of the population in Palestine, "despised their foreign overloads and deeply resented the signs of pagan culture in their ancient homeland. They simply disagreed about how to resist them."[8] This hatred is documented by Alfred Edersheim:

> In truth, the bitter hatred which the Jew bore to the Gentiles can only be explained from the estimate entertained of his character. The most vile, and even unnatural, crimes were imputed them. It was not safe to leave cattle in their charge, to allow their women to nurse infants, or their physicians to attend the sick, nor to walk in their company, without taking precautions against sudden and unprovoked attacks. They should, so far as possible, be all together avoided, except in cases of necessity or for the sake of business. They and theirs were defiled; their houses unclean, as containing idols or things dedicated to them; their feasts, their joyous occasions, their very contact, was polluted by idolatry; and there was no security, if a heathen were left alone in a room, that he might not, in wantonness or by carelessness, defile the wine or meat on the table, or the oil and wheat in the store. Under such circumstances, therefore, everything must be regarded as having been rendered useless.[9]

Although messianic hopes predate Roman occupation, the chaotic religious and political condition of the Jews along the years fueled their messianic hope for liberation from the yoke of Rome. Richard A. Horseley and Johnson S. Hanson describe the situation in which bandits, prophets, and messiahs were common.[10] And the reason for the messianic hopes is based on the fact that "centuries earlier the prophets of Israel had promised a day when the Lord would deliver his people from their pagan rulers and establish his kingdom over the whole earth."[11] This anointed messiah would usher in the kingdom of righteousness and dispel evil and corruption in the world. The perpetual bondage under which God's chosen race lived bred much discontent and frequent riots, especially in Palestine, even during religious feasts (Matt 26:5). And elsewhere, religious riots were common among the Jewish population (Acts 17:5; 19:23, 40; 21:32). Even Paul was falsely accused of stirring up riots among the Jews (Acts 24:5). Acts 5:33–37 suggests that before Jesus came onto the scene, both Theudas and Judas the Galilean saw themselves as messiahs (Acts 5:34–39). This testifies to the level of messianic hopes in Second Temple Judaism that found expression in the many factions and self-styled saviors with their followers. Additionally, passages in the New Testament like John

7. Bruce L. Shelley, *Church History in Plain Language*, 4th ed. (Thomas Nelson, 2013), 4–5.

8. Shelley, *Church History in Plain Language*, 5.

9. Alfred Edersheim, *The Life and Times of Jesus the Messiah* (Macdonald Publishing, 1886), 91–92.

10. Richard A. Horseley and Johnson S. Hanson, *Bandits, Prophets, and Messiahs: Popular Movements at the Time of Jesus* (Winston Press, 1985).

11. Shelley, *Church History in Plain Language*, 5.

6:15 and Acts 1:6 show that almost all the Jews in Palestine felt the yoke of Rome and hoped for political emancipation. The religious dimension of this is our next point.

Palestine Under the Yoke of Religious and Social Turmoil

Heated schisms characterized Palestinian Jews. Major divisions include the Pharisees, the Sadducees, the Zealots,[12] and the mystic sects (the Essenes) who formed the Qumran Community[13] and bequeathed to us the Dead Sea Scrolls. All sects had their devotees. The self-righteous Pharisees and the teachers of the law practiced strict religious pietism and saw themselves as custodians of the Law of Moses (Matt 23:1–3). The Sadducees, largely Hellenized under the Seleucids and eventually becoming the aristocratic class, compromised and allied with their Roman overlords and were thus hated by the Pharisees and teachers of the law.[14] As Gower wrote, "Like the Greeks they rejected traditional beliefs in angels, resurrection, and the providence of God, and became known as Hellenists."[15] Unlike the Sadducees, the Zealots opted for armed conflict in order to liberate themselves from Roman powers.

To a devout Jew, worship of Yahweh was a key component and daily religious ritual. This took place in the home, synagogues, and the temple in Jerusalem. The Gospels record that Jesus frequented the synagogues (Mark 1:21; Luke 4:20; 6:6; John 6:59) and the temple in Jerusalem (Matt 21:12; 24:1; Mark 11:11; 12:35; 14:49; Luke 19:45). The Jews saw themselves as worshippers of the true God—Yahweh. In contrast, both the social and religious life of Rome was anything but godly, as far as a devout Jew was concerned. But as Jensen rightly observes, "The conflicts and struggles of the Jews of that day were mainly of the heart, and the darkness and the sin were overwhelming."[16] Jensen cites James Stalker's description of the Jewish world to which Jesus came as:

> A nation enslaved; the upper classes devoting themselves to selfishness, courtiership, and skepticism; the teachers and chief professors of religion lost in mere shows of ceremonialism, and boasting themselves the favorites of God, while their souls were honeycombed with self-deception and vice; the body of the people misled by false ideals; and seething at the bottom of society, a neglected mass of unblushing and unrestrained sin.[17]

---

12. Reza Aslan, *Zealot: The Life and Times of Jesus of Nazareth* (Random House, 2013); Everett Ferguson, *Backgrounds of Early Christianity*, 3rd ed. (Eerdmans, 2003).

13. See Michael Thomas Davis and Brent A. Strawn, eds., *Qumran Studies: New Approaches* (Eerdmans, 2007); Lawrence H. Schiffman, *Qumran and Jerusalem: Studies in the Dead Sea Scrolls and the History of Judaism* (Eerdmans, 2010).

14. Although the Pharisees and the teachers of the law are often mentioned together in the Gospels and their practices may overlap, they are distinct groups in the sense that the Pharisees were a Jewish sect that emphasized oral traditions and strict moral piety. The teachers of the law were scribes and interpreters of the Law of Moses.

15. Gower, *The New Manners and Customs of Bible Times*, 80.

16. James Stalker quoted in Jensen, *Jensen's Survey of the New Testament*, 49.

17. Jensen, *Jensen's Survey of the New Testament*, 49.

This description can be seen in the light of Jesus's sharp rebuke of the Jews' hypocritical worship (Matt 15:1–19) and his invectives against the self-righteous Pharisees and the teachers of the law (Matt 23:1–39). These were mere "whitewashed tombs, which outwardly appear beautiful, but within are full of dead people's bones and all uncleanness" (Matt 23:27). The citation of this text here must not be understood as a stamp of approval for the supersessionists' agenda, which promotes antisemitism, or the replacement agenda. It is merely a presentation of the biblical narrative. But apart from religious and social upheavals, Palestine was also bedeviled by poverty and diseases.

Palestine Under the Yoke of Poverty and Diseases

According to Robert H. Gundry, "The leveling influence of Judaism reduced stratification in Jewish society, but the chief priests and the leading rabbis helped form an upper class. Farmers, artisans, small businessmen, and their families made up most of the population."[18] The economy of Palestine in the first century was made up of peasant farming. Agricultural products included grapes, grain, figs, and olives. Other economic components were sheep-rearing, fishing, carpentry, hunting, masonry, tent-making, blacksmithing or metal work, merchandise, and physicians.[19] In a land where peasant farming sustained the greater population and in which lack of rain or damage of crops by locusts or other pests could endanger the people and where the mechanized system of farming was the use of oxen for plowing the land, the economy was not too promising. The level of poverty in Palestine at the time of Jesus explains why many people followed him for the sheer miracle of feeding (John 6:26).

Similarly, Jesus healed those who were oppressed by all kinds of diseases (Matt 4:23–25; 11:4–6). An example of the oppressive power of diseases is the healing of the ten lepers (Luke 17:11). Lepers were social outcasts, ostracized from the community because of the contagious nature of their disease. God's command through Moses was, "Anyone with such a defiling disease must wear torn clothes, let their hair be unkempt, cover the lower part of their face and cry out, 'Unclean! Unclean!' And as long as they have the disease they remain unclean. They must live alone; they must live outside the camp" (Lev 13:45–46). Given these conditions, it is not surprising that the mission of Jesus is characterized as freedom for prisoners, recovery of sight for the blind, and release for the oppressed (Luke 4:18).

Palestine Under the Yoke of Power Encounters

At the time of Jesus, exorcism was a common practice (Matt 12:26, 27).[20] The Gospels record that Jesus drove out evil spirits (Matt 12:22; 17:14–21; Mark 1:21–27; 5:1–20). The oppression by evil spirits is recorded in both Mark (5:2–5) and Luke (8:27). As Mark recorded:

---

18. Robert H. Gundry, *A Survey of the New Testament* (Zondervan, 1994), 48.

19. See Jensen, *Jensen's Survey of the New Testament*, 75.

20. Bitrus A. Sarma, *Drums of Redemption: A New Testament Theology for Africa* (HippoBooks, 2023), 101.

> They came to the other side of the sea, to the country of the Gerasenes. And when he had come out of the boat, there met him out of the tombs a man with an unclean spirit, who lived among the tombs; and no one could bind him anymore, even with a chain; for he had often been bound with fetters and chains, but the chains he wrenched apart, and the fetters he broke in pieces; and no one had the strength to subdue him. Night and day among the tombs and on the mountains he was always crying out, and bruising himself with stones. (Mark 5:1–6)

In other instances, the oppression took the form of throwing the victim into fire (Matt 17:14–18). The seizure that Matthew records here is more than ordinary epilepsy, contrary to the Enlightenment school of thought that rejects the idea of demon possession: "And Jesus rebuked him, and the demon came out of him, and the body was cured instantly" (v. 18). He also gave authority to his disciples to drive away evil spirits (Matt 10:1; Mark 6:7; Luke 9:1). The disciples accomplished this mission and came back with excitement because even the demons were subject to them in the name of Christ (Luke 10:17). The exorcisms performed by Jesus and his disciples are a manifestation of the defeat of Satan and evil forces that tormented the people.[21] This is well stated in Peter's message to Cornelius and all his audience: "You know the message he sent to the people of Israel, preaching peace by Jesus Christ—he is Lord of all. That message spread throughout Judea, beginning in Galilee after the baptism that John announced: how God anointed Jesus of Nazareth with the Holy Spirit and with power; how he went about doing good and healing all who were oppressed by the devil, for God was with him. We are witnesses to all that he did both in Judea and in Jerusalem" (Acts 10:36–39).

Palestine Under the Yoke of Gender Inequality

Alvin J. Schmidt asked a penetrating question: "What would be the status of women in the Western world today had Jesus Christ never entered the arena?"[22] According to him, the answer can be found in looking at the status of women in most Islamic countries. Similarly, the low status of women in the Greco-Roman world is well documented. The exception is the upper-class women who enjoyed certain privileges and had social influence in society. Discrimination against women began in early life, such that "A male offspring was her source of prestige and validation, whereas a female child an economic liability, a social burden."[23] That is why female infanticide was common. For example, a Roman soldier wrote home to his wife,

> I urge you, take care of the little one, and as soon as we receive our pay I will send it to you. If by chance you bear a child, if it is a boy, let it be. If it is a girl, expose it.[24]

21. Sarma, *Drums of Redemption*, 101.

22. Alvin I. Schmidt, *How Christianity Changed the World* (Zondervan, 2004), 97.

23. Schmidt, *How Christianity Changed the World*, 99.

24. See Howard Marshall, Stephen Travis, and Ian Paul, *Exploring the New Testament*, vol. 2 (SPCK, 2002), 12; citing Papyrus, Egypt, first century BCE.

Similarly, the status of a Jewish woman in first-century Palestine was lower than that of a man. A woman, for example, "was not qualified to appear in court and was exempt from fulfilling religious duties that had to be performed at stated times (because her first duties were to her children and the home and she might not be in the required state of ritual purity)."[25] The low status of a woman in Jewish society in this period is reflected in the Jewish prayer which says, "Blessed art thou, O Lord our God, who has not made me a woman."[26]

The task of Jewish women included "grinding grain; weaving; making clothes; washing; care of flocks; carrying water; cooking; housecleaning; rearing and educating the children."[27] This means a woman was confined to certain tasks which were considered feminine roles. The men attended to "higher roles" in the family, community, and society.

But Jesus's ministry to women was a decisive departure from the status quo. He related freely with women. Even his disciples marveled that he was talking to a woman (John 4:27). Similarly, many of those who followed and ministered to his needs and the needs of the disciples were women (Luke 8:1–3). He was not ashamed to be associated with women whom society considered outcasts because of their questionable lifestyles (Luke 7:36–50).

From the above, we now turn to similar sociocultural and religious realities in contemporary Africa.

An Analysis of the Sociocultural, Political, and Religious Realities in Contemporary Africa[28]

Africa was once described as the "Dark Continent" by a Welsh journalist and explorer Henry Morton Stanley because he saw the continent as "mysterious," whose "landscapes and cultures were largely unknown to many outsiders until the late nineteenth century."[29] But the Africa of today has been over-explored and exploited, leaving a trail of woes behind in terms of the sociocultural, political, and religious landscape. Many perceive that Africa is still under neocolonialism, bearing the yoke of the West and other world powers. Besides neocolonialism, other sociocultural and religious challenges include political instability and unrest, divisive ethnicity, ethno-religious unrest, gender inequality, corruption, poverty and diseases, and power encounters. Although richly endowed with the best natural and human resources, Africa remains "sick" and burdened with all kinds of sociocultural, political, and religious woes, making her one of the most insecure continents on the face of the earth. A book title such as *Is Africa Cursed?*[30] seems to make sense in the light of the enormous and perennial

25. Ferguson, *Backgrounds of Early Christianity*, 78.

26. Ferguson, *Backgrounds of Early Christianity*, 78.

27. Jensen, *Jensen's Survey of the New Testament*, 75.

28. See Rodney L. Reed, ed., *African Contextual Realities* (Langham Global Library, 2018); Emmanuel Katongole, *The Sacrifice of Africa: A Political Theology for Africa* (Eerdmans, 2011); Rodney L. Reed and David K. Ngaruiya, eds., *God and Creation* (Langham Global Library, 2019).

29. Hamy Huynh, "Shining Light on the 'Dark Continent,'" University of Minnesota, College of Liberal Arts, African American & African Studies, May 28, 2020, https://tinyurl.com/29vm4bfj.

30. Tokunboh Adeyemo, *Is Africa Cursed?* (Christian Learning Material Center, 1997).

challenges that appear to have defied solutions in the continent. The continent of Africa is carrying many yokes.

Africa Under the Yoke of Neocolonialism

Before and during the colonial era, both human and material resources were carted away to Europe and Western nations to enrich their economic development. That is why some African countries are still asking for repatriation of their stolen wealth. But it is argued by some Africans, both secular and religious, that colonialism is still ongoing, whether overtly or covertly. This includes human trafficking, brain drain, economic sabotage, and educational curricula that remain Western, among others. The assertion is that Africa is still under neocolonialism based on the following reasons.

First, the mimicking of Western educational curricula in both the secular and private sectors is believed to be keeping Africa underdeveloped. These outdated curricula are unable to help the African develop the intellectual capacity necessary to solve Africa's sociocultural and religious issues because the learning process does not go beyond remembering and understanding to the vital aspects of analyzing, evaluating, and creating. Without creativity we remain consumers of ideas and products from the West.

Second, some African theologians argue that we inherited theology that is fundamentally Western and colonial in nature. They are advocating for the "Decolonization of Biblical Interpretation in Africa."[31] They rightly reason that while theology—the discourse about God—is universal, the act of theologizing takes place within a context and culture. As a point of departure from the missionaries who condemned the African culture while proclaiming the gospel using their Western worldview and cultural garb, theology must be decolonized through responsible contextualization.

Third, debt burden acquired and carried by African nations is seen as neocolonialism.[32] Many African nations continue to patronize the International Monetary Fund (IMF) and the World Bank in the name of developing their own economies or local infrastructures. But, more often than not, the monies borrowed from these lending agencies are never used for the purposes supposedly intended. Rather, some political elites divert those monies into their personal accounts. These corrupt leaders plunge their nations into the abyss of haunting debt burden. Dambisa Moyo, who defines aid as "the sum total of both concessional loans and grants,"[33] notes that the root problem of Africa's underdevelopment is aid from rich countries to African governments. As she put it succinctly, "It is these billions that have hampered, stifled and retarded Africa's development."[34] As these

31. S. O. Abogunrin, ed., *Decolonization of Biblical Interpretation in Africa* (The Nigerian Association for Biblical Studies, 2008).

32. See Keith Griffin, *International Inequality and National Poverty* (The Macmillan Press, 1978), 8.

33. Dambisa Moyo, *Dead Aid: Why Aid Is Not Working and How There Is a Better Way for Africa* (Farrar, Straus & Giroux, 2009), 26.

34. Moyo, *Dead Aid*, 26.

loans and grants often come with heavy interest rates, the interest keeps accumulating and rising. Unable to pay their debts as scheduled, some African leaders resort to the Paris Club (that is, a group that coordinates between creditor nations and debtor countries on loan repayment plans) to either reschedule their debt repayment period or to reduce debt service dues. When the debts are accumulated, the debtor countries, in particular their future generations, bear the brunt. The creditor governments and agencies lose nothing as the profit from debt servicing is usually high enough to cover whatever they have lent out. This unending servicing of debts is one of the biggest problems for Africa's economic growth and is considered neocolonialism. As Moyo rightly said, "Aid costs money. And unless it's in the form of grants, it has to be paid back, with interest. This point would later come back to haunt many African states."[35] Instead of improved economy, poverty level increases in aid-dependent countries.

Related to the above, the over-dependence on foreign aid[36] is considered another form of neocolonialism. Because of the artificial lack of resources caused by bad governance, poor management, and corruption, many African nations depend on foreign aid to meet urgent domestic needs. An example is the COVID-19 pandemic that saw many African nations running to the West for assistance. This kind of help usually comes with strings attached.

Likewise, the exportation of crude oil and other raw materials can be regarded as neocolonialism. For example, Nigerian refineries have stopped working since the late 1980s. Because of corruption, successive governments failed to revive the refineries. Our crude oil is exported, refined, and sold back to us at an exorbitant price. At the time of writing, the pump price in Nigeria has skyrocketed more than three times in the name of fuel subsidy removal, causing untold hardship to the people because prices of goods went up by the same margin or more.

The fourth sign of neocolonialism is the heavy over-dependence on foreign industries for goods. Local industries like textiles and car assembly companies were strong in Nigeria in the early 1980s. But with collusion with foreign importers, successive governments neglected local industries in favor of foreign goods. This has had adverse effects in terms of employment and inflation as Nigeria has to depend on foreign goods without collateral exports.

Due to the weighty issues above, Africa's freedom remains questionable. This leads us to another challenge for the African continent.

Africa and the Challenges of Political Instability, Insecurity, and Unrest

Political instability and unrest are the bane of most African nations.[37] Martin Meredith chronicles the story of the African continent since independence and paintes a gloomy picture of the political instability and corruption that have characterized most African countries from

35. Moyo, *Dead Aid*, 33.

36. This is supposedly free aid to nations that are struggling financially as distinguished from loans collected with repayment plans.

37. See David J. Francis, ed., *Peace and Conflict in Africa* (Zed Books, 2008).

the time of independence.[38] Based on Meredith's account, the present blatant manipulation of political processes through rigging, the use of political thugs, bribery, ballot snatching, destruction, and killing are not new at all. These evils breed voter apathy and distrust of the entire political process. The exemplary leadership of the late Nelson Mandela of South Africa stands as rare ray of light in the dark political situation of Africa.

The quest to remain in power for life is another factor that breeds political instability and unrest. Most African leaders retain their pre-democratic roots and mentality in which monarchs rule for life. This is not to paint the monarchical system in Africa as evil and democracy as the best. Many African monarchs were good leaders who promoted the well-being of their people and resisted colonialism. Coming from the background of leadership for life, the idea of election for a tenure of a few years is foreign to many African leaders. While they theoretically subscribe to democratic principles, they manipulate the democratic process to fit into their monarchic system of governance. This quest to remain in power at all costs often breeds political unrest as those who want a change of government recruit opposition groups to fight the government. This sometimes results in major conflicts. As Nana K. Poku succinctly puts it, "When weak political systems are added to this . . . catalogue of socio-economic ailments, the outcome is insecurity of ordinary people in circumstances where states—and the international system of states—are either unable to provide protection or are themselves the principal sources of violence."[39]

Africa and the Issues of Divisive Ethnicity and Ethno-Religious Unrest

Divisive ethnicity[40] (also referred to as negative ethnicity) and ethno-religious unrest are formidable forces in Africa. These have three major faces. They include tribalism and ethnocentrism, religious extremism, and political marginalization through ethno-religious divides. Because of their significance in the development and well-being of the continent, we shall devote some time in examining them.

Tribalism and Ethnocentrism[41]

By divine providence, people groups are categorized according to their nationality, race, language, ethnicity, religion, or tribe. Ethnicity relates to ethnic affiliation or ethnic distinctiveness. But tribalism is people finding identity within their own tribal groups to the exclusion of the perceived "outsider." The "outsider" is the one who is not of one's ethnic group. But biblically, it is "from one man he made every nation of men, that they should inhabit the

38. See Martin Meredith, *The State of Africa: A History of the Continent Since Independence* (Simon & Schuster, 2005).

39. Nana K. Poku, "Context of Security in Africa," in *Peace and Conflict in Africa*, ed. David J. Francis (Zed Books, 2008), 92. Poku says that the socioeconomic ailments that breed insecurity are poverty, hunger, diseases, environmental degradation, infant mortality, and illiteracy, among others.

40. Barje S. Maigadi, *Divisive Ethnicity in the Church in Africa* (Baraka Press, 2006).

41. See Bitrus A. Sarma, *Blessed New Humanity in Christ: A Theology of Hope for African Christianity from the Book of Ephesians* (HippoBooks, 2021), 96–102.

whole earth" (Acts 17:26a). This is the basis for loving and respecting "the differentness of other cultures."[42] In other words, belonging to an ethnic group is not the problem. Ethnicity becomes a problem when it turns to ethnocentrism, namely, elevating one's ethnic group and devaluing those considered inferior.[43] Ethnocentrism is responsible for countless deadly conflicts, especially in Africa. The concept of the "outsider"[44] is a global issue but is particularly critical in African society—even in the African church. Because "sin affects every dimension of the human person,"[45] tribal,[46] ethnic, and racial differences often degenerate into conflicts of alarming proportions in the church. As a result, Christian communities and nations have sometimes taken up arms and massacred one another.

But the concepts of "insider" and "outsider" run contrary to the New Testament model of the one body of Christ. The Bible says that in Christ "There is no longer Jew or Greek, there is no longer slave or free, there is no longer male and female; for all of you are one in Christ Jesus" (Gal 3:28). Therefore, tribalism and ethnocentrism are unbiblical and must be condemned by all those who love God and our Lord Jesus Christ.

Religious Extremism

Religion is a broad concept of complex and diverse human engagement with the divine or spiritual reality that controls human life and destiny. It is an organized system of beliefs and practices. As a worldwide phenomenon, religion plays an important role in human culture and relationships. And in every religion there are custodians of beliefs and practices—the clerics or priests. Their qualification may come by virtue of inheritance or special training under tutors. The custodians teach and enforce the beliefs and practices of their religion. Apart from common beliefs and practices that may cut across religions, there may be cardinal creeds within some religious groups that prescribe, in principle, hostility toward others who do not share their beliefs and practices. In recent times, religious extremism has assumed a global dimension because some religious fundamentalists are stressing aspects of their beliefs that are opposed to peaceful coexistence with people who hold different beliefs. For example, Ellis Skolfield shows that the Western world is facing two major problems, namely, apostasy in the church and a militant religion bent on world conquest.[47] For some Islamic extremists, the world must

42. Thomas Schirrmacher, *Racism*, trans. Richard McClary (Culture & Science Publishing, 2012), 60.

43. Brian M. Howell and Jenell Williams Paris, *Introducing Cultural Anthropology: A Christian Perspective* (Baker Academic, 2011), 33.

44. See Adriane Leveen, "Inside Out: Jethro, the Midianites and a Biblical Construction of the Outsider," *Journal for the Study of the Old Testament* 34, no. 4 (2010): 395–417. See also Neil Glover, "Your People, My People: An Exploration of Ethnicity in Ruth," *Journal for the Study of the Old Testament* 33, no. 3 (2009): 293–313.

45. Christopher J. H. Wright, "Biblical Paradigms of Redemption: Exodus, Jubilee and the Cross," in *Transforming the World? The Gospel and Social Responsibility*, ed. Jamie A. Grant and Dewi A. Hughes (Apollos, 2009), 69.

46. Elie A. Buconyori, ed., *Tribalism and Ethnicity* (The AEA Theological and Christian Education Commission, 1977).

47. Ellis Skofield, *Religious Battle Behind the Headlines: Islam in the End Times* (Fish House Publishing, 2007), 131.

belong to their particular creed. As a result, world news headlines report innocent human beings targeted and killed in places of worship, markets, roads, schools, and everywhere with impunity. Some of the world's deadliest terrorist organizations include Hezbollah, the Islamic State of Iraq and Syria (ISIS), the Taliban, Hamas, al-Qaeda, the Islamic Jihad Union (IJU), Al-Shabaab, and Boko Haram. Their quest for global and regional dominance is apparent. Their logic is "to bring every square inch of this planet under submission to the rule of the Qur'an."[48] Their motivation is "altering the conditions around them and changing the country into a new Islamic country."[49] It is a quest for world dominion.[50] One means of doing this is to kill the opponents of this quest. At present many countries in Africa are facing religious extremism. Some West African countries like Nigeria, Niger, and Mali, for example, are facing many security challenges from terrorist groups like Boko Haram and Islamic State of West Africa (ISWAP). Other African countries like Somalia are also facing the dilemma. A recent United Nations headline reads, "Sub-Saharan Africa Is 'New Epicenter' of Extremism."[51]

Radical Islamist groups are motivated by, among other things, the belief that Muslims have "strayed from the pure form of Islam which existed under Muhammad and the first *rashidun* caliphs."[52] And the "extremist" ideology enshrined in their sacred books is the unconditional command "to fight all unbelievers everywhere and at any time."[53] Embedded in such an ideology is the total rejection of anyone who does not share the same creed or ideology. Such ideology sees others as "those who corrupt the land."[54] Typical of this is the propaganda of Abubakar Shekau, a former leader of Boko Haram, who vowed, "By Allah, we will kill whoever practices democracy. . . . What makes you infidels is democracy and western education."[55]

Political Marginalization via Ethno-Religious Divide

Politics refers to activities that are associated with acts of governance such as obtaining legislative or executive powers in a given nation at different levels of governance. And in democratic governments, the means of obtaining legislative or executive power or judiciary is through the ballot box. Therefore, where democracy works, the electorates hold the power and give it to whoever they believe will represent them best.

---

48. R. Albert Mohler Jr., *Culture Shift: The Battle for the Moral Heart of America* (Multnomah Books, 2011), 154.

49. Mark A. Gabriel, *Journey into the Mind of an Islamic Terrorist* (Frontline, 2006), 120.

50. David Zeidan, *Sword of Allah: Islamic Fundamentalism from an Evangelical Perspective* (Gabriel Publishing, 2003), 95–97.

51. Evelyne Musambi, "Sub-Saharan Africa Is 'New Epicenter' of Extremism, Says UN," AP News, February 7, 2023, https://apnews.com/article/islamic-state-group-politics-organized-crime-africa-098f5a2cf237f92d3d1217fade5caf0b.

52. Patrick Sookhdeo, *Unmasking Islamic State: Revealing Their Motivation, Theology and End Time Predictions* (Isaac Publishing, 2015), 27.

53. Yusufu Turaki, *Tainted Legacy: Islam, Colonialism and Slavery in Northern Nigeria* (Isaac Publishing, 2010), 58.

54. Turaki, *Tainted Legacy*, 61.

55. Jonathan Ishaku, *Janjaweed in the Middle Belt: The Menace of Armed Groups in Central Nigeria* (Courier Communications, 2015), 180.

But in the Nigerian context, as in many African nations, elections are never democratic. Rigging, the use of thugs, snatching of ballot boxes, buying of votes, and violence are common. Similarly, most of our "democratic" leaders are dictators and those who have maneuvered their way to power retain it by all means and use such powers to fuel ethno-religious divides for their selfish interests, compounding the political chaos.[56] The political gladiators appeal to religion and ethnicity to achieve their goal of divide and rule.[57] They inject unhealthy religious sentiments that promote divisions and hatred against people of other creeds. And it works. But the worst of this political maneuvering in religious garb is "the political game of ethnic/religious groups that find themselves as a minority in a given area."[58] The minority groups suffer many forms of marginalization. Their children are denied admission into schools. They are refused employment opportunities. They cannot compete for certain political offices. They enjoy less, if any, protection. They are denied the right to obtain certificates of occupancy (C of Os) even for the lands they are able to purchase. They are denied social amenities and many other privileges because the political gladiators who belong to the ruling political/religious enclave reserve the right to treat them that way. This is revealed in the quest for the adoption of *sharia* law in some states of Nigeria by the political class.[59]

What, then, is the fate of a continent fragmented and fractured along religious and ethnic fault lines? Are some of our religious ideologies reconcilable? Do we have any prospects for sustainable unity in Africa? These questions are food for thought as we consider the next yoke.

Africa and the Quest for Gender Equality

As we saw in the Greco-Roman world, women had lower status than men. But the coming of Christianity became the game changer as the Christian faith promoted the equality of humankind and the dignity of women. This is a debatable issue as Christianity bred inequality in some contexts. By contrast, in some traditional matriarchal cultures, women had high social status in the political and religious life of their communities. But as expected in a fallen world, gender inequality persists, and remains a complex and sensitive issue in twenty-first-century Africa, even among some Christians. These issues are usually dictated by culture, religion, and worldviews. And in the light of gender inequality, the women's liberation movement came as a protest against the social discrimination and injustices meted out to women, such as denying education for girls, domestic violence against women, limited access to or absence of jobs for women in the public sector, restriction of women from certain jobs, and the like. Women

56. Yusufu Turaki, *Historical Roots of Ethno-Religious Crises and Conflicts in Northern Nigeria* (Challenge Press, n.d.), 124.

57. Sebastian Elischer, *Political Parties in Africa: Ethnicity and Party Formation* (Cambridge University Press, 2013).

58. Turaki, *Historical Roots*, 123.

59. Jan H. Boer, *Christians and Muslims: Parameters for Living Together*, Studies in Christian–Muslim Relations, vol. 8, part 2 (Essence Publishing, 2009), 129. See Je'adayibe Dogara Gwamna, *Religion and Politics in Nigeria* (African Christian Textbooks, 2010), 56.

(and some men) are raising their voices so that women may be given their rightful positions in all spheres of human endeavor. As a reaction, some men are fighting for the rights of boys.

The African church is also wrestling with the issue of gender inequality. While the Bible teaches that a woman has equal standing with a man before God (Gal 8:28), the issue of gender roles remains debatable among Christians, depending on whether they are egalitarians (emphasis on equality of genders—male and female—and rejection of social hierarchy based on gender) or complementarians (a belief that the two genders play different roles that complement each other). The most controversial figure in the discussion regarding the place of women in the church is the apostle Paul.[60] And "One of the theological conundrums in 1 Corinthians is what Paul says about women in worship (1 Cor 11:1–16; 14:33–35; cf. 1 Tim 2:11–15). Scholars interpret the 'distinctions at worship' implied in the text from their different presuppositions and ideologies."[61] Most feminists and egalitarian interpreters see these texts as arising from their sociocultural contexts and hold that they should be interpreted as such.[62] Therefore, in this view, it is wrong to understand a woman's role in the church in the twenty-first century based on those texts.

To sum up, I have argued in *Drums of Redemption* that from the ministry of Jesus and that of Paul,

> men and women have equal standing before God and share together in the ministry of the gospel. But there is no convincing evidence that Galatians 3:28 abolishes distinctive gender roles. Similarly, it is hard to draw conclusive statements on 1 Corinthians 11:1–16; 14:33–35; 1 Timothy 2:11–15. But we will do well to never let personal prejudices, agendas, ideologies, or presuppositions determine the meaning of the biblical text. Reverent scholarship demands that we submit to the text through the leading of the Holy Spirit.[63]

While differing understandings of women's roles will persist, Christian Africans should clearly teach that treating women as second- or third-class citizens is a gross misrepresentation of God's original plan for man and woman. The unbiblical yoke of inequality is to be thrown away.

Africa Under the Yoke of Corruption, Poverty, and Diseases

Both corruption and poverty are perennial global issues.[64] Vishal Mangalwadi believes that corruption and poverty go together. To prove the correlation between corruption

60. Norbert Baumert, *Man and Woman in Paul: Overcoming a Misunderstanding*, trans. Patrick Madigan SJ and Linda M. Maloney (The Liturgical Press, 1996).

61. Sarma, *Drums of Redemption*, 173.

62. Sarma, *Drums of Redemption*, 176.

63. Sarma, *Drums of Redemption*, 179.

64. See Xavier Massingue, *Theology of Work and Poverty Alleviation in Mozambique* (Langham Monograph, 2013); Ian Senior, *Corruption—the World's Big C Cases: Causes, Consequences, Cures* (The Institute of Economic Affairs, 2006); Kempe Ronald Hope Sr., ed., *Police Corruption and Police Reforms in Developing Societies* (CRC Press, 2016);

and poverty, he cited the Transparency International's Global Corruption Perceptions Index (CPI), whose verdict is that with a rising corruption index as the corruption index rises, the poorer the citizens become.[65] This is because political elites siphon the national resources into personal purses and the corrupt investors put private gain above the welfare of citizens. Corruption has become a monster in some African nations such that fighting it is dangerous.[66] That corruption has become a way of life is portrayed by the rather sarcastic book title, *When Stealing Is Not Corruption*.[67] While it is a global problem, it is believed to hurt the African continent more than other regions of the world because it is "more brazen, and accepted more readily"[68] in Africa.

As highlighted above, corruption breeds poverty. Michael Taylor rightly observes,

> poverty has many causes, some deeply rooted in history. Bad governance, "natural" disasters, personal qualities and cultural practices all contribute. The lack of income and power which characterize poverty also perpetuate it. The global economy with its neo-liberal policies and unequal trading systems is regarded as most to blame. The reasons why some people are poor and others rich are often the same.[69]

Even in modern times and among the rich nations of the world, the problem of poverty persists.[70] Although many African countries are endowed with natural resources, greed, corruption, bad governance[71] and its attendant poor management of resources, and lack of ideas for progress by the leaders have all kept the continent under the yoke of abject poverty. It is estimated that most of the poor people in Africa live on less than US$1 per day. This gross lack means that they are beyond the reach of good medical care, education, food, shelter, and other necessities of life. It is these poor masses that are often manipulated by politicians to either fight or sell their conscience by voting for those who hand them peanuts during electioneering campaigns. When in power, those deceivers never return to give back to those who gave them the power by their votes or make attempts to fulfill their

---

Kempe Ronald Hope Sr. and Bornwell C. Chikulo, *Corruption and Development in Africa: Lessons from Country Case-Studies* (Macmillan Press, 2000).

65. Vishal Mangalwadi, *The Book That Made Your World: How the Bible Created the Soul of Western Civilization* (Thomas Nelson, 2011), 252–253.

66. See Ngozi Okonjo-Iweala, *Fighting Corruption Is Dangerous: The Story Behind the Headlines* (MIT Press, 2018).

67. Nura H. Alkali, *When Stealing Is Not Corruption: Nigeria Under President Jonathan* (Ardo Dembo Publishing, 2015).

68. Bernard Boyo, *The Church and Politics: A Theological Reflection* (HippoBooks, 2021), 177; citing Ignatius Edet, "The Church and Corruption in Africa," *African Ecclesiastical Review* 51–52, no. 4 (December 2009): 625.

69. Michael Taylor, *Christianity, Poverty and Wealth* (SPCK, 2003), 12.

70. Warren R. Copeland, *And the Poor Get Welfare: The Ethics of Poverty in the United States* (Abingdon Press, 1994).

71. Kempe Ronald Hope Sr., *Development in the Third World: From Policy Failure to Policy Reform* (Routledge, 2015), 3.

development promises.[72] This hopeless situation is the reason for the quest for a better life abroad, forcing many to risk their lives on land and sea to get to countries where they think life will be better.[73]

And where poverty is prevalent, diseases are never absent. As a result of poverty, people live in poor environmental conditions that attract diseases. The majority of these people are unable to access good medical care. They suffer and die from diseases that could easily be cured. Because most of these poor masses are unable to send their children to school, the vicious cycle of poverty continues unchecked.

Africa Under the Bondage of Power Encounters

The New Testament is replete with accounts of power encounters and exorcisms. Similarly, power encounters are a formidable challenge in Africa. In the African worldview, the spirit world is made up of both benevolent and evil spirits. In addition, there are people who are "endowed" with knowledge and understanding of the spirit world. This complex unseen world causes fear and anxiety among Africans, including Christians. Therefore, deliverance services are held in some churches and "prayer houses" for the sole aim of delivering people from witchcraft, magic spells, demons, curses, and all kinds of spiritual attacks. In essence, it is believed that every evil that happens to a person has some evil force behind it, and is not just a matter of chance. However, there are cultures who, because of the transactional nature of their worldview, attribute misfortune to the Supreme Being. This Supreme Being rewards those who do good things and punishes those who do wrong. This retribution theology undergirds some cultures' understanding of suffering and misfortune. But more often than not, witches and wizards are blamed for every misfortune. Paul G. Hiebert, R. Daniel Shaw, and Tite Tiénou capture this well.

> Witchcraft is often found in societies in which people explain everything in terms of human actions. They do not believe in "accident," "chance," or "natural causes." They know that a man cut his leg because his ax bounced off the wood and hit it, but their question is why this happened to this man on this occasion when he had been chopping wood for years without accident. In these societies, every misfortune as well as death is blamed on some person, and that person is believed to cause it by means of magic or witchcraft. They believe that modern technology is the result of Western witchcraft. If asked why their witches cannot make cars and airplanes, they answer that their witches actually have this technology, but keep these goods for their exclusive use in their invisible world.[74]

72. See Kempe Ronald Hope Sr., *Poverty and Governance in Africa: Fulfilling the Development Promise* (Palgrave Macmillan, 2008).

73. Sarma, *Blessed New Humanity in Christ*, 19–32.

74. Paul G. Hiebert, R. Daniel Shaw, and Tite Tiénou, *Understanding Folk Religion: A Christian Response to Popular Beliefs and Practices* (Baker Books, 1999), 150. See also Samuel Waje Kunhiyop, *Witchcraft Beliefs and Accusations: A Biblical and Christian Perspective* (Challenge Press, 2019).

A recent encounter with a preacher at a funeral service of an old woman buttresses this worldview. A member of his church was bitten by a snake while working on his farm. The pastor visited him while he was dying from the snake bite. Lamenting the prevalence of witches and wizards in the society, the pastor declared that the snake that had bitten the man was not an ordinary snake. According to him, he asked the dying man if he saw someone on the farm the day the snake bit him. The man responded that his uncle had visited him on that day. The pastor told the man that it was his uncle who had turned into a snake and bitten him! As a result of this worldview, witch hunting and killing is a rising phenomenon in Nigeria. Cases of killings are regularly reported. The victims are men and women, both young and old, who are perceived to be responsible for the death of loved ones.

Because of the fear of invisible evil forces, too many people in Africa, including Christians, live in perpetual fear. This is unscriptural because "There is power in Christ that surpasses all of the powers of the world combined."[75] All evil powers are subject to Christ and to believers because of "the immeasurable greatness of his power for us who believe, according to the working of his great power. God put this power to work in Christ when he raised him from the dead and seated him at his right hand in the heavenly places, far above all rule and authority and power and dominion, and above every name that is named, not only in this age but also in the age to come. And he has put all things under his feet and has made him the head over all things for the church, which is his body, the fullness of him who fills all in all" (Eph 1:19–23). Christians in Africa will be liberated from their fear of evil spirits, witches, wizards, and other forces of darkness as they grasp the meaning of this text and appropriate its application to life by faith. This is believing and living with confidence that nothing could harm them as Christ whom they serve is "far above all rule and authority."

Africa Under the Yoke of Injustice, Oppression, and the Violation of Human Rights

Injustice, oppression, and the violation of human rights are global issues. Injustice is "the act of depriving a person of something to which he or she is entitled as a right and not a privilege."[76] Injustice promotes oppression and human rights violations. Injustice springs from the untransformed heart, described as "devious above all else; it is perverse [desperately wicked]" (Jer 17:9a). As in the days of Noah, "every inclination of the thoughts of their hearts was only evil continually" (Gen 6:5). And to this day, the basic malady in the sinful, unregenerate heart of mankind is the problem of evil with all that is associated with it—wickedness, injustice, corruption, oppression, and the like.

Because of the lack of an efficient justice system in many African countries, oppression and all kinds of violations of human rights take place with impunity. While it is believed that the justice system is the hope of the common person, this perception is gradually being eroded as injustice prevails. The main reason attributed to this is that the justice system has

75. Sarma, *Blessed New Humanity in Christ*, 73.

76. Boyo, *The Church and Politics*, 174.

been corrupted, giving way to impunity. In Nigeria, for example, people are dehumanized, their properties destroyed, and killings take place openly. But the perpetrators of such crimes are above the law because the justice system is under their control. The highest bidder gets "justice," leaving the poor and the oppressed with no place to find redress.

But as salt and light of the world, Christians must be vanguards of justice because God hates injustice and oppression (Isa 59:1–15; Amos 5:7–24). It is our calling to promote righteousness, justice, human rights, and dignity from a biblical standpoint. Unfortunately, the church in Nigeria, for example, seems powerless to confront these evils because most Christians in the corridors of power and outside of it do not live by example. By living contrary to the principles of righteousness, justice, and the promotion of human dignity, the church in Nigeria has lost the moral right to challenge those in power.

Africa and the Challenge of Environmental Degradation

One of the most important issues confronting human existence on planet earth in the twenty-first century is environmental challenges.[77] Environmental crises concern all of us because "our humanity and well-being depends upon the environment."[78] While environmental issues are diverse, the three deadly ones confronting people in sub-Saharan Africa and the entire world include absence of or inefficient waste management resulting in dehumanizing conditions of filthiness, the problem of desert encroachment, and global warming or climate change.[79]

Add to this rapid urbanization without adequate town planning and waste management, and the result is haphazard dumping of refuse that results in a stinking environment, causing diseases and deaths.[80] According to Yinka Adegoke, "Waste management is one of the biggest challenges facing the continent and its fast-growing cities—and has been a problem for a long time."[81] This is caused by rapid urbanization without adequate infrastructure or waste management plans. Shanties and slums are found in many major cities of Africa. These places lack basic amenities such as clean water, light, toilet facilities, good roads, and the like. Most of the dwellers in these places live in dehumanizing conditions.

In addition to the challenges above, human activities such as overgrazing, farming, bush burning, and logging are accelerating the menace of desertification. Similarly, the depletion of the ozone layer due to the emission of carbon dioxide and other gasses is threatening life on planet earth. As we face these threats, namely, filth, desertification, and global warming,

77. See, for example, David G. Horrell, "A New Perspective on Paul? Rereading Paul in a Time of Ecological Crisis," *Journal for the Study of the New Testament* 33, no. 1 (2010): 7.

78. See Alokwu Cyprian Obiora, "Christian and Environmental Sustainability: A Search for Inclusive Response," *An African Journal of Arts and Humanities* 3, no. 1 (January 2017): 74.

79. For a good treatment of dirt, desertification, and climate change, see Bitrus A. Sarma, *Healing the Environment: Christian Ecological Ethics for Africa* (Yakson Press, 2019).

80. See Yinka Adegoke, "When Will Africa's Fast-Growing Cities Get on Top of Their Garbage Problems?," Quartz, March 26, 2018, https://qz.com/africa/1237012/lagos-nairobi-and-accra-are-among-africas-big-cities-to-struggle-with-poor-waste-management.

81. Adegoke, "When Will Africa's Fast-Growing Cities Get on Top of Their Garbage Problems?"

it is quite disturbing that the majority of people seem to lack the right attitude toward environmental issues and the future of the natural habitat in which we live. It is argued that "as stewards of the environment God has given us, it is our responsibility to transform the environment and pass it on to future generations."[82]

From the sociocultural and religious realities above, we now turn to the sociocultural and religious realities in Africa with both retrospective and prospective lenses. The goal is to look at the impact of the gospel in Africa thus far and the journey ahead.

A Retrospective and Prospective View of the Gospel's Impact on Sociocultural and Religious Realities in Africa[83]

While the sociocultural and religious realities of the African continent may be compared to Palestine in the first century, the New Testament is a testament of hope and life in abundance, affecting every element of human society. The year of the Lord's favor in Luke 4:19 is reminiscent of Israel's year of Jubilee in which debts were cancelled and slaves set free.[84] The year signified hope for the poor and hopeless. Therefore, in this retrospective and prospective journey, we shall focus on the impact of the gospel in Africa thus far and envision the Africa of our dreams in light of Luke 4:18–19.

A Retrospective View

Counting the Gains of the Gospel in Africa

The coming of Christianity was the true light shining on people who formerly walked in darkness all over the world, including the African continent, bringing sociocultural and religious transformation on the African landscape. This is not to downplay or mute some of the negative baggage of Western Christianity, such as the equating of Western culture with Christianity, the collaboration of some Western missionaries with the colonizers in promoting the slave trade, the depiction of anything African as evil by some of the missionaries, the barbaric spread of the gospel (such as people coerced to accept Christ) in some places, and the supremacy mentality projected and practiced by some Western missionaries. These reprehensive legacies notwithstanding, our particular concern here is Africa's positive gains as a result of the gospel.

Although there are many areas that could be included, we will limit our discussion to six, namely: family and gender equality, education, health care, economy, and the dignity of human life.

---

82. Sarma, *Healing the Environment*, vi.

83. See Vishal Mangalwadi, *Truth and Transformation: A Manifesto for Ailing Nations* (YWAM Publishing, 2009); Loren Cunningham and Janice Rogers, *The Book That Transforms Nations: The Power of the Bible to Change Any Country* (YWAM, 2007); Sunday B. Agang, Dion A. Foster, and H. Jurgens Hendriks, eds., *African Public Theology* (HippoBooks, 2020).

84. See Darrell L. Bock, *Luke*, IVPNTCS (InterVarsity Press, 1994), 90.

We begin with the family, the bedrock of every society. Before the advent of Christianity, polygamy was the norm of African family life. But Christianity transformed the family by the biblical model of one man one wife. Rather than acquiring a harem for economic and social status, Christians were taught that God's original purpose for marriage was monogamy, as represented in the first marriage (Gen 1:26–27; 2:18–23). In addition, most African societies were patriarchal in nature. Women had inferior status. Sometimes a wife was even less important than the male children she produced! But Christianity taught that both man and woman were created in the image of God and both have equal standing before God (Rom 3:28). Likewise, the Bible provided important roles to be played by different members of the family (Eph 5:21–6:1–4; Col 3:18–25).

The next is "Christianity's imprint on education."[85] Most Christian mission organizations saw the establishment of schools as a priority. Their goal was to help Africans read and write. Eventually, education became a powerful tool for sociocultural and religious transformation. And in following the principle of biblical gender equality, education in mission schools was made available to both males and females. Equally, many of the mission schools were made accessible unbelievers, as education was seen as a means of evangelization. Today, many outstanding figures in Africa, both Christians and non-Christians, have benefitted from Western education provided by mission schools.

Still on education, unemployment, often due to a lack of education, is a "major [cause] of poverty."[86] But good education brings economic empowerment. In the same manner, technology, believed to be the "fruit of biblical worldview,"[87] brings rapid economic development. The most advanced countries of the world today are technologically advanced. The education provided by some Christian schools included the development of basic skills and basic science and technology such as improved agricultural production, local textiles, animal rearing, and more. Also, to be educated in a Christian school was to be taught the biblical ethics of self-discipline, hard work, frugality, and the like. The result is productive living that promotes a person's economic and social status.

Related to education, improved health care is one of the benefits of mission work in Africa. With so much poverty and ignorance, all kinds of diseases plagued the African continent. It is true that many of the Western nations suffered similar kinds of plagues and diseases. But on a comparative scale, Africa had more health-care challenges. Child mortality was high. Leprosy was common. Other diseases like chickenpox, tuberculosis, malaria, measles, and cholera devastated the continent. But motivated by the spirit and love of Christ, mission organizations established hospitals, nursing homes, clinics, dispensaries, and leprosariums. The missionaries believed that Jesus is the "healer of body and soul."[88] People were either treated free of charge or at very low cost because this was considered an act of mercy and part of mission outreach to the unreached.

---

85. Schmidt, *How Christianity Changed the World*, 170.

86. Taylor, *Christianity, Poverty and Wealth*, 13.

87. Mangalwadi, *The Book That Made Your World*, 75.

88. Schmidt, *How Christianity Changed the World*, 151.

Finally, before Christianity came to Africa, tribal wars were common features in many African communities. Ancient hostilities kept communities in perpetual battles. But Christianity taught forgiveness, love for enemies, and respect for human life. Wherever the gospel was fully embraced, barbaric killings stopped. In the same vein, barbaric practices such as throwing away twins in some parts of Africa were stopped. An example worth mentioning is that of Mary Slessor (1848–1915).[89] At the age of twenty-eight, encouraged by her poor widowed mother, Slessor left Scotland to the Calabar region to settle among the Efik people as a missionary (now Akwa Ibom State, Nigeria). At that time, the birth of twins among the Efik people was considered a curse. Natives feared that the father of one of the infants was an evil spirit, and that the mother had been guilty of a great sin. Unable to determine which twin was fathered by the evil spirit, the natives often abandoned both babies in the bush. Slessor adopted every child she found abandoned and cared for them at the Mission House. She also challenged the widespread practice of human sacrifice at the death of a village elder, who, it was believed, required servants and retainers to accompany him into the next world. Slessor was courageous to go even to places where previous male missionaries had been killed.

A Prospective View

Envisioning the Africa of Our Dreams in the Light of Luke 4:18–19

As highlighted above, the African continent is fraught with many sociocultural and religious predicaments that cripple the continent, making it one of the most insecure places for human survival. Is there any hope for Africa? The answer is found in Jesus's mission statement in Luke 4:18–19. The text announces a time of emancipation for those who were held captive in the bondage of sin (cf. Luke 19:10) and its sociocultural and religious implications.

The church is the embodiment of the gospel of Christ, bearing the good news of the abundant life and hope for the marginalized, the poor, the oppressed, and the downtrodden. The good news of the gospel is for body, soul, and spirit. As Melvin Tinker rightly said, "Jesus taught God's love and his followers to love; a love demonstrated by 'deeds' and 'words.' This, it would be argued by many, is sufficient justification for maintaining that it is the task of the church likewise to express the same divine love to a needy world by declaration and deed, evangelism and social action."[90] As the salt and light of the world, the church has the responsibility of transforming the sociocultural and religious structures of society. Influencing governance, education, family, and all the structures that form the bedrock of modern society is part of making disciples of all nations. The church stands the best chance to "anchor public morality"[91]

89. E. E. Enock and J. Chappell, "'Ma,' the Missionary Heroine of Calabar: A Brief Biography of Mary Slessor," 2005 ed., https://www.wholesomewords.org/missions/bioslessor5.pdf.

90. Melvin Tinker, "The Servant Solution: Coordination of Evangelism and Social Action," in *Transforming the World? The Gospel and Social Responsibility*, ed. Jamie A. Grant and Dewi A. Hughes (Apollos, 2009), 147.

91. Rodney L. Reed, "God in the Public Square: The Place of Religion in Shaping Public Morality and Social Cohesion," in *God and Creation*, ed. Rodney L. Reed and David K. Ngaruiya (Langham Global Library, 2019), 205.

and to restructure society. In *How Christianity Changed the World*,[92] Alvin I. Schmidt argues that people must give credit to Christianity for transforming the world in many ways. He enumerates all the beautiful things in the modern world that are rooted in Christianity. These include: the sanctification of human life, elevation of sexual morality, freedom and dignity for women, charity and compassion, hospitals and health care, education, labor and economic freedom, science, abolition of slavery, art and architecture, music, literature, holidays, words, symbols, and expressions. Vishal Mangalwadi shares the same school of thought with Schmidt that the Bible created the soul of Western civilization.[93] The argument here is that the church is the only authentic entity that embodies Christ's vision for world transformation enshrined in Luke 4:18–19. Therefore, the church is endowed with the task of healing Africa's sick sociocultural and religious environment. As the salt and light of the world, the church is the prophetic voice of the nations, opposing and denouncing the strongholds—like ethnocentrism, divisive ethnicity, religious bigotry and extremism, marginalization, greed, self-centeredness, nepotism, and the like—that keep nations backward. She proactively leads the way in nation-building by promoting godly virtues of truth, love, sanctity of human life, hard work, integrity, and love for humanity. The church must be intentional in pursuing her objectives as stated below.

First, all Christians must see themselves as vanguards of truth. God's truth transforms communities, societies, and nations.[94] And contrary to postmodern relativism,[95] God's truth is universal and prevails over falsehood. Christian theologians and all Christians must reject the lies that pervade and keep our nations in bondage. They must denounce the lies that promote killing the unborn, sexual immorality of every kind, and every abominable practice that God hates. Similarly, they must denounce lies from political, religious, and traditional leaders who mislead the people through the craft of deception. They must denounce lies wherever they are found. They must denounce all forms of political correctness aimed at silencing truth. Truth must prevail.

Second, following the example of some of the good missionary initiatives, the church in Africa must strive to eradicate illiteracy in her membership and lead the way in providing the best forms of education in the continent in order to liberate people from spiritual and social blindness. This is because illiteracy is a leading factor in keeping people in bondage. Good education plays a vital role in curing these social and spiritual ailments.

Third, Jesus was countercultural on the issue of gender inequality. Women who were ostracized in society as "sinners" found forgiveness and place in the ministry of Jesus (Luke 7:36–50). The Gospel of Luke narrates at great length the role women played in the birth of Christ (Luke 1–2), his ministry (8:1–3), and his death and resurrection (23:26–30; 24:1–12).

---

92. Schmidt, *How Christianity Changed the World*, 11–14.

93. Mangalwadi, *The Book That Made Your World*. See also Mangalwadi, *Truth and Transformation*; Cunningham and Rogers, *The Book That Transforms Nations*; Agang, Foster, and Hendriks, *African Public Theology*.

94. See Mangalwadi, *Truth and Transformation*.

95. Gene Edward Veith Jr., *Postmodern Times: A Christian Guide to Contemporary Thought and Culture* (Crossway Books, 1994), 16.

Women sponsored his ministry (Luke 8:1–3). Therefore, the church must be the loudest voice in denouncing gender inequality and promoting the dignity of women because they share equal standing with men before God.

Fourth, like Jesus the church must lead the way in fighting abject poverty and hunger. Because the wicked and corrupt leaders use poverty as a powerful tool to cause unrest in society for their own selfish advantage, the church must empower members economically so that they escape the trap of corrupt leaders.

Fifth, Jesus healed the sick. Because one major challenge in many parts of Africa is the failure of governments to provide stable health-care systems, the church can be the best alternative for health-care delivery that is reliable and affordable. Some Christian missions led the way in providing good health care in many parts of Africa. To keep this legacy for the benefit of church and society, health care may continue to form an integral part of the church's mission today. But apart from conventional health care, genuine faith-based healing ministries—as opposed to health and wealth gospel—could go hand in hand with orthodox health care. And against the secularist mindset that rejects the supernatural and the miraculous, we affirm that God still works miracles of healing the sick.

Sixth, to follow the example of Jesus, the church must denounce the trinity of greed, corruption, and injustice in Africa and be an advocate for the equitable distribution of wealth. Christians cannot afford to join the stealing frenzy in the continent, because they are the models of integrity and contentment. The status quo must be resisted, with the church leading the way in adding value to the society rather than subtracting through stealing and other corrupt practices.

Seventh, as part of opposing oppression, the church must stress human dignity from a Christian perspective. All human beings are made in the image of God, and we are all brothers and sisters in that big umbrella. In this sense, no human being can claim to worship the true God, the Father of all, if he/she refuses to treat those created in the image of God as a brother or sister: "Whoever does not love does not know God, for God is love" (1 John 4:8). A person's relation to the true God determines his/her relation with fellow human beings. True love means doing unto others as we would wish them to do unto us. The opposite of love is hatred. Anyone who hates a fellow human being based on ethnicity or religion or race is not connected with the Creator of all. And until the roots of the barbaric forces of hatred are unearthed and destroyed, hope for a united and progressive Africa is an impossible dream.

Eighth, the church must promote the sacredness of life. Human life is sacred. But human life has become far cheaper than animal life in some parts of Africa, where people are now killed for sport. Against those who teach that killing the perceived enemy is the legitimate duty of the faithful, the church in Africa must denounce such barbarism. That every human life is sacred is nonnegotiable truth. Anyone or any ideology or religion that approves and carries out the dehumanization and killing of fellow human beings in the name of God is to be regarded as the foe. The church must utter her prophetic voice in naming that foe and condemn it in totality until Africa is liberated from the dungeon of sociocultural and religious turmoil.

Ninth, Jesus "came and preached peace to you who were far off and peace to those who were near" (Eph 2:17). Therefore, the church must preach peace and promote "ethnic cooperation, solidarity, participation, and recognition of interdependence"[96] in Africa. If God wanted a monolithic society, we would still have one language as it was in Babel (Gen 11:1). Therefore, rejecting others on the basis of ethnic, racial, and religious affiliation does not tally with God's ideal for humanity and the complex matrices of human diversity. A monolithic society neither agrees with the Creator's plan nor the concept of a global village in which we all have a stake.

Conclusion

The gospel of Christ remains "the power of God for salvation to everyone who has faith" (Rom 1:16). From Jesus's mission statement in Luke 4:18, 19, the good news of salvation is holistic, transforming the sociocultural and religious realities of the world. Like the parable of the mustard seed (Mark 4:30–32), the gospel spread as light shining in the darkness from Palestine to the rest of the world. With hindsight, it becomes clear that the gospel transformed many of Africa's sociocultural and religious realities including salvation, family life, education, health care, economy, the dignity of human life, and more. But looking ahead, there remain unconquered grounds and dark spots, such as neocolonialism, political instability, divisive ethnicity, ethno-religious crises, gender inequality, poverty and diseases, power encounters, injustice, corruption, human rights violations, and environmental degradation. As the embodiment of the gospel of light that shines in the darkness, the church in Africa must shine her light on these rather dark spots. Proclaiming the gospel of light that transforms the world is a vital aspect of fighting the good fight of the faith (1 Tim 1:18; 6:12; 2 Tim 4:7).

Therefore, shining the light on Africa's sociocultural and religious landscape means that the church in Africa must be bold to name and fight the foe that is responsible for the realities above. After all, to carry the cross of Jesus also means denouncing social vices. As light penetrating through the darkness, the church must assert that the foe of the African continent is the one who oppresses, marginalizes, kills, and destroys under the cover of religion or ethnic kinship. The enemy is the one who destroys freedom of worship and forces conversion on others (John 10:10). The enemy is the one who degrades women, assigning them lower status than men. The enemy is the one who promotes injustice, corruption, and human rights violations. The enemy is the one who destroys education and promotes illiteracy so that they remain on the highest rung of social stratification while the rest remain subservient. These are the foes all sensible people must fight. For there can be no true nation-building in the atmosphere of discrimination, marginalization, antagonism, and destruction. The church must denounce ethnic prejudice and every form of disunity. Instead, the church in every African country is to promote peaceful coexistence and integration among her members as an example for the world to follow. The church must be different if she is to make a difference in the world. If the church discriminates against people based on tribal or ethnic or racial sentiments, she has no

96. Sunday Bobai Agang, *Impact of Ethnic, Political, and Religious Violence in Nigeria, and a Theological Reflection on Its Healing* (Langham Monographs, 2011), 244.

moral right to accuse the world and endangers her witness to the world about the mission of Christ (John 17:22, 23).

We conclude with this rather bold declaration that the church in Africa, acting as salt and light, is best positioned for the onerous but vital task of transforming the sociocultural and religious landscape of the African continent through the gospel of Christ that offers life in abundance.

Further Reading

Elischer, Sebastian. *Political Parties in Africa: Ethnicity and Party Formation*. Cambridge University Press, 2009.

Grant, Jamie A., and Dewi A. Hughes, eds. *Transforming the World? The Gospel and Social Responsibility*. Apollos, 2009

Hope, Kempe Ronald, Sr., and Bornwell C. Chikulo. *Corruption and Development in Africa: Lessons from Country Case-Studies*. Macmillan Press, 2000.

Ijatuyi-Morphé, Randee. *Africa's Social and Religious Quest: A Comprehensive Survey and Analysis of the African Situation*. Kindle edition. University Press of America, 2014.

Katongole, Emmanuel. *The Sacrifice of Africa: A Political Theology for Africa*. Eerdmans, 2011.

Kirk, J. Andrew. *Civilizations in Conflict: Islam, the West and Christian Faith*. Regnum Books, 2011

Levee, Adriane. "Inside Out: Jethro, the Midianites and a Biblical Construction of the Outsider." *Journal for the Study of the Old Testament* 34, no. 4 (2009): 395–417.

Mangalwadi, Vishal. *Truth and Transformation: A Manifesto for Ailing Nations*. YWAM Publishing, 2009.

Moyo, Dambisa. *Dead Aid: Why Aid Is Not Working and How There Is a Better Way for Africa*. Farrar, Straus and Giroux, 2009.

Sarma, Bitrus A. *Drums of Redemption: A New Testament Theology for Africa*. HippoBooks, 2023.

Senior, Ian. *Corruption—the World's Big C Cases: Causes, Consequences, Cures*. The Institute of Economic Affairs, 2000.

Skofield, Ellis. *Religious Battle Behind the Headlines: Islam in the End Times*. Fish House Publishing, 2007.

Sookhdeo, Patrick. *Dawa: The Islamic Strategy for Reshaping the World*. Isaac Publishing, 2014.

Sookhdeo, Patrick. *Unmasking Islamic State: Revealing their Motivation, Theology and End Time Predictions*. Isaac Publishing, 2015.

Yew, Kuan Lee. *From the Third World to First: Singapore and the Asian Economic Boom*. HarperCollins Publishers, 2011.

CHAPTER TWO

An Introduction to African Biblical Hermeneutics

Elizabeth W. Mburu
Africa International University
Langham Partnership
Nairobi, Kenya

Introduction

HERMENEUTICS IS THE art and science of interpretation. This implies a critical reflection on processes of interpretation and understanding. Biblical hermeneutics has as its goal both the determination of what the biblical text means as well as its contemporary significance. This chapter will cover the motivating factors for Africentric approaches, assumptions, and common characteristics, give a brief overview of Africentric approaches currently in use, provide a closer look at one of these approaches, including two sample texts, and finally conclude with the contribution of Africentric approaches.

Biblical hermeneutics has a long and rich history, beginning with the Levites who assisted Ezra the Scribe (cf. Neh 8:8). Several important early figures in Northern Africa, including Philo, Clement, Origen, and Augustine, also laid a foundation for interpreting the Bible. The history of hermeneutics reveals that the various approaches emphasize different aspects on the continuum of author, text, and reader, or the worlds behind, of, and in front of the text.

It is now certain that all interpretation carries with it a certain ideology or ideologies. Thus, reading from a position of neutrality is impossible. Moreover, given that the Bible is both a literary and a spiritual document, the authors were themselves theologically motivated as they wrote. Thus, ideologies in the text itself as well as from the biblical authors is to be expected. African readers of the Bible often use methods of interpretation that have come from the Minority world. Most Africans are not aware that they are not adopting a "neutral" reading, but a contextual one. This does not imply that readings from the Minority world are to be discarded completely. It simply suggests that readings from the Majority world, that use hermeneutical techniques that consider the worlds behind, of, and in front of the text, are also valid. Like pieces of a jigsaw puzzle, different contextual readings contribute to form a more holistic picture of the biblical text. Africentric approaches are therefore not only valuable but also necessary.[1]

1. For a fuller discussion of Africentric approaches see Elizabeth Mburu, "African Hermeneutics," in *Handbook of Postconservative Theological Interpretation*, ed. Ronald T. Michener and Mark A. Lamport (Cascade Books; Wipf & Stock, 2024), 414–428.

Motivation for Africentric Approaches

The first motivation for Africentric approaches is linked to the rapid growth of the church in Africa. There are now more Christians in Africa (approximately 718 million) than anywhere else in the world. In fact, a Pew Research study predicts that four out of ten Christians will live in Africa by 2060. There is an explosion in the number of denominations and physical church buildings, including mega-churches.[2] The Christian culture is also evident in other ways, such as biblical verses on public transportation and businesses, as well as prayer in the public space. This unanticipated growth has come in four waves. The first wave was the North African and Ethiopian Christianity, which can be traced to the first and fourth centuries respectively. The second wave was the Christianity that accompanied the Portuguese sailors and explorers, beginning in the fifteenth century with Henry the Explorer's European "discovery" of Africa. This came alongside trade, notably trade in African slaves. This would ultimately become a big problem for the spread of the gospel. Up to this period, the view of Christianity as a theocracy had been dominant, either as Protestant nationalism or Catholic Christendom. This would change with the third wave.[3] The third wave, which is sometimes referred to as the modern missionary movement, took place from the eighteenth into the early twentieth century. This wave was birthed from the Great Awakenings in Britain and America, which emphasized "personal conversion and private citizenship in heaven rather than Christendom or Christian nationalism."[4] No Christian witness is neutral and thus hermeneutical approaches that were influenced by the Enlightenment project also found their way to Africa in this third wave. The fourth, and perhaps the most significant, wave is that of the Indigenous church movement which began in the early twentieth century and continues into the twenty-first century. This wave has resulted in the growth of African Initiated Churches, as well as hermeneutical approaches that aim to make the Bible more relevant. These approaches seriously consider the African culture.

A second motivation is the challenges that are linked to this unprecedented growth. Dichotomy, experienced in false teachings and syncretism, has eroded the interpretation that is received and applied by many Christians. For instance, the fastest growing indigenous denomination in Africa today is Neo-Pentecostalism. Neo-Pentecostalism, which has an over-emphasis on power encounters, deliverance from ancestral and other curses, signs and wonders, as well as an emphasis on objects believed to have power, is very attractive.[5] Biblical texts are often skewed, both in interpretation and in application. Moreover, both positive

2. Yomi Kazeem, "Africa Is Set to Be the Global Center of Christianity for the Next 50 Years," Quartz, April 4, 2019, https://qz.com/africa/1587317/how-many-christians-live-in-africa.

3. Mark Shaw and Wanjiru Gitau, *The Kingdom of God in Africa: A History of African Christianity*, rev. and updated (Langham Global Library, 2020), 141.

4. Shaw and Gitau, *The Kingdom of God in Africa*, 140.

5. Matthews A. Ojo, "An Overview of the History of Neo-Pentecostalism in Africa," in *The Abandoned Gospel: Confronting Neo-Pentecostalism and the Prosperity Gospel in Sub-Saharan Africa*, ed. Philip W. Barnes, Bazil Bhasera, Matthews A. Ojo, Jack Rantho, Trevor Yoakum, and Misheck Zulu (AB316, 2021), 19.

and negative aspects of the African worldview(s) are often incorporated uncritically in the process of interpretation.

Syncretism also contributes to this dichotomy. Just as the early church in Africa battled inconsistences, the church in Africa today is confronted by religious syncretism with African Traditional Religions. This is encouraged by a desire to find African identity, which was unfortunately eroded by the colonial-missionary enterprise. Thus, the question, "What does it mean to be Christian and African?" is a difficult one to answer in our constantly evolving contexts. As Mark Shaw and Wanjiru Gitau accurately note, "Despite this explosive shift in Christianity's demographic center, millions of Africans still struggle with what it means to be both African and Christian. Part of the wrestling match has been over the foreignness of Christianity in Africa."[6] This dichotomy is exacerbated by a general lack of discipleship and ignorance of correct doctrine. Africentric approaches are the most suitable way to counteract the growing dichotomy so that an identity that is consistent with the biblical metanarrative emerges.

A third motivation for Africentric approaches is the elimination of the double hermeneutical gap. Most African readers of the Bible experience a double hermeneutical gap when attempting to interpret the biblical text. This occurs when an African reader first attempts to understand the assumptions and worldview(s) underlying methods from the Minority world before entering into the worldview(s) of the biblical text. The biblical authors intended to communicate a message to their original readers, which they passed on in the language and thought-forms of their time. This is the principle of authorial intent. While diachronicity implies that language changes over time, and synchronicity alerts us to the socially conditioned nature of language, unearthing this message is possible. Contextual approaches are therefore important because they address the readers from a position of familiarity as well as relevance. Familiarity is enhanced by the fact that the worldviews represented in the biblical text more closely approximate African worldviews in several aspects. This eliminates the double hermeneutical gap. At the same time, the alterity or "otherness" of the biblical text must be respected and embraced. An African reader of the biblical text should not merely reframe approaches from the Majority world, but should try to conceptualize the text from an Africentric perspective.

Assumptions of Africentric Hermeneutics

Hermeneutics is not static but dynamic and the methods we use must have a theoretical foundation as well as a practical application. This, together with the understanding that neutrality in reading does not exist, implies that all hermeneutics is contextual. After all, readers come to the different texts with their assumptions. To illustrate this, take the story of the tortoise and the hare that is common in many parts of the world. Tortoise challenges hare to a race and naturally nobody expects him to win. However, what he does is to recruit his relatives and place them strategically along the path of the race. Each one jumps out of the bush ahead of hare

6. Shaw and Gitau, *The Kingdom of God in Africa*, 2.

in sequence as the one behind him hides to avoid being seen. At the end of the race, tortoise is the undisputed winner.

Without knowing which rules to apply, or "how to read," one might misunderstand this story to be a criticism of tortoise's deception. Audiences from the Minority world generally arrive at this interpretation. But this story actually teaches that cooperation is necessary in society. It is also a story that emphasizes the importance of honor in an honor/shame culture. It "is an appeal to a higher moral ethic, and that ethic is that a family must work together in unity to see that disgrace never comes to it."[7] Our contextual situatedness leads us to different ways of reading this story. Contextual rereadings are valid because they reveal insights and perspectives we might not otherwise see.

The aim of Africentric hermeneutics is to "decolonize" hermeneutics and separate it from the assumptions of the Minority world. Thus, it tends to be liberational and against the colonial missionary enterprise. It has several common assumptions.

The Bible as Sacred and Powerful

The belief that the Bible is sacred and powerful[8] implies that it is reliable, it can be trusted, it is ultimate truth, and that it was transmitted faithfully. For most Africans, the Bible is a text that they believe embodies power in that it is both, as Gerald West accurately points out, "a tactile object of power and a text of power."[9] It is indeed a living Word, capable of confronting us where we most need it. Africentric approaches recognize that the Bible speaks powerfully into the present. Since the Bible is both a sacred and powerful object and text, it is generally taken at face value. While this is positive, it is sometimes used in the wrong way, much like Christian objects such as crosses and anointing oil, as well as other objects such as handkerchiefs, and so on, are used. These are believed to have power in themselves to bring about healing and/or deliverance, and are therefore used as amulets, fetishes, and talismans. Imprecatory prayers, taken straight from the biblical text, are also believed to have power to change situations.

Faith in God

Interpretation of the Bible in Africa is generally not divorced from faith. Most hermeneutical approaches tend to be confessional not only because of the belief in the sacred nature of the biblical text, but also because of their view of ultimate reality. God plays a significant role in the daily lives of believers. This often stems from the African conception of the Supreme

7. "The Tortoise and the Hare: West African Storytelling, Part I," The Buchele Adventure, January 16, 2008, http://buchele.blogspot.com/2008/01/tortoise-and-hare-african-storytelling.html.

8. For this and the following assumptions, see list in Mburu, "African Hermeneutics," 416.

9. Gerald O. West, "Indigenous Biblical Hermeneutics: Voicing Continuity and Distinctiveness," in *Postcolonial Perspectives in African Biblical Interpretations*, ed. Musa W. Dube, Andrew M. Mbuvi, and Dora Mbuwayesango (Society of Biblical Literature, 2012), 87.

Being, who holds ultimate power over all creation. In actual practice, the spiritual nature of the text is elevated above its historical and literary nature. Because of this, the text is generally approached with trust rather than suspicion, although there are some approaches (as noted below) that employ a hermeneutic of suspicion.

The Holy Spirit as Actively Involved in the Process of Interpretation

Most Africentric approaches hold that the Holy Spirit illumines truth. The Holy Spirit in Africa is generally understood through the lens of dynamism, power encounters, and holism. This paves the way for experiencing the Holy Spirit as a real and powerful entity that is alive and active in the personal lives of believers as well as in the community of faith.[10] Given the view of the Bible as sacred and powerful, no interpretation can be done without the aid of the Holy Spirit. While this is positive and indeed necessary, this may lead to incorrect interpretation because the spiritual aspect is often elevated above the historical and literary. There is also no way to check one's interpretation because one cannot argue with another person's interpretation as long as the Holy Spirit has "confirmed" it. Interpretation may tend to be overly subjective.

The Bible as Functional

Africentric approaches generally emphasize the importance of the sociocultural, political, economic, and religious contexts of the African reader. The word of God is indeed God's unchanging truth and norm for every believer. But how that truth is communicated and understood is not the same in every culture. In other words, these approaches focus on how the text speaks to concrete, contextual realities being experienced by the African people. Functionality implies that the Bible is no longer a foreign object that has been imposed on Africans, but rather a relevant text that allows us to engage in constructive dialogue and find relevant application points.

Common Characteristics of Africentric Hermeneutics

Ideological Orientation

As noted above, all interpretation carries with it a certain ideology or ideologies. Neutrality in hermeneutics, which is one of the negative implications of the Enlightenment, is a myth. Some Africentric approaches engage the text from a position of suspicion. Postcolonial and feminist/womanist approaches in particular hold that there are many conflicting ideologies in the Bible and that some of them are oppressive and should therefore be rejected. However, other Africentric approaches employ a hermeneutic of trust and assign ultimate authority to the Bible. What they all hold in common is that the concrete context of the reader is important and represents the position from which the texts are read.

10. See chapter 6 in this volume on the Gospel of John.

Importance of the World in Front of the Text

All Africentric approaches recognize the importance of the world in front of the text and are thus guided by several contextual concerns, including social, cultural, religious, political, and economic concerns. They recognize that hermeneutics is not just theoretical but also includes general principles and methods implicit in practices of interpretation.[11] They therefore promote understanding and interrogation of African contexts.

Interpretation Is Functional

These approaches view hermeneutics not just as an exercise confined to the academic/intellectual sphere, but as having a transformative impact on individuals and societies. Because it includes ordinary readers at the grassroots level it also includes oral hermeneutical reflection.[12] Thus, hermeneutical principles and practices can be seen in worship, prayer, and preaching.

Decolonizing Approach

As noted above, the aim of these approaches is to decolonize hermeneutics; that is, separating the task of hermeneutics from Minority world assumptions and recognizing that Africentric assumptions are valid. It is providing complementary readings of the same text while at the same time challenging so called "normative" readings. In essence, these approaches conceptualize the process of hermeneutics through contextual lenses. Assumptions from the Minority world, while not monolithic, may include linear reasoning, a greater dependence on scientific methods and therefore more emphasis on neutrality, a more individualistic approach to understanding and representing texts, an anti-spiritualist approach, and a more fragmented view of reality (as opposed to African holism). The goal is to show the relevance of the text to an African audience by bypassing what we have previously been shown through non-Africentric approaches. It is to show that interpretations from the Minority world are not necessarily normative for all cultures and peoples.

Brief Overview of Current Trends

There are several Africentric approaches currently in use in Africa. These approaches are contextual in that they recognize the importance of the African culture and worldview in biblical interpretation, engage the sociocultural, economic, political, and religious backgrounds of the readers, and bring the biblical text to life because, after all, the Bible is meant to be relevant to our everyday situations. These approaches emphasize, in their own ways, a three-way

11. Benno Van den Toren, Elizabeth Mburu, and Samuel Bussey, "Biblical Hermeneutics," in *The Bibliographical Encyclopaedia of African Theology*, January 29, 2021, https://african.theologyworldwide.com/encyclopaedia-bible-in-africa/biblical-hermeneutics.

12. Van den Toren, Mburu, and Bussey, "Biblical Hermeneutics."

dialogue between the worlds behind, of, and in front of the text. As Mbiti accurately noted as early as 1971,

> we have to sing the Gospel in our tunes, set to our music, played on our instruments. I speak metaphorically. We must drum it out with our great drums, on our tom-toms, on our waist-shaped drums, for only these can vibrate and awaken entire villages: the violin is too feeble to awaken the sleeping pagans of our society.[13]

This dialogue therefore removes the barriers that have resulted in many wrongly seeing Christianity as "a white man's religion" and allows Christian Africans to forge an identity that mirrors that of Jesus Christ himself.

The following approaches are from African Theology Worldwide's *Bibliographical Encyclopedia of African Theology*.[14]

1. Ethiopian Hermeneutics. This is based on the *Andemta*, which includes translation and commentary in Amharic on the Bible and related literature written in Ge'ez. It is "an Ethiopian interpretive tradition that comments on biblical texts and patristic writings."[15]
2. African Independent Hermeneutics. Scripture is understood as directly related to the challenges facing Christian Africans and its authority is combined with the authority accorded to African traditions. The physical Bible is itself an object of power.
3. Liberation and Black Hermeneutics. Liberation hermeneutics is characterized by the sequence of see-judge-act in which the understanding of the meaning of the Scriptures begins with an understanding of the context, particularly the realities of oppression and injustice. Epistemological privilege is granted to the poor/oppressed. The book of Exodus is the central focus in exegesis. Black hermeneutics is similar to North American Black theology. It originated in the South African apartheid context of an oppressed majority.
4. Feminist/Womanist Hermeneutics. This focuses on the struggle against the subordination of women in contemporary society, ecclesial, and familial roles.
5. Contextual Bible Study. This foregrounds the role of the ordinary, non-academically trained Bible reader and specifically the reading of Scripture with marginalized communities.

---

13. John S. Mbiti, *The Crisis of Mission in Africa* (Uganda Church Press, 1971), 5.

14. See https://african.theologyworldwide.com/encyclopaedia. For a fuller discussion, see Van den Toren, Mburu, and Bussey, "Biblical Hermeneutics."

15. Abeneazer G. Urga, "Why Did Paul Write Hebrews? Reasons for the Composition of Hebrews in the Ethiopian Orthodox *Tewahido* Church's *Andemta* Commentary Tradition," in *Reading Hebrews and 1 Peter from Majority World Perspectives*, LNTS, ed. Sofanit T. Abebe, Elizabeth W. Mburu, and Abeneazer G. Urga (T&T Clark, 2024), 8.

6. Pentecostal Hermeneutics. This provides a new method of interpretation that is founded on an understanding of the role of the Holy Spirit and the contemporary church in the process of interpretation.
7. Reconstruction Hermeneutics. This emphasizes the interpretation of the Scriptures in the light of political, social, and economic realities. However, the focus is no longer on the fight against the oppressors, but on the collaborative and inclusive task of reconstruction. Rather than Exodus, Deuteronomy, Nehemiah, and the Sermon on the Mount take center stage in biblical interpretation.
8. Postcolonial Hermeneutics. This analyses how literary texts themselves are shaped by "imperialism" and how the subjugated voices of the oppressed can be retrieved.
9. Mother Tongue Hermeneutics. This uses Indigenous language translations of the Bible as resources for interpretation. It focuses on the world in front of the text and is a collaborative, communal task.
10. Inculturation and Intercultural Hermeneutics. These are very similar. Inculturation hermeneutics is a contextual, interdisciplinary hermeneutic that explicitly makes the African context the subject of interpretation. Its goal is sociocultural transformation and its ethos is cultural diversity and identity in reading practices. This method is generally used by Catholic theologians. Intercultural hermeneutics evolved from inculturation hermeneutics. The major development is that while inculturation hermeneutics focuses on the incarnation of the gospel in a culture and the evangelization of that culture, intercultural hermeneutics consolidates a constructive dialogue between the biblical and the African cultures.

Africentric approaches, while valuable, also have several weaknesses.[16] First, they may encourage syncretism. Second, some of the approaches above make the world in front of the text more important than the world of the text and, in many instances, ignore the world behind the text. This is dangerous because the reader runs the risk of imposing meaning on the text. Third, there is the risk of collapsing the two horizons of meaning (that which was intended by the biblical author and significance for the modern reader). Fourth, there is the risk of a canon within a canon. Some Africentric approaches tend to focus solely on specific texts that lend themselves readily to such approaches.

Contextual theologizing is vital for the healthy growth of Christian identity but finding the right balance between contextual relevance and biblical integrity is admittedly a challenge. The contextual approach below factors in the two-sided nature of historical conditioning, namely both the text and the reader stand in two different historical and cultural contexts.

16. See Mburu, "African Hermeneutics," 419.

A Closer Look at an African Hermeneutic

The poem, "The Blind Men and the Elephant," by Godfrey Saxe is a familiar one. Just as the blind men had different perspectives on what they were touching, so too, Africentric approaches such as the one described below provide another perspective on the biblical text. The result is clarity, rather than the confusion which inevitably occurs when Africans are fed a diet of foreign perspectives.

The Four-Legged Stool[17]

There is a growing recognition in African theological circles that one of the reasons we experience dichotomy in our Christian lives is due to a failure to interrogate our cultures and worldviews, thus importing them indiscriminately into our doctrine and practice. This is the premise behind the Four-Legged Stool approach. It is an intercultural hermeneutic. J. G. Van der Watt summarizes intercultural or inculturation approaches not as "a matter of understanding the text primarily within its original context, but understanding the text within the present context of the readers within their reading processes—the text *must* address the reader."[18]

Theoretical Framework

With regards to its theoretical framework, the Four-Legged Stool approach:

1. is an intercultural model that encourages a dialogue between the African context and the biblical context. It focuses on religio-cultural dimensions;
2. is based on the concept of moving from the known to the unknown. It recognizes that parallels between biblical and African cultures and worldviews can be used as bridges to promote understanding, internalization, and application of the biblical text. It is similar to what Jesus and Paul did. Acts 17, Paul's Areopagus speech, is foundational for this approach as it provides a model for how to engage with cultures and worldviews;
3. includes an interrogation of assumptions. It is understood that because readers approach the text from their contextual situatedness, they come with their assumptions. While our assumptions may sometimes aid us in reading the text, we sometimes import them into the text with negative results. At the same time, the various methods that we use in hermeneutics are also based on certain assumptions that must be interrogated;
4. recognizes that African cultures (material and nonmaterial) are a significant tool for the interpretive process. However, this approach goes further by considering the worldviews represented by the reader;

17. Elizabeth Mburu, *African Hermeneutics* (HippoBooks, 2019), 65–89.

18. J. G. Van der Watt, "Johannine Research in Africa, Part 1: An Analytical Survey," *In die Skriflig* 49, no. 2 (2015): 1–14, here 3, emphasis in original.

5. is also similar to some approaches from the Minority world in that it recognizes the value of the theological, literary, and historical contexts of the text. It strives to provide a balanced reading of texts and therefore complements rather than replaces these approaches. However, while there may be some overlap with categories traditionally ascribed to Minority world approaches, the conceptualization of these categories is based on African assumptions;
6. is a three-way dialogue between the "world behind the text," "the world of the text," and "the world in front of the text." Consequently, this approach does not collapse these three worlds. All three stand in a context that must be interrogated. This approach therefore "makes a distinction between meaning (as intended for the original readers) and significance (as applied to the modern reader)."[19]

Steps in the Four-Legged Stool

This approach has five steps which include four legs and the seat. These are parallels to the African context, theological context, literary context, historical context, and application. The legs are not independent of each other and as we gain more information, our assumptions about the text change and our understanding grows.

The first leg primarily involves identifying parallels between the African and the biblical contexts. It is a bridge that allows us to begin to understand the biblical text from a familiar position and to interrogate our assumptions so that we can begin to correct any faulty assumptions that may hinder the interpretive process. This bridge therefore defines the scope or the boundaries within which meaning may be sought. It also guides us in formulating contextually relevant questions of the text. Because of the two-sided nature of historical conditioning, this inter-dynamic process guides us in identifying both points of contact as well as differences with the biblical context. Only when we encourage dialogue between the African and the biblical worldviews, can we determine what is negotiable and what is nonnegotiable. This will help us develop a truly biblical worldview while at the same time retain what is uniquely African.

The second leg is the theological context. While the African approach is holistic, the spiritual dimension of life is more often than not a factor in an African's interaction with the realities around him/her them. This implies that, in Africa, biblical hermeneutics is inseparable from theological reflection, as the emphasis is generally to address contextual realities within our society. Even though the Bible is a literary work, it is primarily a spiritual document. An understanding of the biblical-theological emphases of the text therefore provides the foundational data for the reader, orienting their approach to the interpretation of the text and determining the theological boundaries within which meaning may be sought.

The third leg is the literary context. It defines the boundaries of textual meaning. This is where African cultural resources are incorporated to provide interpretive techniques from

19. Mburu, *African Hermeneutics*, 85.

African oral literature. Here one identifies the genre, literary techniques, language (including lexical, grammatical, and syntactical issues), and the progression of the text as it unfolds, as well as in relation to surrounding texts.

The fourth leg is the historical context. In addition to theological and literary concerns, Africans try to make sense of their lives in relation to the historical and cultural contexts in which events occur. This means that "behind the text" issues provide crucial data in the interpretive process. If authorial intent and determinacy of textual meaning is to be taken seriously, we must respect the alterity or "otherness" of the text.

The final step is the seat, which is where we derive significance. The important feature of meaning as distinct from significance is that meaning (as "boundaries of meaning") is the determinate representation of a text for an interpreter. Significance, on the other hand, is the application to the context of the listener. Here one must deculturize the message, that is separate it from the cultural form in which it is communicated, and express it in terms that we understand in our own African society, as well as distinguish between transcontextual and culture-bound truths.[20]

Application to Sample Texts in the New Testament

Sample Text 1
Narrative (Mark 5:1–20 Healing of the Gerasene Demoniac)

Background

The Gospel of Mark is one of the Synoptic Gospels. It therefore has many similarities with both Matthew and Luke, as well as some differences. Recent scholarship suggests that Mark was the first to put the good news of God's salvation into written form. It is likely that both Matthew and Luke used Mark's Gospel as a basis for their own accounts. This is probably the most relatable gospel for Africans. It is about identity, authority and power, and suffering.[21]

Mark tells a compelling story that artfully unveils who Jesus is, as well as the basis and right understanding of his authority and power. Mark presents us with a Jesus who is relatable in every way and disciples who have weaknesses, just like we do. At the same time, the undeniable power and authority that Jesus demonstrates in every chapter of this fascinating account leave no doubt that Jesus is indeed "the Messiah, the Son of God" (1:1). Mark's Gospel helps us understand the perfect balance between Jesus's divinity and his humanity.

---

20. Adapted with some changes from Seto's model on contextualizing in the Asian society, Wing Luk Seto, "An Asian Looks at Contextualization and Developing Ethnotheologies," *Evangelical Missions Quarterly* 23 (April 1987): 138.

21. For a fuller analysis of the Gospel of Mark see Elizabeth Mburu, "Mark," in *Africa Bible Commentary* (HippoBooks, forthcoming 2025).

Leg 1

Parallels to the African Context

The first parallel is the worldview of holism, which argues that life is integrated. There are no distinctions between the physical and spiritual dimensions of life.[22] In the traditional African worldview, there was no dichotomy existing between faith and nature, between the secular and the sacred, because all of reality was governed by a law of harmony.[23] In other words, there is no separate spiritual and physical reality—there is only one reality. God, the spirits, ancestors, human beings, and objects all live in one world. The African worldview of holism helps us relate to the existence of evil spirits that is found in this text.

The second parallel is the worldview of dynamism. The spirit world is viewed as impersonal, unseen, and unpredictable. The worldview of dynamism argues that those who can manipulate this spirit realm have power to control their lives. The increasing emphasis on demonic oppression, spiritual warfare, healing, and deliverance activities is evidence of the worldview of dynamism at work. Again, this worldview helps us relate to the specific circumstances of demonic oppression and exorcism in this text.

Leg 2

Theological Context

The major theological emphasis in this story is that Jesus is the miracle-working, authoritative Son of God who has authority and power over the natural and spiritual realms. This is the theme that holds this gospel together. There are strategic references to Jesus being the Son of God in various places (1:1, 11, 25, 34; 3:11, 12; 5:7; 9:7; 14:61–62; 15:39). In fact, the Gospel of Mark begins with this theme and ends with it. The author frames his narrative theologically in terms of Jesus being the Son of God. This is no coincidence since Mark's audience was the church in Rome. We know that around that time the Roman emperors were beginning to insist that they be referred to as gods. The Roman context reveals that it was generally believed that Roman emperors, like Vespasian, were divine and could heal.[24] The right understanding of this theological theme allows us to understand this story in the way the author intended. It is meant to challenge the Roman belief in the divinity of emperors. Mark therefore turns his readers' attention away from these false gods to the true Son of God who has authority over the spiritual realm. This theological grid should guide our interpretation.

Leg 3

Literary Context

The events that Mark records revolve around Jesus and therefore reflect that his teachings and miracles happened in a particular historical situation (the life situation of Jesus or *sitz im*

22. Yusufu Turaki, *Engaging Religions and Worldviews in Africa: A Christian Theological Method* (HippoBooks, 2020), 141.

23. Yusufu Turaki, *Foundations of African Traditional Religion and Worldview* (WordAlive Publishers, 2006), 33.

24. Craig A. Evans, "Mark," in *New Dictionary of Biblical Theology*, ed. T. Desmond Alexander, Brian S. Rosner, D. A. Carson, and Graeme Goldsworthy (Intervarsity Press, 2000), 272.

leben Jesu). At the same time, Mark wrote at a much later date and adapted the material for a different historical context (the life situation of the church or the *sitz im leben der Kirche*). One must always consider these two layers in interpretation by first understanding the message to Jesus's audience before moving on to Mark's message for his readers.

There are certain principles that apply in analyzing narratives. A key element is that they involve two distinct but interconnected worlds. There is the world of the narrator and listener (the agents of communication), and the world within the story itself. In interpreting stories, one must understand how these two worlds function and interact to communicate the meaning of the story. Both help to move the story forward to its conclusion. Within the world of the story we have elements such as the plot, setting, style (i.e., repetition, interplay of narration and dialogue, vividness and figurative language), narrative time, and characterization.

The World of the Agents of Communication

Like the other gospels, the Gospel of Mark is anonymous. However, church tradition attributes authorship to Mark, also known as John Mark. Mark was regarded by Peter as his son (1 Pet 5:13) and was an associate of Paul (cf. Acts 12:12, 25; 13:13; 15:37–39; Phlm 24; Col 4:10; 2 Tim 4:11). It is not certain whether he was the young man that fled naked (14:51–52). The first person to identify Mark as the author was Papias, Bishop of Hierapolis (*Interpretation of the Lord's Sayings*, 120/130 CE).[25] Mark himself was not an eyewitness of the events but had Peter as his source and patterned his gospel after Peter's preaching (e.g., Acts 10:36–41). At the same time, it is likely that he had other sources (oral and written) and he also imposed his own style on his work.

Most scholars agree that this gospel was written between 65 and 75 CE but, beyond that, arriving at a specific date has proven difficult given that there are no specific historical events mentioned in the Gospel itself that point to a particular date. Two major factors are considered when arriving at this dating.[26] The first is the context of persecution (e.g., 8:34–38; 10:38–40) which places the Gospel during the time of Nero and after the death of Peter (64–65 CE). Nero was a Roman emperor who promoted his own deification although it was denied at his death by the Senate. He encouraged the use of such titles as "god," "son of god," "lord," "savior," and "benefactor." The second is the Jewish revolt against Rome with the subsequent fall of Jerusalem mentioned in 13:3–37 (66–70 CE) and the last resistance at Masada (73/74 CE). For those who argue against a context of Neronian persecution, 63 or 64 CE has been proposed. However, lack of a precise date does not affect interpretation.

Where did Mark write his gospel? Suggested places include Galilee, the Decapolis, Tyre, Sidon, Syria, the East, Rome, and even Egypt. The Gospel itself provides no clues, but given the relationship between Mark and Peter, tradition associates it with Rome. This might explain why Mark needed to interpret Aramaic expressions (3:17; 5:41; 7:11, 34; 14:36) and Jewish

25. Robert A. Guelich, "Mark, Gospel of," in *Dictionary of Jesus and the Gospels*, ed. Joel B. Green and Scot McKnight (Intervarsity Press, 1992), 514.

26. James A. Brooks, *Mark*, NAC 23 (Broadman Press, 1991), 28.

laws and customs for his audience (e.g., 7:3–5; 14:12; 15:42). The Latinisms (e.g., 12:42; 15:16) may also support Rome, although it must be pointed out that Latin was also spoken outside of Italy and many of the expressions are technical or military terms.[27] Much like the issue of dating, lack of a precise place does not affect interpretation of this gospel.

As with the date and place, it is difficult to determine the destination of this gospel. What is clear from the text is that the audience was unfamiliar with certain forms of Judaism. They were most likely gentiles in Rome. Of all the Gospels, only Mark mentions that Simon of Cyrene was "the father of Alexander and Rufus," evidently well known in Rome (15:12; cf. Rom 16:13). Additional clues are provided in the way time is measured (6:48; 13:35) and the final confession of Jesus's deity by a Roman centurion (15:39). Roman Christians would have found this gospel particularly appropriate to their situation.

Mark's emphasis on suffering and the cross as a precursor to glory suggests that Mark wrote to reassure a struggling community that discipleship entailed suffering and martyrdom but that they too would be victorious in the end.[28] Beyond this, a more overarching purpose can be seen in 1:1—to write the "gospel concerning Jesus Messiah, Son of God." This statement, which "echoes the language of the imperial cult, as seen in the Priene inscription in honor of Caesar Augustus: 'the birthday of the god Augustus was the beginning for the world of the good news,'" is an effective challenge to the imperial myth.[29]

Whether Mark wrote when the threat of persecution was looming, or during the Neronian persecutions when suffering and martyrdom were rife, or even around the time of the fall of Jerusalem, when the city had been sacked and the temple destroyed, it is clear that life was difficult for the early believers. The church was under threat.

The World of the Story

The world of the story includes the genre, literary techniques, language (including lexical and syntactical issues), and the progression of the text as it unfolds, as well as in relation to surrounding texts. Mark's story is divided into three acts: Act I (The beginning of the Gospel; 1:1–13), Act II (The Ministry of Jesus Christ; 1:14–8:26), and Act III (The Passion of Jesus Christ; 8:27–16:8).

Perhaps one of the best metaphors for understanding the role of genre in interpretation is that proposed by E. D. Hirsch. He suggests that genre should be understood as a game. Just as in a game, there are rules that an author follows in writing and that a reader follows in reading.[30] In the last few decades, there have been numerous debates surrounding the genre of Mark. It has been classified variously as a biography, a Hellenistic aretalogy, an entirely new genre, and even compared to the Old Testament historical narratives. At the

27. William Hendriksen, *Exposition of the Gospel According to Mark*, New Testament Commentary (Baker, 1983), 13.

28. Craig L. Blomberg, *The Historical Reliability of the Gospels* (InterVarsity Press, 2007), 121.

29. Evans, "Mark," 268.

30. E. D. Hirsch, *Validity in Interpretation* (Yale University Press, 1967), 72.

same time, Mark also has differences that set it apart from these classifications. Recent scholarship argues that Mark intended to create a new genre that he called a "gospel."[31] Evidence suggests that the most likely genre is theological biography in the style of Old Testament historical narratives.

Mark identifies the plot of his story in his opening statement. It is the "gospel" or "good news" concerning "Jesus, Messiah and Son of God." This plot unfolds through the proclamation of Jesus through his words and actions as seen through Mark's "eyes" (1:14–15; 8:33). The plot develops through a series of conflicts that center around the failure to recognize Jesus's identity and his rejection by various groups of people.[32] This failure is enhanced by what is popularly known as the "messianic secret." The story of the Gerasene demoniac therefore unfolds within this larger plotline. It has an unexpected twist because impure spirits are the ones that unveil Jesus's identity. In terms of the development of the plot, "this story must be read against the backdrop of the dispute between Jesus and the scribes over his exorcisms in 3:22–27."[33]

The spatial setting of this story is the region of the Gerasenes on the eastern shore of the lake (5:1). In the Gospel of Matthew (8:28), the location of the demoniac is identified as Gadara, which was about thirteen kilometers from the lake. This is probably more accurate. The temporal setting is night, when evil spirits were believed to exercise greatest power. This "sets the stage for ancient readers to feel the suspense of the ensuing conflict."[34]

The style is consistent with the storytelling style in the rest of the Gospel. The story is compact and action packed, with vivid graphic descriptions that draw the readers in. The dialogue in this story allows the characters to speak in their "own" voices. Thus, we are given insight into the ideological mentality of the demons that have inhabited the man for such a long time. The main character in this story is Jesus Christ, whose identity is made clear in 1:1. He is the protagonist or the "hero" in the story. The other leading character is the Gerasene demoniac. Those tending the pigs and the people in the region are side characters. The picture that Mark paints of them is not very positive.

Act II, in which this story is found (1:14–8:26) is action-packed, with stories that focus on the teaching and ministry of Jesus, as well as the calling of the disciples. It places more emphasis on Jesus's miracles, which are a demonstration of his power and authority. It is in this act that Mark also introduces and develops the theme of the growing opposition to Jesus.

---

31. For instance, K. L. Schmidt proposed that the Gospels were a new literary genre altogether. D. A. Carson and Douglas J. Moo, *An Introduction to the New Testament*, rev. ed. (Zondervan, 2005), 113, citing K. L. Schmidt, "Die Stellung der Evangelien in der Allgemeinen Literaturgeschichte," in *ΕΥΧΑΡΙΣΤΗΡΙΟΝ: Studien zur Religion und Literatur des Alten und Neuen Testaments*, ed. K. L. Schmidt, FRLANT 19.2 (Vandenhoeck & Ruprecht, 1923), 59–60.

32. David Rhoads and Donald Michie, *Mark as Story: An Introduction to the Narrative of a Gospel* (Fortress Press, 1982), 73–100.

33. Robert A. Guelich, *Mark 1–8:26*, WBC 34A (Nelson Reference and Electronic, 1989), 287.

34. Craig S. Keener, *The IVP Bible Background Commentary: New Testament*, 2nd ed. (InterVarsity Press, 2014), 139.

Analysis of the Story
Mark 5:1–20

From a setting on the sea (4:31–41), where Jesus demonstrates his power over the physical elements, Mark takes us back to land, to the region of the Gerasenes on the eastern shore of the lake (5:1). It is still night, and in this scene, Jesus and his disciples encounter a demon-possessed man who was living in the tombs. As is the case in many African communities today, Jews regarded tombs as unclean and believed that they were inhabited by demons.[35] Robert Guelich notes that "the scene accentuates the man's condition. Defiled by living among the tombs, himself inhabited by an 'unclean spirit,' he lived in a gentile land marked by its herd of swine."[36] This was therefore an appropriate place for this man to live. The surprising thing about him was his extraordinary strength. Not even chains could confine him! (5:2–4). It was obvious he was in anguish for he was alienated from society and spent nights and days crying out and cutting himself with stones (5:5). All human interventions had failed to deliver him from his torment.

The text does not record the man asking for Jesus's help, but Jesus in his compassion gives it all the same by commanding the impure spirit to leave the man (5:8). Kneeling before Jesus, he acknowledges him as "Ιησοῦ υἱὲ τοῦ θεοῦ τοῦ ὑψίστου" (Jesus, Son of the Most High God). This was a typically gentile expression (5:7; cf. 1:1). The use of this title and the subservient attitude from spirits that could exercise such superhuman strength in a man is further evidence of Jesus's authority and power. It is also another account where impure spirits accurately identify Jesus.

Surprisingly, Jesus asks the impure spirit for his name, which he gives as "Λεγιὼν" (Legion; 5:9). While a legion consisted of about five thousand men in military terms, this figure is probably not literal but hyperbolic. In many church settings in Africa, where demon exorcism is a part of church life, ministers spend hours trying to get demons to identify themselves by name. However, this is not Jesus's usual mode of operation and his approach here is the exception rather than the rule. Since the man has no control over himself, Jesus cannot get to him without first removing the obstacle of the impure spirit.

The impure spirit's request not to be sent out of the area but into a nearby herd of pigs is an acknowledgment that his/their fate lies in his hands (5:12). In ancient times, demons were associated with particular local areas.[37] Some cultures in Africa are familiar with territorial spirits that have power and authority over designated areas. Any move away from these areas will result in a loss of power. Surprisingly, Jesus gives them permission to go into the pigs, which promptly run into the lake and are drowned (5:13).

In the Jewish culture, pigs were considered unclean animals so this detail emphasizes the gentile setting of the story. It is puzzling why Jesus opted to send the demons into the pigs whereas in other exorcisms he doesn't send them into animals. Scholars suggest that the extent of the possession was so great that the man would have been severely harmed as they exited. Or perhaps he wanted the people to see his power through the physical evidence of the

35. Keener, *IVP Bible Background*, 140.

36. Guelich, *Mark 1–8:26*, 287.

37. Keener, *IVP Bible Background*, 140.

expulsion. Set in this context of impurity, the expulsion of the unclean spirit signifies "Jesus' authoritative deliverance in the land of the Gentiles."[38] Jesus's authority and power are thus seen in the demons' subservience to him.

The story has a surprising twist. When the people hear the report and see the evidence of Jesus's mighty work in the demoniac, they are afraid. Rather than welcome Jesus, they plead with him to leave (5:14–17). The reader will recall that this man could not be restrained but now here he was, sitting calmly and in his right mind. The contrast is undeniable. Such a demonstration of power and authority over the forces of evil and about two thousand pigs without a clear understanding of who was yielding it might have been one source of fear. Alternatively, as is the case in many agricultural communities in Africa where livestock is a financial commodity, this would have been a great loss to the owners. Perhaps this is another reason why the people wanted nothing to do with Jesus.

The contrast between the herdsmen and the healed man is clear. He, understandably, seems to have more insight than they do and desires to follow Jesus (5:18). Rather than allow this, Jesus sends him instead as the first missionary in that area and as a participant in his mission (5:19). This is a surprising detail to the reader who has come to expect secrecy surrounding Jesus's miracles. The "messianic secret," or Jesus's command to various characters to keep silent about his identity, is a major motif in Mark's Gospel. The probable reason for the lack of secrecy here is that, unlike the Jews, a primarily gentile audience would not have been likely to understand that it was God that had done these things without it being told to them clearly. They would have attributed it to a magician.[39] Moreover, unlike the miracle-conscious Jews in his own country, the gentiles were not likely to be a political danger and a spiritual hindrance to his mission once they knew who he was.[40]

Although Mark does not tell us whether the people responded positively, they were amazed at his testimony (5:20). The word used, "ἐθαύμαζον," is literally "they were marveling." It is probably an ingressive imperfect which can be translated "they began marveling," with the implication that the action continued.

And, as for the now healed demoniac, he recognized Jesus's cleansing and saving work "and knew himself to be the recipient of God's saving mercy (19). No-one could make such an equation except by the revelation of the Holy Spirit (1 Cor 12:3) and therefore, he was truly a disciple, even if not permitted to follow Jesus literally."[41] Since the people had asked Jesus to leave, he was the only witness left in this area to preach about the kingdom.

Leg 4

Historical Context

The context surrounding ancient exorcism texts reveals that it was standard practice for exorcists to address impure spirits by the names by which they could be subdued. Ancient exorcism

38. Guelich, *Mark 1–8:26*, 283.

39. Keener, *IVP Bible Background*, 140.

40. R. G. Gruenler, "Mark," in *Evangelical Commentary on the Bible*, vol. 3 (Baker Book House, 1995), 774.

41. R. A. Cole, *Mark: An Introduction and Commentary*, vol. 2 (InterVarsity Press, 1989), 158–163.

texts also show that "Ancients were familiar with demons pleading for mercy or other concessions when they were about to be defeated (e.g., **1 Enoch* 12–14; Testament of Solomon 2:6)."[42]

Seat

Application

What is the meaning of the text for Mark's original readers? Although the first few chapters focused on a primarily Jewish audience, this account reveals that Jesus's mission is universal (cf. 7:24). Even gentiles can be the beneficiaries of his salvific ministry as its impact begins to be felt amongst the gentiles in its spread to the region of the Decapolis, a concentration of ten Hellenistic cities. This account reminds the reader of the establishment of God's sovereign rule through Jesus, demonstrated in the parable of the binding of the strong man (3:27).

What about its application for African readers today? As the miracle-working son of God who has power over the spiritual realm, believers can live in freedom, recognizing that demonic oppression has no power in their lives. The belief in dynamism that undergirds the African worldview can be reframed in light of who Jesus is and what he does. Evil spirits are under his authority, and witchcraft has no power over a Christian individual and community. Moreover, the Gospel is universal and is superior to all African Traditional Religions.

Sample Text 2
Letter (1 John 3:11–15)

Apart from Ethiopia, which had a precolonial letter-writing custom, letters, in written form, are a relatively recent category for African literature. Most of the instances we have come from the postcolonial period. This is understandable, given the oral nature of communication in traditional Africa. In more recent times, and with the growth in literacy, letter-writing gained popularity, particularly as more and more people moved away from their traditional homes into the cities and even out of the country. However, even in preliterate Africa, it was still possible to communicate information orally. Of course, in the globalized society in which we live today, letters have largely been replaced with emails and text messages.

Background[43]

First John, until the twentieth century, was attributed to the apostle John, the beloved disciple of Jesus and the brother of James. Both external and internal evidence point to Johannine authorship. Although he is not identified by name, similarities between 1 John and the Gospel exist. Early Christian tradition attributes 1 John to the apostle John. A number of relevant texts include those of Irenaeus (d. 202 CE), Dionysius of Alexandria (d. 265 CE),

42. Keener, *IVP Bible Background*, 140.

43. For a fuller analysis of 1 John, see Elizabeth Mburu, Judy Wang'ombe, Caroline Seed, and Josephine Mutuku, *1,2,3 John*, Windows on the Text, ed. Ida Glaser and Martin Accad (Langham Global Library, forthcoming).

and Tertullian (d. after 220 CE). 1 John has no stated recipients and was therefore meant to be circulated to a number of churches. Its date of authorship is affected by that of the fourth Gospel. While there is no consensus about its dating, it was most likely written between 85 and 95 CE from Ephesus, before John's exile to the island of Patmos and after the destruction of Jerusalem and the temple in 70 CE. It was written after the fourth Gospel as the author seems to assume that the readers are familiar with the Gospel.

Analysis of the Text

First John 3:11–15 is the center of the chiastic structure of 1 John and thus carries the main message.[44] The first half builds up toward this message based on the Cain and Abel narrative and the second half of the sermon moves away from the main idea, repeating the ideas of the first half and adding more depth and explanation to them. In the previous section, John has exhorted readers on the need to avoid the temptation to live sinfully.

Leg 1

Parallels to the African Context

The growth of the church in Africa is complicated by a troubling dichotomy. One of the major issues is the false teaching being taught by religious leaders, the most prominent being the prosperity health and wealth gospel. While it appears to teach a holistic view of life, this is not the case. This gospel has rapidly transitioned to Neo-Pentecostalism. Its popularity is probably associated with the African transactional understanding of God, worldviews of holism and dynamism, as well as a growing consumerism. It emphasizes power encounters, deliverance from ancestral and other curses, signs and wonders, as well as an emphasis on objects believed to have power.[45] Even mission-founded churches have begun to align with the theology and ecclesiology of Neo-Pentecostalism. The issue with Neo-Pentecostalism, apart from its deceptive doctrine, is that it encourages religious syncretism. This is exacerbated by wrong doctrine with regards to Christology and pneumatology. Thus, while its teachings may not align directly with the secessionists' teaching that John is confronting in this text, the core issue of idolatry that is exemplified in Cain (1 John 5:21) is clearly evident.

The second parallel is community. Africans have a strong sense of community. Relationships are important and maintaining these relationships is a part of the kinship system that reflects our traditional African worldviews. Because of the worldview of holism, maintenance of these relationships extends beyond the living to the living dead (including ancestors) and the unborn. The basic African view with regard to people was that the individual existed only because others existed. This philosophy, known as Ubuntu, reflects the African conception of what it

---

44. Mburu et al., *1,2,3 John*, n.p.

45. Matthews A. Ojo, "An Overview of the History of Neo-Pentecostalism in Africa," in *The Abandoned Gospel: Confronting Neo-Pentecostalism and the Prosperity Gospel in Sub-Saharan Africa*, ed. Philip W. Barnes, Bazil Bhasera, Matthews A. Ojo, Jack Rantho, Trevor Yoakum, and Misheck Zulu (AB316, 2021), 19.

means to be human and determines the I-Other dynamic.[46] However, even given this worldview of Ubuntu, "othering" still rears its ugly head. The law of kinship determines "insiders" and "outsiders."[47] Insiders are determined by sociocultural identity markers and "othering" often leads to fractured church communities, much like what is described in the text under study.

Leg 2

Theological Context

The main idea in this section is the Hebrew story of the first two brothers, Cain and Abel.[48] As in previous sections, John makes his point using contrasts. The story is given a central place in the sermon in 1 John 3:11–12. Using the illustration of Cain and Abel, John provides a concrete example of the love/hate, light/darkness, truth/lies contrast that he expounds on throughout his sermon. The core issue in this text is love and this contrast forms a sharp antithesis between genuine believers and the secessionists. It demonstrates that the absence of Christian love in the community of faith is akin to murder. The absence of love also contrasts sharply with the example of Jesus Christ, who gave up his life as a demonstration of his love (cf. 1 John 3:16).

Leg 3

Literary Context

Genre

Again, as with all interpretation, it is important to identify the genre of a given work to identify what rules will apply. First John more closely resembles the genre of sermon. This section lies at the centre of what is essentially a prophetic midrash on Genesis 4:1–16,[49] or perhaps more accurately, is written in a midrashic style. The prophetic midrash is an interpretation of current events through ancient Torah themes.[50]

Elements

The second step in interpreting a letter is to identify the elements that constitute a letter. Although the general format points to the genre of letter, 1 John does not have a salutation or a closing, and neither is there a greeting as was the convention of letters of the time. First John 3:11–15 is found in the main body.

---

46. See chapter 6 in this volume on the Gospel of John for a more complete analysis.

47. Yusufu Turaki, *Engaging Religions and Worldviews in Africa: A Christian Theological Method* (HippoBooks, 2020), 168.

48. For this emphasis, see Mburu et al., *1,2,3 John*, n.p.

49. Anthony Royle, "1 John as Midrash Pesher on Genesis 1–4: Eschatological Typology, Structure and Early Christian Polemics," Conference Paper, The British New Testament Society Conference at the University of Manchester, September 6, 2014.

50. Jacob Neusner, *What Is Midrash?* (Wipf & Stock, 2014), 7–12.

Function

The third step is to identify the function of the letter under analysis. The letters of the New Testament were occasional documents, generally written to address specific situations in the churches. An important implication, therefore, is that, as much as is possible, they must be understood within their specific historical contexts. From 1 John it is clear that the readers "appear to have been members of a number of churches in fellowship with the church of which the author was a member."[51] They were encountering people who had seceded from the author's church and were propagating an aberrant form of the Gospel (2:18–27). The author regards the readers as those whose fellowship with him is under threat and he therefore writes to confront these false teachers and to give his readers assurance of salvation (5:13).

Context

What is the surrounding context of 1 John? Schism, which had probably never crossed the readers' minds, had occurred in the community of faith. The severing of relationships would have been excruciating. Although Keener suggests that John wrote "to encourage Christians expelled from the synagogues,"[52] it is more likely that it was because of the trauma of the internal schism that had occurred in the community (1 John 2:18–19). As Painter points out, the Jews are not mentioned at all by John.[53] What is evident is John's palpable grief at what was happening to the community of faith, those whom he regarded as his "dear children." In addition to this, the remaining members may even have begun to doubt their own faith as they considered whether those who had left were right. Thus, the readers were probably also tempted by the heresy of compromise advocated by the false prophets, as well as idolatry, which was a constant threat in the Roman Empire.[54]

Analysis of the Text

1 John 3:11–15

> 11 For this is the message you have heard from the beginning, that we should love one another.

The word "for" (ὅτι) that begins this verse is an explanatory conjunction. In the previous verse (3:10), John has just given the credentials that distinguish between children of God and of the devil. Now he connects this to the defining feature in the community of faith, that is love. The word "message" appears only twice in this sermon (1:5). Why does John use the first-person plural in 1:5, but the second-person plural form here? The implication is that in

51. Colin G. Kruse, *The Letters of John*, PNTC, 2nd ed. (Eerdmans, 2020), 15.

52. Keener, *IVP Bible Background*, 706.

53. John Painter, *1, 2, 3 John*, SP 18 (Liturgical Press, 2008), 24.

54. Keener, *IVP Bible Background*, 706.

1:5 it is a theological proposition, whereas here it is an ethical obligation.[55] It is probably best not to make such a sharp distinction because, for John, doctrine and practice are intertwined.

This message is not new and John writes that they have heard it from the beginning (ἀπ' ἀρχῆς; 1:1; 2:7). Here, "beginning" refers to the start of their Christian lives and as encapsulated in the Torah. As Marshall rightly points out, "John is appealing to the traditional nature of the message to emphasize its importance and its truth to his readers who may have been tempted to ignore it in view of the bad example presented by John's opponents."[56] This "looking back" appeals to the traditional African perspective of time. The past was important because it served to provide direction for the present. Even now, there is a resurgence of traditional values because many believe that is the only way to recover their lost identities.

The following clause that begins with the conjunction "that" (ἵνα) is a content clause that provides details regarding the content of "the message." This is to love one another (2 John 4–6). In 1:5, "the message" had to do with the nature of God as light and therefore the two are part of the same message. Love for one another is not a new idea. In 2:7–11, John explains that love is an "old yet new" command and that those who love their brothers and sisters live in God's light and truly know him. The source of the commandment to love one's fellow Jews is found in Leviticus (19:18). A visible lack of love in the community probably motivated John to reiterate this message. While he does not use the imagery of light and darkness here, clearly it is those who love who are in the light. While love should begin in the community of faith (2:10; 3:10, 14; 4:20f.), it is likely that in this verse John also extends this command to include love for those outside the faith.

> 12 We must not be like Cain, who was from the evil one and murdered his brother. And why did he murder him? Because his own deeds were evil and his brother's righteous.

John's negative example of Cain illustrates the nature of love and shows that lack of love originates in the evil one. In his gospel, John notes that Jesus relegates the Jews who refused to believe in him to the family of the devil (John 8:44). Love and hatred therefore typify righteousness and sin respectively.[57] Although there are several allusions throughout the sermon, this is the only time John makes direct reference to the Old Testament. It is likely that John's readers were familiar with this story.

A core aspect of the Jewish worldview was an abhorrence for violence, particularly in the form of killing (Exod 20:13). Brotherly care and responsibility were taken for granted but Cain failed in this when he killed his own brother, Abel (Gen 4:1–16). John uses the analogy of brothers because a similar situation is reflected in the community to which he was writing. The African worldview of Ubuntu works much in the same way. Taking care of "insiders," those who are determined by sociocultural identity markers, is expected in the community.

55. Stephen S. Smalley, *1, 2, 3 John*, WBC (Thomas Nelson Publishers, 1984), 182.

56. I. Howard Marshall, *The Epistles of John*, NICNT (Eerdmans, 1978), 276.

57. Smalley, *1, 2, 3 John*, 183.

However, there is no such obligation where "outsiders" are concerned and "othering" often leads to fractured church communities.

Rather than repent of his mistake, Cain directed his negative emotions toward his brother. Cain's murderous act is evidence that he was of "the evil one." In Jewish thought, Cain was a "stereotypical prototype for wickedness" (Jubilees; 1 Enoch; Wisdom of Solomon 10:3) and later Rabbinic sources claimed that Cain's father "was a bad angel, even the devil himself."[58] John connects hatred of one's brother to murder akin to Cain's.

John takes the precedent of Cain to illustrate how heinous lack of love is. The word used here for "murdered" (ἔσφαξεν) is very strong. It means "butchered." Its vividness, which is not captured in our English translation, conveys the violence of Cain's act.

John then asks an unexpected rhetorical question which he then promptly answers. John's interpretation of Cain's act is missing in the Genesis story and Cain's motives are not clearly explained. John explains it as a contrast between Cain's own evil deeds and his brother's righteous ones. There are several sources outside the Old Testament which propose that Cain's act of murder was inspired by the devil (Apocalypse of Abraham 24.5; Apocalypse of Moses 3.2; Testament of Benjamin 7.5).[59] The writer of Hebrews views Cain's actions as stemming from jealousy and that Abel had faith whereas Cain did not (Heb 11:4). Yarbrough notes that "Cain's behavior and underlying attitude were the utter antithesis of love. John uses Cain, the epitome of treachery (cf. Jude 11), as an example of how God's people must not regard each other."[60]

While a failure to love does not always lead to literal murder, John probably takes this thought from Jesus's words in Matthew (Matt 5:21–28). His readers must recognize the implications of Jesus's teaching and that hatred is in essence "embryonic murder."[61] Moreover, Cain's attitude of hatred is in complete contrast to the attitude of love required of all God's children (2:10; 3:14). Even more importantly, it stands in complete contrast to Christ who is pure and righteous and who loves to the point of his own death (3:2–7, 16).

[13] Do not be astonished, brothers and sisters, that the world hates you.

This verse begins with the prohibition not to be astonished or surprised (NIV) (μὴ θαυμάζετε). It can also be rendered "do not marvel." It is likely that the secessionists, who once identified themselves with the church but are now antichrists and hence part of "the world" (2:18–19), had already begun to act with hostility toward the genuine Christians they had left behind. Kruse notes that it is surprising that this verse follows the stress on love between fellow Christians in the previous verse.[62] However, it is not so surprising when one recognizes that it follows the logical train of thought that began in verse 12. Thus, Cain epitomizes "the world"

58. Keener, *IVP Bible Background*, 712.

59. Robert Yarbrough, *1–3 John*, BECNT (Baker Academic, 2008), 199.

60. Yarbrough, *1–3 John*, 198.

61. Marshall, *The Epistles of John*, 277.

62. Kruse, *The Letters of John*, 145.

(ὁ κόσμος), namely those who are hostile to God and under the power and influence of the "evil one."

John generally uses "children" when addressing his readers. The use of "brothers" (ἀδελφοί; rendered brothers and sisters in our text) here is therefore a little unusual, but because John is emphasizing mutual love between fellow Christians, it is entirely appropriate. Jesus himself warned his disciples that they would be hated by "the world." After all, they hated him first (Luke 21:17; John 7:7; 15:18). The verb "to hate" (μισέω) is quite strong. It is also emphatic, coming as it does at the beginning of the clause in the Greek, and serves to show the "fundamental opposition which exists between believers and the world."[63] Although John does not explicitly use the "two ways" language common in Jewish thought, the similarities are obvious.

> [14] We know that we have passed from death to life because we love the brothers and sisters. Whoever does not love abides in death.

After the brief warning of verse 13, John returns to the theme of mutual love amongst fellow Christians. Verses 14 and 15 are tightly connected and provide an argument for the identity of genuine Christians. There are three steps in John's argument:[64] (1) The evidence of spiritual life is love of fellow Christians; (2) The converse is true in that the evidence of death is lack of love; (3) Hatred of a fellow Christian is murder. This last point is an intensification of the first two steps and is found in verse 15.

The verb used for "we know" (οἴδαμεν; 2:20–21) is an affirmation of what genuine Christians profess.[65] Passing from death into life is another way of referring to the eternal life that one possesses in Christ (1:2; 2:24–25). This is very different from the African conception of the afterlife in which the living dead and ancestors continue to be a part of the community. The verb "we have passed out of" can also be rendered "we have crossed over" (μεταβεβήκαμεν). It is used metaphorically and vividly represents the "transition from the world of hatred and death to the realm of love and life."[66] It has close connections to the formulation in John 5:24 and thus can be interpreted in a similar way. The perfect tense indicates a past action that has abiding results in the present, as is characteristic of then Johannine already-but-not-yet manner of representing the Christian life. John is therefore stating that love for fellow Christians is simply a natural outflow of salvation and of the love of God in a Christian.

This brings us to the second step of his argument, namely that the converse is also true. Those who do not love "abide in death." As in previous instances, the use of the present tense reflects an ongoing state. John uses the word "abide" in relation to Christians and Christ (2:6). However, here, it is related to death, in which case eternity is in view. As is characteristic of the Johannine style, life and death, love and hatred are presented as contrasts. The lack of

63. Smalley, *1, 2, 3 John*, 186.
64. Smalley, *1, 2, 3 John*, 187.
65. Yarbrough, *1–3 John*, 200.
66. Smalley, *1, 2, 3 John*, 188.

love demonstrated by the secessionists reveals that they had never left the realm of death and consequently never had any claim to eternal life.

> [15] All who hate a brother or sister are murderers, and you know that murderers do not have eternal life abiding in them.

This verse concludes the third step in the argument. It is an allusion to the illustration of Cain and Abel given earlier (3:12). Going beyond the outward actions, John reveals the heart attitude of the one who hates. He begins with the characteristic "all who" (πᾶς ὁ; 3:3, 4, 6, 9, 10) which reflects personal responsibility in community. As he has already implied (3:12, 13), hatred makes one a murderer and therefore subject to the same judgment. As in verse 13, John uses the word "brother" (ἀδελφὸς; rendered brother and sister in our text) to refer to Christians in general with the assumption that love also extends to those outside the community.

The word John uses for "murderer" (ἀνθρωποκτόνος) is "man-killer." In the New Testament, this word occurs only here and in John 8:44 where Jesus uses it to describe the devil. In other ancient literature, this word "did not refer to murder in general, but to those acts of killing which were considered to be particularly repugnant including, but probably not limited to, the sacrifice and/or devouring of a human victim."[67] The familial language comunicates that this violent killing of a family member is just as repugnant as human sacrifice and/or devouring of the victim.[68] Earlier, John had mentioned "children of the devil" (3:10) and also aligned Cain with the devil (3:12). It is not surprising that he describes Christians who do not love one another as "murderers."

In addition to alluding to the Cain and Abel story, John is also referring to Jesus's words in Matthew where Jesus connects anger and murder (Matt 5:21–22). As we have seen throughout this section, murder is related to evil and hatred and is completely opposed to righteousness and love. Such people cannot therefore have eternal life abiding in them. In using this imagery of hatred and murder, John is not suggesting that those who do not love have committed murder in the same sense that Cain murdered Abel. What he is doing is presenting the readers with an either/or imagery, the kind that is found in the Sermon on the Mount. Like Jesus, he is also using hyperbole to make his point.[69] There is no neutral ground. Christians must understand that a lack of love is hatred in God's eyes.

Leg 4
Historical Context

The two brothers motif is one that is also found in Jewish culture. The background to this motif forms a valuable point of contact in understanding the text in this section. Love for

67. John Byron, "Slaughter, Fratricide and Sacrilege: Cain and Abel Traditions in 1 John 3," *Biblica* 88, no. 4 (2007): 527.

68. Byron, "Slaughter, Fratricide and Sacrilege," 527.

69. Yarbrough, *1–3 John*, 201.

each other was expected from every individual Jew.[70] The converse was the injunction against hatred of one's fellows, unless that person was the *rasha*, the evil doer.[71] Apart from loving fellow Jews, love amongst fraternal brothers was also key (Jubilees 20:2, 12, 22:3).[72] Brothers were expected to love one another and were seen as responsible for each other.

Kruse points to the second-century BCE text, Benjamin 7:1–5, and the first- or second-century CE text, Apocalypse of Abraham 24:3–5, to show that Cain's act of killing his brother is regarded as an act "inspired by the devil (Beliar/the crafty adversary)."[73] In the Jewish culture, "brotherly love" and "living in peace" are synonymous.[74]

Seat

Application

What is the meaning of this text for the original readers? John uses the Cain and Abel story, a story of two brothers, to emphasize that the current situation was analogous to the situation between Cain and Abel. The secessionists, who were causing such sharp divisions in the church that it had caused a schism, were actually like Cain, who did not worship God in the right way and was therefore an idolater who belonged to the evil one. A Christ-centered love lies at the heart of genuine Christianity and true fellowship. Given the hatred that was in the community to which John was writing, it was obvious that his readers had not grasped this yet.

What is the meaning of the text for African believers today? Clearly, the frequent "othering" that we experience, either because of our ethnic, gender, sociocultural, economic, or political differences, is not tenable. If love is truly at the core of genuine Christianity, then any attitudes or actions that do not reflect love actually negate one's claim to be a Christ-follower and put one squarely in the camp of the idolater. Idolatry has at its core the failure to acknowledge the centrality of Christ. This is a shocking truth because Christians often use the word "idolater" when speaking of those practicing African Traditional Religions, Islam, Hinduism, and other religions. No genuine fellowship in the church can be achieved without genuine love.

Conclusion

This chapter covered several aspects of Africentric approaches, including the motivating factors for Africentric approaches, assumptions and common characteristics, a brief overview of Africentric approaches currently in use, and a closer look at one of these approaches, including two sample texts.

70. Norman Lamm, "Loving and Hating Jews as Halakhic Categories," *Tradition* 24, no. 2 (1989): 98.

71. Lamm, "Loving and Hating Jews," 98.

72. Atar Livneh, "'Love Your Fellow as Yourself': The Interpretation of Leviticus 19:17–18 in the Book of Jubilees," *Dead Sea Discoveries* 18, no. 2 (2011): 181.

73. Kruse, *The Letters of John*, 144.

74. Livneh, "Love Your Fellow as Yourself," 184.

Given that all interpretation is contextual, Africentric approaches have a place in the field of biblical hermeneutics in general. They have several contributions to make.[75] First, they speak to African contextual realities. The text is no longer a foreign object that has been imposed on us, but rather a relevant text that allows us to engage in constructive dialogue and find relevant application points. Second, they confront dichotomy and syncretism by allowing for dialogue between the biblical and African contexts, thus exposing wrong doctrine and practice. Third, they allow for fresh insights from the biblical texts. They provide a different way of reading that complements other readings, thus reflecting the global character of the church. Fourth, rather than relegate hermeneutics to the domain of academics/intellectuals, they make it possible for ordinary readers to participate actively in Bible interpretation. Fifth, because they promote understanding and internalization of biblical truths within the African context, the potential for transformation of society is increased. Sixth, they promote understanding and interrogation of African contexts and awareness of our religious spaces. This is important because Africa is very pluralistic and religious spaces are quite porous. And finally, they allow for a redefinition of Christian African identity based on biblical criteria. African identity markers are therefore not determined by African Traditional Religion, culture, or even African worldviews.

Further Reading

Abraha, Tedros. "Andemta." In *Encyclopaedia Aethiopica*, vol. 1, edited by Siegbert Uhlig. Harrassowitz, 2003.

Adamo, David T. "The Task and Distinctiveness of African Biblical Hermeneutic(s)." *Old Testament Essays* 28, no. 1 (2015): 31–52.

Anderson, Allan H. "African Initiated Church Hermeneutics." In *Initiation into Theology: The Rich Variety of Theology and Hermeneutics*, edited by Simon Maimela and Adrio Konig. J. L. van Schaik, 1998.

Bediako, Kwame. "Biblical Exegesis in Africa: The Significance of the Translated Scriptures." In *African Theology on the Way: Current Conversations*, edited by Diane B. Stinton. SPCK, 2010.

Chipenda, Jose B, André Karamaga, J. N. K. Mugambi, and C. K. Omari. *The Church of Africa: Towards a Theology of Reconstruction*. All Africa Conference of Churches, 1991.

Dube, Musa W. "Talitha Cum Hermeneutics of Liberation: Some African Women's Ways of Reading the Bible." In *The Bible and the Hermeneutics of Liberation*, edited by Alejandro F. Botta and Pablo R. Andiñach. Society of Biblical Literature, 2009.

Dube, Musa W., Andrew M. Mbuvi, and Dora Mbuwayesango, eds. *Postcolonial Perspectives in African Biblical Interpretations*. Society of Biblical Literature, 2013.

Kyomya, Michael. *A Guide to Interpreting Scripture: Context, Harmony, and Application*. HippoBooks, 2010.

Loba Mkole, Jean-Claude, and Ernst R. Wendland, eds. *Interacting with Scriptures in Africa*. Acton Publishers, 2005.

Manus, Ukachukwu C. *Intercultural Hermeneutics in Africa: Methods and Approaches*. Acton Publishers, 2003.

Mburu, Elizabeth W. *African Hermeneutics*. HippoBooks, 2019.

Mugambi, Jesse N. K., and Johannes A. Smit, eds. *Text and Context in New Testament Hermeneutics*. Acton Publishers, 2004.

75. Mburu, "African Hermeneutics," 419.

Nel, Marius. *An African Pentecostal Hermeneutics: A Distinctive Contribution to Hermeneutics*. Wipf & Stock, 2018.

Nthamburi, Zablon J., and Douglas Waruta. "Biblical Hermeneutics in African Instituted Churches." In *The Bible in African Christianity: Essays in Biblical Theology*, edited by Hannah W. Kinoti and John M. Waliggo. Acton Publishers, 1997.

Sugirtharajah, Rasiah S., ed. *Voices from the Margin: Interpreting the Bible in the Third World*. Orbis, 1991.

West, Gerald O. *Contextual Bible Study*. Cluster, 1993.

CHAPTER THREE

The Gospel of Matthew

Bitrus A. Sarma
ECWA Theological Seminary Kagoro
Nigeria

François Batuafe Ngole
Catholic University of Congo
Congo

Introduction

THE GOSPEL ACCORDING to Matthew occupies a strategic place in the biblical canon. It serves as a basic framework for comprehending the concept of promise-fulfillment as the narrator portrays the birth, life, ministry, death, and resurrection of Jesus as the definitive fulfillment of the Jewish Scriptures. And from the African context, Matthew's Gospel lays a robust foundation for addressing Christian discipleship, ethics, mission, tribalism, oral traditions (orality), violence, and miracles. However, African scholarship is yet to fully engage some of these fundamental facets from Matthew's Gospel for their contextual relevance in the African milieu. This chapter is aimed at filling this gap. The authors investigate these features and their import for African Christianity using theological and contextual approaches. The methodological process is threefold, namely, contextualization, decontextualization, and recontextualization. The first is to evoke African sociocultural data; the second is to shed light on the same subject in the Gospel according to Matthew; and the third is to critically analyze African biblical realities from a theological and intercultural perspective.

Matthew has been described as the gospel for the church. The first reason is its explicit mention of the church (Matt 16:18; 18:17). The second is its contents and structure, suggesting that the book was designed as a "training manual"[1] for Matthew's community of believers. The third is the Gospel's liturgical use by the early church as attested by some church fathers.[2] Just as Matthew focused on the needs of his Jewish-gentile audience, the church in Africa resonates with many of the issues that the Gospel of Matthew addresses. One of the major challenges identified in African Christianity is depreciating moral values arising from inadequate discipleship. This decline in ethical principles and standards has given rise to the perennial problems of divisive ethnicity and tribalism, communal hostilities, violence, unforgiving

1. Craig S. Keener, *The IVP Bible Background Commentary: New Testament* (InterVarsity Press, 1993), 45.

2. Luke Timothy Johnson, *The Writings of the New Testament* (Fortress Press, 1999), 187.

spirit, retaliation and genocide, and a rising divorce rate. Another critical issue is pretentious religiosity, which Jesus sternly warned against (Matt 6:1–18). Similarly, the practice of holistic mission as exemplified in the ministry of Jesus seems to be grossly inadequate in African Christianity. Therefore, the essence of this introductory chapter is utilizing Matthew's Gospel in engaging some of these concerns.

But the main discourse in this chapter is preceded by some important background matters, such as the historical framework, the literary characteristics of the Gospel, the overall structure, and some major theological themes. These provide the basic framework for understanding Matthew's narrative. It is followed by investigating Matthew on the concept of Christian ethics or values (*ubuntu*) projected in the Sermon on the Mount. According to Mungi Ngomane, Ubuntu "encompasses all our aspirations about how to live life well, together. We feel it when we connect with other people and share a sense of humanity; when we listen deeply and experience an emotional bond; when we treat ourselves and other people with the dignity they deserve."[3] In other words, Ubuntu "recognizes the inner worth of every human being—starting with yourself."[4] Ubuntu is the golden rule (Matt 7:12) in African conception. Simply put, "the key premise and lesson of *Ubuntu*" is "to recognize and affirm one another's common humanity."[5] The goal is to underscore Matthew's significance for African Christian culture and ethics. With the same objective in mind, we explore Christian mission in Africa. Accent is placed on the holistic nature of mission as found in the Gospel of Mathew and how this applies to Christian mission in Africa. Also probed in the chapter are crucial concerns about orality, tribalism, violence, and the place of miracles in the context of African Christianity.

Introductory Matters

Historical Setting

This section answers four questions: Who wrote the Gospel according to Matthew? To whom was it written? When was this gospel written? Where was it written?

Authorship

The Gospel according to Matthew is anonymous, with no mention of the author's name. Tradition attributed it to Matthew, also called Levi (Mark 2:14), in the second century CE.

3. Mungi Ngomane, *Everyday Ubuntu: Living Together, the African Way* (Harper Designs, 2019), 10. For more on Ubuntu, see James Ogude, ed., *Ubuntu and the Reconstitution of Community* (Indiana University Press, 2019); Leonhard Praeg and Siphokazi Magadla, eds., *Ubuntu: Curating the Archive* (University of KwaZulu-Natal Press, 2014); Drucilla Cornell and Nyoko Muvangua, eds., *Ubuntu and the Law: African Ideals and Postapartheid Jurisprudence* (Fordham University Press, 2012).

4. Ngomane, *Everyday Ubuntu*, 13.

5. Mark Mathabane, *The Lessons of Ubuntu: How an African Philosophy Can Inspire Racial Healing in America* (Skyhorse Publishing, 2018), 17.

He is identified as one of Jesus's disciples and apostles (Matt 10:3) and was a tax collector (Matt 9:9; 10:3). Eusebius of Caesarea reports the words of Papias of Hierapolis, who said that Matthew had put together the *logia* or words (of Jesus) in Hebrew dialect (of the Hebrews) and each person interpreted them as he could.[6] However, this Aramaic or Hebrew proto-gospel cannot be found. The original text was written in Greek. The characteristics of this gospel, in particular its interest in the Torah and its mastery of Jewish traditions, suggest that the author of the Gospel according to Matthew was a Jewish Christian.

Recipients

The first community for which this gospel was intended was made up mainly of Jewish Christians, with a few gentile-Christians. As a book addressing a community made up of both Jews and gentiles, it is described as a "Handbook for a mixed church under persecution."[7]

Date and Place of Writing

In order to hypothesize the date of writing, certain prerequisites must be taken into consideration: First, the reference to the destruction of the temple in Jerusalem in 70 BCE (Matt 23:37–39; 24:1–31); second, the dynamics of the mission, first limited to Israel, then open to the nations (Matt 10:5–6; 14:34–36; 15:21–28; 28:16–20); and finally, the active role of the Pharisees in the conflict with Jesus and his disciples, as well as the violence suffered by the Christians, point to a period when Christians' frequenting of Jewish synagogues was becoming increasingly problematic, just before the Hebrew canon of the Bible was established in 90 CE. So the Gospel according to Matthew is said to have been written between 80 and 90 CE, first in Jerusalem, then in a Jewish Christian community in Palestine. While this late dating may be plausible, views from some scholars regarding earlier dating (50s to 70s) still persist and are worth considering.[8]

Literary Characteristics

To better understand Matthew's Gospel, it is essential to recognize specific literary characteristics.

Gathering the material into blocks: The overall organization of this book is based above all on the grouping of the material into narrative and discursive blocks. There are five main discourses:[9] the Discourse on the Mount (Matt 5–7); the Missionary Discourse (Matt

6. See Eusebius, *Hist. eccl.* 3.39.16.

7. Robert H. Gundry, *A Survey of the New Testament*, 3rd ed. (Zondervan, 1994), 159.

8. Leon Morris, *The Gospel According to Matthew*, PNTC (Apollos, 1992), 8–9; R. T. France, *The Gospel of Matthew* (Eerdmans, 2007), 18–19; Robert H. Gundry, *A Survey of the New Testament*, 3rd ed. (Zondervan, 1994), 161.

9. W. D. Davies, and D. C. Allison, *A Critical and Exegetical Commentary on the Gospel According to Saint Matthew*, vol. I, *1–7*, ICC (T&T Clark, 1988), 59; see also Donald A. Hagner, *Matthew 1–13*, WBC 33A (Word Books, 1993), l–lii.

10:1–11:1); the Parabolic Discourse (Matt 13); the Ecclesial Discourse (Matt 18); and the Eschatological Discourse (Matt 24–25). The narrative blocks consist mainly of the accounts of Jesus's childhood and the preparation for his public ministry (Matt 1–4), the section on miracles (Matt 8–9), Jesus's itinerary from Galilee to Jerusalem (Matt 11:2–12:50; 14–17; 19–23); and the account of his passion, death, and resurrection (Matt 26–28).

Repetition: Repetition, one of the characteristics of Semitic literature, is well exploited in the Gospel according to Matthew.[10] This includes, for example, the concluding formulas of the great discourses (Matt 7:28; 11:1; 13:53; 19:1; 26:1), the introductions of the fulfilment quotations (Matt 1:22–23; 2:15,17–18, 23; 4:14–16; 8:17; 12:17–21; 13:35; 21:4–5; 27:9–10); summaries (Matt 4:23; 9:35; 11:1); the inaugural kerygma of John the Baptist (Matt 3:2; 4:17); the expression Ἀπὸ τότε ἤρξατο (*apo tote erxato*) (Matt 4:17; Matt 16:21); the withdrawals of Jesus due to the violence suffered by John the Baptist (Matt 4:12; 14:13); the statements on the divine filiation of Jesus (Matt 3:17; 16:16; 17:5); the power of the keys given to Peter and the community (Matt 16:18; 18:18); the *syntagm* βασιλεία τῶν οὐρανῶν (*basileia tôn ouranôn*) which occurs thirty-two times; and the term δικαιοσύνην (*dikaiosynē*) (Matt 3:15; 5:6, 10, 20; 6:1, 33; 21:32).

Rabbinic techniques: The example is the title "Emmanuel" (Matt 1:23) and its semantic extension "I am with you always, to the end of time" (Matt 28:20), which forms an *inclusio*.[11] Similarly, the first and last occurrences of the word "justice" constitute an inclusio (Matt 3:15 and 21:32). Others include chiasm (see Matt 8:28–9:1), concentric constructions (see Matt 6:1–18), and numerical schemes to organize its material (see the conclusion of the genealogy with 3x14 generations: Matt 1:1–17).

Structure

The structure of the Gospel of Matthew is contentious and no consensus has been reached.[12] Some scholars caution against "imposing an outline on Matthew."[13] One of the reasons for the open-ended structure is that the Gospel of Matthew does not provide markers that would serve as an outline for the book.[14] And according to Bauer, the differing views on Matthean structure stem "from the application of diverse methodologies to the question of Matthew's structure."[15] Bauer believes that the solution is in literary criticism because it focuses on the final form of the text. This means that the arrangement of the final text gives it its structure. This structure, according to Bauer, is as follows:

10. Davies and Allison, *A Critical and Exegetical Commentary on the Gospel According to Saint Matthew*, 88–92; Ulrich Luz, *The Theology of the Gospel of Matthew*, trans. J. Bradford Robinson (Cambridge University Press, 1995), 4.

11. Davies and Allison, *A Critical and Exegetical Commentary on the Gospel According to Saint Matthew*, 92–93; Luz, *The Theology of the Gospel of Matthew*, 4–5.

12. David R. Bauer, *The Structure of Matthew's Gospel: A Study in Literary Design* (Almond Press, 1996), 7.

13. Robert H. Gundry, *Matthew: A Commentary on His Literary and Theological Art* (Eerdmans, 1982), 10.

14. R. T. France, *The Gospel of Matthew*, NICNT (Eerdmans, 2007), 2.

15. Bauer, *The Structure of Matthew's Gospel*, 7.

1. Jesus's birth and infancy narrative (1–2);
2. Jesus's preparation for ministry (3:1–4:11 //Mark 1:1–13);
3. 4:12–15:20 Jesus's ministry and teaching in Galilee (//Mark 1:14–7:23);
4. Jesus's ministry outside Galilee (15:21–18:35 //Mark 7:24–9:50);
5. Jesus's journey to Jerusalem (19:1–20:34//Mark 10);
6. Jesus's last days (21–28//Mark 11:16:8).[16]

And based on the above arrangement of materials closely related to Mark, some argue that Matthew's structure is derived from Mark's narrative framework.[17] Following the above structure, but without necessarily leaning on source criticism which suggests that Matthew depended on Mark for his structure, we offer an abridged structure of the Gospel according to Matthew in five main parts.[18]

Part I: Prologue (Jesus's childhood: Matt 1–2)
Part II: Jesus's Galilean ministry (4:12–15:20)
Part III: Jesus's ministry outside Galilee (15:21–18:35)
Part IV: Jesus on way to Jerusalem (19:1–20:34)
Part V: Jesus's Passion Week and Resurrection (21–28)

Theological Themes in Matthew

Matthew's Gospel is replete with weighty theological themes. These themes are interwoven in his narrative scheme. They include Christology, the kingdom of heaven, the church, and promise-fulfillment. Other significant themes are faith and practice and the issue of justice. We will examine each of these briefly.

Christology

Christology is the main theme of the Gospel according to Matthew. The author from the very beginning presents Jesus as the Messiah, the Son of David (Matt 1:1). The first aim of Matthew's account is to show that Jesus, through his teachings and actions, is the Messiah who fulfils the promises made by God to Abraham and Israel. He is Immanuel, the God present in the midst of his people Israel (Matt 1:23; 18:20; 28:20). Jesus is essentially the crucified Messiah. His story unfolds in a dramatic way and conflict occupies a central place in it.[19] From childhood to the cross, the conflict between Jesus and the religious and political authorities

16. Bauer, *The Structure of Matthew's Gospel*, 7.

17. Johnson, *The Writings of the New Testament*, 188; Gundry, *A Survey of the New Testament*, 161.

18. François Batuafe Ngole, *Evangiles synoptiques: Introduction à la lecture scientifique* (L'Harmattan, 2023), 64. See also France, *The Gospel of Matthew*, 3.

19. J. D. Kingsbury, *Matthew as Story* (Fortress Press, 1988), 3.

rises to a crescendo until he is put to death, a sign of his rejection by Israel, as happened to the prophets of old. But God sides with Jesus and raises him from the dead on the third day. Matthew interprets Jesus's controversial journey using the typology of the Servant of God from the book of Isaiah, to show that his suffering and death play a saving role for those who believe in him.

The Kingdom of Heaven

The kingdom of heaven is Jesus's main message in this gospel. John began his ministry by calling his audience to repent in view of the imminence of the kingdom of heaven ἡ βασιλεία τῶν οὐρανῶν[20] (Matt 3:1–2). Jesus began his ministry with the identical call for repentance in anticipation of the kingdom of heaven (Matt 4:17). This theme is explained by the teachings (speeches, parables) and miracles. It is a gift from God (Matt 5:1–12) that man must seek (Matt 6:33) by practicing charity toward the least of these (Matt 25:31–46). This reign is historical, at work in this world, and eschatological, awaiting its completion at the end of time (Matt 24–25). The righteousness of the kingdom of heaven means obedience to God's will and the gift of salvation.

By announcing the kingdom of heaven, Jesus was "evoking the story of Israel and her destiny."[21] This is placing the announcement of the kingdom within Israel's messianic hopes and the establishment of God's kingdom on earth (Acts 1:6). Daniel M. Doriani rightly noted that the people in Jesus's day had concrete images of what the kingdom of God meant. "To them, 'the kingdom is at hand' meant God would soon make his reign evident on earth. If God begins to reign, then Rome no longer reigns; the end of Rome's political and economic dominance is nigh."[22] This is reflected in the account of Matthew 20:20–24, with the disciples arguing and lobbying for honorable seats in the kingdom. That the imminence of the kingdom is a dominant theme at the time of Jesus is reflected in Zechariah's prophetic utterance (Luke 1:68–75). With the birth of John the Baptist, the forerunner of Jesus Christ, the time for salvation from enemies had come. But as we examine the Gospel of Matthew, the kingdom of God is both present and future as depicted in Bitrus A. Sarma's *Drums of Redemption*.[23] George E. Ladd refers to it as "presence of the future."[24] The kingdom was manifest in the ministry of Jesus (Matt 11:1–6; cf. Luke 17:21). But it was still future and its realization becomes one of the disciples' supplications (Matt 6:10).

---

20. Kingdom of heaven and kingdom of God are used as interchangeable terms. See Craig S. Keener, *Matthew*, IVPNTCS (InterVarsity Press, 1997), 41.

21. N. T. Wright, *Jesus and the Victory of God* (SPCK, 1996), 200.

22. Daniel M. Doriani, *Matthew*, REC (P & R Publishing, 2008), 85.

23. Bitrus A. Sarma, *Drums of Redemption: A New Testament Theology for Africa* (Hippo Books, 2023), 80–81.

24. George Eldon Ladd, *The Presence of the Future: The Eschatology of Biblical Realism*, rev. ed. (Eerdmans, 1974).

Ecclesiology

The word ἐκκλησία (*ekklesia*) appears twice in Matthew's Gospel (Matt 16:18; 18:17). The word ἐκκλησία was used in a broad sense to mean an assembly of people, either for political or other purposes. But it has come to be used as congregation or community of believers in Christ. The Church of Matthew is the community of Emmanuel; it lives in the permanent presence of the Lord, until the end of time (Matt 28:20; 18:20). It is inclusive and universal as well as exclusive as there are criteria for belonging. In his conception of the church, Matthew places great value on the weaker categories: He identifies the Lord with the least of these (Matt 25:31–46); he makes children models and evaluation criteria for anyone who wants to enter the kingdom of heaven (Mt 18:1–10); the simple are the beneficiaries of revelation (Matt 11:25–27). The church is a community of brothers, disciples of Jesus, and children of the Heavenly Father (Matt 5:16, 48; 6:4, 9, 14, 18; 7:9; 23:8). Matthew insists on forgiveness (Matt 6:14–15; 18:21–35) and fraternal correction (Matt 18:15–20). The church is compared to an edifice built on the rock of the apostles, with Peter as its head, to whom the keys are given (Matt 16:17–19). Finally, the church is missional (Matt 10; 28:16–20).

Theology of Fulfillment

A distinctive feature of the Gospel of Matthew is his "consistent emphasis on Jesus's role as the fulfillment of the hopes of Israel."[25] In the first Gospel, the story of Jesus Christ fulfils the prophecies of the Old Testament.[26] The God of Jesus Christ is the God of Abraham, the God of Isaac, the God of Jacob, the protagonist of the history of salvation from one Testament to the other. Matthew interprets Jesus by situating him above all in his Jewish origins (Matt 1:1–17) and in the perspective of the promises God had made to David's descendants (Matt 1:18–2:12). The fulfillment of the Scriptures as a hermeneutical key makes it possible to define the relationship between the two Testaments. This means that the Old Testament served as precursor, foreshadowing the life of Christ as the New Testament bears witness. For Matthew, Jesus did not come to abolish the Law of Moses, but to fulfill it, to reveal its full meaning (Matt 5:17–19). This unity of the two Testaments is due to the uniqueness of the God who guides the history of salvation. The relationship between the Old and New Testaments is therefore dialogical. On the one hand, Matthew interprets Jesus in the light of the Scriptures; on the other, he reinterprets the Scriptures in the light of Jesus Christ. This implies that the New Testament continues God's salvific purposes for the world as fulfilled in Jesus Christ. At the same time, there is discontinuity with regards to the Old Testament's legalistic righteousness such as sacrifices or observance of special

25. George E. Ladd, *A Theology of the New Testament*, rev. ed. (Eerdmans, 1993), 221.

26. Bitrus A. Sarma, *Hermeneutics of Mission in Matthew: Israel and the Nations in the Interpretative Framework of Matthew's Gospel* (Langham Monographs, 2015), xi, 1.

days and ceremonies. So while the two Testaments are one, there are also contrasts with regards to covenant relationship between Yahweh and Israel and relationship between God and believers in Christ.

Faith as Orthopraxis (Right Practice)

According to Matthew, Jesus's audience is divided into two blocks. He contrasts those who believe with those who do not (Matt 21:25, 32). The criteria for this discernment are practical. The Discourse on the Mount insists on *praxis* (as defined below) as a condition of access to salvation. Indeed, ποιεῖν (to do) has justice as its object (Matt 6:1); this verb also structures the golden rule (Matt 7:12) and characterizes Scripture (the Law and the Prophets) by its practical purpose (Matt 7:12). Similarly, in the metaphor of the tree and its fruit, the verb ποιεῶ (to do) advocates action as the criterion for evaluating the so-called prophets (Matt 7:15–20). The end of the Discourse on the Mount marks the *climax* of the practical aspect of all Jesus's teaching (Matt 7:21–27). Matthew contrasts, on the one hand, "saying Lord, Lord" with "doing (ποιῶν) the Father's will" (Matt 7:21), and on the other hand, "listening and putting into practice (ποιῶν) the words of Jesus" (Matt 7:24) with "listening without putting into practice (μὴ ποιῶν) the words of Jesus" (Matt 7:26). By virtue of the programmatic scope of the Discourse on the Mount (Matt 5–7), the objective literary data concerning the putting into practice of God's will (Matt 21:31a) raise implications.

In Matthew 7:21–28, Jesus's words express God's will. In the final instructions of the Discourse on the Mount (Matt 7:21–27), as in the application of the parable of the father with his two children (Matt 21:28–32), the author establishes a consistent link between "doing God's will" and entering into the kingdom of God (Matt 7:21; 21:31). The teachings of Jesus and John the Baptist express the will of God, and consequently, faith understood as the putting into practice of the divine will (Matt 21:23–32) means welcoming John and Jesus as eschatological messengers and recognizing in their ministries the expression of the divine will. The focus on acting (ποιῶν) in accordance with God's will defines faith as *orthopraxis*. The pragmatic connection between faith and *praxis* is situated in the perspective of the theology of works that Matthew develops in his Gospel from the preaching of John the Baptist and Jesus. For John the Baptist, the practice of works worthy of conversion is the only way to escape God's wrath (Matt 3:7–10). For the Matthean Jesus, "good works" testify to the Christian's divine filiation in the eyes of the world (Matt 5:16); they are the only criterion of prophetic and charismatic authenticity (Matt 7:15–20). Furthermore, putting Jesus's words into practice is the foundation of any solid Christian life and the only way to be saved from the tribulations of the eschatological age (Matt 7:21–27). The Last Judgment once again highlights *praxis* as the criterion for evaluation and the condition for admission or not to the inheritance of the kingdom of God (Matt 25:31–46). The primacy of *orthopraxis* implies that, in the Matthean perspective, the authenticity of faith is verified by the *praxis* of God's will expressed in the ministries of John the Baptist and Jesus (Matt 3:8–10). The disciples of Jesus must avoid the "sin of *hearing* but not doing his words concerning the Father's will. Otherwise, they too will fall under judgment."[27]

Justice

Justice is an important theological theme in Matthew's Gospel. It has been the subject of several studies. According to Chris Marshall, "Justice has to do with honoring the rights and entitlements of people, especially in conflict situations."[28] This includes the exercise of legitimate power for fair and equitable distribution of benefits and penalties. As Marshall rightly says, "Biblical justice touches on every aspect of life—the personal and the social, the public and the private, the political and the religious, the human and the non-human—and therefore requires a variety of translation terms to encompass its various applications."[29] Matthew defines justice as obedience to God's will and the gift of salvation. The term "justice" (rendered "righteousness" in NRS and NIV) recurs seven times. The reader will find it only on the lips of Jesus (Matt 3:15; 5:6, 10, 20; 6:1, 33; 21:32).[30]

According to Marshall, biblical righteousness is "doing, being, declaring, bringing about what is right."[31] From a biblical perspective, justice is rooted in God's attributes (Psalm 89:14) and corresponds to his righteousness, holiness, and faithfulness. Christian justice goes beyond retribution for wrongs done to include, inextricably, right relationship between God and man (Mic 6:8; Matt 22:34–40). This is to say that God is not only a just God, he demands righteous and just dealings among his chosen people. From the life and teaching of Jesus, true justice encompasses love, peace, compassion, fairness, and restoration (restorative justice). As Marshall aptly put it, "doing justice in the Bible conveys the idea of righting what has gone wrong, of restoring things to a condition of 'rightness' or righteousness.'"[32] For Christian Africans to reflect God's justice, they must learn to live right with God and fellow human beings by practicing fairness, love, forgiveness, compassion and promoting peace and

---

27. Gundry, *Matthew*, 133, emphasis in original.

28. Chris Marshall, *The Little Book of Biblical Justice: A Fresh Approach to the Bible's Teaching on Justice* (Good Books, 2005), 7.

29. Marshall, *The Little Book of Biblical Justice*, 11.

30. See the following studies: G. Strecker, *Der Weg der Gerechtigkeit: Untersuchung zur Theologie des Matthäus* (Vandenhoeck & Ruprecht, 1962); B. Przybylski, *Righteousness in Matthew and His World of Thought* (Cambridge University Press, 1980); J. M. A. Castaño Fonseca, *Δικαιοσύνη en Mateo: Una interpretación teológica a partir de 3,15 y 21,32*, TG.ST 29 (GBP, 1997); R. Deines, *Die Gerechtigkeit der Tora im Reich des Messias: Mt 5,13–20 als Schlüsseltext der matthäischen Theologie*, WUNT (Mohr Siebeck, 2005); François Batuafe Ngole, *L'accomplissement de toute Justice: Approche pragmatique du procès dialogique entre Jésus et Jean-Baptiste dans l'Évangile de Matthieu*, Publications Universitaires Européennes, Série XXIII: Théologie (Peter Lang, 2017).

31. Marshall, *The Little Book of Biblical Justice*, 11.

32. Marshall, *The Little Book of Biblical Justice*, 12.

reconciliation.[33] Similarly, to promote justice in Africa, the church is to be involved in "formulation of sociopolitical theology that enhances justice."[34]

Reading Matthew in Africa

Joe Kapolyo succinctly delineated five contextual issues in the Gospel according to Mathew "with many lessons to teach Africa today."[35] These include leadership in which Jesus is depicted as perfect teacher and leader. Other concerns addressed in Matthew's Gospel are mission, living in community, Christian values, and the cost of discipleship. In addition to these, we will examine the perennial challenge of tribalism with regards to African community life. Other matters discussed in this chapter are orality and miracles.

Matthew and Christian Ethics (Ubuntu) in Africa

What is the foundation for African Christian culture and morality? It is argued here that the African reading of the Gospel according to Matthew can help to make *Ubuntu* an evangelical culture. Jesus is a Master of *Ubuntu*. The Discourse on the Mount can be very useful in comparing the Gospel and *Ubuntu*. The notion of *ubuntu*, as a principle of excellence and a foundation of values,[36] is a point of dialogue between African culture and the Gospel according to Matthew. For several decades now, particularly since the end of apartheid, African researchers have been studying *Ubuntu* to understand and explain the principles of African culture. From all these studies, it emerges that "*Ubuntu* is not just a concept or a notion, it is fundamentally a culture, a philosophy, an ethic, even a theology."[37] In its essence, *Ubuntu* is the culture of excellence, of living together harmoniously. This culture is reflected in the human and social values it promotes: "*Ubuntu* is the sum of virtues and values."[38] The values promoted are manifold and serve to build peaceful coexistence: friendship, solidarity, compassion, sharing, respect, helpfulness, community, love, mercy, forgiveness, benevolent reciprocity, and so on.

But it is observed that many converts to Christianity or Islam cling to their traditional beliefs and assumptions "that determine how they act morally."[39] While many scholars "disapprove of Jesus' theology," they "laud his ethical teaching, finding in it an enduring

33. See Samuel Peni Ango, "Christianity, Justice and Forgiveness in the African Church Experience," *Kagoro Journal of Theology* 5, no. 1 (2023): 138–160.

34. Bernard Boyo, *The Church and Politics: A Theological Reflection* (HippoBooks, 2021), 175.

35. Joe Kapolyo, "Matthew," in *Africa Bible Commentary* (WordAlive, 2006), 1131.

36. We define values here as "underlying, fundamental beliefs and assumptions that determine behavior." Samuel Waje Kunhiyop, *African Christian Ethics* (HippoBooks, 2008), 5.

37. A. Kabasele Mukenge, "Editorial: *Ubuntu*, une philosophie à se réapproprier," *Cahiers des religions africaines* n.s. 2, no. 4 (December 2021): 5.

38. J. Mbayo Mbayo, "Le principe bumuntu," *Cahiers des religions africaines* n.s. 2, no. 4 (December 2021): 34.

39. Kunhiyop, *African Christian Ethics*, 5.

significance."[40] We argue, therefore, that the Gospel of Matthew provides the foundation for African Christian ethics and Jesus's Sermon on the Mount is the rudimentary framework for ethical principles for the Christian. This sermon (Matt 5–7; cf. Luke 6:17–49) is considered Jesus's blueprint for the values and ethics of the kingdom of heaven. It is believed that the accounts in both Matthew and Luke "were spoken *one* time and constitute *one* sermon."[41] The site of the sermon designated as "on the mountain" in Matthew or "on a level place" in Luke is clarified that the sermon was either preached on a mountain-plain or that he chose his disciples while they were on the mountain but then descended to a plain where he performed the miracles of healing the sick. After that, he returned to the mountain top and sat down to preach.[42] Another submission is that the title "Sermon on the Mount" is a misleading delineation because there is no place that could be specifically pointed out as the mountain in question. This view maintains that the level place to which Jesus descends (Luke 6:17) "supports a reference to a setting generally in the hill country rather than on a mountain-top."[43]

But our primary concern at the moment is not the site of the sermon but the ethical values and practices derived from it. The Sermon on the Mount set the disciples of Jesus as distinct from the rest of humankind with the unique designation as the salt and light of the world (Matt 5:13–16). As Richard B. Hays noted, "The Sermon on the Mount calls for a life of uncompromising rigor in discipleship."[44] Hence, to enter the kingdom of heaven, their righteousness must go beyond that of the scribes and the Pharisees (Matt 5:20). First is the Beatitudes (Matt 5:2–12). These Beatitudes express the values of the kingdom of heaven. Their similarities with apocalyptic literature and the Dead Sea Scrolls are well attested.[45] The Qumran Beatitudes speak about the blessings of those who walk according to the law "and do not adhere to perverted paths."[46] Matthew's Beatitudes "reveal key character traits that God approves in his people."[47] These character traits are countercultural as they stand in contrast to what the culture had believed to be signs of blessings from the Lord.

Second is their ethical principles (Matt 5:17–7:27). The stringent requirements of the kingdom include some paradigm shifts in the interpretation and application of the Law of Moses. Jesus is the personification of the law and provides the interpretation that is in keeping with the heart of the law and the mind of God. Matters of particular ethical concerns reinterpreted include taming anger (Matt 5:21–26) and lust (Matt 5:27–30). Morris says that like the command not to murder, "Jesus is concerned with the inner state that leads to action and does

---

40. Ladd, *A Theology of the New Testament*, 119.

41. William Hendrickson, *The Gospel of Matthew*, NTC (The Banner of Truth Trust, 1974, repr. 2006), 260, emphasis in original.

42. Hendrickson, *The Gospel of Matthew*, 260.

43. France, *The Gospel of Matthew*, 157.

44. Richard B. Hays, *The Moral Vision of the New Testament: A Contemporary Introduction to New Testament Ethics* (T&T Clark, 1996), 97.

45. David L. Turner, *Matthew*, BECNT (Baker Academic, 2008), 146.

46. Florentino Garcia Martinez, *The Dead Sea Scrolls Translated: The Qumran Texts in English*, trans. Wilfred G. E. Watson (Eerdmans, 1992), 395.

47. Turner, *Matthew*, 147.

not simply prohibit the outward deed."[48] Jesus teaches that the righteousness of the kingdom of heaven is the ideal of excellence and perfection that Christians should pursue: "Be perfect as your heavenly Father is perfect" (Matt 5:48). The demand for perfection is motivated by the exemplary nature of God, whom Christians must imitate (Matt 5:45, 48). The evangelical justice that Jesus teaches means respect for the life and dignity of others: "Thou shalt not kill" (Matt 5:21ff., KJV). The golden rule, "whatever you want others to do for you, do also for them" (Matt 7:12), is the principle of reciprocity, so important to *Ubuntu*. The text of the Last Judgment promotes the values of solidarity with those who suffer and of hospitality (Matt 25:31–46). Matthew 18 indicates the importance and the demands of community life: attention to the very young, to children, forgiveness and reconciliation. Fraternity (Matt 23:8) and helpfulness (Matt 20:24–28) are all Gospel values that build community life. Ubuntu is committed to the principle of exemplarity. In the Gospel according to Matthew, Jesus is a master who teaches by example. The disciple does no more than imitate the master. From Matthew's perspective, the Gospel does not abolish the Ubuntu, but fulfils it (Matt 5:17). In this theology of fulfilment, the *Ubuntu* is called to be open to the Gospel, especially in its vertical dimension, that is, the relationship with the Holy Trinity.

An equally weighty issue is the common practice of divorce (Matt 5:31–32), which was permitted under Moses because of the hardness of the people's hearts (Matt 19:1–9). Apart from the grounds of adultery, "Jesus accepts no excuse for divorce."[49] For divorce was never God's intention from the beginning. This strict ethical stance is what R. T. France refers to as Jesus setting "the tone for the process of re-education in the revolutionary values of the kingdom of heaven."[50] The disturbing nature of this teaching is seen in the disciples' reaction. For them it would be better to remain celibate than to marry under such conditions (Matt 9:10). Paul added another dimension on the issue of divorce and remarriage with regards to one who is married to an unbeliever (1 Cor 7:13–16). If a man or woman has an unbelieving spouse[51] who is willing to stay in the marriage union, the believing spouse must not divorce him or her. Paul's reason is that the unbelieving spouse may be sanctified by the believing spouse. But if the unbelieving spouse chooses to leave, the believing spouse is under no obligation to stay with him or her. From both Jesus and Paul, marriage and divorce are weighty matters, hence the highlights below.

The first is the issue of adultery. This is critical for African Christianity in a global village turning amoral. But it must be made clear that the issue of marital infidelity applies to both males and females. This unethical living is backed by legislations in some countries. Among the issues that stand out are abortion, sexual perversion, and illicit sex. Biblical morality is jettisoned as outdated. Doriani observes that the Western world is increasingly questioning

48. Morris, *The Gospel According to Matthew*, 527.

49. Craig L. Blomberg, "Matthew," in *Commentary on the New Testament Use of the Old Testament*, ed. G. K. Beale and D. A. Carson (Baker Academic, 2007), 23.

50. France, *The Gospel of Matthew*, 713.

51. Considering the pioneering work of the gospel by Paul in Corinth, it may be assumed that this is the case of the wife or husband coming to faith in Christ while the other does not. This often happens even in the African continent, especially among Muslim converts.

biblical teachings. People argue that while laws against adultery may have been necessary in the past for social reasons, those laws are no longer relevant because women are now liberated and educated and can handle problems of birth outside marriage through contraceptives, abortion, and the rest. With those laws outdated, "People should be free to choose their own lifestyle."[52] As we live in a global village, the mindset that rejects biblical standards as too strict, outdated, and unfit for the new age has infiltrated the entire world. And we need to point out that marital infidelity would include pornography and every form of sexual gratification outside marriage. While it is increasingly difficult for the church in Africa to adhere strictly to biblical principles of divorce in the midst of poverty, HIV/AIDS, and infidelity in the continent, biblical standards and principles remain normative at all times and places. Christians are called to be the salt and light of the world (Matt 5:13–16) and never to conform to the pattern of the world (Rom 12:2).

The second debilitating concern as highlighted above is the increasing divorce rate in the world and in Africa. As Samuel W. Kunhiyop writes, "Issues related to marriage, divorce and remarriage will continue to dominate the life of the church and community in Africa."[53] Jesus clearly forbids divorce (Matt 5:31–32) and explained to the Pharisees that Moses permitted divorce (Deut 24:1–4) on the grounds of the people's stubborn hearts (Matt 19:7–9). But the rate of divorce in the world, even among Christians, is increasing. Divorce is considered "a consequence of lust and discontent."[54] Biblically, marriage is a life-long relationship. According to Jesus, divorce is adultery unless it is as a result of a spouse's unfaithfulness. Therefore, one of the ways the church in Africa may serve as an example to the world is strict adherence to this principle of life-long relationship. And this is achieved through fidelity and commitment to marital vows to stay married until death do them part. What African Christianity must wrestle with is taking the word of God seriously at its face value, applying the truth that God hates divorce (Mal 2:16, KJV).[55] Kunhiyop's recommendations are worth considering, especially where marriage cannot be salvaged.[56] Divorce must be seen as the last resort. In summary, just as Jesus challenged Jewish attitude to divorce and remarriage, Christian Africans must not take lightly the issue of divorce and remarriage.

The third important issue from the African context is Jesus's injunction not to resist (μὴ ἀντιστῆναι) an evil person but to love the enemy. It is observed that "Here Jesus even more clearly sets aside a fundamental Mosaic law."[57] While the legal "tit-for-tat" system required that a wrong done against an individual or group of people be paid back in the same measure, Jesus gave a radically different interpretation that is opposed to the norm. Most would probably agree that "There are few commands in the Bible that clash more with our natural inclination

52. Doriani, *Matthew*, 153.

53. Kunhiyop, *African Christian Ethics*, 258.

54. Doriani, *Matthew*, 160.

55. The translation of this verse is contested because of the ambiguity in the Hebrew structure surrounding the subject of the verb "hates." For instance, NIV translates this as "The man who hates and divorces his wife."

56. Kunhiyop, *African Christian Ethics*, 258.

57. Blomberg, "Matthew," 26.

to protect our person and our honor than the commands found in Matthew 5:38–42."[58] But from the African context, how do we apply this in matters of religious and ethnic conflicts? How do we apply his teachings on loving a neighbor when the neighbor is from a hated ethnic group? In response, we argue that if Jesus is the Christian's model, his "deeds interpreted his words, above all at his trial."[59] As recorded in Isaiah 50:6–8, Jesus did not defend himself at his trial even when slapped and spat on (Matt 26:67; 27:30; cf. John 19:9–11; Mark 14:65). The Bible does not forbid resisting all evil as we are commanded to resist the devil (Jas 4:7; 1 Pet 5:9). This implies that resisting evil could be done in such a way that it does not amount to personal vendetta (Rom 12:19–20).

The fourth issue, related to the above, that deserves attention for African Christianity is loving the enemy (Matt 5:43–48). From the African context, people are not hated only for their religious beliefs; they are hated for their tribal and ethnic affinities.[60] Stanley N. Mutunga observed that the lingering on of major tribal animosities after decades or even centuries of Christianity brings to the fore a fundamental question: "What is involved in conversion to Christ?"[61] Mutunga's concern is that if true conversion brings automatic racial and tribal harmony, why the lingering social and cultural differences in the so-called Christian nations? That makes intentional discipleship a critical priority. When Christians are unable to see their true identity in Christ, their allegiance inevitably leans toward their familiar blood affinities. That is why Jesus taught that true discipleship involved loving him more than father, mother, wife, children, and brothers (Matt 10:37; Luke 14:26). Similarly, Jesus taught that the true mother, father, and brother are those who do the will of God (Matt 12:46–50; Mark 3:31–35; Luke 8:19–21). Jesus redefines true kinship.

In addition to the above, the disciples must shun practices like taking of oaths (Matt 5:33–37), retaliation (Matt 5:38–42), and hating their enemy (Matt 5:43–48). As we shall see below, loving the enemy is probably one of the most difficult demands among the ethical principles of the kingdom of heaven, especially in the context of the growing animosity and violence against the church.

These ethical principles of the kingdom of heaven extend to matters of almsgiving (Matt 6:1–4). Against the practices of the day when giving acts of charity were done publicly by some to impress onlookers, Jesus warned that such behavior is hypocritical and does not attract blessings from God. Instead, true giving is done in secret, "And your Father who sees in secret will reward you" (6:4). Jesus's stern warning against giving to impress people could be applied to some Christian politicians in the Nigerian context. During political campaigns, most politicians like to impress people in social and church gatherings with proud announcements of their donations and love the loud claps that follow. And some of the donations are mere pledges that are never redeemed. In the same vein, prayer is not a public display of piety (Matt 6:5–15). It is

58. Doriani, *Matthew*, 175.

59. Doriani, *Matthew*, 179.

60. Barje S. Maigadi, *Divisive Ethnicity in the Church in Africa* (Baraka Press, 2006).

61. Stanley N. Mutunga, "Toward A Wa Kwetu Without Strangers," in *Tribalism and Ethnicity*, ed. Elie A. Buconyori (The AEA Theological and Christian Education Commission, 1977).

a personal communion with the unseen God who rewards such devotion, and the same applies to fasting (Matt 6:18). The rest of the Sermon on the Mount deals with: the priority of the kingdom rather than the pursuit of earthly treasures and mundane things (Matt 6:19–34); judging others (Matt 7:1–6); asking (Matt 7:7–11); living by the "golden rule" (Matt 7:12–14); and a stern warning against impostors, who are recognized by their fruit (Matt 7:15–23).

The Sermon on the Mount is concluded by a call for practical application of the message preached. The proof of receiving his teaching is doing them (ποιεῖ αὐτούς). He uses the example of the two foundations (Matt 7:24–27; cf. Luke 6:46–49). So, how is the Sermon on the Mount to guide African Christian morality? We do not intend to treat all of the ethical principles outlined by Jesus. But there are critical issues that demand urgent attention for African Christianity.

Matthew and Discipleship in Africa

The Gospel of Matthew may well be regarded as a manual for Christian discipleship as it is replete with the concept of discipleship (4:8; 5:1; 8:21, 25; 9:10, 11, 14, 19, 37; 10:1, 42; 11:1). The calling of the twelve was primarily a call to discipleship (Matt 5:18–19; cf. Mark 3:14). The Great Commission was a charge to make disciples (Matt 28:19–20). But who is a disciple and what is discipleship? A disciple (μαθητὴς) is a learner, an apprentice, who stays close to the master and watches him or her at his or her occupation in order to acquire and perfect their own knowledge and skills. Therefore, discipleship is the process of learning under a tutor or mentor. True discipleship hardly takes place by proxy.[62] Therefore, for about three-and-a-half years, Jesus's disciples walked with him. They saw and heard him preach, teach, heal the sick, cast out demons, raise the dead, and perform many other functions. They saw him disputing with and denouncing the Pharisees and teachers of the law (Matt 12:1–14; 15:1–9; 21:23–27; 23:1–36). They also saw him embrace "sinners" (Matt 9:10–13; 11:19) and explain that he came for the lost sheep of the house of Israel (Matt 10:6; 15:24; cf. Luke 15:4). Finally, they saw him accused falsely, humiliated, crucified, and saw him die on the cross.

But why is discipleship of primary significance? In Matthew's Gospel, the kingdom of God is expanded through discipleship.[63] David J. Bosch sees mission in Matthew as disciple-making.[64] From Jesus's example, embedded in discipleship is fishing for men and women (Matt 4:19), embracing the values of the kingdom (Matt 5–7), carrying one's own cross, and following him (Matt 16:24; cf. Luke 9:23). That is the essence of discipleship. From these features of discipleship, of particular significance for African Christianity is the need to embrace fully the values of the kingdom of heaven as Jesus expressed them in the Sermon on the Mount. The goal of Christian discipleship is growing in Christ "until we all reach unity in the faith and in the knowledge of the Son of God and become mature, attaining to the whole measure of the fullness of Christ" (Eph 4:13).

62. Sarma, *Drums of Redemption*, 76.

63. Sarma, *Drums of Redemption*, 98–101.

64. David J. Bosch, *Transforming Mission: Paradigm Shifts in Theology of Mission* (Orbis Books, 2007), 56–83.

And the critical need for discipleship in Africa is the observation that the rapid numerical growth of the church in Africa is not quite commensurate with her spiritual maturity. Many Christian Africans are doctrinally and morally ill-equipped to face the battles of the Christian life.[65] The result is that many who profess faith in Christ remain infantile and are therefore easy prey in the hands of masqueraders who peddle the gospel for profit. From the Nigerian context, our cities and towns are full of both mega and small churches. Some of the practices in many of the churches, however, are anything but biblical. Instances of ministers of the gospel extorting money from the worshippers by dubious means are rampant. In a particular church worship service, a pastor was said to have used anointing oil to draw a circle on the ground. He then told the worshippers that he received a fresh revelation that anyone who would jump into the circle with a particular amount of money was actually jumping into his/her prosperity. The eyewitness, who was a pastor from another church, confirmed that when the service was over the minister who concocted that scheme told fellow ministers that they must act that way to ensure that the people did not return home with their money. Another example is a pastor who bathed himself in a drum of water and gave the same water for his members to drink in order to receive their prosperity. There are many other unethical and immoral behaviors of pastors which are reported in the media. Similarly, patronizing "prayer houses" is a common feature in Nigerian Christianity. Some of the owners and operators of these prayer houses behave more like African magicians or witch doctors than Christian clergy. Practices like bathing clients in streams in the night, using special perfumes, and wearing particular garments to attend their meetings are quite common. But the level of patronage from the general public and church members is indicative of the amount of ignorance among believers.

The implications of the above for African Christianity are that even the demographic shift of professing Christians from the Minority world to the Majority world does not seem to give African Christianity the advantage of being the global center of Christianity because it lacks the missional, theological, and ethical moorings to engage the world. The point is that immature Christians lack the capacity to advance the gospel of Christ by evangelizing and influencing the national or global culture.[66] From the example of Jesus and his disciples, those who will disciple the nations must undergo adequate discipleship training themselves.

Matthew and Missions in Africa

It is commendable that more African churches are involved in missions than ever before. There are hundreds of mission organizations founded and sponsored by Africans. They are engaged in the mission task both within their countries and abroad. Similarly, some Africans in the diaspora are playing a significant role in reverse mission.[67] Among the diaspora missionaries

65. Bitrus A. Sarma, *Blessed New Humanity in Christ: A Theology of Hope for African Christianity from the Book of Ephesians* (Hippo Books, 2021), 123.

66. J. P. Moreland and William Lane Craig, *Foundations for a Christian Worldview* (InterVarsity Press Academic, 2003), 5.

67. See, for example, Jehu J. Hanciles, *Migration and the Making of Global Christianity* (Eerdmans, 2021); Dana L. Robert, *Christian Mission: How Christianity Became a World Religion* (Wiley Blackwell, 2009), 74–75.

are people who went to Europe and other Western countries to study but remained there.[68] According to Matthew 9:36–10:4, "Jesus commissioned his disciples to begin replicating his work of preaching, teaching and healing."[69] Healing is part of Jesus's mission (Matt 8:17).[70] But Jesus did not limit himself to teaching and healing. He also fed the hungry, an event recorded by all four Gospels (Matt 14:13–21; Mark 6:30–34; Luke 9:10–17; John 6:1–15). This indicates that Jesus's mission is holistic, reaching out to body, soul, and spirit. It is in line with his mission statement in the Gospel of Luke which states,

> *The Spirit of the Lord is upon me,*
> *because he has anointed me*
> *to bring good news to the poor.*
> *He has sent me to proclaim release to the captives*
> *and recovery of sight to the blind,*
> *to let the oppressed go free,*
> *to proclaim the year of the Lord's favor. (Luke 4:18–19)*

Modeling Jesus, Christian mission in Africa is to be holistic, taking into account the multifaceted challenges in the continent. A key text often used as the motivation for mission in Africa is Matthew 28:18–20. But more often than not, the emphasis is on evangelism and counting the number of "converts" as the evidence of fulfilling the Great Commission. This may be a good starting point. But the omission in the commission is the neglect of what Jesus exemplified for his disciples—a holistic approach. Bosch's expression of this is "an all-inclusive mission" and asserts that Jesus's mission "embraces both the poor and the rich, both the oppressed and the oppressor, both the sinners and the devout. His mission is one of dissolving alienation and breaking down walls of hostility, of crossing boundaries between individuals and groups."[71]

Christian mission, when embraced from such a holistic standpoint, has more far-reaching positive effects than is understood and pursued by the church in Africa.[72] As Banning Liebscher put it, the Great Commission (Matt 28:18–20) is essentially "to disciple nations, transform society, and see the glory of the Lord cover the earth."[73] Liebscher's supposition is that we cannot heal the land without transforming culture. Therefore, healing the land is transforming culture. And healing the land takes place in the family, religion, economy, education, government, arts and media, science and technology. According to Liebscher, "whoever commands and controls those mountains sets the agenda and atmosphere in society."[74] This means that

68. Robert, *Christian Mission*, 74.

69. Craig L. Blomberg, *Jesus and the Gospels: An Introduction and Survey* (Apollos, 1997), 285.

70. Keener, *Matthew*, 177.

71. Bosch, *Transforming Mission*, 28.

72. Brian Woolnough and Wonsuk Ma, eds., *Holistic Mission: God's Plan for God's People* (Regnum Books International, 2010).

73. Banning Liebscher, *Jesus Culture: Living a Life That Transforms the World* (Destiny Image Publishers, 2009), 58.

74. Liebscher, *Jesus Culture*, 59.

for Christian mission to serve as a tool for healing Africa, these "mountains" are to be engaged and transformed by Christian values. This may seem too utopian, but we only need to take a look at the impact of Jewish Christian faith and values in the world.[75] The point is that if the Great Commission is interpreted in light of the entire Gospel of Matthew and the mission of God as the "Bible's grand narrative,"[76] we see a holistic approach to mission.

Matthew and African Orality

Rabbis taught oral traditions.[77] Although Matthew's mixed community needed a written manual "for Gentile converts,"[78] orality still resonates in the African context. In African orality,[79] the palaver and the griot are keys to the reading of the Gospels. The palaver is an oratorical institution used either to forge alliances or to resolve conflicts within the community. Its main actors are the elders, masters of the art of oratory and guardians of ancestral traditions. Indeed, "when a chief, judge or witness takes the floor in an African palaver, what he says carries an authority under his social status."[80] The palaver takes place in public, under the palaver tree. Several studies agree on the main characteristics of the palaver: orality, circularity of speech through the change of interlocutors, reference to tradition and history through proverbs, anecdotes and parables, and sign language. As a result, the palaver is an instance of intergenerational discourse and is essentially wisdom-oriented.

The use of proverbs, parables, and anecdotes gives the African palaver an esoteric and popular character. As for the griot, he is a traveling storyteller, sometimes considered as having magical powers. His role is based on the sacredness of orality because, according to African traditions, the griot-storyteller not only masters the art of storytelling but is invested with the power to recount the collective memory, made up of genealogies, ancestral biographies, and the history of the clan.[81]

The Gospel according to Matthew can enter into dialogue with African orality through the conflict resolution procedure. In the ecclesial discourse (Matt 18), the proposal to resolve conflicts in the community corresponds to the African palaver. This process considers several levels of community mediation: first, oneself, one or two other brothers, the church or the assembly (Matt 18:15; 16:17). These different levels of mediation invite the wrongdoer, or

75. See Alvin I. Schmidt, *How Christianity Changed the World* (Zondervan, 2004); Vishal Mangalwadi, *The Book That Made Your World: How the Bible Created the Soul of Western Civilization* (Thomas Nelson, 2011); Vishal Mangalwadi, *Truth and Transformation: A Manifesto for Ailing Nations* (YWAM Publishing, 2009); Loren Cunningham and Janice Rogers, *The Book That Transforms Nations: The Power of the Bible to Change Any Country* (YWAM, 2007).

76. Christopher J. H. Wright, *The Mission of God: Unlocking the Bible's Grand Narrative* (InterVarsity Press, 2006).

77. Keener, *IVP Bible Background Commentary*, 45.

78. Keener, *IVP Bible Background Commentary*, 45.

79. In 2021, African researchers published a work that gives an account of African orality: A. Ngengi Mundele, E. Wabanhu, and J. C. Loba Nkole, *Bible and Orality in Africa: Interdisciplinary Approaches* (Bicam-Cebam, 2021).

80. François Batuafe Ngole, "L'oralité performative dans la Bible: Approche pragmatique et contextualization," in *Bible and Orality in Africa*, 142.

81. Cf. François Batuafe Ngole, *La Bible au cœur de l'interculturalité: les enjeux de la tribalité, de l'oralité et des migrations en Afrique* (Presses de l'Université Catholique du Congo, 2023), 54–55.

rather the sinner, to acknowledge his wrongdoing or sin. For forgiveness and reconciliation, the offence committed must be acknowledged by its perpetrator, for without the truth, there is no solid basis for reconciliation. The purpose of the mediation that leads to reconciliation is none other than the recovery of a member of the community, who must return to the path of brotherhood. The conclusion of this exhortation (Matt 18:18) reveals another dimension of the reconciliation process. The power of the keys reserved for Peter (Matt 16:19–20) is also exercised by the assembly (Matt 18:18), which now has a deliberative voice. There are some implications to be drawn from this. First, the sovereign community has the power to evaluate the results of the reconciliation process and decide the offender's fate in relation to the group. It can exclude him if he persists in his evil, and reinstate him if he converts and admits the fault he has committed against his brother. Second, it turns out that the *vox ecclesiae* is the *vox Dei* (the voice of the church is the voice of God). Matthew shows that reconciliation with God also involves reconciliation with the community.

The application of this gospel in the African context finds its inculturation in the palaver, where orality contributes to conflict resolution, reconciliation, and the re-establishment of fraternity in the community. *Ubuntu* is one of the organizing principles underpinning the African palaver. "The societal interest in the concept of *Ubuntu* dates back to its evocation in the process of reconciliation of the South African peoples after the end of apartheid."[82] The example of South Africa fits in well with the evangelical spirit of forgiveness and reconciliation that Matthew promotes in the community. So the marriage between *Ubuntu*, the African palaver, and Matthew 18:15–18 is a path to be explored to enrich African orality with gospel values.

From an African perspective, the Matthean narrator plays the role of the griot. He recounts the life of Jesus, just as the African griot recounts the story of the ancestors of a clan. For the African griot, the aim is to invite the younger generations to follow the teachings and imitate the virtues of the ancestor in question. The work of Christology in African theology has already opened up this reading by attributing to Christ the title of proto-ancestor.[83] In Africa, the ancestral story is sacred, because the ancestor is an intermediary between the divine and the tribe. Many Africans recognize this story as part of their own identity. Hence the griot is the narrator of the collective memory. This category evokes the consecration of orality. The griot is consecrated in African tradition as the bearer and communicator of the sacred memory of a people, from one generation to the next. This figure of orality can serve as a reference point for understanding the importance of the oral tradition in communicating the faith since the beginnings of Christianity. Matthew would therefore be understood as an African griot, endowed with the mission of communicating the collective memory of nascent Christianity by telling the story of Jesus. The genealogy that opens Matthew's Gospel (Matt 1:1–17), the teachings and miracles, and the end of Jesus's life recounted by Matthew are similar to African

82. A. D. Bonyanga Bokele, "Les impératifs moraux de *bomoto* comme humanitude," *Cahiers des religions africaines* n.s. 2, no. 4 (December 2021): 57.

83. But this is not to be understood as one who came in the blood and lineage of sinful African ancestors. Jesus is one with God and cannot be equated with African ancestors.

genealogies and biographies transmitted orally by the African griot. This way of telling the story of Jesus by referring to that of his ancestors reflects the African conception of life as participation in the vital energy (spiritual force that is associated with the ancestors) or the vital life force[84] regarded in some African traditions as the communion of the living with the ancestors, namely, members of the clan in fellowship with their living dead. The well-being of the community is dependent on this vital life force. The Gospel parables (Matt 13) are a form of communication that is close to African culture, where proverbs, anecdotes, and tales are important cultural resources for communicating life lessons.

Matthew and Negative Ethnicity in Africa

In a continent with some two thousand tribes, the Gospel according to Matthew could contribute to the construction of open tribal identities. Africans construct their identity by referring to tribalism, which means "the natural fact or awareness of belonging to a tribe."[85] In fact, the African tribe is defined on the basis of several criteria: "the awareness of being descendants of a common ancestor, the sharing of a cultural and traditional heritage (rites of birth, marriage, funerals, initiation); the use of the same language; the sharing of eating habits, social traditions (patriarchal, matriarchal)."[86] The tribe highlights the importance of the community, the family, and the bond of brotherhood that unites the various members. It implies a conception of life as participation with the living dead. The tribal reality is also a place of education in solidarity and communion. The religious impact of tribalism lies in the worship (and/or veneration) of ancestors:[87] "the main cult in traditional African religion is to the ancestors."[88]

The real problem facing Christian communities in Africa is that of identity-based withdrawal or tribalism. This scourge is a severe gangrene, ruining the management of public institutions and giving rise to deadly conflicts between different ethnic groups. Tribalism affects ecclesiology in Africa, where crises caused by tribal conflicts or tribalism are multiplying. For this reason, reading the Gospel according to Matthew in an African context should enable us to explore the path of universal brotherhood and sisterhood beyond tribalism.

Ethnic identity is taken into account in Matthew's story. Above all, belonging to the tribe of Judah is a reason that confirms Jesus's messianic identity (Matt 1:20; 2:6). In fact,

84. In the African context, the living and the dead are inextricably linked. The dead ancestors provide the life force necessary for sustaining the living while the living venerate the ancestors until they too go to join them in the land of the living dead.

85. C. Dimandja Eluy'a Kondo, "Un pas vers une nouvelle conscience sociale et politique," *Les incidences de la tribalité: les nouvelles rationalités africaines* 3, no. 11 (1998): 334.

86. François Batuafe Ngole, *La Bible au cœur de l'interculturalité: les enjeux de la tribalité, de l'oralité et des migrations en Afrique* (Presses de l'Université Catholique du Congo, 2023), 37.

87. It is interesting to read Charles Nyamiti, *Jesus Christ, the Ancestral of Humankind: Methodological and Trinitarian Foundations*, Studies in African Christology 1 (The Catholic University of East Africa, 2005).

88. B. Akotia, "Pourquoi les peuples d'Afrique noire connaissent Dieu sans lui rendre un culte? Les enjeux du culte africain," *Cahiers des religions africaines* n.s. 1, no. 1 (April 2020): 39.

"according to the evangelist Matthew, Jesus's birth in the tribe of Judah fulfils the Scriptures (2 Sam 7:16; Mic 5:1). This means that Jesus's belonging to the tribe of Judah is an argument that confirms that he is the Messiah."[89] However, Jesus, Son of David and Son of Abraham (Matt 1:1) is the Son of God and universal savior. His Jewish background did not prevent Matthew from presenting him as the Messiah sent by God to save all humanity. However, Matthew's community, made up mainly of Jews, underwent a form of missionary conversion demanded by the universalism of salvation. The first Gospel bears traces of a certain tension between those who thought that the mission should be limited to the people of Israel and those who advocated opening up the mission to the gentiles: "Do not go the way of the Gentiles" (Matt 10:5) and "Go and make disciples of all nations" (Matt 28:19). The final tone of the Gospel is universal. It "speaks against racial, religious, social, political, and ethnic divides, especially in the final commission to disciple all the nations."[90] We can see that this community has become aware of its universal mission, above and beyond ethnic or racial identity-based divisions. The inclusivism of salvation is thus the key to rereading African tribalism. The salvation that Jesus brings is intended for "all the tribes of Israel" (Matt 19:28) and "all the tribes of the earth" (Matt 24:30). To build open tribal identities, Matthew advocates brotherhood and sisterhood (Matt 23:8), based on God's paternity toward all (Matt 5:48; 6:9; 23:9). As a result, the encounter of Africans with the Gospel according to Matthew is a true path of conversion toward the communion and unity of African tribes around Christ, who is recognized as the proto-ancestor. The evangelical perspective is also at the service of interculturality. Matthew's community was made up of Jews and gentiles. Matthew's challenge also concerns the prejudices that sometimes form barriers between ethnic groups. Matthew shows that the God of Jesus Christ, who is none other than the God of Abraham, Isaac, and Jacob, the ancestors of Israel, is the only God to whom humanity must give worship. In Jesus, then, African worship and/or veneration, offered to the ancestors, is called upon to be purified by redirecting it to the adoration of the true God. This perspective rejects any form of religious syncretism, which is very present in African Christianity.

Matthew and Violence in Africa

Africa resonates with the history of violence:[91] the slave trade, slavery, colonization, genocide, massacre, mutilation, human trafficking, Christian martyrs, apartheid, war, and migratory phenomena. These situations, which continue to scar Africa's collective memory, bring the modern audience closer to Matthew's Gospel.

89. Ngole, *La Bible au cœur de l'interculturalité*, 44.

90. Sarma, *Hermeneutics of Mission in Matthew*, 209.

91. See Emmanuel Katongole, *The Sacrifice of Africa: A Political Theology for Africa* (Eerdmans, 2011), 125–131. See also Bitrus A. Sarma, "Living in an Age of Violence and Anxiety in Africa: A Biblical Response," *Kagoro Journal of Theology* 5, no. 1 (2023): 1–30.

Similarly, Matthew is addressing a community living under Roman domination and also facing persecution, not forgetting the tragedy of the destruction of the temple in Jerusalem in 70 CE (cf. Matt 24).[92] From a literary point of view, the story is full of action verbs that evoke violence: to kill or destroy (Matt 2:16; 10:21); to hand over (Matt 4:12; 10:17, 19, 21; 26:2); to persecute (Matt 5:11, 12; 10:23); to scourge (Matt 10:17; 20:19; 23:34). Matthew also recounts scenes of violence, such as Herod's massacre of the children (Matt 2:13–21), the beheading of John the Baptist (Matt 14:1–12), and Jesus's passion (Matt 26–27). What is more, the story of Jesus is a real drama, because he is subjected to violence from beginning to end, that is, from the cot to the cross (Matt 2:13–21; Matt 26–28). The hermeneutical background to this violence suffered by Jesus can be found in the history of Israel, which was the victim of violence in Egypt, Babylon, and even in Israel with the Persians, Greeks, and Romans. Matthew also shows that Jesus's disciples are sent on mission into a violent world, ready to persecute them (Matt 5:11, 12; 10:17, 19, 21, 23, 27).

Against a backdrop of violence, the Gospel proclaims peace, seen as the fruit of forgiveness and reconciliation. Matthew firmly believes that forgiveness and reconciliation are the only effective means of breaking the cycle of violence. Human forgiveness is first and foremost *imitatio Dei* (imitation of God). Matthew insists that we must forgive in order to be forgiven by God: "For if you forgive others their trespasses, your heavenly Father will also forgive you; but if you do not forgive others, neither will your Father forgive your trespasses" (Matt 6:14–15). Jesus abolished the Law of Talion in the name of evangelical forgiveness, which extends to love for one's enemies (Matt 5:38–42). In ecclesial discourse, forgiveness and reconciliation occupy a central place (Matt 18). Without abolishing the right of victims to social justice, the Evangelist Matthew considers that, over and above the penal sanctions of positive law, only Christian forgiveness offered by victims to their tormentors constitutes an effective remedy against violence and a real guarantee of reconciliation and lasting peace. The African journey of the Gospel according to Matthew can be a path of forgiveness and reconciliation for a new beginning.

The Paschal perspective with which Matthew interprets violence is an avenue for African appropriation of his own violence accumulated over the course of history. For Matthew, the story of the massacre of the children and the flight of Jesus, Mary, and Joseph into Egypt is a midrash (from the Hebrew *darash*, meaning "to search" or "investigate," the term is an interpretive technique for the Hebrew Bible, often using analogy, that is, identifying similarities or drawing inferences) of the exodus and exile (Matt 2:13–21). These catastrophic moments for the people of the Covenant were a painful preparation for liberation from slavery and oppression. Given that the passion-death-resurrection cycle of Jesus has the Jewish Passover as its hermeneutical framework, it follows that his passage from death to life fulfils the exodus and rebirth of Israel after exile (Matt 26–28). These stories should encourage Africans to tell their own stories of slavery and exile, with a view to committing themselves, in faith in God

92. See Richard A. Horsley and John S. Hanson, *Bandits, Prophets, and Messiahs: Popular Movements at the Time of Jesus* (Winston Press, 1985), 29–47; Alfred Edersheim, *The Life and Times of Jesus the Messiah* (Macdonald Publishing, 1886).

the liberator, to the advent of the African Passover. The Passover that Africa needs is also historical, because the Gospel must remain the Good News that liberates from oppression, war, and all sorts of evils that debase Africa.

Matthew and Miracles in Africa

The causes of illness in Africa are often metaphysical.[93] An African generally interprets illness as a curse, the origin of which would be a sorcerer or evil spirits. Illness can also be a reprimand for behavior that goes against traditional customs. But death could also be an act of the Supreme Being (God), especially when people die in their ripe (old) age. Apart from physical illnesses, this interpretation also applies to sterility and other life difficulties. The proclamation of a miracle-working God is very popular in Africa. It also influences the conception of Christian salvation by a large part of the population. Hence the healing of an illness, over and above medical practices, is a miracle, the fruit of supernatural forces. That is why Africans turn to the healer-fetishist, whom they believe to be endowed with supernatural powers to ward off evil spells and free people from evil possessions, of which illness is the expression. The witch doctor knows how to handle the witch, a sign of his friendship with the genie, the spirit that dwells in nature and reveals remedies to him.[94] Healing is achieved through a ritual performed by the healer. To prevent possible evil attacks, some Africans wear charms or amulets around the loins or neck, or keep them in the house. The message about Jesus's healing miracles might have sounded to some Africans like their superstitious beliefs. This might have contributed to the reception of Jesus and his gospel among some Africans. Similarly, this might have been responsible for the popularity of the gospel of miracles in Africa. And one of the consequences of this is the marketing of miracles of healing and exorcism. We can say that the misconception of miracles is one of the distortions of Christianity in Africa. But how can we engage the Gospel according to Matthew regarding miracles from a biblical perspective? That is our next point of discussion. We affirm that miracles of healing and exorcism were among Jesus's main activities: "Jesus went throughout Galilee, teaching in their synagogues and proclaiming the good news of the kingdom and curing every disease and every sickness among the people" (Matt 4:23; cf. 9:35). In Matthew 8–9, the author recounts several of Jesus's miracles: healing of a leper (Matt 8:1–4); healing of a centurion's child (Matt 8:5–13); multiple healings (Matt 8:16–17); the storm calmed (Matt 8:23–27); expulsion of demons from the Gadarenes (Matt 8:28–34); healing of a paralytic (Matt 9:1–8); healing of a woman with bleeding and resurrection of a synagogue leader's daughter (Matt 9:18–26); healing of two blind men (Matt 9:27–31); healing of a mute demoniac (Matt 9:32–34).

Unlike those who dismiss healing based on their Enlightenment and liberal persuasion, the above passages show that healing was an essential component of Jesus's holistic ministry. As

93. Paul G. Hiebert, R. Daniel Shaw, and Tite Tiénou, *Understanding Folk Religion: A Christian Response to Popular Beliefs and Practices* (Baker Books, 1999), 150. See also Samuel Waje Kunhiyop, *Witchcraft Beliefs and Accusations: A Biblical and Christian Perspective* (Challenge Press, 2019).

94. Cf. Akotia, "Pourquoi les peuples d'Afrique noire," 42.

D. A. Carson said, "Jesus' miracles are bound up with the inbreaking of the promised kingdom (8:16–17; 12:22–30; cf. Luke 11:14–23). They are part of his messianic work (4:23; 11:4–6) and therefore the dual evidence of the dawning of the kingdom and of the status of Jesus the King Messiah."[95] Therefore, to dismiss miraculous healing does not represent biblical Christianity.[96] The problem is that in the African context many people reduce Jesus to the one who meets their need for healing without a personal relationship with him as their Lord and Savior. This misconception of miracles helps to strengthen superstition, at the risk of turning Christianity into a kind of amulet that gives power to the one who wears it without a living relationship with Jesus himself. Yet Jesus's miracles are signs of the coming of the kingdom of heaven among us (Matt 12:28). Miracles are never an end in themselves. From Matthew's perspective, the miracles play a christological role, helping to reveal Jesus's messianic identity. To communicate this conviction, the author uses several messianic titles: κύριος (Lord: Matt 8:2.5. 8); υἱὸς τοῦ ἀνθρώπου (Son of Man: Matt 8:20; 9:6); υἱὸς θεοῦ (Son of God: Matt 8:29); and υἱὸς Δαυίδ (Son of David: Matt 9:27). Except for the title Son of Man used by Jesus himself, the others fall under the "block of faith" (Matt 8:10, 13, 26; 9:2, 22, 28, 29). The narrator contrasts this block of faith with another opposing group that engages in dispute against Jesus (scribes: Matt 9:1–8; Pharisees: Matt 9:10–13; disciples of John the Baptist: Matt 9:14–17), some of whom consider Jesus's power to be of demonic origin (Matt 9:34; especially the Pharisees).

Some of the effects of Jesus's miracles are amazement and curiosity of the people about his identity (Matt 8:27; 9:8, 33). The narrator thus draws the reader's attention to the strict link between emotion and discursive enunciation. From a pragmatic point of view, the miracles transform the attitude of the witnesses and trigger a new understanding of Jesus's identity, which is directly linked to God. The quotation from Isaiah 53:4 interprets Jesus's miracles as the fulfillment of the servant figure who bears the sins of his people (Matt 8:17). The figure of Isaiah's servant is vital for understanding the Christology of the first Gospel. In addition to the explicit quotations from Isaiah 53:4 (Matt 8:17) and Isaiah 42:1–4 (Matt 12:18–21), there are numerous allusions to the figure of the servant: Isaiah 42:1 (Matt 3:17; 17:5); Isaiah 50:6 (Matt 26:67; 27:30); Isaiah 53:7ff (Matt 20:28; 26:28; 27:12–14.38). The quotation from Hosea 6:6, "I desire mercy and not sacrifice," which appears twice in the first Gospel (Matt 9:13; 12:7), helps to formulate Jesus's messianic identity. The characterization of Jesus as the "physician" (Matt 9:12) with divine authority to forgive sins (Matt 9:1–8) interprets his behavior as an *imitatio Dei* (imitation of God), in the sense of the manifestation of God's mercy toward sinners.

Conclusion

This chapter has focused on the significance of the Gospel of Matthew for African Christianity. As a manual that addressed the concerns of Matthew's mixed community of Jews and

95. D. A. Carson, "Matthew," in *The Expositor's Bible Commentary*, vol. 8 (Regency Reference Library, 1984), 36.

96. Johana Kariuku Gitau, "A Theology of Spiritual Power in African Christianity," in *African Contextual Realities*, ed. Rodney L. Reed (Langham Global Library, 2018), 25.

gentiles, the Gospel according to Matthew has laid a firm foundation for tackling many of the issues confronting the church in Africa. Some of these critical contextual challenges include increasing moral decadence, inadequate discipleship, and a fragmented approach to Christian mission. By using theological and contextual approaches, the authors have concluded that the Gospel of Matthew is invaluable in comprehending and applying Christian values as Jesus delineated in the Sermon on the Mount. But not only does the Gospel according to Matthew speak unequivocally on African Christian ethics, it also lays down the principles for holistic Christian mission. Although Jesus came to save humanity from the scourge of sin (Matt 1:21), He reached out holistically by meeting the people's spiritual, physical, and emotional needs by preaching the gospel of the kingdom, healing the sick, casting out demons, raising the dead, and feeding the hungry. He demonstrated that the package of salvation is interconnected—touching soul, body, and spirit. He who bore the sins of the people also healed their diseases and supplied their daily bread. And just as he commissioned his followers to make disciples of all nations (Matt 28:18–20), the church in Africa is responsible in carrying out the same mandate.

Similarly, for a continent plagued by divisive ethnicity, tribalism, and violence, the Gospel of Matthew provides the Christian alternative not only for peaceful coexistence as taught and demonstrated by Jesus's nonviolent approach to aggression and conflicts, but also demonstrates that Christians have the vantage position of peacemakers (Matt 5:9). They teach and exemplify the virtues of love, peace, forgiveness, and reconciliation, thereby making the church the true salt and light in a troubled world.

Further Reading

Aghaegbuna, E. O. N., and R. H. Horton. *St. Matthew's Gospel.* Edward Arnold, 1982.

Ajani, Ezekiel Oladapo Aremu. "The Kingdom of God and Its Missiological Imperatives for the Contemporary African Christian Mission." *Ogbomoso Journal of Theology* 12 (2007): 117–135.

Anyaeche, Jude O. "The Canonical Implications of Matthew 19:6 for Christian Marriage in Nigeria." In *The Bible and Theological Reflections*, edited by Ignatius M. C. Obinwa and J. O. Iheanyi. Hanging Gardens Publishers, 1995.

Arnold, Eberhard. *Salt and Light: Living the Sermon on the Mount.* Plough Publishing House, 2007.

Batuafe Ngole, François. *L'accomplissement de toute Justice: Approche pragmatique du procès dialogique entre Jésus et Jean-Baptiste dans l'Évangile de Matthieu.* Publications Universitaires Européennes. Série XXIII: Théologie. Peter Lang, 2017.

Batuafe Ngole, François. *Evangiles synoptiques: Introduction à la lecture scientifique.* L'Harmattan, 2023.

Beale, G. K. *Handbook on the New Testament Use of the Old Testament: Exegesis and Interpretation.* Baker Academic, 2012.

Blomberg, Craig L. *Matthew.* NAC 22. Broadman Press, 1992.

Bohr, Richard. *Jesus' Plan for a New World: The Sermon on the Mount.* St. Anthony Messenger Press, 1996.

Carson, D. A. *Jesus's Sermon on the Mount and His Confrontation with the World: A Study of Matthew 5–7.* Baker Books, 1987.

Clarke, Howard. *The Gospel of Matthew and Its Readers: A Historical Introduction to the First Gospel.* Indiana University Press, 2003.

Holladay, Carl R. *A Critical Introduction to the New Testament: Interpreting and Meaning of Jesus Christ*. Expanded ed. Abingdon Press, 2005.

Kapolyo, Joe. "Matthew." In *Africa Bible Commentary*. WordAlive, 2006.

Kinoti, Hannah W. "Matthew 5:1–12: An African Perspective." In *Return to Babel: Global Perspectives on the Bible*, edited by Priscilla Pope-Levison and John R. Levison. Westminster John Knox Press, 1999.

Nolland, John. *The Gospel of Matthew: A Commentary on the Greek Text*. Eerdmans, 2005.

Onwu, Nlenanya. "Righteousness in Matthew's Gospel: Its Social Implications." *Bible Bhashyam* 13, no. 3 (1987): 151–178.

Pennington, Jonathan T. *Heaven and Earth in the Gospel of Matthew*. Brill, 2007.

Powell, Mark Allen, ed. *Methods for Matthew*. Cambridge University Press, 2009.

Rukundwa, Lazare S., and Andries G. Van Aarde. "Revisiting Justice in the First Four Beatitudes in Matthew (5:3–6) and the Story of the Canaanite Woman (Mt 15: 21–28): A Postcolonial Reading." *HTS Teologiese Studies/Theological Studies* 61, no. 3 (2005): 927–951.

Sarma, Bitrus A. *Hermeneutics of Mission in Matthew: Israel and the Nations in the Interpretative Framework of Matthew's Gospel*. Langham Monographs, 2015.

Staples, Jason A. *The Idea of Israel in Second Temple Judaism*. Cambridge University Press, 2021.

Ukpong, Justin S. "The Problem of the Gentile Mission in Matthew's Gospel." *Vidyajyoti* 59, no. 7 (1995): 437–438.

Yoder, John Howard. *The Politics of Jesus*. 2nd ed. Eerdmans, 1994.

CHAPTER FOUR

The Gospel of Mark

Bekele Deboch Anshiso
Ethiopian Graduate School of Theology
Ethiopia

Introduction

FROM THE BEGINNING to the end of Mark's narrative, Jesus is portrayed as the central figure or the major subject of the Gospel in which the evangelist persuades his readers to understand his real identity as the Son of God (Mark 1:1, 11; 3:11; 5:7; 9:7; 15:39) and the Son of Man (Mark 8:31; 9:9, 12, 31; 10:33, 45; 14:21 [2x], 41). "Unlike the Gospel of John, for instance, where major themes are made explicit, Mark has much more *implicit* major themes, requiring readers to enter into the drama of the Gospel in order to understand its meaning."[1] For instance, Mark believes that Jesus's identity as the Son of God is the central theme of his Gospel, but he writes about it in a less obvious way than the popular expectations of his time.[2] Thus, in order to communicate to his readers about Jesus's divine identity, Mark underlines the idea of the glory and suffering of Jesus as clues to his full identity. One of the outstanding features in Mark's Gospel is the way he places alongside one another the powerful deeds of Jesus in chapters 1–8 and the suffering and death of Jesus in chapters 9–16.[3]

This chapter will briefly discuss some introductory matters including Markan priority, authorship, style, date, readers, and place of composition. Next, keeping modern African readers in mind, I will examine major themes in the Gospel within its context and the ways that they intersect and interconnect with African cultures, worldviews, and realities.

---

1. James R. Edwards, *The Gospel According to Mark*, PNTC (Eerdmans, 2002), 12–13; see also Bekele D. Anshiso, *Jesus's Identification with the Marginalized and the Liminal: The Messianic Identity in Mark* (Langham Monographs, 2018), 1.

2. It is obvious that Mark in the beginning of his narrative mentioned Jesus's Sonship (1:1); however, even though the same is also mentioned by God in 1:11 and 9:7 and by the demons in 3:11 and 5:7, until the Roman/gentile centurion clearly announced in this title (Mark 15:39), there was no one among human beings who had declared him the Son of God.

3. See Anshiso, *Jesus's Identification with the Marginalized and the Liminal*, 2.

Priority of Mark

In the history of Christianity, early church fathers of the second century, for instance, Irenaeus, Clement of Alexandria, Origen, Jerome, and Eusebius, believed that of the three Synoptic Gospels, the Gospel of Matthew was written first because it was placed first in the New Testament canon with a great emphasis on Jesus's fulfillment of the Old Testament promises.[4] They believed that Mark was a later and shorter account with a similar basic message to Matthew and Luke.

However, later scholars questioned Matthean priority and were persuaded that Mark was the first written Gospel, and Matthew and Luke are later expansions of Mark.[5] In a similar vein, this chapter argues that Mark is the first written account among our canonical gospels even though it is put as the second gospel in the canonical order.

Authorship

Similar to other canonical gospels, the author of the Gospel of Mark is not clearly identified, except by the normal expression, the "Gospel according to Mark." However, as preserved by Eusebius, the first reference to the author of Mark's Gospel comes from Papias, bishop of Hierapolis. According to Eusebius, Papias stated that even though he was not an apostle, the second Gospel derives from Mark who was a faithful interpreter of Peter. Papias's testimony informs us that although not in entirely chronological order, Mark wrote all he remembered accurately and tried to make no false statements.[6] Thus, one assumes that Mark would have had access to many different sources, particularly to someone who was actually with Jesus and Jesus's eyewitness. If so, apostle Peter fits this argument since he was the first and the last person who was mentioned in Mark's narrative. Peter is also a major character who acts in the whole narrative next to Jesus. In other words, it is rightly suggested that the tradition considers that this Gospel was Mark's arrangement and reshaping of the teaching and preaching of Peter.[7]

Mark, also known as John Mark, was the son of a Christian woman in whose house the early church gathered in Jerusalem (Acts 12:12).[8] He was the same person who evangelized in Africa, particularly in Egypt, and who planted apostolic churches there and eventually became the first bishop of Alexandria.[9] Even though it is not possible to provide clear evidence about the issue, Jerusalem appears to be the site of the Last Supper (Acts 1:13–14 and Mark 14:14). Moreover, in various events John Mark is mentioned in association with some prominent figures, such as Barnabas and Saul, as an assistant during the first missionary journey (Acts 12:25; 13:4).

---

4. See Robert Stein, *Mark*, BECNT (Eerdmans, 2008), 15–16.

5. See Stein, *Mark*, 16.

6. See Eusebius, *Hist. eccl.* 339.15.

7. See Stein, *Mark* 5; see also Victor Babajide Cole, "Mark," in *Africa Bible Commentary*, ed. Tokunboh Adeyemo (HippoBooks; WordAlive Publishers; Zondervan, 2006), 1197–1198.

8. See Thomas C. Oden, *The African Memory of Mark* (InterVarsity Press, 2011), 21–22, 52.

9. See Edwards, *Mark*, 6, see also Eusebius, *Hist. eccl.* 2.16.

Further, Thomas Oden argues that Mark was born in Cyrene of Africa (as a diaspora Jew), and was related to the apostle Peter and completed his gospel-journey in Alexandria where he died a martyr's death. In short, according to Oden, even though the Gospel of Mark is not only a story of one continent, Africa, it can be considered in some sense to be a story about Africa, and Mark, who understands and shares the pain of Africans, is an African evangelist and author.[10]

Style

Finally, regarding the style Mark used to write his Gospel, Victor Babajide Cole argues that it is unique among other Synoptic Gospels in conveying a sense of urgency, and Mark adopted "an uncommon approach to common accounts."[11] Edwards also argues that since Mark utilized sophisticated styles such as the use of irony, special motifs of insiders-outsiders, commands to silence, and the journey, Mark must be considered as a skilled literary artist and theologian because he used all these styles and arts in order to portray a profoundly theological conception of Jesus as the authoritative yet suffering Son of God.[12]

Further, we believe that Mark had heard Peter teaching and preaching the gospel during his time in Rome. He also knew Peter's speech about the controlling and governing power of the Holy Spirit to enable human writers of Scripture to record the prophecy (2 Pet 1:20–21). In other words, even though the gospel writers including Mark used various styles and methods to record their accounts according to their audiences and cultures, the ultimate governor of the Scriptures is the Holy Spirit.

Place of Composition, Date, and Readers

The date of the composition of Mark is ambiguous, precisely because we cannot see any evidence about its date either in the Gospel itself or in other canonical gospels. The traditional theory, however, indicates that it was written in Rome in the late 60s CE by John Mark. However, having discussed various points of views and suggestions by scholars and theologians, James R. Edwards concludes that a combination of external and internal data appear to point to a composition of Mark in Rome between 64 and 70 CE, likely in the year 65.[13]

The readers of Mark's Gospel are the church in Rome, the gentile readers. The writer explains the Jewish customs and traditions (Mark 7:2–4; 15:42) and translates Aramaic and Hebrew words and phrases into Greek equivalents (3:17; 5:41; 7:11, 34; 10:46; 14:36; 15:22, 34). This indicates that the readers are mainly gentiles in Rome. Furthermore, even though there were a few elites (2–3%) among Mark's readers, most of his audience (80%)

10. See Oden, *The African*, 11–12, 20–21, 29, 139–140.

11. Cole, "Mark," 1197.

12. See Edwards, *Mark*, 2–3; also Stein, *Mark*, 16.

13. See Edwards, *Mark*, 6–9.

were common people and the rest were poor or destitute and outcast.[14] Finally, focusing on the second section of the Gospel, Mark seems to be interested in explaining the suffering and death of Jesus and the persecution of his followers (Mark 8:34–38; 13:9–13) which was the great concern of Roman Christians who should know that Jesus is not only the glorious Son of God but also the suffering and dying Son of Man followed by glorious resurrection. Simply put, most Africans also experience suffering, persecution, and many afflictions in various ways; nevertheless, it can strengthen their faith and finally they will be resurrected.

Outline

- Jesus Christ the Son of God and divine Messiah (Mark 1:1–8:21)
  - Jesus, the glorious Son of God and the Lord around Galilee (Mark 1:1–45)
  - Jesus's mighty acts and opposition from religious authorities and unbelief (Mark 2:1–6:6a)
  - Jesus's mission and mighty acts were misunderstood (Mark 6:6b–8:21)
- Jesus, the suffering Son of Man on the way to Jerusalem (Mark 8:22–16:8)
  - Recognizing and following Jesus on the way to the cross (discipleship) (8:22–10:52)
  - The death and resurrection of Jesus, the Son of Man and the Son of God (11:1–16:8)

Points of Contact with African Realities

Jesus, the Son of God as Servant

We see that having demonstrated Jesus's glorious Messianic activities through miracles in and around Galilee in the first part of Mark's narrative (Mark 1:1–8:30), the same evangelist tells us that Jesus must undergo great suffering and shameful death in Jerusalem (Mark 8:31–16:8). In other words, Mark affirms that the kingdom which was accomplished by the crucifixion of the one who brings it and the cross must go together. Therefore, the Son of God as servant is the key to understanding the full identity of Mark's Jesus.[15]

The reader understands that, most likely, Mark is trying to show that for Jesus the coming of the kingdom entailed both an extraordinary experience of power as well as an experience of suffering and affliction. The two halves of the Gospel therefore underscore two central features of Jesus's identity, the Messianic Son of God and the suffering Son of Man. Thus, New Testament scholars have had different views about Mark's Son of God and Son of Man. Some (e.g., William Wrede, Rudolf Bultmann, Burton Mack)[16] think that the idea of the Son

14. See Anshiso, *Jesus's Identification with the Marginalized and the Liminal*, 24–32.

15. See Anshiso, *Jesus's Identification with the Marginalized and the Liminal*, 1n2.

16. William Wrede, *The Messianic Secret*, trans. J. C. G. Grieg (Attic, 1971), 216–218, 230; Rudolf Bultmann and K. Kundin, *Form Criticism: Two Essays on New Testament Research*, trans. Frederick C. Grant (Harper and Brothers, 196) 71; Burton L. Mack, *A Myth of Innocence: Mark and Christian Origins* (Fortress, 1988), 289–290.

of God and divine messiahship of Jesus in Mark's narrative is an invention of the evangelists and of the early church for their own theological agendas, because Jesus did not think that he was the Messiah. In their view, that was the reason why Jesus rejected Peter's and other disciples' confession as the messiah (Mark 8:31–33).

Others (e.g., Theodor Weeden, Norman Perrin)[17] think that Jesus was/is the suffering and dying Son of Man and the servant rather than the divine Son of God. They also believe that what Jesus said and taught in the second part of Mark's narrative beginning at 8:31 is to correct his first disciples' wrong belief and confession of him because for these scholars Mark is correcting the title "Son of God" in the first part of Mark with the "Son of Man" in the second.

Finally, N. T. Wright rightly argues that Jesus himself thought that he was the Messiah and his first followers understood and declared him to be the Messiah (Mark 8:29–30). So, for Wright, the reason why Jesus's messiahship in the first section was kept secret is because there was a political connotation associated with this title in first-century Jewish territory.[18] Thus, Jesus was cautious about revealing his identity as the Messiah precisely because of the danger that it would not be understood as he intended it and would thus actually hinder his ministry. Put simply, Jesus was concerned not to be misunderstood in terms of current Jewish expectations. He wanted to define his role for himself, rather than be slotted into a readymade role.[19] Therefore, I argue that it is impossible to split Mark's narrative into two as though its first part is about his divinity and the second part is his humanity since both halves speak of his divine Sonship and suffering servanthood and the vindicated Son of Man.[20] So, how can a figure of such transcendent power and authority be at the same time one who suffers such weighty humiliation?

In the history of the world and in many cultures and religious traditions, it is unthinkable for a person to be a divine King/Messiah and servant at the same time. The Ethiopian proverb ሰማይ አይታረስም ንጉሥ አይከሰስም ("The sky is not to be ploughed; the king is not to be accused") indicates that it is difficult to reconcile the concepts of kingship and servanthood in the same person in both political and religious circles, because unlike servants, kings are known as glorious people with supreme power and authority over others.

Unfortunately, unlike ordinary people in African churches, nowadays, on various TV channels,[21] we see some charismatic preachers some of whose followers polish their shoes while they are preaching in glorious pulpits. Their great mansions, expensive cars, and many other material possessions make them unique among others not as servants but as kings and lords over others.

---

17. Theodor Weeden, *Mark: Tradition in Conflict* (Fortress, 1971), 65–67; Norman Perrin, "The Christology of Mark: A Study in Methodology," in *A Modern Pilgrimage in New Testament Christology* (Fortress, 1974a), 104–121.

18. N. T. Wright, *Jesus and the Victory of God*, Christian Origins and the Question of God, vol. 2 (Fortress, 1996), 529–530, 539, 495–497.

19. See Anshiso, *Jesus's Identification with the Marginalized and the Liminal*, 215.

20. For full argument and understanding of the issue by different scholars, read my work in Anshiso, *Jesus's Identification with the Marginalized and the Liminal*, 7–13.

21. For more information see http://gnnliberia.com/2020/03/25/covid-19-will-be-over-march-27th-whether-we-like-it-or-not-tb-joshua-declares.

Nevertheless, Mark tells us that in the revelation of Jesus as both the suffering servant and the messianic Son of God the heavens are ripped open and God himself steps into history (Mark 1:9–12). Therefore, believers in Africa need to understand Mark's Jesus not only as the divine Son of God or a great supernatural figure but also as the real historical figure who suffered and died; in doing so, he is able to understand and share the pains and afflictions of Africans in various ways.

So, Mark the African evangelist and author tells them that the Son of God of Mark 1:1, 11; 9:7, and 15:39 is the Son of Man who did not come to be served, but to serve, and to give his life as a ransom for many (Mark 10:45). Mark's Jesus, thus, is to be understood as a real person through whom the history of Israel's destiny has come to climax in saving the world.

Disciples and Discipleship

In Jesus's days, in the Greco-Roman world the term "disciple" or "discipleship" was used in various institutions such as religious, philosophical, and political circles, indicating that leaders of those institutions had "followers committed to their causes, teachings and beliefs."[22] So one understands that, as in our time, in the first century students come to their teachers to follow and learn or to imitate them in some ways. In contrast, Jesus, the unique Messiah who needs unique followers for his unique purpose and goal, by his own initiative called his first followers to be with him and to prepare them for his mission (Mark 3:13). So Jesus is unique.

The Greek term μαθητής (*mathetes*) and Hebrew terms *talmid* and *limmud* have similar connotations indicating the relationship between the followers and the masters or students and teachers. Furthermore, in Ge'ez, the Ethiopian ancient language, and in the modern Tigrigna, "disciple" means a little but well-trained child of his master. Generally, any disciple may depart from his master for various reasons but a child cannot leave his father. In other words, in Ge'ez and Tigrigna, a disciple is more than a follower but is also a child who is well trained and so remains with and imitates his father/mother.[23] Similarly, in many African traditions there are leaders and followers as well as students and teachers. For instance, in the southern section of Ethiopia there are some Muslim religious groups called *Gariba*.[24] They travel from place to place, following their leaders, seeking something temporal to eat and drink.[25] They obey whatever their local leaders order them to do.

Likewise, some local priests in the Ethiopian Orthodox Tewahido Churches (EOTC), as well as local preachers in many Protestant/Pentecostal groups, travel from place to place with their followers. Using some Christian jargon, they imitate the performance of miraculous activities such as healing the sick and casting out demons. They also imitate preaching the word

22. M. J. Wilkins, "Disciples; Gospels," in *The IVP Dictionary of the New Testament* (InterVarsity Press Academic, 2004), 310.

23. ደስታ ተክለ ወልድ፣ *መጽሃፈ ሰዋሰው፤ ወመዝገበ፤ ቃላት ሐዲስ።* (አርቲስቲክ ማተሚያ ቤት 1948 በኢትዮጵያውያን አቆጣጠር)፣ ገጽ 380.

24. In Amharic these religious groups are called ገሪባ.

25. This includes political leaders and their party cadres as well.

of God in beautiful words. Nevertheless, contrary to the word of God, instead of preaching the Christ crucified, they start to collect money or material possessions for themselves from the poor and destitute. Many of their followers may or may not know who their leaders really are, what the object of their beliefs is and for which purpose they have been following their masters.

Many of them know is that they are following a well-known and attractive person who imitates the performance of something unique and from whom they expect something material such as food, drinks, and money. Simply put, even though this is not always the case, the purpose of some leaders and preachers and their followers, in my opinion, is personal gain rather than following the Christ crucified.

Furthermore, the followers of some preachers wish to copy some spiritual gifts/activities to imitate their leaders. Likewise, many of the followers of those superficial preachers are proud of claiming, "my pastor/bishop or a man or woman of God anointed me; or I am anointed by him/her." Even though this has been a worldwide problem from the very beginning, nowadays it is particularly true of some African preachers, whose focus is on personal gain rather than expanding the kingdom of God.

As the central theme of this study, I will attempt to describe true discipleship as a cross-bearing life and humble servanthood for the whole Christian world, rather than seeking special honor and privilege for oneself. Discipleship in Mark's Gospel is a crucial element to be learned and applied in the context of African/Ethiopian Christian churches, since, for some immature Christians, strong leadership by popular figures is thought to be the most important position or rank, rather than humble servanthood following the example of the crucified Jesus.

Furthermore, although we cannot find the explicit term "leader" or "leadership" in our four gospels, in Mark Jesus has something in mind to prepare humble and servant leaders through his supremely exemplary life and teaching. He did not openly teach his disciples that their roles would be as leaders but rather, as rightly suggested, "he desires that they lead as he leads—proceeding down the road of self-sacrifice."[26] Jesus summoned and repeatedly instructed them to be faithful followers in the way of the cross. In his teaching, we find that the biblical leadership (which is servanthood in Mark 9:35; 10:42–44) is completely different from the leadership of the world which seeks elevation to the highest position above others. In other words, the ways of leadership in the eyes of God and in the eyes of this world are different, even opposite, because unlike this world, the people of God are directed to follow the crucified Messiah by rejecting all pretense to status and high position.

Before beginning his teachings on Jesus's identity as the suffering servant, Mark brings Jesus's question to his first followers: "Who do people say that I am?" (Mark 8:27). Mark records that the people responded according to the common view of the day which indicates "that the various opinions about Jesus had not changed since the early stages of Jesus's ministry—John the Baptist, Elijah, one of the prophets."[27] The answer given in Mark 8:28 is

26. Ben Witherington III, *The Gospel of Mark: A Socio-Rhetorical Commentary* (Eerdmans, 2001), 437.

27. Alan Cole, "Mark," in *New Bible Commentary: 21st Century Edition*, ed. D. A. Carson, R. T. France, J. A. Motyer, and G. J. Wenham (InterVarsity Press, 1994), 964.

also similar to what Herod heard of Jesus in Mark 6:14–15, in which Herod saw Jesus as John the Baptist while others regarded Jesus as Elijah returned.

In other words, similar to our days in African churches, people from diverse backgrounds have various views about Jesus. Some try to associate him with popular religious leaders, prophets, and so-called men and women of God. However, all these points of view concerning Jesus's true identity are inadequate, even incorrect.[28]

Next, in light of people's various opinions about him, Jesus asks the disciples, "But what about you?" (Mark 8:29). In doing so, Jesus wanted to know their personal understanding of who he really was/is. Peter, answering for the other disciples, acclaims Jesus as the "Christ" (Mark 8:29), which means the Messiah. But after Jesus spoke of his suffering, death, and resurrection for the first time in Mark 8:31, Peter rebuked Jesus and urged him not to say anything about his suffering and death (Mark 8:32) because it was strange and unexpected for this to happen to messianic figures of the Old Testament and the first century.[29] Put simply, both ordinary people in 8:28 and Peter and his friends in 8:29 put Jesus in the same category with popular figures of the Old Testament and the Jewish messiahs of the day, while in reality Jesus was and is the uniquely anointed Son of God with the unique purpose and goal of serving and saving many (Mark 10:45).

Peter's confession of Jesus as the Christ was not wrong since his concern for his Lord was great, but in Peter's rebuke (Mark 8:32) Jesus sees the temptation of Satan to grab power and status rather than walking the difficult road to the cross. This happened because Peter and the disciples could not understand that the way of men—which seeks to achieve a high position for oneself—contradicts the will of God which is the way of the cross (Mark 8:33).

Thus, since Jesus vehemently rebuked Peter for announcing him as the Christ, there must be a problem, because Peter's understanding of Jesus's true messiahship is not fully correct; and Jesus's subsequent teaching shows that he is correcting Peter's misunderstanding regarding his real identity as both the glorious Son of God and the suffering Son of Man whose ultimate goal was his death and glorious resurrection.

Hence, African churches need to know that in the second half of Mark's narrative, Jesus redefined or reinterpreted his messiahship in terms of his own suffering, crucifixion, and vindication; so his style of messiahship is totally unique. In other words, he is to be understood not as the Christ of popular expectation as the powerful Messiah, or a Davidic king who destroys his enemies and the enemies of Israel, but as the one who, unexpectedly, spoke of his suffering, death, and rising in terms of the Son of Man.[30] So, with this new teaching of

28. William Lane, *The Gospel of Mark*, NICNT (Eerdmans, 1974), 290.

29. Regarding the messianic figures in the Old Testament and in the first century, unlike Mark's Jesus, there have been some people who appointed themselves, or claimed to be messiahs, or whose followers have declared that they were messiahs. See Anshiso, *Jesus's Identification with the Marginalized and the Liminal*, 101; Michael F. Bird, *Are You the One Who Is to Come? The Historical Jesus and the Messianic Question* (Baker Academic 2009), 50–52.

30. In Mark, Jesus did not use any glorious titles for himself, such as the Son of God, the Messiah, the Christ, the Lord or Master, but just the "Son of Man" who suffers, dies, is buried, and rises in glory. This Jesus is to be followed by his true followers rather than introducing oneself as so-called prophets, apostles, men and/or women of God of Africa.

Jesus, Peter was confused because this was not what he thought should happen to the expected Messiah of Israel.

Moreover, after Jesus began his new teaching, identifying himself as the suffering Son of Man close to the beginning of the second half of Mark's Gospel, during the transfiguration, God's command comes to the disciples, "This is my Son, whom I love. Listen to him!" (Mark 9:7). Here Jesus took Peter, John, and James with him up to the mountaintop, where they were given an extraordinary experience. Then Jesus appeared with two great prophets (Moses and Elijah) of Israel's history in the Old Testament. Then Peter suggested making three temporary dwellings, one for each of them. In doing so, he categorized three of them (Moses, Elijah, and Jesus) on a great and equally glorious level, thinking that these three were the three great figures of the messianic age. In doing so, Peter had already recognized Jesus to be the anointed king Messiah (Mark 8:29) and Elijah as the high priest of the renewed Israel. Moses, then, would be the greatest of the prophets in this reconstituted Israel.[31] So, Peter makes his poor suggestion of honoring each of them with some sort of tent.

Nevertheless, Peter's thoughts are sharply contradicted by the divine voice. By ignoring Moses and Elijah, God decisively distinguished Jesus from these Old Testament figures and specifies him as his beloved son: "This is my Son, whom I love. Listen to him" (Mark 9:7), confirming what he had already said to Jesus at his baptism (Mark 1:11). This singles out Jesus as unique since Moses and Elijah are God's servants; Jesus is God's beloved Son (Mark 12:6) so that his disciples follow him with a clear vision of his identity.

When the three disciples look around, they see that Moses and Elijah have disappeared, or were taken up in the overshadowing cloud, but Jesus is still there with them so that his followers should listen to and obey his subsequent teachings, particularly focusing on the significance of his death and resurrection.

In other words, even though the phrase "Listen to him" indicates the teachings of Jesus's whole life and ministry, in this context, it is about his new teaching concerning his rejection, suffering, unique death, and resurrection. Moreover, even though Moses and Elijah did not face a bitter suffering in their own days, they did not face a shameful death like Jesus would endure.[32] Put simply, unlike Moses and Elijah who were just servants, Jesus's unique status as the Son of God led him to his death and ultimate victory of resurrection. Thus, as the early addressees of Mark's Gospel, African churches need to know Jesus and follow him on the way through suffering, expecting victorious resurrection afterwards.

Finally, similar to the failure of the first disciples of Jesus to understand him, his mission, and the grace of God shown to them through Jesus's constant teachings on true discipleship, the African churches need to learn that although failure in discipleship is not unexpected,

---

31. See Anshiso, *Jesus's Identification with the Marginalized and the Liminal*, 139.

32. In other words, as indicated above, it is a reminder that, unlike Jesus's shameful death, Elijah did not die but was taken up in the overshadowing cloud, and Moses's grave was unknown.

God's mercy is our final hope to follow Jesus to the end, as exemplified in the way Jesus deals with Peter, the spokesman of the disciples (Mark 14:66–72; also 16:7).

Miracles

It is true that the matter of miracles or works of power and magical activities is a big issue worldwide, particularly in Africa, and similarly in many Asian countries and their cultures. So we know that from the time of the ancient world, there have been many people who were thought to be miracle workers, some of whom are often known as magicians, and others who are considered as religious miracle workers, even using Jesus's name (Mark 9:38; Matthew 7:22–23). Thus, thinkers of different times, including the present, have tried to define, interpret, and practice the concept of both phenomena (Magic-Miracle) in various ways. For instance, John D. Crossan argues, "I hold, in summary, that Jesus, as a magician and miracle worker, was a very problematic and controversial phenomenon not only for his enemies but even for his friends."[33] Morton Smith, who is skeptical toward the gospel tradition, also concludes that Jesus himself was not different from magicians. Even though he argued that "miracle working is the most authentic part of the Jesus tradition,"[34] he explained Jesus's works of power along magical lines. In other words, these thinkers do not believe that Jesus is the divine Messiah who is able to perform miracles by himself. Put simply, unlike his contemporaries, Jesus was not dependent on anyone or anything; rather, he did all divine activities by his own power rather than any other source.

However, many gospel scholars and theologians agree that Jesus of Nazareth performed great miracles.[35] Craig Keener affirms that "Jesus's summary of his miracle working . . . clearly indicates that he believed himself a miracle worker."[36] Craig Evans also contends that healing and exorcism miracles were essential parts of Jesus's proclamation of the kingdom of God. In other words, Jesus's works of power (miracles) and verbal proclamation of the gospel go together.[37] It is also recorded that Jesus invited his first followers to preach, to cast out demons and to perform genuine miracles for the expansion of the kingdom of God (Mark 3:14–15). Put simply, for both Jesus and his first followers, preaching the gospel verbally as well as performing works of power support each other

33. John D. Crossan, *The Historical Jesus: The Life of a Mediterranean Jewish Peasant* (Harper, 1991), 311; see also Marcus Borg, *Jesus, A New Vision: Spirit, Culture, and the Life of Discipleship* (Harper & Row, 1987), 67.

34. Morton Smith, *Jesus the Magician* (Harper & Row, 1978), 128; see also John M. Hull, *Hellenistic Magic and the Synoptic Tradition*, SBT 2.28 (SCM, 1974), 78.

35. See Barry Blackburn, "The Miracles of Jesus," in *Studying the Historical Jesus: Evaluations of the State of Current Research*, ed. Bruce Chilton and Craig A. Evans (Brill, 1998), 362; see also Eric Eve, *The Jewish Context of Jesus' Miracles*, JSNTSup 231 (Sheffield Academic, 2002), 360.

36. Craig Keener, *Miracles: The Credibility of the New Testament Accounts* (Baker Academic, 2011), 22.

37. Craig Evans, *Fabricating Jesus: How Modern Scholars Distort the Gospel* (InterVarsity Press, 2008), 141.

while announcing the kingdom of God so that the people of God do the same for the same purpose and goal.

We also need to know that there were magicians, religious leaders, and preachers who were treated as miracle workers before and after Jesus's lifetime in the Jewish and Greco-Roman worlds.[38] In other words, whereas there are many genuine miracle workers following in Jesus's footsteps, nowadays, in certain charismatic movements[39] we observe that there are many pretenders or fake wonder-workers, as a result of which many ordinary people have been confused. Thus, the need exists to distinguish between genuine acts of power following Jesus's example in order to expand the kingdom of God on earth[40] and fake pretenders whose focus is on their own personal gains.

Hence, we understand that as an evangelist and author who knows the needs of the people, Mark wrote this gospel to help the people of God rethink the unique nature of Jesus's miracles and some techniques of magicians and so-called miracle workers whose tricky activities confuse the church of God and destroy the faith of many.

Therefore, it is important to explore how Mark portrays the miracles of Jesus in his narrative and some magical elements and gestures reported in the Gospel which have also been used in some African charismatic movements. Then, contrary to the superficial magical techniques of Jesus's contemporaries and activities of some charismatic movements in Africa, we will discuss the uniqueness of the miracles of Mark's Jesus and their significances.

As Paul Achtemeier says, "it is quite natural . . . among the important things Jesus did was the working of 'miraculous,' or 'acts of power'. . . . More than any other of our four Gospels, Mark's narrative is filled with stories of such acts by Jesus."[41] In other words, the fact that Mark devoted most of his Gospel to recording miracles is unquestionable. Nevertheless, a few questions that must be raised are: Which miracles are recorded by Mark in his narrative? What is the significance of all these miracles in Mark's teaching? And what is the unique nature, purpose, and goal of Jesus's miracles in Mark, unlike his contemporary magicians and deceitful miracle workers of our days?

Before discussing their significance, it is necessary first to list, in Table 4.1, what sort of miracles Mark reports and put them in four categories rather than trying to explain each story. In Mark we see nature miracles, healing miracles, casting out demons (exorcism), and raising of the dead.

---

38. Two Jewish charismatic figures of the first century BCE—Honi and Hanina Ben Dossa and Apollonius of Tyana of the Hellenistic divine men tradition—are good examples.

39. In saying so, I am not generalizing all charismatic and/or Pentecostal movements, but am referring to some who perform fake miraculous activities in the name of Jesus for their own personal gains.

40. For instance, Keener provides various examples of the performance of genuine miracles in various parts of Africa, not only from among charismatic/Pentecostal movements but also from mainline churches (see Keener, *Miracles*, 309–338).

41. Paul Achtemeier, *Mark*, Proclamation Commentaries (Fortress Press, 1986), 85; see also Keener, *Miracles*, 23–24; John Wilkinson, *The Bible and Healing: A Medical and Theological Commentary* (Eerdmans, 1998), 65.

Table 4.1. List of Miracles in Mark.

Nature miracles	Stilling the storm (Mark 4:35–41), feeding 5,000 and 4,000 people (6:30, 8:1), walking on the water (6:48), and withering the fig tree (11:12–14, 20–25)
Healing miracles	Healing the leper (Mark 1:4), Peter's mother-in-law (1:30–31), the sick in the evening (1:32), the paralytic (2:3–12), the hemorrhaging woman (5:25–29), a man with a withered hand (3:1–5), the gentile woman's daughter (7:24–30), the epileptic boy (9:17–19), many people (6:1–5), two blind men (10:46–52), a deaf-mute (7:31), and a blind man at Bethsaida (8:22–26)
Casting out demons (Exorcism)	Casting out unclean spirits (1:23–26; 3:11) and a demon entering a herd of swine (Mark 5:1)
Raising of the dead	A ruler's daughter (Mark 5:22–42)

Then, what is the significance of all these miracles in Mark? Is it to astonish others and be appreciated by others as a result of which Jesus will get great fame and wealth as some African preachers think? Not at all! But rather, as suggested, "his deeds manifest the kingdom, his words define it."[42] The prime reason for miracles in Mark is to proclaim the coming sovereign rule of God on earth. Suzanne Henderson also rightly adds that:

> from the beginning of his ministry, Mark's Jesus encounters adversarial forces in the form of sickness and demonic possession . . . and . . . even natural powers . . . [and] . . . he launches a decisive campaign against the powers that would prevent the full establishment of God's rule upon the earth.[43]

Thus, unlike some superficial miraculous activities in some deceitful movements, first, nature miracles in Mark indicate Jesus's victory and authority over natural elements and powers of chaos and the eschatological provision of peace and security even in the midst of trouble. For instance, the miracle of the feeding of thousands indicates Jesus's ability to provide for the needs of his followers even when they are in a desperate condition. Ultimately it points to God's eschatological Messianic feast[44] or provision, so that all African believers, too, learn to trust in him for all of their needs.

Second, as N. T. Wright said "the effect of these cures . . . was not merely to bring physical healing . . . but to reconstitute those healed as members of the people of Israel's god,"[45] the ultimate goal of healing miracles was not simply to relieve physical pains, but to heal and set free all those who trust in God from the ultimate enemies (Satan and sin). Jesus saw healing

42. Donald A. Hagner, "Synoptic Gospels," in *New Dictionary of Biblical Theology*, ed. Brian S. Rosner, T. Desmond Alexander, Graeme Goldsworthy, and D. A. Carson (InterVarsity Press, 2000), 127.

43. Suzanne W. Henderson, *Christology and Discipleship in the Gospel of Mark* (Cambridge University Press, 2006), 256.

44. See Henderson, *Christology*, 175–176.

45. N. T. Wright, *Jesus and the Victory of God* (SPCK, 1996), 192.

miracles "as part of the inauguration of the sovereign and healing rule of the covenant God of Israel, and welcoming sinners to the renewed membership of the true people of God."[46] Thus, "the reader can always take Jesus's ministry of healing as dealing not only with sickness but also with sin through forgiveness,"[47] because Mark in 2:12 tells us that as the agent of God and God himself, Jesus is able to heal from both physical disease and sin through forgiveness.

Furthermore, in Mark 7:27 when the gentile woman expressed her faith in him, Jesus performed a miracle from which one learns that Jesus's miraculous activities are not only for the benefit of Jews (Mark 5:33), but also for gentiles.[48] In other words, as David Wenham and Steve Walton write, "an important ingredient in the miracles was faith: he healed in response to peoples' faith, he was limited by lack of faith."[49] Put simply, unlike the activities of some pretending miracle workers of our day everywhere, particularly in Africa, peoples' faith is a very important theme for the real miraculous ministry to be successful.[50] Nevertheless, we need to understand that Jesus is not always dependent on our faith to do all his divine activities.

Further, as Graham Twelftree points out "the nature of faith that Mark is describing through *Jarius' request is not in Jesus simply as wonder worker but as a healer and saviour*."[51] So unlike the term "faith" proclaimed by the prosperity gospel preachers, here it "indicates that Jesus is a divine life giver, who is able to grant entry to the future kingdom."[52] Finally, although the ultimate purpose of healing miracles in different forms is to proclaim God's reign, it is also true that Jesus did them because he cared about the people in need, and he had the power to act out of that compassion.

Third, casting out demons (exorcism) indicates Jesus's ultimate victory over Satan, the real enemy of all human beings. In doing so, the reader knows that Jesus was engaged in the eschatological battle against Satan, the enemy of God and his people. Twelftree sees Jesus's exorcism miracles "as primarily one of a battle against Satan and his minions . . . [and] the first stage of the destruction of the kingdom of Satan and the arrival of the expected kingdom";[53] and finally Jesus won the ultimate victory. Therefore, the people of God in Africa should know that Satan is a disarmed and defeated enemy such that the followers of Jesus should know that they are victorious in him.

Fourth, the raising of the dead in 5:21–43 shows us the power of Jesus over death, and that he is able to give eternal life to those who believe in him. Further, having demonstrated Jesus's divine authority over sin through forgiveness, over illness through healing, over demons through exorcism, and over natural chaos and over physical death, which are seen as

46. Wright, *Jesus and the Victory of God*, 192; also David Wenham and Steven Walton, *Exploring the New Testament* (SPCK, 2001), 107–108.

47. Graham Twelftree, *Jesus the Miracle Worker: A Historical and Theological Study* (InterVarsity Press Academic, 1999), 65.

48. Twelftree, *Jesus the Miracle Worker*, 79–80.

49. David Wenham and Steve Walton, *Exploring the New Testament* (SPCK, 2001), 104.

50. Henderson, *Christology*, 252–253.

51. Twelftree, *Jesus the Miracle Worker*, 73, emphasis in original.

52. Twelftree, *Jesus the Miracle Worker*, 73.

53. Twelftree, *Jesus the Miracle Worker*, 357.

manifestations of ultimate death, Jesus, the unique Messiah, has revealed his supreme authority over death itself through his own death[54] and followed by glorious resurrection. Therefore, the death of Jesus is not a sign or symbol of his failure or defeat on the cross but rather the ultimate victory of God over death itself,[55] and Mark's "Jesus is the crucified but victorious King-Messiah."[56]

However, similar to some Jewish holy men and Hellenistic divine men traditions of the first century, as well as some superficial preachers in African charismatic movements, why did Mark's Jesus use some religious and traditional elements and gestures[57] of the day while performing miracles? Regarding this, it is not correct to conclude that two actions that are similar in external features must have an identical meaning and significance. They may have their own meanings within their own social and cultural contexts. So, Jesus used gestures and techniques during his healing miracles; particularly physical touch, which he had in common with his contemporaries. Nevertheless, Jesus was not dependent upon these techniques since in general he used a simple command, sometimes even in his physical absence. In other words, unlike his contemporaries in the first century and superficial miracle workers in some parts of Africa, Jesus of the gospels is unique and so not dependent upon techniques since he was able to perform miracles by himself even from a distance (Matt 8:6–10; Luke 7:6–10).

For instance, as recorded in Mark 5, Jesus did not refuse the act of touching by the hemorrhaging woman during her miraculous healing but emphasized that her faith was a great instrument of her healing. In showing the power that is conveyed through bodily contact we see that Mark is correcting any magical understanding when he accentuates the role of faith.[58] In doing so, Jesus reinterpreted the actual means of her healing from the ritual action of magic to faith in Jesus.[59]

Likewise, Jesus utilized saliva and spitting when he healed people (Mark 7:33; 8:23). Thus, as indicated above, both Smith and John M. Hull conclude that by utilizing saliva and spitting on his patients during his healing ministry, Jesus is not different from his contemporary magicians.[60] However, since the Markan Jesus healed the blind and the deaf, sometimes with and the other times without saliva and since the gesture of using saliva has no evidence in the

---

54. See Peter G. Bolt, *Jesus' Defeat of Death: Persuading Mark's Early Readers* (Cambridge University Press, 2003), 10–11, 271, 279.

55. Wright, *Jesus and the Victory of God*, 609–610.

56. David Seccombe, *The King of God's Kingdom* (Paternoster Press, 2002), 577–578, 601.

57. Further, even though there are some ritual elements and gestures with their own meanings and significances in their contexts, we see some examples such as baptismal rites (Mark 1:9–11) and a story of a group of women who came to Jesus's tomb to perform burial anointing rites (Mark 16:1–8). There are also mentions of uncleanness and ritual washing (Mark 7:1–5), as well as three stories of healing rituals (Mark 5:1–20, 25–34, 35–43). Also, healing people through anointing and hand-laying practices are mentioned (Mark 1:31, 41; 5:25–34, 41; 6:5; 7:31–35; 8:23, 25; 9:27; 14:3).

58. John Paul Meier, *A Marginal Jew: Rethinking the Historical Jesus*, vol. 2 (Doubleday, 1994), 709.

59. R. Guelich, *Mark 1–8:26*, WBC 34 (Word, 1989), 148.

60. See Smith, *Jesus the Magician*, 128; Hull, *Hellenistic Magic and the Synoptic Tradition*, 78.

ancient world as a means to heal deafness, it is unlikely to conclude that Jesus shares these gestures and techniques with magicians and other imitators to perform miracles.

On the question of touching Jesus or being touched by him for healing, it seems that the people who were trying to touch him thought that he had magical power and believed that if they touched him, they would be healed. Nevertheless, since Jesus healed many with and without using gestures or rituals, but only by mentioning their faith in him, touching Jesus or being touched by him must not be considered as essential for his divine activities. So, I argue that due to their previous beliefs in deities and in traditional magic practices, some gentiles may have come to Jesus hoping that he would do the same thing, but Jesus healed and saved them because of their faith in him, rather than their traditional expectations, even though he did not totally ignore their expectations based on faith in him.

Contrary to some African superficial "miracle workers" and "healers" who use a variety of objects such as holy oil, their own sweat, their hands, saliva, anointed water, and holy leaves and fruits from plants, we see that Jesus heals and saves many even in his physical absence from a distance (Matt 8:6–10; Luke 7:6–10). Thus, rather than putting his hands or other objects on people for healing, Jesus's physical contact in Mark should be understood not as religious/traditional power, but as a symbol of spiritual contact or of an intimate relationship between Jesus and the healed people who have faith in him.

Finally, the miracles of Jesus in Mark are distinct from other traditional miraculous activities of his contemporaries and those who have been perceived as miracle workers in invented forms in some religious movements because Mark's Jesus is the unique Messiah whose purpose and goal are unique. So, in Mark's view, the major purpose and goal of miracles is to help African believers gain an insight of Jesus not only as a great miracle worker of the day and/or unique among other miracle workers but also he himself is the miracle/sign. In other words, unlike other fake miracle workers of various eras, the main purpose of Jesus's miracles in Mark is primarily to point to his identity as the Son of God. Put simply, Jesus's miracles were central to who he was/is; so he is more than his miraculous activities.

The Cross of Christ in Ethiopian Christianity and the Gospel of Mark

As Oden said, "The roots of African Christianity lie in Mark."[61] It is also possible to think that Mark was interested in writing about the significance of the cross of Christ. Thus, it is likely that the Ethiopian Orthodox Tewahido Church (EOTC) in Africa was instigated in the early fourth century[62] by two captive brothers (Frumentius and Edesius).[63] These brothers moved from Alexandria in Egypt to Aksum/Axum in the northernmost part of Ethiopia. Since then, the tradition of the cross has been practiced and celebrated by the EOTC every

61. See Oden, *The African Memory of Mark*, 12.

62. See Jon Abbink, "The Cross in Ethiopian Christianity: Ecclesial Symbolism and Religious Experience," in *Routledge Companion to Christianity in Africa*, ed. Elias Kifon Bongmba (Routledge, 2016), 122–140, here 123.

63. Ghelawdewos Araia, "The Ethiopian Orthodox Tewahido Church: History, Doctrine, and Challenges," *Institute of Development and Education for Africa (IDEA)*, November 20, 2017: 2.

year on September 27 because they claim that a portion of the cross of Christ was found in northern Ethiopia. The term *Meskel* or *Mesqel* (መስቀል) is the Tigrigna and Amharic word for "the cross" transliterated from Ge'ez to Latin script. So, from the very beginning of the history of Christianity in Africa, the issue of the cross has been very important.[64]

Both the EOTC and some from the Ethiopian Evangelical Church (EEC) join the celebration of the cross every year in the middle of September. But although each of these Christian faith traditions claims to believe in the cross, they think and practice various things in different forms in their own traditions. For instance, whereas the EOTC believe that the wooden cross which was buried at Golgotha by the Jews was found on September 27 and they celebrate it with great religious sensitivity and traditional activities, the EEC discourages the veneration of crosses. They do not carry and/or display it as a living symbol of the cross of Christ, other than occasionally using it symbolically in religious activities in their assemblies. In other words, even though each of these Christian traditions claims to believe in the cross of Christ and speak of it in their congregations, they both think about and practice it in different ways according to their own traditions.

Similar to the EOTC, the cross has been celebrated among several groups in southern Ethiopia, where Protestant denominations dominate, and in the southwest, where several different groups or tribes live.[65] They celebrate the Meskel/cross in various religious activities, traditions, and languages for various reasons. Some of them do have their own traditional religious practices, while others claim to be members of the EOTC but without knowledge of its doctrines. Still others think that they are members of the Protestant churches but without enough knowledge of Jesus, who was crucified for the salvation of the world.

Many in the EOTC and other evangelical churches in the southern part of the country claim that Meskel is the celebration of the cross, but without understanding Jesus the crucified Messiah. They include some traditional religions while calling the event Meskel and celebrating it in the same month of the year, September. During the event, they dance and sing special songs in their own cultures and languages while celebrating the holiday. In doing so, they associate it with aspects of their society's cultural and social life rather than the cross of Christ.

However, how does Mark think of and teach about the cross of Christ? First, the readers of Mark know that the concept of the death of Jesus on the cross is indicated not only in the second half of the Gospel wherein the Passion Narratives are recorded and reported, but there are also some indications of his coming, suffering, and death in the early chapters of the Gospel. Morna Hooker explains that Mark links the suffering and death of Jesus with others before and after Jesus's death, particularly with the fate of John the Baptist. Although it is not clearly stated as such, if we read the whole story, we understand that the first hint

64. Agizachew Tefera, ዐጼ ዘርዓ ያዕቆብ እና አባ እስጢፋኖስ በኢትዮጵያ ቤተ ክርስቲያን ታሪክ (Zer'a Yaqob and Aba Estifanos in the Ethiopian Church History) (Rehobot Printers, 2023), 127–133.

65. Instances in the southern area are Kambata, Haddiya, Gamo Gofa, Wolayita Dawuro, Gurage, and Mareko, among others, and in the western section of the country, Shakicho, Kaficho, Yem, and Konta.

of the coming suffering and death of Jesus and its significance is indicated in Mark 1:14.[66] The verb in Greek, παραδοθῆναι, that Mark uses when describing the arrest of John, is the same verb he used later to describe Jesus's being handed over into the power of evil in 9:31, 10:33, and 15:1–15. Likewise, it is the verb he uses about Judas's betrayal of Jesus (3:19; 14:10, 18, 21, 42, 44). In other words, what happens to John and what happens to Jesus in the whole story is similar, although the manner of their death was different.[67] John Stott also affirms that "from Jesus' youth, indeed even from his birth, the cross cast its shadow ahead of him."[68]

Second, even though he does not directly mention the term "the cross," in the heart of his passion-narrative Mark mentions the rejection, suffering, death, and resurrection of Jesus (Mark 8:31–9:1, 31–41; 10:33–45). Here all of the teachings are organized around three passion-resurrection predictions.

Third, during Jesus's death on the cross, we see the three hours of darkness which bring Jesus to speak of his experience of abandonment by God: Ελωι ελωι λεμα σαβαχθανι ("My God, my God, why have you forsaken me"; 15:34). This is the only phrase that Jesus spoke from the cross in Mark rather than in other Gospels.

The language Jesus used to express his abandonment on the cross in verse 34 is not only about the heaviness of the darkness but also his forsakenness by God. In this regard, scholars raise some questions regarding which language Jesus used to speak of his forsakenness. However, whatever language Jesus spoke (whether it was Hebrew or Aramaic), it was the language of the common people in the first century.

Further, Jesus's cry on the cross must be understood as his total self-identification with all people that are affected by sin as a result of which they experience God's absence. So Jesus bore the sins of the world while he underwent extreme suffering as "a ransom for many" (Mark 10:45), being abandoned not only by human beings but also by his Father.

Fourth, the proclamation of the Roman centurion during Jesus's death on the cross (Mark 15:39) reveals that crucifixion shows us what it means for God to be God precisely because the divine identity of Jesus as the Son of God is ultimately "revealed not only in his deeds of divine authority, nor merely in his coming participation in God's cosmic rule, but also in his godforsaken death."[69]

In other words, unlike other fake miraculous activities and the traditional expectations of the day, Jesus entered into the shame of humanity and experienced its horror through crucifixion, and finally won victory over its power through resurrection. Thus, the crucified

---

66. Morna Hooker, *Not Ashamed of the Gospel: New Testament Interpretations of the Death of Christ* (Eerdmans, 1994), 47–49.

67. See Anshiso, *Jesus's Identification with the Marginalized and the Liminal*, 75.

68. John Stott, *The Cross of Christ* (InterVarsity Press, 1986), 17, 28.

69. Richard Bauckham, *Jesus and the God of Israel: God Crucified and Other Studies on the New Testament's Christology of Divine Identity* (Eerdmans, 2008), 266; see also Anshiso, *Jesus's Identification with the Marginalized and the Liminal*, 80.

Jesus would mightily deliver his people from the power of the evil one and give them total victory over death on the cross.

Finally, Mark's readers should know that following after Jesus involves crucifying oneself for the sake of Jesus and the Gospel. Regarding one's taking up his/her cross, whilst some think it is a literal or the wooden cross, others think that it is metaphor about the cross of Christ. When the whole context is taken into consideration, it seems to be a literal/material object (the tree), in some cases, and metaphorical in others.

In Mark 8:31, Jesus's prediction is about his own literal death, although the means of his death was not specified until Mark 15. In Mark 8:35 the first followers of Jesus were told that they might have to lose their lives through suffering martyrdom for the sake of Jesus, because carrying crosses and literal death by crucifixion was familiar for those who rebelled against Roman authority. The person who was crucified was publicly displayed, given the lowest possible status, and humiliated before the world.[70] It is this status in the eyes of the world that Jesus says that his followers must assume for themselves.

Nevertheless, it is difficult to take the words "the cross" fully literally because it may lose its universal relevance to the life of most followers of Jesus. Best said, "the next part of the command, 'follow me' . . . envisages a process, and not a short journey to the place of execution."[71] Thus, it seems that the intention of Jesus is not only for his few followers to die literally but to illustrate the fact that to follow him is a process. Best rightly stresses that *the command* of Jesus to take up the crosses is not only to his smaller group but also to the larger crowd; therefore, he is not saying that all the crowd should face martyrdom, because some of them who were standing there would not experience death at the present time.[72] Moreover, "Jesus does not speak of his disciples being *nailed* to crosses, only of their *taking* crosses."[73]

However, during our talk on this issue, Stephen Wright, my former instructor and mentor, argued that presumably any bystanders who saw someone "take up" a cross would know that they were on their way to being nailed to it; so it should be true of Jesus and his followers.[74]

Thus, others think that taking up crosses must not be understood metaphorically as meaning patience, endurance of persecution, and discomfort for Jesus's sake, since those who want to follow him might lose their lives.[75] In other words, when Jesus talks about taking up one's cross, for his contemporaries, it could have been taken literally or by others as a metaphor. Therefore, Mark's readers are reminded to be ready to suffer the threat of crucifixion literally. It is also worth believing that taking up one's cross means the absolute renunciation of all forms of status in the eyes of the world for the sake of Jesus and the gospel.

---

70. Dennis M. Sweetland, *Our Journey with Jesus: Discipleship According to Mark* (Michael Glazier, 1978), 307; see also Lane, *The Gospel of Mark*, 307.

71. Ernest Best, *Disciples and Discipleship: Studies in the Gospel According to Mark* (T&T Clark, 1986), 8.

72. See Best, *Disciples and Discipleship*, 8.

73. Robert Gundry, *Mark: A Commentary on His Apology for the Cross* (Eerdmans, 1993), 436, emphasis in original.

74. This was Stephen Wright's suggestion during our private email discussion on September 26, 2024.

75. R. T. France, *The Gospel of Mark: A Commentary on the Greek Text* (Paternoster Press, 2002), 340.

An African Gospel

Developing from four points of contact with African reality, Mark's readers realize that his Gospel is an African gospel. For Africans, each point of contact here is directly associated with a major message of the Gospel's essential aspect rather than just similarly related ideas.

In contrast to the secular world's leaders in general and many African church leaders and preachers in particular, it is Mark's Jesus who is able to become servant-king. Thus, first of all, it is crucial to know Jesus fully and his agenda on earth before coming to the position of leadership at any level. It is also possible to understand that Mark's Jesus has been rebuking many of us in Africa to stop self-promotion and self-acclamation in order to become great and superior leaders over others rather than serving others humbly as he did. What we learn from the exemplary life and ministry of Mark's Jesus is that the secret of greatness in the reversal value of the kingdom of God is humble servanthood (Mark 10:43–44).

Therefore, the disciples of Jesus in Africa are called to follow Jesus with a clear vision of his real identity to serve him and his people, humbly. The way of discipleship is to help and serve others rather than being served by others and benefiting in a material way from the people we serve (Mark 10:29–30). Furthermore, since Jesus called his first disciples to be with him and to perform miraculous activities (Mark 3:13–19), we Africans are invited to do the same thing as he did; however, we have to be sure of the major purpose of all miracles which must reveal Jesus himself who is the Son of God and the Servant.

Even though some Africans who claim to be Christians may utilize the symbols of the cross in various forms and for various purposes, such as beauty, protection from demonic forces, and to distinguish themselves from other religious groups, and so on, the cross of Christ must be understood and remembered as the place of the victory of God through Jesus's suffering and shameful death because his godforsaken death became the climax of his revelation not only to Africans and Jews but also to the whole of humanity. And it "transfers the place of God's presence from its hiddenness in the holy of holies to the openly forsaken cross of the dead Jesus."[76] It is also precisely through the godforsaken death of Jesus on the cross that the barriers were broken down and even gentiles could recognize the true identity of Jesus as the Son of God (15:39).[77] In short, Jesus's death on the cross has changed a place of shame into the place of glorious victory of God in Jesus's resurrection.

Conclusion

Mark tells us, that Jesus is not only the glorious Son of God with extraordinary actions, but also the real historical person who presented himself as the suffering Son of Man. In doing so, Mark's Jesus must be recognized as Yahweh himself in person, and his coming as Yahweh's coming (Mark 1:2–3). Thus, I would like to challenge all Christian Africans, including Ethiopians, to rethink Mark's Jesus as the servant-king, whose unique identity is revelation to

76. Bauckham, *Jesus and the God of Israel*, 267.

77. See Anshiso, *Jesus's Identification with the Marginalized and the Liminal*, 86.

those who have eyes to see. So, those who identify themselves with him as his disciples, both men and women, are expected to follow him on the way he underwent to the victory of God on the cross.

Likewise, since Jesus is one of a kind in his being as well as his divine actions, we do not need to put him on the same level with any of the Old Testament figures, New Testament close friends, including his family members, or current so-called prophets, apostles, and miracle workers in Africa. Jesus is unique.

Further Reading

Achtemeier, Paul. *Mark*. Proclamation Commentaries. Fortress Press, 1986.

Anshiso, Bekele. *Jesus's Identification with the Marginalized and the Liminal: The Messianic Identity in Mark*. Langham Monographs, 2018.

Bauckham, Richard. *Jesus and the God of Israel*. Eerdmans, 2008.

Best, Ernest. *Disciples and Discipleship: Studies in the Gospel According to Mark*. T&T Clark, 1986.

Bolt, Peter. *Jesus' Defeat of Death: Persuading Mark's Early Readers*. Cambridge University Press, 2003.

Cole, Victor Babajide. "Mark." In *Africa Bible Commentary: A One-Volume Commentary Written by 70 African Scholars*, edited by Tokunboh Adeyemo. WordAlive Publishers; Zondervan, 2006.

Edwards, James. *The Gospel According to Mark*. Eerdmans, 2002.

France, R. T. *The Gospel of Mark: A Commentary on the Greek Text*. Paternoster Press, 2002.

Gundry, Robert. *Mark: A Commentary on His Apology for the Cross*. Eerdmans, 1993.

Henderson, Susanne. *Christology and Discipleship in the Gospel of Mark*. Cambridge University Press, 2006.

Keener, Craig. *Miracles: The Credibility of the New Testament Accounts*. Baker Academic, 2011.

Lane, William. *The Gospel of Mark*. NICNT. Eerdmans, 1974.

Oden, Thomas. *The African Memory of Mark*. InterVarsity Press, 2011.

Sweetland, Dennis. *Our Journey with Jesus: Discipleship According to Mark*. Micheal Glazier, 1987.

Twelftree, Graham. *Jesus the Miracle Worker: A Historical and Theological Study*. InterVarsity Press Academic, 1999.

Witherington, Ben III. *The Gospel of Mark: A Socio-Rhetorical Commentary*. Eerdmans, 2001.

Wright, N. T. *Jesus and the Victory of God*. SPCK, 1996.

CHAPTER FIVE

The Gospel of Luke

Michael F. Wandusim
University of Münster
Germany

Introduction

To PRESENT AN African introduction to the Gospel of Luke is both challenging and innovative. Innovative in the sense that there are hardly any such introductions based on the unique African experience of Christianity and the dynamic engagement of the Bible on the continent.[1] Therefore, this volume is a valuable opportunity to address this gap in scholarship. It is, however, challenging because what we know as Africa today is a vast continent, with fifty-four countries with diverse ethnic groups and cultures. Consequently, it is not possible to present an introduction to the third Gospel that takes cognizance of all relevant experiences and issues in Africa. In light of these limitations, the introduction presented here will be situated in West Africa, with Ghana serving as a specific case study. By implication, all the relevant issues and examples that will be cited to bring into dialogue the major themes of the Gospel of Luke will be from the Ghanaian context. It is evident that, even in the case of Ghana, the contextual hermeneutical resources used here do not represent the full spectrum of the country's ethnic groups. Nevertheless, the "good news" is that some of the issues discussed below may resonate with readers from various African contexts.

Historical Background

Authorship

The third gospel of the New Testament currently bears the title, Κατὰ Λουκᾶν, "according to Luke," implying that it was written by Luke. However, the book itself is formally anonymous; it does not state its author by name. Why then the name Luke? This is based on church tradition in the second century which attributed this Gospel to Luke, a companion of Paul and also, Luke the physician. The earliest Christian sources to make this attribution are Irenaeus and the Muratorian Canon, followed by Clement of Alexandria, Tertullian, Origen,

1. A helpful bibliography of African scholarship on the Gospel of Luke is provided by African Theology Worldwide: https://african.theologyworldwide.com/bibliography/4497488.

and Eusebius.[2] The name itself occurs three times in the New Testament: Colossians 4:4; 2 Timothy 4:11; Philemon 24. Current critical scholarship on the Gospel is, however, divided on this traditional attribution. Those who side with church tradition that it was written by Luke the physician, a companion of Paul, present at least four points of their argument: the title of the Gospel, the second-century church tradition, a particular interpretation of the we-passages found in Acts 16:10–28:16, and the so-called "medical language" that the Gospel exhibits.[3] Those who hold a contrary view, especially that he was a companion of Paul, dispute these points by raising doubts about the originality of the current title of the Gospel (including that of the other Gospels), the reliability of church tradition, offer different interpretations of the we-passages of Acts, and find the medical-language argument as not unique to Luke in the ancient context.[4] Because of its anonymity, this debate remains in the realm of speculation. Therefore, the discussion of authorship tends to focus on the text itself, maintaining "Luke" for purposes of discussion and reference. This is what this introduction will do also. The author will be referred to as "Luke," while the book itself will be referred to as "the Gospel of Luke."

Basing the determination of authorship on the text is essential because the author refers to himself in the first person in the preface of the Gospel, 1:1–4, and dedicates it to a named individual, "most excellent Theophilus" (cf. Acts 1:1). This implies that truly it was written by someone whom the original recipient(s) would have known. It becomes clear from this that the same author is behind Acts.[5] Based on 1:1–4 and the contents of the rest of the Gospel, therefore, some scholars argue that the author of the Gospel of Luke could have been a gentile Christian[6] of the second/third generation (maybe previously part of the *God-fearers* of Acts), who was well educated, with a good command of the Greek language, well versed in the Septuagint (LXX), and situated in the upper-middle class of the Hellenistic society.[7]

That it was written anonymously, however, should not present any major barrier to its interpretation because, as M. Eugene Boring has rightly asserted, it stands in the tradition of the biblical narratives which were all produced anonymously and for which acceptance or

2. M. Eugene Boring, *An Introduction to the New Testament: History, Literature, Theology* (Westminster John Knox Press, 2012), 588–590. Cf. Mikeal Carl Parsons, "The Third Gospel and the Acts of the Apostles," in *The Cambridge Companion to the New Testament*, ed. Patrick Gray (Cambridge University Press, 2021), 134–139.

3. Boring, *An Introduction to the New Testament*, 588.

4. See Boring, *An Introduction to the New Testament*, 588–589; Reinhard Feldmeier, "Die Synoptischen Evangelien," in *Grundinformation Neues Testament: Eine bibelkundlich-theologische Einführung*, ed. Karl-Wilhelm Niebuhr, 5th ed. (Vandenhoeck & Ruprecht, 2020), 116; Mark Allan Powell, *Introducing the New Testament: A Historical, Literary, and Theological Survey*, 2nd ed. (Baker Academic, 2018), 163–166.

5. Hence, categories such as Luke-Acts and Luke's double work or volume. Recent debates on these categories are discussed in Parsons, "The Third Gospel and the Acts of the Apostles," 144–148; Knut Backhaus, "Luke-Acts: A Theory in Turmoil," *Early Christianity* 15, no. 1 (2024): 5–24, https://doi.org/10.1628/ec-2024-0003.

6. Cf. Michael Wolter, *The Gospel According to Luke: Luke 1–9:50*, trans. Wayne Coppins and Christoph Heilig, BMSEC (Baylor University Press, 2016), 1:11, who thinks of Luke as growing up in a Jewish family.

7. See Boring, *An Introduction to the New Testament*, 575, 577, 590; Feldmeier, "Die Synoptischen Evangelien," 113–115; Parsons, "The Third Gospel and the Acts of the Apostles," 134–139.

rejection was decided on the basis of content and not authorship.[8] Similarly, the Ghanaian setting is replete with many folktales transmitted orally through several generations without claim to a single authorship. For example, such popular Ghanaian tales as the *Ananse Stories* and the myth about how *Nyame* (the creator God) became distant from human dwelling[9] have been told in ways that their moral content become the object of interpretation and reception more than their authorship or origin.[10]

Audience and Provenance

Just like the question of authorship, that of audience and place of composition of the Gospel are uncertain. Regarding audience, however, Luke clearly states Theophilus as the recipient (1:3) and indicates the purpose of writing as providing a reliable account of the Jesus story from which Theophilus could gain certain knowledge of the things he has been instructed (1:4). However, exactly who and where Theophilus was is unclear. Such an individual, if not a literary creation of Luke, could belong to the upper class of society given that the author addresses him as "most excellent Theophilus" (κράτιστε Θεόφιλε).[11] Nevertheless, it could be that the Gospel in actual fact was meant for a larger Christian audience and that Theophilus could have been that "wealthy patron" who sponsored it, given the cost implications involved in producing such a voluminous work.[12] Based on its content and style, it is also speculated that the author had a gentile Christian audience in mind, coupled with an eye on non-Christians of the upper class for whom he tries to mediate the Christian gospel.[13]

No certain knowledge exists about the provenance of the Gospel. Some suggested locations include Antioch, Ephesus, and Rome, with Rome mostly favored because of the geographical constitution of the narrative of the two volumes (i.e., Luke-Acts), which begins in Jerusalem in the east and ends in Rome in the west.[14] The geographical scope of the narrative suggests a universal focus with a universal audience in mind. This is implied in the universalistic nature of Luke's genealogy of Jesus in Luke 3:23–38. For instance, in contrast to the genealogy of Jesus presented by Matthew (1:2–17), which is primarily Jewish-centered with Jesus as the "son of David, the son of Abraham" (Matt 1:1),[15] Luke traces Jesus's genealogy beyond these

8. Boring, *An Introduction to the New Testament*, 588.

9. Kwame Gyekye, *African Cultural Values: An Introduction* (Sankofa Publishing, 1996), 8.

10. See Ekaputra Tupamahu, "The Gospel of Luke," in *An Asian Introduction to the New Testament*, ed. Johnson Thomaskutty (Fortress Press, 2022), 104–105, who has made similar observations in the Indonesian context.

11. Cf. Acts 23:26; 24:3; 26:25.

12. See Powell, *Introducing the New Testament*, 163–166.

13. Feldmeier, "Die Synoptischen Evangelien," 115–116; Powell, *Introducing the New Testament*, 165–166.

14. See Boring, *An Introduction to the New Testament*, 590–594; Wolter, *The Gospel According to Luke*, 1:12.

15. Admittedly, Matthew's inclusion of the four gentile women (Tamar, Rahab, Ruth, and the wife of Uriah, in Matt 1:3, 5–6) in addition to Abraham (who is "an ancestor of a multitude of nations," Gen 17:4, and in whom "all the families of the earth shall be blessed," Gen 12:3) anticipates Jesus's universal significance beyond Israel (cf. Matt 28:18–20).

key Jewish figures to include Adam, who is referred to as "son of God" (Luke 3:38).[16] Luke thus universalizes his Jesus narrative by making it relevant for both Jewish and non-Jewish audiences.

Again, as was stated in relation to authorship, lack of knowledge of original audience and location of the text does not pose any barrier to its interpretation in Ghana. Precisely because many Ghanaian folktales, including religious ones, have been traded down the ages without such details, they continue to be told and their content finds new appropriations. The same is the case with the Gospel of Luke.

Date

The date of authorship is equally unknown. The majority of scholarly speculations on the issue converge on the period from 80 CE to 90 CE based on two important assumptions—that Luke relied on Mark dated in the early 70s CE and that he was not yet aware of the Pauline corpus.[17] Other contending views date it in the period 90–120 CE on the basis that Luke could have known Josephus's works, that of the Pauline corpus, and that Luke's community was no longer facing persecutions related to the reigns of emperors Nero and Domitian.[18] All this remains conjectural and each exegete has to take a reasonable stand depending on prior exegetical assumptions. Ultimately, a date after 70 CE is favored here on the premise that Luke certainly used Mark, and granted that Mark was probably written in the 70s, a date after this time makes sense. Nevertheless, for our contextual reading of the Gospel of Luke in Ghana, this speculation has fewer hermeneutical implications, since the reception of oral traditional stories relies less on their compositional dates and more on their ethical content for their current audience.

Outline

Lukan scholarship presents several narrative outlines to the Gospel based on different criteria. Michael Wolter explains the issue as follows: "[Luke] narrates the structuring markers of his story. This fact, however, is also the reason why no two commentaries have the same outline for the Gospel of Luke. Every outline is brought to the Lukan story of Jesus from outside and is therefore already part of its interpretation. Accordingly, an outline is a text that the commentator writes."[19] Doubtless, Luke presents his Jesus story differently from his co-synoptics (Mark and Matthew) which is informed by his theology, purpose, and literary style. These parameters underlie the outline below.[20]

16. This in effect traces Jesus's descent back to God and thus underscores his divine sonship stated earlier in Luke 1:32, 35; 3:22.

17. Boring, *An Introduction to the New Testament*, 587; Feldmeier, "Die Synoptischen Evangelien," 118.

18. Boring, *An Introduction to the New Testament*, 589.

19. Wolter, *The Gospel According to Luke*, 1:19.

20. Cf. Feldmeier, "Die Synoptischen Evangelien," 110; Boring, *An Introduction to the New Testament*, 568.

1:1–4	Preface
1:5–2:52	The birth narratives (John, Prophet of the Most High and Jesus, Son of God)
3:1–9:50	The ministry of Jesus in Galilee and Judea
9:51–19:44	Jesus's journey to Jerusalem (the *travel narrative*)
19:45–24:53	The ministry of Jesus in Jerusalem (Passion, Easter, and Ascension)

The Lukan story of Jesus so outlined narrates the unfolding of the salvation history of God which was promised in the Scriptures of Israel and which reached its decisive point in the life and ministry of Jesus, the Son of God. Moreover, everything took place within a historical time and space (3:1–2), directed by God through the Holy Spirit. Composing his Jesus story in this manner, Luke exhibits unique features incomparable to the canonical Gospels. These include his special interest in the Holy Spirit, his understanding of the kingdom of God as proclaimed by Jesus, his centering of marginalized actors (women, poor, sinners, etc.), and his key emphasis on prayer. These unique elements will be brought into creative hermeneutical dialogue with societal and religious developments in contemporary Ghana.

Luke in the West African Context

It has been a consistent feature of African biblical scholarship to read biblical texts in light of sociocultural, economic, and political realities in Africa.[21] Undergirding this orientation is the acknowledged "hermeneutical advantage" that African readers of the New Testament possess due to the close affinities that exist between the biblical worldviews and that of Africa.[22] Thus, the worldview underlying the Jesus story in the Gospel of Luke, where the spiritual (unseen) and physical spheres of existence interpenetrate each other is easily discerned in Ghana.[23] Therefore, the following presentation highlights hermeneutical resources within the Ghanaian context that can facilitate an African understanding of the Gospel and also indicates hermeneutical implications, especially in cases where Luke challenges an existing contextual issue in Ghana. Admittedly, the discussion aims less at exhausting the selected issues and more at stimulating further contextual investigations on them in West Africa.

21. Gerald West, "Biblical Hermeneutics in Africa," in *African Theology on the Way: Current Conversations*, ed. Diane B. Stinton, SPCK International Study Guide 46 (SPCK, 2010), 22; Andrew M. Mbuvi, "African Biblical Studies: An Introduction to an Emerging Discipline," *Currents in Biblical Research* 15, no. 2 (2017): 152–155; Michael F. Wandusim, "The Bible and Its Interpreters: Assessing the Future of Biblical Interpretation from a West African Context," in *What Does Theology Do, Actually? Exegeting Exegesis 2*, ed. Phillip A. Davis Jr., Daniel Lanzinger, and Matthew Ryan Robinson (Evangelische Verlagsanstalt, 2023), 235–236.

22. See Werner Kahl, "The Power of Interpretation—the Interpretation of Power: The Gospel and the Bible as Contested Spaces in Global Christianity," in *Mission and Power: History, Relevance and Perils*, ed. Atola Longkumer, Jørgen Skov Sørensen, and Michael Biehl, vol. 33 (Fortress Press, 2016), 54–57, https://doi.org/10.2307/j.ctv1ddcrhd.8; Kwame Bediako, *Christianity in Africa: The Renewal of a Non-Western Religion*, Trends in African Christianity (Regnum Africa, 2014), 252–255.

23. See John S. Pobee, *Toward an African Theology* (Abingdon, 1979), 43–52; Elizabeth Mburu, *African Hermeneutics* (Langham Global Library, 2019), 21–64.

Jesus, the Holy Spirit, and Charismatic Renewal in Ghana

As previously stated, the Holy Spirit features significantly in Luke's Jesus story. A statistical investigation using πνεῦμα alone indicates that Luke uses the word more frequently than the other New Testament authors.[24] Out of the seventy-eight occurrences of the word in the Synoptic tradition, Luke alone takes a greater portion of thirty-six.[25] Admittedly, πνεῦμα in the New Testament does not always mean Holy Spirit. Indeed, depending on the context and qualifiers used, it could mean "wind," "breath," "ghost," "soul," "evil or unclean spirits," and "the (Holy) Spirit" (Luke 8:29; 9:42, 24:37, 39; John 3:8; Heb 1:7; 2 Thess 2:8).[26] Yet it is instructive to note that the majority of the cases in the Gospel of Luke refers to the Holy Spirit.[27] In all, much of the Spirit's activity is concentrated in 1:5–4:19; namely, the background narrative preceding Jesus's public ministry. In the rest of the Gospel, the Spirit recedes into the background, appearing in the *travel narratives* a few times (10:21; 11:13; 12:10).

In the background narrative, Luke assigns significant functions to the Spirit. The Spirit is that active divine presence that is responsible for filling certain individuals with divine power and inspiration to act or speak in certain ways in relation to the unfolding salvation of God. That the Spirit is responsible for inspired speech/prophecy can be seen in relation to characters like Elizabeth (1:41–45), her husband Zechariah (1:67–79), and Simeon (2:25–32). In the case of Elizabeth, the visit of Mary occasions her pneumatic experience (1:41c), which is immediately followed by her inspired utterance in 1:42–45. Luke demonstrates the connection between the pneumatic experience of being "filled with the Holy Spirit" and prophesying much clearer in the case of Zechariah's *Benedictus*[28] (1:67–79). Here he uses the expression "was filled with the Holy Spirit" (ἐπλήσθη πνεύματος ἁγίου) and connects it with prophesying, so that verses 68–79 are supposed to be understood as the result of the pneumatic experience in verse 67. Simeon's *Nunc Dimittis*[29] can equally be seen to be the result of the Holy Spirit because of the three-fold mention of the Spirit in 2:25–32. Ultimately for Luke, all these speeches have one agent behind them, the God of Israel, who through his Spirit bears witness to his promised salvation that he is about to accomplish in Jesus.

Apart from being responsible for inspired speech, the Holy Spirit commissions and provides the driving force behind the ministries of John the Baptist and Jesus. From being

24. Michael F. Wandusim, "The Holy Spirit in West African Christianity: A Case Study in Ghanaian Christianity," in *Geist: Phänomenologie - Religionsgeschichte - Theologie. Ein Kompendium*, ed. Benjamin Schliesser, Reinhard Feldmeier and Jörg Frey, WUNT 542 (Mohr Siebeck, 2025), 1153–1174.

25. Robert Morgenthaler, *Statistik des neutestamentlichen Wortschatzes*, 3rd ed. (Gotthelf, 1982), 133; Paul Hoffmann, Thomas Hieke, and Ulrich Bauer, *Synoptic Concordance: A Greek Concordance to the First Three Gospels in Synoptic Arrangement, Statistically Evaluated, Including Occurrences in Acts*, vol. 3 (Walter de Gruyter, 2000), 225.

26. See BDAG, 832–836; Horst Balz and Gerhard Schneider, eds., *Exegetisches Wörterbuch zum Neuen Testament*, 3rd ed. (Kohlhammer, 2011), 282.

27. Hoffmann, Hieke, and Bauer, *Synoptic Concordance*, 225. Cf. Wandusim, "The Holy Spirit in West African Christianity."

28. Meaning "blessed," technically a of song of praise and thanksgiving. It comes from the first words of Luke 1:68 in the Biblia Sacra Vulgata (the Latin Bible): "Benedictus Deus Israhel . . ." ("Blessed be the God of Israel . . .").

29. Meaning, "now let depart" which are the first words of Simeon's prayer in the Latin Bible.

filled with the Holy Spirit in his mother's womb (1:15) to becoming great in spirit (1:80), Luke makes it clear that John is decisively called and empowered by God, like the Old Testament prophets, to prepare the way for his in-breaking salvation through Jesus. Likewise, yet differentiated, the Holy Spirit is ultimately responsible for Jesus's existence and the power behind his entire earthly ministry. He is called "the Son of God" (υἱὸς θεοῦ) because the Spirit is responsible for his conception (1:35). Moreover, the divine confirmation of this status at baptism is equally linked to the Spirit (3:22). Furthermore, Luke demonstrates that Jesus's ability to defend his divine sonship in the temptation narrative (4:1–13) is equally the work of the Spirit. For it is the prior "full of the Holy Spirit" (ἐπλήσθη πνεύματος ἁγίου) and being "led by the Spirit *in* the wilderness" (ἤγετο ἐν τῷ πνεύματι ἐν τῇ ἐρήμῳ, 4:1) that accounts for the triumph over the devil. Additionally, it is in the Spirit's power that Jesus returns from the wilderness (4:14) to begin his public ministry from 4:16 onwards. Narrated this way, Luke makes it explicit that the Jesus we meet in power and in suffering is Spirit-filled and Spirit-driven. In other words, he is the one through whom God is acting to bring about his promised salvation. This could account for the reason why the Spirit recedes to the background in the rest of his Gospel, because all that is happening after 4:14, 18, in Luke's view, should be understood as having the Spirit behind it as the driving force.

It is worth underlying that Luke contrasts the *Holy* Spirit with other spirits he terms as *unclean* or *evil* spirits who are responsible for various sicknesses in their human hosts (4:33, 36; 6:18; 7:21; 8:2, 29; 9:42; 11:24). However, the bearer of the Holy Spirit, Jesus, drives out the unclean/evil spirits from the human hosts as part of proclaiming the good news of the kingdom of God (9:1–2; cf. 11:20)

A West African reading of the Gospel of Luke will identify with Luke's pneumatology, especially with the aspects of inspired utterance and empowerment. Luke's pneumatology will in most cases be affirming Ghanaian Christian experience since the early twentieth century. This is because the history of West African Christianity in general and Ghanaian Christianity in particular cannot be properly understood without considering the charismatic renewal movements that emerged in the early twentieth century, which resulted in schisms of some mission-founded churches and the subsequent emergence of the so-called African Instituted Churches (AICs), like the Twelve Apostles Church, Musama Disco Christo Church, the Saviour Church, the Apostles' Revelation Society, the Eternal Sacred Order of Cherubim and Seraphim Society, Aladura (Church of the Lord), African Faith Tabernacle Congregation, and later the Pentecostal-charismatic churches.[30] The charismatic renewal movements emphasized the essential role of the Spirit in Christian experience and, in West Africa, was led by prophetic figures who were seen as bearers of the Spirit, foremost among them being Prophet Wade Harris of Liberia.[31] Today, the dominance of Pentecostal-charismatic Christianity is largely to

30. See Michael Wandusim, *The Lord's Prayer in the Ghanaian Context: A Reception-Historical Study*, SBR 20 (De Gruyter, 2021), 122–136.

31. See Cephas Narh Omenyo, *Pentecost Outside Pentecostalism: A Study of the Development of Charismatic Renewal in the Mainline Churches in Ghana*, Mission: Missiologisch Onderzoek in Nederland 32 (Uitgeverij Boekencentrum, 2002), 67–71; Bediako, *Christianity in Africa*, 91–93.

be explained by the fact that these churches championed the need for pneumatic experiences in Christian worship such as speaking in tongues, healing and deliverance, prophecy, and so on, which are all strictly linked to the activity of the Spirit. An important religious expression in this Christianity is "anointing of the Spirit" (cf. 4:18) which is defined as "the 'empowering presence of God' that makes things happen. . . . It is the power of God in action."[32]

The appropriation of pneumatic experiences was not only facilitated by the translation of the Bible into West African mother tongues,[33] but importantly also the reading of texts like the Gospel of Luke. This validated existing "primal pneumatology"[34] which carried with it the belief in the existence of benevolent and malevolent spirits who could possess human and nonhuman beings for good or evil. For instance, among the Ewes of southeast Ghana, it is known that spirits of local deities (*trɔ*) could call a person into priesthood through possession and also spirit possessions (in Lukan terms, "fullness" or "in-filling") could produce inspired utterances.[35]

The charismatic renewal movements impacted the religious and socioeconomic spheres of Ghana in several ways. For instance, their activities led to the Pentecostalization of mission-founded churches and the emergence of Pentecostal-charismatic megachurches. These mega-sized churches have made significant contributions to the education sector in Ghana by setting up schools and university colleges, and also investing in the area of health through their construction of health facilities. Nonetheless, as is common with new religious movements, charismatic renewal activities have also given rise to certain excesses that can be termed as *commercialization of pneumatic experiences* in some sections of Ghanaian Christianity. This is exemplified in such practices as the sale of anointing oil, anointed water, anointed church paraphernalia, religious consultation fees, and "sowing seed" (i.e., monetary donations) into the life of the "anointed" man or woman of God for prosperity. These practices ultimately benefit self-seeking pastors who engage in them to the detriment of their members. However, in my view, such excesses in Ghanaian Christianity are due to a disconnect between pneumatology and Christology which Luke holds together in his Gospel and even in Acts. Consequently, a contextual reading of the Gospel should be dynamic and critical.

Jesus, the Kingdom of God, and Politics in Ghana

It is not for nothing that Luke couples his pneumatology with Christology, because the Spirit-conceived, -filled, and -empowered Jesus (1:35; 4:1, 14) has proclaiming "the good news of the kingdom of God" as his mission on earth (4:43; 8:1), which he also shares, in a limited sense,[36]

32. Kwabena J. Asamoah-Gyadu, "Anointing Through the Screen: Neo-Pentecostalism and Televised Christianity in Ghana," *Studies in World Christianity* 11, no. 1 (2005): 22.

33. See Bediako, *Christianity in Africa*, 66.

34. I use this in a nontechnical sense to mean the traditional religious understanding of and belief in the existence and working of various spirit entities in West African societies.

35. See Birgit Meyer, *Translating the Devil: Religion and Modernity Among the Ewe in Ghana*, International African Library (Edinburgh University Press, 1999), 67–68, https://doi.org/10.1515/9781474471008.

36. They will assume full responsibility after Easter as Luke makes it clear in Acts.

with his disciples (9:2). Indeed, the Jesus yet to be born is declared as king whose kingdom will have no end (1:32–33). Thus, for Luke, in Jesus's life and ministry, the kingdom of God is effectually present.[37] His words and deeds embody the reality of the kingdom (11:20; 17:20–21). Understood this way, it should be noted that Jesus's teachings, exorcisms and healings, mediation of forgiveness, association with the otherwise socially marginalized, and miracles become means by which the reality of the kingdom is experienced in the here and now. In this vein, Boring argues, "the time of Jesus is the time of the presence of the kingdom on earth."[38] Nevertheless, Luke also presents the kingdom in terms of future expectation (19:11; 22:16, 18; 23:51) and even of prayer (11:2). In other words, the kingdom that was once present with the Spirit-filled and -driven Jesus, will reappear at the parousia in power at the end of time.[39] Relatedly, it is in this context that one should understand Luke's soteriology—that the promised salvation is not achieved only on Good Friday on the cross, but through the life and ministry of Jesus, the Son of God, people experience God's salvation here and now.[40]

Embodying the kingdom in words and deeds, however, presents a spiritual duality in which the kingdom of God is confronted by "cosmic anti-God powers" whom Luke associates with Satan or the devil (4:1–13).[41] Apart from the devil, anti-God powers are personified in demons/unclean spirits who are responsible for different kinds of sicknesses in human beings. But clearly, for Luke, the presence of the kingdom in Jesus means defeat for Satan and his cohorts. Hence the proclamation of the kingdom goes hand in hand with healings and exorcisms (9:1–6; 10:9, 17). Moreover, because the time of Jesus's public ministry is the time of the presence of the kingdom, Satan is completely absent (4:14–22:2) and only makes an appearance again (after departing in 4:13) at the dying moments of Jesus's ministry (22:3). It is, however, important to note that the Satanic confrontation in the temptation narrative subtly permeates the rest of the narrative, manifesting in demonic outcries and hostilities from Jewish groups such as the Pharisees, scribes, lawyers, and Jewish leaders. This culminates in Judas's betrayal, which Luke explicitly interprets as the work of Satan (22:3).

It can be reasonably assumed that readers of the of Gospel of Luke in West Africa will have no difficulty comprehending the kingdom of God as embodied in Jesus, given the significant similarities between the cosmology projected in the narrative and the primal worldview prevalent in the subregion. Indeed, Ghanaian readers will relate easily to the connection established between diseases and anti-God spiritual entities because they believe that certain sicknesses, especially those which are protracted and medically difficult to cure, are caused by malevolent spirits such as witches. Hence, the phenomenon of prayer camps (discussed

37. Boring, *An Introduction to the New Testament*, 599.

38. Boring, *An Introduction to the New Testament*, 606.

39. Boring, *An Introduction to the New Testament*, 606.

40. There are diverse views on Luke's soteriology. See Timothy W. Reardon, *The Politics of Salvation: Lukan Soteriology, Atonement, and the Victory of Christ*, LNTS 642 (T&T Clark, 2021). Also, Boring, *An Introduction to the New Testament*, 608; Christfried Böttrich, "Lukas in neuer Perspektive," *Evangelische Theologie* 79, no. 2 (1 April 2019): 114–129, https://doi.org/10.14315/evth-2019-790206.

41. Parsons, "The Third Gospel and the Acts of the Apostles," 149; Boring, *An Introduction to the New Testament*, 559.

below) and healing/deliverance practices are prevalent in Ghanaian Christianity, particularly among Pentecostal-charismatic churches. Although influenced by the traditional religious culture, these practices emerged from and are sustained by reading, especially in the mother tongue, such gospel stories as the Gospel of Luke, where the proclamation of the kingdom of God is coupled with casting out demons who cause various sicknesses and discomfort to human beings.

Beyond the spiritual implications of the kingdom of God, there are also the political implications. Indeed, it is central to Luke's narrative theology that Israel's God is presented as the Lord over universal history and that God determines how it ultimately ends through his divine plan as set forth in Scripture and operationalized in Jesus of Nazareth (1:5–52).[42] This explains why, unlike other evangelists, Luke consciously embeds his Jesus narrative in the ongoing (political) history of the ancient world as dominated by Rome by making explicit references to two Roman emperors and their provincial representatives: Caesar Augustus, Quirinius (2:1), Caesar Tiberius (Augustus's successor), Pontius Pilate, Herod Antipas, and Philip (3:1).[43] And it should be noted that the term βασιλεία itself can be rendered "empire." Therefore, references to the imperial context imply that the proclamation of the kingdom of God embodied in the life and ministry of Jesus was happening in a colonial context where the people of God, under political subjugation, were longing for when God would finally bring about their restoration, that is, independence (Acts 1:6; Luke 1:69–74; 2:25; 17:20; 19:11; 23:51; 24:21). That is a background that a West African reading of the Gospel will not fail to recognize due to the century's long history of Western colonial and imperial domination of the subregion. While formal colonialism, in the political sense, has long been overthrown in West Africa, starting with Ghana in 1957, neocolonial practices still perniciously exist in different avatars through the Bretton Woods Institutions, Western multinational corporations, and "digital empires" like Facebook, Google, Apple, and so on.[44] Neocolonialism in Africa at large takes the form of economic domination, imbalanced international relations, political interference, and cultural subjugation.[45] In that light, the promised kingdom that brings down the powerful (neo)colonialists from their thrones while uplifting the lowly, sending the rich away empty while filling the hungry with good things (1:52–53) should be hermeneutically engaged in a West African reading of the Gospel of Luke.

Moreover, even though he largely portrays Roman officials, and by extension the Roman Empire, in a positive light, Luke shows at various points that proclaiming and embodying the kingdom of God implies proclaiming a new/alternative kingdom to Rome. Such instances of inference include: his use of ἀσφάλεια (certainty, security) in 1:4 (cf. 1 Thess 5:3) which is

42. Boring, *An Introduction to the New Testament*, 556–558.

43. See the so-called "six-fold synchronization" in Luke 3:1–2.

44. Cf. R. S. Sugirtharajah, "Introduction: The Bible, Empires, and Postcolonial Criticism," in *The Oxford Handbook of Postcolonial Biblical Criticism*, ed. R. S. Sugirtharajah (Oxford University Press, 2022), 4, https://doi.org/10.1093/oxfordhb/9780190888459.013.37.

45. A helpful discussion is provided by Ifeanyi John Obikwelu, Gérard-Marie Messina, and Andy Chukwuemeka Odumegwu, "The Effects of Neocolonialism on Africa's Development," *PanAfrican Journal of Governance and Development* 4, no. 2 (2023): 3–35.

reminiscent of the *Pax Romana*; the declaration of Jesus as king (1:32; 19:38); and the declaration that the kingdoms of the οἰκουμένης (*oikoumenēs*) (i.e., the civilized world, Roman Empire) are in the hands of the devil (4:5–8), which obviously implies that Jesus's kingdom is of God.[46] In addition, for Luke, the kingdom of God presents an alternative view of the exercise of (political) power, which he indicates through the obvious redaction of his source in 22:24–27 (cf. Mark 10:42–45).

Furthermore, the theme of reversal of status is central to the character of the God whose kingdom is proclaimed: he favors the humble and scatters the proud, brings down the powerful from their thrones and uplifts the lowly, fills the hungry with good things and sends the rich away empty handed (1:47–53); he centers those who are at the margins of political, economic, and social constellations, seeks the lost, and justifies the humble. The status-reversal theme is set down in a radical form in the Sermon on the Plain (6:20–36). Thus, in reality, the kingdom as Jesus embodies it in his life and ministry upsets existing social orders by turning them upside down.[47]

In postcolonial West Africa, therefore, a reading of Luke's theology of the kingdom of God as potentially anticolonial, decolonial, and socially liberative is hermeneutically relevant. It entails factoring into the exegetical process such socioeconomic and political issues as high levels of public sector corruption, frequent coup d'états, frequent unconstitutional maneuvers to perpetually hold on to political power, and local collusion with Western and Eastern (China) neocolonial and imperial elements that sustain the subtle domination of the cultural, economic, and political spheres of Africa.[48]

Jesus, Women, and Gender Discourse in Ghana

Concern for and centering of the otherwise socio-religiously marginalized actors in the Jesus story—women, so-called tax collectors and sinners, and the poor—is distinctive of Luke. This is doubtlessly consistent with his status-reversal theology, according to which the God of history, present in Jesus's life and ministry by means of the Spirit, turns his gracious attention to the poor, marginalized, and repentant, and through that pulls them to the center of divine and social attention and sends the powerful, rich, and privileged to the margins, especially if they refuse to use their privileged status to enhance the lot of the marginalized.

It is important to observe that the women characters in the Gospel of Luke are not only present, but they also take on significant roles. Right in the opening section of the Gospel, Elizabeth (1:5–7, 24–25, 40–45, 57–60), Mary (1:26–39, 46–56; 2:5–7, 19, 51), and Anna (2:36–38) are given active roles in the unfolding drama of God's promised salvation. They qualify to be enabled by the Spirit (specifically Elizabeth and Mary) to participate in the

46. See Boring, *An Introduction to the New Testament*, 562.

47. Feldmeier, "Die Synoptischen Evangelien," 119.

48. Various suitable contextual hermeneutical approaches exist in African biblical scholarship for this purpose. See Frederick Mawusi Amevenku and Isaac Boaheng, *Biblical Exegesis in African Context* (Vernon Press, 2022); Mburu, *African Hermeneutics*, 65–89; Mbuvi, "African Biblical Studies," 160–164; Wandusim, *The Lord's Prayer in the Ghanaian Context*, 140–155.

history of salvation alongside their male counterparts like Zechariah (1:5–23, 67–79), Joseph (2:4–6, 16), and Simeon (2:25–35). This is all the more striking when compared with Matthew and Mark. Additionally, the women/female characters in the Gospel of Luke are presented as worthy recipients of the salvific effects of the kingdom of God mediated through Jesus. This includes divine compassion in the case of the widow of Nain (7:11–17; v. 13a ἐσπλαγχνίσθη ἐπ' αὐτῇ); forgiveness of the sinful woman (7:36–50; cf. 5:17–26); as well as healing and deliverance (4:38–39; 8:2, 40–56; 13:10–17). Furthermore, women are depicted as providing (material) support for Jesus and his disciples (8:2).[49] Relatedly, they are portrayed as faithful disciples as they follow Jesus from Galilee till his burial in Jerusalem (23:55–56).[50] In addition, alongside the Pharisees (7:36; 11:37), women also become hosts of Jesus, as the case of Martha and Mary indicates (10:38–42). Moreover, they appear as characters in Jesus's parables on the kingdom of God (13:20–21) and the lost coin (15:8–10).[51] The parable of the lost coin particularly underscores Luke's "gender-inclusive theology."[52] That Luke is intentional about including women characters in his story is confirmed by the frequent paralleling of stories with male and female characters.[53] Further, they become prime and credible witnesses of the resurrection on the first Easter day (24:1–11). Their credibility as witnesses is seen from the perspective of the narrator and the readers, because in the narrative world of the text their report is not believed (24:11). Finally, and more importantly, they are *recognized* through identification by *name* which serves to concretize and particularize their identity. Thus, we meet women like Elizabeth (named alongside her husband), Mary, Anna (all three in 1–2), Mary Magdalene (whom Luke describes as having seven demons cast out from her, cf. Mark 16:9), Joanna, Susanna (8:2–3), and Martha and Mary (10:38–39). Viewed from the patriarchal context of the first century, the recognition of women in the Gospel of Luke serves to mainstream them in the Jesus story, which is an expression of Luke's status-reversal theology. That notwithstanding, it has been observed that women are not part of the chosen twelve apostles (6:13–16) and also "the female image of God" in 15:8–10 is still situated in a patriarchal, domestic setting.[54]

A Ghanaian reading comes to the Gospel with a mixed perception of women. On the one hand, the Ghanaian context highly prizes the female figure because women are thought to provide care and hold society together. Like Elizabeth and Mary, they play procreative and nurturing roles that sustain communities over generations,[55] hence, the feminine epithet

49. Scholarly opinions differ on the kind of *diakonia* rendered by the women. See Wolter, *The Gospel According to Luke*, 1:331.

50. Paul John Isaak, "Luke," in *Africa Bible Commentary: A One-Volume Commentary Written by 70 African Scholars*, ed. Tokunboh Adeyemo (WordAlive Publishers; Zondervan, 2006), 1244.

51. See also Luke 18:1–8.

52. Tupamahu, "The Gospel of Luke," 123.

53. See Powell, *Introducing the New Testament*, 174; Boring, *An Introduction to the New Testament*, 582–583.

54. Tupamahu, "The Gospel of Luke," 123. See also Melanie A. Howard, "Recent Feminist Approaches to Interpreting the New Testament," *Currents in Biblical Research* 20, no. 1 (1 October 2021): 72–73, https://doi.org/10.1177/1476993X211047300.

55. See Wandusim, *The Lord's Prayer in the Ghanaian Context*, 171.

Ɔbaatanpa, which literally means "good mother."[56] When Afua Kuma in her *Jesus of the Deep Forest*[57] describes Jesus as *Ɔbaatanpa* she underscores her understanding of Jesus as one who identifies with women and who at the same time transcends gender.[58] Additionally, women hold religio-cultural and political positions as traditional priestesses,[59] Christian pastors, and queen mothers in traditional, political settings. For instance, Yaa Asantewaa, a former *Edwesohemaa* (i.e., Queen Mother of Ejisu of the erstwhile Asante Empire in Ghana), is forever eulogized as an "epitome of African womanhood and resistance to European colonialism" due to her role in the last British–Asante war in 1900/1901 (the so-called Yaa Asantewaa War).[60] Moreover, among the Asante of Ghana the *Asantehemaa* (queen mother) plays a nominating role in the process of enstooling (i.e., installing) a new *Asantehene* (king of Asante).[61] Regarding Lukan gender-inclusive theology, the Ga of southern Ghana refer to God as *Ataa-Naa Nyonmo* ("Father-Mother God") to illustrate the genderlessness of God. All this, among others, provides a hermeneutical bridge between gender discourse in the Gospel of Luke and in Ghana. On the other hand, however, the marginalization of women through social change, patriarchal cultural elements cemented through missionary Christianity, and eclectic reception of the Bible means that Luke's gender-inclusive theology presents a challenge to the Ghanaian context. Such concrete expression of female marginalization as high levels of gender inequality in education, income, employment, and public leadership roles, thus requires hermeneutical attention in a West African reading of the Gospel. Concretely, this implies carefully integrating into our exegesis of the Gospel of Luke insights from theological reflections of African women theologians—both academic and popular—who see in the nativity narrative of Luke 1–2 their experiences, fears, and hopes reflected and centered in the salvation history of God.[62]

Jesus, the Poor, and Poverty in Ghana

Just like women, the poor equally receive great narrative attention in the Gospel of Luke. This operates within the larger Lukan theme of money and possession or the rich and the poor.[63]

---

56. See Philip T. Laryea, "Mother-Tongue Theology: Reflections on Images of Jesus in the Poetry of Afua Kuma," *Journal of African Christian Thought* 3, no. 1 (June 2000): 50.

57. Afua Kuma, *Jesus of the Deep Forest: Prayers and Praises of Afua Kuma*, trans. Jon Kirby (Asempa Publishers, 1980). The Akan version is entitled, *Ayeyi ne mpaebɔ: Kwaebirentuw ase Yesu*.

58. See Laryea, "Mother-Tongue Theology," 50.

59. Among the Ewes of southeast Ghana, see Meyer, *Translating the Devil*, 67.

60. T. C. McCaskie, "The Life and Afterlife of Yaa Asantewaa," *Journal of the International African Institute* 77, no. 2 (2007): 178.

61. See Beverly J. Stoeltje, "Asante Queen Mothers in Ghana," in *Oxford Research Encyclopedia of African History* (Oxford University Press, 2021), 1–32, https://doi.org/10.1093/acrefore/9780190277734.013.796. Cf. Laura S. Grillo, "African Rituals," in *The Wiley-Blackwell Companion to African Religions* (Blackwell, 2012), 122–123.

62. See Mercy Amba Oduyoye, *Introducing African Women's Theology*, Introductions in Feminist Theology 6 (Sheffield Academic Press, 2001), 51–65.

63. A helpful discussion is provided by Outi Lehtipuu, "The Rich, the Poor, and the Promise of an Eschatological Reward in the Gospel of Luke," in *Other Worlds and Their Relation to This World*, ed. Tobias Nicklas, Joseph Verheyden,

Within this theme, the status-reversal theology operates forcefully in ways that mean the poor are favored by God and the rich are rejected, especially those who do not care for the poor. Already, this is overtured in the *Magnificat*[64] (1:46–55), where God fills the hungry with good things (πεινῶντας . . . ἀγαθῶν) and sends the rich away empty (πλουτοῦντας κενούς). Thereafter, Jesus indicates in his inaugural sermon in Nazareth that his ministry was about bringing good news to the poor (4:18; πτωχοῖς). Accordingly, the poor become God's "favorite" in Jesus's ministry; for instance, in the Sermon on the Plain (6:17–49), the poor and hungry are blessed (vv. 20–21), but the rich and full are cursed (vv. 24–25). That Luke here has the literal poor and rich in view is evident by contrasting his material with Matthew 5:3–12, where Matthew qualifies the poor with the phrase "in spirit" (v. 3) and does not mention the rich at all in his Beatitudes. Moreover, the poor man Lazarus (πτωχὸς δέ τις ὀνόματι Λάζαρος, 16:20) is blessed in eternity (16:22), but the rich man who did not care about poor Lazarus at his gate is cursed with eternal torment after death (16:23–24).

The rich only become recipients of eschatological blessings so long as they use their riches to help the poor.[65] For instance, the leading Pharisee is admonished by Jesus to invite, among others, the poor as dinner guests instead of the rich (14:1, 12–14). Moreover, the rich ruler is asked to sell his possessions and distribute the proceeds to the poor and receive treasure in heaven (18:18–23), and, lastly, Jesus conferred salvation on Zacchaeus (19:9) only after the latter declared his readiness to relinquish half of his possessions to the poor (19:8). In contrast, those who are absorbed by their riches and possessions without care for the poor are excluded from eschatological blessing and consigned to eternal suffering, as chiefly depicted in the story of the rich man and Lazarus (16:19–31). The rich fool in 12:16–21 equally stands in the same light.

Ultimately, Luke has a communal understanding of wealth which should be used to enhance the lot of the poor and not cherished. Likewise, in Ghana, as is true of other parts of Africa, less well-off relatives are not to be left unsupported. Rich family members are expected to demonstrate social solidarity by caring for the poor ones, including those beyond the nuclear family.[66] It is in this vein that the following saying among the Kusaas of northeast Ghana makes sense: *omi du'am*, literally "he/she knows family." It is used in a context where a person supports not only their biological siblings, but also other kin members. This communal value is, of course, threatened by social change, urbanization, and the so-called prosperity gospel

---

Erik M. M. Eynikel, and Florentino García Martínez (Brill, 2010), 229–246; Paul J. J. van Geest, "The Fundamental Paradox in Luke's Perception of Money and Property," in *Themes and Texts in Luke-Acts: Essays in Honour of Bart J. Koet*, ed. Bert Jan Lietaert Peerbolte, Caroline H. C. M. Vander Stichele, and L. van Wieringen, Studies in Theology and Religion 31 (Brill, 2023), 13–27.

64. Meaning "magnifies," taken from the first word in Luke 1:6b in the Latin Bible.

65. Luke's view of money and property presents a paradox where, on the one hand, these two, without using them to help the poor, are hindrances to salvation, and on the other hand, some of the virtues preached by Jesus presuppose having money and property. Van Geest, "The Fundamental Paradox in Luke's Perception of Money and Property," 13–27.

66. Jean-Claude Loba-Mkole, "The Social Setting of Jesus' Exaltation in Luke-Acts (Lk 22:69 and Ac 7:56)," *HTS Teologiese Studies/Theological Studies* 61, no. 1/2 (October 9, 2005): 298, https://doi.org/10.4102/hts.v61i1/2.441.

which tends to express an individualistic view of riches and success.[67] While the Ghanaian communal understanding of wealth provides a hermeneutical bridge to the Gospel of Luke, a reading of the Gospel will also have to reckon with the fact that close to three million Ghanaians currently live in "extreme poverty"[68] and thus must be centered in socioeconomic development discourse and policy making.

Jesus, Prayer, and Prayer Camps in Ghana

It is equally distinctive of Luke that he presents Jesus as a person of prayer from the beginning to the end of his ministry. He has accordingly been labeled "the evangelist of prayer."[69]

That Luke makes prayer a central part of his Jesus story is confirmed by the fact that he opens his Gospel with a prayer scene at the Jerusalem temple and has prayer as the last words of Jesus on the cross (23:46). It is also attested by the redaction (editing) of his sources. For example, in the baptismal narrative (3:21–22), whereas Mark 1:9–11 and Matthew 3:13–17 have the descent of the Spirit as a post-baptismal experience without mentioning prayer, Luke inserts prayer as the prior activity to the descent of the Holy Spirit upon Jesus after baptism.[70] Even though the prayer theme is set at the beginning of the Gospel, its further development is focused on Jesus so that our discussion here would give more attention to prayer in the life and ministry of Jesus.

Nonetheless, brief remarks on the infant narrative (1:5–2:52) are relevant. In this section, the Jerusalem temple is the place of prayer[71] and prayer as a religious activity is a mark of the ideal, pious Israel represented by Zechariah and Elizabeth, as well as Simeon and Anna. Moreover, prayer is presented here as efficacious and set in the context of God's eschatological fulfillment of Israel's hopes.[72] The temple experience of Zechariah is, for instance, clear evidence that his prayer has been answered (1:13), yet the answer to his prayer, being the birth of John the Baptist, has more far-reaching implications because John will be a key figure in God's salvation history, as 1:14–17, 76–79 indicate.[73] In the case of Anna (2:36–38), her dedicated prayer (and fasting) is remarkable. Her devout prayer life centers on the temple as a place of prayer and her prayer is connected with the eschatological hopes of Israel (2:38).

67. Michael F. Wandusim, "Reception of the Lord's Prayer in Pentecostal-Charismatic Christianity in Ghana," *Journal of the Bible and Its Reception* 9, no. 1 (April 13, 2022): 93, https://doi.org/10.1515/jbr-2020-0011.

68. Doris Dokua Sasu, "Ghana: People in Extreme Poverty by Area 2016–2023," Statista, accessed April 20, 2024, https://www.statista.com/statistics/1245342/number-of-people-living-in-extreme-poverty-in-ghana-by-area.

69. Geir O. Holmås, "Prayer, 'Othering' and the Construction of Early Christian Identity in the Gospels of Matthew and Luke," in *Early Christian Prayer and Identity Formation*, ed. Reidar Hvalvik and Karl Olav Sandnes, WUNT I (Mohr Siebeck, 2014), 102.

70. The grammar and syntax of Luke 3:21–22 strongly suggest that the Spirit's descent is a post-baptismal event during prayer. So also, Geir O. Holmås, *Prayer and Vindication in Luke-Acts: The Theme of Prayer Within the Context of the Legitimating and Edifying Objective of the Lukan Narrative*, LNTS 433 (T&T Clark, 2011), 85–86.

71. Cf. Luke 19:45–46 where the temple's original purpose is inverted. See also Holmås, "Prayer," 106–107.

72. Holmås, *Prayer and Vindication*, 65–76.

73. See Holmås, *Prayer and Vindication*, 70–71.

In the rest of the Gospel (3:1–24:53), Luke structures his presentation of prayer in the life and ministry of Jesus in two ways. In one breath, he portrays Jesus as consistently seeking close personal fellowship with his Father in prayer (mostly in lonely places) in crucial stages of his life such as: baptism (3:21–22); before the choice of the twelve apostles (6:12); before Peter's disclosure of his messianic identity (19:18); on the mount of transfiguration (9:28–29); before teaching on prayer (11:1); at the Mount of Olives before his passion (22:41–44);[74] and at death on the cross (23:34,[75] 46). In addition to these, Luke makes remarks on Jesus's prayer at other points of his narrative (5:16; 10:21–22; and 22:32). It is noteworthy that references to Jesus's unflinching devotion to prayer cut across his ministry both in power (especially the Galilean phase) and in suffering (the Jerusalem phase); from initial acceptance, through increasing opposition to outright rejection and death in Jerusalem.[76] Remarkably, in all these references Jesus is the only one portrayed as actually praying.[77] In another breath, we observe Luke's paraenetic (instructive) presentation of Jesus's teaching on prayer to his disciples (6:28; 10:2; 11:1–13; 18:1–8; 21:36; 22:40, 46). The remarkable aspect of this didactic dimension is that it is consciously presented as an outgrowth of Jesus's prayer life.[78] Both aspects are inextricably linked together, such that the instruction on prayer is enforced by the exemplary character of the portrait of Jesus as a person of prayer. A prime example is the teaching of the Lord's Prayer (11:1–4). Prayer, then, has implications for discipleship. Next to radical self-denial, among others, it becomes a distinctive mark of discipleship in the Gospel of Luke.[79]

Scholarly views vary in interpreting this dual yet interconnected Lukan data on prayer.[80] For our purposes, we will adapt Geir O. Holmås's interpretation that Luke sought with Jesus's prayer life to pursue an apologetic aim by indicating that God validated Jesus as Israel's messiah and savior.[81] This will, however, be reframed to underline the fact that, just like the Holy Spirit in the Gospel of Luke, prayer mediated God's presence in the life and ministry of Jesus so that what he did and said were divinely effectuated through that constant communion with God.

This view is precisely important because a reading of the Gospel of Luke in Ghana will not escape such contextual issues as the role of prayer in religio-cultural settings and the pervasive presence of prayer camps. The phenomenon of prayer camps in Ghana has been the subject of several studies.[82] They are considered as "supernatural intervention centres"

74. There are text critical issues with Luke 22:43–44. See Holmås, *Prayer and Vindication*, 107.

75. Luke 23:34 is marked as an early insertion into the textual tradition.

76. See Holmås, *Prayer and Vindication*, 79, 81.

77. Holmås, *Prayer and Vindication*, 77.

78. See also Holmås, "Prayer," 103.

79. Cf. Holmås, *Prayer and Vindication*, 115.

80. See various studies on the subject in Holmås, *Prayer and Vindication*, 4–16.

81. Holmås, *Prayer and Vindication*, 78.

82. See Francis Benyah, "Prayer Camps, Mental Health, and Human Rights Concerns in Ghana," *Journal of Religion in Africa* 51, no. 3–4 (2 March 2022): 283–308, https://doi.org/10.1163/15700666-12340207; Jocelyn Edwards, "Ghana's Mental Health Patients Confined to Prayer Camps," *The Lancet* 383, no. 9911 (4 January 2014): 15–16, https://doi.org/10.1016/S0140-6736(13)62717-8.

where people with diverse problems—illness,[83] marriage, barrenness, economic difficulties, visa acquisition difficulties, career and business crises—visit to engage in prayer and fasting and other ritual activities with the aim of attracting God's intervention.[84] They are usually situated on the outskirts of towns and cities, with some located on mountains.[85] Moreover, depending on their denominational affiliation and/or history of emergence, they are mostly led by a charismatic person (with assistants) who is believed to be anointed (i.e., empowered) by the Holy Spirit in a special way to help visitors find solutions to their problems.[86]

The relevant aspect of this phenomenon for our discussion of the Gospel is the underlying understanding of prayer. Largely, within a Pentecostal-charismatic orientation, prayer is understood as having "performative powers" capable of attracting divine intervention against evil powers believed to be the cause of the problems of visitors to prayer camps.[87] Essentially, this understanding is shaped by the underlying primal worldview of mystical causality and the role of imprecatory prayers in traditional religious settings that are aimed at securing a good life.[88] The effectiveness of prayer (and fasting) is, therefore, foregrounded in prayer camps, just as the notion of a sacred place for effective prayer is equally present. Hence, visitors expect to experience results after visiting such sacred places of prayer. Studies on prayer camps have not only attested to their attraction of regular visitors, but have also documented instances of human rights abuses in these camps, particularly those that provide residency for visitors to stay for a period of time.[89]

Essential Lukan parallels to this phenomenon are the efficacy of prayer, remote places/mountain(s) as places of prayer, and the assurance of answered prayers. However, a contextual reading of Luke's prayer theme urges a rethinking of the understanding of prayer that undergirds prayer camps. The cross has to be integrated into this understanding, for just as Luke doubtlessly situates prayer in the power phase of Jesus's ministry, so does he equally make prayer a central part of the suffering phase of his ministry. Consequently, it is not only the results-oriented dimension of prayer that should be emphasized, which has the latent effect

83. Mental health seems to dominate. See Francis Benyah, "Prayer Camps, Healing, and the Management of Chronic Mental Illness in Ghana: A Qualitative Phenomenological Inquiry," in *Spiritual, Religious, and Faith-Based Practices in Chronicity: An Exploration of Mental Wellness in Global Context*, ed. Andrew R. Hatala and Kerstin Roger (Routledge, 2021), 173–194.

84. Kwabena J. Asamoah-Gyadu, *Contemporary Pentecostal Christianity: Interpretations from an African Context* (Regnum Africa, 2013), 51; Wandusim, *The Lord's Prayer in the Ghanaian Context*, 131–132. See also Benyah, "Prayer Camps, Mental Health, and Human Rights Concerns in Ghana," 284.

85. See also Edwards, "Ghana's Mental Health Patients Confined to Prayer Camps," 15.

86. See Benyah, "Prayer Camps, Mental Health, and Human Rights Concerns in Ghana," 284.

87. Asamoah-Gyadu, *Contemporary Pentecostal Christianity*, 35, 40; Wandusim, "Reception of the Lord's Prayer," 87.

88. See Eric N. Osei-Akoto, "God 'Has Not Left Himself without Witness . . .': Evidences of the Witness of God in the Akan Pre-Christian Heritage of Prayer," *Journal of African Christian Thought* 20, no. 1 (June 2017): 49–56.

89. See Edwards, "Ghana's Mental Health Patients Confined to Prayer Camps"; Benyah, "Prayer Camps, Mental Health, and Human Rights Concerns in Ghana."

of generating a quick-fix attitude to prayer, but also the role of prayer in providing divine enablement in *enduring* suffering as a path to glorification should equally be articulated.

Conclusion

In sum, the foregoing sections offered an exegetical and hermeneutical introduction to the Gospel of Luke on selected themes. The aim has been to bring the Gospel's distinctive thematic issues into creative dialogue with contextual issues in West Africa, with Ghana as a specific context. Some of the unique Lukan themes that are discussed include the Holy Spirit as the reason for Jesus's being and the driving force behind his earthly ministry; the kingdom of God as a spiritual, political, and social force of God's presence in Jesus's ministry; the centering of women and the poor in the ministry of Jesus; as well as the portrait of Jesus as the praying messiah. The discussion of these issues takes as discursive dialogue partners corresponding contextual issues in Ghana, such as charismatic renewal movements, politics, gender discourse, poverty, and prayer camps.

Admittedly, there is much in the Gospel of Luke that could not be addressed in this introduction. Similarly, there are more contextual issues in Ghana that qualify as hermeneutical dialogue partners with Luke that could not be covered here. That is simply because of the breadth of the Gospel material on the one hand, and the sheer impossibility of representing all elements of a particular country in one limited discursive space like this chapter. However, it is my hope that, by this attempt, students of the Gospel of Luke interested in a contextual reading will be inspired to carry the conversation further in detail and in new directions. When and where that occurs, the events that were fulfilled among Lukan Christians in the ancient world (Luke 1:1) would be fulfilled anew among us today in a hermeneutical sense.

Further Reading

Bediako, Kwame. *Christianity in Africa: The Renewal of a Non-Western Religion*. Trends in African Christianity. Regnum Africa, 2014.

Benyah, Francis. "Prayer Camps, Mental Health, and Human Rights Concerns in Ghana." *Journal of Religion in Africa* 51, no. 3–4 (2 March 2022): 283–308. https://doi.org/10.1163/15700666-12340207.

Boring, M. Eugene. *An Introduction to the New Testament: History, Literature, Theology*. Westminster John Knox Press, 2012.

Grillo, Laura S. "African Rituals." In *The Wiley-Blackwell Companion to African Religions*, edited by Elias Kifon Bongmba. Blackwell, 2012.

Holmås, Geir O. *Prayer and Vindication in Luke-Acts: The Theme of Prayer Within the Context of the Legitimating and Edifying Objective of the Lukan Narrative*. LNTS 433. T&T Clark, 2011.

Isaak, Paul John. "Luke." In *Africa Bible Commentary: A One-Volume Commentary Written by 70 African Scholars*, edited by Tokunboh Adeyemo. WordAlive Publishers; Zondervan, 2006.

Loba-Mkole, Jean-Claude. "The Social Setting of Jesus's Exaltation in Luke-Acts (Lk 22:69 and Ac 7:56)." *HTS Teologiese Studies/Theological Studies* 61, no. 1/2 (October 9, 2005): 291–326. https://doi.org/10.4102/hts.v61i1/2.441.

Mahali, Faustin. *The Concept of Poverty in Luke in Perspective of a Wanji from Tanzania*. Erlanger Verlag für Mission und Ökumene, 2006.

Oduyoye, Mercy Amba. *Introducing African Women's Theology*. Introductions in Feminist Theology 6. Sheffield Academic Press, 2001.

Reardon, Timothy W. *The Politics of Salvation: Lukan Soteriology, Atonement, and the Victory of Christ*. LNTS 642. T&T Clark, 2021.

Ukpong, Justin S. "The Parable of the Shrewd Manager (Luke 16:1–13): An Essay in Inculturation Biblical Hermeneutic." *Semeia* 73 (1996): 189–210.

Wandusim, Michael F. *The Lord's Prayer in the Ghanaian Context: A Reception-Historical Study. The Lord's Prayer in the Ghanaian Context*. SBR 20. De Gruyter, 2021. https://doi.org/10.1515/9783110730579.

Wolter, Michael. *The Gospel According to Luke*. Translated by Wayne Coppins and Christoph Heilig. Vols. 1–2. BMSEC. Baylor University Press, 2016, 2017.

CHAPTER SIX

The Gospel of John

Elizabeth W. Mburu
Africa International University
Langham Partnership
Nairobi, Kenya

Introduction

THIS CHAPTER ON the introduction to the Gospel of John will focus on an intercultural methodology that involves reading from a context (both African and biblical) and reading into a context (African). It will address issues related to the worlds in front of, behind, and of the story—all three worlds stand in a context that must be interrogated. The first two sections will focus on the worlds behind and of the story since they provide the context within which all African realities should be addressed. The third section will address the world in front of the story by highlighting themes that arise from African contextual realities that are paralleled in the Gospel of John.[1] The last section will provide a Johannine response to the issues raised in the section on the world in front of the story.

In order to avoid a double-hermeneutical gap, this approach is based on the Four-Legged Stool model, which builds on the concept of moving from the known to the unknown.[2] It recognizes that parallels between African and biblical cultures and worldviews can be used as bridges to promote understanding, internalization, and application of the biblical text. It therefore has an intercultural dialogue as its basis. This approach allows the otherness of the biblical text to stand in its own right, while at the same time bringing it closer to the African reader by highlighting the points of contact. This intercultural dialogue also serves to affirm, confront, and/or correct the assumptions that African readers bring to their reading of the text.

World Behind The Story

This section will discuss introductory issues behind the world of the story that give greater insight into the world of the narrator, listeners, and events in the Gospel of John. Due to its limited scope, this chapter assumes certain conclusions regarding the historical background

1. My methodology, described in Elizabeth Mburu, *African Hermeneutics* (HippoBooks, 2019), generally begins with the world in front of the text. Although I have maintained the same theoretical and conceptual framework, I have reorganized the steps to conform to this volume's guidelines.

2. Mburu, *African Hermeneutics*.

and composition of the Fourth Gospel, while at the same time conceding that there is by no means a consensus on most of these issues.[3]

The world behind the story is what is referred to as the "world of the agents of communication" in African stories, which includes the narrator and the listener.[4] The date, location, and purpose are also addressed here.

Narrator

In biblical narratives, the narrator is usually the same as the author. Both external (Polycarp, Irenaeus, Eusebius) and internal evidence point to authorship by one of the twelve disciples. Following the approach initially proposed by Westcott, it is likely that the author was a Jew, of Palestinian origin, an eyewitness, an apostle, the beloved disciple, John, the son of Zebedee and the brother of James (the two were nicknamed "Sons of thunder" by Jesus, cf. Matt 10:2).[5] He was an early disciple of John the Baptist, was part of the inner circle of Jesus's disciples (Matt 17:1; Mark 14:33), and was present at the transfiguration (Matt 17). Bauckham points out that it is also likely that he was known to his readers and served as a guarantor of the oral tradition that stemmed from Jesus's ministry. The more common understanding that this Gospel is formally anonymous may not therefore be appropriate.[6]

Listeners

The listeners are also usually the same as the original readers. Scholars have disagreed as to whether the original readers were Jews or gentiles. The narrator's emphasis on the new temple and conflict with synagogues (16:2), as well as an emphasis on Pharisees, suggests a primarily Jewish audience. It is likely that "their opposition is somehow related to the opponents his readers face in their own communities."[7] Although it is written to a Jewish audience, it nevertheless has a universal flavor.

Date and Location

Tradition suggests that John wrote from Ephesus, where he had served as bishop, probably around 85–95 CE. It is likely, without downplaying other factors, that the destruction of the temple in 70 CE, the gentile mission, and the inevitable rise of false teaching, particularly Gnosticism, constitute significant events prompting the writing of this Gospel.[8] In

3. For an overview, see the discussion in D. A. Carson and Douglas J. Moo, *An Introduction to the New Testament*, rev. ed. (Zondervan, 2005), 225–284.

4. Mburu, *African Hermeneutics*, 108–109.

5. B. F. Westcott, *The Gospel According to John* (Eerdmans, 1975), v–xxviii.

6. Richard Bauckham, *Jesus and the Eyewitnesses: The Gospels as Eyewitness Testimony* (Eerdmans, 2006), 300–302.

7. Craig S. Keener, *The IVP Bible Background Commentary: New Testament*, 2nd ed. (Intervarsity Press, 2014), 246.

8. Andreas. J. Köstenberger, "The Destruction of the Second Temple and the Composition of the Fourth Gospel," *Trinity Journal* 26, no. 2 (Fall 2005): 205–242.

addition, the christological confessions (such as that of Thomas) provide a clue that this Gospel was written at a time when the emperor cult was gaining in strength, and Domitian was its focus.

Purpose

All the four gospels reveal distinct theological motivations and the Gospel of John is no exception. It has a clearly articulated purpose statement that reveals that the author has carefully selected certain material pertaining to Jesus to convince his readers that "Jesus is the Christ, the Son of God" (John 20:30–31). Hence, it seems that his intention is not only to engender faith in Jesus, but also to encourage those already in the faith.

Having discussed the world behind the story, let us turn to the world of the story.

World of the Story

The world of the story includes matters that arise from the text itself, such as genre, style, structure, and distinctive features. They serve as crucial hermeneutical devices in the process of interpretation.[9] This section will also address Johannine themes that are paralleled by the world in front of the story. As is the case with all the Gospels, the life situation of Jesus (*sitz im leben Jesu*) and that of the church (*sitz im leben der kirche*) must be considered.

Genre

Genre is a crucial hermeneutical device in understanding any text. It provides us with the "rules" that the author followed in composing the work, rules that s/he intends the readers or hearers to follow. Scholars are not in agreement as to which genre best fits this Gospel. It has been characterized as a biography (*bios*), an aretalogy, history, a novel, Greek drama, a new literary form, narrative, narrative Christology, Jewish Trial, and even a Jewish theodicy.[10] While all these have merit, its undisputed salvation-historical dimension suggests that it is likely a theological biography communicated in the historical narrative style characteristic of the Old Testament. There are also embedded genres of various kinds, all playing differing roles within the larger setting of the Gospel.

Style

John uses a number of literary and structural devices to weave his story. However, there are a few that are significant because they contribute a great deal to the comprehension of this Gospel. Of particular note are his use of editorial comments, misunderstandings, double

9. Mburu, *African Hermeneutics*, 109.

10. For a discussion of these various options, note especially the discussions by Craig S. Keener, *The Gospel of John: A Commentary*, 2 vols. (Hendrickson, 2003), 1:4–11; Robert Guelich, "The Gospel Genre," in *The Gospel and the Gospels*, ed. P. Stuhlmacher (Eerdmans, 1991), 173–208.

entendre, irony, symbols, *inclusios*, chiasms, and metaphorical language. He also includes contrastive dialogue (which reveals the speakers' ideological mentalities) and characterization.

Plot development in this Gospel is structured around both the recognition and the lack thereof of Jesus's identity. Hence, as in the other Gospels, it reflects "conscious plotting," that is, the deliberate arrangement of material by the author that reflects his understanding and interpretation of the life and ministry of Jesus.[11] The plot revolves around Jewish feasts, festivals, and religious symbols, and their fulfillment in Jesus Christ, not only as the promised messiah, but also as the Son of God (20:31–31). As Jobes points out, "By the time the fourth gospel was written the defense of Jesus' identity had moved beyond his credentials as the Messiah . . . to the level of his unique relationship with God the Father."[12]

Structure

This Gospel has a generally linear, chronological sequence that displays a repetitive pattern. There is characteristic repetition and development of multiple themes (that are introduced in the prologue, 1:1–18), as well as the use of chiasms and parallel constructions. Conscious plotting also means that John sometimes rearranges chronology (e.g., the temple cleansing in 2:12–25). Scholars have proposed numerous structures but the one that seems to best allow the text to speak for itself includes a five-part outline: Prologue (1:1–18), Book of Signs (1:19–10:42), Transition (11:1–12:50), Book of Glory (13:1–20:31), Epilogue (21:1–25).[13]

Prologue	1:1–18	
Book of Signs	1:19–51	Introduction
	2:1–10:42	Jesus's public ministry
Transition	11:1–12:50	
Book of Glory	13:1–17:26	Jesus's final ministry to the twelve
	18:1–20:9	Jesus's arrest, crucifixion and burial
	20:10–31	The Risen Lord
Epilogue	21:1–25	

Distinctive Features (as Compared with the Synoptic Gospels)

When read alongside the Synoptics, the Gospel of John adds depth to their accounts. This is the most interpretive of all the gospels, as John's intent is to explain the spiritual significance of Jesus as the Messiah and the Son of God (20:31). Thus, the narrator often interprets statements from his more theologically advanced and motivated post-resurrection vantage point.

11. R. Alan Culpepper, *Anatomy of the Fourth Gospel: A Study in Literary Design* (Fortress Press, 1983), 85–88.

12. Karen H. Jobes, *John: Through Old Testament Eyes* (Kregel Academic, 2021), 16.

13. This is the structure proposed by Raymond E. Brown, *The Gospel According to John*, AB 29A (Doubleday, 1966), 1:cxxxix, and adopted by numerous scholars today.

Only in this Gospel is the title of God explicitly designated to Jesus (1:18; 20:20). It has an already-but-not-yet inaugurated eschatology, as well as a unique approach to the Holy Spirit. Unlike the Synoptics, it has no miracles but includes seven signs which serve to authenticate Jesus as the sent Son (2:1–11, 13–22; 4:46–54; 5:1–18; 6:5–14; 9:1–7; 11:1–45) and seven "I Am" statements (6:35; 8:12; 10:7; 10:11, 14; 11:25; 15:1). It also has no birth account, genealogies, parables, or demon exorcisms. Instead, it includes longer discourses, such as Jesus's encounters with Nicodemus and the Samaritan woman (3–4) and the Farewell Discourse (13–17). There are several allusions to the Old Testament, with Jesus presented as replacing revered figures, and as the fulfillment of Old Testament prophecy and the Jewish cultus.[14]

Key Theological Themes

The Gospel of John has several key theological themes that resonate with African contextual realities. These include the identity of Jesus, the person of the Holy Spirit, community, spiritual blindness, and fullness of life. These themes unfold in line with John's theological and narrative purpose.

Identity of Jesus

Numerous scholars have noted that this gospel has a very high Christology and its plot revolves around the conflict between belief and unbelief in Jesus's identity. A clue to John's view of Jesus's identity is first seen in the prologue. The prologue begins with an allusion to the creation account of Genesis 1, thereby setting "the story of the significance of Jesus within the realm of the divine."[15] John refers to Jesus as "the Word" (ὁ λόγος), which, in Hebrew thought "referred to the Lord's revelation of himself through the prophets."[16] The fact that he took on flesh does not mean that he was no longer the divine λόγος.

The genre of the prologue differs from the narrative style in the rest of the Gospel. Suggestions regarding its genre include Hebrew poetry, interspersed with prose comments at various points, or even poetry that has a Gnostic root. It is more likely that it is rhythmical or elevated prose. This piece of embedded genre has an emphatic function, focusing the reader on the message that follows in the main narrative. It also formulates the conclusion that Jesus is the preexistent Word made flesh and the only one with authority to give eternal life.[17] Notably, John records Jesus's self-designation as the Son of Man (1:51; 3:13; 8:28; 13:31; cf. Dan 7:13–14; Num 21:8–9; Isa 42:13), thus highlighting his divine identity.

John makes several allusions and references to Old Testament concepts and people, showing that Jesus's identity must be understood as the fulfillment of the Old Testament.

14. For more on John's relation to the Synoptics and its contribution, see Carson and Moo, *An Introduction to the New Testament*, 257–264, 276–278.

15. Jobes, *John*, 31.

16. Jobes, *John*, 31.

17. Elizabeth Mburu, *Qumran and the Origins of Johannine Language and Symbolism* (T&T Clark, 2010), 39.

Katanacho notes that "John not only connects us to Moses, the manna, and the wilderness, but he also rereads these traditions, declaring that Jesus is the bread, the source of water, and the light."[18] Several Old Testament motifs can also be traced back to Old Testament figures such as Moses, David, Elijah, Jacob, Daniel, and Isaiah. Casselli argues convincingly for the presentation of Jesus in this Gospel as the fulfillment of the Law, as eschatological Torah. This is based on John's use of the Exodus narrative, the connection of Jesus with Moses, and in particular the representation of both as the word of God, wisdom, truth, as well as the familiar images of life and light, bread, water, and wine.[19] Thus, light and darkness imagery, which harks back to the Old Testament and other Jewish literature (Gen 1; Isa 9:2; 50:10; Ps 107:10, 14; Qumran literature), as well as water symbolism, pervade John's retelling of the story of Jesus.

Another clue to Jesus's identity is John's identification of Jesus as the fulfillment of the symbolism inherent in the Jewish cultus, its feasts, festivals, and symbols. Theologically, these can be traced back to Moses and the exodus. Thus, the Sabbath, Passover, Dedication, and Tabernacles are significant clues. Jobes notes that the "lamb of God" metaphor, previously not used of the Messiah, is reminiscent of the Old Testament sacrificial system. It may be alluding to the Passover lamb of Exodus 12, the Suffering Servant of Isaiah 53, or perhaps the apocalyptic lamb of Revelation 4.[20] It thus has implications for substitutionary atonement. Another key example is Jesus's death during Passover week which reveals that Jesus is the prototype of the Jewish Passover (19:14). Thus, Judaism is merely a preparatory phase that anticipates the coming of the Messiah.

Jesus's identity is also revealed in the way John structures his narrative around the Jewish institutions and feasts. Note the following statement by Katanacho about the Jewish understanding of holy space:

> If the people lost the temple, they would lose their identity, history, blessings, stability, and religious life and would live in exile and alienation. Losing the temple was like crucifixion without resurrection. It was the death of God and the victory of evil.[21]

The temple, like circumcision and the Sabbath, was a key identity marker of the Jewish people. Thus, the prominence that he places on the account of the temple cleansing (2:12–25) communicates that Jesus, in his death and resurrection, is the true embodiment and replacement of the Jerusalem temple (2:21).

Another significant clue is in John's inclusion of signs, not miracles (2:1–11; 2:13–22; 4:46–54; 5:1–18; 6:5–14; 9:1–7; 11:1–45). These point to a new exodus and authenticate Jesus's claim as God's true representative. Carson notes that "Jesus' miracles are never simply naked displays of power, still less neat conjuring tricks to impress the masses, but *signs,*

18. Yohanna Katanacho, *Reading the Gospel of John Through Palestinian Eyes* (Langham Preaching Resources, 2020), 40.

19. Stephen J. Casselli, "Jesus as Eschatological Torah," *Trinity Journal* 18, no. 1 (Spring 1997): 15–41.

20. Jobes, *John*, 35.

21. Katanacho, *Reading the Gospel of John Through Palestinian Eyes*, 26.

*sign*ificant [*sic*] displays of power that point beyond themselves to the deeper realities that could be perceived with eyes of faith."[22] Through the inclusion of these signs, John shows that Jesus is the fulfillment of Old Testament prophecy and the Jewish cultus. In at least two of these signs (5:1–18; 9:1–7), Jesus redefines the Jewish understanding of holy time by fulfilling the purpose of the Sabbath. Thus, John rereads "holy time in light of the coming of the Christ."[23]

The "I Am" sayings are perhaps the biggest clue to Jesus's identity. Many scholars have noted that this phrase alludes to God's self-revelation to Moses (Exod 3:14). Each of these statements reveal different facets of Jesus's self-understanding. The first "I Am" statement (6:35) reveals that Jesus is the true, genuine bread who provides eternal life. Although Keener points out that this statement "alludes directly to divine wisdom,"[24] some scholars view the motif of wisdom as peripheral, seeing the connections more in terms of prophecy and fulfilment, along typological lines.[25]

The second statement (8:12) is in a section that has the repeated motif of testimony and that displays characteristics common to a trial or lawsuit. This statement must be understood against the imagery of light that was introduced in the prologue (1:4, 5, 9). Jewish tradition used "light" as a symbol for God or his presence, as well as associated "life" with the light of God's word.[26] Jesus is the fulfilment of Old Testament expectations and allusions, as well as the one who ushers in the new creation. The symbolism of Jesus as light also alludes to the wilderness tradition. As the true light, Jesus is the only means of salvation.

In the third statement (10:7), Jesus refers to himself as the gate for the sheep, the only protection against thieves and robbers. This is an allusion to the true Old Testament prophets and Ezekiel 34, as well as a condemnation of the Pharisees and chief priests. As the gate, Jesus offers salvation, safety, and satisfaction to anyone who would enter through him.[27] This is followed by a shift in metaphor in which Jesus refers to himself as the good shepherd, the fourth statement (10:11, 14). In Palestine, sheep would often be exposed to attacks by wild animals. As the embodiment or fulfillment of the good shepherd prophecy,[28] he cares for the sheep, lays down his life for them, and brings in others to join the flock.

What prompts Jesus's fifth statement is Lazarus's death (11:25). In line with Judaism of the time (except the Sadducees), Martha believed in the bodily resurrection of the dead at the end.[29] This statement reveals that only Jesus has authority and power over life and death. The raising of Lazarus, as well as Jesus's own resurrection, validate his claim and show that he is indeed God's true representative, the long-awaited Messiah. This sign also echoes themes of

22. D. A. Carson, *The Gospel According to John* (Eerdmans, 1991), 175.
23. Katanacho, *Reading the Gospel of John Through Palestinian Eyes*, 36.
24. Keener, *The Gospel of John*, 682–683.
25. Carson, *The Gospel According to John*, 289.
26. Jobes, *John*, 33.
27. Samuel Ngewa, "John," in *Africa Bible Commentary* (HippoBooks; WordAlive Publishers, 2006), 1299.
28. Katanacho, *Reading the Gospel of John Through Palestinian Eyes*, 56.
29. Keener, *The IVP Bible Background Commentary*, 283.

the new creation and that Christ, as the second Adam, solves the problem of death brought by the first Adam.[30]

The sixth statement (14:6) is an answer to Thomas's question about the way to the Father. Way, truth and life are also associated with the Torah in Judaism, and by the Qumran community which referred to itself as "the Way," because of its strict adherence to the Law. By saying he is "the way," Jesus is representing himself as the fulfillment of the Law; by saying he is "the truth," Jesus reflects his awareness that he is the full revelation and embodiment of the redemptive purpose of God;[31] and by saying he is "the life," he means that he is the one who possesses life and is the only one with the authority to impart it (cf. 1:4; 3:15; 4:13; 6:54; 10:28).

The final statement (15:1) is found in the extended metaphor of the vine (15:1–11) which is the core of the Farewell Discourse. The imagery of the vine reflects Old Testament references to Jews. Jesus is thus the true and genuine vine as opposed to Israel, the unfaithful vine (cf. Jer 2:21; Ezek 15:1–8; 19:10–14; Ps 80:9–16).[32] The emphasis of this metaphor is not on the branches, but on the vine. Jesus is the center of this entity, just as he is the center in the metaphor of the flock in chapter 10. Only he completely measures up to God's ideal.

The Holy Spirit

John's teaching on the Holy Spirit overlaps with other New Testament teaching elsewhere but also introduces the unique terminology of Paraclete and Spirit of Truth (see 14–16; cf. 1 John 2:1). The Holy Spirit is first introduced at Jesus's baptism (1:32) as a testimony to John the Baptist that Jesus is indeed God's Son. Reference to the Holy Spirit also appears in conjunction with "water" (3:5). Additionally, the symbolism of water is also used of the Holy Spirit (4:10–15; 7:37–39). The appositional linking of "Paraclete," "the Spirit of Truth," and the "Holy Spirit" shows they have the same referent.

In the Farewell Discourse (13–16), Jesus informs his disciples that the direct access to him that they had previously enjoyed would change with his departure. Several scholars have pointed out that the genre of 13:31–16:33 is farewell speech or testament resembling Moses's final words in Deuteronomy.[33] This reflects John's propensity for Old Testament connections. In chapter 14, Jesus promises "another Paraclete," one who would not only be with them, but would also live in and among them (14:16–17). The term "Paraclete" (παράκλητος) is often used in a legal sense in secular Greek to refer to a legal assistant or advocate. Later Rabbinic writings associated the role of advocate with the Holy Spirit (*Lev. Rab.* 6.1 on Lev 5:1).[34] Similarities

30. Katanacho, *Reading the Gospel of John Through Palestinian Eyes*, 61.

31. George E. Ladd, *A Theology of the New Testament* (Eerdmans, 1993), 303.

32. C. K. Barrett, *The Gospel According to St. John: An Introduction with Commentary and Notes on the Greek Text*, 2nd ed. (SPCK, 1978), 472–473.

33. Keener, *The Gospel of John*, 2:896–897.

34. See Johannes Behm, "παράκλητος," in *Theological Dictionary of the New Testament*, ed. Gerhard Kittel and Gerhard Friedrich, trans. Geoffrey W. Bromiley (Eerdmans, 1967), 5:803.

with regard to the judicial role or the personal character of the Paraclete are also found in late Jewish literature (particularly the Qumran literature and *T. Jud.* 22.1–5).[35]

The use of "another" suggests that Jesus is the first Paraclete (cf. 1 John 2:1), showing that there is overlap in terminology attributed to Jesus and the Holy Spirit. The difference is that the epistle has a legal nuance, whereas the Gospel clearly means "encourager" or "comforter." Nevertheless, there is a close connection in that "the comfort afforded by the paraclete is in its essence *because* he intercedes on our behalf before the Father, putting right our relationship with God at the time of the judgement of our sin."[36] The giving of the Paraclete is intimately tied to Christ's own death and exaltation (7:39; 14:15, 26; 15:26; 16:12). He is sent by both the Father and the Son (14:17, 26; 16:7), and he comes to indwell believers, uniting them to both the Father and the Son (14:15–20, 23) in a manner never experienced before. His presence is a permanent presence as anticipated in the Old Testament prophets (14:16; see Joel 2:28; cf. Acts 2:17–21).

This abiding presence is identified as having yet another purpose (cf. 14:26). He has the task of teaching the disciples all things, reminding them of everything that Jesus has taught them. From prior contexts it is clear that Jesus's teaching must be understood as the ultimate revelation from God. The Paraclete discloses prior teaching given by Jesus, illuminating it and making it understandable to the disciples. Whitacre rightly points out that Jesus acts "as the organ of communication between God and a person."[37] The role of the Spirit in this context is similar to that of the Spirit of prophecy in the Old Testament.

The Spirit of Truth also bears witness to the truth that Jesus both embodies and reveals (15:26). This statement is also found in the legal context of testimony. The future work of the Spirit of Truth would be to aid and guide the witnessing ministry of the disciples in their words and deeds. He passes on only what he hears from Jesus and not new revelation, contra Burge who proposes that, in addition, "the Spirit works creatively in the church, bringing a new prophetic word."[38] Rather than predictive prophecy, "the Paraclete . . . also enables the believers to boldly testify for Jesus, recognizing that it is the world, and not the believers, that is really on trial before God."[39] As in 14:26, this role most closely resembles that of the Spirit of prophecy in the Old Testament.

The designation "Spirit of Truth" is significant given that Jesus self-identified as the "Truth" in 14:6. In 1 John 5:6, John notes that the Spirit is the truth. It thus shows continuity between Jesus and the Spirit. Betz rightly proposes that "truth" is a mark of the divine being.[40] It is opposed to error/delusion/deception (1 John 4:6). Only those who know the Spirit of Truth can accept or receive Jesus—the world cannot. While this indwelling probably refers

35. See Raymond Brown, "The Paraclete in the Fourth Gospel," *New Testament Studies* 13 (1967): 121.

36. Jobes, *John*, 230.

37. Rodney A. Whitacre, *John*, IVPNTCS 4 (InterVarsity, 1999), 358–359; M. E. Boring, "The Influence of Christian Prophecy on the Johannine Portrayal of the Paraclete and Jesus," *New Testament Studies* 25 (1978): 113–123.

38. Gary M. Burge, *Interpreting the Gospel of John* (Baker Books, 1992), 452.

39. Keener, *The Gospel of John*, 2:1024.

40. Otto Betz, *Offenbarung und Schriftforschung in der Qumransekte*, Wissenschaftliche Untersuchungen zum Neuen Testament, 6 (Mohr Siebeck, 1960), 60.

to the community of believers as a whole, his inner presence in individuals is also necessary since it is only inwardly that believers are able to understand the Spirit and his activity.

Presenting the Spirit's activity with respect to the world as a legal battle or cosmic trial, John records that another key role would be to convict the world concerning sin, and righteousness and judgment (16:8). The use of the word "he will convict" or "convince" (ἐλέγξει) in this verse is similar to its use in 8:46. Büchsel points out that although this word carries the sense of education and discipline in the LXX, in the New Testament it has a narrower sense and is always used with regard to showing someone their sin and bringing them to repentance.[41] It therefore has a forensic tone, with the legal role of the Paraclete being to convict the unbelieving world on the grounds of its unbelief in Jesus, of Jesus's righteousness, and of its own certain judgment incurred due to its failure to believe in Jesus.

Community

The prologue provides the foundation for how John understands community. As noted above, it is an embedded genre that introduces themes that are expounded on in the rest of the Gospel. The prologue introduces us to Jesus and shows "the preexistence of Christ as the Son of God who was with God and who was God before the universe began."[42] Thus the theme of community is grounded in the eternally existing relationship between God the Father, Son, and Spirit. There are several other instances in the rest of the narrative where Jesus talks about him and the Father being one (10:30; 14:10; 17:10, 11, 21, 22, 23). Indeed, there is a unity of purpose exemplified in both of them sending the Holy Spirit (14:17, 26; 16:7). This unity can also be seen in the glorification of the Father through Jesus's death/exaltation and in Jesus's pronouncement that he shares God's name (17:1, 5, 11). Within this mutual indwelling and relational intimacy, there is also diversity demonstrated in the roles that each member plays.

A significant way in which community in the Godhead is expressed is seen in how Jesus, as the sent Son, faithfully represents the interests of his Father (3:17, 34; 5:23). Their purpose is one and this unifies them. Schlatter notes the crucial role of the motif of the "sent son" in Johannine thought in that "John uses the Son concept to delineate the basis, manner, and extent of Jesus' rule."[43] He is the only way to the Father and by having been with him, the disciples both know and have seen the Father (14:6, 7). This theme of "sent son" has a legal flavor. As the "sent son" Jesus is able to function as a unique delegate on his Father's behalf. The farewell prayer in chapter 17 also reveals that Jesus is both the sent son and the sender.[44]

---

41. Friedrich Büchsel, "ἐλέγχω," in *Theological Dictionary of the New Testament*, ed. Gerhard Kittel, trans. Geoffrey W. Bromiley (Eerdmans, 1964), 2:473–474.

42. Jobes, *John*, 17.

43. Adolph Schlatter, *The Theology of the Apostles: The Development of New Testament Theology*, trans. Andreas J. Köstenberger (Baker Books, 1998), 129–130.

44. Herman Ridderbos, *The Gospel of John: A Theological Commentary*, trans. John Vriend (Eerdmans, 1997), 547.

John's Gospel redefines "community" in terms of family. In this regard, the prologue is crucial. John 1:12–13 constitutes the climax of the prologue and therefore best reflects the purpose of the Gospel (cf. 20:30–31). Those who believe in Christ are given the right to become children of God. Therefore, as Ridderbos points out, "The privilege of being children of God is special and exclusive. It is not a natural quality that every human being has as a creature of God; nor is it the inalienable right of Israel as 'his own' (cf. 8:42)."[45] The true community in Johannine terms is the spiritual family of God. It is an exclusive category.

At the same time, community is also redefined in terms of inclusivity. The story of the Samaritan woman in chapter 4 exemplifies how Jesus breaks down barriers of ethnicity and gender in his embracing of the hated Samaritans. She serves both as a foil and, like a number of other individuals, as a mirror, reflecting Christ's image in different ways.[46] Through his dialogue with the woman, Jesus redefines holy space and time by relocating both the locus and the manner of worship (4:23, 24), revealing that he, as the eschatological hour, is the only means of access to God. People of all ethnicities, genders, socioeconomic classes, political orientations, and so on, are invited to become part of this new community.

It is in the Farewell discourse (13–16) that the new community begins to take on a more defined shape. However, it is only after Jesus's final prayer that John records Jesus officially commissioning the disciples as the newly constituted community (20:22). Their task is to testify to the truth, just as Jesus himself was sent into the world to do the same. Those in this new community are therefore held together by a common mission.

The metaphor of the vine (15:1–8) is an apt description of what community means. It is modeled after the example of the union that exists between Jesus and his Father.[47] Hence, in order to be considered part of this corporate unity, the disciples must remain in Christ. "Remain" (μένω), used eleven times in this section, is indicative not simply of that moment in which one enters into a relationship with Christ, but of continued dependence on him.[48] The exhortations to love, obey, and be united are only possible if one remains in him. The very structure of the Farewell Discourse leads to the understanding that Jesus is the locus of the newly constituted people of God. As Whitacre points out, "The identification of the people of God with a particular nation is now replaced with a particular man who incorporates in himself the new people of God composed of Jews and non-Jews."[49] The outward expression of this new community of faith is the bearing of fruit, which is in itself based on a relationship of dependence on Jesus. The context suggests that the bearing of fruit refers to a life of consistent Christian discipleship.

The theme of community is exemplified in the prayer of Jesus. Structurally, this final prayer is not part of the Farewell Discourse. However, in terms of its contents, it mirrors 13:1–35 with its central theme of oneness of Father, Son, and believers. It is divided into

45. Ridderbos, *The Gospel of John*, 46.

46. See Brown, *The Gospel According to John*, 1:176; Ridderbos, *The Gospel of John*, 152.

47. Barnabars Lindars, *John* (JSOT Press, 1990), 490.

48. Keener, *The Gospel of John*, 2:1000.

49. Whitacre, *John*, 372.

three general sections: a prayer for himself (vv. 1–5), a prayer for his disciples (vv. 6–19), and lastly, a prayer for all believers (vv. 20–26). In this prayer, Jesus provides his followers with a missionary paradigm.[50] We are co-reconcilers with God and Christ. Apart from mission, one of the main themes that stands out in this prayer is that of unity, primarily "the eternal unity of Father and the Son in its relation to the incarnation and the temporary (and apparent) separation which the incarnation involved,"[51] but also a unity amongst believers, and between believers, Jesus and the Father. This prayer reveals that community is both historical as well as contemporary.[52] Genuine community has implications for the mission of God. It is a double testimony to the world in that it demonstrates, first, that the sending of Jesus came from God himself; second, just as God loved the Son, he displays the same kind of love to believers everywhere; and finally, Jesus provided his followers with a missionary paradigm.[53] We are co-reconcilers with God and Christ.

Spiritual Blindness

The theme of spiritual blindness runs like a thread throughout the whole gospel. However, this theme is epitomized by several Jewish religious leaders. The first is Nicodemus, an authority of the law (3:1–20). Like the story of the Samaritan woman which follows, this story serves to reveal yet another aspect of the author's portrayal of Christ. Nicodemus, too, serves as a foil. Although Nicodemus was an authority on the Law, and he acknowledges that Jesus had been sent by God (3:2), he seemed to have a difficult time understanding Jesus (3:3–4). Keener points out that "it never occurs to him that someone Jewish would need to convert to the true faith of Israel."[54] Hence, he assumed that Jesus was speaking about physical matters. Jesus's purpose is to bring him to a deeper awareness of his identity and the only path to a relationship with God. Thus, as Carson notes, "Even for a Nicodemus, there must be a radical transformation, the generation of new life, comparable with physical birth."[55]

The second is Caiaphus, the high priest during the events surrounding Jesus (John 11:49–50; 18:14). He and Annas had had Jesus arrested and questioned (18:1–27), then passed him off to the Roman governor, Pilate, for questioning. The motives behind Jesus's arrest were religio-political and revolved around the preservation of the land and Jewish identity.[56] There is double irony in this situation. The first is pointed out by Carson:

---

50. Andreas J. Köstenberger, "The Challenge of a Systematized Biblical Theology of Mission: Missiological Insights from The Gospel of John," in *Studies on John and Gender: A Decade of Scholarship*, Studies in Biblical Literature 38 (Peter Lang, 2001), 156–157.

51. Barrett, *The Gospel According to St. John*, 500.

52. Marianne Meye Thompson, "John," in *Dictionary of Jesus and the Gospels*, ed. Joel B. Green, Scot McKnight, and I. Howard Marshall (Intervarsity Press, 1992), 382.

53. Andreas J. Köstenberger, "The Challenge of a Systematized Biblical Theology of Mission: Missiological Insights from The Gospel of John," *Missiology* 23, no. 4 (1995): 445–464.

54. Keener, *IVP Bible Background*, 255.

55. Carson, *The Gospel According to John*, 190.

56. Katanacho, *Reading the Gospel of John Through Palestinian Eyes*, 72.

> The Jews take elaborate precautions to avoid ritual contamination in order to eat the Passover, at the very time they are busy manipulating the judicial system to secure the death of him who alone is the true Passover.[57]

John cleverly brings out the second irony involved in having this death sentence passed against Jesus. The intention of the Jews was to get rid of what they perceived as a threat against them. They also desired to discredit Jesus's claims about himself by having him die under the curse of God (cf. Deut 21:23). However, death by crucifixion was exactly the kind of death Jesus had predicted for himself and the only means of ensuring the fulfillment of God's plan of salvation for mankind. Their spiritual blindness was a barrier to understanding the very Scriptures over which they were custodians.

The third is the Jewish religious establishment in general. Although they thought that their ethnic heritage as Abraham's descendants was enough, they were wrong. Indeed, "From John's perspective, . . . A Jew could not benefit from the Abrahamic blessings without Jesus Christ."[58] The story of the man born blind (John 9) is perhaps the best illustration of this theme. John demonstrates how Jesus "opens the eyes of the blind" to the truth that he teaches and that he embodies. The irony of this narrative is that Jesus was operating on two levels—the first was the literal opening of the blind man's eyes; the second was that of pointing out the spiritual blindness of the Pharisees, which was evidence of their estrangement with God, regardless of their ethnic identity. This story, which took place on the Sabbath, is one of Jesus's signs. John uses both light and water imagery to establish that the Feast of Tabernacles is fulfilled in Jesus and that the messianic age has arrived. These two symbols point to God's divine presence and the Lord's provision of water from a rock.[59] The retribution theological background of this story is evident. The disciples, like most Jews of the day, believed that there was a correlation between sin and suffering. One could be punished not just for one's own sins, but also for the sins of others.[60] Because the Pharisees had no physical disabilities and they kept the Sabbath, they wrongly believed that God approved of them. Through this healing, Jesus corrected their wrong assumptions. Sometimes God allows suffering so that his work might be revealed in people's lives. The Pharisees, who put stock in their Scriptures, their knowledge of God, and their ethnicity as Jews, did not recognize their spiritual blindness, which only Jesus could cure.[61]

Fullness of Life

Fullness of life is explicitly related to reception of Jesus in the shepherd metaphor of chapter 10. As the good shepherd, Jesus has come to grant fullness of life, both in the present and in

57. Carson, *The Gospel According to John*, 589.

58. Katanacho, *Reading the Gospel of John Through Palestinian Eyes*, 44.

59. Jobes, *John*, 139.

60. Carson, *The Gospel According to John*, 362.

61. Ngewa, "John," 1299.

eternity, to those that believe in him (10:10; cf. Ezek 34). The fulfilment motif in John is also evident in this theme. Jobes states that as the promised messianic shepherd who would die an atoning death for all humankind, "Jesus came to bring his people into that abundant life in the present as the start of an eternal life that will one day be lived out in the ultimate fulfilment of Ezekiel's visions."[62] Fullness of life in John is therefore contingent upon identity—Jesus's identity and the identity of the readers.

In John 8:31–38, which has the repeated motif of testimony and thus displays characteristics common to a trial or lawsuit, Jesus's identity is once again in question. The notion of testimony was crucial in Jewish society. Although self-witness was regarded as invalid in both Jewish and Hellenistic legal proceedings,[63] Jesus nevertheless testifies in his own defense against the religious authorities. There may be in this context an implicit contrast between the power of Jesus's revelation and the law. An understanding of the Feast of Tabernacles is important for understanding Jesus's words about liberation in this context—it alludes to more than political freedom.[64] In view of the Johannine concept of sin, it refers to "freedom existentially as liberation from the realm of sin and death, from the darkness of an existence remote from God (cf. 8:12), from the ordinary unsaved situation of man in 'this world' (see 8:23)."[65] Jesus, therefore, introduces a revolutionary understanding of the path to fullness of life, one that is embodied and personal. It is based on a redefinition of identity—from ancestry and ethnicity to belief in him.

Another key element in considering the question of fullness of life is that of the relationship between obedience and sacrifice. John demonstrates that for Christ, obedience leads to sacrifice, and there is no sacrifice without obedience (12:27–36). The setting of the story is the Passover feast (cf. 11:55, ἐν τη ἑορτη), which finds its genesis in the Exodus account (Exod 12:1–28). The narrator's presentation of Jesus as the fulfillment of the symbolism inherent in the Jewish cultus and sacrificial system provides the backdrop to this text. John has, throughout the Gospel, been consistent regarding Jesus's character. Obedience to the father has been his top priority (cf. 4:32). The question in 12:27 that follows Jesus's expression of anguish is a rhetorical question that reveals that obedience is costly. It also reveals that, for Jesus, obedience and sacrifice are inextricably intertwined. God honors Jesus's impending sacrifice on the basis of a life lived in obedience, but the obedient life was always headed toward sacrifice. The benefits of Jesus's death encompass glorification (of both Father and Son?), authentication of the Son, dethronement of the prince of peace, and the taking away of sin resulting in salvation and reconciliation for all mankind. His death and resurrection are the only basis for true fullness of life, in the present and in eternity. Nevertheless, as Jobes points out,

> The exultation of Jesus on the cross inaugurates a new world order where God's judgement has been fully executed and where there is no place for the reign of evil.

---

62. Jobes, *John*, 176.

63. Rudolf Schnackenburg, *The Gospel According to St. John* (Seabury Press, 1980), 2:120.

64. Gerald L. Borchert, *John 1–11* (Broadman & Holman, 1996), 407.

65. Schnackenburg, *The Gospel According to St. John*, 2:206.

> Although the new world has been inaugurated in this age, it will be fully realized only by the promised new heavens and new earth (Isa 65:17; Rev 21:1).[66]

Having looked at the worlds behind and of the story, we turn our attention to the world in front of the story.

World in Front of the Story

This section will focus on prominent issues in African contextual realities that find a parallel in the themes addressed above. These are the identity of Jesus, the Holy Spirit, community, spiritual blindness, and fullness of life.

Identity of Jesus

The question of who Jesus is for the average African believer is generally answered from the perspective that is deeply relevant to the lived experiences of the African people. An approach that encourages an abstract, philosophical Christology that is difficult to be grasped by the ordinary reader of the Bible is generally rejected. Thus, while ontological dimensions may arise, it tends to focus more on functionality. Pobee, who rightly argues for a cultural consideration in Christology in Africa, affirms that it is "important who the African is, because homo Africanus is encountered by Christ as he or she is."[67]

African Christology is generally divided into two categories: Christologies of liberation and Christologies of inculturation.[68] African Christologies of liberation reflect elements that are similar to Latin American liberation theologies with more emphasis on cultural and religious values and less on secular and Marxist ideologies. Christologies of inculturation include ancestral and non-ancestral categories. While this twofold categorization of Christology is useful, it is limiting. Apart from liberation and inculturation, other existing paradigms such as reconciliation, reconstruction, symbolic and oral paradigms, charismatic, restorative, market-theology, and rural-ministry, which do not fit this narrow characterization, should also be considered. As an example, Kä Mana, who views reconstruction as the overriding paradigm in twenty-first-century African theologies, integrates other motifs "of identity, inculturation, reconciliation and liberation thereby reconstructing Africa as well as the world, in accord with humane requirements."[69] Another example is Jesse Mugambi's reconstructive Christology which identifies "Christ as guest."[70]

---

66. Jobes, *John*, 201.

67. John Pobee, *Skenosis: Christian Faith in an African Context* (Mambo Press, 1992), 15.

68. The following brief summary is from Julius Gathogo, "Reconstructive Hermeneutics in African Christology," *HTS Theological Studies* 71, no. 3 (2015): 2–6, https://doi.org/10.4102/hts.v71i3.2660.

69. Gathogo, "Reconstructive Hermeneutics in African Christology," 5.

70. Jesse N. K. Mugambi, *From Liberation to Reconstruction: African Christian Theology After the Cold War* (East African Educational Publishers, 1995), 9.

Another way of categorizing African Christologies is cultural and functional.[71] The cultural trend (which overlaps with inculturation) argues that African culture must be taken seriously. Only by interacting with the African culture can the Christian faith become meaningful in the African context. The functional trend places more emphasis on Jesus's function or work than on his person or nature. This approach aims to communicate that Christ is relevant (counteracting an over-spiritualized gospel), Christ is present (not in some super-spiritual realm), and Christ is current.[72]

These categorizations have given rise to various christological titles that resonate with the church in Africa. While these are not limited to the Gospel of John, they are nevertheless important in helping us situate ourselves in the current African context of studies related to Jesus Christ. Some examples of christological titles proposed by African scholars include Liberator (Takatso Mafokeng, Allan Boesak, Jean Marc Ela, Laurenti Magesa, T. Souga, L. Tappa, M. A. Oduyoye, and E. Amoah, to name a few), Chief, Master of Initiation (championed originally by Anselme Titianma Sanon), Healer (Anne Nasimiyu-Wasike), Ancestor (Charles Nyamiti [brother-ancestor] and Benezet Bujo [proto-ancestor]), and Victor (John Mbiti).[73] Other titles arise from specific readings of texts. For instance, Jesus as revealer, liberator, unifier of the church, ultimate curse-remover, high priest, and healer.[74]

Since the titles given to Jesus Christ stem from categories that have arisen from African lived experiences, they are highly relevant and form a useful bridge for understanding. However, not all these categories lead to a right and proper understanding or worship of Christ. Take for instance, the category of Christ as ancestor or proto-ancestor which arises from African culture and cosmology. While the mediatory role of Christ may seem to parallel that of African ancestors, and is thus a useful link, the nature of the mediation that Christ engages in is qualitatively different and therefore superior. In a critique of the ancestor Christology category, Mokoathi rightly notes, even as he acknowledges that some like Pobee affirm the supremacy of Christ, that "the parallelism of Jesus with ancestors does not seem to do justice to Jesus' eminence and role as our redeemer."[75]

Functional approaches to Christology are to be applauded because they recognize the real presence of Jesus Christ in daily life. They also expose the gap in Western theologies which tend to de-emphasize the value of functionality in theology. Nevertheless, they tend to be limited and the failure to integrate both functionality and ontology renders some of the categories inadequate.

---

71. Charles De Jongh, "Contemporary Trends in Christology in Africa," *South African Baptist Journal of Theology* (2008): 3.

72. De Jongh, "Contemporary Trends in Christology in Africa," 6.

73. See Elizabeth Mburu, "Exploring the Multidimensional Nature of Christology in Galatians," in *Who Do You Say That I Am? Christology in Africa*, ASET Series, ed. Rodney L. Reed and David K. Ngaruiya (Langham Global Library, 2021), 61–62.

74. See Rodney L. Reed and David K. Ngaruiya, eds., *Who Do You Say That I Am? Christology in Africa*, ASET Series (Langham Global Library, 2021).

75. Joel Mokoathi, "Jesus Christ as an Ancestor: A Critique of Ancestor Christology in Bantu Communities," *Pharos Journal of Theology* 99 (2018): 5.

The Holy Spirit

The Holy Spirit in Africa is generally understood through the lens of dynamism, power encounters, and holism. The spirit world remains very real for most Africans such that spiritual activity (including the existence of angels and demons) and the invisible dimension of faith are never doubted. However, it is viewed as impersonal, unseen, and unpredictable. The worldview of dynamism argues that those who can manipulate this spirit realm have power to control their lives.

Having this worldview means that many Christian Africans live in fear of the power of witchcraft and demons over their lives. Moreover, there is rarely a rationalistic explanation for the things that happen in nature. This perspective means that one cannot change their circumstances through any power of their own since only a stronger power can defeat a lesser one. This naturally leads to a desire for an all-consuming power that "exerts an enormous influence on morality and ethics and on the relationship between humans and spirit beings and supernatural powers or forces."[76] This power is obtained from ritual manipulation, the laying on of hands, encountering a spirit being, and contact with persons of superior religious status or even their personal items such as clothing.[77]

Dynamism paves the way for experiencing the Holy Spirit as a real and powerful entity that speaks and acts in a tangible way. In general, the church in Africa has a strong belief that the Holy Spirit is alive and active in the personal lives of believers as well as in the community of faith. Hearing the voice of the Holy Spirit speak into one's circumstances is hardly ever doubted. Like the early Christians of Acts, many Christians in Africa believe that the Holy Spirit is directing their everyday lives as he builds his church. The presence and activity of the Holy Spirit in worship services is taken for granted, as is his ability to heal, perform miracles, and exorcisms. The increasing emphasis on demonic oppression, spiritual warfare, and healing and deliverance activities is evidence of the worldview of dynamism at work. As McDonald points out, even in non-Pentecostal/charismatic churches, "Christians are at war with spiritual forces, and our tumultuous services revolve around that conflict through declarations and exorcisms."[78] The understanding of the Holy Spirit as a power capable of defeating the powers of darkness is indeed a strength in the church in Africa.

However, because the Holy Spirit is generally understood within the framework of the worldview of dynamism, this sometimes leads to an abuse of the Holy Spirit and his role. It is becoming more common for some church leaders to treat the Holy Spirit like a puppet to be manipulated for their gain. In many instances, an encounter with the Holy Spirit may be used solely as a means of experiencing power encounters, miracles, signs, and wonders.

---

76. Yusufu Turaki, *Foundations of African Traditional Religion and Worldview* (WordAlive Publishers, 2006), 35.

77. Turaki, *Foundations of African Traditional Religion and Worldview*, 35.

78. Scott McDonald, "Spiritual Powers," in *The Abandoned Gospel: Confronting Neo-Pentecostalism and the Prosperity Gospel in Sub-Saharan Africa*, ed. Philip W. Barnes, Bazil Bhasera, Matthews A. Ojo, Jack Rantho, Trevor Yoakum, and Misheck Zulu (AB316, 2021), 54.

Community

What does "community" imply in Africa? For traditional Africans, community included the living, the living dead (including ancestors), and the unborn. Rites and rituals spanning from birth to death were an important part of entering into and maintaining communal identity. Questions about self within such a framework provide challenges in understanding the role of an individual within community. This is because the basic African view with regard to people was that the individual existed only because others existed. Thus, one cannot conceive of personal freedom and autonomy without regard for the community.[79]

Although many scholars concede that the Ubuntu philosophy is difficult to define, its most basic expression aptly encapsulates the African communal solidarity: "I am because we are and, since we are, therefore I am."[80] Ubuntu is in essence a unifying worldview in that it captures the essence of what it is to be human for an African. It therefore recognizes that human beings can never exist in isolation, but must coexist in relationship with others. This unity in life (or vital union) "is the bond joining together, vertically and horizontally, beings living and dead; it is the life-giving principle in all. It is the result of communion, a participation in the one reality, the one vital principle that unites various beings."[81] It therefore defines our perspective on the I–Other dynamic.

Individuals were expected to maintain a balance in all their relationships. This resulted in a kinship system that was a crucial organizing factor in society as it provided the principles of social differentiation and social organization that guided all of life within the community.[82] This was important because horizontal relationships had to be established before the vertical relationship could take effect. Mugambi points out that, "The strong belief in the maintenance of the balance of relationships also implied that any action leading to the breakdown of harmony . . . was considered to be at the same time an offence against all those beings who formed this network of relationships."[83] This community structure served to promote healthy codependence and peaceful coexistence. It also ensured that one avoided offending both humans and spirits alike, as any violation of community norms and values led to shame and dishonor.

However, even given this worldview of Ubuntu, "othering" still rears its ugly head. This is because of the law of kinship, which determines and distinguishes between "insiders" and "outsiders."[84] Insiders are determined by ethnic identity, which is so strong that the "other" is often regarded in dehumanizing terms. This insider–outsider paradigm results in negative ethnicity expressed through ethnic rivalries that often lead to violent conflicts. Unfortunately,

79. John S. Mbiti, *Introduction to African Religion* (Praeger Publishers, 1975), 175.

80. John S. Mbiti, *African Religions and Philosophy* (Heinemann, 1970), 44.

81. Vincent Mulago, "Traditional African Religion and Christianity," in *African Traditional Religions in Contemporary Society*, ed. Jacob K. Olupona (Paragon Publishing House, 1991), 120.

82. Turaki, *Foundations of African Traditional Religion and Worldview*, 37.

83. J. N. K. Mugambi, *African Heritage and Contemporary Christianity* (Longman Kenya, 1989), 62.

84. Yusufu Turaki, *Engaging Religions and Worldviews in Africa: A Christian Theological Method* (HippoBooks, 2020), 168.

ethnic identity frequently overshadows Christian identity. As a result of "othering," many churches in Africa are formed along sociocultural identity markers, such as ethnicity, rather than doctrinal commonalities. In addition, issues of gender equity are prominent because the patriarchal structure that undergirded African traditional societies continues to have its influence. The Christian community is often fractured.

This framework of community has been eroded in recent years, although it still holds true in many rural African communities today. Modernization (and postmodernization), urban mobility, and globalization have brought with them the breakdown of the community structure and the growth of individualism. This is becoming even more pronounced with the increasing influence of social media, which has radically changed how relationships are defined. A positive aspect of this erosion is the gradual realignment and eventual watering down of ethnic identity. However, this too has its negatives since it has led to the decrease of cultural diversity.

Living in this increasingly individualistic environment has had an effect on many modern Africans. Nevertheless, community ties are still experienced, particularly during funerals and weddings. Moreover, virtual social platforms have made it easy for anyone with a smartphone to join a virtual community. Such are rapidly taking over face-to-face interactions. Consequently, while individualism may prevail in some areas, the framework of community is still a part of the everyday life of most modern Africans.

Spiritual Blindness

The church in Africa, which is currently going through explosive growth, also has a troubling dichotomy. This landscape is further complicated by a rapidly changing digital and globalized context. Alongside the sound teaching, there are many deceptive doctrines being taught by religious leaders. The most prominent false teaching is the prosperity health and wealth gospel. On the surface at least, it appears to teach a holistic view of life. Its proponents promote a "health and wealth," "word-faith," or even "name it and claim it" theology. The background to churches that teach this doctrine is Pentecostal and charismatic. However, not all churches with this orientation teach about prosperity. There are many healthy, genuine, gospel-centered churches that emphasize the work of the Holy Spirit, and genuine healings and exorcisms do occur without an overemphasis on the financial aspect.

The prosperity health and wealth gospel is rapidly morphing into Neo-Pentecostalism. The African traditional understanding of God, which is transactional rather than relational, as well as our holistic worldview, make it quite attractive. The worldview of holism argues that life is integrated. There are no distinctions between the physical and spiritual dimensions of life.[85] In the traditional African worldview, there was no dichotomy existing between faith and nature, between the secular and the sacred, because all of reality was governed by a law of harmony.[86] Apart from the worldview of holism, another reason why Neo-Pentecostalism

85. Turaki, *Engaging Religions*, 141.

86. Turaki, *Foundations of African Traditional Religion and Worldview*, 33.

is growing so rapidly is the worldview of dynamism. It influences how Africans "assess the potency or efficacy of a new religion or ritual practice."[87] Consequently, Neo-Pentecostalism, with its overemphasis on power encounters, deliverance from ancestral and other curses, signs, and wonders, as well as an emphasis on objects believed to have power, is very attractive.[88] It is also fueled by a growing materialism, which has normalized consumerism.

Neo-Pentecostal theology and ecclesiology have also shaped mission-founded Protestant churches. Churches that have this philosophical and theological orientation have a huge influence not only on the continent, but in their many diaspora churches in Europe and the United States. The African understanding of the Holy Spirit within this framework of holism and dynamism is a positive contribution to the global church, particularly in countering Enlightenment assumptions. This perspective demonstrates, particularly to those who have relegated the work of the Spirit in the church to the background, the very real power, presence, and activity of the Holy Spirit in everyday life and worship.

Nevertheless, alongside this spiritual awakening and growth, Neo-Pentecostalism and its attendant doctrines are having a detrimental effect on the healthy growth of the church in Africa. There are also many thriving cults that often have a similar philosophy. Moreover, African religious spaces are extremely porous. As Galgalo points out, we are capable of "participating in Islam, one form or another of Christianity, and African traditional rituals all in one day without fear of self-contradiction."[89] The result is that the inclusion of syncretistic beliefs and cultural practices that are not aligned with biblical truth is fast becoming an integral feature of many churches. Sanneh described this as "the unresolved, unassimilated, and tension-filled mixing of Christian ideas with local custom and ritual."[90] While syncretism is a universal problem, religious syncretism is more dangerous. Syncretism is attractive because it reinforces a sense of identity and ownership of faith. In a rejection of the identity imposed by "others," many Christian Africans seek to redefine their identity by looking back to their traditional religious practices and worldviews. This results in the subversion and disintegration of a genuine Christian faith. While an outsider might be critical of the way in which such practices are reshaping Christian identity in Africa, and indeed the syncretistic end products ought to be shunned, an insider recognizes the yearning within to "find ourselves."

Contextual theologizing is vital for the healthy growth of Christian identity but finding the right balance between contextual relevance and biblical integrity is a challenge. The belief in a retribution theology, intermediaries, spiritual powers, and witchcraft that is so evident in our churches betrays a theological framing that is more aligned with African traditional religious worldviews than a biblical worldview.[91] Many African pastors can be compared to

87. Turaki, *Foundations of African Traditional Religion and Worldview*, 35.

88. Matthews A. Ojo, "An Overview of the History of Neo-Pentecostalism in Africa," in *The Abandoned Gospel: Confronting Neo-Pentecostalism and the Prosperity Gospel in Sub-Saharan Africa*, ed. Philip W. Barnes, Bazil Bhasera, Matthews A. Ojo, Jack Rantho, Trevor Yoakum, and Misheck Zulu (AB316, 2021), 19.

89. Joseph Galgalo, *African Christianity: The Stranger Within* (Zapf Chancery, 2012), 27.

90. Lamin Sanneh, *Whose Religion Is Christianity? The Gospel Beyond the West* (Eerdmans, 2003), 44.

91. Joseph Galgalo, "Syncretism in African Christianity: A Boon or a Bane," in *African Contextual Realities*, ed. Rodney L. Reed, ASET Series (Langham Global Library, 2018), 84–85.

witch doctors in the way in which they practice their craft. Christian objects such as crosses and anointing oil, as well as other objects such as handkerchiefs, and so on, are used as amulets, fetishes, and talismans, and are believed to have power in themselves to bring about healing and/or deliverance. Practices such as traditional burial rites, which ensure that the dead successfully pass on to the realm of the living dead/ancestors, may sometimes be practiced alongside a Christian burial service without any visible conflict. Clearly, the very gospel we claim to believe in stands endangered as we embroil ourselves in syncretistic doctrines and practices.

Fullness of Life

Fullness of life in Africa is related to the worldviews of holism and dynamism. Numerous scholars have suggested that the world, for the African, is a monosectional reality.[92] In other words, there is no separate spiritual and physical reality—there is only one reality. God, the spirits, ancestors, human beings, and objects all live in one world.

The belief in impersonal powers and spirit beings (both nonhuman as well as the spirits of the ancestors) was assumed. These spirit beings were either good or evil, depending on whether they brought blessings or curses.[93] They played a more significant role in daily life than the Supreme Being. While the spirit realm was a reality, only specialized individuals such as medicine men, rainmakers, mediums, diviners, sorcerers, magicians, witches, and those with the ability to manipulate spirit beings could access it. They served as mediators between the physical and the spiritual realms.[94] Restoration of ontological balance was driven by a worldview of dynamism, rather than love, and could only be achieved by sacrifice via the mediators.

A major aspect with regards to the experience of fullness of life is suffering. If there was suffering in a community, one could find answers by determining where relationships had broken down. Relational breakdown was bound to result in swift judgment in the form of disease and other natural catastrophes. And since there was no equivalent of Satan, when misfortune came the community would investigate who had offended God, the spirits or the ancestors.[95] This they did through diviners. Apart from the human element, evil spirits were also believed to destroy harmony in the community.

Many Christian Africans continue to operate within this worldview of holism. Crises are generally approached from a spiritual perspective since physical and spiritual realities go hand in hand. Nevertheless, many struggle with leading fulfilled lives. Life has become fragmented in this postmodern, globalized age. Fullness of life has been reduced to material prosperity and power in society. The prosperity health-and-wealth gospel feeds into this as Christians are taught in their various churches that "they can live a life of spiritual and material abundance

92. Mugambi, *African Heritage*, 78.

93. Turaki, *Foundations of African Traditional Religion and Worldview*, 25.

94. Turaki, *Foundations of African Traditional Religion and Worldview*, 26.

95. Mugambi, *African Heritage*, 62.

in the world,"[96] often without interrogating the biblical texts from which these promises are made.

As a corollary, the failure to experience fullness of life or holistic abundance is attributed to personal failure, witchcraft, or even the activity of demons. Note the following quote from Ojo: .

> Prosperity preachers also insist that Christians enter into the realm of prosperity based on an individual understanding of God's promises because God has given humans access to the Abrahamic covenant. Hence, one's salvation launches one into the realm of God's abundance (i.e. material benefits are the result of exercising faith). Christians who are not prospering could be harbouring unbelief or are unaware of God's promises and the laws of success, or maybe they are not paying their tithes, have accepted the lies of the devil, or are bogged down by sin and curse.[97]

Interestingly, the sentiments expressed in the quote above also seem to have close connections with an African worldview of retribution, a transactional relationship with God, as well as consumerism. In times of suffering, some Christians have opted to draw from the worldview of dynamism by consulting witch doctors to counter the attack, rather than depend on God for help.

An additional deterrent to understanding or experiencing fullness of life stems from the African perspective of time. It leans toward an over-realized eschatology in its conceptualization of past, present, and future. For some, time is two-dimensional. It consists of a long past, a present, and virtually no future.[98] For others, the future exists but is merely a continuation of the present. It is referred to as the potential present.[99] This perspective continues to influence many Christian Africans. Both these definitions help us understand that the Western concept of time as linear, with an indefinite past, present, and indefinite future did not exist in traditional African thinking. The past is more important because present circumstances can always be explained by looking to the past.

What about the "future"? A belief in fate meant that one's destiny was fixed and could not generally be changed although supernatural powers could hinder individuals from realizing their destiny.[100] The idea of history progressing toward an ultimate goal is also absent in African thinking. Mugambi points out that "as long as man maintains his proper relations with fellow men and with nature, the universe will continue as it has always done, unless of course, God chooses to change the course of events."[101] This naturally leads to the failure to

96. Matthews A. Ojo, "The Prosperity Gospel Among Neo-Pentecostals in Africa," in *The Abandoned Gospel: Confronting Neo-Pentecostalism and the Prosperity Gospel in Sub-Saharan Africa*, ed. Philip W. Barnes, Bazil Bhasera, Matthews A. Ojo, Jack Rantho, Trevor Yoakum, and Misheck Zulu (AB316, 2021), 30.

97. Ojo, "The Prosperity Gospel," 30.

98. Mbiti, *African Religions*, 78.

99. Mugambi, *African Heritage*, 83.

100. Turaki, *Foundations of African Traditional Religion and Worldview*, 40.

101. Mugambi, *African Christian Theology*, 127.

grasp the eschatological significance of the Christian life. Fullness of life is reduced to past and present, without recognizing that the future, with its eternal rewards or punishments, are the natural consequence of human life.

This section focused on the world in front of the text by highlighting key themes that arise from African contextual realities that are paralleled in the Gospel of John. The next section will provide a Johannine response to the world in front of the story.

Johannine Response to the World in Front of the Story

This section will provide a response to the themes raised in the world of and in front of the story through John's theologically motivated retelling of the story of Jesus.

Identity of Jesus

Christological categories that stem from an Africentric understanding are relevant, particularly because they recognize the real presence of Christ in our contextual realities. Nevertheless, while African categories such as Liberator, Chief, Master of Initiation, Healer, Ancestor, and so forth, are a useful starting point, they are deficient in that they do not present a robust understanding that captures both the ontological and functional aspects of Jesus Christ. Jesus is the eternal, preexistent Word, the full revelation and embodiment of the redemptive purpose of God, the fulfillment of Old Testament prophecy and the Jewish cultus, the only one with life and the power to give it, and the only one who lives up to God's ideal. John's post-resurrection perspective reveals that Jesus's incarnation was not a mere appearance on earth but a real entering into human life and flesh, and that only one who was truly divine *and* human could be the true redeemer of the human race.

Holy Spirit

The worldviews of dynamism, holism, and power encounters, while useful, are just a small part of how the Holy Spirit ought to be understood. A correct understanding of the person of the Holy Spirit is essential so that he is not misunderstood and taken as some kind of talisman that is more in line with African traditional religious beliefs. The Holy Spirit is an encourager, comforter, advocate, he indwells believers and communities of faith and unites them with the Father and the Son, he teaches and bears witness to revealed truth, he convicts of sin and helps believers in their witnessing.

Community

The African conception of Ubuntu, the unifying worldview of what it means to be human, is a useful starting point for understanding "community." It has many positive aspects; however, it is limited because it promotes "othering" along defined identity markers. Community for John is redefined in terms of unity of purpose, spiritual family, it derives its existence from

Jesus, it is exclusive as well as inclusive, and it consists of a web of interrelationships in which unity in diversity is experienced. John demonstrates what he means by "community," and that Jesus inaugurates a (new) community by breaking the barriers of the existing status quo and requiring belief in him as the only criterion for entry.

Spiritual Blindness

The worldviews of holism and dynamism, and the transactional understanding of ultimate reality, lead to a theological framing that is more aligned with African traditional religious practices, hence encouraging syncretism. Spiritual blindness in John is characterized by a failure to understand the Scriptures, an inadequate understanding of God, sin, and the path of salvation, and an overestimation of Jewish ethnic identity. In particular, while sin in Africa has traditionally been understood as the relational breakdown between the physical and the spiritual realms, it is more than that. Sin in Johannine terms is the failure to believe in Christ, salvation is more than just a restoration of the ontological balance between the spiritual and the physical realms, and God does not save us through our sacrifices or our right actions. Salvation is always based on our acceptance of Christ and his redemptive work.

Fullness of Life

The African worldview of holism is positive in that it assumes a harmonious and peaceful coexistence with and within the physical and spiritual realms. Nevertheless, it is limited because it fails to consider that fullness of life is characterized by true freedom. For John, fullness of life implies that one understands that Jesus is the only one authorized to liberate us from slavery to sonship. Because he represents the Father and is the sent Son of God, he is the only one who can break the chains of bondage to sin. Belief in Christ entails a holistic salvation that engenders genuine fullness of life, now and in eternity, and that negates a transactional and self-serving relationship with God. Through him, believers have been moved from the kingdom of Satan into the kingdom of God. Moreover, because he chose to liberate us by entering into our human existence, we are assured that he liberates us not from a distant, transcendent plane of existence, but from within our own circumstances.

Conclusion

This chapter on the introduction to the Gospel of John focused on an intercultural methodology. The first two sections focused on the worlds behind and of the story in order to provide the context within which similar themes in the African context could be addressed from a biblical-theological perspective. The third section addressed the world in front of the story by highlighting how themes that arise from African contextual realities, and that are paralleled in the Gospel of John, are understood. These included the identity of Jesus, the Holy Spirit, spiritual blindness, community, and fullness of life. The last section provided a Johannine response to the themes identified in the world in front of the story.

As the reader confronts the text from his/her contextual situatedness, the text also confronts the reader and affirms assumptions that enhance faith and/or corrects those that hinder a genuine Christian faith. The African culture and worldview can be used positively to enhance understanding of the biblical text. However, this has its limitations, and insights gleaned from such analyses need to be refracted through the Johannine lens. Such an approach has great potential in enhancing faith that is both biblical and African.

Further Reading

Barnes, Philip W., Bazil Bhasera, Matthews A. Ojo, Jack Rantho, Trevor Yoakum, and Misheck Zulu, eds. *The Abandoned Gospel: Confronting Neo-Pentecostalism and the Prosperity Gospel in Sub-Saharan Africa*. AB316, 2021.

Bauckham, Richard. *Jesus and the Eyewitnesses: The Gospels as Eyewitness Testimony*. Eerdmans, 2006.

Borchert, Gerald L. *John 1–11*. Broadman & Holman, 1996, 2002.

Boring, M. E. "The Influence of Christian Prophecy on the Johannine Portrayal of the Paraclete and Jesus." *New Testament Studies* 25 (1978): 113–123.

Burge, Gary M. *Interpreting the Gospel of John*. Baker Books, 1992.

Carson, D. A. *The Gospel According to John*. Eerdmans, 1991.

Culpepper, R. Alan. *Anatomy of the Fourth Gospel: A Study in Literary Design*. Fortress Press, 1983.

Galgalo, Joseph. *African Christianity: The Stranger Within*. Zapf Chancery, 2012.

Jobes, Karen H. *John: Through Old Testament Eyes*. Kregel Academic, 2021.

Katanacho, Yohanna. *Reading the Gospel of John Through Palestinian Eyes*. Langham Preaching Resources, 2020.

Keener, Craig S. *The Gospel of John: A Commentary*. 2 vols. Hendrickson, 2003.

Mbiti, John S. *Introduction to African Religion*. Praeger Publishers, 1975.

Mburu, Elizabeth. *African Hermeneutics*. HippoBooks, 2019.

Mugambi, J. N. K. *African Heritage and Contemporary Christianity*. Longman Kenya, 1989.

Ngewa, Samuel. "John." In *Africa Bible Commentary*. HippoBooks; WordAlive Publishers, 2006.

Reed, Rodney L., ed. *African Contextual Realities*, ASET Series. Langham Global Library, 2018.

Reed, Rodney L., and David K. Ngaruiya, eds. *Who Do You Say That I Am? Christology in Africa*. ASET Series. Langham Global Library, 2021.

Sanneh, Lamin. *Whose Religion Is Christianity? The Gospel Beyond the West*. Eerdmans, 2003.

Schnackenburg, Rudolf. *The Gospel According to St. John*. 2 volumes. Seabury Press, 1980.

Turaki, Yusufu. *Engaging Religions and Worldviews in Africa: A Christian Theological Method*. HippoBooks, 2020.

Turaki, Yusufu. *Foundations of African Traditional Religion and Worldview*. WordAlive Publishers, 2006.

CHAPTER SEVEN

The Book of Acts

Daniel Nii Aboagye Aryeh
Perez University College
Ghana

Introduction

THE BOOK OF Acts is a critical resource that gives considerable information concerning how the early church began, missionary activities, fellowship, persecution, pneumatology, ecclesiology, ethnicity, and theology. It is an indispensable resource for the study of early Christianity and church life. It serves as a bridge between the Gospels and the Epistles and demonstrates how the disciples of Jesus continued the mission of Jesus. The book can be largely divided into two main parts: (1) the mission led by Peter, which is mainly centered in Jerusalem (Acts 1–12); and (2) the mission to the gentiles led by Paul to other nations (Acts 13–28). These two missionary activities have generated common and related themes that have been discussed by many scholars of Acts.[1]

Various commentaries and studies on Acts are limited to reflections and examinations of the world behind and the world of the text of the book. While these are significant and seminal works that contribute toward the understanding of the background and features of the book, they leave out the component of the world in front of Acts. Many studies that focus on the world in front of the book are restricted to early Christianity to the fifth century CE. This does not often include the contemporary church situations. This creates challenges for contemporary readers of Acts whose interests are not mainly historical but rather focus on how the themes in Acts reflect religious and philosophical worldviews in their contexts for effective and dynamic Christian living, and scholarship. In other words, they pursue consolidation of early Christian practices and norms in their indigenous and contemporary contexts. Analyzing the contemporary world of the reader in front of the text or themes in Acts "involves a process

1. Dennis D. Sylva, "The Meaning and Function of Acts 7:46–50," *Journal of Biblical Literature* 106, no. 2 (1987): 261–275; Mark Reasoner, "The Theme of Acts: Institutional History or Divine Necessity in History?," *Journal of Biblical Literature* 118, no. 4 (1999): 635–659; Gary Gilbert, "The List of Nations in Acts 2: Roman Propaganda and the Lukan Response," *Journal of Biblical Literature* 121, no. 3 (2002): 497–529; Laura Nasrallah, "The Acts of the Apostles, Greek Cities, and Hadrian's Panhellenion," *Journal of Biblical Literature* 127, no. 3 (2008): 533–566; Ryan S. Schellenberg, "The First Pauline Chronologist? Paul's Itinerary in the Letters and in Acts," *Journal of Biblical Literature* 134, no. 1 (2015): 193–213.

of SIGNIFICATION in the act of reading. The reader must make key decisions about what the text says"[2] in his/her context or life settings today.

John D. K. Ekem argued that the Arab raid of North Africa succeeded in the seventh century CE because the Christian faith was not established in the Indigenous life settings of the people. For example, the Berber language, which was dominant, has Indigenous religious and philosophical concepts and artifacts from which the Christian faith and its tenets in the early church could be deduced. However, Christianity in North Africa was mainly expressed in the Latin language and philosophy, which was alien to many of the Indigenous North African Christians. The Eastern Church was resilient to the raid due to the fact that it was expressed in the Coptic language and Indigenous philosophies.[3] When the themes of early Christianity find identity with Indigenous realities in receptor cultural norms, it consolidates the critical themes and issues in the receptor culture. In this way, it gradually becomes synonymous with the Indigenous practices without adulterating the faith. In academic parlance, the receptor culture explores how certain theological themes in Acts are reflected in Indigenous religious traditions and philosophical concepts. This may provide answers to how an African Indigenous person may perceive and read Acts. It will find domesticated concepts and themes for effective Christian scholarship in Africa and increasingly minimize conflicting themes between Acts and African realities of life, holistic nurture, and scholarship.

This approach to the study of themes in Acts and African realities is eclectic. The comparative and evaluative methods of African biblical studies have been engaged. This chapter will seek to compare themes in Acts with themes in African religious settings and philosophy. It deviates from other forms of the comparative method where themes in the book of Acts were compared with themes in Greco-Roman and Ancient Near East (ANE) religions that may share a direct relationship with themes in Acts.[4] The evaluative method of African biblical studies applied in this study reflects the approach of Justin S. Ukpong that emphasizes the implications of the distinctions between themes in the Bible and how they resonate with African life and thought through thematic analysis and African realities.[5] This approach and method will help develop a balanced perspective of themes in Acts and Africa to demonstrate their degree of significance.

This chapter will delve into the critical themes in Acts and explore how these themes resonate with the realities of life and nurture in the African context. The study is outlined thus: (1) the authorship of Acts; (2) recipients of Acts; (3) date of composition; (4) genre; (5) outline

2. W. Randolph Tate, *Handbook for Biblical Interpretation: An Essential Guide to Methods, Terms, and Concepts*, 2nd ed. (Baker Academic, 2012), 474, capitals in original.

3. John David Kwamena Ekem, *Early Scriptures of the Gold Coast (Ghana)* (St. Jerome Publishing; Edizioni di Storia e Letteratura, 2011), 1–2.

4. Olugbemiro Olusegun Berekiah, "African Biblical Studies in Retrospect and Prospect: A Reflection on the Practice and Praxis of Biblical Studies in Africa," in *The Present State and the Future of Biblical Studies in Africa: Essays in Honour of Samuel Oyinloye Abogunrin*, ed. S. O. Abogunrin, J. D. Gwamna, A. O. Dada, and Hope E. Amolo (Zenith BookHouse, 2017), 70–87.

5. Justin S. Ukpong, "Inculturation as Decolonization of Biblical Studies in Africa," in *Decolonisation of Biblical Interpretation in Africa*, ed. S. O. Abogunrin, and J. O. Akao (NABIS, 2005), 32–50.

and rhetoric; (6) themes and points of convergence and divergence with African realities; and (7) conclusions. The points of convergence and divergence with African realities are the main focal points of the chapter. It will discuss how the themes of mission, wealth distribution, pneumatology, ethnicity, dispute resolution, miracles, persecution, religion, and politics in Acts reflect African realities. These themes will be analyzed with the *Adinkra*[6] symbols of Africa to reflect on their values, goals, and cultural heritage to the themes in Acts. This chapter seeks to demonstrate that themes in Acts that resonate with African realities are not limited to religious practices but are also embedded in philosophical arts and symbols.[7] This study posits that some themes in Acts are not unique to early Christianity or the Christian faith. Hence, their authority to influence Christian life and thought is not solely due to the fact that they are contained in Acts or were the core values of early Christianity. They can be traced in some Indigenous religious and philosophical tenets in Africa that sometimes predate the book of Acts. This makes some themes in Acts resonate in African cultures although it must be noted that the authority of these African themes on a believer is qualitatively different from that of the biblical themes because of their source.

Introductory Matters

Authorship and Recipient of the Book of Acts

The authorship of Acts is not in doubt. The reason is that the internal evidence in the prologue of the book states: "In the first book, Theophilus, I wrote about all that Jesus did and taught from the beginning" (Acts 1:1). The phrase τὸν μὲν πρῶτον λόγον ("in the first writing") demonstrates that the author of the first writing to Theophilus is the same author as the book of Acts, which is the second book. The prologue of the Gospel of Luke mentioned Theophilus being the recipient of the Gospel concerning the ministry activities of Jesus: "After his suffering he presented himself alive to them by many convincing proofs, appearing to them during forty days and speaking about the kingdom of God" (Acts 1:3 NRS). Hence, Luke, a physician, a companion of Paul, and also a historian is the author of the book of Acts. This has been the traditional and most acclaimed view on the authorship of Acts.[8] It is not clear why Luke would dedicate ink and papyri to write a two-volume book to Theophilus. It begs the question: Does Luke have a special relationship with Theophilus, Jesus, or the disciples? Is Luke a leader in the early church? Or has Theophilus been targeted for conversion to the Christian faith by Luke? Regardless of the answers to these questions, it is clear that Theophilus is a wealthy person due to his position and it is likely that he was a patron of Luke.

6. *Adinkra* is an Akan term that refers to symbols that express philosophical, cultural, social, and traditional concepts and aphorisms of the Akan people of Ghana. They are often found in fabrics and hangings in many palaces and traditional settings in Ghana.

7. John S. Mbiti, *Introduction to African Religion*, 2nd ed. (Heinemann Educational, 1991), 26, 38–39; Kwame Gyekye, *African Cultural Values: An Introduction* (Sankofa Publishing, 2003), 125–136.

8. Mark Allan Powell, *Introducing the New Testament: A Historical, Literary, and Theological Survey* (Baker Academic, 2009), 147.

Besides the prologues of both the Gospel of Luke and Acts that demonstrate a connection to the same author, there is also thematic continuity of Luke in Acts. The themes of disciples, the Spirit, welfare, and mission can be traced in direct continuity.[9] The themes of discipleship, mission, welfare, and the operation of the spirits are critical themes in many pieces of religious literature in the Greco-Roman context in which the New Testament was composed. Although Acts is addressed to Theophilus, the content implies that it can be read to or read by other audiences who become the implied readers and listeners of Acts. The tone of the book depicts conversion and establishment in the Christian faith. The use of orality in the inclusive personal plural "we" toward the end of Acts demonstrates that the author identifies with the actors in the narratives where he is a witness. While it could also be a direct and verbatim quotation from a written source that the author is referring to, there is no proof to show this. That notwithstanding, the "we" narratives could be a conventional literary device to make the book sound and appear very active to implied readers.[10]

Date of Composition and Genre

Since Luke authored both the Gospel of Luke and Acts, it is believed that Acts was written just after the Gospel of Luke. Therefore, Acts was written in the mid-80s CE. This date is based on the assertions of Josephus that it could not have been written later.[11] Unfortunately, the history contained in the book ended in the 60s CE, leaving out the destruction of the temple, the persecution by Nero, the death of James (the brother of Jesus), and so on. This leaves room for some scholars to argue that the book was written in the early 60s.[12] However, this argument would mean that the date of the Gospel of Luke ought to be moved to a date before the 60s, which is not historically conceivable. Others posit a date beyond the mid-80s to mid-90s.[13] The date of mid-80s to mid-90s is proposed to make a case for the nonreportage of the destruction of the temple in the 70s and the end of the ministry of Paul in Acts.

There are three major sources for the collection of information for the composition of Acts: (1) An Aramaic document that describes the activities of the early church in Jerusalem (1–12); (2) a tradition of the church in Antioch, which is used to compose the narratives concerning Stephen and Barnabas (Acts 6:1–8:4; 11:19–30; 12:25–25:35); and finally (3) a travel diary that recorded the travel activities of Paul.[14]

The genre of Acts is regarded as a theological history embedded in a pneumatological milieu. It is a genre that was popular in the Greco-Roman World, but the uniqueness

9. Reasoner, "The Theme of Acts," 635–659.

10. Mikael Winninge, "The Gospels and The Acts of the Apostles," in *Jesus, the New Testament, & Christian Origins: Perspectives, Methods, Meanings*, ed. Dieter Mittrnacht and Andres Runesson (Wm. B. Eerdmans, 2021), 233–280.

11. H. C. Thiessen, *Introduction to the New Testament* (Eerdmans, 1964), 184; Robert G. Gromacki, *New Testament Survey* (Baker Academic, 2009), 150.

12. Gromacki, *New Testament Survey*, 150.

13. Winninge, "The Gospels and The Acts of the Apostles," 260.

14. Powell, *Introducing the New Testament*, 195.

of Acts is that the genre is influenced by Christology and pneumatology. Luke did not totally deviate from the literature genres of his day. These histories are often biased to celebrate persons who have achieved religious milestones and to condemn persons who failed to achieve set religious and cultural standards. Often, these types of works were written by the public affairs unit of a religious group or movement.[15] This is what gave impetus to Dibelius and Bultmann to argue that the miracle narratives of Jesus and other early church leaders that have been documented were written to defy those persons and to say that the miracles did not happen.[16] Even though the case may be correct that a disciple of Apollonius—Philostratus in the third century CE—organized narratives in private to portray Apollonius as a miracle worker, this is not the case for Jesus and his disciples. The genre of Acts is a history that is infused with religious rhetoric to persuade the implied readers to leave their erstwhile religions to join the Christian faith. Though it does not explicitly condemn other religions, it praises the Christian faith, encouraging the admiration of implied readers.

Structure and Outline

The outline of the book of Acts demonstrates the narrator's objective to showcase the works of the apostles through the empowerment of the Holy Spirit. The outline follows:

- Preface and preliminary issues of Acts (1:1–26)
  - Preface (1:1–5)
  - The ascension of Jesus (1:6–11)
  - The selection of Mattias to replace Judas Iscariot (1:12–26)
- The birth of the early church (2:1–47)
  - Descent of the Holy Spirit on the 120 with the evidence of speaking in tongues (2:1–13)
  - Preaching of Peter after the descent of the Holy Spirit (2:14–47)
- Ministry in Jerusalem (3:1–8:3)
  - Healing, and preaching in the temple by Peter (3:1–26)
  - Persecution, miracle, generosity and unity of purpose (4:1–8:3)
- Ministry in other jurisdictions (8:4–12:24)
  - The mission of Philip to Samaria (8:4–40)
  - Conversion and preaching of Paul in Damascus (9:1–31)
  - Peter's Gentile mission, persecution, and the Church in Antioch (9:32–12:24)

---

15. Stephen J. Patterson, *The Gospel of Thomas and Jesus* (Polebridge, 1993), 110; Martin Hengel, *The Four Gospels and the One Gospel of Jesus Christ* (Trinity, 2000), 169–207; Michael D. Goulder, "Is Q a Juggernaut?," *Journal of Biblical Literature* 115, no. 4 (1996): 667–681.

16. Rudolf Bultmann, *The History of the Synoptic Tradition*, trans. John Marsh (Basil Blackwell, 1963), 210; Stephen S. Travis, "Form Criticism," in *New Testament Interpretation: Essays in Principles and Methods*, ed. I. Howard Marshall (Paternoster Press, 1977), 126–138.

Ministry to the ends of the earth (12:25–20:38)
The mission of Paul and Barnabas, and persecution (12:25–14:28)
Controversy and Council decision (15:1–35)
The mission of Paul and Silas, and persecution (15:36–20:38)
The arrest and trials of Paul (21:1–28:31)

The outline of the book of Acts emphasizes repetitive rhetoric to persuade readers that the work of the apostles is motivated by the influence of the Holy Spirit, which did not negate persecution and suffering. The Holy Spirit inspired the apostles and the early church to preach, support the needy among them, perform miracles, and have supernatural experiences. However, the end of the lives of the major characters in Acts—Peter and Paul—were not mentioned. It may depict to readers that missionary work under the influence of the Holy Spirit is a sacrificial life. The narrator was interested in the activities of the apostles and the early church, not how the lives of the major characters ended.

Theological Themes in Acts and Their Point of Contact with African Realities

The book of Acts is rich in many theological themes that also demonstrate strong points of contact and relevance with African realities. The themes indicate contrapuntal (simultaneous but unique) information to implied readers concerning the activities of the apostles and the early church. The worth of related and revolving themes in Acts is that they can be grouped together under the Holy Spirit, mission in Jerusalem and other jurisdictions, welfare, miracles, and persecution. It emphasizes a reading that harmonizes the themes and resonates with contemporary church life in Africa.

The Holy Spirit

Among the books of the New Testament, Acts is the book that shows the descent of the Holy Spirit as a new-era dispensation. This makes it a critical book in the study of the Holy Spirit in the New Testament.

> The sequel to Luke's Gospel, Acts, begins with the story of the migrants from Galilee who settled in Jerusalem to receive the promise of the Father after Jesus ascended into heaven. At the feast of Shavuot (Pentecost), which occurred ten days after Jesus's ascension into heaven, many Diaspora Jews and proselytes witnessed the power of the Holy Spirit descend on the 120 Galileans who became Jesus's disciples. They did not seem to be mere visitors on a religious pilgrimage.[17]

17. Gani Wiyono, "Reading the Pentecostal Interpretations of the Book of Acts Contrapuntally: A Response to Ekaputra Tupamahu," *Pneuma* 46 (2024): 223.

These 120 persons became the first group of people on whom the Holy Spirit descended, without racial, cultural, and social discrimination. This historic event is replicated by the Holy Spirit in other mission locations in Acts. "There was implicitly a role for the Holy Spirit in preparing the right person to carry the gospel amid the first-century Graeco-Roman world."[18] The Holy Spirit is the empowering agent for ministry activities in Acts. In other words, he is an indispensable member of the godhead for mission and ministry. The descent of the Holy Spirit validates the credentials of Jesus—that his promise of the Holy Spirit is not vague. It also makes Jerusalem a critical center of religious activities in the first-century religio-cultural setting.[19]

The coming of the Holy Spirit and influence on the apostles and the early church is to motivate them to pursue the agenda of Jesus and the task of the disciples to continue the work of Jesus. The Holy Spirit is to help the apostles and the early church fulfill the mission of Jesus to bring salvation to all creation. The mission began in Jerusalem and continued to other parts of the world in fulfillment of the instruction of Jesus: "But you will receive power when the Holy Spirit has come upon you; and you will be my witnesses in Jerusalem, in all Judea and Samaria, and to the ends of the earth" (Acts 1:8). Acts 1:8 is central to the missionary activities and movement of the key missionary characters—Peter and Paul.[20] The audience on the day of Pentecost were believed to have traveled to their various cities to spread the message of the Gospel. The apostles would have to select additional leaders to handle the administrative issues of the early church to enable them to focus on missionary ventures (Acts 6:1–7).

The missionary activities experienced the conversion of others to join the early church based on the preaching of the apostles and the miracles they performed. These miracles reflect the continuation of the ministry of Jesus, which is characterized by miracles.[21] The witnessing assignment of the apostles in Acts 1:8 is not only in words but deeds of power. The preaching (words) of the apostles and the early church involved recontextualization of some Hebrew Bible texts and sayings of Jesus to prove that Jesus is the Messiah. The recontextualization and some miracles performed to prove that Jesus is the Messiah led to persecution mainly by Jews. Nevertheless, the persecution further led to the spread of the Gospel (Acts 8:1–25).

The Holy Spirit is a central theme in Acts. It is the fulfilment of a promise by Jesus that came to pass (Luke 24:49). The Holy Spirit's role in Acts can best be observed by its dynamic presence in the ministries of the apostles and members of the early church through speaking in tongues, preaching, miracles, and prophecy. The promise of the descent or outpouring of the Holy Spirit on the disciples was made by Jesus at the time when the disciples inquired concerning how they would fare in his absence. Jesus did not answer the ethnic and political

18. Wiyono, "Reading the Pentecostal Interpretations of the Book of Acts Contrapuntally," 224.

19. Powell, *Introducing the New Testament*, 197–205.

20. Daniel Nii Aboagye Aryeh, "Mission: An Expositional Analysis of Acts 1:8 and Mission in Some Ghanaian Market Places," in *The Bible, Cultural Identity, and Missions*, ed. Daniel Berchie, Daniel Kwame Bediako, and Dziedzorm Reuben Asafo (Cambridge Scholars, 2016), 264–287; Paul Kang-Ewala Diboro and Boniface Kwaku Blewusi, "Implications of Acts 1:8 for Ghanaian Neo-Pentecostal Missiology," *E-Journal of Humanities, Arts and Social Sciences* 2, no. 12 (2021): 191–209; Robert P. Menzies, *Empowered for Witness* (T&T Clark, 2005), 202.

21. James B. Shelton, *Mighty in Word and Deed: The Role of the Holy Spirit in Luke-Acts* (Wipf & Stock, 2018), 125.

questions of the disciples but gave a promise and an assignment (Acts 1:8). The implied narrator appears to have engaged in the genre of farewell speech of some patriarchs in the Hebrew Bible that are characterized by speeches of blessings, judgment/punishment, and assignments. For example, when Isaac was old and was convinced that he might die any moment, he requested a favorite dish from Esau to bless him before he departed. Jacob cunningly met the requirements and got the blessing instead of Esau (Gen 27). In the last days of Jacob, he assigned Joseph under oath to make sure that he was not buried in Egypt; thereafter, Jacob blessed Joseph, and later blessed all his children (Gen 47:27–49:33). The blessings Jacob bestowed on his children when he was about to die appeared to be prophetic. He told them what would happen to each of them and how they would relate to each other after his departure/death. When Joseph realized that he was getting closer to dying, he made the Israelites swear an oath to carry his bones to the promised land (Gen 50:22–26). It is a system where by the dying prominent person gives an assignment to the living to carry out a mission on his/her behalf. Jesus wanted his mission to be perpetuated by the disciples; hence, he promised that the Holy Spirit would empower them.

The promise of the Holy Spirit was not limited to the original disciples of Jesus. Peter, the leader of the disciples, extended it to include anyone who later believed in Jesus and was baptized (Acts 2:38–39). It is an honor for the later believers to be found worthy and to be grafted in to the blessing and task of the disciples. Therefore, the Samaritans, gentiles in the house of Cornelius, and the Ephesian believers are duly qualified to receive the Holy Spirit just like the disciples (8:14–28; 10:44–48; 19:1–7). This is a syllogistic (premise that gives logical justification for a conclusion) progression that would provide the empowerment for effective witnessing in Jerusalem, Samaria, and to the ends of the world (Acts 1:8).[22]

The descent of the Holy Spirit on the day of Pentecost was accompanied by fire, wind/breath, and sound (2:1–4). The "fire and sound" reflects the concept of the preface element to the manifestation of the Spirit of Yahweh in the Exodus account in the Hebrew Bible. The presence of Yahweh with Moses on Mount Sinai was prefaced and described as יְהוָ֗ה כְּאֵ֣שׁ ("a devouring fire") (Exod 24:17). The manifestation of God to Moses in the call narrative is through the fire of the burning bush without consumption (Exod 3:1–12). The Israelites were led through the wilderness during the night by a pillar of fire (Exod 13:21). When the Israelites consecrated themselves to meet God close to Mount Sinai, the presence of God was preceded by קֹלֹ֨ת וּבְרָקִ֜ים (sounds and lightning/fire) (Exod 19:16). In addition to the Exodus account, Elijah's experience with God at Mount Horeb was prefixed by wind, fire, and sound (1 Kgs 19:11–18). Key religious leaders of Israel—Moses and Elijah—who represent the Law and the Prophets, have earlier experienced the presence of God with such prefixes. This phenomenon would possibly convince the audiences, who were Jews and familiar with the happenings in the Hebrew Bible, to accept that God has acted through the same indicators that announce his immanent presence.

The themes of promise, confession, and spirit manifestation correlate with African realities. Although death has varied causalities, many elderly persons approaching their death will

22. Aryeh, "Mission: An Expositional Analysis of Acts 1:8," 264–287.

call members of the family or close relatives to reveal hidden treasures of the family to them and hand over ancestral instructions and relics in their possession.[23] The living who receive and inherit these instructions, blessings, and relics are expected to observe all the instructions religiously. Failure to observe them attracts the punishment of the ancestors. The promise of the Holy Spirit in Acts and the mission is not associated with punishment if the apostles fail, but ancestral stipulations are accompanied by threats of punishment to persons who fail to strictly observe them. Failure to observe them is considered to be flouting the ancestral assignments. In addition to this, people who have committed some evil deeds are pressured by their ancestors to confess them before they die. This practice is aimed at warning the living to eschew evil.

The manifestation of spirits is rife in African cosmology. The spirits of the ancestors, deities, and others manifest through their priests/priestesses by speaking in unknown languages that have to be interpreted by the attendants to the audience. In Akan traditional religion and social location, the *Ɔkomfoɔ* (traditional priests/priestesses) sometimes speak in unknown languages when the spirits of the deity descend upon them and the *Asɔfoɔ* (attendant at the shrine) interprets it to the seekers.[24] Among the Yoruba people of Nigeria, the diviners who use the Ifa system of divination are trained in "interpreting sounds and using seances by means of which they or their medium get in touch with the spirit world."[25] Although the presence of the Spirit is felt through sound or natural elements that make noise, speaking in unknown languages under the influence of the manifestations of the Holy Spirit in Acts appears similar to that of the Yoruba Ifa system of divination. However, there are some differences. There was no interpretation of the unknown languages spoken on the day of Pentecost, but the audience understood the apostles in their native languages. In African cosmology, there are trained shrine attendants who interpret the unknown language of the deities/spirits to the seekers. In both cases, the Spirit (or spirits where African cosmology is in view) propels the speaking of unknown languages. The manifestation of the Spirit in speaking in tongues and unknown languages in Acts is seen in the experiences of neophyte Christians, while in Africa spirits communicate through established traditional priests/priestesses. In the African context, the manifestations of deities/gods/spirits are based on specialization. There are spirits of water, thunder, fire, and wind, among others.[26] The preface elements of the Holy Spirit, such as wind/breath and fire in Acts, will be interpreted by African traditionalists as multiple spirits' manifestations.

The promise of the Holy Spirit and its fulfillment on the day of Pentecost may be compared to the wisdom behind *Adinkra* symbols that seek to teach through vivid symbols in print, arts, and culture that are popular in Ghana, the Ivory Coast, and other parts of

23. Mbiti, *Introduction to African Religion*, 118–122.

24. John D. K. Ekem, *Priesthood in Context: A Study of Priesthood in Some Christian and Primal Communities of Ghana and Its Relevance for Mother-Tongue Biblical Interpretation* (SonLife Press, 2008), 43–49.

25. T. N. O. Quarcoopome, *West African Traditional Religion* (African University Press, 1987), 83.

26. Mbiti, *Introduction to African Religion*, 70–76.

Africa. The symbols may be different in other African countries but have similar meanings.[27] The three *Adinkra* symbols of *Akoben*, *Akoma Ntoaso*, and *Agyin Dawuru* are critical in this theme. The symbol of *Akoben* is a form of horn that represents "a call to action, readiness to be called to action, readiness, and voluntarism."[28] The gathering and readiness of the disciples to receive the Holy Spirit while gathered at one location may be likened to *Akoben,* with the sign of the wind and tongues of fire and readiness for action. Therefore, in African philosophical discourse, the wind and tongues of fire as seen in Acts have some similarities to *Akoben*, which calls for the action of speaking in tongues (*xenolalia*) and preaching to convert others to the Christian faith. However, there are distinctive features between the wind and tongues of fire as seen in Acts and *Akoben*. The wind and tongues of fire on the day of Pentecost are initiated by the Holy Spirit who is the third person of the Godhead. It is originated by the Holy Spirit without human involvement but empowers humans to receive power as the fulfillment of a promise. *Akoben* is solely an initiation by traditional authorities to call for action by citizens.

The meaning of *Akoma Ntoaso* is related to *Akoben* by giving a sense of purpose that amplifies *Akoben*. *Akoma Ntoaso* is the "joining of hearts. A symbol of agreement, togetherness and unity or a charter."[29] *Akoma* refers to the heart and *Ntoaso* is joining together to proceed or progress. The implied narrator of Acts 2:1 underscores the fact the disciples were united in purpose. The phrase πάντες ὁμοῦ (Acts 2:1) depicts being together geographically based on a prior instruction that led a group to agree and be of like mind. The African would call the house the disciples were gathered in *Akoma Ntoaso*: a location that fosters the joining of the hearts. This unity of purpose was not limited to the day of Pentecost but continued in the ongoing ministry of the disciples.

The experience of the Holy Spirit on the day of Pentecost resonates with the symbol of *Agyin Dawuru*. The phrase *Agyin Dawuru* literally means *Agyin*'s gong. It is a symbol that commemorates the alertness, faithfulness, and dutifulness of a gong bearer of the Asantehene called *Agyin*.[30] The symbol is to honor *Agyin* for his gong-beating work for the Asantehene. The term *Dawuru* means proclamation. The disciples were honored for being obedient to be gathered at one location with one heart and expectation of the descent of the Spirit. Peter preached (*Dawuru*) after the reception of the Holy Spirit. This resonates with how *Agyin* received the message of the Asantehene and went on to proclaim it to the citizenry, though it does not suggest that the proclamation or preaching by Peter on the day of Pentecost is the direct equivalence of *Dawuru*. While they have similarities, there are also some significant differences in terms of content, purpose, and effect. The content of Peter's preaching is focused on repentance to salvation. It is not limited to a particular ethnic group or people. *Dawuru* is directed to a group of people within the jurisdiction of a traditional ruler and the content is existentialism. The purpose of Peter's preaching is to express the love of God to God's creation,

27. Mbiti, *Introduction to African Religion*, 26.

28. https://www.adinkrasymbols.org (accessed May 2, 2025).

29. https://www.adinkrasymbols.org.

30. https://www.adinkrasymbols.org.

while the purpose of *Dawuru* is to demonstrate the authority of the traditional ruler over the subject and to announce his/her instructions. The effects are that the preaching of Peter called the audience to leave their erstwhile religious affiliation to belong to or join the Christian faith. *Dawuru* maintains the audience in their existing religious affiliation or adds to it.

There are some significant differences between the concept of the Holy Spirit and spirits in the African religio-cultural setting. The Holy Spirit is the third person of the Godhead, who shares a similar status with God and Jesus Christ.[31] Spirits in the African traditional setting are not members of the Godhead but the manifestation of dead persons and deities that are considered below the status of the supreme being.[32] These spirits are defined within the confines of a clan, ethnic group, or family. They do not share the same status as the Holy Spirit.

Mission in Jerusalem

Acts is considered a missionary piece that did not leave out Jews as persons who need missionary proclamation. It is based on the instructions in Acts 1:8 which mentions Jerusalem being among the places mentioned for mission. It demonstrates the universal "enduring evidence of the church's global missionary task."[33] Missionary activities started in Jerusalem on the day of Pentecost when the Holy Spirit descended on the disciples with them (120 persons). Missionary activities in Jerusalem were dominated by the preaching and miracles of Peter. Missionary activities are characterized by (1) intertextual interpretation of Scripture to give support to Jesus as the Promised Messiah; (2) the mission also spread to some gentile communities; (3) biblical Jewish religious venues such as the temple precinct and the synagogues were the targeted areas for mission; and (4) Jews were the main target for conversion to the Christian faith. The structure clearly shows a well-organized mission where the message was persuasively crafted from the Scripture of the audience to invite them to join the Christian faith. The message was sent to the targeted audiences in their respective religious settings. This may be due to the fact that many of the members of the early church were Jews and were familiar with the Septuagint version of the Hebrew Bible.

The way messages were crafted and conveyed in Acts bears some similarity with how they are handled in the African context. In a polytheistic African context, such as that of the Akan, the main focus is on proclaiming a message from the deities/spirits to avert impending disaster/calamity, often as a result of the nonperformance of rituals or taboos committed.[34] The religious intermediaries make a proclamation or the religious intermediary informs the chief of the community (traditional political head) to cause a proclamation to be made. Among

31. Patrick Schreiner, *Acts* (Holman Reference, 2022), 10–12.

32. Mbiti, *Introduction to African Religion*, 70–78.

33. Jerry Michael Ireland, "The Missionary Nature of Tongues in the Book of Acts," *PentecoStudies* 18, no. 2 (November 20, 2019): 200–223.

34. Peter K. Sarpong, *People Differ: An Approach to Inculturation in Evangelisation* (Sub-Saharan Publishers, 2002), 104.

the Gbeabo people of Liberia, this religious intermediary is "the official mouthpiece of the chief,"[35] which is different from the linguist who speaks for the chief during a gathering in the palace. The offender of the taboos is expected to respond to the proclamation by reporting to the shrine for rituals to appease the gods. The offender is warned to repent and not to repeat the act.[36] The proclamation is not directed at enlightening people to leave their erstwhile religious affiliation to join a new religion which is being proclaimed. In other words, no religious belief is considered to be fundamentally superior to the other; they simply work to meet the needs of adherents. Rather, nonperforming deities are neglected and the performing ones are upheld with timely sacrifices and rituals offered to them.[37] The rejection of a deity is dependent on one's observation of the performance of the deity, not a proclamation to reject that deity. There is no exclusivist approach to religion in the African traditional context. Hence, while the message of Jesus is proclaimed among some Africans with emphasis on the rejection of erstwhile religions, there is a danger that the message of Jesus may be accepted in addition to other religious beliefs and practices.

The *Adinkra* concept of *Agyin Dawuru* provides a bridge that helps us understand the mission in Jerusalem. In African philosophical and religious discourse, proclamation is limited to subjects of a king/chief/priest, and so on. *Dawuru* is aimed at informing citizens concerning impending issues (either favorable or unfavorable), the solutions to avert the unfavorable situation, and what can be done to experience the favorable news. These mass announcements/proclamations may include foreigners who live within the jurisdiction of the king/chief/priest. The Fantes of Ghana have a proverb that reads *adi wo fia oye* ("it is good to have good things in one's house"), implying the need to attract good things and fortunes to one's home and prevent evil from coming home. Since most of the disciples were Jews, they felt the need to proclaim the good news to their own people before moving out.

The enterprise of proclamation to co-indigenes as a priority brings to mind the symbol of *Nkyinkyim*. *Nkyinkyim* has varied philosophical connotations, but the meaning that is applicable in this case is "a symbol of dedication to service,"[38] that begins at home or in the formative years by a journey through life's ups and downs. While undertaking proclamation to co-indigenes, the proclaimer learns the art of persistence and resilience for when he/she is confronted with life challenges in the future within or outside his/her jurisdiction. Hence, the preaching work in Jerusalem would be understood by Africans as somewhat similar to *Dawuru* and *Nkyinkyim,* to administer what is good to co-indigenes and prepare for life challenges further afield.

The mission that is mainly concentrated in Jerusalem witnessed miracles (3:1–10; 5:12–16; 9:32–43). The biblical Jewish worldview accepts the occurrence of miracles in the natural

35. Lamin Sanneh, *Translating the Message: The Missionary Impact on Culture* (Orbis Books, 2009), 235.

36. Mbiti, *Introduction to African Religion*, 144–147.

37. J. Kwabena Asamoah-Gyadu, "Spirit and Spirits in African Traditional Religions," in *Interdisciplinary and Religio-Cultural Discourses on a Spirit-Filled World*, ed. Veli-Matti Kärkkäinen, Kirsteen Kim, and Amos Yong (Palgrave Macmillan, 2013), 41–54.

38. https://www.adinkrasymbols.org; Mbiti, *Introduction to African Religion*, 39.

world. It does not dichotomize between the physical and the spiritual realms. Both realms are considered to play complementary roles for the betterment of human life. The limitation of health facilities and personnel are also contributing factors to the patronage of the services of miracle workers in the ancient world and even today.[39] The miracles in the Jerusalem mission were directed at solving health impairments that rendered the victims incapacitated and economically impotent, since health conditions often have corresponding economic and social status effects. The miracles affirmed that Jesus was a miracle worker, which is why his disciples could also perform miracles. The overall impact of the miracles was that they drew others to believe in Jesus and join the Christian faith.

The miracles in Acts restored the victims to health, a good economic trajectory, and social status, and they also increased the prominence of the apostles. The situation of the crippled man at the Beautiful Gate rendered him economically deprived such that he had to rely on the benevolence of others to survive. He was expecting money from Peter and John. The healing miracle would offer him the opportunity to pursue other economic ventures. A chiasmus structure can be deduced from the miracles that were performed in the Jerusalem mission, which attempts to emphasize the miracles performed by the apostles.

A Peter healed the crippled man at the Beautiful Gate (3:1–10).
B The apostles healed many (5:12–16).
A^1 Peter healed Aeneas (9:32–43).

Although the miracles started and ended with Peter, the plot shows that the apostles, not only Peter, could perform miracles.

Miracles are a critical component of religion in African traditions. Mission among Indigenous peoples is often miracle-focused. A performing deity is a deity that performs miracles that include healing and exorcism. These miracles are usually procedural through the administration of substances and relics given by the priests/priestesses. The miracles build confidence in the efficacy of the priests/priestesses and the deities.

Performing miracles for co-indigenes is expressed in the *Adinkra* symbol of *Asaawa*. It is represented by four sweet berries also referred to as "Miracle Berries,"[40] believed to have emerged as a solution in difficult situations. A miracle is considered as serving sweet berries to co-indigenous people. It expresses the concept of religious ethics in the African context, which required staying in constant relationships with the deities for miracles to take place. This reflects the concept of the symbol *Aban* as a fortress, "a symbol of strength, seat of power, authority, and magnificence."[41] The person who receives miracles is considered as having the attention of the deities and being protected from shame, while the miracle worker is the most

39. Daniel Nii Aboagye Aryeh, "Discipleship as Empowerment for Faith-Sharing an Healing Theory in Luke 9:1–6: Appropriation for Contemporary Christianity in Ghana," *Trinity Journal of Church and Theology* 20, no. 2 (September 2020): 43–68.

40. https://www.adinkrasymbols.org.

41. https://www.adinkrasymbols.org.

powerful religious person. However, in Acts, the attention and praise is given to the God who performs the miracle through the apostles, not to the apostles themselves.

Miracles in Other Contexts in Acts

Missionary activities to other jurisdictions rather than Jerusalem were led by Peter and Paul. The mission is composed of preaching and performing miracles similar to the mission in Jerusalem. The early church, which was limited to some Jews and had been considered as a strand of Judaism, turned out to be more than that. It had no ethnic or geopolitical limitations. In other words, Judaism was not a prerequisite to becoming a Christian.

Peter struggled to accept the divine invitation to go and preach to Cornelius and his household due to ethno-geopolitical considerations. However, Peter realized that "I truly understand that God shows no partiality, but in every nation anyone who fears him and does what is right is acceptable to him" (Acts 10:34b–35). This statement is a critical turning point for the mission to the ends of the world. The mission to the ends of the world is to extend the blessings and love of God to the rest of the world with equal access and opportunity, which is different from Jewish proselytism where the proselyte did not have equal rights with the Jew.[42]

The mission to the ends of the earth involves the performance of miracles. The miracles in the mission to the ends of the earth share a similar structure and emphasis with the miracles in the Jerusalem mission.

A Paul healed a crippled man (14:8–20).
B Paul performed many miracles such that his aprons and handkerchiefs were taken to the sick and they were healed (19:11–20).
A[1] Paul healed the father of Publius and others (28:1–10).

The emphasis is on the fact that Paul and even articles of clothing from Paul could perform miracles. The mission to the ends of the world that was led by Paul and supported by Barnabas had the strategy of starting in the synagogue. In many towns and cities that Paul and Barnabas went to, they first and foremost identified a synagogue and visited it during worship days when they would be asked to make a statement, which they eventually took advantage of to preach the gospel of Jesus Christ (Acts 13:4–12, 14–51; 14:1–7; 17:1–21; 18:1–11, 18–23; 19:8–10). This is not unique to Paul and Barnabas. It was the norm for Jesus to visit synagogues to read the Scriptures and to also perform miracles (Matt 9:35–38; Mark 1:21–28; Luke 4:31–38). The synagogue played a central role in the mission of Jesus and that of Paul and Barnabas to the ends of the earh. Indeed the mission in Jerusalem was concentrated on

42. Martin Goodman, *Mission and Conversion: Proselytizing in the Religious History of the Roman Empire* (Clarendon Press, 1994); Shelly Matthews, *First Converts: Rich Pagan Women and the Rhetoric of Mission in Early Judaism and Christianity* (Stanford University Press, 2001); E. P. Sanders, *Judaism: Practice and Belief: 63 BCE–66 CE* (Trinity Press International, 1992); Louis H. Feldman, "Conversion to Judaism in Classical Antiquity," *Hebrew Union College Annual* 74 (2003): 115–156; Christoph Stenschke, "Mission in the Book of Acts: Mission of the Church," *Scriptura* 103 (2010): 66–78.

Jewish religious buildings.[43] Jesus, the disciples, Paul, and Barnabas had unfettered access to the synagogue because they were themselves Jews.

Miracles performed for non-indegenes in the African traditional context have no limitations as long as the seekers have accepted to observe all the instructions given by the priest/priestess. Although miracles in the African context attract others to the shrine and the priest/priestess, the seeker is not required to desert their erstwhile religious affiliation. The miracle does not necessarily precede proclamation. Just as Paul was seen as a mystery figure by the people of Malta, so are the miracle workers of African Traditional Religions considered.

In rhetorical parlance, mission activities in Jerusalem and the other parts of the world expressed emphasis through repetition of pattern. Repetition in rhetoric is often directed toward the buttressing of a phenomenon to persuade implied readers of the values of the repeated issue.[44] There is a repetition of the general pattern of proclamation being followed by miracles in Acts. This deviates from the norm of Jesus as captured in the Gospels and argues that the miracles were aimed at attracting the crowd for the proclamation of the teaching concerning the kingdom of God.[45] The reverse order is experienced in Acts within the same context in Jerusalem, where Jesus earlier ministered, as well as in a different context (Samaria and other parts of the world) where Jesus did not personally extend his ministry. The repetition of proclamations preceding miracles demonstrates the emphasis of the ministry of the early church in Acts motivated by Acts 1:8 with the key term of μάρτυρος (witness); although the performance of miracles can be considered as a form of witnessing, the emphasis is on proclamation. In the African terrain of proclamation and miracles in a religious context, there is no specific pattern that is similar to the pattern in Acts. Miracles are emphasized above proclamation because religious conversion is a minor theme in African Traditional Religions and culture.

The Centrality of Welfare

There were more poor members in the early church than rich ones; therefore there was the requirement for a welfare system to provide for their needs (Acts 2:43–47; 3:32–37; 5:1–11). New religious movements appear to be attractive to the poor if they propose solutions to their existential challenges. It does not mean that new religious movements do not attract the wealthy; they do, but not easily because the rich already have streams of provision for their

43. Jordan J. Rya, "The Kingdom of God and the Assembly of the People: The Role of the Synagogue in the Aims of Jesus" (PhD diss., McMaster University, 2016), 48; James C. Miller, "The Jewish Context of Paul's Gentile Mission," *Tyndale Bulletin* 58, no. 1 (2007): 101–115; Silas Turrang Dogara, "The Synagogue as Locus of Ministry in Luke-Acts: A Socio-Historical Study of Luke 4:16–30" (PhD diss., Stellenbosch University, 2020).

44. Aristotle, *Rhetoric*, Book I, trans. W. Rhys Robert; David B. Gowler, "Socio-Rhetorical Interpretation of Text and Its Reception," *Journal for the Study of the New Testament* 33, no. 2 (2010): 191–206; Daniel Nii Aboagye Aryeh, "Ethnicity, Miracle, and Lepers in Luke: Inner Textures Analysis of Luke 17:11–19," in *Troubling Topics, Sacred Texts: Readings in Hebrew Bible, New Testament, and Qur'an*, ed. Roberta Sterman Sabbath (Walter de Gruyter, 2021), 493–516.

45. George Henry Hubbard, "The Message of the Miracles to the Modern Minds," *The Biblical World* 42, no. 4 (October 1913): 204–213; Udo Schnelle, "The Signs in the Gospel of John," in *John, Jesus, and History: Glimpses of Jesus Through the Johannine Lens*, ed. Paul N. Anderson, Felix Just, and Tom Thatcher (SBL Press, 2016), 3:231–244.

daily needs and so may not feel the need for more. The welfare system of the early church in Acts was crafted with the concept of appealing to the few wealthy members to give in support for the basic needs of the poor members. It became the devoted responsibility of the wealthy members to consistently give in support to the needy members. Does this welfare system put a hardship on the wealthy and make the needy lazy and reliant on the magnanimity of the wealthy? Would it discourage the wealthy from joining the church and encourage the poor to join the church?

The narrator indicated that the first or founding members of the early church in Acts after the preaching of Peter on the day of Pentecost (2:43–47) were generous to church members from a lower socioeconomic bracket. Hence, the rich "would sell their possessions and goods and distribute the proceeds to all, as any had need" (Acts 2:45). It is legitimate to ask how the poor got their basic needs met before they became members of the church. They were likely engaged in peasant and menial daily work for the affluent and wealthy in society.[46] Because the early church met frequently, it was difficult for the poor to attend to their daily work to earn money for their daily needs. In Acts 2:43–47, it appears that the wealthy voluntarily sold their possessions to support the needy without a request by the leadership of the church. However, the wealthy could not do so without approval from the leadership of the church (Acts 4:35). The early church welfare system expanded from helping the poor in the same congregation to helping other congregations affected by famine (11:27–30). The selling of properties by the wealthy to support the needy in the early church seems to have been limited to the church in Jerusalem and does not seem to have been the practice in other churches, though in Antioch sacrificial contributions were made by the members of the church not for the poor in the church but to mitigate the effect of famine in the church in Judea (Acts 11:22–30).

The wealthy and the poor in the ancient Mediterranean world had a relationship of reliance on each other for a common good. The wealthy needed the poor peasants to undertake menial domestic work, construction, and agricultural work. This served as a source of income and sustenance for the poor.[47] This relationship continued in the church in a varied manner where the poor did not necessarily have to work for the wealthy for payment for their daily sustenance but they did because they saw each other as brothers/sisters in the church. The wealthy voluntarily sold their properties and the proceeds were distributed to the poor in the church.

Well-being is critical to the communal lifestyle in Africa. Africans are required to work legitimately to acquire wealth to give to the poor, which is a key aspect of community.[48] The rationale for wealth is not its accumulation while one's neighbors do not have daily provision of their basic needs. The wealthy person who does not support the welfare of the poor is

46. Ernest van Eck, "In the Kingdom Everybody Has Enough: A Social-Scientific and Realistic Reading of the Parable of the Lost Sheep (Lk 15:4–6)," *HTS Teologiese Studies/Theological Studies* 67, no. 3 (2011): 1–10.

47. Ernest van Eck, "When Neighbours Are Not Neighbours: A Social-Scientific Reading of the Parable of the Friend at Midnight (Lk.11:5–8)," *HTS Teologiese Studies/Theological Studies* 67, no. 1 (2011): 1–14; Van Eck, "In the Kingdom Everybody Has Enough," 1–10.

48. Kwame Gyekye, *African Cultural Values: An Introduction* (Sankofa Publishing, 2003), 95–100.

considered to have ill-gotten wealth. Feeding the poor authenticates that one's wealth had been gotten legitimately and for good purposes. Therefore, wealth is not limited to individual comfort and satisfaction but also is to be used for the welfare of the poor in society. Providing for the basic needs of the poor by the wealthy is a form of poverty reduction.[49] In other words, the economic power of the wealthy has been extended to the benefit all members of the church, which implies their influence in church life.

African society was defined and built on communal structures where the poor and wealthy in society complemented each other. This is expressed in the proverb "a man must depend for his well-being on his fellow man,"[50] which seeks to draw attention to the fact that no human is an island concerning issues of well-being. The Akan of Ghana have a maxim that reads: *osikani mpo, paniɛ hia nu* ("even the wealthy may require a needle"). In other words, the rich in society may need the smallest domestic item; the rich need the services of the poor. The relationship between the rich and the poor provides communal balance and mutual aid. Hence, welfare in the African context goes beyond religious considerations in Acts where the welfare system appeared to have been concentrated largely on members of the Jesus movement/church. The African system of welfare was accessible to the immediate and some extended members of the community from the rich to the poor and vice versa.[51]

Well-being is expressed in the *Adinkra* symbol of *Adwo*, which means calmness, "peace, tranquility, and quiet."[52] It is a symbol of two oval-shaped objects facing each other vertically in equal measure. *Adwo* is expressed in a communal lifestyle where the wealthy give to the poor to have a calm, peaceful, and quiet society. It demonstrates the African traditional philosophy of Ubuntu that underscores the interrelatedness of all persons and their shared responsibilities to each other and to the environment. It is mainly driven by kindness and care for the supply of the basic needs of the other.

The system of welfare demonstrated by the early church in Acts may be understood by many Africans as a selective welfare system on the grounds that: (1) the narrator of Acts mainly indicated that the rich sold their properties to provide for the needs of the poor in the church. Arguably, the selling of properties by the rich to give toward the needs of the poor in the church could be precipitated by the notion of Maranatha (the imminent second coming of Jesus) that the early leaders of the church preached. Some understood this teaching to discourage property ownership and wealth accumulation; (2) the welfare is limited to members of the church, not the entire society. Hence, it is sectarian, while the African welfare system is communal and embedded in the social lives of all the people; and (3) selling essential properties for the provision of the basic needs of the poor is not often experienced in the African context of welfare. Essential properties such as houses, lands, and so on could be sold or auctioned to help hire the services of an expert when one is involved in a potentially incriminating case or

49. Rabiatu Ammah, "Islam and Poverty Reduction Strategies Attempts at Dealing with Poverty in the Ghanaian Muslim Community," *Ghana Bulletin of Theology* 2 (2007): 3–20.

50. Gyekye, *African Cultural Values*, 34.

51. Gyekye, *African Cultural Values*, 99.

52. https://www.adinkrasymbols.org.

to pay for compensation to save the community from an impending calamity as a result of a taboo someone has committed. The theme of well-being in Acts is narrower than welfare in the African context.

The proposition of some resemblance between the welfare system of the early church in Acts and African realities of life shows some degree of mutuality between the first century CE church and the African traditional understanding and practice of welfare. Significantly, the system of welfare in Africa is mainly experienced among rural community members. It is not the same in urban areas, where the sense of African community is gradually fading out. This may be due to heightened levels of security and modern architecture that do not allow easy entry into a neighbor's house. It could also be due to capitalism, materialism, and consumerism that have become the norm in many African urban communities.

Expansion of Leadership

The disciples could not effectively lead the congregation due to welfare issues and the preliminary assignment to go and preach the gospel (6:1–7; 1:12–26; 9:16–17; 9:26–31; 13:1–3; 15:36–41; 16:1–5). In other words, they were not endowed to manage the congregation but to convert non-Christians to the faith of Christianity. The selection of additional leadership was based on specific criteria of how long the candidates had been in the faith and the influence of the Holy Spirit in the life of the candidates.

The early church selected individuals to replace others (1:12–26), serve a role in the congregation (6:1–7), go to uncharted jurisdictions to convert non-Christians to the faith (9:16–17; 9:26–31; 13:1–3), and be assistants to the apostles on mission (15:36–41; 16:1–5). Besides the assistants, all the other selections have the input of the community of Christians and key leaders of the church. Leadership in the early church is for the candidate to perform a specific role in the mission of the church and attract others to the church. The dominant criterion is charismatic endowments. Hence, some of the six (Stephen and Philip) selected as leaders to handle welfare issues in the church in Jerusalem were later found preaching and performing miracles to draw others to the faith. The charismatic requirement may be due to the promise and reception of the Spirit on the day of Pentecost.

Leadership in Africa is typically by dynasty or charismatic endowments. Traditional political leadership is by ancestral lineage, while leadership in the religious milieu is based on evidence (*charisma*) of being called by the deities. The leaders "serve as the link between their fellow human beings on one hand, and God, spirits, and invisible things on the other."[53] The link or bridge is the ability to communicate with the divine on behalf of the subjects and to receive responses to their existential needs because traditional religion is largely existential in approach. The charisma of the religious leader represents the efficacy of the deity. Leadership succession is often the responsibility of the deity, who endows the individual with spiritual abilities. Since leaders of traditional religions do not often meet together corporately, leadership is exercised at the shrine to mediate for the subjects.

---

53. Mbiti, *Introduction to African Religion*, 153.

Leadership and selection of leaders in Acts resonates with the *Adinkra* symbol of *Adinkrahene* which is represented by a spiral of varied layers. The term *Adinkrahene* means the king/chief of *Adinkra*. It is the king of all the *Adinkra* symbols which connotes that all other *Adinkra* symbols came into existence because of the leadership, inspiration, and charisma of *Adinkrahene*.[54] It depicts the concept of leadership as the ability to mentor and train others to take up leadership positions. Hence, the disciples of Jesus who assume the position of apostles in Acts would be considered as *Adinkrahene* in traditional *Adinkra* philosophy and through them, others were brought into leadership positions in the early church. However, apostles may refer to learners who have undergone training and have been sent out for mission to establish themselves. It does not demonstrate an independence from the message or training notes of the master. *Adinkrahene* connotes the concept of a king that has become a king of kings of *Adinkra*. While apostle demonstrates service in humility, *Adinkrahene* denotes service in royalty.

In another breath, selecting individuals to serve in a religious capacity is mostly not the duty of the community of the adherents of the shrine or deity. The deity selects the person through some manifestation or action of the candidate that reveals he should be selected to serve.[55] In other words, human involvement in the selection process is limited. In Acts, the congregation had a critical role in the selection of their leaders. This way of selecting leaders demonstrates that leadership in Acts is service to the congregation and then to God; hence, the congregation has critical inputs based on the evidence of the influence of the Holy Spirit in the words and deeds of the candidate. Leadership in traditional African religio-cultural context is service to the deity followed by service to the adherents of the deity. While there are some differences, both Acts and African Traditional Religious contexts show that God, for the former, and the deity, for the latter, both have a central role in the selection of a chosen candidate.

Contextualizing the Gospel

Contextualization is a problem that is associated with new converts that are deeply committed to their erstwhile religious and traditional norms to the point that they find it difficult to disassociate from them because of their cultural identity and anthropological definition of the individual. Contextualization raises questions of religion and cultural identity. Although religious beliefs and practices constitute a person's identity and sense of humanity, should religious conversion include the neglect or total departure from one's ethnocultural identity? What are the criteria for accepting new religious norms against ethnocultural traditions?

The early church was initially considered a strand of Judaism because Jesus and many of his followers were Jews. They met at Jewish synagogues and observed Jewish religious and cultural traditions without any hindrances (Acts 13:4–12, 14–51; 14:1–7; 17:1–21; 18:1–11, 18–23; 19:8–10). They began to encounter critical challenges when Christianity began to expand to gentile territories whose erstwhile religion and ethno-cultural norms conflicted with those of believers from a Jewish background who initially formed the majority membership of the early church

54. Mbiti, *Introduction to African Religion*, 39.

55. Gyekye, *African Cultural Values*, 7.

(Acts 6:1–2). Circumcision existed among the gentiles before it became a covenant between God and the Israelites.[56] However, it was not obligatory among the gentiles as it was for the Israelites. Some Jewish Christians from Judea insisted that gentile converts to Christianity must undergo Jewish circumcision to become Christians. This matter created tension among the gentile Christians which had to be dealt with by the council of the early church in Jerusalem (15:1–35).

The council concluded that if the Holy Spirit can be released to the gentiles in their uncircumcised state just as he can be to Jews, there is no need for circumcision because salvation is by the grace of Jesus (15:11). In other words, circumcision is an ethnocultural Jewish identity marker and anthropological feature which non-Jewish persons do not need to practice. This proposition of the council was reinforced with the recontextualization of Amos 9:11–12. The decision of the council presupposes that becoming a Christian does not necessarily disassociate a convert from their ethnocultural and anthropological norms. It emphasizes the contextualization of the Christian faith in varied contexts without neglecting the core values of the Christian faith. Religious conversion must not force an individual to lay aside their ethnocultural and anthropological identity and make this a requirement for salvation. However, unrighteous ethnocultural beliefs and practices must be transformed by the good news. For example, the ethnocultural beliefs and practices that intend to keep women and children in perpetual subjugation and obnoxious practices where innocent children are forced to serve shrines for the sins (mistakes) of their parents or grandparents should be done away with.

Although there is competition among traditional religious leaders in Africa to prove who is the most powerful, which occasionally leads to problems and disagreements, issues of doctrinal problems hardly occur. This is due to the polytheistic nature of some religions in Africa. One is not often required to leave one's erstwhile religious affiliation or religious practice before access to the benefits from a new deity is granted. Various religious beliefs and practices can be syncretized without conflict. Therefore, the conflicts regarding ethno-traditional beliefs and practices would not pose challenges to the African context but caution is needed to ensure that syncretism is avoided.

Supernatural Experiences

Personal encounter with the divine is a critical component of supernatural experiences in the early church (Acts 8:26–40; 9:1–19; 10:1–33; 12:6–19; 16:6–10). These supernatural encounters are experiences with angels, Jesus Christ (the risen Lord), and a divine voice that mainly gives guidance to the preaching of the good news, clarification on ethnocultural issues, and deliverance from danger. Often, the individuals who experience these divine encounters are in a state of trance or dream where they do not have much control over what is happening. Supernatural experiences in the early church were limited to situations where human intervention was not able to achieve the needed results in good time. Angelic encounters facilitate the proclamation of the good news (8:26–40; 10:1–14); and encounters with angels provide for

56. D. Doyle, "Ritual Male Circumcision: A Brief History," *Journal of the Royal College of Physicians of Edinburgh* 35 (2005): 279–285.

deliverance from prison (5:17–21; 12:6–19). These divine experiences served as encouragement for the apostles to continue the mission in the midst of difficult situations.

The supernatural experiences reflect the experiences of some key religious leaders in the Old Testament (Gen 18:1–15; Exod 3:1–12; 1 Sam 3; 1 Kgs 9:1–14; 19:11–18; Isa 6; Jer 3:6–25; Ezek 1–3) and Jesus in the Gospels (Matt 3:13–17; 4:1–11; 17:1–13; Mark 1:9–11, 12–13; 9:2–8; Luke 3:21–22; 4:1–13; 9:28–36). In supernatural encounters where the religious leaders (particularly prophets) engage with a group of divine entities in a discussion of a critical issue, it is referred to as a "divine council" meeting which leads to tasks being assigned to the prophets or encouraging them to overcome a pending persecution.[57] It adds to the credentials of the prophet that God is concerned about the task of mission. The heavenly hosts come in to help when human capability is critically challenged or limited in the face of impending issues. Jesus had similar experiences at his temptation (Matt 4:11; Mark 1:13) and on the Mount of Transfiguration (Luke 9:28–36). The supernatural experiences that were noted in the Old Testament continued with Jesus and the early church. It is a trajectory that seeks to argue that the God that acted in history is still in operation in the early church. However, supernatural experiences with divine beings are not the preserve of Judaism and the early church.

Supernatural experiences with divine beings (spirit beings and God) in Acts have both similarities to and differences with traditional African religions' encounters with the supernatural. Supernatural experiences with the divine are rife in some African Traditional Religions. These are not limited to religious intermediaries; ordinary people could have similar experiences, which are determined by the deity. For example, if a deity decides to call someone for service, the deity can encounter the person at any time without notice.[58] Just as the mission of the early church started after the experience with the Holy Spirit, in many African contexts, one cannot start a mission until an encounter with the deity that indicates a calling to serve in a particular capacity. The experience with the deity by the would-be traditional priests/priestesses sometimes results in the candidate becoming somewhat insane. In other words, the behavior of the candidate is not normal to humans. He/she is then sent for diagnosis to determine the specific deity that was encountered and then begins training into the priesthood. For example, in the Akan traditional religion, persons who exhibit tendencies or behaviors that depict being called by a deity for service are sent to the Akonnedi shrine in Larteh, in the eastern region of Ghana. The priestess in charge of Akonnedi then discerns the deity that is inviting the candidate for service and the course of training.[59] After graduation, the deity periodically has encounters with the priest/priestess for further instructions and guidance.

Ancestral spirits can manifest and speak through any member of the family. This phenomenon may happen during funerals but may occur on other occasions as well. At a funeral

---

57. Samuel A. Meier, *Themes and Transformations in Old Testament Prophecy* (InterVarsity Press, 2009), 19–27.

58. For details, see Kofi Asare Opoku, "Training the Priestess at the Akonnedi Shrine," *Institute of African Studies Research Review* 6, no. 2 (1970): 34–50, available at African e-Journal Project, http://digital.lib.msu.edu/projects/africanjournals.

59. Opoku, "Training the Priestess at the Akonnedi Shrine."

in Asebu, Winneba, in the central region of Ghana, the spirit of the dead person (yet to be buried) was said to have come upon a lady of about twenty-six years of age and she began to confess/reveal those who had killed him (the dead person). She mentioned the names of people who were perceived to be witches and sorcerers in the community and how they should be dealt with.[60] The spirit of the deities and ancestors could also have an encounter with anyone, particularly hunters, at any time. "Hunters could meet spirit beings in the forests. The origin of the *Kundum* dance and festival can be traced to an encounter a hunter had during one of his hunting expeditions in the night. The hunter, who was a native of Aboadze, was reported to have been taught how to dance *Kundum* by the leader of the dwarfs called Afoakye for a period of one month."[61] This makes supernatural experiences a central issue in traditional religion in Africa because the concept of community in the African context includes the living, the yet-to-be-born, the ancestors, and the spirit beings. The lack of supernatural encounters with the divine constitutes a defective community. The concept of community that exists in Acts and African traditional religio-cultural and social context serves as a good bridge between the two.

Both are communities where the Holy Spirit or spirit entities are counted to be part of human society. However, the Holy Spirit is the third person of the Godhead. The Holy Spirit has no physical abode such as a shrine. The Holy Spirit cannot be bought. Spirit entities or deities in many African Traditional Religions are limited to specific clans or ethnic groups. They can be bought and reside in specific locations.

Persecutions

Persecution is a critical theme in the book of Acts. Although it is not a palatable situation, it can be understood from the perspective that Jesus had earlier informed the disciples concerning the issue of being rejected or thrown out (Luke 9:1–6; 10:1–12). Therefore, the idea of persecution was not new or strange to the apostles. It seems that persecution after the departure of Jesus was more grievous than when Jesus was physically present with the disciples. The main reason for the persecution is the proclamation of the apostles that the promise of the Messiah is fulfilled in the person of Jesus. Jews, who were one of the primary audiences of the apostles, strongly disagreed with the teaching that Jesus fulfills messianic expectations.

The leaders of the early church made frequent references to the Septuagint in their preaching because it was the most popular religious document of many Jews in the first century CE and the majority of the apostles, if not all, were Jews.[62] The claim that Jesus is the promised Messiah, which most Jews did not accept, became the cause for persecution. Some Jews felt the need to resist the proclamation of the Gospel by the apostles, which they thought was distorting the concept of the promised Messiah (4:1–31; 5:17–42; 6:8–7:60; 8:1–3; 9:23–25;

60. Author observation at Asebu, a community near Perez University College, February 17, 2018.

61. Daniel Nii Aboagye Aryeh, *Biblical, Traditional, and Theological Framework for Understanding Christian Prophetism in Ghana Today* (Wipf & Stock, 2018), 19.

62. John David Kwamena Ekem, *Early Scriptures of the Gold Coast (Ghana) the Historical, Linguistic, and Theological Settings of the Gã, Twi, Mfantse, and Ewe Bibles* (Edizioni di Storia e Letteratura; St. Jerome Publishing, 2011), 1–3.

12:1–19; 14:1–7, 19–21; 16:16–40; 22:22–27:44; 28:17–22). The persecution was not caused by the preaching about Jesus as the promised Messiah but also by miracles performed by the apostles in the name of Jesus (Acts 3). The persecution progressed to arrest ordinary persons who accepted and believed in Jesus as the promised Messiah (Acts 9). Hence, it is a holistic persecution concerning any person or activity related to Jesus.

There is competing rivalry between shrines and traditional religious leaders in many African contexts. The competition often develops into persecution where opposing shrines fight for the elimination of the other so that the dominant shrine can have more patronage.[63] That notwithstanding, persecution in some African Traditional Religions can be experienced when a shrine is suspected to be working against the welfare of the community in which it is located or is promoting witchcraft activities. This fuels actions by the traditional political leaders and the entire community to expel the shrine and its leaders from the community. The actions that expel the shrine and its leaders from the community are sometimes interpreted by others who subscribed to the shrine as a persecutory act. However, the action to expel is intended to protect the entire community from evil; hence, it is difficult for the members of the community to call it persecution. In other words, malevolent shrines/cults are not welcome in the community even if they interpret expulsion to be persecution.[64] This is a major difference with the persecution experienced by the early believers. While the concept of persecution may be similar, the motivation and effects are not. In Acts, persecution served as a catalyst for the spread of the gospel "to the ends of the earth."

Conclusion

To a large extent, it can be argued that many themes in Acts reflect African realities, with some variations and differences. It implies that the first-century early church culture has some commonality with twenty-first-century African society. It emphasizes the relevance of the early church culture in contemporary times. Belief in the activities of God or the Holy Spirit in the natural world is critical. This is a central theme that connects the two epochs of themes, thereby attracting other themes of affinity. The commonalities flow naturally with Africans and resonate with some of their religious, social, and cultural themes. Point to the fact that Africans are more likely than others to accept Acts and the entire Bible as the authoritative religious document that guides life and nurture.

The commonalities identified between some themes in Acts and the African context of church or religion do not imply that there are no differences or gaps. There are economic, social, cultural, anthropological, ecclesiological, and other differences between the early church in the first century CE as recorded in Acts and contemporary life in Africa. However, the

63. Kwame Gyekye, *An Essay on African Philosophical Thought: The Akan Conceptual Scheme*, rev. ed. (Temple University Press, 1995); Mark Hill and Thomas J. Hellenbrand, "Religious Persecution in Africa: Nigeria, Algeria, and Eritrea," *Notre Dame Law Review Reflection* 97, no. 3 (2022), https://ndlawreview.org/wp-content/uploads/2022/06/Hill-Cropped-1.pdf.

64. Peter K. Sarpong, *Peoples Differ: An Approach to Inculturation in Evangelisation* (Sub-Saharan Press, 2002), 96–106.

principles governing the themes of the Holy Spirit, mission, miracles, welfare, leadership, contextualization, supernatural experiences, and persecution can be adapted and applied in the contemporary church in Africa for life and nurture.

This chapter also demonstrates that themes in Acts are not only found in the first-century CE church. They are general themes with varied concentrations. Many of the themes in Acts can be observed in different times and places, notably, for the purpose of this chapter, in African traditional societies. It calls for an African approach to these themes, with an amalgamation of methods to isolate a specific theme in Acts and how it resonates with particular African realities for an in-depth study. Since the African context is wide and contains various nuances, it is recommended that singular studies of themes should be considered with specific African contexts.

Further Reading

Adadevoh, Dela. "He Went on His Way Rejoicing: The Salvation Experience of an African Executive: Acts 8:26–40." *Africa Journal of Evangelical Theology* 20, no. 2 (2001): 209–214.

Adelakun, Adewale J. "Civil Disobedience and Democratic Sustainability in Nigeria: A Study of Acts 5: 17–42." *Ilorin Journal of Religious Studies* 6, no. 1 (2016): 17–30.

Botha, P. J. J. "Community and Conviction in Luke-Acts." *Neotestamentica* 29, no. 2 (1995): 145–165.

Dali, Samuel D. "What If . . . Reverse Mission: Rhetoric or Reality? Matthew 28:18–20 and Acts 1:8." *Brethren Life and Thought* 63, no. 2 (2018): 50–56.

Du Toit, Philip L. G. "Was Paul Fully Torah Observant According to Acts?" *HTS Teologiese Studies/ Theological Studies* 72, no. 3 (January 1, 2016): 1–9.

Igba, Jacob T., Risimati S. Hobyane, and Henk G. Stoker. "Salvation in Acts 16:16–40: A Socio-Historical Exploration of the Graeco-Roman Understanding. Research." *HTS Teologiese Studies/Theological Studies* 75, no. 3 (2019): 1–7.

Keener, Craig S. *Acts*. New Cambridge Bible Commentary. Cambridge University Press, 2020.

Mumo, Paul Kisau. "Acts of the Apostles." In *Africa Bible Commentary: A One-Volume Commentary Written by 70 African Scholars*, edited by Tokunboh Adeyemo. WordAlive Publishers; Zondervan, 2006.

Onongha, Kelvin. "Acts 1:8—A Paradigm for Mission in West-Central Africa." *Journal of Adventist Mission Studies* 5 no. 2 (2009): 61–73.

Polhil, John B. *Acts*. NAC. Broadman Press, 2001.

Schreiner, Patrick. *Acts*. Holman Reference, 2022.

Williams, Jeremy. "Acts and Whiteness: Response." Paper presented to Society of Biblical Literature annual meeting, San Antonio, Texas, November 19, 2023.

CHAPTER EIGHT

The Letter to the Romans

Jean-Claude Loba Mkole
University of the Free State
United Bible Society
Kenya

Introduction

IN ADDITION TO the introductory matters, the present chapter will highlight the Letter to the Romans's historical background and tackle its content from three perspectives—beginning, body, and conclusion—before ending with an epilogue.

This introduction aims to present the Letter to the Romans as an intercultural ecological epistle written by the Hellenistic Jew rhetor, intercultural mediator, and ecologist Paul. The thesis of Romans consists of expanding Paul's gospel, identified as the word of God, the word of Jesus, and the power for the salvation of every believer because the justice of God manifests itself from his faithfulness to the faithfulness of the believer (1:16–17). In fact, lack of faithfulness from the end of the believer has dramatic consequences, culminating in all sorts of vices (1:18, 22, 28). It is a theological exercise that targets literary critics of the word of God, religion scholars or theologians, and people who promote environmental integrity in Africa. It is an African introduction, as it focuses on faith interactions between Paul and Africans by birth, citizenship, residence, or profession.[1] "African scholars" who wrote on Romans are few. They include Origen (Alexandria), Augustine (Bishop of Hippo), John William Colenso (Bishop of Natal), Andrie du Toit (University of Pretoria), Cilliers Breytenbach (Berlin University), David Kasali (Africa International University/Université de Grand Ben), Jean-Claude Loba Mkole (University of Pretoria/University of the Free State), and some others. This comment interacts extensively with the views of two of them: one white pastor (Bishop Colenso) and one Black theologian (Professor Kasali). They have produced valuable commentaries that may easily fall into oblivion, but they yet deserve close attention from the readers of Romans. Kasali's well-argued commentary is available in the prestigious collective work entitled *The Africa Bible Commentary*, produced by evangelical theologians. Jonathan A. Draper (University of KwaZulu-Natal) edited and published the commentary by Colenso and made it more accessible for interested readers. As a result, Robert Jewett has dedicated his commentary

1. Cf. Jean-Claude Loba Mkole, "Paul and Africa?," *HTS Theological Studies* 67, no. 1 (2011): 1–11.

on Romans to Colenso and saluted him as "the first to suggest that Paul aimed to overcome prejudice against allegedly inferior peoples."[2] He argued as follows:

> By placing the argument of Romans in opposition to imperial claims of European colonists in South Africa, he showed that Paul defended the status of the ancient inferiors comparable to the "Zulus and Kafirs" of the nineteenth-century Africa and thus that the righteousness of God was impartial.[3]

Nonetheless, the target readers consist of the African audience at large and theologians in particular. This target audience in general is not an experimental field or informants for testing or applying a theory but constitutive parts of understanding and interpreting Romans from their traditional (religious) backgrounds and church culture frames, and contemporary life experiences. In fact, "as an act of communication . . . the transmission of faith is not a unilateral process: we must not underestimate the relationships that are established between the actors in this communication, where 'the receiver cooperates as much as the sender in the process of signification.'"[4] Moreover, focusing on Afro-Christian audiences and interpretations implies going beyond the geographical boundaries of the continent to embrace other people due to human and faith interconnectedness. In this introduction, Africa means the continental geographical area called by this name, which the African Union divided into six regions: Southern Africa, Central Africa, Eastern Africa, Western Africa, Northern Africa, and Diaspora Africa. Nevertheless, the efforts undertaken by Africans to understand and convey the truth expressed in the letter to the Romans should transcend Africanity because the truth of faith, ethics, and discipline must be one regardless of the diversity and location of the interpreters.

Method

Guided by intercultural ecojustice hermeneutics, this introduction highlights the ecojustice hermeneutic principles in each rhetorical section of Paul's Letter to the Romans and simultaneously engages with three frames of reference. The ecojustice hermeneutic principles include worth (intrinsic value of a being), interconnectedness (interdependence), voice (expression), purpose (goal or objective), mutual custodianship (stewardship), and resistance (resilience).[5]

2. Robert Jewett, *Romans: A Commentary* (Fortress Press, 2007), xv.

3. Jewett, *Romans*, xv; cf. J. William Colenso, *Commentary on Romans*, reprint of the 1861 ed., ed. with an introd. Jonathan A. Draper (Cluster Publications, 2003), 195–196.

4. Olivier Riaudel, "Fides qua creditur et Fies quae creditur: Retour sur une distinction qui n'est pas chez Augustin," *Revue Théologique de Louvain* 43 (2012): 170 (my translation); cf. Denis Willepelet, *L'avenir de la catéchèse* (De l'atelier—Lumen Vitae, 2003), 89.

5. Norman C. Habel, *Readings from the Perspective of Earth*, ECB 1 (Sheffield Phoenix Press, 2017); Michael Trainor, *About Earth's Child: An Ecological Listening to the Gospel of Luke*, ECB 2 (Sheffield Phoenix Press, 2017), 5; Tonstad K. Sigve, *The Letter to the Romans: Paul Among the Ecologists*, ECB 7 (Sheffield Phoenix Press, 2017), xi–xiii.

They constitute the fundamental values of ecological justice (abbreviated as ecojustice), though this study will focus more on interconnectivity. The present introduction also reflects the patterns of Kinshasa school of thought, which since 1961—the year of my birth—started demonstrating the possibilities and ways of particular or contextual theologies[6] led by inculturation/liberation,[7] reconstruction,[8] or intercultural interpretive paradigm.[9]

The intercultural analysis involves a constructive dialogue with three cultural frames of reference: original sacred text cultures, intermediate church cultures, and contemporary cultures. Among other things, it posits Jesus, recorded in the Gospels, as the ultimate epistemological privilege and authority that illuminates the truthfulness of any interpretive stand of sacred texts.[10] Consequently, the intercultural approach evokes one or some of Jesus's sayings that may confirm or contradict its conclusive findings. In an African contemporary culture, it can interact with scholars or ordinary readers of the chosen text. This intercultural commentary will highlight the views expressed by "African" scholars, that is, people associated with Africa by birth, citizenship, or profession. Accordingly, it engages African contexts through Colenso and Kasali and compares their views with the author's analysis of the Pauline letter in its original canonical text. The choice of these authors is not exclusive, but encourages the reader to include others in his or her intercultural dialogue with Romans.

Introductory Matters

Authorship

In the beginning of the Letter to the Romans (1:1), Paul introduces himself as δοῦλος Χριστοῦ Ἰησοῦ, κλητὸς ἀπόστολος ἀφωρισμένος εἰς εὐαγγέλιον θεοῦ ("slave of Christ Jesus, called an apostle, set apart for the gospel of God").[11] This introduction, combined with other literary indices within and outside the current letter, positions Paul as an author, a persecutor, or a preacher (2 Pet 3:15–16; Acts 7:58–28:31). His birth date is unknown,

---

6. Cf. Pope Francis, *Ad Theologiam Promovendam* ("To promote theology"), November 1, 2023, www.vatican.va/content/francesco/it/motu_proprio/documents/20231101-motu-proprio-ad-theologiam-promovendam.html.

7. Alphonse Ngindu-Mushete, *Thèmes majeurs de la théologie africaine* (L'Harmattan, 1989); Benezet Bujo and Juvevan Ilunga Muya, eds., *African Theology. The Contribution of the Pioneers*, 3 vols. (Paulines Publications Africa, 2003–2013).

8. Ntumba Tshiamalenga, "Les quatre moments de la recherche philosophique africaine aujourd'hui," *Bulletin de Théologie Africaine* 3 (1981): 71–80; Kä Mana, *Théologie africaine pour temps de crise: Christianisme et reconstruction de l'Afrique* (Karthala, 1993).

9. Jean-Claude Loba Mkole, "Intercultural Constructions of the New Testament: Epistemological Foundations," *HTS Teologiese Studies/Theological Studies* 77, no. 2 (2021): 1–8, https://doi.org/10.4102/hts.v77i2.6739; Jean-Claude Loba Mkole, "Inculturation and Interculturality: A Paradigm Transmutation in Theology," *Hekima Review* 65 (2022): 9–26.

10. Jean-Claude Loba Mkole, "The Social Setting of Jesus' Exaltation in Luke-Acts (Lk 22:69 and Ac 7:56)," *HTS Teologiese Studies/Theological Studies* 78, no. 4 (2005): 297; Jean-Claude Loba Mkole, "Jesus: The Apex of Biblical Canons," *HTS Teologiese Studies/Theological Studies* 78, no. 4 (2022): 1–8, https://doi.org/10.4102/hts. v78i4.7189.

11. All the translations are mine, unless otherwise stated.

although it was most likely in the "first decade AD."[12] He died in Rome around 65–67 CE. He acquired his Jewish identity and Roman citizenship from his parents, who were Jews and Roman citizens (Acts 22:25–29; 16:37; 23–27). His profile rightly fits a "product of the confluence of three cultural orientations—Jewish, Hellenistic Greek, and Roman."[13] Nevertheless, he is even more than that, as he acquainted himself with Arabs when he spent fourteen years in Arabia (Gal 1:17; 2:1) and Africans during his journeys (cf. Mark in Acts 15:37) and Romans (cf. Rufus and his mother in Rom 16:23). He is also an ecologist: "Paul is among ecologists in the Judeo-Christian sacred texts. His ecological guild is made up of the patriarchs, priests, and prophets (Rom 1:16–17; cf. Hab 1:4; Rom 5:12–21; 8:19–22; cf. Gen 1–31; Rom 15:8–12; cf. Isa 11:1–10)."[14] However, Paul's concern for the environment reflects more of his adherence to ecological principles of compassion, awareness of the world, and sensitivity to the plight of others, championed by Jesus, of whom he claims to be the slave (Rom 1:1).[15]

Date and Readership

Paul finished and dispatched the Letter to the Romans before traveling from Jerusalem to Rome as a prisoner. The immediate timeframe and space that are in a better position for the writing or dictation of this letter seem to be Corinth, where Paul met Prisca (or Priscilla) and Aquila (Acts 18:1–2) and spent eighteen months with them (Acts 18:11). Then he departed from Corinth after the hearing before Gallio (18:12–18). The Gallio Inscription allows scholars to date the departure to Rome within the twelve months, from July 1, 51 to July 52. Consequently, Robert Jewett concludes:

> When one calculates the subsequent events in his career, taking account of details in the letters and the realities of travel in the ancient world, this brings him to 56–57 CE as the final winter in Corinth (1 Cor 16:6) when the letter to the Romans was probably conceived and dictated.[16]

The letter identifies its addressees or readers as all those beloved of God, called saints in Rome (1:1). Andrie du Toit regards the idea of the Roman "church of the catacombs" as a myth.[17] For him, the first Roman Christians came together in the everyday living quarters of better-off households, where they met in the main room of an apartment (*insula*), spacious enough to

12. Joseph A. Fitzmyer, "Paul," in *The New Jerome Biblical Commentary*, ed. Raymond Edward Brown, Joseph A. Fitzmyer, and Ronald E. Murphy (Prentice Hall, 1990), 1332.

13. Ben Witherington III, *Conflict and Community in Corinth: A Socio-Rhetorical Commentary on 1 and 2 Corinthians* (Eerdmans, 1995), 1.

14. Tonstad, *The Letter to the Romans*, 18.

15. Tonstad, *The Letter to the Romans*, 18.

16. Jewett, *Romans*, 19–20.

17. Andrie du Toit, *Focusing on Paul: Persuasion and Theological Design in Romans and Galatians* (De Gruyter, 2007), 508.

accommodate about fifteen to twenty-five persons. Such would have been the meeting place in the home of Aquila and Prisca. Jewish synagogues also served as a starting point for preaching the Christian gospel (Acts 11:19–20; 13:5, 14; 14:1–6; 17:1–7, 10, 17; 18:4–7, 19–21, 26; 19:8–9). House churches recorded in Romans 16 are namely the ones in the home of Aquila and Prisca (16:5), the home of the "Asyncritus" group (16:14), and those around Filogus, Julia, and others (16:15).

Literary Genre

The Letter to the Romans is an epistolary genre shaped by Greco-Roman rhetoric. Generally, the Greco-Roman rhetoric operated in three modes (forensic, deliberative, and epideictic). Each mode had a particular function, though these modes could overlap. The forensic mode focuses on the past and deals with accusations and defense. With its future orientation, the deliberative mode seeks persuasion and dissuasion. The epideictic mode addresses a present situation using praise or blame to approve or reject some values. The overall function of rhetoric is to arouse emotions associated with pathos (stronger feelings like anger, fear, and pity) and ethos (gentle emotions such as laughter). A rhetorical piece comprises four or six parts: *exordium* (opening), *narratio* (matter at stake), *partitio* or *propositio* (thesis), *probatio* (argument/proof), *refutatio* (refutation), and *peroratio* (recapitulation/conclusion).[18]

Outline

Scholars generally do not question the epistolary nature of the letter to Romans. However, they dispute whether it is a doctrinal treatise, a situational letter,[19] or a contextualized document.[20] Admittedly, the beginning, the body, and the end of the letter to the Romans display a characteristic feature of a "letter-missive," an epistolary genre in which the relationship between the author and the addressee receives less expansion than the writer's thought.[21] The subdivision of the Judeo-Christian sacred texts in chapters and verses is a late phenomenon. However, the words used by Paul at the beginning and end of the writing pinpoint their epistolary nature. Therefore, a content structure in line with the epistolary literary genre could be the most appropriate one. As a result, we have opted to follow the structure proposed by Robert Jewett:[22]

Exordium, *narratio* and *propositio* (Rom 1:1–17)
Probatio (Rom 1:18–15:13)
Peroratio (Rom 15:16–16:27)

18. Witherington, *Conflict and Community*, 43–44.

19. Cf. Jewett, *Romans*, 42; Frank J. Matera, *Romans* (Baker Academic, 2010), 8.

20. Udo Schnelle, *Apostle Paul: His Life and Theology*, trans. Eugene Boring (Baker Academic, 2003), 305.

21. Simon Légasse, *L'épître de Paul aux Romains*, Lectio divina Commentaires 10 (Cerf, 2002), 38.

22. Cf. Jewett, *Romans*, vii–xix.

Thematic Comments

Introduction (Exordium)
Ecology, Salvation, and Justification (Rom 1:1–17)

African Target Culture

The name of Paul (Rom 1:1) manifests the worth or intrinsic value of the person who bears it. Through its Hebrew counterpart שָׁאוּל, Paul's name confers to him the value that a Benjaminite Jew would attribute to King Saul of the tribe of Benjamin as, in other passages, Paul confirms that he was a Benjaminite like King Saul with whom he shares the same name and the same clanic group (Rom 11:1; Phil 3:5). The interconnectedness between the beings (and in one case, the thing) named or alluded to in the introduction (1:1–7) include Paul, Christ Jesus, God, the Holy Spirit, Paul (a slave of Jesus Christ, apostle, set apart for the gospel of God), prophets, holy writings, David, the Romans (God's beloved in Rome called saints), and gentiles.[23]

In African cultures, the names provide the bearers with a web of identity information: ethnic, clanic or family affiliations, circumstances such as date or place of birth, social ranks, or other meanings. In Kenya, a name starting with the letter O (for male) or A (for female) generally identifies the person as a member of the Luo tribe. Among some Ghanaian tribes (e.g., Akan), a name associates the bearer with the day of his or her birth. For the Indrŭ people of DR Congo, a name may signal the place of birth, social rank, family, clan, ethnicity, or the totem of the bearer. As an illustration, the name Loba—which literally means a male person who possesses the word (*lo*) or a discourse master—indicates the Northern Lendu/Bhale/Ndrŭ or a Nilo-Saharan origin of the bearer. His second name, Mkole (meaning born in Muko locality or a member of Muko clan) connects him with the Southern Lendu/Bhale/Ndrŭ together with Muko and Zadhu clans, who traditionally belong to Walendu-Bindi chieftainship (DR Congo). While the Southern and Northern Lendu/Bhale/Ndrŭ inhabit DR Congo, others live in Uganda. The (I)ndrŭ live, think, and act as intercultural or interconnected entities among themselves and others *mutatis mutandis*. Basic concepts of interculturality include: *nganda* ("kin": nuclear and extended family members who should not marry each other), *ambɛlɛ* (any person with whom the marriage is possible), *ɔdhɨ* ("friend"), *alo* ("covenantal friend"), *olo* ("guest"), and *ɔmbvŭ* ("enemy"). The enemy may reconcile with the others and enter into a different type of interpersonal relation. A Ndrŭ's worth goes hand in hand with his or her relations or interconnectedness, starting with the parents. For the Ndrŭ, the most common question concerning someone's identity is not about his academic qualifications, profession, or social status. The person who introduces another one should answer the question: Whose son or daughter is he or she? The name will then connect with the family, clan, and ethnic affiliations of the bearer. A Ndrŭ is an intercultural being and justice consists of living in harmony with others.

---

23. Cf. Du Toit, *Focusing on Paul*, 232.

Though some of their languages are not mutually intelligible, they claim to originate from the common ancestor Ndrŭ, who migrated from Egypt southward. One of the known Ndrŭ ancestors is Mutuni (Chad), who could constitute a link with Lucy (Kenya), Toumai (Sahelanthropus tchadensis), the son of Seth, the son of Adam, the son of God. To paraphrase David Dawson, Adam, the first man, inspired Moses to understand and put the Torah, or the word of God, into writing. Thus, since the beginning of the creation, the word of God, the order of things, and their meaning have been embedded in human cultures, including languages.[24] Archaeological, linguistic, and historical evidence attest to the anteriority of the Negro-African culture whereby the Proto-Nilo-Saharan language would be the most ancient one and ancestor to Ancient Egyptian and Hebrew, both spoken by Moses.[25] However, to avoid miscommunication, spiritual wanderings, and idolatries, God sent consecutively his only Son, Jesus Christ, and the Holy Spirit to be the ultimate interpreter and mediator of his will to humanity.[26] Horizontally, the Ndrŭ intermingle with the pygmies, Bantu and Nilo-Saharans (Nilotic and Sudanic) tribes. One of the Ndrŭ traditions attest the following:

> Our elders' stories tell us that we are one among the many groups worldwide whose origin is traced to the Northern part of Africa. We moved as one large group of Ndrukpa people (then called Ndrŭ) from our cradle in Egypt in the Northern part of Africa as all other people were migrating for various reasons.[27]

Furthermore, the first name Jean-Claude links the same above-mentioned bearer with a French Jesuit Saint Claude La Colombière (1641–1682), Hebrew name Johannah ("God is gracious") and the Latin Claudius ("lame"). Names in their original languages are not meaningless labels, but culturally and ecologically bound identifiers. They constitute intercultural ecojustice devices, serving to identify and connect the bearers with visible and invisible worlds within an ecosystem of horizontal and vertical relations, which include human beings, nature, and

24. David Dawson, *Allegorical Readers and Cultural Revision in Ancient Alexandria* (University of California Press, 1992), 88; The Cross-Cultural Foundation of Uganda (CCFU), *The Oral History, Customs and Traditions of the Ndrukpa* (Ndrukpa Kingdom, 2019), 8.

25. Cheikh A. Diop, *Nations nègres et culture: De l'antiquité négro-égyptienne aux problèmes culturels de l'Afrique noire d'aujourd'hui* (Editions Présence Africaine, 1955), 27–64; Cheikh A. Diop, *Antériorité des civilisations nègres: Mythe ou vérité historique* (Présence Africaine, 1967), 13–26; Cheikh A. Diop, *Civilisation ou barbarie: Anthropologie sans complaisance* (Présence Africaine, 1981), 12; Joseph Ki-Zerbo, *Histoire de l'Afrique noire d'hier à demain* (Editions Hatier International, 1972), 43–56: Théophile Obenga, *L'Afrique dans l'antiquité: L'Egypte pharaonique-Afrique noire* (Présence Africaine, 1973), 53–90; Théophile Obenga, *L'Égypte, la Grèce et l'école d'Alexandrie. Histoire interculturelle dans l'Antiquité: Aux sources égyptiennes de la philosophie grecque* (Editions L'Harmattan, 2005), 21–98; Luka Lusala lu ne Nkuka, *L'influence de la philosophie égyptienne sur la philosophie grecque* (Éditions de l'Érablière, 2015), 15–18; Luka Lusala lu ne Nkuka, *De l'origine égyptienne des Bakongo: Étude syntaxique et lexicologique comparative des langues r n Kmt et kikongo*, vol. 1 (Éditions de l'Érablière, 2020); Luka Lusala lu ne Nkuka, *Introduction au kamitisme* (Éditions de l'Érablière, 2023), 23–24.

26. Cf. Jean-Claude Loba Mkole, "Intercultural Hermeneutics of the Words of God in Africa," in *Nexus Between History, Theology, and Cultures*, ed. Paul Béré (Gregorian and Biblical Press, 2025).

27. The Cross-Cultural Foundation of Uganda (CCFU), *The Oral History*, 8.

God. In brief, a name is a key cultural or intercultural identifier when understood from its original settings. Accordingly, the name Paul identifies him as a person connected with his cultural or intercultural milieu and other persons, including the divine and human, as explicitly stated in the beginning of the letter. Each person represents at least a culture and his or her personal relations with other people or cosmic elements make him or her an intercultural and ecological subject.

John W. Colenso considers the words of verse 16 ("the power of God unto salvation to everyone that believeth," KJV) as "the very keywords of the whole epistle."[28] According to him, Paul—in this verse—brings three points. First, "the salvation is wholly of God, wrought by His power, bestowed by his Love, of His own free grace in the Gospel, and therefore to be meekly and thankfully received as His gift, not arrogantly claimed as a matter of right."[29] Second, salvation "is meant for Jew and Gentile alike, for all that believe, without any special favour or distinction."[30] Third, salvation "is to be received by faith alone, by 'all that believe,' by simply taking God at His word and trusting in His Love, not to be sought by a round of ceremonial observances or acts of legal obedience."[31]

Andrie du Toit tackles the topical theme of justification in Romans (1:16–17) as one of the ethical indicators of the faith essentials. These essentials, according to him, consist of existence in faith (Rom 1:16–17, 12; 11:20; 12:3, 6; 14:22–23) and justification that transforms the believers into the citizens of Graceland (Rom 5:1–2, 9; 8:30). They command four ethical indicators, namely obedience of faith (Rom 1:5; 10:16; 15:18; 16:19; see also 1 Thess 1:3; Gal 5:16), righteous living (Rom 1–6), sanctification (Rom 1:7; 8:27; 12:13), and love (Rom 5:5; 13:8–10; 14:15; see also Gal 5:13–6:10).[32]

David Kasali highlights three things that Paul wants his addressees to know about him: he was a servant of Jesus Christ, called to be an apostle, and set apart for the Gospel of God (1:1). He also contends that the central theme of Romans is the Gospel that Paul is eager to preach to the Romans, which is "the proclamation of God's power to transform people's lives" (1:16–17). Paul had already had a life transformation experience on the road to Damascus (Acts 9:1–22).[33] In Romans (1:16–17), he defines the Gospel as the power of God, which—in his view—leaves no room for shame (1:16a), as he connects it with salvation for everyone who believes (1:16b). God's salvation plan rhymes with his justice to bring humankind into a relation with God and set a standard for human behavior. Kasali stresses that "God's justice cannot be attained through observance of law but only by faith (1:17; Hab 2:4; Gal 3:11). By responding in faith to the gospel message, believers will attain eternal life and experience the

28. Colenso, *Commentary on Romans*, 29.

29. Colenso, *Commentary on Romans*, 29.

30. Colenso, *Commentary on Romans*, 29.

31. Colenso, *Commentary on Romans*, 29.

32. Du Toit, *Focusing on Paul*, 372–376.

33. David M. Kasali, "Romans," in *Africa Bible Commentary: A One-Volume Commentary Written by 70 African Scholars*, ed. Tokunboh Adeyemo (HippoBooks; WordAlive Publishers; Zondervan, 2006), 1351.

fullness of life in Christ."[34] In African traditions, faith entails less a verbal proclamation or a statement (creed). It is more a matter of holistic faithfulness to God, fellow humans, and nature that the people experience unceasingly. Prayers and sacrifices serve to maintain this cosmic harmony and repair the transgressions.

From the views of African cultures and African scholarship, the introduction (Rom 1:17) highlights Paul's intercultural connectedness or ecological interconnectedness within the framework of divine salvation or justification. Right from his name and those of the beings/thing mentioned, Paul displays a web of intercultural, cosmic, or ecological connectedness. This interconnectedness involves Christ Jesus, God, the Holy Spirit (on divine side), and Paul (a slave of Jesus Christ, apostle, set apart for the gospel of God), prophets, holy writings, David, Romans (God's beloved in Rome called saints), and gentiles (on human side). The salvation or justification—is wholly of God (Colenso). It transforms the believers into the citizens of Graceland (Du Toit), which is the eternal fullness of life in Christ (Kasali). Each African believer may use their web of vertical and horizontal relations to (re)discover their intercultural identity and the call for participating in the mission of sharing the word of God.

Original Canonical Culture

The starting point (*terminus a quo*) and the end (*terminus ad quem*) of the introduction form an *inclusio* framed by the term "God": εἰς εὐαγγέλιον θεοῦ (1:1) and δικαιοσύνη γὰρ θεοῦ (1:17). Paul's presentation also delineates this section as a literary unit: his self-designation (Παῦλος) (1:1) and personal statement (Οὐ γὰρ ἐπαισχύνομαι τὸ εὐαγγέλιον) (1:16-17). The content of this unit revolves around Paul and the Gospel of God. This literary unit contains three discrete epistolary sections: the prescript (1:1–7), the thanksgiving section (1:8–12), and the body-opening section (1:13–17).[35] The prescript or *exordium* includes the sender's name and status (1:1), confession (1:2–4), apostolic credentials (1:5), address (1:6–7), and salutation (1:7).[36]

The introduction of the letter abounds with authoritative credentials and references, which are intercultural and ecological. According to the intercultural method, the references and credentials in the introduction of the letter represent three frames of culture reference: the divine culture created by God, his Son Jesus Christ, and the Holy Spirit (1:1–17); an ancient faith community culture made up of the prophets (1:2); and a contemporary culture represented by the author and his target audience (Romans, Jews, and gentiles, cf. 1:7, 14–16). All these references exhibit ecological principles. They are worthy and interconnected. They have a voice and purpose and participate in offering mutual custodianship, resistance, and "compassion."[37]

34. Kasali, "Romans," 1353.

35. Du Toit, *Focusing on Paul*, 225; Matera, *Romans*, 26.

36. Jewett, *Romans*, 99.

37. Tonstad, *Romans*, xiii.

The author Παῦλος (1:1) is the one already known in Acts as Σαῦλος (Saul) (7:58; 8:1, 3; 9:1, 8, 11, 22, 24; 11:25, 30; 12:25; 13:1, 2, 7, 9). The form Σαῦλος is a Greek transliteration of the Hebrew שָׁאוּל ("asked for") with some modifications at the beginning and end of the name. The Greek alphabet, having no equivalent for the Hebrew letter shin (שׁ), has rendered it by a close sound, the letter sigma (σ, ς), and added two letters (ος) to accommodate it with the Greek nomenclature. In this way, שָׁאוּל became Σαῦλος, though some readings might suggest that the Hebrew שָׁאוּל matches the Greek Παῦλος.[38] Accordingly, the name Παῦλος aligns with the preference of Roman citizen parents of Jewish origin who enjoyed giving their children names that would resemble those of the native Romans.[39] In the same vein, Paul would have later on followed "the typical tripartite name of a Roman citizen, such as Gaius Julius Paulus" or Lucius Sergius Paulus or Paullus (cf. Acts 13:6–12) and introduced himself as Παῦλος δοῦλος Χριστοῦ Ἰησοῦ, κλητὸς ἀπόστολος (Paul, servant of Christ Jesus, apostle called).[40] Transliterated in Latin as Paulus (small, tiny), this name could evoke a baby or—as the Acts of Thecla describes—"a man small in size."[41] Even if Jesus used the name שָׁאוּל/Σαῦλος/Σαούλ when he called Paul on the way to Damascus (Acts 9:4x2; see also 9:17; 13:21; 22:7x2; 26:14x12), the apostle somehow resisted this appellation and preferred the name Παῦλος. This designation shows more suitability with a Roman audience, while keeping its Jewish connection with שָׁאוּל through the Greek Σαῦλος/Σαούλ. Nonetheless, Paul associates himself with Christ as his slave and as an apostle whom he called. Consequently, Paul will resist everything and deliver his mission as slave and apostle throughout his ministry, preaching the gospel of Jesus and the reign of God until Rome (Acts 28:30–31). It seems to be his nickname, as implied in Acts 13:9 (Σαῦλος δέ, ὁ καὶ Παῦλος). From Acts 13:9 onward, the name Σαῦλος shifts to Παῦλος (128 times). All the letters attributed to him and 2 Peter 3:15 refer to him not as Σαῦλος, but Παῦλος (Rom 1:1, 1 Cor 1:1; 2 Cor 1:1; Gal 1:1; Eph 1:1; Phil 1:1; Col 1:1; 1 Thess 1:1; 2 Thess 1:1; 1 Tim 1:1; 2 Tim 1:1; Titus 1:1; Phlm 1:1).

The thanksgiving (1:8–12) strengthens the existing relationship but adds new references. The latter include an expression of gratitude to God and service to him by the proclamation of his Son's gospel, praise of the Romans for their faith acclaimed in the whole world, longing for a face to face meeting, mutual sharing of spiritual gifts or encouragement of faith.[42] The body-opening section (1:13–17), which contains the *narratio* (1:13–15) and the *propositio* (1:16–17), encompasses the following references: brothers in an inclusive sense, harvest of the fruit, Romans (1:13), Greeks and barbarians, wise and foolish (1:14), eagerness to proclaim the gospel to those in Rome, the righteous (15), not ashamed of the gospel,

38. Cf. Craig S. Keener, *Acts: An Exegetical Commentary*, vol. 2 (Baker Academic, 2013), 1444.

39. Keener, *Acts*, 1444.

40. Jewett, *Romans*, 99.

41. Julia A. Snyder and Elliot Ritzema, "Acts of Thecla," in *The Lexham Bible Dictionary*, ed. John D. Barry, David Bomar, Derek R. Brown, Rachel Klippenstein, Douglas Mangum et al. (Lexham Press, 2016).

42. Cf. du Toit, *Focusing on Paul*, 227, 232.

which is the power of God for the salvation of every believer (16), the righteous (just), and faithfulness (1:17).

In the *narratio*, Paul explains his intention to visit Rome and the hindrance encountered, his motivation for reaping some fruit such as logistical support for the mission in Spain (1:13; cf. 1:24, 28),[43] and his aim of preaching the gospel among the Romans and other gentiles (1:15; cf. Acts 27:23–27).[44] Subsequently, the *propositio* (1:16–17) defines the gospel as "the power of God for the salvation of all those who believe, for in it, the justice of God is revealed." In the two previous occurrences of the gospel (good news) in Romans 1:1–17, this term relates to God (1:1) and Jesus (1:9), but brings a new semantic definition in a collocation that associates the term with the justice of God.

In the rest of the letter, the term "gospel" appears in association with Paul (2:16; 16:25); disobedience (10:6); enemies of God (11:28); God (15:16); Christ (15:19). These occurrences show that the gospel that Paul or other evangelists proclaim (1:15; 10:15; 15:20) is the gospel of Jesus Christ (1:9; 15:19) and God (1:1; 15:16). More precisely, in Romans, the gospel of Paul, the gospel of God, and the gospel of Jesus Christ are synonymous and interchangeable. Furthermore, in the canonical dispensation, they are also synonymous with νόμος/ תּוֹרָה and λόγος τοῦ θεοῦ/Χριστοῦ (Mark 1:45; 2:2). As I argued elsewhere, "the origin of νόμος is divine in the view of Exod 12:1–12 // 43–51, which John 1:1–18 echoes in the hymn to λόγος and expands in the Hellenistic Judaism of the first century . . . in the original culture of the sacred texts represented by MT and LXX, בדבר / λόγος / ῥῆμα / might be the most inclusive expression to represent different meanings shared by תּוֹרָה / קח / חֻקָּה /."[45] Other Christian canonical authors have done the same (cf. Mark 1:45; 2:2; Acts 15:7; 20:24). Furthermore, the proclamation of the gospel or apostleship appeals for the obedience of faith (Rom 1:1, 5; 10:17); differently put, the obedience of faith is a response to the proclamation of faith.

It is vital to note that Jesus is the ultimate incarnation of the word of God who came not to abolish the former expressions of divine revelation but to fulfill them (cf. Matt 5:17; John 1:1–18). God is one (Deut 6:4; Mark 12:19; Gal 3:20). He "is the apex of the Word of God because he embodies the totality of God's revelation (cf. Col 1:19)."[46]

Paul felt compelled or obliged (ὀφειλέτης) to preach the same gospel to all the nations (1:5), called of Jesus Christ or Christians (κλητοὶ Ἰησοῦ Χριστοῦ, 1:6), God's beloved ones in Rome (1:7), brothers (1:13), Greek and Barbarians, wise and foolish (1:14), in brief Jews and gentiles (1:16). The Afro-Christians in Rome such as Rufus, son of Alexander and his mother (Mark 15:21; Rom 16:13), and those who followed Paul's missionary trips from elsewhere, were undoubtedly eager to hear what this man of God and apostle of Jesus would say about

43. Jewett, *Romans*, 130.

44. Beverly Roberts Gaventa, "'To Preach the Gospel': Romans 1,15 and the Purposes of Romans," in *The Letter to the Romans*, ed. Udo Schnelle (Peeters, 2009), 179.

45. Jean-Claude Loba Mkole, "Intercultural Translation Criticism of the LXX Nomos," *Journal for Semitics* 32, no. 2 (2023): 1–9.

46. Loba Mkole, "Jesus," 1–9.

the word of God. The Jewish community and Afro-Christians in Alexandria would have been among those who were expecting Paul[47] to visit them, as he did or intended to do for other Jewish diasporas like the one in Spain (15:24, 28). Africans generally and gradually open themselves up to listen to God's messengers or prophets visiting them from afar, even if they suspected them to be a threat or welcomed them as a chance.[48]

The *propositio* alone contains the half of the six occurrences of the word πίστις in the letter's introduction (1:1–17). Its meaning includes confidence, faithfulness, faith, belief,[49] or trustfulness.[50] However, translating it as "faithfulness" in 1:16–17 may convey a more accurate sense, involving the faithfulness of God and the believer, each according to his capacity. Accordingly, the translation of 1:16–17 (Οὐ γὰρ ἐπαισχύνομαι τὸ εὐαγγέλιον, δύναμις γὰρ θεοῦ ἐστιν εἰς σωτηρίαν παντὶ τῷ πιστεύοντι, Ἰουδαίῳ τε πρῶτον καὶ Ἕλληνι. δικαιοσύνη γὰρ θεοῦ ἐν αὐτῷ ἀποκαλύπτεται ἐκ πίστεως εἰς πίστιν, καθὼς γέγραπται, Ο δὲ δίκαιος ἐκ πίστεως ζήσεται) could read: "For I am not ashamed of the gospel: it is the power of God for salvation to everyone who believes, to the Jew first and also to the Greek, for in it the justice of God is revealed from faithfulness for faithfulness, as it is written, 'the just will live by faithfulness'" (cf. Hab 2:4: Heb 10:38).[51] This nuanced translation offers new and pertinent insights compared with the Vulgate, post-Reformation Scripture texts, or the interpretations warranted by most *sola fide* debate competitors: God's faithfulness covers what pertains to him as the one who is, who was, and who is coming (Rev 1:4; cf. Exod 3:14). The believer's faithfulness involves faith in God and its essentials, such as obedience of faith, righteous living, sanctification, and love. In 1:1–17, the term πίστις appears six times (1:5, 8, 12, 17x3) with different nuances (polysemic meaning): obedience of faith (1:5), your faithfulness (1:8), each other's faithfulness (1:12), from faithfulness (1:17) to faithfulness (1:17), by faithfulness (1:17). Paul used this stylistic devise of polysemy elsewhere with the term παρθένος in 1 Cor 7:25–40. It appears six times (7:25, 28, 34, 36, 37, 38): female and male virgins (7:25; cf. Rev 14:4), female virgin (7:28, 34), virginity (7:36, 37, 38).[52]

In short, in the original culture, the *propositio* (1:16–17) defines the gospel as "the power of God for the salvation of all those who believe, for in it, the justice of God is revealed." In the two previous occurrences of the gospel (good news) in Romans 1:1–17, this term relates

47. Loba Mkole, "Paul and Africa?," 6.

48. Oscar Bimwenyi-Kweshi, *Discours théologique négro-africain: Problème des fondements* (Présence Africaine, 1981), 263–299; Claude Ozankom, "End of a Period of Discussion on the Possibility of African Theology," in *African Theology in the 21st Century: The Contribution of the Pioneers*, ed. Bénézet Bujo and Juvenal Ilunga Muya (Paulines Publications Africa, 2002), 118–145.

49. B. H. McLean, *New Testament Greek: An Introduction* (Cambridge University Press, 2011), 124.

50. Troels Engberg-Pedersen, "Gift-Giving and God's Charis: Bourdieu, Seneca and Paul in Romans 1–8," in *The Letter to the Romans*, ed. Udo Schnelle (Peeters, 2009), 100.

51. See already Tonstad, *Romans*, xiii, 15; Tonstad quotes Richards B. Hays, *Echoes of Scripture in the Letters of Paul* (Yale University Press, 1989), 36–40.

52. Chrys C. Caragounis, *New Testament Language and Exegesis: A Diachronic Approach* (Mohr, 2004), 299–316; Jean-Claude Loba Mkole, "Translating παρθένος in 1Cor. 7:25–38," *Hekima Review* 54 (2016): 144–155.

to God (1:1) and Jesus (1:9), but brings a new semantic definition in a collocation that associates the term with the justice of God. This understanding of faith complements the one from African scholars by emphasizing the meaning of faithfulness instead of faith (πίστις). It explicitly embodies the ethical dimension of faith without introducing any doctrinal bias.

Body (Probatio)
Proofs of the Gospel as the Power of God for Salvation (1:18–15:13)

African Target Culture

The heart of Paul's argument in the body revolves around the universal need for salvation, which God already provided through his Son Jesus Christ to redeem Jews and gentiles from the consequences of their sins and usher them to lead transformed lives. In the Negro-African traditions, salvation implies life in abundance experienced through peace, harmony, or order with God, ancestors, nature, and fellow human beings. Such order is "part of the Divine plan."[53] The transgression of this order will bring God's wrath or ancestors' punishments in form of soil's or women's barrenness, diseases, famine, floods, infants' or youngsters' mortalities, and the like. Only heads of the households or community priests can offer sacrifices to God through ancestors for the restoration of the lost order. Salvation in African religion depends less on faith confession, and more on life experience in which the human (living, unborn, or dead), nature, and the divine form integral parts of the harmonious life in its fullness.[54]

In present-day Africa, one may notice the emphasis on the transformed life. As an illustration, research on transformed lives among evangelical clergy and nonclergy leaders in Africa who have the most influence or impact[55] includes Pastor Dinis Eurico (Angola), Dr. David Koudougueret (CAR), and Bishop John Bosco (Kenya). To get this result, the respondents were asked to rate each leader on a Likert scale on the basis of the following: (1) skill at work; (2) wisdom and knowledge of the local context; (3) ethical integrity; (4) love and service; (5) positive reputation; (6) inspiring teamwork and community mobilization; (7) efficiency in use of resources; and (8) training other leaders.[56] These qualities have been condensed in three sections: qualities of effective leadership; areas of impact; and training. Qualities of effective Christian leadership were assessed in view of church commitment, vocational excellence, community connectedness, cultural flexibility, endurance under hardship, lifelong learning,

---

53. Laurent Magesa, *African Religion: The Moral Traditions of Abundant Life* (Paulines Publications Africa, 1998), 54.

54. See Magesa, *African Religion*, 55, referring to Charles Nyamiti, *The Scope of African Theology* (Gaba Publications, 1973), 20.

55. David K. Ngaruiya, "Characteristics of Influential African Christian Leaders," in *African Christian Leadership: Realities, Opportunities, and Impact*, ed. J. Robert Priest and Kirimi Barine (Orbis Books, 2017), 29–47.

56. Ngaruiya, "Characteristics of Influential African Christian Leaders," 29–30.

empowering mentorship, embrace of technology, and passion for civic engagement.[57] Areas of influence that were considered involve: drug abuse prevention; children and youth education; sex education and the fight against HIV/AIDS; entrepreneurship; music; and church leadership development.[58] Lastly, the training of African Christian leaders encompasses knowledge acquired from their childhood home and from their educational background, broadening experience through travel and seminars.[59]

Colenso argues that from 1:18, the apostle undertakes a crucial task: "The pious Jew at Rome, or Jewish proselyte, like Nicodemus of old, had no idea that he too, like any poor 'sinner of the Gentiles,' as by his natural birth under the curse, needed God's forgiveness, God's righteousness."[60] Paul's primary objective is to guide the sinner to realize his or her position before God and comprehend that "there will be no room for the Gospel of God's love to enter in and possess his whole heart and being."[61] The rest of the body of the letter goes on to explore this universal need for salvation.

For Kasali, the body of the letter includes the following sections: the Gospel's heart as justification by faith (1:18–4:25); the assurance and hope of salvation (5:1–39); Israel not to blame God's justice (9:1–11:36); and the transformed life of believers (12:1–15:13).[62] According to him, justification by faith (1:18–3:20; 3:21–4:25) implies that God is a just judge who acquits the just who live by faith and condemns the wicked, since his justice will not leave sin unpunished. The wrath of God against sin becomes clear "when we see the level of corruption and perversion in our time, where often wealth is concentrated in the hands of a few, where criminals go free because they pay bribes and where the masses remain poor and unprotected."[63] Kasali suggests a way forward by asserting that God is the "righteous" judge and the church must represent his interests on earth and "be at the centre of the fight against these evils."[64]

In addition, justification by faith means that God's salvation is available through faith in Jesus Christ alone (3:21–31), as prefigured by Abraham (4:1–25). Therefore, there is no more ground for boasting (3:27–28), no more racial or tribal divisions (3:29–30), and no more struggling to meet the requirements of the Law (3:31).[65]

57. Ngaruiya, "Characteristics of Influential African Christian Leaders," 33–38.

58. Ngaruiya, "Characteristics of Influential African Christian Leaders," 38–41.

59. Ngaruiya, "Characteristics of Influential African Christian Leaders," 41–44, see also Christophe Munzihirwa, *La houe, la vache le mwami: Mode de production agro-pastoral et changement des structures socio-politiques* (Karthala, 2023); Florence Muindi, *The Pursuit of His Calling: Following in His Calling* (Integrity, 2008); Florence Muindi and Charlie Vittitow, *Teach a Man to Fish: Engaging the Local Church to Create Sustainable, Transformational Missions* (Tyndale House, 2024).

60. Colenso, *Commentary on Romans*, 37.

61. Colenso, *Commentary on Romans*, 37.

62. Kasali, "Romans," 1350.

63. Kasali, "Romans," 1354.

64. Kasali, "Romans," 1354.

65. Kasali, "Romans," 1357.

As a result, the justification by faith in Christ alone provides the assurance and hope of salvation (5:1–8:39) in different areas: end of hostility with God, peace and hope (5:1–5); demonstration of God's love through the death of Jesus Christ (5:6–11); universal applicability of justification (5:12–21); freedom from bondage to sin (6:1–13); freedom from bondage to the Law (7:1–25); and blessings and security live in the Spirit (8:1–39).[66]

Furthermore, this justification by faith shows Israel that God's justice is not to blame (9:1–11:36). The three chapters explain in detail how God chose the people of Israel to receive the gospel but rejected it. However, the apostle also warns "Gentile believers not to boast or look down on the few Jewish believers in the Church."[67] In fact, despite the unbelief of Israel (9:1–5), God preserves Israel as his chosen people (9:6–13), exhibiting his sovereignty over human inclinations (9:14–29). Nevertheless, he established Jesus Christ as the only way to salvation (9:30–10:21), whom the remnant, chosen by grace, accepted (11:1–10). Therefore, the future of Israel (11:11–32) lines up with God's purpose in its temporary rejection (11:11–24), which is a wise way of salvation for all Israel and all gentiles (11:25–32). Praise to God for his wisdom (11:33–36)![68]

The justification by faith prompts ethical implications culminating in the transformed life of the believers (12:1–15:13), which translates into total consecration (12:1–2), humility and service in the Body of Christ (12:3–8), love in social relationship (12:9–21), submission to civil authority (13:1–7), love as the fulfillment of the Law (13:8–10), living as Children of Light (13:11–14), and living in unity (14:1–12).[69] In concluding this section, "Paul asks God to fill the Roman Christians with joy and peace so that they *may overflow with hope by the power of the Holy Spirit* (15:13)."[70]

In summary, salvation in the traditional Negro-African cultures implies harmony between fellow humans (unborn, living, and dead), with nature, and God. For postcolonial Africa, the notion of salvation rhymes with the justification by the faithfulness of God (Father-Son-and-Spirit) and the believers (Colenso, Kasali), as expressed through transformed lives (Kasali). The faithfulness of God and the human being (believer) becomes a key term connecting the notion of salvation in traditional and postcolonial Africa (Negro-African Christianity). This faithfulness may account for the traditional harmonious life and justification by Christ.

Original Canonical Culture

The body of the letter (1:18–15:13) deals with four proofs of the gospel as the power of God: the wrath of the God of justice (1:18–4:25); the life in Christ as a new system of honor (5:1–8:39); the triumph of the divine justice in the gospel mission (9:1–11:36); and the living

66. Kasali, "Romans," 1359–1364.

67. Kasali, "Romans," 1364.

68. Kasali, "Romans," 1364–1368.

69. Kasali, "Romans," 1368–1374.

70. Kasali, "Romans," 1374, italics in original.

together in accordance with the gospel (12:1–15:13).[71] The first proof starts with an observation about the wrath of God revealed from heaven against all ungodliness and lawlessness of those who by their wickedness suppress the truth (1:18). It ends with a wishful statement: "May the God of hope fill you with all joy and peace in believing, so that you may abound in hope by the power of the Holy Spirit" (15:13). Some of the key references mentioned in the introduction of the letter feature in this section and hold it as a bigger literary unit in which an alarming start (wrath of God, revealed from heaven, ungodliness, wickedness, suppression of the truth) gives way to a happier ending, involving the God of hope, joy, peace, faith, power, and the Holy Spirit. The arguments that led to such transformation form parts of the four proofs of the power of the gospel for the salvation of the believer, the justice of God revealed through faithfulness to faithfulness (1:16–17).

The first proof (1:18–4:25) shows the evidence of how the gospel or word of God expresses his impartial justice. In other words, the revelation of the wrath of God accounts for his justice, communicated through his gospel or word.[72] Besides, from the beginning, the argument sets forth the intercultural and ecological nature of the actors involved: God from heaven, men in their wickedness, and the created world (1:18–32). God relates to men through his act of creation and justice or wrath against their wickedness because he punishes the wicked and rewards the just (1:26–28; cf. Prov 13:21). However, men and women relate to God in a perverted manner (1:19–32): idolatry (1:18–23) and wickedness, through which they also relate to each other (cf., lusts of hearts leading to impurity and bodily dishonor in 1:24–27, and all sorts of vices in 1:28–32).[73]

Those vices include evil, covetousness, malice, envy, murder, strife, deceit, craftiness, gossiping, slander, God-hating, insolence, haughtiness, boastfulness, evil inventors, rebellion against parents, foolishness, faithlessness, heartlessness, and ruthlessness (1:31; cf. 1 Cor 6:9–10). Such perversions result from the wrath of the God of justice. In this case, his justice manifests in punishing the unbelievers by giving them up to enjoy the consequences of suppressing the truth and relying on their self-declared wisdom (1:18, 22, 28). However, only God, the Father of all compassion, will bring salvation to humankind (cf. Rom 2:4; 3:26; 5:15–21; 9:1–11:33; 12:1).[74] In Gal 5:16–21, Paul calls such vices the works of the flesh and adds a warning: "Those who do such things will not inherit the reign of God" (Gal 5:21). Facing dissensions within the Corinthian community (1 Cor 1:10–31), Paul reminded them that God "is the source of your life in Christ Jesus, whom God made our wisdom, our righteousness and sanctification, and redemption" (1 Cor 1:30).[75] The Synoptic Gospels and other canonical authors translate the concept of the justice of God into the love

71. Cf. Jewett, *Romans*, viii–ix.

72. Cf. Légasse, *L'épître*, 113.

73. Cf. Légasse, *L'épître*, 113.

74. Cilliers Breytenbach, "Charis and Eleos in Paul's Letter to the Romans," in *The Letter to the Romans*, ed. Udo Schnelle (Peeters, 2009), 277.

75. Wilfried Okambawa, *Paulus und Sophia: Eine exegetische-rhetorische Untersuchung zu 1 Kor 1,10–31* (Peter Lang, 2003), 367.

of God (cf. Matt 22:34–40; Luke 10:25–28; Mark 12:28–36; John 3:16; 14:21, 34; 15:9, 12, 17; Jas 1:12; 2:5; 2:8; 1 Pet 1:8, 22; 2:17; 3:10; 1 John 4:7–12, 20–21; 5:1–2; 2 John 1:5; 3 John 1:1; Rev 1:5; 3:9). The author of Hebrews views the royal throne of Jesus as eternal and his scepter of justice as the scepter of his reign, for he loved justice and hated lawlessness or wickedness (Heb 1:9; also 5:13; 7:2; 11:7, 33; 12:11). In this context, Jesus appears as "the final revelation, 'heir of all things,' agent of creation, the radiance of God, the bearer of God's nature, sustainer of the universe, priest-victim, enthroned Messiah, and superior to angels (Heb 1:1–4)."[76]

In the light of ecojustice principles, the evildoers have tempered their worth by changing the natural function of their bodies (1:26–27), contrary to what God intended when he created humankind as male and female, and in his image and resemblance (Gen 1:26–27). The effect of interconnectedness shows up when earthly evil actions attract the wrath of the God of justice from heaven (1:18). While the noises of the evildoers and cries of their victims attract God's wrath, Paul's voice—like a prophet (cf. 1:1)—denounces and condemns them or explains how they condemn themselves by ignoring God and exchanging his glory with the images of mortal beings (1:23). They have therefore perverted the purpose of their creation by God, which is to know, love, and serve him above all and avoid evil (cf. Exod 20:1–17; Deut 5:5–21). Unfortunately, they offered mutual support in evildoing and destroyed all the pillars for resisting evil, such as knowing, thanking, and honoring God (1:21) or respecting the intrinsic worth of each other (1:26–27).[77] Nonetheless, it is worthwhile to note that Paul already alludes to the resurrection of Jesus as the highest argument for the justice of God (1:4; 6:5; 8:29; cf. 1 Cor 15:1–58). As Jean Bosco Matand puts it:

> So, the content of the mystery that Paul proclaims to the Gentiles is the very resurrection of Christ, the resurrection of the dead and the salvation of all men in him, the work of God alone. For Paul, proclaiming this Gospel of the resurrection of Jesus Christ means proclaiming the power of God to save everyone who believes (Rom 1:16). Evangelising means proclaiming that there is only one true God in whom we must believe and on whom we must rely, the one who raised Jesus from the dead. He is still the one who can raise the dead and call them into being (2 Cor 2,9; Rom 4,17).[78]

76. Abeneazer G. Urga, *Intercession of Jesus in Hebrews: The Background and Nature of Jesus' Heavenly Intercession in the Epistle to the Hebrews*, WUNT 2/585 (Mohr Siebeck, 2023), 161.

77. Karl Barth, *The Epistle to the Romans*, trans. Edwyn C. Hoskyns (Oxford University Press, 1933), 37, describes the situation in the following terms: "The power of God is power—unto salvation. In this world men find themselves to be imprisoned. In fact the more profoundly we become aware of the limited character of the possibilities which are open to us here and now, the more clear it is that we are farther from God, that our desertion of Him is more complete (i. 18, v. 12), and the consequences of that desertion more vast (i. 24, v. 12), than we had ever dreamed. Men are their own masters. Their union with God is shattered so completely that they cannot even conceive of its restoration. Their sin is their guilt; their death is their destiny; their world is formless and tumultuous chaos, a chaos of the forces of nature and of the human soul; their life is illusion. This is the situation in which we find ourselves."

78. Jean-Bosco Matand Bulembat, *Noyau et enjeux de l'eschatologie paulinienne: De l'apocalyptique juive et de l'eschatologie hellénistique dans quelques arguments de l'apôtre Paul* (De Gruyter, 1997), 289 (my translation).

After depicting a gloomy picture caused by the wrath of the God of justice at the beginning of the first proof section (1:18–4:25), the apostle goes on to show the ways that the gospel as the power of God is lived out in the subsequent sections: life in Christ as a new system of honor (5:1–8:39); the triumph of the divine justice in the gospel mission (9:1–11:36); and living together according to the gospel (12:1–15:13).[79] The details of these sections, which will require more space than the one allocated to the current brief introduction, continue to display the intercultural and ecological interactions between the characters involved.

The understanding of the universal need of salvation in the original canonical culture and the African target culture is similar: The consequences of the wrath of God are manifest in the Letter to the Romans and in Africa through unethical lifestyles. However, the transformation caused by the proclamation of the gospel among Paul's intended audience in Rome replicates itself in current Africa.

Conclusion (Peroratio)
Appeal for Cooperation in Gospel Mission (15:14–16:24)

Contemporary African Culture

In the concluding section, Paul summarizes the missional purpose of his proposed trip to Spain via Rome as fulfilling the call of preaching or sharing the gospel with the gentiles (Rom 1:15; 15:24, 28). Postcolonial Christian Africa is embarking on the same mission, starting with themselves. In his message delivered to Africans in Kampala on July 31, 1969, Pope Paul VI started by borrowing from the words of Paul to the Romans (16:6): "All the Churches of Christ greet you." Then, identifying his audience as the "living members of the Catholic Church" (not only Roman Catholic Church), because they are "Christian and Africans," he challenged them in the following terms: "You Africans are missionaries to yourselves."[80] The awareness of this call is gaining momentum in current Africa. Florence Muindi and Charlie Vittitow map out the landscape of this new way of understanding the mission in Africa and Global South:

> Indigenous leaders in the Global South are positioned and culturally equipped to fulfil integral wholistic missions in their own communities, countries, and continents. . . . The shifting missions landscape may also be an opportunity to reassess your personal calling. We are still commissioned to go and make disciples of all nations. But how we do it may be up for review. This may be an appropriate time to reappraise what God is doing and how he is inviting you to partner with him.[81]

79. Cf. Jewett, *Romans*, viii–ix.

80. Pope Paul VI, Eucharistic celebration at the conclusion of the symposium organized by the bishops of Africa. Homily on 31 July 1969, Kampala (Uganda), https://www.vatican.va/content/paul-vi/en/homilies/1969/documents/hf_p-vi_hom_19690731.html (last accessed November 21, 2024).

81. Muindi and Vittitow, *Teach a Man to Fish*, 237–238, 242.

Partnering with God involves the realization and materialization of divine, human, and cosmic interconnectedness in which the wholistic harmony epitomizes the gospel of salvation or justification.

In the concluding section of the letter (15:14–16:27), Colenso starts by indicating that Paul is making clear that his addressees do not need these words from him. Consequently, this situation emboldened him to write more freely to them in discharge of his duty as an apostle and remind them of what they already know. He delivers this ministry in confidence placed not in himself but in the Lord (15:14–17). According to Colenso, the end of the section (16:26–27) echoes the same message. It reminds:

> his readers once more of what he has told them all along, namely, that the Gospel, which he had to preach, was no new message, but only a more clear and full declaration of that "righteousness of God," which He as a Faithfull Creator, had prepared for His creatures, in his infinite counsels, before the foundations of the world were laid,—a revelation of that "mystery of godliness" in Christ Jesus, by which that righteousness is bestowed by the grace of God upon mankind,—a mystery which had been hidden hitherto.[82]

However, by his command, God has now made this mystery known to all the nations for the obedience of faith in full accordance with Jewish prophetical Scriptures, as shown by the apostle throughout his epistle. For Draper, Colenso's exegesis of the Letter to the Romans puts a "new emphasis on natural religion and conscience: All human beings experience the Fatherhood of God, have access to the gift of salvation given in Christ and are called by the creator Spirit to an ethical life by the conscience given to every human being."[83] As a result, "the Christian has no ground for pride or for a sense of superiority. For Colenso, the Epistle was specifically written by Paul to counter feelings of racial privilege and pride."[84]

Original Canonical Culture

Paul's concluding remarks (15:14–16:27) contain a recapitulation of his missionary calling (15:14–33), recommendations or commendations, greetings, and an epistolary benediction (16:27). All the characters representing the divine culture (God, Jesus, and the Holy Spirit), ancient culture (prophets) and contemporary culture are still active in this last section of the letter. Paul conveys his feeling of the presence and action of the divine culture members by mentioning the grace given to him by God (15:14; also 15:16, 17, 30, 32, 33; 16:20, 26, 27) to be a minister of Christ (15:16; also 15:17–20, 29–30; 16:3, 5, 7, 9, 10, 16, 18, 24, 25, 27) by the power of the Holy Spirit (15:19, 27, 30). His interaction with the ancient culture

82. Colenso, *Commentary on Romans*, 270.

83. Jonathan A. Draper, ed., "Introduction," in John William Colenso, *Commentary on Romans* (Cluster Publications, 2004), xxxiii.

84. Draper, "Introduction," xxxiii.

reappears through the mention of the prophetic writings through which God disclosed his hidden mystery (16:26).

Some members of his contemporary culture benefit from an explicit mention for recommendation, commendation, or greetings. Fifteen of them stem out of personal acquittances: Prisca, Aquila, Epaenetus, Mary, Andronicus, Junia, Ampliatus, Urbanus, Stachys, Apelles, Tryphaena, Tryphosa, Persis, Rufus, and Rufus's mother. Ten others might be leaders of the Roman house church: Herodion, Asyncritus, Phlegon, Hermes, Patrobas, Hermas, Philologus, Julia, Nereus, and Olympas. Other members are anonymous, though Paul knows the names of their leaders: the church in the house of Prisca and Aquila (16:5a), those among the slaves of Aristobulus (16:10b), those among the slaves of Narcissus (16:11b), the brothers who are with Asyncritus et al. (16:14b), the saints who are with Philologus et al. (16:15b).

Furthermore, Paul extends to his addressees the greetings from his coworkers in Corinth: Gaius, Erastus, and Quartus (16:23). Paul's explicit target audience displays a web of different national or ethnic cultures of which the Hellenists constitute the majority, followed by those of Roman origin (Ampliatus, Urbanus, Julia, Prisca) and Jewish origin (Mary, Aquila, Junia, Herodion),[85] including Africans of Jewish origin (Rufus and his mother) from Libya (cf. Mark 15:21; Acts 2:10; 13:1–3).[86] As Thomas Oden puts it: "By definition, those who had been living for centuries on the African continent are rightly called Africans."[87] Among other Africans whom he could have in mind but who were not in Rome, Paul would also include John Mark from Cyrene, who was his missionary companion (Acts 19; 12:25; 15:37–39; Col 4:10–11; Phlm 24; 1 Pet 5:13). However, his mention of prophetic writings made known to all the nations (16:26) undeniably engage all the spokesmen of the word of God.

In the light of ecojustice principles, the concluding section of the letter (15:14–16:27) provides a more positive image of the addressees. The latter acquired some values in tandem with their human intrinsic worth because they are full of goodness, filled with all knowledge, and able to instruct one another (15:14). They do not need any new teaching except a bold reminder of what they are and ought to be (15:15). The section reaffirms the interconnectivity of all the actors already mentioned in the introduction of the letter (1:1–17) and who represent the divine culture, ancient culture, and Paul's contemporary culture in 15:15–16:27. Then, Paul associates his Corinthian coworkers' voices to greet the Roman audience, even if he alone goes on to extend to them personalized greetings, commendations, recommendations, and warning.

The addressees seem to have understood their purpose of being holy and leading a life of obedience to God and justice (1:5–7), which they strive to achieve by being good, knowledgeable, and supportive toward each order (15:14). Yet, they do need a continual strength or power as spelled out throughout Paul's Gospel, the preaching of Jesus Christ, and the gospel of God (15:14–16) to keep making their offering acceptable and sanctified by the Holy Spirit (15:17)

85. Jewett, *Romans*, 953.

86. Thomas C. Oden, *The African Memory of Mark: Reassessing Early Church Tradition* (InterVarsity Press Academic, 2011), 18.

87. Oden, *The African Memory*, 18, 21.

and to avoid the dissenters (16:17). Thus, Paul comes to terms with mutual custodianship as he is willing to exchange spiritual gifts with the Roman community when he arrives (15:17, 30–32). He also evokes an example of material sharing regarding the charity campaign in favor of the saints of Jerusalem (16:25–29). Finally, Paul seems to capture in four expressions (obedience of faith, goodness or justice, wisdom in goodness and purity toward evil) the type of resistance he anticipates from his audience: "For while your obedience is known to all, so that I rejoice over you, I would have you wise as to what is good and guileless as to what is evil" (16:19).

The concluding part of the letter in its original canonical culture resonates in the religious life of the target African culture. In view of African scholars and Paul, the Letter to the Romans is not a new message to Romans or Africans, but it puts a new emphasis on natural religion and conscience while emphaszing that salvation is only by faith in Jesus Christ. "All human beings experience the Fatherhood of God, have access to the gift of salvation given in Christ and are called by the creator Spirit to an ethical life by the conscience given to every human being."[88]

Epilogue

Saul, mostly known by his nickname Paul (Acts 13:9), which suits him as a Roman citizen (of Jewish origin), is the author of this Letter to the Romans. He dictated it to Tertius (Rom 16:21) while in Corinth around 56–57 CE. He intends to remind the Romans of the gospel they have already received. Accordingly, he takes this opportunity to expand the thesis according to which the gospel is the power of God for the salvation of every believer because the justice of God manifests itself from his faithfulness to the faithfulness of the believer (1:16–17). The lack of faithfulness from the believers has dramatic consequences, culminating in all sorts of vices (1:18, 22, 28). In support of the central thesis, Paul lays down four arguments or proofs: the gospel expresses the impartial justice of God (1:18–4:25); living in Christ as a new system of honor (5:1–8:39); the triumph of divine justice in the gospel mission (9:1–11:36); and living together according to the gospel (12:1–15:13). In his concluding remarks, Paul rejoices over the fact that his addressees had been leading a life of justice, as they are full of goodness, knowledgeable, and able to instruct themselves (15:14). Nevertheless, they do need a continual strength or power as spelled out throughout Paul's Gospel, the preaching of Jesus Christ, and the gospel of God (15:14–16) to keep making their offering acceptable and sanctified by the Holy Spirit (15:17) and to avoid the dissenters (16:17).

Primary sources from the canonical or church culture frame and African contemporary culture frame hold similar and dissimilar views about the content of the Letter to the Romans. All agree that Paul mainly emphasizes and develops the meaning of the gospel and the justice of God in his Letter to the Romans. However, in the same letter, he extends the notion of the justice of God to embrace its manifestations, such as his wrath, mercy, and love. Other canonical authors of Jesus's movement have translated the notion of the justice

88. Draper, "Introduction," xxxiii.

of God into the love of God. Nevertheless, the result will be the same: joy and peace (Rom 15:13). Regarding the meaning of justification by faith or better faithfulness, representatives from different culture frames hold diverse opinions. In Kasali's views, the justification by faith (1:18–3:20; 3:21–4:25) implies that God is a just judge who acquits the just who live by faith and condemns the wicked, since his justice will not leave sin unpunished. For him, corruption and perversion, criminality, and unwarranted poverty indicate the wrath of the God of justice against sin. He suggests a way forward by asserting that God is the "righteous" judge; the church must represent his interests on earth and "be at the centre of the fight against these evils."[89]

The response from the faith communities to take responsibility in promoting environmental justice might account for new commitments such as *Laudato Si'*,[90] Earth Bible Commentary Series, or the UN Environment Faith for Earth Initiative, and others. The ball is now in the court of African believers! Incidentally, for most Africans, environmental integrity would be less a matter of law (lest a natural one), faith, or justice than of being. In their worldview, leading a life of justice or ecological integrity (Rom 1:16–17; 8:18–31) would entail being faithful in the sacred web of their relationship to God, themselves, Jesus Christ, and the cosmos. This web of interculturality and integrity is what—forms a bridge to Paul's Letter to the Romans (Rom 15:16). Accordingly, let us keep living the baptismal commitment, which is the visible evidence of our faith in Christ, by avoiding counter-testimonies and promoting everything that enforces life in all respects, remembering that Jesus came for us to have life abundantly (John 10:10). He also insisted on the need for conversion (Mark 1:15), which is the backbone for spiritually and socially transformed lives. Constantly growing conversion backed by divine and human faithfulness (justice) should be the way forward for Africans in their endeavors to be missionaries to their own people and beyond.

Further Reading

Andria, Solomon. *Romans*. Africa Bible Commentary Series. WordAlive Publishers; Zondervan, 2012.

Barth, Karl. *The Epistle to the Romans*. Translated by Edwyn C. Hoskyns. Oxford University Press, 1933.

Bimwenyi-Kweshi, Oscar. *Discours théologique négro-africain: Problème des fondements*. Présence Africaine, 1981.

Colenso, J. William. *Commentary on Romans*. Reprint of the 1861 ed. Edited, with an introduction, by Jonathan A. Draper. Cluster Publications, 2003.

Du Toit, Andrie. *Focusing on Paul: Persuasion and Theological Design in Romans and Galatians*. De Gruyter, 2007.

Heliso, Desta. *Pistis and the Righteous One: A Study of Romans 1:17 Against the Background of Scripture and Second Temple Jewish Literature*. WUNT 2/235. Mohr Siebeck, 2007.

Jewett, Robert. *Romans: A Commentary*. Hermeneia. Fortress Press, 2007.

89. Kasali, "Romans," 1354.

90. Pope Francis, *Laudato Si': Encyclical Letter of the Holy Father Francis on Care for Our Common Home* (Paulines Publications Africa, 2015).

Kasali, David M. "Romans." In *Africa Bible Commentary: A One-Volume Commentary Written by 70 African Scholars*, edited by Tokunboh Adeyemo. WordAlive Publishers; Zondervan, 2006.

Légasse, Simon. *L'épitre de Paul aux Romains*. Cerf, 2002.

Luther, Martin. *Lectures on Romans*. In *Luther's Works*, vol. 25, edited by Hilton C. Oswald. Concordia, 1972.

Origen. *Commentary on the Epistle to the Romans*. Trans. Thomas P. Scheck. The Catholic University of America Press, 2001.

Schnelle, Udo. *The Letter to the Romans*. BETL CCXXVI. Peeters, 2009.

Thomas Aquinas. *Commentary on the Letter of Saint Paul to the Romans*. Translated by Fabian R. Larcher. Aquinas Institute; Emmaus Academic, 2020.

Tonstad, K. Sigve. *The Letter to the Romans: Paul Among the Ecologists*. EBC 7. Sheffield Phoenix Press, 2017.

CHAPTER NINE

The First Letter to the Corinthians

Vuyani S. Sindo
Stellenbosch University
George Whitefield College
South Africa

Introduction

QUESTIONS OF IDENTITY are questions that continue to be dominant in Christian communities across the globe, particularly in areas such as self-identification, leadership, sexuality, and family life. Christian Africans are not immune to these questions and often struggle to find answers to them. Some African scholars argue that Africans must return to the precolonial African social norms to find their true identities. In contrast, others say that precolonial Africa is long gone and buried and that the very nature of colonialism meant the destruction of people's identities, heritage, and social memory. This chapter argues that in his First Letter to the Corinthians, Paul sought to shape the Corinthian Christ followers' identity in light of the Christ event. The Corinthians had derived their identity and praxis from Greco-Roman society instead of Christ. Paul wrote the letter to help the community come to terms with their in-Christ identity. The chapter suggests that Paul's First Letter to the Corinthians can help us navigate these realities as first-century Corinthian society experienced its fair share of colonialism and destruction. It attempts to elucidate Paul's teachings in 1 Corinthians on Christian identity, arguing that the in-Christ identity should be salient amongst Christ's followers without them losing their previous identities completely. Those previous identities have been transformed in Christ, to the point that Paul can remind the community that they do not belong to themselves but belong to Christ, and therefore they are to honor Christ in their bodies (1 Cor 6:19–20).

Authorship

First Corinthians 1:1–3 follows the traditional style of Greek letter-writing where the author introduces himself and then identifies who the intended audience is, followed by the greeting. In verse 1, Paul is introduced as an author, and then there is a mention of the brother Sosthenes. There are no scholarly disputes about Paul's authorship of the letter. As early as 95 CE, Paul's authorship was affirmed by the early church fathers such as Clement of Rome and the "second-century church fathers such as Ignatius and Polycarp."[1] The only debate is about Sosthenes's role in its composition; was he simply a co-sender or a scribe? It is not uncommon for Paul to mention co-senders in his writings. An example of this can be found in 1 Thessalonians 1:1 and 2 Thessalonians 1:1, where Paul mentions Silas and Timothy as co-senders. In other Pauline letters, we also see that Paul mentions scribes who helped him write the letter (i.e., 1 Cor 1:1; 2 Cor 1:1; Phil 1:1; Col 1:1; 1 Thess 1:1; 2 Thess 1:1; Phlm 1).[2] Usually, when Paul uses a scribe to write the letter, he adds his classic signature toward the end of the letter, where he writes the greeting with his own hands and states, "I, Paul, write this greeting with my own hand" (1 Cor 16:21; see also Gal 6:11; Col 4:18; 2 Thess 3:17). Thus, it is clear that Paul wrote 1 Corinthians using a scribe but I do not think that Sosthenes was the scribe. Sosthenes was a respected synagogue ruler who was persecuted in Corinth for his faith in Jesus Christ, according to Acts 18:17. Paul might have mentioned him to state he was with him and agreed with the contents of his letter. Paul calling him a brother suggests that the church knew him, and the dominant use of the first-person singular in 1 Corinthians 1:1–2:6 suggests that Paul is the author.[3]

Dating

Paul wrote 1 Corinthians in Ephesus (1 Cor 16:8) during his third missionary journey, probably in 54 or 55 CE, if we give room for his lost letter that is mentioned in 1 Corinthians 5:9 and for the ministry of Apollos in Corinth.[4]

The Quest for Identity

The more I study the book of 1 Corinthians, the more I realize there is nothing new under the sun, especially when it comes to identity questions. On October 6, 2015, Wesley Morris of the *New York Times* wrote an article entitled "The Year We Obsessed Over Identity."[5] In this article, Morris demonstrated people's obsession with identity in 2015. However, questions about identity did not only emerge in 2015, nor were they limited to that year. Questions about identity have persisted throughout all generations and have been with us since time immemorial. Rooted in the questions of identity is one's sense of worth and purpose. Modern

1. Dachollom Datiri, "1 Corinthians," in *Africa Bible Commentary: A One-Volume Commentary Written by 70 African Scholars*, ed. Tokunboh Adeyemo (WordAlive Publishers; Zondervan, 2006), 1403.

2. For the use of scribes by Paul, see David B. Capes, Rodney Reeves, and Randolph E. Richards, *Rediscovering Paul: An Introduction to His World, Letters, and Theology* (Apollos, 2007), 68–82.

3. Paul Gardner, *1 Corinthians*, ZECNT (Zondervan Academic, 2018), 56.

4. For a detailed analysis of the other factors that are crucial for the dating of 1 Corinthians, such as the edict of the proconsul Gallio, see Vuyani S. Sindo, *Paul as a Prototype and Entrepreneur of Christian Identity: An Investigation into Leadership and Identity in 1 Corinthians 1–4* (Langham Academic, 2024), 107–109.

5. Wesley Morris, "The Year We Obsessed Over Identity," *New York Times*, October 6, 2015, https://www.nytimes.com/2015/10/11/magazine/the-year-we-obsessed-over-identity.html.

philosophers such as René Descartes laid the foundations for how people in the West perceived their sense of identity when he famously wrote, "I think, therefore I am." Generally speaking, people in the West tend to describe their identity individualistically and emphasize one's mental capacity and feelings, in other words, "to thine own self be true."[6] This sense of defining one's identity is entirely different from how Africans typically perceive themselves and their identities.

By and large, Africans tend to reject the individualistic view of the self and see themselves in light of the communities they belong to, in other words, the individual self is viewed in light of a collective self. For example, my name and surname come last when I meet my fellow Black South Africans. When I introduce myself, my collective self, my clan name tends to be at the forefront of my self-identification. I often describe myself as Umqoco, UZikhali, UJojo, UTiyeka, Butsolobentonga, and Mbizana before I say I am Vuyani Sindo. This means that my communal identity takes more precedence in my self-identification than for most people in the West. In South Africa, this is often captured by the Ubuntu philosophy, "I am because we are," which is radically different from the Western ways of self-identification which are primarily individualistic. Within the Ubuntu philosophical system, individuals find their identity and existence within the "whole interwoven structure of the immediate family, the extended family, and the entire community."[7]

Bruce J. Malina argued that the early Jesus followers had collective self-identification, just like Africans.[8] The community is the soul of Africa, and personal identity is derived from that community.[9] However, this can be problematic for Jesus Christ's followers in the African context, just like it was for the early Jesus followers in Corinth during the time of the apostle Paul. When an African converts to Christianity, some things could estrange them from their community, such as abstaining from ancestral veneration and polygamy, which are prevalent in some communities. This estrangement can lead to an identity crisis and alienation from their community. It can raise questions about what being a Christian in Africa means. The Pauline community at Corinth faced struggles similar to those which Africans experience sometimes about their identity. I hope that this chapter, which functions as an introductory investigation of 1 Corinthians, will provide preliminary contours that can help shape African Christian identity.

Approach

Much has been written as an introduction to 1 Corinthians, but these treatments tend to mainly focus on sociohistorical analysis without bridging the context and content of the letter

---

6. To quote a line from William Shakespeare's play, *Hamlet*, act 1, scene 3.

7. Abraham M. M. Mzondi, "'Two Souls' Leadership: Dynamic Interplay of Ubuntu, Western and New Testament Leadership Values" (PhD diss. University of Johannesburg, 2009), 48.

8. Bruce J. Malina, *Timothy: Paul's Closest Associate* (Liturgical Press, 2008), 3–4.

9. Augustine Shutte, *Philosophy for Africa* (University of Cape Town Press, 1993), 11.

to the current realities of Africa. I seek to revisit the discussion, paying particular attention to identity formation discourse in 1 Corinthians using social identity theory (SIT) in conjunction with sociohistorical analysis to bridge that gap. I do this with the hope of applying the letter of 1 Corinthians to the African context. Social identity theory is primarily concerned with intragroup and intergroup dynamics in any given community and will be used here to analyze these dynamics within the text of 1 Corinthians. However, this can easily be anachronistic; hence, sociohistorical and grammatical analysis must precede this methodological framework.

Henri Tajfel developed SIT, and he is known as the father of this theory. He defined SIT as:

> that part of an individual's self-concept which derives from his [*sic*] knowledge of his membership of a social group (or groups) together with the value and emotional significance attached to that membership . . . however rich and complex may be the individuals' view of themselves in relation to the surrounding world, social and physical, some aspects of that view are contributed by the membership of certain social groups or categories. Some of these memberships are more salient than others; and some may vary in salience in time and as a function of a variety of social situations.[10]

Human beings generally tend to define themselves in terms of the group they belong to. We tend to feel good about how well our group is doing against other groups. This definition gives us the three interrelated dimensions of social identity theory: the cognitive dimension, the evaluation dimension, and the emotional dimension.

This chapter will first consider the socio-historical context of 1 Corinthians that shaped the social identity of the early Christ followers, then I consider three points of contact which should shape the identity of Christians in Africa.

Historical Context of 1 Corinthians

In this section, my aim is threefold: First, I want to describe the social context of Corinth; secondly, I want to investigate the Corinthian Christian community; third, I want to identify the underlying cause of the problems in 1 Corinthians.

As stated above, I am reading 1 Corinthians through the lens of identity formation discourse. In order to effectively and responsibly make use of the social-scientific categories of SIT with regard to the ancient biblical text, we must first pay careful attention to the original socio-historical context of 1 Corinthians. Thus, I now first want to consider the socio-historical context of Corinth.

---

10. Henri Tajfel, *Human Groups and Social Categories: Studies in Social Psychology* (Cambridge University Press, 1981), 255.

The City of Corinth and Its Social Context[11]

My task in this section is to accurately depict the city of Roman Corinth and reconstruct its configuration and identity. I do this with the view that it will shed more light on the dynamics in the Pauline community at Corinth—which will be explored subsequently.[12]

Scholars such as Engels say, "The problems that Paul encountered at Corinth were a reflection of the nature of the city's people,"[13] while David A. deSilva writes that "Many of the specific problems which Paul must address in both [Corinthians] letters radiate from the more basic issue of the believers' continued allegiance to their primary socialisation."[14] Based on what these scholars say, it thus seems important to address the issue of the social description of the city of Corinth first.

Corinth Before Roman Destruction

The city of Corinth was an important city in the ancient world due to its great location, its good agricultural land, and its wealth. Located approximately halfway between Athens and Sparta, Corinth occupied the strip of land that connects the Peloponnese with the Greek mainland.[15] Corinth was important for controlling trade between Asia and Rome. Its two harbors, Lechaeum on the Corinthian Gulf and Cenchreae on the Saronic Gulf, made the city an essential link between the east and the west, enabling traders to negotiate the dangerous oceans around the southern tip of the Peloponnese (Cape Malea).[16] Cicero,[17] describing Corinth's ideal location for navigational purposes, wrote, "It was situated on the straits and in the very jaws of Greece, in such a way that by land it held the keys of many countries, and . . . it almost connected two seas, equally desirable for purposes of navigation, which were separated by the smallest possible distance."[18] Corinth became very wealthy due to its advantageous location.[19]

---

11. Portions of this chapter stem from my monograph, Sindo, *Paul as a Prototype and Entrepreneur of Christian Identity*.

12. A reconstruction of Roman Corinth is not without its fair share of difficulties. See further Craig Steven de Vos, *Church and Community Conflicts: The Relationships of the Thessalonian, Corinthian, and Philippian Churches with Their Wider Civic Communities*, SBLDS 168 (Scholars Press, 1999), 179.

13. Donald W. Engels, *Roman Corinth: An Alternative Model for the Classical City* (University of Chicago Press, 1990), 110.

14. David A. deSilva, "Let the One Who Claims Honor Establish That Claim in the Lord," *Biblical Theology Bulletin* 28, no. 2 (1998): 61–74. See also Robert D. Keay, "Paul the Spiritual Guide: A Social Identity Perspective on Paul's Apostolic Self-Identity" (PhD diss., St. Andrews University, 2004), 266.

15. For the history of the origins of the name of Corinth and the general description of the city see Pausanias (*Descr.* 2.1–14); Strabo (*Geogr.* 8.6.23).

16. Strabo, *Geogr.* 8.6.20.

17. Cicero, *Agr.* 2.87.

18. Strabo, *Geogr.* 8.6.20

19. Strabo, *Geogr.* 8.6.19–20; Homer, *Il.* 2.570.

It was great not just because of its geographical location; it was also rich because of the quality of its soil. According to Cicero, Corinth had the "most excellent and productive land,"[20] and, apparently, the "wealth of Corinth was legendary."[21] When I think of the geographical advantage of Corinth and the quality of its soil, it makes me think of the continent of Africa, which is often described in these terms. It makes me think of the opportunities that are in this continent but are missed due to people's confusion about their identities, which now tend to be derived from their colonial masters.[22] But I digress. The location of Corinth is perhaps one of the reasons why Paul chose this city as the strategic location for one of his churches; it was ideally located to ensure that his gospel could influence people from many different areas. Jerome Murphy-O'Connor notes that "the intense traffic in all directions assured [Paul] of superb communications. He could not have chosen a more suitable base for his move into Europe."[23] According to Favorinus, the list of the people who visited Corinth included "traders or pilgrims or envoys or passing travellers."[24]

Corinth, however, endured a devastating tragedy in 146 BCE, after the city and the Achaean League proclaimed war on Rome's ally, Sparta. Lucius Mummius destroyed Corinth for its role in the war.[25] Most of the ancient reports suggest that many of the men of the first Corinth were killed, while the women and children were sold into slavery.[26] After the Romans' destruction, the city lay desolate for many years. It was only rebuilt by Julius Caesar as a Roman colony in 44 BCE, shortly before his death.[27] Some scholars claim that the new Corinth became the capital of the Roman province of Achaia.[28] The newly rebuilt Corinth was named Colonia Laus Julia Corinthiensis (Colony of Corinth in Honor of Julius) in honor of Julius Caesar. Craig S. de Vos notes that, upon colonization, the city was rebuilt extensively, old surviving buildings were refurbished, and it was made to be a thoroughly Roman city; its South Stoa, measuring 500 feet, was one of the "longest buildings in Greece,"[29] while its *agora* (marketplace) was amongst the largest in the Roman Empire.[30]

---

20. Cicero, *Agr.* 1.5.

21. Strabo, *Geogr.* 8.6.19–23.

22. For more on this, see Stephen Ocheni and Basil C. Nwankwo, "Analysis of Colonialism and Its Impact in Africa," *Cross-Cultural Communication* 8, no. 3 (2012): 46–54.

23. Jerome Murphy-O'Connor, "The Corinth That Saint Paul Saw," *Biblical Archaeologist* 47 (1984): 147–159, 148.

24. Favorinus, Dio Chrysostom, *Disc.* 37.8.

25. Cicero, *Agr.* 1.5.; Pausanias, *Descr.* 2. 1.2.; Strabo, *Geogr.* 8.6.23; Diodorus Siculus, *Hist.* 27.1; 32.4.5.

26. Pausanias, *Descr.* 7.15.1–16.9.

27. Strabo, *Geogr.* 8.6.23.

28. V. Henry T. Nguyen, *Christian Identity in Corinth: A Comparative Study of 2 Corinthians, Epictetus and Valerius Maximus* (Mohr Siebeck, 2008), 122; Mark T. Finney, *Honour and Conflict in the Ancient World: 1 Corinthians in Its Greco-Roman Social Setting* (Bloomsbury, 2012), 54.

29. De Vos, *Church and Community*, 182.

30. Timothy B. Savage, *Power Through Weakness: Paul's Understanding of the Christian Ministry in 2 Corinthians* (Cambridge University Press, 1996), 36.

Corinth Rebuilt

The new Corinth became distinctly Roman and had a strong resemblance to Rome, in terms of ethos, cultural identity, and laws. This was also evident in its architecture, which resembled Italian cities (that is, Pompeii).[31] Both De Vos and V. Henry T. Nguyen note that the new colonizers made a deliberate effort to make sure that Corinth resembled Rome and not the surrounding Greek cities.[32] Even its new name, Colonia Laus Julia Corinthiensis, was a clear attempt by the Romans to distinguish Corinth from its erstwhile Greek format. Bruce W. Winter, observes the Roman influence on the culture of Corinth: "Whether rich or poor, bond or free, the cultural milieu which impacted life in the city of Corinth was *Romanitas*. This does not mean that there were no ethnic minorities, but it does mean that the dominant and transforming cultural influence was Roman."[33] In contrast to other Roman colonies, the newly rebuilt Corinth was inhabited mostly by poor Romans and freed slaves, whose socioeconomic status was only marginally better than that of the slaves;[34] Pausanias and Philo also speak of this.[35] James Walters says that the new "Corinth was settled by 12,000–16,000 colonists."[36]

During Paul's time, Corinth had already regained its prominence. It had become a prosperous city and was an important trade, banking, and financial center. The resumption of the Isthmian Games, the second most important games after the Olympics, meant that Corinth became a hub of tourist activity.[37] These games were held in the spring of 51 CE, and Murphy-O'Connor notes that it was most likely during the time of the proconsul Gallio (cf. Acts 18:12).[38] Since Paul stayed in Corinth for about eighteen months (cf. Acts 18:11), he was probably in Corinth during the time of these games, or at least during the preparations for, or aftermath of, the games. Some scholars believe these games influenced Paul's imagery of an athlete in 1 Corinthians 9:24–25.[39] The games meant there was a great demand for people like Paul, Priscilla, and Aquila, who possessed tent-making skills (cf. Acts 18:1–3). During the games, visitors from abroad were housed in tents, and the shopkeepers moved into the

31. Nguyen, *Christian Identity in Corinth*, 122; Finney, *Honour and Conflict in the Ancient World*, 54.

32. De Vos, *Church and Community*, 182; Nguyen, *Christian Identity in Corinth*, 122.

33. Bruce W. Winter, *After Paul Left Corinth: The Influence of Secular Ethics and Social Change* (Eerdmans, 2001), 22.

34. Donald A. Carson, Douglas J. Moo, and Leon Morris, *An Introduction to the New Testament* (Zondervan, 1992), 263.

35. Pausanias (*Descr.* 2.1.2.) notes that the new "Corinth [was] no longer inhabited by any of the old Corinthians, but by colonists sent out by the Romans."

36. James Walters, "Civic Identity in Roman Corinth and Its Impact on Early Christians," in *Urban Religion in Roman Corinth: Interdisciplinary Approaches*, ed. Daniel N. Schowalter and Steven J. Friesen (Harvard University Press, 2005), 402.

37. Jerome Murphy-O'Connor, *The Theology of the Second Letter to the Corinthians* (Cambridge University Press, 1991), 6.

38. Murphy-O'Connor, *The Theology of the Second Letter*, 6.

39. Murphy-O'Connor, *The Theology of the Second Letter*, 7.

city to supply the needs of the visitors, using tents to display their products.[40] The games also provided an excellent opportunity for someone like Paul to evangelize.

Religion in Rebuilt Corinth

Religious pluralism was prevalent in Corinth owing to its location and the resultant diversity of its population (1 Cor 8:5). According to Murphy-O'Connor, archaeological findings in the ruins of Corinth reveal temples and shrines that attest to the worship of a large number of different gods and goddesses.[41] These ranged from the Greek gods to the Egyptian gods and goddesses such as Isis and Serapis, as well as emperor cult worship. However, evidence points to the dominant worship of the Greek gods such as Apollo, Athena, Tyche, Aphrodite, Dionysos, Artemis, Cybelle, Poseidon, Asclepios, Demeter and Kore, Hera, Argaea, Zeus, and others. Most of these Greek gods and goddesses were associated with fertility; this is perhaps why Paul had to repeatedly address sexual immorality amongst the Corinthians (cf. 1 Cor 5, 6, and 7).

What is absent from the archaeological data is material concerning the Jewish presence in Corinth. However, the historical data indicates that a large and vibrant Jewish community was at Corinth in the first century CE[42] and that this community included those who followed Jesus Christ. Vuyani S. Sindo notes that "one does not know how much can be made from the fact that at Corinth, emphasis was placed on the harmony of all religions and their compatibility with other religions."[43] Mark T. Finney thinks that the Judeans were "held in contempt by the wider community or were targets of ethnic prejudice."[44] He thinks that this better explains why, for example, when the Corinthian Judeans brought the case before the proconsul Gallio regarding Paul, Gallio refused even to hear the case. In Acts 18, the reason given for Gallio's dismissal of the case is that he refused to be drawn into a controversy within the Judean sect. Finney notes that it is possible that "Gallio's dismissal of the case may have been due not only to its nature but also to the weak Judean influence in Corinth."[45] Finney further notes that this "highlight(s) negative civic attitudes towards Judeans."[46] Thus, for example, when Sosthenes the synagogue-ruler was severely beaten, Gallio was unconcerned.

Sindo notes, "Religion in Roman-Corinth was an integral part of life and impacted heavily on the cultural, social, political and commercial realities of everyday life."[47] It is worth noting though that people were less concerned with different religious formations' specific proclivities, and were more concerned with the favor of the gods. This resulted in an unwelcome

40. Murphy-O'Connor, *The Theology of the Second Letter*, 7.
41. Murphy-O'Connor, *The Theology of the Second Letter*, 5.
42. Philo, *On the Embassy to Gaius*, 281–282.
43. Vuyani S. Sindo, "A Socio-Rhetorical Approach to the Pauline Theology of Reconciliation in 2 Corinthians" (MA thesis, North-West University, 2014), 82.
44. Finney, *Honour and Conflict in the Ancient World*, 57.
45. Finney, *Honour and Conflict in the Ancient World*, 56.
46. Finney, *Honour and Conflict in the Ancient World*, 56.
47. Sindo, "A Socio-Rhetorical Approach," 82.

consequence for the Jewish community, as their religion emphasized purity and a separation of oneself from pollution by gentile "idolatrous worship."[48]

Corinth and the Prizing of Boasting

As was noted earlier, many scholars believe the attitudes in Corinth and its social make up were part of the wellspring of the particular issues the church faced. Chief among these was the tendency toward pride and boasting.

Corinth was a cosmopolitan city of great beauty, and its buildings were a matter of pride in antiquity. Loyal citizens would sacrifice large sums of money to support elaborate building schemes,[49] and "their sole reward was the proud boast of a finer agora, a grander temple."[50] This was reward enough for both the rich and the poor alike, as "boasting in one's city was a matter of personal standing."[51] Kate C. Donahoe notes further that boasting and honor were part and parcel of the culture of the times and that the "people of Corinth frequently expressed their honor and civic pride through benefactions, abilities, and positions of leadership."[52] Donahoe observes that "Honor is the public recognition of [social] status" that can either be inherited through family, gender, or birth order or earned through achievements, virtues, and public roles.[53] Honor can be gained or lost through one's actions and public recognition.[54] Boasting and chasing honor were so pervasive in the Greco-Roman world and Corinth in particular that people "erected inscriptions praising their own accomplishments, contributions to building projects, and social status."[55] The evidence of chasing honor in Corinth could be seen through a "plethora of temples, statues, buildings, monuments, theatres, and baths."[56] Thus, "the beauty, prominence, and stature of Corinth no doubt incited pride in its residents."[57] Hence, it comes as no surprise that the Pauline congregation at Corinth had a tendency toward boasting (1 Cor 1:31; 3:21; 4:7; 5:6; 13:3) because this was a key feature of the society in which they lived.

So far, in this section, Corinth has been depicted as a strategic location, which made it possible for Paul's message to reach the known world. I also noted that the Corinth that Paul saw was still a young city with shallow roots, which meant that he had a better chance of getting a hearing there. However, this section has also demonstrated that while Corinth was a land of opportunity, some of its cultural practices collided with Paul's message.

---

48. Sindo, "A Socio-Rhetorical Approach," 82.

49. Dio Chrysostom, *Tumult.* 2–4.

50. Savage, *Power Through Weakness*, 25.

51. Savage, *Power Through Weakness*, 25.

52. Kate C. Donahoe, "From Self-Praise to Self-Boasting: Paul's Unmasking of the Conflicting Rhetoric-Linguistic Phenomena in 1 Corinthians" (PhD diss., University of St. Andrews, 2008), xvii.

53. Donahoe, "From Self-Praise to Self-Boasting," xvii.

54. Donahoe, "From Self-Praise to Self-Boasting," xvii.

55. Pausanias, *Descr.* 2.2.8; 2.7.2–5; 2.10.1, 3, 5, 7. cf. Donahoe, "From Self-Praise to Self-Boasting," xviii.

56. Donahoe, "From Self-Praise to Self-Boasting," xviii. See also Andrew D. Clarke, *Secular and Christian Leadership in Corinth: A Socio-Historical and Exegetical Study of 1 Corinthians 1–6* (Brill, 1993), 31.

57. Donahoe, "From Self-Praise to Self-Boasting," xviii. cf. Dio Chrysostom, *Isthm.* 8, 21.

The Corinthian Christian Community

In this section, I want to investigate Paul's relationship with the Corinthian community and use the book of Acts to formulate the logical and chronological sequence of Paul's movements.[58] Particular attention will be given to Paul's second missionary journey, as it was during this period that he made contact with Corinth and founded the church.

Paul's relationship with the Corinthians is a multifaceted affair that lasted approximately seven years (50–57 CE), and encompassed several visits, letters, and reports. When one reads 1 and 2 Corinthians, one can see that there was constant interaction between Paul and this community. Paul sent letters to them and they also wrote to him (1 Cor 5:9; 1 Cor 7:1). Paul mentions a previous letter in which he taught the Corinthians not to associate with immoral members who claim to be a brother or sister (1 Cor 5:9–11). Similarly, in 2 Corinthians 2:4, he refers to another letter that he wrote out of great distress and anguish of heart. If one takes these two letters together with the two surviving letters we have, it is fair to estimate that Paul, at the very least, penned four letters to the Corinthian church.[59] There also seems to be evidence that Paul returned to Corinth at least once after his initial one-and-a-half-year visit (1 Cor 16:3; 2 Cor 1:15–2:1; cf. Acts 18:11). Paul made three visits[60] to the Corinthians; the first visit of Paul to Corinth is the one mentioned in Acts 18:1–10, and the second visit is normally described as the painful visit (1 Cor 16:5–8; cf. 2 Cor 2:1). The third visit is inferred by Paul in 2 Corinthians 12:14, 20–21, and 13:1–2 (together with evidence from Acts 20:2–3). Members of the Corinthian church visited Paul and reported activity within the church to him (1 Cor. 1:11; 16:17). Lastly, Paul sent Timothy to Corinth (1 Cor 4:17; 16:10; 2 Cor 1:1).

According to Acts 18:1–17, Paul first came to Corinth near the end of his second missionary journey in 50 CE, after his arrival from Athens (a journey that would have taken him three days on foot as it was about 85 km). Acts 18:1–2 states that upon Paul's arrival at Corinth, he stayed with Aquila and Priscilla, working with them as a leatherworker during the week and preaching in the synagogue on the Sabbath days.[61] Acts 18:2 states that Aquila and Priscilla had recently come to Corinth as a result of Claudius's edict. Only upon the arrival of Silas and Timothy from Macedonia does Paul devote himself to preaching and teaching for most of the time (Acts 18:5). Perhaps Silas and Timothy brought him financial support

58. For a chronology of Paul's missionary journeys and their dating, see Stanley E. Porter, *The Apostle Paul: His Life, Thought, and Letters* (Eerdmans, 2016), 50–60; Jerome Murphy-O'Connor, *Paul: A Critical Life* (Clarendon Press, 1996), 1–31.

59. Scholars debate whether these two letters are incorporated in 1 and 2 Corinthians; for a discussion of this, see John C. Hurd, *The Origin of 1 Corinthians* (Mercer University Press, 1983), 235–237; N. H. Taylor, "The Composition and Chronology of Second Corinthians," *Journal for the Study of the New Testament* 14, no. 44 (1991): 67–87, 71, 75–79; Anthony C. Thiselton, *The First Epistle to the Corinthians* (Eerdmans, 2000), 36–40; David G. Horrell, *The Social Ethos of the Corinthian Correspondence: Interests and Ideology from 1 Corinthians to 1 Clement* (T&T Clark, 1996), 89–91.

60. Donahoe, "From Self-Praise to Self-Boasting," 7.

61. Ronald F. Hock, *The Social Context of Paul's Ministry: Tent Making and Apostleship* (Fortress Press, 1980), 50.

from the churches in Macedonia, and this enabled him to free up more time for evangelism (cf. 2 Cor 11:8–9; Phil 4:15).

This, however, was not a smooth period of ministry. Opposition arose among the Jews, and Paul moved his preaching to the house of Titus Justus, a God-fearer (Acts 18:6, 12–18); he lived next door to the synagogue. Owing to Paul's ministry, Crispus, the ruler of the synagogue, was converted (Acts 18:8; 1 Cor 1:14), along with many of the Corinthians, and thus the Corinthian church was established. It was during this time that Sosthenes embraced Christianity and as a result the crowd turned against him and beat him in front of the proconsul Gallio, who showed no concern (Acts 18:8; 1 Cor 1:1). It is the same Sosthenes who was with Paul in Ephesus when Paul wrote to Christ's followers in Corinth (1 Cor 1:1). Paul stayed in Corinth for about a year and a half after he founded the church (Acts 18:11); he left a vibrant church that continued to grow (Acts 18:18–19; 20:31). But this church tended to be susceptible to outside influences and it is to this that I turn now. What happened after Paul left this community?

Problems in Corinth

After Paul Left the Congregation

Most New Testament scholars tend to agree with Margaret Mitchell that Paul in 1 Corinthians sought to unify the community fraught with several issues such as division and factionalism.[62] Scholars are, however, divided about the underlying causes of the problems in 1 Corinthians.

In 1 Corinthians 1–4, Paul deals with the issue of divisions which arose as a result of a preference for particular leaders (1 Cor 1:12). However, there is no consensus amongst scholars regarding the issues that Paul is seeking to address in the whole of 1 Corinthians, or the reasons that the Corinthians preferred one leader over others, and why some in the congregation rejected Paul as their leader, even though Paul had founded the congregation. Who is to be blamed for all the issues that arose after Paul left Corinth? Paul W. Barnett notes that no conflict is recorded in Acts 18 within the congregation when Paul founded the Corinthian church.[63] When Paul wrote 1 Corinthians in 55 CE, his letter indicated much strife within the community. He notes that the crisis reached a particularly heightened point when writing 2 Corinthians in 56 CE. Several other letters mentioned by 1 and 2 Corinthians also indicate that all was not well in Corinth (1 Cor 5:9–10; 2 Cor 7:8). The nagging question scholars have to deal with is: What went wrong in this congregation? Some scholars believe that the problems that Paul experienced in 1 Corinthians resulted from foreign teachers coming to Corinth, while others argue that Paul is also to be blamed.

Traditionally, when scholars consider this section, they approach it theologically and seek to identify Paul's opponents in the Corinthian church, particularly those mentioned in 1 Corinthians 1–4.[64]

62. Margaret M. Mitchell, *Paul and the Rhetoric of Reconciliation: An Exegetical Investigation of the Language and Composition of 1 Corinthians* (John Knox, 1991).

63. Paul W. Barnett, *The Corinthian Question: Why Did the Church Oppose Paul?* (Apollos, 2011), 15–20.

64. Oh-Young Kwon, *1 Corinthians 1–4: Reconstructing Its Social and Rhetorical Situation and Re-Reading It Cross-Culturally for Korean-Confucian Christians Today* (Wipf & Stock, 2010), 387; Hurd, *The Origin of 1 Corinthians*, 95–113.

One of the problems, though, that one has to contend with when trying to identify the opponents of Paul in 1 Corinthians 1–4 is that, unlike 2 Corinthians and Galatians, there is a lack of clear, organized opposition to Paul from the outside, or from inside for that matter, in 1 Corinthians. For instance, Gordon Fee, who tries to identify Paul's opponents in 1 Corinthians, has conceded that "quite in contrast to 2 Corinthians and Galatians, this letter [1 Corinthians] yields little or no evidence that the church has been invaded by the outsiders."[65] Due to this lack of opposition to Paul from the outside, Mitchell has argued very strongly that "Pauline scholarship should not simply talk about Paul's 'opponents' in 1 Corinthians in the same way as is done in the case of 2 Corinthians or Galatians, where Paul's own description of the situation justifies such language."[66]

When scholars consider the issues behind 1 Corinthians, it is important to note that they look at 1 Corinthians in its own context and do not impose the setting of other Pauline correspondence onto this letter. Walters has rightly observed that in 1 Corinthians, "there is curious lack of references to conflict with outsiders, even though references to contact between insiders and outsiders are more common in 1 Corinthians than in any of Paul's other letters."[67] Walters observes that the Pauline community moved freely and even received invitations to dine with people outside this community (1 Cor 8:7–13; 10:27–11:1). It also seems that the outsiders moved freely within this community as well (cf. 1 Cor 14:23–25). Is it possible that the causes of the issues in 1 Corinthians result from the congregation's social interaction with the Greco-Roman world?

I want to propose that at the heart of the underlying problems in 1 Corinthians were the issues of identity, not theology, that gave rise to the tension between Paul and his congregation at Corinth (1 Cor 1:12; 4:3, 6, 18–20; 9:3; 10:29–30; 14:37).[68] The fundamental issue that Paul is dealing with in 1 Corinthians is the secular influences of the previous gentile identity upon the Corinthian community. In 1959, Johannes Munck argued that divisions in Corinth were understood best in the light of the social milieu of Roman Corinth.[69] He said that the issue behind 1 Corinthians was that the "Corinthians regarded the Christian message as wisdom like that of the Greeks, the Christian leaders as teachers of wisdom, themselves as wise, and all this as something to boast about."[70] Munck contends that what Paul is doing in 1 Corinthians is to spell out the implications of the Gospel, which is counter-cultural.[71] He says: "Paul asserts, on the contrary, that the Gospel is foolishness, that the Christian leaders are God's servants whom God will judge, that the Corinthians are of the flesh and therefore

---

65. Gordon D. Fee, *The First Epistle to the Corinthians* (Eerdmans, 2014), 51.

66. Mitchell, *Paul and the Rhetoric of Reconciliation*, 302.

67. Walters, "Civic Identity in Roman Corinth," 397–399. cf. John M. G. Barclay, "Thessalonica and Corinth: Social Contrast in Pauline Christianity," *Journal for the Study of the New Testament* 47 (1992): 49–74.

68. For a most recent review of this question, see Brian J. Tucker, *You Belong to Christ: Paul and the Formation of Social Identity in 1 Corinthians 1–4* (Pickwick, 2010), 14–31.

69. Johannes Munck, "The Church Without Factions: Studies in 1 Corinthians 1–4," in *Christianity at Corinth: The Quest for the Pauline Church*, ed. Edward Adams and David G. Horrell (John Knox, 2004), 68–69.

70. Munck, "The Church Without Factions," 68.

71. Munck, "The Church Without Factions," 68.

without wisdom, and that none of this redounds to the glory of any human being, but that he who boasts is to boast of the Lord."[72]

Winter, on the other hand, says that the root cause of the problems in 1 Corinthians was secular influences upon the young Christian community.[73] Similarly, Tucker also argues that Paul's "main concern was the formation of the Christ-movement around the Mediterranean basin."[74] He goes on to say that the issue in 1 Corinthians is that "some in Corinth were continuing to identify primarily with key aspects of their Roman social identity rather than their 'in Christ' identity and this confusion over identity positions contributed to the problems within the community."[75]

Based on what these scholars have observed, it seems that the transmission of the secular cultural norms into the Pauline community at Corinth had a devastating effect on the life of the community, and gave rise to all the issues that Paul had to address. Even scholars who had previously thought that the root cause of the problems in the Corinthian correspondence was mostly theological have now conceded that secular influences also had a significant role. Thiselton has now acknowledged that the problems in 1 Corinthians are a result of both secular influences upon the community and theological misconceptions.[76]

The picture that emerges from the scholars who see secular influences as an underlying cause of the problems is that identity is the major issue with which the Corinthians were grappling, and their perception of identity influenced their conduct. If in 1 Corinthians Paul deals with the issues of identity, particularly Greco-Roman cultural influences upon the Pauline community, then Roy E. Ciampa and Brian S. Rosner are stating the same concern theologically when they say "[1] Corinth[ians] consists primarily of a confrontation with the church over purity concerns in general and two vices in particular."[77] Since sexual immorality and idolatry were the two vices that were perceived by the Jewish people as being consistent with the identity and the behavior of gentiles, it seems that the major issue in 1 Corinthians is about identity. Or, at the very least, in 1 Corinthians Paul responds theologically to culturally driven issues. But what does Paul hope to achieve by his theological response to these social issues? My argument here is that at the heart of Paul's response is his desire to see that the identity of this community at Corinth aligns itself with their identity in Christ.

Summary of the Issues and Structure in 1 Corinthians

After Paul left Corinth, he received an oral report from Chloe's people that there was division and quarrelling amongst the Corinthians (1 Cor 1:10–11). He also received letters from the Corinthians in which the Corinthians raised certain matters with him that he needed to

72. Munck, "The Church Without Factions," 68.

73. Winter, *After Paul Left Corinth*, 4.

74. Tucker, *You Belong to Christ*, 13.

75. Tucker, *You Belong to Christ*, 13; also Donahoe, "From Self-Praise to Self-Boasting," xiv; Savage, *Power Through Weakness*, 64.

76. Thiselton, *The First Epistle to the Corinthians*, 40; cf. David E. Garland, *1 Corinthians* (Baker Academic, 2003), 8.

77. Roy E. Ciampa and Brian S. Rosner, *The First Letter to the Corinthians* (Eerdmans, 2010), 21.

respond to (1 Cor 7–16). The latter is marked by the Περὶ δὲ ὧν ἐγράψατε ("now concerning the matters which you wrote about") formula, which is found in 1 Corinthians 7:1 and repeated in 7:25; 8:1; 12:1; 16:1, 12 as Περὶ δὲ). Broadly speaking, there seem to be five issues that come out in the letter, which also inform my structure:[78]

Division and quarrelling (report from Chloe's people) (1:1–4:21)
Confusion about sexuality (5–6)
Marriage, singleness, and divorce (7)
The use of one's rights in relation to food offered to idols (8–10)
Confusion about the gifts of the Spirit and chaotic church services (11–14)
Confusion about the resurrection and the letter closing (15–16)

We have examined how Paul came to learn of the issues at Corinth as well as the structure of his argument; we will now consider points of contact between the Corinthian context and contemporary African realities.

Points of Contact Between 1 Corinthians and African Realities

Looking at 1 Corinthians, one soon discovers that the Pauline community at Corinth confronted cultural issues that the church in Africa also encounters. Due to the occasional nature of 1 Corinthians and its corrective nature, the following section will also deal with issues that need to be addressed within the church in Africa. This section will limit its investigation to only three broad issues as it seeks to apply 1 Corinthians to African realities. These are (1) disunity in the church caused by personality cults, (2) sexuality and identity, and marriage, and (3) food offered to idols.

Personality Cults and Disunity

For our first point of contact I will look at personality cults. A personality cult can be broadly understood as a situation wherein a group derives its identity (and impetus or reason for existing) from a charismatic leader or a person they perceive to embody their set of values.[79]

Within the African context, personality cults tend to be centered around the glorification and allegiance to the so-called "man/women of God." Thus, in Africa prosperity preachers and their ministry styles tend to be similar to the personality cults that were prevalent in Corinth.

78. It is beyond the scope of this chapter to examine considerations regarding the literary integrity and theological unity of 1 Corinthians. I have written about this elsewhere, see Sindo, *Paul as a Prototype*, 122–148.

79. Britannica defines a "cult of personality" as follows: "a deliberately created system of art, symbolism, and ritual centred on the institutionalized quasi-religious glorification of a specific individual." Rebecca M. Kulik, "Cult of Personality," *Encyclopedia Britannica*, December 20, 2024, https://www.britannica.com/topic/cult-of-personality.

Personality Cults in the African Context

The prosperity gospel movement is one of the fastest-growing Christian movements within the African continent and the world. Its exponential growth has been experienced all over the world.[80] The movement is mostly led by people who claim that they have a unique connection with God. They claim to have received a special message from God tailored to address people's fundamental needs, such as health, wealth, and overall well-being. This proposition holds particular appeal given the socioeconomic circumstances of their followers in the African continent.

Many attendees of these congregations come from economically disadvantaged backgrounds, a demographic often intersecting with racial identity in South Africa, where many Black people are subjected to abject poverty due to the legacy of apartheid. Within South Africa, a large population of Black people live below the poverty line. According to the World Bank's April 2020 report, "Poverty & Equity Brief," for South Africa, "approximately 55.5 percent (30.3 million people) of the population is living in poverty at the national upper poverty line (~ZAR992 [=54 USD]) while a total of 13.8 million people (25 percent) are experiencing food poverty."[81] These socioeconomic factors gave rise to the popularity of the prosperity gospel movement within the continent. However, poverty is not the only reason for the popularity of the prosperity gospel in South Africa; lack of access to health care is another driving factor. Marius Nel observes that in countries such as Nigeria, Kenya, Cameroon, Ghana, the Ivory Coast, Uganda, and South Africa, where the prosperity gospel movement is growing, there is a high rate of unemployment, poverty, and diseases, with state institutions failing (due to corruption) to meet the needs of the population.[82] These sentiments are also shared by the authors of the Lausanne Theological working group on the prosperity gospel in point four of the 2010 statement, where they wrote:

> We recognize that Prosperity Teaching flourishes in contexts of terrible poverty; and that for many people it presents their only hope, in the face of constant frustration, the failure of politicians and NGOs, etc., for a better future, or even for a more bearable present.[83]

Through personality cults the prosperity gospel capitalizes on humanity's primal longing for an escape from these dire circumstances. It offers hope to those in desperation, pledging a

80. Dan Lioy, "The Heart of the Prosperity Gospel: Self or the Savior?," *Conspectus* 4, no. 1 (2007): 41–64, here 42.

81. Victor Sulla, "Poverty & Equity Brief Sub-Saharan Africa: South Africa," World Bank Group, April 2020, https://databankfiles.worldbank.org/public/ddpext_download/poverty/33EF03BB-9722-4AE2-ABC7AA2972D68AFE/Global_POVEQ_ZAF.pdf.

82. Sulla, "Poverty & Equity Brief," 1–2.

83. Lausanne Theology Working Group, "A Statement on the Prosperity Gospel," Lausanne Movement, January 16, 2010, https://lausanne.org/content/a-statement-on-the-prosperity-gospel.

path out of poverty and illness. Prosperity gospel preachers peddle the promise of liberation through their teachings and lifestyles, asserting that unwavering faith and sacrificial giving are essential for achieving similar blessings.

That message is attractive and appealing to desperate people, especially people who are influenced by the African worldview. Elizabeth Mburu writes that within the African worldview people believe that suffering is a consequence of displeasing God or the ancestors.[84] Normally, people within this cultural context would consult witch doctors (*Sangomas*), diviners, or traditional healers to remedy the situation. In these consultations, people normally seek "power in order to manipulate the spirit realm, and thereby gain control over their lives."[85] The prosperity gospel preachers have now stepped into that space, offering their own remedies and exhibiting their power through their expensive lifestyles and their powers over the demonic forces.[86]

Apart from the reasons noted above, there are also spiritual reasons that make the movement attractive, such as spiritual protection and emphasis on the experience of intimacy with God. Some scholars have argued for similarities between the prosperity gospel and African Traditional Religions.[87] Just like within African Traditional Religions, prosperity gospel preachers sell religious artifacts believed to have the power to change people's fortunes. These religious artifacts tend to have their names or faces branded on them.[88] The leaders of this movement claim to have a special relationship with God akin to that of the *Sangomas*, who claim power and special access to the ancestors. This, in turn, has encouraged a tendency toward personality cults within the movement, with some of the teachers claiming that speaking out against them will bring about a curse.[89] Within the prosperity gospel movement, leaders sometimes demand absolute loyalty from their congregations, and the church members tend to describe their identity by their association with a particular prosperity gospel teacher. This brings about a culture of division and competition amongst the followers of the different so-called men/women of God. Interestingly, it is precisely the personality cult that Paul sought to challenge amongst the Corinthians.

---

84. Elizabeth Mburu, *African Hermeneutics* (HippoBooks, 2019), 55.

85. Mburu, *African Hermeneutics*, 55.

86. Vhumani Magezi and Peter Manzanga, "Prosperity and Health Ministry as a Coping Mechanism in the Poverty and Suffering Context of Zimbabwe: A Pastoral Evaluation and Response," *In die Skriflig* 50, no. 1 (2016): 1–10.

87. Magezi and Manzanga, "Prosperity and Health Ministry as a Coping Mechanism," 5–6. See also Conrad Mbewe, who expresses a similar point, "Nigerian Religious Junk!," *A Letter from Kwabata* (blog), February 20, 2011, http://www.conradmbewe.com/2011/02/nigerian-religious-junk.html.

88. See Leo Igwe, "TB Joshua and Covid-19 Anointing Water," News Ghana, January 6, 2021, https://newsghana.com.gh/tb-joshua-and-covid-19-anointing-water, about T. B. Joshua and COVID-19 anointing water.

89. Ben Ezeamalu and Ogechi Ekeanyanwu, "Chris Oyakhilome Warns Members Against Speaking Against Man of God; Suspends Pastor," Premium Times, September 15, 2014, https://www.premiumtimesng.com/news/top-news/168164-chris-oyakhilome-warns-members-against-speaking-against-man-of-god-suspends-pastor.html?tztc=1; cf. REON International, "Pastor Chris Oyakhilome: Don't Criticize Men of God (Must Watch)," YouTube Video, March 31, 2021, https://www.youtube.com/watch?v=PoRxkbflHDM.

Personality Cults in Corinth

As seen already above in 1 Corinthians 1–4, Paul deals with a report from Chloe's people who informed him about quarrels (ἔριδες, 1 Cor 1:11) which resulted in division because of the community's preference for one leader at the expense of the other (1 Cor 1:10–12; 3:4–5). In 1 Corinthians 3:3 Paul returns to the subject of division and quarrelling. An issue of identity and belonging was at the heart of the issues of division and quarrelling.[90] This becomes apparent when we consider 1 Corinthians 1:12: "I follow Paul," or "I follow Apollos," or "I follow Cephas," or "I follow Christ" (both ESV and NIV). Mary Katherine Birge provides a rationale why Ἐγὼ δὲ could be translated as "I belong."[91] She writes that "the word 'belong' is a dynamic equivalent for the verb 'to be' accompanied by a noun in the genitive case, e.g., Ἐγὼ μέν εἰμι Παύλου, 'I belong to Paul' (3:4) . . . 'to express that a thing belongs to another.'"[92] Thus, a better translation here is: "What I mean is that each one of you says, 'I belong to Paul,' or 'I belong to Apollos,' or 'I belong to Cephas,' or 'I belong to Christ.'"[93] The issue here in 1 Corinthians 1:12 and in 1 Corinthians 3:4 (where Paul writes: "For when one says, I belong to Paul, I belong to Apollos, are you not mere human beings") is that the community, rather than deriving their identity from Christ, were identifying with certain subgroups within the community. Winter, Birge, and Abraham J. Malherbe observe that the cultural influences behind the slogans "I belong to Paul" and "I belong to Apollos" (as an expression of loyalty for preferred leaders) were a result of continued Greco-Roman cultural influences upon the community.[94] Chong notes that the "term *I belong*" was used in the Greco-Roman world as a way of self-identification.[95] I remember a few years ago seeing a bumper sticker that read, "I belong to T. B. Joshua." I was so shocked that a Christian would put that on their car, seeming to value the prophet more than Jesus. This is the same thing that was happening in Corinth. Hence, just like people in Africa who belong to the prosperity gospel leaders, the Corinthians were deriving their identities from their preferred leaders.

Personality-centered cultural politics played a crucial role in the community's preference for one leader at the expense of the other.[96] Winter suggests that the Corinthians were influenced by the Sophist tradition of teacher/pupil relationships in the Greco-Roman world.[97]

---

90. Tucker, *You Belong to Christ*, 15.

91. Mary K. Birge, *The Language of Belonging: A Rhetorical Analysis of Kinship Language in First Corinthians* (Peeters, 2002), 14.

92. Birge, *The Language of Belonging*, 14.

93. Interestingly, Isaiah 44:5 (LXX) and Acts 27:23 use a similar Greek construction (τοῦ θεοῦ εἰμι ἐγώ) which is very similar to 1 Corinthians 1:12, but what I find interesting is that the NIV and ESV translate it as "I belong to God" instead of "I follow God" as they have done with 1 Corinthians 1:12.

94. Winter, *After Paul Left Corinth*; Birge, *The Language of Belonging*, 10; Abraham J. Malherbe, *Social Aspects of Early Christianity* (Wipf & Stock, 1983), 69.

95. Timothy Kh Chong, *Strategies in Church Discipline from 1 Corinthians: A Chinese Perspective* (WestBow Press, 2016), 31, emphasis in original.

96. Winter, *After Paul Left Corinth*, 31.

97. Winter, *After Paul Left Corinth*, 31–43.

He notes that during Paul's days the Sophists were held in high honor by some and viewed as the most skillful public speakers of the day. They spoke in secular gatherings and had a large public following. Further, the Sophists ran very expensive public performance schools where "they trained the next generation of the social elite to argue in the criminal and civil courts and debate in the secular assemblies."[98]

In these Sophist schools, pupils, expressing their belonging and loyalty to their teachers, modeled themselves after their Sophist teachers. This is because the student was seen as the disciple of the teacher. In this regard, they modeled themselves after their teachers, "not only in terms of the oratorical style of the teacher but also in the way that the disciple spoke, dressed, and even walked."[99] Winter notes that the Corinthians applied to Paul, Apollos, and possibly Peter the same cultural norms that "governed the relationship of secular pupils and their elitist teacher."[100]

Another important feature of the Sophist schools which must have influenced relationships within the church at Corinth is that the students tended to play teachers against each other. Teachers would also compete against each other in order to win more disciples.[101] Students were encouraged to be loyal to their teachers, and the way in which they expressed that loyalty was that they needed to be zealous for the honor of their teachers. They did this by promoting the oral attributes and "educational prowess" of their teachers.[102] This created strife, as the act of promoting one's teacher also meant that one had to highlight the deficiencies of the other teacher. Scholars believe that Paul alludes to this cultural practice in 1 Corinthians 3:3 when he criticizes the Corinthians for their jealousy and strife. Hence, Paul views what the church was doing with respect to claiming to belong to him or Apollos as "acting like mere human beings" (1 Cor 3:3–4). He views their behavior as inconsistent with their identity in Christ, and being worldly, because they used secular Sophist categories to assess him and Apollos.

The problem with the church members in Corinth is that they were committing idolatry in adopting the wisdom of the day.[103] This is a danger that we can easily fall into, even in our own day and age. The issue in 1 Corinthians 1:12 and 3:4 is the community's failure to grasp that they "belong to God alone and to claim otherwise is idolatry."[104] This is the same danger that faces the church in Africa. To counter this danger of idolatry, Paul penned 1 Corinthians 1:1–9 to remind the community that their identity is rooted in Christ.

In 1 Corinthians 1:1–9, Paul also sets the agenda for the whole epistle. In these verses, he reminds the Corinthians about the salient aspects of their group identity and also of his status as an apostle. Richard A. Horsley notes that the opening and thanksgiving section

98. Winter, *After Paul Left Corinth*, 33.

99. Winter, *After Paul Left Corinth*, 33.

100. Winter, *After Paul Left Corinth*, 31.

101. Winter, *After Paul Left Corinth*, 36–37; cf. Chong, *Strategies in Church Discipline*, 32.

102. Winter, *After Paul Left Corinth*, 39.

103. Birge, *The Language of Belonging*, 10–11.

104. Birge, *The Language of Belonging*, 11.

of Paul's letters does not merely follow ancient letter-writing conventions but also contains Paul's extended rhetoric that introduces the major themes of the argument to be expounded in the body of the letter.[105] From the outset, Paul invites the Corinthians to participate in the conversation about his identity-formation agenda. This becomes clear when considering the "in Christ" and the "calling" terminology that Paul uses in 1 Corinthians 1:1–9 as the basis of the salient in-group identity.

In the epistolary prescript of 1 Corinthians 1:1–3, Paul describes his identity and that of his recipients in Christ's terms.[106] Social identity scholars say the more someone's core identity is switched on, the more likely that person will act in a manner consistent with their identity. Thus Paul rebukes those who might have thought they belong to him or Peter or Apollos by reminding them that they belong to Christ and him alone. Later, in 1 Corinthians 3:5–9, Paul reminds the Corinthians that both he and Apollos are simply servants through whom the Corinthians came to believe. To view them otherwise would be to follow the wisdom of this age.

First Corinthians 1:17–25 demonstrates that this age's wisdom is diametrically opposed to godly wisdom. Within the African continent the tendency is to elevate personalities who demonstrate the power of the Holy Spirit either through their rhetorical abilities or miracles. However, Paul would argue that that kind of emphasis might empty the cross of its power (cf. 1 Cor 1:17). As we have already seen, the Corinthians valued eloquent wisdom. But Paul is clear in 1 Corinthians 1:17 that God sent him to preach the gospel "not with eloquent wisdom, so that the cross of Christ might not be emptied of its power."[107] In this verse, Paul argues that the gospel's power does not lie in how eloquently he presents it. Paul believes that the emphasis on rhetorical eloquence, which was the preferred choice of wisdom by the Corinthians, actually dilutes the message about the cross of Christ, and it might empty the gospel of its power to save people. Verse 17 acts as a bridge that links 1 Corinthians 1:18 to what precedes it. In fact, this link is established by the conjunction of verse 18, which reads: "For the message about the cross is foolishness to those who are perishing, but to us who are being saved it is the power of God."

What emerges in this verse and the following is that Paul is making a contrast between "wisdom of speech" with "word of the cross." Paul argues that the gospel of King Jesus, understood as the gospel or the word of the cross, is diametrically opposed to human wisdom. The latter places too much emphasis on the personality of the leader, while the former is all about God. The cross is scandalous and divisive; it divides humanity into two. There are those who will look at the cross and see it as utter foolishness, while for others it is the power of God. Christian Africans need to embrace this foolish gospel and stop chasing the so-called men/women of God, lest they lose their salvation by ignoring King Jesus.

105. Richard A. Horsley, *1 Corinthians* (Abingdon Press, 1998), 39.

106. Sin Pan Daniel Ho, "'Cleanse Out the Old Leaven, That You May Be a New Lamp': A Rhetorical Analysis of 1 Cor 5.1–11.1 in Light of the Social Lives of the Corinthians" (PhD diss., University of Sheffield, 2012), 297.

107. The Bible references below are all from the New Revised Standard Version Updated Edition—NRSVUE.

Personality cults have no place amongst the people of God. They are divisive and can move us away from Jesus. Personality cults reveal the spiritual immaturity of those who claim to belong to other human beings (1 Cor 3:1–4). In 1 Corinthians 1:13, Paul asks a very important question of that kind of people: "Is Christ divided? Was Paul crucified for you? Or were you baptised in the name of Paul?" Paul wants the Christians to understand that the Lord Jesus Christ created this community, not the Christian leaders.

Sexuality and Marriage

In this point of contact I will first examine sexuality and identity within Corinth, looking at Paul's response and how his teaching can be applied to the contemporary African church. Second, I examine the teaching on marriage in 1 Corinthians, bringing it into discussion with some communities within the African context.

Sexuality and Identity

As indicated in the introduction to this chapter, some people, in defining their identities, tend to focus on their own feelings and desires. The *zeitgeist* at this point in history, particularly for people in the West, can be described as being true to themselves. This has been particularly so in the area of sexuality.[108] In 1 Corinthians 5:1–6:20, Paul spells out for the Corinthians how their new identity in Christ results in a new lifestyle, especially in relation to how one views one's body. The main issue that 1 Corinthians 5–6 deals with is the failure of the community to fully recognize that being in Christ, or the new identity that the Corinthians have in Christ, means "a complete break with the old mores and patterns of social relationship and with all self-indulgent behaviour."[109] In 1 Corinthians 5:1–13, Paul deals with an area of compromise by the Corinthians in that they failed to act in line with their identity in Christ, something that the church in Africa is also not immune to.

The church in Africa, when it comes to the issues of sexuality, tends to be very conservative and is known for its stance, particularly against same-sex marriage, relying extensively on 1 Corinthians 6:9–10 in its opposition. In 2023, this was brought to the world's attention when the church of Uganda welcomed decisive anti-homosexual bills on the continent of Africa.[110] While this stance has been welcomed in some quarters within the broader church, this caused tensions within the Anglican Communion, with the archbishop of Canterbury,

108. For more on the change in people's views on areas of sexuality, please see Phillip Hammack and Liam Wignall, "Sexual & Gender Diversity in the 21st Century," *Current Opinion in Psychology* 52, no. 5 (2023): 101616.

109. James D. G. Dunn, *Beginning from Jerusalem: Christianity in the Making*, vol. 2 (Eerdmans, 2008), 101; cf. Douglas J. Moo, *A Theology of Paul and His Letters: The Gift of the New Realm in Christ* (Zondervan Academic, 2021), 121.

110. For more on this, see Francis Martin, "Church of Uganda 'Grateful' as Harsh New Anti-Homosexuality Law Is Approved," *Church Times*, May 30, 2023, https://www.churchtimes.co.uk/articles/2023/2-june/news/world/church-of-uganda-grateful-as-harsh-new-anti-homosexuality-law-is-approved.

Justin Welby, criticizing the Ugandan church,[111] deepening the rift within the Anglican Communion, and resulting in the language of "us" versus "them" within the church.[112] While the church in Africa is known for its clear stance against same-sex marriage, I question if the church is as clear and decisive when dealing with the sexual immorality of heterosexual people within the church. After all, the vice list of Paul is inclusive of all sexual sins (1 Cor 6:9–10).

In this section, I want to draw out some implications of Paul's teachings for Christ's followers in Africa regarding the area of sexuality in general. I must first establish the context for 1 Corinthians 5–6 before I look at the implications of Paul's teachings for the African context.

In 1 Corinthians 5:9–13, Paul seems to want to clear up confusion about one of his previous letters (which has been lost to us). It seems like the church in Corinth had clearly misunderstood Paul's teachings in his previous letter. In 1 Corinthians 5:9–11 we read:

> I wrote to you in my letter not to associate with sexually immoral persons, not at all meaning the sexually immoral of this world, or the greedy and swindlers, or idolaters, since you would then need to go out of the world. But now I am writing to you not to associate with anyone who bears the name of brother or sister who is sexually immoral or greedy or an idolater, reviler, drunkard, or swindler. Do not even eat with such a one.

It seems like the Corinthians had completely misapplied his teaching and reversed his intentions; instead of separating themselves from sinful believers, they were separating themselves from sinful unbelievers and tolerating sin in their midst.[113] Craig L. Blomberg notes that it is striking how conservative Christians have seemed to do the same in recent centuries.[114] Paul hears disturbing news about the church in Corinth, presumably from Chloe's people (1 Cor 5:1–13; cf. 1 Cor 1:11). It is reported to him that a Christian man within the community is having sex with his father's wife (presumably his stepmother), something that is clearly prohibited by both the Old Testament law (Lev 18:7–8) and Greco-Roman law—which frowned upon incest (Cicero, *Clu.* 15). The shocking thing is that not only are the Corinthians tolerating this sin, but Paul says he is informed that they are proud (1 Cor 5:2). It is not clear from 1 Corinthians 5:1–2 what exactly the Corinthians are proud of.

Both Gordon Fee and Douglas Moo believe that the Corinthians were proud of the man's sin.[115] I do not agree with this view, however, I think a much more plausible explanation is the

---

111. Harriet Sherwood, "Justin Welby Criticises Ugandan Church's Backing for Anti-Gay Law," *The Guardian*, June 9, 2023, https://www.theguardian.com/world/2023/jun/09/justin-welby-criticises-ugandan-church-backing-for-anti-gay-law.

112. Aljazeera, "Ugandan Anti-LGBTQ Law Deepens Anglican Church Rift on Gay Rights," June 14, 2023, https://www.aljazeera.com/news/2023/6/14/ugandan-anti-lgbtq-law-deepens-anglican-church-rift-on-gay-rights.

113. Craig L. Blomberg, *From Pentecost to Patmos: An Introduction to Acts Through Revelation* (B&H Publishing, 2006), 174.

114. Blomberg, *From Pentecost to Patmos*, 174.

115. Fee, *The First Epistle to the Corinthians*, 221–22; Moo, *A Theology of Paul*, 121.

one suggested by Andrew Clarke,[116] John K. Chow,[117] and Ciampa and Rosner,[118] who argue that the Corinthians were not necessarily proud of the man's sin; rather, they were proud of his social status. That is, even though he was clearly in contravention of the Greco-Roman laws regarding incest, nothing happened to him.[119] Paul uses his apostolic authority and calls up on the church to act against such an immoral, unrepentant brother. In other words, Paul calls on the congregation to exercise church discipline (1 Cor 5:3–5, 7–8). Paul is concerned with the purity of the church (1 Cor 5).

One of the advantages that the church in Africa has is that due to the communal nature of African society, people tend to know everyone's business. There is no such thing as a "private" life. However, due to the socioeconomic challenges on the continent, the church can easily fall victim to the patronage system. In the twenty-four years that I have been Christian, I have never seen a wealthy Christian being placed under church discipline, while the church easily exercises the right of church discipline over ordinary or average-income Christians.

Now, it is quite possible that the wealthy Christians I know are very godly, and I pray that is the case. Looking at 1 Corinthians 5, though, I think pastors have to be extremely careful in how they exercise church discipline, lest they show favoritism to the rich. In 1 Corinthians 5:9–13, Paul ends the section with the exhortation for the whole church to act against sexual immorality within the church, instead of focusing on those outside the church.

Paul returns to the subject of sexual immorality in 1 Corinthians 6:12–20, particularly focusing on the members of the congregation visiting prostitutes. A lot has been written in recent times about how technology has changed the "sex work industry."[120] Gone are the days when most prostitutes stood at street corners selling their bodies, and those buying their services were visible to the whole community. In our time, it can all be done secretly, with an app or a website.[121] Africa is not immune to these vices as well.

In the Greco-Roman world, there was a rite of passage from boyhood to manhood which was known as the *toga virilis*.[122] During this rite of passage, sexual immorality was the norm

116. Clarke, *Secular and Christian Leadership in Corinth*, 73–88.

117. John K. Chow, *Patronage and Power: A Study of Social Networks in Corinth* (Sheffield Academic Press, 1992), 130–140.

118. Ciampa and Rosner, *The First Letter to the Corinthians*, 203.

119. Incest was treated as a criminal offence under Roman law, the punishment for which could even include death or exile to an island, see Gaius, *Inst.* 1.63; Paulus, *Opinions* 2.26.

120. For more on this, see the following articles: Jacob Berstein, "How OnlyFans Changed Sex Work Forever: OnlyFans Has Put X-Rated Entertainment in the Hands of Its Entertainers. Call It the Paywall of Porn," *New York Times*, February 9, 2019, https://www.nytimes.com/2019/02/09/style/onlyfans-porn-stars.html; Alexandra Sifferlin, "There Is Now an App for Prostitution," *Time*, April 22, 2014, https://time.com/72218/there-is-now-an-app-for-prostitution.

121. See Thérèse Bernier, Amika Shah, Lori E. Ross, Carmen H. Logie, and Emily Seto, "The Use of Information and Communication Technologies by Sex Workers to Manage Occupational Health and Safety: Scoping Review," *Journal of Medical Internet Research* 23, no. 6 (2021): e26085. https://doi.org/10.2196/26085.

122. Plutarch, *Mor.* 37 C-D; Bruce W. Winter, "The 'Underlays' of Conflict and Compromise in 1 Corinthians," in *Paul and the Corinthians: Studies on a Community in Conflict. Essays in Honor of Margaret Thrall*, ed. Trevor J. Burke and J. Keith Elliott (Brill, 2003), 144.

among young men, who would sleep with prostitutes. The consequence of coming of age meant that the young men (around the age of eighteen years old) were now allowed to "recline at the banquets and were also exposed to 'its attendant perils.'"[123] These banquets were often marked by what Winter calls the "'intimate and unholy trinity' of eating and drinking and sexual immorality."[124]

Coincidentally, amongst African peoples there are similar rites of passage from boyhood to manhood that are often marked by male circumcision. In this chapter I will focus on the Xhosa nation with their rite, *ulwaluko* (male circumcision).[125] During this rite of passage in the Xhosa culture, the young men think about what it means to be a man and the sacrifices that they ought to go through to support their families.[126] This rite of passage culminates with the young men coming back from the bush, which is a momentous occasion for the families as, even in recent times, many die during this rite of passage. Like the unholy trinity of Corinth, the coming home celebration (*Umgidi*) is often marked by a feast of food and alcohol. However, Mawethu Ncaca, in his study, has also observed that there is an ugly side to this rite of passage. He argues that the Xhosa initiation schools seem to "contribute to women being portrayed as (sexual) objects."[127] After the young men have completely healed, they are encouraged by the other young men to sleep with women in order to test if their male sex organ functions properly, a practice commonly referred to as *ukubulala ihlola*.

Paul challenges the practice of sleeping with prostitutes by the young men during the rite of passage by reminding the young men that sleeping with a prostitute means that they are united to her and also that such actions were fornication (1 Cor 6:13, 16). This would not have gone down well with the Corinthians who, according to Winter, defended their actions with the catchphrases "all things are permitted for me" and "'food is for the belly, and the belly is for food,' and by implication 'sex (fornication) is for the body, and the body is for sex' (fornication)."[128] These catchphrases were self-justifying maxims for "the notorious conduct of the Corinthian Christians at dinners."[129]

These feasts were characterized by gluttony, drunkenness, and sexual immorality. The wealthier the patron, the more extravagant they would be. Winter tells a story of the banquet hosted by the president of the Isthmian Games, who made use of the traveling brothels to cater for the guests at his parties.[130] In elite parties, it was customary for the host not only to provide food for the appetites but also prostitutes for sexual appetites. According to 1 Corinthians

123. Winter, *After Paul Left Corinth*, 89–90.

124. Winter, *After Paul Left Corinth*, 88.

125. For more on this Xhosa custom, see the documentary by Mayezenke Baza, "Ndiyindoda: I Am a Man," Aljazeera, January 3, 2013, https://www.aljazeera.com/program/people-power/2013/1/3/ndiyindoda-i-am-a-man. See also Mawethu Ncaca, "Yithi Uyindoda! (Say, You Are a Man!)" (MA diss., Stellenbosch University, 2014).

126. Richard Bullock, "It's Hard to Be a Man," *Africa Geographic*, May 29, 2015, https://africageographic.com/stories/xhosa-circumcision-ritual-south-africa-its-hard-to-be-a-man.

127. Ncaca, "Yithi Uyindoda!," 4.

128. Winter, *After Paul Left Corinth*, 88, cf. Winter, "The 'Underlays' of Conflict and Compromise," 144.

129. Winter, *After Paul Left Corinth*, 88.

130. Winter, *After Paul Left Corinth*, 88.

6:12–20, it seems that the Corinthians took part in these parties and had sex with the prostitutes within a dining context.[131]

Sexual freedom was defended philosophically in the Roman world by philosophers like Cicero who poured scorn on any call for sexual abstinence (except for incest and contravention of their Roman-Greco law).[132] Some scholars see this extravagant food and alcohol consumption, along with sexual immorality and license, as characteristic of gentile identity, particularly the vice of sexual immorality.[133] Therefore, this practice demonstrates the continued cultural influences of the Greco-Roman world upon the Pauline community at Corinth (1 Cor 6:12–20). As we conclude our examination of the original gentile context of Paul's audience and our African context regarding sexual immorality—specifically addressing young men in this case—we can see Paul's teaching in 1 Corinthians should inform young Christian men to value their identity in Christ in the midst of societal pressure.

What becomes clear in 1 Corinthians 6:12–20 is that Paul desires that all in the church in Corinth understand the implications of their physical (somatic) and spiritual (pneumatic) identity in Christ.[134] In this section, Paul wants the Corinthians to understand that, since their identity is in Christ, their bodies belong to Christ and are identified with Christ (1 Cor 6:15). What is fascinating in Paul's description of the Corinthians' identities here is that their bodies are not identified as the property of Christ; rather, they are the members of Christ (μέλη Χριστοῦ). This presents a strong link between the identity of the Corinthians and that of Christ; it is an intimate relationship.[135] Thus, their actions of visiting prostitutes are not consistent with their identity in Christ. To drive home this point, Paul asks them a pertinent question: Shall I then take the members of Christ and unite them with a prostitute? Since their identity is in Christ, their bodies are exclusively for his use, which precludes them from visiting prostitutes. Their "in Christ" identity is mutually exclusive of πορνεία (sexual immorality).

What seems to be clear in 1 Corinthians 6 is that the Christian community at Corinth seems to not have fully understood the implications of their identity in Christ. They seem to have been heavily influenced by the Greco-Roman world; the vice of sexual immorality, which was a characteristic of gentile identity, seems to have had a grip on the Pauline community at Corinth. The church in Africa will do well to dedicate a concerted effort in helping church members (not the world) to understand the implications of their identity when it comes to issues of sexual purity. Since believers are people whom God has set apart for himself, they should not need to be told to flee idolatry and sexual immorality (1 Cor 6:18; 10:7–8, 14)! In these and other areas, Paul had to urge them to guard their life as God's community, protecting it from the world's corrosive influences; the same is true for the church in Africa.

---

131. Winter, *After Paul Left Corinth*, 88.

132. Winter, "The 'Underlays' of Conflict and Compromise," 144–145; Cicero, *Cael.* 20.48.

133. For more on this see Judith Lieu, *Christian Identity in the Jewish and Greco-Roman World* (Oxford University Press, 2004), 104; Roy E. Ciampa, "Flee Sexual Immorality: Sex and the City of Corinth," in *The Wisdom of the Cross: Exploring 1 Corinthians*, ed. Brian S. Rosner (Apollos, 2011), 100–133; Ciampa and Rosner, *The First Letter to the Corinthians*; "Structure and Argument"; Ho, "Cleanse," 17–19.

134. Alistair S. May, *The Body for the Lord: Sex and Identity in 1 Corinthians 5–7* (T&T Clark, 2004), 110.

135. May, *The Body for the Lord*, 110–111.

Marriage

So far, I have looked at the treatment of sex in relation to incest and sex with prostitutes, focusing on Paul's prohibitions. Paul now turns to answer the questions that Corinthians had written to him about (1 Cor 7:1–16:4); here Paul puts forth a positive vision of sex.[136] David Wenham thinks that part of the issue at Corinth might have stemmed from some in the congregation misunderstanding Paul's teachings, particularly when it came to 1 Corinthians 7.[137] He says that the people who were "advocating for Christian celibacy," and recommending that those who were married should separate (i.e., 1 Cor 7:1, particularly if they were married to unbelievers, cf. 1 Cor 7:13–16), probably drew this view from an incorrect understanding of Paul's teaching regarding marriage and sexual practice (cf. 2 Cor 6:14–7:1).[138]

He also states that some in the Corinthian congregation might have advocated celibacy because they thought that what they were teaching was in line with Jesus's teachings in Luke 20:35. He says: "The Corinthians certainly thought that they have arrived at 'that age' [the age that is promised in Luke 20:35] (possibly even to the resurrection of the dead), and so it made sense to conclude that sex was no longer appropriate for people who were now 'in the Spirit' and for whom bodily life was unimportant."[139]

Whatever one chooses as a backdrop of 1 Corinthians 7, what becomes clear in this chapter is that Paul advocates for a positive view of sex within marriage, whether or not a believer is married to a nonbeliever. In fact, 1 Corinthians 7:2–5 makes it clear that sex within marriage is one of the ways that will help a married couple not to fall into the sin of sexual immorality. While 1 Corinthians 7 covers a variety of topics, such as marriage, divorce, engagement, and slavery, here I will limit the discussion to the topic of marriage. To try to be more inclusive of the broader African context, in preparation for this section, I asked my six South Sudanese students, who have over twenty years of Christian ministry experience combined, to explain to me how marriage is understood in the Dinka community. The following is the summary of how they view marriage in their context, focused on four key areas:

1. The first element that became clear to me was that, amongst the Dinka people, marriage is not a choice but an obligation rooted in a belief that marriage ensures the continuity of the family line. The emphasis on the continuity of the family line is so strong that when a child dies, whether as an infant or adult, the parents of the deceased child must find a spouse for one of the siblings of the deceased,[140] who will then bear another child to continue the lineage and memory of the deceased child, even if the infant died before they were given a name. This practice extends even to infants who die before being named, referred to as *Amuom*,

136. See May, *The Body for the Lord*, 205–267.

137. David Wenham, "Whatever Went Wrong in Corinth?," *The Expository Times* 108, no. 5 (1997): 140.

138. Wenham, "Whatever Went Wrong in Corinth?," 140.

139. Wenham, "Whatever Went Wrong in Corinth?," 140.

140. In the case of no siblings, the father can take another wife.

which means "anonymous," if the baby is a boy. In such cases, a spouse is still sought to ensure the continuation of the child's lineage. Should the deceased child be female, her brother(s) will marry a woman to bear offspring in her name.

2. Second, when a Dinka man dies after marrying, leaving behind a widow, the responsibility of caring for her falls upon one of his brothers. Caring entails providing for her material needs and continuing the deceased's lineage by fathering children with her. Even if the deceased husband had children before his death, his widow remains under the care of his brothers, with whom she may bear additional children if she is of childbearing age.
3. Dinka culture stipulates that men or women who are mentally ill or physically incapable of marrying will still be provided with a spouse. In such cases, the father or brother is responsible for fathering children on their behalf. Similarly, if a woman cannot conceive, her husband may take another wife to ensure the continuity of his lineage.
4. The concept of male heirs holds immense significance within the Dinka community, to the extent that even women who have only borne daughters are considered barren. In such instances, husbands are encouraged to marry additional wives to secure male heirs.

Within the context of the Dinka culture, 1 Corinthians 7, especially verses 7–9, would sound very strange, as Paul in these verses suggests that singleness is a good thing for the sake of the gospel. Also, 1 Corinthians 7:2, when looked at carefully, is countercultural: "But because of cases of sexual immorality, each man should have his own wife and each woman her own husband." Blomberg notes that Paul, in this verse, is not saying that "each person should acquire a spouse, but each married person should continue to have sexual relations with his or her spouse."[141] Within the marriage context, sex is to be celebrated and enjoyed in a mutually beneficial manner (1 Cor 3–5). Christian marriages are marriages of mutual benefit, where both partners are equal. Blomberg notes that, throughout chapter 7, Paul "issues exactly parallel commands to both husband and wives, treating them as fully equal to each other."[142] The wife is not simply a utility to continue a family line; she is an equal member of the family who has authority over her husband's body, just like the husband has authority over his wife's body. To protect the purity of the family, Paul encourages consensual sex within the context of marriage (1 Cor 7:5). He understands that for the sake of spiritual discipline, the couple might abstain from sex. Still, he encourages them to do this for a short time, lest one of the partners are tempted to look for sex elsewhere (1 Cor 7:5–6).

Paul turns his attention to the widows and the unmarried (1 Cor 7:8–9). In this case, he encourages both the unmarried and the widows to consider celibacy for the sake of the gospel (cf. 1 Cor 7:32–35, 40). Interestingly, he counts himself amongst this group, which has led

141. Blomberg, *From Pentecost to Patmos*, 176.

142. Blomberg, *From Pentecost to Patmos*, 176.

some scholars to speculate that he must have been a widower.[143] But even with this group, he advises marriage for those who cannot control their passions. In some African cultures, levirate marriages are still a common practice. These marriages are designed to protect the widow and her children after the death of her husband.[144] Daniel Bediako, in his article, provides a helpful summary of the levirate marriages within the African context.[145] In the list that he gives, I just want to focus on his first point, that of the wife who is inherited as part of her late husband's property. This practice seems to be against the spirit of mutuality that Paul was advocating for within the Christian marriage context. The wife is an equal partner to the husband and not a possession of the husband.

Food Offered to Idols

In our final point of contact, Paul addresses the subject of food offered to idols (1 Cor 8:1, 4, 7–10; 10:19), which suggests that the church in Corinth wrote him a letter asking for his advice (1 Cor 8:1). This section may seem irrelevant for people who live a modern urban or suburban life where meat is easily available and accessible through the supermarkets. This was not the case for the many poor people in the Greco-Roman world, just like for many people who live in the poorer parts of the African continent. In the first-century Greco-Roman world, meat mostly came from pagan temples. The leftover meat was sold in the markets after the animal was sacrificed inside the temple. In many African rural areas, especially amongst subsistence farmers, meat is mostly available after the slaughter of an animal in a ritual context for the veneration of the ancestors. The question of whether Christians should eat meat offered to idols is a hotly debated subject within the continent of Africa; as well as whether or not Christians should participate in such ceremonies.[146]

Just like in Africa today, this seems to have raised questions and divided the church in Corinth. Should Christians eat meat that was offered to idols?[147] The church was divided into two groups regarding the issue of food offered to idols; there were those in the community who were described as the weak (1 Cor 8:7, 9–10) who refused to eat meat sacrificed to idols, and those whom we may call the strong (even though there is no such description in the text), who saw that there was nothing necessarily wrong in eating the meat offered to idols.[148] The second group is marked by knowledge; they know that "no idol in the world really exists" and

143. Blomberg, *From Pentecost to Patmos*, 177.

144. Ogolla Maurice, "Levirate Unions in Both the Bible and African Cultures: Convergence and Divergence," *International Journal of Humanities and Science* 4, no. 10 (2014): 287–292. It's worth noting that while this custom is supposed to be practiced in order to protect property rights of the widow, it is sometimes used to simply acquire more property for the men involved.

145. Daniel K. Bediako, "Levirate Marriage: Ancient Near Eastern, African, and Biblical Perspectives" (draft), https://www.academia.edu/44644036/Levirate_Marriage_ANE_Africa_and_Bible, 5–9.

146. For more on this see Choon Sup Bae and P. J. Van der Merwe, "Ancestor Worship: Is It Biblical?," *HTS Theological Studies* 64, no. 3 (2008): 1299–1325.

147. Moo, *A Theology of Paul*, 131.

148. Blomberg, *From Pentecost to Patmos*, 177.

that "there is no God but one" (1 Cor 8:4). The latter group is arrogant, they had a mantra—"all of us possess knowledge" (1 Cor 8:1)—and they use their knowledge as a license to sin. Paul responds to them with a rebuke by reminding them that the most important Christian virtue is love. He writes, "Knowledge puffs up, but love builds up" (1 Cor 8:1). Paul lays out a principle of how the Christians with knowledge were to act toward their weaker brothers and sisters (1 Cor 8:4–13).

In many ways, Paul agrees with their knowledge that there is but one God and that there is nothing inherently wrong in eating meat that was previously sacrificed to idols (1 Cor 8:4–6, 8). Still, he disagrees with their self-centered assertion of their "rights" and their loveless indifference to the needs of the "weak." Paul wants the knowledgeable group to be careful in the use of their knowledge and freedom and not to cause the younger or weak believers to fall into sin (1 Cor 8:7, 9–13). Paul uses himself as an example of how he let go of his rights and privileges for the sake of others and for the gospel (1 Cor 9). Paul wants the community at Corinth to be marked by the same attitude. But the question still remains: Should Christians eat meat that was previously sacrificed to idols? Traditionally, in answering this question, scholars have argued that Paul sees no problem in principle with eating meat that was previously offered to idols (1 Cor 8:4–6; 10:25–26, 30). However, he recognizes that there are three different settings in which such meat can be encountered: at the market (1 Cor 10:25), in the homes of non-Christians (1 Cor 10:27), and in meals held at pagan temples (1 Cor 8:10; 10:20–21).

Paul seems to indicate that what believers should do depends on the situation concerned, which includes whether a "weak" brother is likely to see you dining at a temple (1 Cor 8:10) or to be troubled that the meat you are eating as a dinner guest was sacrificed to idols (1 Cor 10:28–30).[149] Within the African context—especially among Xhosas—there are ancestral veneration ceremonies where Christians will encounter circumstances within which they might find themselves fellowshipping with unholy spirits (1 Cor 10:14–22). In this context, Paul's advice for Christians would be to avoid partaking in that ceremony and the food involved in it.[150] Paul reminds the Corinthians of their fellowship and identity in Christ—particularly in their partaking in the Lord's Supper (1 Cor 10:16–17). This table fellowship with the Lord is exclusive and calls for loyalty and, therefore, the rejection of any practice that compromises this (1 Cor 10:20–22).

Conclusion

This chapter has argued that Paul's First Letter to the Corinthians deals with the issues of identity formation. The church in Corinth was struggling to understand the implications of their identity in Christ. As a result, they failed to display to the world what Christ's followers

149. For more on this, see Joël Delobel, "Coherence and Relevance of 1 Cor 8–10," in *The Corinthian Correspondence*, ed. Reimund Bieringer (Leuven University Press, 1996), 182–186.

150. This parallels with Paul's injunction in 1 Corinthians 5:11; 6:18 that one should remove oneself from certain situations in order to remain faithful.

look like. Instead, they reflected Corinthian society. In this chapter, I have examined three points of contact between the Corinthian church and the church in Africa. I did this in order to show how Paul's Letter to the Corinthians is relevant for the African context as Christians in this continent are also dealing with questions of identity.

Further Reading

Adewuya, J. Ayodeji. *1 Corinthians: A Pastoral Commentary*. Wipf & Stock, 2019.

Adewuya, J. Ayodeji. "The Spirit in 1 Corinthians: Spiritual Formation and Giftedness." *Pneuma* 43 no. 3/4 (2021): 485–495.

Barrett, C. K. *The First Epistle to the Corinthians*. Hendrickson Publishers, 1968.

Blomberg, Craig L. *1 Corinthians*. NIVAC. Zondervan, 2009.

Ciampa, Roy E., and Brian S. Rosner. *The First Letter to the Corinthians*. PNTC. Eerdmans, 2010.

Datiri, Dachollom. "1 Corinthians." In *Africa Bible Commentary: A One-Volume Commentary Written by 70 African Scholars*, edited by Tokunboh Adeyemo. WordAlive Publishers; Zondervan, 2006.

Fee, Gordon D. *The First Epistle to the Corinthians*. Rev. ed. Eerdmans, 2014.

Gardner, Paul. *1 Corinthians*. ZECNT. Zondervan Academic, 2018.

Garland, David E. *1 Corinthians*. BECNT. Baker Academic, 2003.

Kim, Yung Suk, ed. *1 and 2 Corinthians*. Fortress Press, 2013.

Lockwood, Gregory J. *1 Corinthians*. CC. Concordia Publishing House, 2010.

Oropeza, B. J. *1 Corinthians*. NCCS. Cascade Books, 2017.

Sindo, Vuyani S. *Paul as a Prototype and Entrepreneur of Christian Identity: An Investigation into Leadership and Identity in 1 Corinthians 1–4*. Langham Academic, 2024.

Winter, Bruce W. *After Paul Left Corinth: The Influence of Secular Ethics and Social Change*. Eerdmans, 2001.

Wright, N. T. *Paul for Everyone*. Presbyterian Publishing Corporation, 2004.

CHAPTER TEN

The Second Letter to the Corinthians

Tibebu Teklu Senbetu
Mekane Yesus Seminary
Ethiopia

Introduction

THIS CHAPTER OFFERS a selected thematic commentary of 2 Corinthians from an Ethiopian perspective. Such an approach is critical, allowing us to comprehend the text's significance for communities in Africa facing distinctive challenges and aspirations. This epistle mainly teaches endurance amidst trials within the church and outside of the church. Many Christian communities in Africa are facing various kinds of suffering—poverty, conflict, corruption, and injustice—which are all lived realities in Ethiopia as well. This epistle is vital to this community so that Christian Africans may endure suffering, uphold the gospel's truth, advocate for justice and maintain Christian unity. In this introduction, therefore, I will connect Paul's message to the Corinthians with modern African realities, drawing the divine message of the text for Christians in Africa today.

Introductory Matters

Historical Background

Ancient Corinth became an important city because of its strategic location for both military and trade purposes.[1] Corinth soon became a wealthy city because of its many ports and resources, which welcomed new ideas and social mobility. However, Lucius Mummius destroyed the city in 146 BCE.[2] In the year 44 BCE, when Julius Caesar came to power, he rebuilt the city as part of a Roman colony, and it became a center of attraction for a diverse population, including Romans, Greeks, and Jews.[3] Although Corinth was a part of Greece in ancient times, it later became a Roman colony. Despite being a Roman colony, Corinth remained connected with Greek religion, philosophy, and the arts during Paul's time.[4] The

1. Jerome Murphy-O'Connor, *St. Paul's Corinth: Texts and Archaeology*, 3rd ed. (Liturgical Press, 2002), 3.

2. Paul Barnett, *The Second Epistle to the Corinthians*, NICNT (Eerdmans, 1997), 1–4.

3. Raymond F. Collins, *Second Corinthians: Commentary on the New Testament* (Baker Academic, 2013), 3.

4. J. Ayodeji Adewuya, "The People of God in a Pluralistic Society: Holiness in 2 Corinthians," in *Holiness and Ecclesiology in the New Testament*, ed. Kent E. Brower and Andy Johnson (Eerdmans, 2007), 202.

city of Corinth had a mixture of Greco-Roman culture that brought people from all over the world and its strategic significance attracted people for political, economic, social, and religious activities.

The city of Corinth was also known for its immorality, sexual impurity, and idolatry. One of the examples of these immoralities is an indulgence in incest, a sin even condemned among the pagan communities (1 Cor 5:1–2). We also read about other immoralities stated in the text itself, such as Corinthian Christians having fellowship with gentiles and becoming part of idol worship and fornication (1 Cor 6:12–20; 10:14–22). Although the gentiles in Corinth were converted and became Christians, they did not abandon their gentile practices. Paul stated that they were behaving in a worldly manner, and their maturity as followers of Christ was still in its infancy (1 Cor 3:1–3).

This epistle also mentions Paul's previous correspondence with the church in Corinth. He referred to this letter as "the sorrowful letter," which seems to have caused anguish to the Corinthians. Paul attempted to visit the Corinthians to address the issue and settle the matter in person (2 Cor 2:4; 7:8–12). Scholars propose that Paul wrote at least four letters to the Corinthians, with two of these letters now lost. Among them, the "sorrowful" letter is identified as the third. While some suggest that 2 Corinthians 10–13 may represent this missing letter, there is no substantive evidence to validate this claim. In this lost letter, we see Paul's efforts to restore his relationship with the Christians in Corinth and defend his apostolic authority. Paul was concerned that the Corinthians were bieng led astray by false teachers who claimed superior apostolic authority over Paul's apostleship.

Author

The internal evidence in the text itself affirms Pauline authorship, along with his coworker, Timothy (2 Cor 1:1; 10:1). Internal evidence of consistent use of distinct Pauline expressions or styles, such as "in Christ" (2 Cor 2:14; 5:17) and "God who raises the dead" (2 Cor 1:9), alongside Paul's autobiographical details concerning his sufferings (2 Cor 11:23–28) and his profound concern for the churches (2 Cor 11:28), strongly support the conclusion that the letter reflects Paul's unique theological style and personal experiences, affirming his authorship.

Moreover, the majority of New Testament scholars, including Murray Harris and George Guthrie, have asserted that 2 Corinthians is written by the apostle Paul.[5] Despite widely accepted Pauline authorship and the unity of the epistle, a few biblical scholars question Pauline authorship of parts of the epistle. D. A. Carson, Douglas Moo, and Guthrie, although they do not agree with the conclusion of the following scholars, acknowledge the arguments of Hans Dieter Betz, Joseph Fitzmyer, Richard Hurd, and Robert Jewett, who question Pauline authorship and literary integration of specific section of 2 Corinthians, such as 2 Corinthians

5. George H. Guthrie, *2 Corinthians*, BECNT (Baker Academic, 2015), 26–27; Alfred Plummer, *A Critical and Exegetical Commentary on the Second Epistle of St. Paul to the Corinthians* (T&T Clark, 1915), xi; Murray J. Harris, *The Second Epistle to the Corinthians* (Eerdmans, 2005), 1–2.

6:14–7:1; 8–9; 10–13.[6] For instance, Betz argued against Pauline authorship of 2 Corinthians 6:14–7:1, For him, this section could be an "interpolation," which might be either a fragment from the lost letters (1 Cor 5:9) or some other sources unauthorized by Paul.[7] However, prominent scholars such as Paul Barnett, Carson and Moo, and Guthrie himself affirm that the unit is authentically Pauline, arguing that it is integral to Paul's message in addressing specific needs in Corinth.[8]

Therefore, we can conclude that 2 Corinthians is a letter written to the Christian community in Corinth and is traditionally attributed to Paul the apostle as a single and unified epistle. The historical context of the text addresses diverse issues describing a challenging connection between Christians in Corinth and Paul, called to be an apostle of Jesus Christ. Paul had to address the problem by defending his apostleship and the message he delivered while seeking true reconciliation with the Corinthians.[9]

The Recipients

The recipients of the second epistle to the Corinthians were Christians living in the ancient Greek city of Corinth and to all the saints throughout Achaia (2 Cor 1:1). After Paul had planted a vibrant Christian church in Corinth and left the city, various issues against Paul's teaching had arisen among the Christians. There were false teachings (2 Cor 2:17; 4:2–4; 11:3–4, 13–15; 12:11–12), divisions within the Christian community (2 Cor 2:5–11; 13:11), questions about Paul's apostolic authority (2 Cor 3:1–3; 10:7–11; 11:5–6), issues concerning Christian suffering (2 Cor 1:3–7; 4:7–12, 16–18; 6:3–10; 11:23–29; 12:7–10), forgiveness and reconciliation (2 Cor 2:5–11; 5:18–21; 6:11–13; 7:8–13), a call for disassociation from unbelievers (2 Cor 6:14–18), the need for Christian holiness (2 Cor 6:14–18; 7:1; 10:3–5), Christian charity (2 Cor 8:1–15; 9:6–15), and many more. Regardless of these challenges, Paul continued to show responsibility and concern for the Christians in Corinth, showing the importance of forgiveness and reconciliation among believers. He also admonished the Corinthians to uphold the true gospel he preached to them. Paul's divine message reaches a wider audience, including both the original recipients in Corinth and Christian readers through generations, exhorting believers to maintain the truth of the Gospel.

Date

Scholars agree that the date for Second Corinthians is toward the early second half of the first century. Since the first epistle to the Corinthians was written while Paul was in Ephesus,

6. D. A. Carson and Douglas J. Moo, *An Introduction to the New Testament*, 2nd ed. (Zondervan, 2005), 438–444.

7. Hans Dieter Betz, "2 Corinthians 6:14–7:1: An Anti-Pauline Fragment?," *Harvard Theological Review* 66, no. 1 (1973): 88–108.

8. Barnett, *The Second Epistle to the Corinthians*, 17–26.

9. Barnett, *The Second Epistle to the Corinthians*, 28–29; see also Mark A. Seifrid, *The Second Letter to the Corinthians* (Eerdmans, 2014), 287.

shortly before Pentecost, in late spring (Acts 16:8), around 55 CE, the second epistle would most likely have been written a few months or a year later, between 56–57 CE.[10]

Occasion and Purpose

In his letter Paul states the occasion that led him to defend his apostleship with a primary focus on his call and service to the Christians and his mission to the gentiles (2 Cor 1:1; 3:5–6; 4:1–2; 5:18–20; 10:13–16). After Paul left Corinth, some agitators came to question his apostleship and confused the Corinthians, claiming super apostleship authority against Paul (2 Cor 11:4–5:12:11). Due to this new teaching, Paul encountered opposition and confrontation from the Corinthians, which resulted in a painful visit earlier, followed by a tearful letter, and the decision to postpone any more visits to Corinth in order to avoid further damaging their relationship (2 Cor 1:23–2:1). Nevertheless, Paul rejoiced greatly after hearing from Titus, whom he met in Macedonia, that the Corinthians had received the letter and repented (2 Cor 6:6–9). Encouraged by this news, Paul urged the Corinthians to live according to their new identity as members of the new covenant (2 Cor 7:5–16). For Paul, living a life worthy of the Gospel is not a matter of choice for Christians; rather it is the Corinthians' expression of their identity as members of the new covenant.

Paul had various issues to deal with in the church at Corinth. As stated above, some groups of people had attempted to invalidate his apostleship, which led Paul to sharply rebuke the agitators and demonstrate the source of his apostolic authority by referring to himself as "Paul, an apostle of Christ Jesus by the will of God" (Παῦλος ἀπόστολος Χριστοῦ Ἰησοῦ διὰ θελήματος θεοῦ) (2 Cor 1:1; cf. 12:12). Indeed, in his defense of his apostolic authority, his primary concern is not ultimately his authority but rather to safeguard the message and the true Gospel that he had delivered to the Corinthians. Paul proved his responsibility and capacity to carry the Gospel because God had chosen him and given him the capacity to be a minister of the New Covenant (2 Cor 3:5–6). Moreover, Paul proposes a financial collection to support the church in Jerusalem (2 Cor 8:1–15). To maintain the unity of all believers, Christians in Corinth should demonstrate their love for one another through their financial support (2 Cor 9:1–15). Such cooperation goes beyond easing the financial burden and challenges the Christians in Jerusalem faced; it also validates the strong bond of unity each part of the body has in Christ Jesus beyond cultural and social boundaries.

Outline

Second Corinthians has various sections, themes, and divisions. However, the following structure is a general outline of the epistle.

10. Carson and Moo, *An Introduction to the New Testament*, 447–448.

1:1–12 Introduction
2:12–7:16 Paul's principles of action in his ministry
8:1–9:15 Collection for the poor at Jerusalem and recommendation for Christian charity
10:1–13:14 Paul defends his apostleship and closes the epistle with exhortation and conclusion

The Unity of 2 Corinthians

The fragmentary nature of 2 Corinthians fired a hot debate among biblical scholars. For example, texts such as 2 Corinthians 2:13–14 and 7:4–5 are considered broadly as a large fragment inserted in to 2 Corinthians. Further secondary collections of fragments are apparent, when one considers the tone, style, and content shifts between chapters 9 and 10. These variations led some scholars to argue whether 2 Corinthians might be a letter containing combined fragments from different Pauline letters to the church in Corinth, or if the narrative breaks are intentional stylistic choices of the apostle Paul, as a single author, rather than an indication of fragmentary sources.[11]

With due respect to the scholarly debate, I would rather argue for the unity of 2 Corinthians because the apparent disruption and style change of the epistle could be due to the broader context of the rhetorical strategies and the changing nature of Paul's conversation with the church in Corinth over an extended period. A single epistle can address various issues using multiple approaches.

Reading 2 Corinthians from an African Perspective

In the opening verse of 2 Corinthians (2 Cor 1:1–2), Paul reaffirms his apostolic authority with a strong reference to God as the one who called him for the specific ministry, "an apostle of Christ Jesus by means of the will of God." Paul's call was legitimate and divinely ordained leadership associated with God's will to serve and protect the well-being of the community. Paul's affirmation of his apostolic authority in the beginning sets a strong background to the theological and sociocultural discussion in the subsequent chapters. Moreover, the opening verses deeply connect to the African context where leadership authority is connected to one's integrity, and commitment to the position, community, and shared identity plays a significant role. Leadership and authority in African contexts are evaluated and continually affirmed through genuine service, integrity, and the ability to take risks, standing firm in the shared values and norms within the African context. Paul's description of the source of his apostleship and the defense of his ministry in the face of opposition reflects the challenges of maintaining

11. Harris, *The Second Epistle to the Corinthians*, 50; Randolph Richards, *Paul and First-Century Letter Writing: Secretaries, Composition and Collection* (InterVarsity Press, 2004), 25; Ben Witherington III, *Conflict and Community in Corinth: A Socio-Rhetorical Commentary on 1 and 2 Corinthians* (Eerdmans, 1995), 329; Frederick J. Long, *Ancient Rhetoric and Paul's Apology: The Compositional Unity of 2 Corinthians* (Cambridge University Press, 2004), 230.

integrity and leadership in such tough circumstances. He underlined the need for collective healing and transformation through unity and good leadership when facing social, political, and spiritual struggles.

Consequently, in the following discussion, I will begin to demonstrate how prominent African leaders like Gudina Tumsa and Tsehay Tolosa, as key figures in the Evangelical churches of Ethiopia, effectively utilized their God-given leadership opportunities. Just like Paul, these two people promoted justice and boldly proclaimed the liberating power of the Gospel, even at the risk of their own lives. Then, I will incorporate unique African traditions that help integrate the Gospel and either maintain or reframe the African worldviews in the process of contextualizing the Gospel to African context and practice. During each discussion, I include passages from 2 Corinthians to support the argument instead of offering the typical verse-by-verse exegetical descriptions already addressed by many other scholars.

Challenges in Leadership
The Testimony of Gudina Tumsa and Tsehay Tolessa

In 2 Corinthians 4, Paul describes the nature of authentic ministry in the midst of various challenges. He emphasizes sincerity (2 Cor 4:1), acknowledges trials faced in ministry (2 Cor 4:8–9), and highlights the paradoxical strength found in weakness (2 Cor 4:16). Despite hardships, he points to the power of God in salvation (2 Cor 4:7) and encourages focusing on eternal truths—not on what is seen, but on what is unseen. This implies directing attention away from temporary afflictions and toward the eternal glory and promises of God (2 Cor 4:18).

Paul states that Christians inevitably experience suffering for the sake of their belief. He says, "We are afflicted in every way, but not crushed; perplexed, but not driven to despair; persecuted, but not forsaken; struck down, but not destroyed; always carrying in the body the death of Jesus, so that the life of Jesus may also be made visible in our bodies" (2 Cor 4:8–10). He repeatedly describes his persecution and faithfully proves his apostolic authority by sharing in and representing the suffering of Jesus Christ (2 Cor 1:1–8; 6:3–13). He lists out the kinds of suffering he experienced; he was beaten, imprisoned, stoned, shipwrecked, had sleepless nights, went without food, and so on (2 Cor 11:24–29). Despite all hardships, Paul remained faithful to his call and continued preaching the Gospel and encouraging Christians to share in the suffering life of Christ.

The affliction Paul stated is comprehensive, signifying various forms of suffering that Christians may face for the sake of their faith. Despite the afflicting nature of Christians' suffering, the epistle also promises that this same suffering can produce patience and endurance. Paul notes, "And not only that, but we also boast in our sufferings, knowing that suffering produces endurance, and endurance produces character; and character produces hope" (Rom 5:3–4). Christians not only share in Christ's suffering; they also enjoy the comfort of God that overflows from Christ. He notes, "For just as the sufferings of Christ flow over into our lives, so also through Christ our comfort overflows" (2 Cor 1:5). Despite the severity of the suffering Paul is experiencing, he still thanks God because such experiences will benefit others in comforting them with the comfort Paul himself has experienced. This implies that both vocation and lived experiences are indispensable for effective ministry. Vocation and call provides the foundation for the ministry, while experience develops one's compassion and wisdom, and enhances the ability to serve with authenticity and impact. In other words, a person who has passed through challenges can effectively comfort others, sharing his or her experience of how God has helped him or her overcome the affliction and remain faithful in the midst of suffering. Linda Belleville correctly notes, "His [Paul's] primary concern is to show the Corinthians that their lives are intertwined so that what impacts Paul impacts Corinthians and vice versa. It is for their benefit, he says, that he encounters trouble."[12]

Unlike many popular preachers in Ethiopia today, Paul fulfilled his apostolic mission with authority and humility. Paul depended on the power of the Gospel and God's provision whenever facing challenges and becoming physically and emotionally weak. The Gospel's power is demonstrated in times of weakness, and Paul believes that the weight of suffering in this life will be exchanged for an eternal weight of glory in the next. Thus, Paul's call to the apostolic ministry of the Gospel significantly differs from the prevailing health-and-wealth teachers or the so-called "apostles" in our context today. According to Paul's teaching, the fullness of life, health, and wealth do not mean the absence of suffering. Instead, God gives his children endurance and comfort in the midst of their infirmity. It is their "thorn in the flesh," allowed in their lives to produce humility so that they may depend on God's power for help. Paul notes, "In order to keep me from becoming conceited, I was given a thorn in my flesh, a messenger of Satan, to torment me" (2 Cor 12:7). The health-and-wealth movement proponents preach that Christians suffer due to a lack of genuine faith, and they believe that a Christian with firm faith remains resistant to sicknesses and suffering. They try to hide their personal afflictions and claim that they are doing well as a sign of a higher standard of spirituality. However, this teaching of Paul invalidates a blind denial of any form of suffering in the life of Christians.

God provides strength for those who trust in him in times of difficulty. Paul's concept of trusting God in times of suffering and various hardships to find true comfort in faith reminds us of the life and testimony of the late Rev. Gudina Tumsa in Ethiopia. Rev. Gudina and his wife Tsehay Tolessa's lives and testimonies can serve as modern-day examples of steadfast faith and commitment to the Gospel in the midst of persecution. Rev. Gudina (Ethiopian naming style prefers to go by first name with titles than a family surname) is a prominent figure in the history of evangelical churches in Ethiopia, particularly in the Ethiopian Evangelical Church Mekane Yesus. Some call him "the Bonhoeffer of Africa,"[13] and he is well respected

12. Linda L. Belleville, *2 Corinthians* (InterVarsity Press, 1996), 56.

13. Paul Wee, "Dietrich Bonhoeffer and Gudina Tumsa: Shaping the Church's Response to the Challenges of Our Day," in *Church and Society: Lectures and Responses*, ed. The Gudina Tumsa Foundation (WDL-Publishers 2010), 15–51; see also Abeneazer Gezahegn Urga, "'The Bonhoeffer of Africa': Rev. Gudina Tumsa's Life, Theological Emphases and Contributions to the Ethiopian Church," paper presented at the southeast regional Evangelical Missiological Society meeting at Columbia International University, Columbia, South Carolina, March 18, 2017.

and remembered for his faithfulness to the point of martyrdom for the sake of the Gospel, promoting justice and upholding human dignity, and bravely becoming a voice for the voiceless.

Rev. Gudina Tumsa was born in Boji in 1929. His parents were members of an Ethiopian Orthodox Tewahido Church. His parents did not want to send him to school; rather they wanted him to serve his parents in tending sheep and farming. Nevertheless, Gudina had a great passion for education and insisted on pursuing education. Against their will, his parents sent Gudina to a local primary school owned and run by Lutheran Christians.[14] While studying at the primary school, the gospel was introduced to him, and he decided to follow Jesus. He realized that Jesus is more powerful than the traditional evil spirits. From that time on he began to refuse to participate in the sacrifices offered to spirits and worship practices performed under a tree in his village.

Following his conversion, Gudina began living out the gospel and immediately took the bold step of cutting down the traditional sacred tree, under which the villagers and his parents used to sacrifice to and worship spirits.[15] The community in his village, Boji, got angry and stood against Gudina and his parents for his strange act against the existing traditions and customs. According to the villagers, Gudina's act of cutting the sacred tree would bring calamities such as earthquakes, floods, and illness to the villagers. Although he anticipated the devastating reaction of the villagers, including his parents, Gudina had taken bold steps in trusting God's divine delivering power to rescue him from the hands of his opponents. Finally, as the opposition grew, Gudina had to flee from his hometown and live with his uncle in a different city.

The gospel Gudina heard at an early age at primary school began to grow in his life. Finally, Gudina decided to study theology to be a pastor and messenger of the good news. He served as executive general secretary of the Ethiopian Evangelical Church Mekane Yesus (EECMY) for about a decade (1960–1970). Gudina was the first leader of the EECMY who combined both the gospel and social concerns in Ethiopia as integrated aspects of humanity that should not be detached from one another. However, Gudina served as a prominent church leader during a time when social and economic issues were becoming the center of interest. Dr. Estifanos Tesemma correctly identified Rev. Gudina's focus on understanding human nature noting, "Knowing the danger of this socio-economic view of human beings, Rev. Gudina developed an approach to understanding of human nature from an informed theological-anthropological perspective."[16]

Gudina Tumsa had his theological education at Luther Theological Seminary, St. Paul, USA (1963–1966), during the Civil Rights Movement established by Martin Luther King Jr. His theological position and understanding would have been deeply influenced by this US Civil Rights Movement.[17] He would also have been influenced by the racial discrimination

14. Aud Saeveras and Tsehay Tolessa, *The Fiery Furnace: The Life and Witness of Teshay Tolesa, the Wife of Reverend Gudina Tumsa* (Gudian Tumsa Foundation, 2023), 25–26.

15. Saeveras, *The Fiery Furnace*, 25–26.

16. Estifanos Tesemma, "Gudina Tumsa's Approach to Human Rights: A Dialogue Between Anthropology and Christology," *Global South Theological Journal* 2, no. 2 (2023): 11–25, here 11.

17. Urga, "'The Bonhoeffer of Africa."

in America which led him to address such discrimination and injustice through the teaching of the gospel. Gudina returned to Ethiopia with his experiences of racial issues and injustice in America, determined to stand against similar practices in Ethiopia.

During Gudina's time, the Ethiopian government was influenced by the Marxist-Leninist ideology for about seventeen years (1974–1991). This regime heavily suppressed churches, religious institutions, and all other civic organizations that advocated for civil rights, social justice, and human rights. Due to the harsh treatment, which often extended to the assassination of those who challenged the government's authority, none of the religious leaders across denominations confronted the authorities. It was during this time that Gudina became the first critic of the oppressive policies of the Marxist-Leninist military government. He stood against the government's interferance in church affairs, espousing the necessity of separation of church and state. He strongly resisted cooperating with the government in the request to align with the its Marxist oppressive ideology that denied the existence of God. According to him, human beings are not just material beings; rather, they are holistic and personal beings, and the church should be a voice for the voiceless and promote justice and human dignity since humans are created after God's image and likeness.

Gudina's deep commitment to justice and the set principles for his ministry put him in sharp conflict with the communist regime in Ethiopia. He consistently experienced harassment, arrests, and physical and verbal abuse that put his life in danger. On July 28, 1979, Gudina was kidnapped by the government's security forces and was killed. Like apostle Paul, who had endured multiple persecutions and sufferings for the sake of the gospel (2 Cor 11:23–28), Gudina also endured numerous persecutions, imprisonments, and torture for promoting human dignity and advocating for human rights. As Paul exhorts believers to live a godly life and yet expect persecution from this world, Gudina exemplified this truth when he remained steadfast in his faith despite the grave dangers posed by the communist regime in Ethiopia.

Thus, Gudina's theological message and life testimony are a living reality that communicates a profound message to African leaders. The message of the gospel of Christ is not just spiritual; rather, it addresses the holistic aspect of human life. African leaders should follow in the footsteps of Gudina in speaking the truth of the gospel regarding human rights and advocating for human dignity. His sacrificial death remains an existing fact that helps young leaders in Ethiopia count the cost of discipleship.

After the martyrdom of her husband, Mrs. Tsehay Tolessa was left to look after their six children alone, while living under consistent scrutiny and intimidation by the communist government in Ethiopia. Since the government recognized the enduring influence of her husband and the perceived threat of his legacy in Ethiopian Evangelical church history, the government authorities targeted Tsehay in an attempt to silence her. However, Tsehay continued witnessing about Gudina's legacy, advocating his values and principles. Although Tsehay was persistently forced to renounce her husband's legacy publicly, she boldly refused and instead treasured the values and principles for which her husband had lived and died. She was arrested several times and also imprisoned for ten years because of her strong resistance to injustice (1979–1989).

Despite these trials, and even because of them, Tsehay was strengthened to continue living out the gospel and the principles her husband had maintained. Tsehay became a symbol of resilience, inspiring her family and Christian women and men in Ethiopia with her ability to stand firm in faith and endure suffering while remaining faithful to Christian values and teachings. This reminds us of Paul's message to the Corinthians, "We are afflicted in every way, but not crushed; perplexed, but not driven to despair; persecuted, but not forsaken; struck down, but not destroyed; always carrying in the body the death of Jesus, so that the life of Jesus may also be made visible in our bodies" (2 Cor 4:8–10). Her life is a witness to this divine truth, reminding us of the transformative power of faith in the face of Christian suffering and persecution.

Both Gudina and Tsehay are treasured in the history of Ethiopian Christianity and remembered for their unwavering faith and commitment to the gospel. Even though they experienced strong persecution and suffered violently, they endured trials for the sake of their beliefs and the one who called them to the ministry of the gospel. The current generation in Africa can learn much from their experience and be motivated to carry out the mission task of the church in making disciples of all nations, standing firm in their Christian faith even in times of political, economic, and social challenges.

Likewise, apostle Paul's writings in 2 Corinthians provide insights into the challenge of leadership, especially in the context of suffering and perseverance. He consistently emphasizes the challenging nature of leadership, where trials and opposition are inevitable (2 Cor 4:8–10). However, despite these challenges Paul relied on God's strength as the source of his ability to endure hardship while remaining steadfast in faith. More importantly, Paul highlights that God provides comfort in times of trouble, not only for the benefit of leaders, but so that they can also extend that comfort to others. Paul said, "Blessed be the God and Father of our Lord Jesus Christ, the Father of mercies and the God of all consolation, who consoles us in all our affliction, so that we may be able to console those who are in any affliction with the consolation with which we ourselves are consoled by God." (2 Cor 1:3–5). For Paul, leadership is not just about guiding others but also about bearing the burden of their struggles and offering support in times of difficulty. Such endurance and perseverance will also lead to the ultimate reward, which overshadows temporary trials (2 Cor 4:16–18). Paul's testimony affirms that while leadership may be filled with misfortune, it also carries the potential for spiritual development and eternal consequence.

Forgiveness and Reconciliation in the African Context

Paul's message of forgiveness and reconciliation is the central theme of the message of the Gospel. In 2 Corinthians 5:18–21, Paul says, "All this is from God, who reconciled us to himself through Christ, and has given us the ministry of reconciliation; that is, in Christ God was reconciling the world to himself, not counting their trespasses against them, and entrusting the message of reconciliation to us. So we are ambassadors for Christ, since God is making his appeal through us; we entreat you on behalf of Christ, be reconciled to God. For our sake he made him to be sin who knew no sin, so that in him we might become the righteousness of God." After God reconciled himself to the world, he also called Christians to this ministry of reconciliation. The complete aspect of biblical reconciliation is vertical reconciliation, God reconciling with human beings in Christ Jesus, and horizontal reconciliation, a reconciliation human beings need to maintain with other fellow creatures.

In the Ethiopian context, the experience of forgiveness and reconciliation goes beyond mere theological concepts because they are particularly critical for practical living. In other words, the history of the country reveals ethnic diversity, political instability, and also religious hostility. To such a country, like Ethiopia, Paul's message of forgiveness and reconciliation is a lived reality. Religious institutions possess significant potential to drive societal change. However, the prophetic engagement of the church and church leaders in advocating for justice, equality, reconciliation, and peace has frequently been insufficient.

African churches should embody their role as ambassadors of Christ, delivering the message of peace and reconciliation to their communityies. Due to the current political unrest in Ethiopia, the Ethiopian government has invited various stakeholders, and religious and civil societies to foster national reconciliation and lead peace initiatives. The churches' engagement in peace-building and reconciliation processes should be intentional, and the Christian community in Ethiopia has to take the initiative to combat discrimination.

Currently, the Ethiopian government facilitates a platform for national dialogue, peace, and reconciliation. The current government contrasts with the time of the communist government that led to persecution during Gudina Tumsa's era, when Christians faced widespread cruelty. The active government-led persecution has now significantly diminished, though localized instances of religious persecution continue to occur in some areas. Thus, Ethiopian evangelical churches should use the privilege of religious freedom and actively engage in helping the government find the root cause of the conflicts.

Most of the time, reconciliation takes place without addressing the root cause of the problem, and then the same conflict continues. National reconciliation requires a deep study and research on the current ethnic tensions, which might have been intensified by the ethnic-based federalism in the country. Getachew Gelebo Guyo has convincingly argued that "the ethnocentric mindset resulting from the ethnic-based federalism in Ethiopia has challenged the unity in the body of Christ and become the basis for the brutal conflicts in the Gumaide area. Christians are unable to live the life of the community of saints and be active in the ministry of reconciliation."[18] In this context, forgiveness cannot be superficial or imposed; it must involve a process of truth-telling, justice, accountability, and compensation to the victims.

18. Getachew Gelebo Guyo, "The Effect of Ethnic Federalism on the Ministry of the Church and Unity of Christians in South Ethiopia: The Case of EECMY Gumaide Parish" (MTh thesis, Mekane Yesus Seminary, Addis Ababa, May 2023).

The evangelical church leaders in Ethiopia must preach the true message of forgiveness. God has called the church for the ministry of reconciliation, making all parties responsible for their mistakes and enforcing compensation to the victims. In particular, those who are vulnerable must feel secure and protected regardless of their ethnicities and political orientations. African leaders and churches should act across theological and political boundaries to promote genuine reconciliation and bring peace and security to their society. Even though most African countries have communal life orientations and various social traditions, they still experience violence, corruption, and injustice. Thus, Africans should emphasize and promote their positive social customs and conflict resolution traditions alongside their political constitutions. It is essential to integrate these cultural frameworks with efforts addressing the historical and political causes of divisions, conflicts, and ethnic and religious extremism. African leaders should understand and promote peace, development, and unity as the foundation for justice and truth.

The social custom known as *Shimagele* is an excellent example of a cultural peace-building tradition, fostering reconciliation between conflicting individuals, families, tribes, and communities in Ethiopia. A mediation process is led by senior and influential individuals respected within the country. Due to the high reputations and reservations of the *Shimagelewoch* to publicly associate with any political or ethnic groups, it is often effective in reconciling families, groups, and societies in conflict.

In Ethiopian culture, *Shimagelewoch* are respected because of their rich experience and wisdom, especially in mediating between groups and individuals in conflict. They facilitate an environment that is convenient to both conflicting parties, giving the same time and respect for all to present their complaint. According to this tradition, after the parties in conflict and the elected leaders have an open discussion and the peace settlement is done, the whole community in that village celebrates the occasion with the slaughtering of an animal. The shed blood is considered a sign of covenant renewal, and all the attendees, including their families, eat together by feeding (*gursha*) one another as a symbol of forgiveness and reestablishment of strong friendship. Such an experience echoes Christ's sacrificial death to reconcile the Creator with his creation so that the broken covenant relationship might be renewed.

The *Gaddaa* System, a traditional democratic system, is another significant cultural conflict resolution and peace-building structure that has been functional in Ethiopia for centuries. This tradition is the social, political, economic, and cultural governance framework of the Oromo community. As a unique and indigenous independent association, it regulates political, social, cultural, and ceremonial activities. The system is unique because it is formed based on a seniority or age-grade system in which leadership and responsibilities are rotated every eight years among different age sets, known as *Gaddaa* classes. The rotation of leadership ensures a balance of power and representation of the same ethnic group, whose members come from various regions within the county. The fair cycle of power precludes any single group from dominating governance so as to dominate the minority. The leaders of the *Gaddaa* System are called *Abbaa Gaddaa*, translated as "fathers of *Gaddaa*."

These elders are elected for a certain period and make vows in front of the community to keep all the rules and laws during their leadership. The *Gaddaa* has a significant role in making decisions, writing constitutions, and preparing bylaws alongside other community leaders. They are elected by vote to serve a maximum of two terms, highlighting the democratic principle of the system. One of the significant factors of the system is its emphasis on conflict resolution efforts to maintain peace and solidarity within the community. The *Gaddaa* system also uplifts the value of telling the truth, mutual respect, and open dialogue between conflicting groups and families. Within the system, there are laws known as *Aadaa* and *Seera* that fairly uphold human dignity, offer protection for women and children, and promote communal harmony. It also gives guidelines to manage economic resources and social orders, dealing with ethnic conflicts.

African governments could learn from the *Gaddaa* system and adopt it into their constitutions. Even if this system is currently only functional for the Oromo community in Ethiopia, I strongly suggest that other ethnic groups and communities adopt and contextualize their basic principles of conflict resolution and peacemaking resolution. Integrating this tradition into the contemporary federal government in Ethiopia and beyond will connect native wisdom to minimize ethnic tensions and build a healthy and productive community.

Paul's exhortation in 2 Corinthians 6:1–2, where he urges believers not to receive God's grace in vain but to act now—"Behold, now is the favorable time; behold, now is the day of salvation"—resonates with the urgency of the current Ethiopian situation. Church leaders are called to step into this moment with courage and prophetic clarity. To efficiently encourage forgiveness, reconciliation, and peace in Ethiopia, both community-based approaches and institutional efforts within and outside of the church must work together. This approach will create a good platform to bridge traditional practices with theological and social imperatives that address the deeper roots of conflict and division. The desire for national reconciliation in Ethiopia cannot be effective unless the leading religious leaders actively and intentionally become part of the process. Religious institutions in Ethiopia are not isolated institutions that remain unaffected by the conflict. Thus, religious leaders should take a significant role in helping the government achieve national dialogue and reconciliation. This divine model of reconciliation calls for a justice that is restorative rather than retributive, aiming to rebuild broken relationships and create a more just and equitable society.

Rethinking Paul's Call for Separation in the Ethiopian Context

Paul advises the Corinthians to distance themselves from worldly associations, which could harm their close relationship with God, Paul, and their involvement in his ministry (2 Cor 6:14–7:1). The Corinthians were misled by Paul's opponents, who preached a different gospel than what Paul had taught them. In 2 Corinthians 2:17, Paul contrasts himself with those who misused God's word for personal gain, thus requesting the Corinthians not to follow and trust such false apostles. Then, in 2 Corinthians 4:2, he indirectly warns against those who distort God's Word and commands. In all these verses and the current section, in 2

Corinthians 6:14–7:1, Paul sets the stage for the strong and explicit critique against false apostles in 2 Corinthians 11:13–15, saying, "For such men are false apostles, deceitful workmen, disguising themselves as apostles of Christ. And no wonder even Satan disguises himself as an angel of light. So, it is not strange if his servants also disguise themselves as servants of righteousness. Their end will correspond to their deeds." These texts reflect his ongoing concern for the Corinthians to remain grounded in the true gospel of Christ and reject those who might lead the Corinthians astray.

Additionally, in 2 Corinthians 6:14–7:1, Paul uses the temple imagery in his argument to encourage them to dissociate from worldly affairs. Barnett argues that Paul's restriction to distance or dissociate themselves is a prohibition of participation in the temple cult.[19] Paul told the Corinthians that they are the temple of the Holy Spirit (2 Cor 6:16). The temple of God and idols have nothing in common, and the Corinthians are strongly rebuked and instructed not to associate with pagan table fellowship or participate in their communal worship setting (2 Cor 6:17–18). In the new dispensation, Christians are holy and sanctified by the Holy Spirit individually and collectively. They are called not to associate with such idolatrous worship and table fellowship in the context of eating food sacrificed to idols. Therefore, Paul employs this comparison with idols to instruct the Corinthians about upholding holiness as God's people and as a temple of God, in which the Holy Spirit dwells permanently.[20]

About the current text, I would like to mention one social practice in Ethiopia known as *Iddir* that many evangelical Christians avoid partaking in, applying this text of Paul in 2 Corinthians 6:14–7:1. Some evangelical Christians in Ethiopia use this text to condemn and dissociate themselves from an essential social association. *Iddir* is an association that connects and strengthens the social life of the people in Ethiopia.[21] People from different ethnic and religious backgrounds become part of the association to help each other when one's loved one dies. It is a form of social support system where members of the community come together to collectively provide financial assistance, food, and other forms of support to help cover the expenses associated with funerals and provide assistance for the bereaved family. *Iddir* is typically formed within neighborhoods, villages, or communities, and membership is open to individuals who contribute regular dues to the association. The gathering provides essential support of various kinds, especially during times of mourning. The community gathers to spend time with the bereaved and offers financial contributions, food, and other forms of assistance to grieving families. The members are expected to spend a minimum of one week with the mourning family to help them be comforted and feel loved.

---

19. Barnett, *The Second Epistle to the Corinthians*, 341.

20. Barnett, *The Second Epistle to the Corinthians*, 337–358; see also Coulibaly Issiaka, "2 Corinthians," in *African Bible Commentary: A One-Volume Commentary Written by 70 African Scholars*, ed. Tokunboh Adeyemo (WordAlive Publishers; Zondervan, 2006), 1431.

21. Dejene Aredo, "Informal and Semi-Formal Financial Sectors in Ethiopia: A Study of the Iqqub, Iddir, and Savings and Credit Co-Operatives," Centre for the Study of African Economies (University of Oxford, 1993), 1–68.

Although this communal solidarity is distinct from moral impurity, some Christians in Ethiopia argue that Paul's command to "be separate" from non-Christians should extend to every association, including participation in *Iddir*. However, a careful study of the holiness concept in Paul does not command social segregation. Paul's primary criticism of the Corinthians should not be interpreted and applied to every social association, especially those associations that strengthen African communal living that do not contradict the basic principles of Christian ethics. On the contrary, such social gatherings are a good opportunity for Christians to present the gospel through active love and care for the desperate. It allows Christians to address fundamental human needs and promote justice, unity, love, and compassion. It also enables congregations to foster goodness and resist injustice, violence, oppression, and immoral practices that may threaten the community's well-being.

Paul's primary concern is that the Corinthians should dissociate themselves from false apostles who came up with human wisdom and led many Christians astray to live immorally. Moreover, Paul rebuked the Corinthians for associating with idol worship, sexual immorality, and table fellowship in the context of idol worship. Such association directly hurts their relationship ultimately with God and their relationship with Paul. He reminds them that their body belongs to the Lord and they are the temple of the Holy Spirit and are expected to live a life worthy of their calling and the gospel. However, the correct understanding of Paul's message in the text does not prohibit Ethiopian social gatherings in *Iddir*.

The Concept of Holiness

Paul's Epistles emphasize the doctrine of holiness as a crucial factor when dealing with human beings' relationship with God and their relationships with one another and other creatures. Paul addresses such themes of holiness by advising Christians in Corinth to remain unconnected with anyone or anything that contradicts the message of the gospel (2 Cor 6:14–7:1). Paul calls believers to avoid being "yoked" with unbelievers, highlighting the incompatibility between righteousness and wickedness, light and darkness, Christ and Belial. He further uses the temple imagery to emphasize the need to keep the body holy as a dwelling place of God and his Spirit.

When we speak of holiness, one must differentiate the holiness God has granted believers through Christ Jesus and the holiness each Christian is instructed to pursue. Tibebu T. Senbetu categorized the biblical concept of holiness as *divine* and *human* holiness, noting, "Whenever Paul mentions holiness in his epistles, he refers to either the divine holiness that has been fully manifested to humankind through Christ or the holiness that has been accomplished in humans."[22] Paul is urging Christians to actively seek holiness in their daily life. They should sanctify their mind, body, and spirit from any kind of defilement. This holiness is functional in their relationship with other human beings and

22. Tibebu Teklu Senbetu, "The Ethiopian Orthodox Tewahedo Church's Interpretation of Ἀναξίως in 1 Cor. 11:27–29 in Relation to Worthy Admission to the Eucharist in Light of Ritual Jewish Purity Laws Embedded in Its Qeddassé and Tradition" (PhD diss., Saint Louis Concordia Seminary, 2022), 188–192.

creatures. Paul says in 2 Corinthians 7:1, "Since we have these promises, beloved, let us cleanse ourselves from every defilement of body and spirit, bringing holiness to completion in the fear of God." Tibebu notes, "Paul encourages believers to pursue a life of holiness, and to reorient themselves in their thoughts and actions by demonstrating and perfecting holiness as they reflect God's moral purity in their life and heart,"[23] whereas the passive holiness, which Tibebu states as the "divine holiness," is the holiness that only God possesses. It is the holiness associated with our salvation through the work of Christ Jesus that becomes ours in faith.

The immediate reason Tibebu distinguishes between human and divine holiness is that believers in Ethiopia most often conflate them, utilizing them interchangeably. This confusion has led many to mistakenly associate human holiness with works-based righteousness, ultimately shaping their understanding of salvation in a way that is both flawed and misinformed. Nevertheless, Paul's appeal for human holiness is bound within the principle of faith alone and grace alone. According to Paul's Epistles, believers have already been justified and made holy, and salvation has already been secured for them. After believers' conversion they have become new creatures and a new humanity has been formed in the resemblance of Christ Jesus. Paul clearly states, "For it is by grace you have been saved, through faith—and this not from yourselves, it is the gift of God—not by works, so that no one can boast" (Eph 2:8–9). He also states how believers in Corinth become God's people, sanctified in Christ Jesus and called to be holy (1 Cor 1:2). Believers spiritually become the temple of God in whose heart the Holy Spirit dwells. God no longer dwells in the handmade building; rather the gathered community who begins to exercise their holiness is the true temple in whom God continually dwells. After Paul mentions that the Christian's body is the temple of God, he goes on in Romans 12:1–2 to exhort them to serve God with whole-body devotion. In 2 Corinthians 6:16–18, Paul also underscores how Christians become the temple of the living God, in whom the Holy Spirit is indwelling. Then, he urges them to live holy lives by separating themselves from impurity and dedicating their entire being to God. Such appeal directly shapes the exhortation in Romans 12:1–2, where Paul urges believers to offer their bodies as a living sacrifice, holy and pleasing to God, as an act of spiritual worship. The imagery of God's temple highlights the sacred responsibility of believers to honor God not only in spirit but also in their bodies tangibly in a way that reflects the holiness of God.

Therefore, believers are already made holy through God's work in Christ Jesus, without condition or exception. Our saving holiness is not something to be achieved via good works, but a reality to be embraced by faith and faith alone. Nevertheless, while this passive holiness is a gift given by God, Christians are still called to live in alignment with the holiness of God. Believers' pursuit of holiness is not merely a human effort but is by God's will for them. While saving holiness is already accomplished through divine action, Christians must continually maintain and stay in this state of holiness through self-examination, repentance, and a life shaped by the truth of the gospel.

23. Senbetu, "Ἀναξίως in 1 Cor. 11:27–29," 189.

Christian Charity

The commonly held African culture that upholds the spirit of unity, collective identity, and strong collaboration to achieve shared values, norms, and goals resonates with Paul's command for partnership between Christians in Corinth and Jerusalem as members of God's family. The principle of Christian giving makes it apparent that grasping the underlying concepts of reciprocity, community, and human flourishing requires a thorough understanding of the ancient Greco-Roman friendship motives.

In ancient Rome, if people were rich and powerful, it was seen as proof that they were good people and deserved their position. This belief came from Greek philosophy, which said that being good (ἀγαθός) came from having certain qualities like virtue (ἀρετή).[24] Since wealthy people could do good things with their money, they were considered virtuous.[25] This meant that people with high status were seen as deserving of their power and wealth, while those with low status were also thought to deserve their place in society. Everyone was expected to act a certain way toward others based on their status.

In the Greco-Roman world, friendships were mostly between equals, but later it became acceptable for someone of higher status to be friends with someone of lower status in a form of giving charity.[26] This led to a mix of friendship and patronage, where one person might help the other and give charity because they were friends, not only because they had power over them. John Chow analyzed the social structures of patronage in ancient Corinth and their influence on the early Christian community, and notes, "The social structure of patronage was fundamental in organizing social relationships in Corinth, influencing not only economic and political spheres but also religious life." He explores the dynamics of patron–client relationships, but he does not focus on the writings or philosophies of Cicero and Seneca; instead, his primary focus is to show how these ancient social networks impacted the Corinthian church.[27] Even though some thinkers like Cicero and Seneca still believed that true friendship should be between equals, they were worried that friendship was losing its moral value.[28] They thought real friendship should be about supporting the community and living a virtuous life, not just

24. Andrew D. Clarke, *Secular and Christian Leadership in Corinth: A Socio-Historical and Exegetical Study of 1 Corinthians 1–6*, AGJU 18 (Brill, 1993), 23–24; Steven S. H. Chang, "Fund-Raising in Corinth: A Socio-Economic Study of the Corinthian Church, the Collection and 2 Corinthians" (PhD diss., University of Aberdeen, 2000); and see Anthony Edward Carreras, "Aristotle's Ideals of Friendship and Virtue" (PhD diss., Rice University, 2011), 172–211; see also Julia Annas, "Virtue and Eudaimonism," in *Virtue and Vice*, ed. Ellen Frankel Paul, Fred D. Miller Jr., and Jeffrey Paul (Social Philosophy and Policy Foundation, 1998), 37–55.

25. Ruth Whiteford, "Friendship and Gift in 2 Corinthians 8–9: Social Relations and Conventions in the Jerusalem Collection" (PhD diss., Concordia Seminary, 2018), 25–26.

26. Bruce W. Winter, *After Paul Left Corinth: The Influence of Secular Ethics and Social Change* (Zondervan, 2001), 184–206.

27. John K. Chow, *Patronage and Power: A Study of Social Networks in Corinth*, JSNTSup 75 (JSOT Press, 1992), 33–34.

28. Whiteford, "Friendship and Gift in 2 Corinthians 8–9," 62–72; Cicero, *Cicero*, trans. D. R. Shackleton Bailey, 32 vols., LCL (Harvard University Press, 1913–2010), 1.5; 6:21–22; 22.84; 23; and see also Seneca, *Epistles*, trans. Richard M. Gummere, 3 vols., LCL (Harvard University Press, 1917–1925), 6.3.

personal gain. Despite their concerns, they knew that people did not always live up to these ideals, and they talked about how people behaved wrongly in their friendships. Christians should be a light in the world and be there for those who are struggling

Paul's theology of charity begins from the selfless giving character exhibited in the Macedonian churches. Before Paul dives into his message, he focuses on the role of the grace of God granted to the church of Macedonia that enabled them to give cheerfully beyond their ability (2 Cor 8:1). Paul intentionally talks about God's χάρις (grace) and how this grace influencesd the Macedonians.[29] He believes that because of God's grace, the Corinthians will also experience reconciliation. The grace of God given to the Macedonians had a great impact on their willingness to support and share in the suffering of other parts of the body of Christ, which is the church. Paul says, "For during a severe ordeal of affliction, their abundant joy and their extreme poverty have overflowed in a wealth of generosity on their part" (2 Cor 8:2). Grace is central in relationships, and since the Corinthians have received God's grace, they should also be generous in giving to the collection. This χάρις becomes a major theme in chapters 8 and 9. Paul is proud of the Corinthians and wants them to feel affirmed because they listen to his leadership. Paul could have used other words like "gift," but "grace" means more to him as it is not just about receiving gifts; it is about the whole cycle of giving, receiving, being thankful, and showing gratitude. God's χάρις gives the Macedonians the power to give to others.

Paul applauds the believers in the Macedonian churches for their sacrificial giving, regardless of their poverty. He witnessed their generosity, saying that "For, as I can testify, they voluntarily gave according to their means, and even beyond their means" (2 Cor 8:3). The Macedonian church's sacrificial giving reflects the African ethos of prioritizing the community's needs over personal gain. The South African saying, "I exist because you exist," expresses the concept in African communal living that strengthens interconnectedness and underscores the need for unity regardless of diversity. The philosophy of Ubuntu is often expressed through the proverb *Umuntu ngumuntu ngabantu* ("I am because we are"), or it could mean a person is a person through other persons.[30] John Mbiti notes, "The individual can only say: 'I am, because we are; and since we are, therefore I am.' This is a cardinal point in the understanding of the African view of man."[31] It is a philosophical and ethical principle deeply rooted in many African cultures, particularly in southern Africa, including countries like Zimbabwe and Zambia, to mention a few. According to Ubuntu philosophy, each individual is seen as an integral part of a larger community. In other words, their wholeness is defined by the security and comprehensiveness of existing among others. Therefore, one's activities and choices should consider the effect on the whole community. The principles of Ubuntu also direct and determine interpersonal associations, governance, and social values. The philosophy of Ubuntu is naturally manifested in human beings caring for others, showing sympathy, and significantly showing mercy and forgiving each other. It promotes human dignity and mutual respect

29. Whiteford, "Friendship and Gift in 2 Corinthians 8–9," 90–102.

30. John S. Mbiti, *African Religion and Philosophy* (Anchor Books, 1970), 141.

31. Mbiti, *African Religion and Philosophy*, 141.

in the communal journey to build a community that pursues justice. In cases of conflict, Ubuntu pursues forgiveness and reconciliation rather than immediately imposing any form of punishment. It incorporates not just people's communal interaction with one another; it also integrates human beings' acceptable and protective interaction with the entire environment. Ubuntu emphasizes a peaceful coexistence and promotes harmony with the environment through human stewardship.

Therefore, the Ubuntu concept, rooted in African society and culture, underscores friendly coexistence, including respect for the environment through human stewardship. Scholars like John Mbiti have underlined the interconnectedness and the shared responsibility for each other's well-being. Such understanding aligns with the Christian concept of charity described in 2 Corinthians. Charity is not only an act of kindness but also promotes the well-being of others within the community. Just as Ubuntu teaches that one's humanity is intertwined with the well-being of others, charity in 2 Corinthians underscores the importance of mutual care, solidarity, and support for one another. It also fosters a harmonious and compassionate community. Both perspectives highlight the significance of shared commitment and harmony as foundational components for a thriving society.

Conclusion

Second Corinthians demonstrates a sound theology of reconciliation and servanthood leadership, which echoes deeply with the African ethos of collective commitment to peace-building. Paul repeatedly emphasizes his willingness to bear adversity, resistance, and persecution for the sake of the gospel (2 Cor 6:4–10; 11:23–28). Such sacrificial leadership calls us to recognize African figures such as Rev. Gudina Tumsa and his wife, Tsehay Tolessa, who demonstrated Christ-like servanthood by offering their lives for the gospel. Their continuing legacies remind African leaders that leadership is not a pursuit for personal benefit but a sacred calling to serve others faithfully, promote justice, and champion equality, outwitting ethnic and socioeconomic barriers.

We have also seen how apostle Paul's ministry of reconciliation, in 2 Corinthians 5:18–20, delivers a sound theological framework for dealing with the ethnic factions and conflicts familiar to the history of Ethiopia. Paul calls for Christians to act as ambassadors of reconciliation in the contemporary African context, exhorting Christian leaders to take a visionary role in advocating for national peace, unity, and solidarity. For instance, the current Ethiopian government's podium for national conversation provides an occasional and essential opportunity for the evangelical church to participate and lead in these efforts. By incorporating the gospel's message of forgiveness and reconciliation, Ethiopian church leaders can model a counternarrative to the recurring factions and animosity.

Moreover, Paul's focus on restorative justice and community-building efforts resonates with the Ethiopian traditions of *Shimegelena* and the *Gadaa* system. These two Indigenous traditions of reconciliation and administration align with Paul's theology of the church as a unified body of Christ where the well-being of one part of the body impacts the whole body of

Christ, which is the church (2 Cor 8:13–15). The African practice of mutual and communal support, demonstrated in local systems such as *Iddir*, resonates with the Macedonian churches' charitable acts for the Jerusalem church (2 Cor 8:1–5). Such connections indicate the biblical principle of community and the African spirit of belonging to each other by recongnizing that one's identity is bound up in the well-being of others.

Finally, Paul's call for holiness uses temple metaphors to reinforce holiness and detachment from worldly practices (2 Cor 6:16–18). This is a clear challenge to Christian Africans and leaders, because a call to holiness is not merely private purity but a loyalty to the embodiment of God's justice and righteousness in our private and public lives. The teaching of Second Corinthian's not only aligns with Africa's long-standing practices of peace-building and collective cautiousness and care but also challenges the church to exceed its boundaries and embody the transformative power of the gospel. Thus, Paul encourages African leaders and Christians to become agents of peace and justice, promoting unity in diversity and proclaiming the hope of the gospel to a divided and hurting world.

Further Reading

Adewuya, J. Ayodeji. *Holiness and Community in 2 Cor 6:14–7:1: Paul's View of Communal Holiness in the Corinthian Correspondence*. StBL 40. Peter Lang, 2005.

Adewuya, J. Ayodeji. "The People of God in a Pluralistic Society: Holiness in 2 Corinthians." In *Holiness and Ecclesiology in the New Testament*, edited by Kent E. Brower and Andy Johnson. Eerdmans, 2007.

Barnett, Paul. *The Second Epistle to the Corinthians*. NICNT. Eerdmans, 1997.

Barrett, C. K. *The Second Epistle to the Corinthians*. Reprint. BNTC. Hendrickson, 1993.

Belleville, Linda L. *2 Corinthians*. InterVarsity Press, 1996.

Best, Ernest. *Second Corinthians*. Interpretation. John Knox Press, 1987.

Betz, Hans Dieter. "2 Corinthians 6:14–7:1: An Anti-Pauline Fragment?" *Harvard Theological Review* 66, no. 1 (1973): 88–108.

Betz, Hans Dieter. *2 Corinthians 8 and 9: A Commentary on Two Administrative Letters of the Apostle Paul.* Hermeneia. Fortress Press, 1985.

Carson D. A., and Douglas J. Moo. *An Introduction to the New Testament*. 2nd ed. Zondervan, 2005.

Chang, Steven S. H. "Fund-Raising in Corinth: A Socio-Economic Study of the Corinthian Church, the Collection and 2 Corinthians." PhD diss., University of Aberdeen, 2000.

Chow, John K. *Patronage and Power: A Study of Social Networks in Corinth*. JSNTS up 75. JSOT Press, 1992.

Collins, Raymond F. *Second Corinthian*. Paideia. Baker Academic, 2013.

Coulibaly, Issiaka. "2 Corinthians." In *African Bible Commentary: A One-Volume Commentary Written by 70 African Scholars*, edited by Tokunboh Adeyemo. WordAlive Publishers; Zondervan, 2006.

Garland, David E. *2 Corinthians*. NAC 29. B&H, 1999.

Kruse, Colin. *2 Corinthians*. TNTC. InterVarsity Press, 2007.

Martin, Ralph P. *2 Corinthians*. WBC 40. Word Books, 1986.

Mbiti, John S. *African Religion and Philosophy*. Anchor Books, 1970.

Murphy-O'Connor, Jerome. *St. Paul's Corinth: Texts and Archaeology*. 3rd ed. Liturgical Press, 2002.

Richards, Randolph. *Paul and First-Century Letter Writing: Secretaries, Composition and Collection*. InterVarsity Press, 2004.

Scott, James M. *2 Corinthians*. NIBC. Hendrickson Publishers, 1998.

Seifrid, Mark A. *The Second Letter to the Corinthians*. Eerdmans, 2014.

Senbetu, Tibebu T. "The Ethiopian Orthodox *Tewahedo* Church's Interpretation of Ἀναξίως in 1 Cor. 11:27–29 in Relation to Worthy Admission to the Eucharist in Light of Ritual Jewish Purity Laws Embedded in Its *Qeddassé* and Tradition." PhD diss., Concordia Seminary, Saint Louis, 2022.

Seneca. *Epistles*. Translated by Richard M. Gummere. 3 vols. LCL. Harvard University Press, 1917–1925.

Tesemma, Estifanos. "Gudina Tumsa's Approach to Human Rights: A Dialogue Between Anthropology and Christology." *Global South Theological Journal* 2, no. 2 (2023): 11–25.

Wee, Paul. "Dietrich Bonhoeffer and Gudina Tumsa: Shaping the Church's Response to the Challenges of Our Day." In *Church and Society: Lectures and Responses*, edited by The Gudina Tumsa Foundation. WDL-Publishers, 2010.

Whiteford, Ruth. "Friendship and Gift in 2 Corinthians 8–9: Social Relations and Conventions in the Jerusalem Collection." PhD diss., Concordia Seminary, 2018.

Winter, Bruce W. *After Paul Left Corinth: The Influence of Secular Ethics and Social Change*. Zondervan, 2001.

Witherington, Ben III. *Conflict and Community in Corinth: A Socio-Rhetorical Commentary on 1 and 2 Corinthians*. Eerdmans, 1995.

Scott, James M. *2 Corinthians*. NIBC. Peabody: Hendrickson Publishers, 1998.
Seifrid, Mark A. *The Second Letter to the Corinthians*. PNTC. Grand Rapids: Eerdmans, 2014.
[illegible] "The [illegible]" [illegible]
[illegible] 2012.
[illegible] University Press, 1987.
[illegible] "[illegible]: A Dialogue Between Anthropology and [illegible]," [illegible] no. 2 (2023): [illegible]
[illegible]
[illegible] 2010.
[illegible] Relations and [illegible] to the [illegible] 2016.
[illegible]
[illegible]

CHAPTER ELEVEN

The Letter to the Galatians

Gesila Nneka Uzukwu
Nasarawa State University
Nigeria

Introduction

THE LETTER TO the Galatians remains one of the most controversial, but also key, theological letters written by Paul. Paul's theological exposé in Galatians highlights Paul's rejection and condemnation of the misunderstanding of external signs of religiosity or external characteristics of rituals and practices as the defining power, mission, and purpose of religion. The discourses in Galatians highlight how the some false teachers (that is, a group of early Christian teachers who advocated that for gentiles to be accepted as Christians they would need to adopt Jewish customs and laws, especially circumcision, dietary restrictions, and observance of the Jewish Sabbath and festivals) perceived Christianity as a continuation of Judaism. Galatians is known for its reaction to the demands of these false teachers (called Judaizers), and its outright rejection of false or legalistic claims over Christianity. With its emphasis on the fulfillment of God's promise, Paul's letter to the Galatians domesticates the gospel of Christ as sufficient in fulfilling the function and purpose of the promise God granted to Abraham, revealing the christological continuity between the promise God made to Abraham and its fulfillment in the gentile mission. In light of these theological persuasions, scholars have argued that without the strong words of Galatians, Christianity would not have remapped its boundaries and would have remained a branch of Judaism. In addition, the words of Galatians have further opened Christianity to the gentile world, and its subsequent impact on the constructs and appropriations of liberation hermeneutics.

As with other Pauline letters, Galatians provides us with an interpretative lens to understand Christianity's relations with religio-cultural aspects of other cultures and religions. It is important to note, however, that Galatians does not readily highlight the nature and content of possible cultural or theological points of interaction and contact with the gentile world since Paul's primary concern was on the impact of the influence of the Judaizers. Any reading of Galatians that ignores the contextual character and influence of Paul's engagement with certain aspects of both Jewish and gentile religio-cultural worldviews undoubtedly misses out on the best of Galatians.

Given that Galatians is one of the significant writings of Paul that emphasizes the communal, universalistic, collaborative, and unitarian character of the people of God, this study considers how Paul's ideological constructs about the Law, the Abrahamic promise, Christian baptism, the sense of Christian unity, the place and nature of ethnic, gender, and social diversities, and the manifestations of the Spirit reverberate with the situational aspects of African communities. In the first section, I shall briefly address preliminary questions about the authorship, audience, date, place, structure, and outline of the letter. In the second part of the chapter, I will engage certain specific social and theological claims of Galatians that have distinctively shaped African Christianity, seeking to understand how Paul's letter to the Galatians can be used as a textual and hermeneutical lens through which we can address the African realities, as well as the inherent limitations of Galatians for an African context.

Introductory Matters

Authorship

The authorship of Galatians has never been contested since the letter discloses the writer (Paul claims to have written the letter with his own hands, 6:11). The letter also bears personal information about Paul, including his identity and mission (1:1, 11–12), missionary experiences and struggles (1:13–2:14; 4:13–14), and parting greetings and admonitions typical of Paul's letters (6:18). Theologically, Galatians projects Paul as its author as the text contains distinctive styles and themes associated with Paul's writings, such as the Law, the promise to Abraham, and justification not by works of the Law, but through faith in Jesus Christ.

Recipients

There are two alternative theories for the recipients of Galatians: that Paul is either addressing the group of Christians living in the northern part of the Roman province of Galatia, or the group of Christians living not only in the geographical district of Galatia in the north, but extending to the geographical districts of Lycaonia, Pisidia, and part of Phrygia in the south.[1] Neither of these positions affect the literary interpretation of the text. What is important is that by reading the letter to the Galatians, we can highlight related issues for an African audience.

Occasion and Purpose

Paul's letter to the Galatians, believed to have been written about 54–55 CE but perhaps composed earlier, around 48 CE (that is, if it was written before the Council of Jerusalem in 49 CE), was an occasional letter written in response to a particular theological problem

1. Ernest DeWitt Burton, *A Critical and Exegetical Commentary on the Epistle to the Galatians*, ICC (T&T Clark, 1968), xxi–xxiii; J. Louis Martyn, *Galatians: A New Translation with Introduction and Commentary*, AB 33A (Doubleday, 1998), 282.

that arose in the church of Galatia after the Galatians had been converted through Paul and received the Spirit of Christ (3:1–5). Drawing from Paul's own words, a certain group of teachers/preachers had come to Galatia and preached a gospel different from Paul's (see Gal 1:6–10). The theological issue (especially as described in Gal 3:1–12; 5:2–12) was the demand on the Galatians to adopt certain aspects of the Mosaic Law—especially circumcision and commitment to Israel's Torah—for them (the Galatians) to complete their conversion to the God of Israel. Although scholarship has questioned the identity of the false teachers (that is, Paul's opponents in Galatia)—whether they could be called the "Judaizers," "teachers," "some of Paul's own Gentile converts who veered into heresy," or Paul's own victims at the time of his persecution of Christians—a take-home point here is that Paul was against the message preached by these intruders. In his opinion, their gospel was both false and enslaving.[2] In reaction to the false teaching of the intruders, Paul enjoins the Galatians to live by the Spirit and the works of the fruit of the Spirit (see 5:16–26).

Structure of Galatians

Galatians has at least four identifiable literary divisions: (1) a thematic division that follows the thesis and arguments raised in the letter,[3] (2) a rhetoric division that builds on Paul's methodical approach to Galatians,[4] (3) a literary division that delineates Galatians as a letter,[5] and (4) a division based on the argumentative nature of the text.[6] These several ways of structuring Galatians, scholars argue, demonstrate some of the difficulties in compressing the different individual elements of Galatians into a larger unit of thought. While this observation may seem problematic for a reader, it delineates the universal and multidimensional nature of the letter to the Galatians as it opens it to wider explorations and conversations with varied realities about Christian formation, gospel, and mission.

It is in keeping with these pluralities of understanding that we can thematically structure Galatians to assert and appropriate the representations of religious values, teachings, beliefs, and practices found in both Christian and African religious traditions. For a critical reflection of Galatians for an African audience, the literary division proposed is structured to provide starting points for thematic reflection on the meaning and place of Galatians in African Christianity.

2. Richard B. Cook, "Paul and the Victims of His Persecution: The Opponents in Galatia," *Biblical Theology Bulletin* 32 (2002): 182.

3. See for instance, Martyn, *Galatians*, 24.

4. Hans Dieter Betz, "The Literary Composition and Function of Paul's Letter to the Galatians," *New Testament Studies* 21 (1975): 353. This article is also incorporated in his Hans Dieter Betz, *Galatians: A Commentary on Paul's Letter to the Churches in Galatia*, Hermeneia (Fortress Press, 1984), 16–23. See also D. F. Tolmie, "The Rhetorical Analysis of the Letter to the Galatians: 1995–2005," *Acta Theologica Supplementum* 9 (2007): 1–28; Walter G. Hansen, *Abraham in Galatians: Epistolary and Rhetorical Contexts*, JSNTSS 29 (Sheffield Academic Press, 1989), 59–60.

5. D. Mitternacht, "A Structure of Persuasion in Galatians: Epistolary and Rhetorical Appeal in an Aural Setting," *Acta Theologica Supplementum* 9 (2007): 64–75.

6. Mika Hietanen, *Paul's Argumentation in Galatians: A Pragma-Dialectical Analysis*, LNTS 344, ed. Mark Goodacre (T&T Clark, 2007), 175–179.

Salutation (1:1–5)
Body of the letter (1:6–6:10)
    There is no other gospel than the gospel of Christ (1:6–2:21)
    Living in the promise of the Spirit (3:1–29)
    Becoming children of God (4:1–20)
    The allegory of Hagar and Sarah (4:21–31)
    Set free to live by the Spirit (5:1–6:10)
Signature line and summing-up of arguments (6:11–18)

Key Themes of Galatians for an African Audience

In order to understand how Paul's defense in Galatians can speak ideologically and religiously to an African audience, one must look at how the letter can provide suggestions and points of interactions regarding questions about African Christianity, identity, and the notion of belongingness. It is an attempt to understand the place of Christian theology in African society vis-à-vis the place of African traditions in African Christianity. Since the coming of Western Christianity to Africa, Africans have lived and continue to live in a world of competing ideologies between Christianity and African spirituality.

Beginning from the early periods of Christianity's presence in Africa, Africans have struggled to understand and be at home with Christian teachings, especially with Christian theologies that are at variance with African cosmology and worldviews. Various methods that were used to explain Christianity to most traditional African societies reflected the colonial mindset. They were condemnatory of African Traditional Religions and worldviews at best, and destructive of the culture at worst. Some of the early transmitters of the Christian faith refused to seriously engage African traditions at the level of African cosmologies, epistemologies, and philosophy. This way of projecting and transferring the Christian faith did not have a deep impact on the religio-cultural world of traditional Africans and African life. In the wake of new missionary approaches and biblical methods of interpretation, a major shift has characterized the reception of Christian missions and practices in Africa. Scholars have sought new ways to appropriate Christianity with African cosmology. Despite the newer scholarship, there are still aspects of Christian theology that are yet to be fully understood and integrated into certain elements of African perspectives.

As Michael Matthew notes, after almost two centuries of Christianity's presence on the African soil, the Christian faith still struggles to entrench itself into African concerns and realities or to create new values that would replace the pre-Christian values of African Traditional society.[7] An African reading of Paul's letter to the Galatians is an invitation to critically analyze the letter in a shared perspective, investigating how the letter's representations of Christian theology can interact, engage, and dialogue with African traditions, religions, beliefs, and practices. Speaking of the Catholic Church and its approach to the Christian

7. Matthew Michael, *Christian Theology and African Traditions* (Wipf & Stock, 2013), 8.

mission, Teresa Okure comments that "it is impossible to plant the gospel firmly in any culture at any age without this process of inculturation, understood as 'the intimate transformation of authentic cultural values through their integration in Christianity and the insertion of Christianity in the various human cultures.'"[8]

In light of the above observations, my rereading of Galatians is an attempt to engage Paul's theologies that shaped the basic tenets of the Christian faith. This chapter seeks to address theological themes—such as theology of the Spirit, Paul's view of the Law, promise and faith of Abraham, faith in Christ Jesus, baptism, slavery and freedom, ethnic, social, and gender identities—to look at how these Christian theologies can make sense for an African audience.

Circumcision or Remaining Authentically Christian

One of the key topics of Galatians is Paul's discourses on circumcision. Galatians could be called the letter about Paul's stand toward circumcision. According to Paul, circumcision as an identity marker is not necessary for gentile inclusion in the community of Christians or to be part of God's people. To dissuade the Galatian believers from accepting circumcision, Paul argues the following: In Galatians 2:1–3, Paul spoke about the fact that Titus was not compelled to be circumcised although he was Greek. In 2:11–16, Paul rebuked Peter for compromising his stand on the gospel, for giving the gentile Christians the impression that they are somehow inferior to Jewish Christians. In 5:1–11, Paul emphasized that there is no distinction between one who is circumcised and one who is not, that circumcision makes no difference for those in Christ. He warned the Galatians that by allowing themselves to be circumcised, they are under the yoke of slavery (5:1–6). And in 6:11–16, Paul finally condemned circumcision as having no value.

Paul had called the message of circumcision the "other Gospel" (1:6–9), not because circumcision was a Judeo-traditional tribal mark used for identifying a particular group of people or a tribal rite used for a particular group, but because there were religio-cultural ideological presuppositions embedded in the notion of circumcision. In Paul's view, circumcision was a marker of exclusion, a divisive barrier that runs counter to the vision of unity. Circumcision was a divisive element in the way it was being used by the Judaizers because created false divisions and imposed unnecessary religious barriers within the early Christian community. In context, Paul was insisting that the Galatian believers should not feel compelled to adopt such Jewish customs to be fully accepted as believers in Christ.

There are three points from the circumcision faction that can be highlighted for an African audience. First, Paul's rejection of circumcision aimed at emphasizing authentic Christianity. Authentic Christianity was Paul's vision for all Christians, whether Jewish Christian, Greek, African, Asian, American, and so on. Keeping external religious practices like circumcision and observing certain days, feasts, or rituals do not make one an authentic Christian. And neither do ethnic background, gender, class, or cultural practices qualify as an identity marker for a Christian. The many conflicts and divisions among Christian Africans are not

8. Teresa Okure, "Contemporary Perspectives on Women in the Bible," *Bulletin Dei Verbum* 53 (1999): 4–11, 8.

whether they profess faith in Christ but situations that stem from doctrinal practices, founded and unfounded accusations about external religious practices and rituals, legalism (religious rules and rituals are more emphasized than faith in Christ in some Christian communities), historical claims to superiority and originality, lack of sincerity and openness, and above all greed and corruption.

To remain authentic to the faith, Paul tells both the Galatian Christians and, by extension, the present readers of Galatians to avoid judging others by their faithfulness to external markers and instead focus on their faith and relationship with Christ. For Paul, faith in Christ equalizes every believer and unites them as one in Christ. Faith in Christ Jesus, and not circumcision, liberates one from enslaving legalistic practices and external rules and frees one to walk in the freedom and grace that comes from a relationship with Christ.

Second, in critiquing the use of circumcision as an identity marker, Paul highlights the received apostolic tradition as the true foundation of Christian faith, which has nothing to do with being either Jewish or Greek, slave or free, or having a male or female identity, nor with religious or social cultural assumptions. The purity of the apostolic tradition lies in the fact that it was revealed by Jesus and Jesus is the fulfillment of all aspirations of human and cosmic universal longing. Jesus did not reveal his gospel for any particular people, nation or language, but for all of humanity. Paul speaks in Galatians that his Gospel is rooted in the revelation of Christ, and not of any human origin, source, or context (1:11–12). This is the very tradition that Paul says, "But even if we or an angel from heaven should proclaim to you a gospel contrary to what we proclaimed to you, let that one be accursed!" (1:8–9).

The idea that Paul's Gospel is rooted in the revelation of Christ and not of any human origin is one of the fundamental themes of Paul's writings, particularly emphasized in his letter to the Galatians. The gospel as a Christ-centered revelation is devoid of the use of any traditional values, fabricated religious categories, rituals, and identity markers as standards to shape and define Christianity. It is true that Christian theology has been developed or is rooted in culture, but to apply certain human social, religious, or cultural criteria as definitive means of salvation fall under the "other gospel" as Paul categorizes it. Although Paul emphasizes that his Gospel was given by direct revelation, he also sought to confirm that it aligned with the revelation (teaching) other apostles had received (2:1–2).

The third point is the question: How can an African Christian merge being an authentic African Christian and being true to the apostolic tradition, that is, being truly African and truly Christian? The interest in how an African can be truly African and truly Christian is raised here because of the contemporary state of African Christianity. Despite the growth of Christianity in Africa, the enthusiasm for and the impact of the Christian religion in African communities like Nigeria is gradually waning, especially among the young. Christianity is gradually losing its foothold and impact on African soil as some Christians are raising important questions about the nature and identity of Christianity, especially the Christianity that has become an avenue for material exploitation, human rights abuses, various forms of atrocities, spiritual degradation, and the major source behind some political, ethnic, and religious problems.[9]

As mentioned earlier, there are certain aspects of Christian teachings that are yet to find their roots in African soil and the African reality. The Christian faith that was brought to some African countries (like Nigeria) was a form of Western Christianity that knowingly or unknowingly introduced hierarchical thinking, the subjugation of African peoples and culture, and oftentimes colluded with colonialism. One of the negative effects of colonialism on Christianity was the inheritance of structures of a religion that were foreign to the African, with Western liturgies, languages, and customs, that led to the perception that Christianity was a "foreign" religion. Within this context, being a Christian for most Africans is about behaving, speaking, dressing, praying, and singing like the Westerner. Where Christianity is conceived in such material notions, it results in a very limited comprehension of the theological message and meaning of the gospel of Christ. The implication is that many Christian Africans, especially the younger generation, lack a profound grasp of the truth of the gospel, which leads to shallow faith and, by extension, a shallow understanding of African identity, spirituality, and epistemological worldviews.

Unfortunately, this lack of integration has led to a certain disconnect between Christian teaching as a way of life and African thinking and worldview as another way of life. The African religious worldview promotes good health, wealth, and abundant living as indices of one being in good relationship with the spirits/divine being, while the Christian theology of the cross appears to be somewhat at variance with the African reality. Without a true engagement of the African reality and given the lack of a genuine Christian teaching in many churches, some preachers of the faith have struggled to mediate the theological crisis. We have some preachers and teachers who emphasize materialism, self-centeredness, wealth, success, personal gain, and abundant life. Some have become particularly obsessed with legalism, doctrines, and rituals over the simple gospel of love of Christ and neighbor. Others have used their ministry as a platform for promoting their ego, attaining self-glory, fame, or control over others. Yet others without solid grounding in Scripture and the teachings of the church have become susceptible to heretical ideas and false teachings, misrepresenting both the Scripture and the apostolic tradition.

The letter to the Galatians speaks of authentic Christianity. Paul wanted the Galatians to feel at home with their unique identity and embrace Christianity as a spiritual reality. An African does not need to erase their African identity to be a Christian. Christianity is not embedded with or inherently tied to any culture, people, language, or race. One of the core messages of Christianity is its universality, meaning that it transcends cultural, geographical, ethnic, gender, and social boundaries. The essence of Christianity is spiritual and personal transformation through faith in Christ, not an erasure of one's unique cultural, ethnic, biological, or physical identity. Embracing Christianity doesn't require adopting certain customs or

9. Gesila N. Uzukwu, "Crisis of Faith: Today's African Christians and Mami-Wata (Mother-Water) Spirituality," *Journal of Ecumenical Studies* 59, no. 2 (Spring 2024): 161–167.

values, as though they are the single way to salvation. To be truly African, we need to uphold Christianity through our languages, arts, customs, and values that have shaped us as Africans, and historical narratives that make us Africans. Being truly Christian is to live a life rooted in the teachings of Jesus Christ and the gospel—emulating Christ's example by loving God, loving one's neighbor, and serving others. As Christians, we are committed to keeping the apostolic tradition, that is, to the teachings and practices passed down from the apostles of Jesus Christ, seen as the authentic deposit of faith.

Christology and Freedom Theology in Galatians

Among the different projections of Christ in Galatians, the notion of freedom in Christ presents interesting starting and finishing points for an understanding of the identity and role of Christ in the letter to the Galatians. Although there are various themes that posit Christ in Galatians—Christ as one who commissioned Paul's mission (1:1), one who gives peace (1:3), who underwent death on the cross (2:19–3:1, 13; 6:12–14), seed of Abraham (3:16), and the one who fulfils the Abrahamic promise (3:14, 21–22)—all these themes evoke contexts that narrow down to the theme of freedom.

First, Paul's freedom theology hangs on his understanding of Christ as one who liberates the Galatian audience from the particularities of Jewish culture, which, according to Paul, generate stereotypes, divisions, and exclusion at various levels, and can lead to exploitation and intimidation (cf. 2:4–5; 3:23–29; 4:4; 5:1–6). Second, Paul's message of freedom in Christ highlights Christ as a voice that dissents from and resists the imposition/bondage of the law and its requirements as a necessary means to be a sharer in the Abrahamic promise. Third, the message of freedom in Galatians points to Christ as one who liberates his people from enslavement and fear of the unknown, especially fear of unknown spirits, spiritual beings, and fearful elements of the world (4:1–7).[10] With all these at stake, Paul summarizes his persuasive message of freedom in the words: "For freedom Christ has set us free; stand firm therefore, and do not submit again to a yoke of slavery" (5:1).

10. By reading almost every paragraph in Galatians, one can observe that Paul's description of the image and role of Christ is foundational to everything he says to the Galatians. The message to the Galatians begins and ends with Christ (1:1; 6:18); in Gal 1:11–2:21 Paul defends his apostleship and Gospel and argues that his apostleship and Gospel came through Jesus Christ and God the Father (1:1–2:21); in 6:1 he reproves the Galatians for turning away from the gospel and exhorts them to remain true to the gospel because it is the gospel of Christ (1:6–12) and was received from Jesus Christ (1:12); the freedom that the believers enjoy is the freedom they have in Christ Jesus (2:4; 5:1–15); the law is not a means of salvation because the death of Christ has redeemed us from the curse of the law (2:15–21; 3:10–14); gentile believers are now included into Abrahamic inheritance because Christ is identified as the seed of Abraham to whom the promise of inheritance was made (3:15–18, 23–29); and what was promised to faith in Jesus Christ is now given to those who believe (3:21–22); the barrier between Jews/gentile, slave/free, male/female is broken because they have been baptized in Christ and made one in Christ (3:23–29); Paul's exhortation to the believers is that they should become like Christ (5:1–[12]–6:10); Gal 2:20; 6:12–15 speaks of the death of Christ and its saving significance. Overall, Galatians is a Christ-centered letter with about thirty-nine occurrences of either the single use of *Christos*, *Iēsous Christos*, or *kurios Iēsous Christos*. H. Bachmann and W. A. Slaby, eds., *Concordance to the Novum Testamentum Graece of Nestle-Aland, 26th Edition, and to the Greek New Testament*, 3rd ed. (De Gruyter, 1987), 899, 1922.

Situating freedom Christology against the background of an African Christian audience evokes previous African scholarly theological perceptions about Christ. Much of African scholarship on the question of "what it means for the man Jesus to be the Messiah for the African" draws on discourses that portray Jesus as a liberator.[11] The liberation motif seems to offer an interesting perspective for contemporary African religious thought on Galatians, given that the emphasis on the liberative approach falls on how religion, culture, and rituals have been used to oppress and enslave people, and to deny them their rights and privileges. As a response, some African women scholars have appropriated the gospel of Christ and the gospel of liberty implicit in Christianity as a strong motivating force in their struggle for liberation.[12]

A few studies have gone beyond the issue of gender to capture the challenging situations of Africa as a continent that has been sociopolitically enslaved, and seek a rereading of the gospel to address the political context of African society.[13] Here studies are interested in using the liberation theology of Galatians to critique the African struggles against colonial and neocolonial marginalization, oppression, exploitation, unjust power structures, systemic poverty, and inequality. Although studies have continued to use the "Christ as the Liberator" paradigm to speak to the African realities, John S. Mbiti and Andrew Mbuvi have their reservations. In their opinion, any articulation of African liberation Christology should not be equated with the "Western constructions of a Christus Victor ('Christ the Conqueror') or liberator model"—the militant and powerful Christ who brings light to the "dark continent" of Africa and has served to enable colonial structures of oppression, exploitation, and domination.[14]

Significantly, Paul's letter to the Galatians has remained one of the key New Testament texts used to defend the African christological discussion on liberation. Carrie Pemberton summarizes how the theology of Galatians 3:28 has occasioned the rise of theological discussions on Christian reconstruction of gender identity, cultural identities, the decentralization of male hierarchies, African liberation in church dogmatics, praxis, and cultural memory, aimed at ending hostility and forming a new identity in Christ.[15]

---

11. James Okoye identified four models of African Christologies; the comparative, systematic, liberationist, and community-oriented approaches. This basic division does not encompass the vastness and diversity of opinions that have emerged from an understanding of Christ within the context of the African culture, but we have picked up here ideological frameworks that can shed light on the contextual-hermeneutical relationship between the classical Christologies of Galatians and the African Christology. See also James Okoye, "African Theology," in *Dictionary of Mission: Theology, History, Perspectives*, ed. Karl Muller, Theo Sundermeier, Stephen B. Bevans, and Richard H. Bliese (Orbis, 1997), 12–14.

12. Teresia Hinga, "Jesus Christ and the Liberation of Women in Africa," in *The Will to Arise*, ed. Mercy A. Oduyoye and Musimbi Kanyoro (Orbis, 1992), 183–194; Mercy Amber Oduyoye, "Feminist Theology in an African Perspective," in *Paths of African Theology*, ed. Rosino Gibellin (Orbis, 1995), 176.

13. Jean-Marc Éla, *My Faith as an African* (Orbis, 2009).

14. John S. Mbiti, "Some African Concepts of Christology," in *Christ and Younger Churches: Theological Contributions from Asia, Africa and Latin America*, ed. Georg Vicedom (SPCK, 1972), 55; Andrew M. Mbuvi, *African Biblical Studies: Unmasking Embedded Racism and Colonialism in Biblical Studies* (Bloomsbury T&T Clark, 2023), 182.

15. Carrie Pemberton, *Circle Thinking African Woman Theologians in Dialogue with the West* (Brill, 2003), 170–183.

Furthermore, besides the language of freedom and liberation, Paul's Christology in Galatians also highlights the universal Oneness of all people and nations, and Christ as the Universal One that brings universal unification of humanity. From his beliefs of the Jewish God as the One True God of all peoples who has promised to gather Jews and gentiles into one people of God and of humanity as one family through Abraham, Paul appeals to Christ as the Master/Lord who has the power to free people from the particularities of ethnicity, gender, and class, and unite them all in one common faith.[16]

One of the most precious possessions of Christianity is the significant number of both African men and women that have accepted the Christian faith, thanks to the faith and resilience of the first and subsequent generations of Western missionaries to Africa. The population of Christian Africans is evidence not only of the success of the history of Christianity and its belief system, but also of the fulfilment of the Abrahamic promise. In the use of Pauline theology and other theologies of Sacred Scripture, Christians have successfully continued to spread the gospel of unity of identity and brotherhood of all who are baptized in Christ, bringing to fruition and fulfilment the covenant of promise of Genesis 15 and 17 (LXX), which Paul takes up in Galatians 3:14–29.[17]

Ethnic, Gender, and Social Differences Among Christian Africans

At the heart of the letter to the Galatians is the message of overcoming human, religio-cultural, ethnic, and gender differences through the one identity in Christ (Gal 3:26–29). Paul's explanation that anyone who is in Christ Jesus is clothed with Christ's identity is an exhortation for unity and reconciliation among peoples of various cultures, ethnicities, races, genders, and social statuses. Here, Paul speaks about overcoming the assumed privileges set for the Jews against the gentiles, male against female, and free persons against slaves. In his opinion, Christ's identity deconstructs the specific privileges attached to gender, status, and ethnic backgrounds, and the use of religious, ethnic, social, or gender differences to exclude some people from the community of believers and appropriate rights to others. Galatians 3:26–29 is interpreted as the *magna carta* of Christian liberty and unity not only for the Galatians, but also for present and future Christians. But how can it work in an African context?

In our present time, Christianity has cross-culturally and universally spread through all the nooks and crannies of Africa and many have embraced the faith. While there is a teeming population of Christian Africans today, the problem is not whether believers have accepted Christ but the level of integration of the Christian message into people's lives and moral conduct. During the early Christian mission to Nigeria and elsewhere in Africa, Christian missionaries fought hard to see that their converts accepted the Christian message. As already pointed out, it was an aggressive missionary approach aimed at deconstructing and replacing Indigenous beliefs, spiritualities, and systems of powers, which in their old dispensation

16. Daniel Boyarin, *A Radical Jew: Paul and the Politics of Identity* (University of California Press, 1994), 13–25.

17. Gesila Uzukwu, *The Unity of Male and Female in Christ: An Exegetical Study of Galatians 3.28c in Light of Paul's Theology of Promise*, LNTS 531 (Bloomsbury T&T Clark, 2015), 198–200.

emphasized shared values such as peace, love, social cohesion, and community unity. More so, the introduction of different religions to Africa—Christianity, Islam, and newer religious movements—had the potential of bringing about divisions among peoples and communities because of conflicts of interest, morals, values, and traditions.

Aside from the problem of foreign religions, there are also certain beliefs and attitudes of African religious spiritualities that have religiously and culturally divided peoples and communities along ethnic, gender, age, and social differences. For instance, in many African societies, belief in witchcraft, sorcery, and the power of spiritual leaders (witch doctors or diviners) to cast spells, curse, or control people's lives has caused a lot of harm to individuals and communities. Persons have been burnt at the stake, others ostracized or maimed, on the assumption that they were witches or sorcerers. Caste systems, which are practiced in some African societies, have historically been a source of division, discrimination, ostracization, unequal treatment, and limited opportunities for peoples assumed to be members of the so-called "Untouchables."

We also have destructive social and political habits, such as corruption, social injustices, and political polarization, where the community or group that wins takes all, and there is an unequal distribution of natural resources and wealth and a lack of accountability, all of which have given birth to a culture of impunity, division, greed, and injustice within many African societies. These social vices have reinforced a spirit of division and hatred among Christian Africans and non-Christians alike and have created multiple crises that ultimately hamper the purpose of the Christian faith and mission in Africa. This situation has also hindered a full understanding and realization of the mission of freedom, unity, and equality for all races, genders, and classes.[18]

Furthermore, division is precipitated along ethnic and gender lines. In Nigeria, for instance, membership of most churches is comprised of people from different tribes and communities. Be that as it may, there are cases where church membership is dominated by two, or three, tribes, giving room to ethnic domination, unhealthy competition, discrimination, and people being treated as minority groups. The problem can grow to the extent that people are not given fair opportunities to integrate in the affairs of the church. There are also cases where gender differences are the focus, and this creates problems. Certain Christian communities do not incorporate inclusive leadership structures that welcome people of

18. Although Christianity has brought about a lot of changes in the lives of Africans and in Africa as a continent, the earlier histories of Christianity in Africa—of colonial-missionary demonization of the Africans and the African reality, collusion of mission and trade, political negotiations and manipulation, involvement in sex crimes, corruption, instigating ethnic tribal quarrels—have an undeniable impact on African Christianity up until this day. The coming of different Christian denominations, such as the Roman Catholic and the mainline Protestant churches, and of Islam, left Africa as a battle space for these major religious groups who were already competing for memberships, social relevance, and attention. So right from the beginning there were crises that planted or distorted the church's original mission and purpose, especially that of freedom, equality, and unity. See Toyin Falola, *Understanding Ogbu Kalu: Christianity and Culture in Africa* (Pan Africa University Press, 2019), 25–26, 69–70; Mbuvi, *African Biblical Studies*, 113–114.

different backgrounds and genders into leadership positions, which in a sense underpins and enforces an ecclesiology of unequal membership.[19]

With these many issues in African society the question is: How can an African Christian fully understand and realize the mission of freedom, unity, and oneness in Christ? A Nigerian Christian, for instance, living in an oppressive multicultural, social, religious, and class situation will have problems understanding how Paul's message of unity and freedom can be negotiated. The situation becomes even more problematic when some preachers of the faith bear false witness and teach false spirituality that undermines the entire message of Christ preached through Paul. In some churches in Nigeria, for instance, there is a high level of corruption, selfishness, or self-centeredness that exists among believers. Pastors and preachers alike engage in the commoditization of God and holy objects, preaching the false gospel of prosperity, and the spiritualization of money and wealth (to mention a few). Each of these elements has in one way or the other brought about actual situations of discrimination, oppression, exploitation, quarrels, division, and disunity in the believing community, while spreading the wrong understanding of Christianity to the outsider. In this way, the message of Christ is spreading not only for the right but also the wrong reasons.

Of course, a significant part of the negative attitudes and biases toward persons based on their ethnic, gender, or social differences is indeed rooted in sin. Sin distorts relationships and leads people to treat others with prejudice, discrimination, and a lack of compassion. These are attitudes that contradict the gospel of love, equity, equality, justice, and unity. In his letter to the Galatians Paul pointed out how sin is an influential force that separates persons from persons, and persons from God because sin keeps people in bondage—whether the bondage of the law (3:19–25), of the flesh (5:19–21), or of legalism (5:4). A life in sin is a life without the Spirit. It is true to say that colonial powers, structures, and religion exacerbated ethnic, social, and gender differences in African society; but it is also the case that our cultural traditions and norms have contributed to strengthening the divisions and placing limitations on people.

The Christian faith that came to the African continent did not build and promote the strong sense of oneness, unity, and of overcoming of differences as preached by Paul, but it is also the case that Africa was not built on the notion of universal oneness and unity as preached by Paul. Prior to the coming of Christianity, Africans' notion of unity and oneness was very much influenced by the notion of tribal unity—a people that "shares a common distinctive culture, religion, language, and other connecting links."[20] Paul's message of unity has universal merits despite one's religious affiliation, and it can undo every religio-cultural tradition or norm that contributes to division, conflict, or factionalism among believing Christians and communities. As we try to uphold the Christian message of unity, inclusivity, freedom, and the oneness of the believers in Christ, there are some African belief systems and ideologies

19. James O. Adeyanju and Ben O. Bello, "Argument Against Ethnicity: Conflicts and Divisions in the Church in Nigeria Using the Ethical and Theological Imperatives of Ephesians 4:1–6," *Light in a Once-Dark World* 1 (2019): 196–199.

20. Aloysius M. Lugira, *World Religions: African Traditional Religion* (Chelsea House, 2009), 136.

that can serve to help us better understand the African worldview, what defines religion for an African, and how Christianity can bridge the gap.

The starting point in these interactive theologies is for African Christian theology to embrace the African Ubuntu philosophy that "involves charity, sympathy, caring, sensitivity to the needs of others, respect, consideration, patience and kindness" as the inevitable step to reading and understanding the message of Galatians 3:26–29.[21] The idea that, in Christ, "there is no longer Jew or Greek, slave or free, male and female" must begin with an acknowledgment and respect of differences, reaching out in love to people without condemning their humanity, speaking to Christians the language of charity, sympathy, care for the needy, respect and consideration of differences, patience, and kindness. It is only when we have love, care, and respect for one another that we can begin to discuss how faith in Christ deconstructs or overcomes polarities of ethnicity, social class, nationality, and gender differences.

Baptism and the African Identity Phenomenon

Baptism occupies a central place in the theology of Galatians. Although the word βαπτίζω (*baptizō*) appears once in Galatians (probably indicating that it is not a primary focus), it does play a significant theological role in (1) Paul's argument about the nature of his Gospel, (2) Shaping the Christian life, practices, ethics, and mission, and (3) Deconstructing the polarities of ethnicity, social class, nationality, and gender differences, and bringing people together into one body in Christ and in the Abrahamic promise (Rom 6:1–14; 1 Cor 1:10–17; 10:1–13; 12:12–31; 15:29–34; Gal 3:26–29). In addition, Paul's treatment of baptism in Galatians is closely tied to his central theme of justification by faith, not by works of the Law, particularly Mosaic Law.

Beyond the argument on the theological importance of baptism in Galatians is the question of the pre-Pauline tradition behind the baptismal reference in Galatians 3:26–29, and particularly of the garment imagery ("putting on Christ") in 3:27. Scholarly historical debates, although not conclusive in themselves, have suggested that the garment imagery formula harks back to either the initiation ritual found in Hellenistic mystery cults, the clothing of the first human in a garment of light, or the Roman *toga virilis* ceremony that marks a boy's coming of age.[22] Although reviewing these hypotheses lies beyond the scope of this chapter of particular relevance is the suggestion that the "putting on" imagery parallels an initiation ceremony.[23]

Underlining the relevance of baptism for an African audience begins with the representation of baptism as a moment of spiritual initiation, where the one baptized is initiated

21. Nonceba Nolundi Mabovula, "The Erosion of African Values: A Reappraisal of the African Ubuntu Philosophy," *Inkanyiso: Journal Human & Social Science* 3, no. 1 (2011): 41.

22. For scholarly list and discussion, see J. Albert Harrill, "Coming of Age and Putting on Christ: The Toga Virilis Ceremony, Its Paraenesis, and Paul's Interpretation of Baptism in Galatians," *Novum Testamentum* 44, no. 3 (2002): 252–253. See also Sarolta A. Takács, *Isis and Sarapis in the Roman World*, Religions in the Graeco-Roman World 124 (E. J. Brill, 1995), 163.

23. Dennis R. MacDonald, *There Is No Male and Female: The Fate of a Dominical Saying in Paul and Gnosticism*, HDR 20 (Fortress Press, 1987), 5–16.

into membership of the community of believers. At baptismal rituals, the baptized takes up a new identity that is characterized by Christ himself, puts on a character after that of Christ, symbolically united with Christ, and participates in unity with all who are called Christ's followers. One of the core theological messages of baptism is that it obliterates differences among people of different races, cultures, traditions, and genders (Gal 3:28). Thus, baptism is the visible demonstration of the Christian life in terms of salvation, but also in terms of membership in the local and universal church.[24]

Second, baptism represents a moment of spiritual purification, transformation, and regeneration. The baptismal reference in Galatians 3:26–29 does not only speak of baptismal initiation but also of the transformative and efficacious power of the Spirit in the life and identity of the believer. This understanding of baptism is connected to the fact that the presence and action of the Spirit are indispensable to the reception of baptism. While Paul does not specifically use the term "baptism of the Holy Spirit" in Galatians 3:27, the connection he makes between the baptismal theology of Galatians 3:27 (of being "clothed with Christ") and the reception of the Spirit (3:1–5) and life in the Spirit (Gal 5:16–25) implies that the new identity and life in Christ are powered by the Spirit. This observation can be attested in other parts of Paul's letters where he speaks of being baptized by one Spirit into the one body of Christ (1 Cor 12:13), of having the spirit of Christ as an essential aspect of belonging to Christ (Rom 8:9–11, 14–16), or of becoming adopted as "sons" of God by virtue of the Spirit of Christ in the hearts of the believers (Gal 4:6–7). The implication is that the experience of the Holy Spirit is an indispensable presence in the initial initiation (marking believers' entrance into the body of Christ) and continuing life in Christ (living a life empowered by the Spirit).

Baptism as an initiation rite is performed by all Christians. It is interesting to note that there are various types of baptism found across the different Christian traditions or denominations. There is "infant baptism" which is practiced by the Roman Catholic Church, Eastern Orthodox Church, Anglican/Episcopal Church, and some Lutheran and Methodist churches. In addition, there is "adult baptism" or "the believer's baptism," which comes from individuals who have made a personal decision to be baptized and follow Christ, practiced by Baptist churches, Pentecostal churches, Evangelical denominations, and some nondenominational churches. Furthermore, there is "Spirit baptism" (that is, baptism in the Holy Spirit). Pentecostal, Charismatic, and some Evangelical churches emphasize this. Identifying these different baptisms as rooted in the gospel of Christ reflects the depth and diversity of Christ's message and acknowledges the adaptability of Christianity to the different life situations and environments of every Christian.

Given that baptism is practiced as a ritual that initiates believers into the body of Christ and unites Christians into one identity with Christ, baptism has also stood as a source of division, as evidenced within some African Christian communities. There are cases where some Christian communities do not recognize one another's Christian baptism. This situation can create tension among believers, leading to either the invalidation of the baptism and "rebaptizing (or, in their understanding, baptizing) persons already baptized in another church"

24. Millard Erickson, *Christian Theology* (Baker Academic, 2013), 1086.

or the ostracization of some Christian communities at an ecumenical level.[25] According to Michael Root and Risto Saarinen, baptism has not always guaranteed unity. On the contrary, it "changes into a highly confessional or even confessionalistic, self-preserving exercise that in fact is more divisive than unifying."[26] Rather than always being a source of unity, baptism can be "one of the stumbling blocks to Christian unity, due to the variety of baptismal practices and understandings among the churches today."[27]

Besides the problem of the unity of members, controversies also dominate the understanding of the experience of the Spirit at baptism. The presence of diversity of Christian traditions—ranging from mainline Protestant and Catholic denominations to Pentecostal, charismatic, and African Instituted churches—mark significant contributions to the nature, character, and growth of Christianity in Africa, but also add to the layers of controversy surrounding the problem of different understandings of baptism and the experience of the Spirit. For instance, there has been major controversy between traditional denominations (like Catholics and Anglicans) that see baptism (including infant baptism) as a complete rite that is accompanied by the Holy Spirit and charismatic and Pentecostal churches that advocate a separate "baptism of the Holy Spirit" or a "second blessing" as a fulfillment of the presence of the Holy Spirit.[28] These differences of interpretation of the presence of the Spirit can sometimes lead to tensions within Christian communities.

The idea that baptism has not always provided the foundational structure of unity among Christian Africans raises a serious problem because it envisages a situation where some believers are yet to grasp the goal of Christian baptism. Beyond the comprehension of the biblical and theological emphases on baptism, there is also the need to underline the significance of baptism through the cultural lens. For an African audience, the significance of baptism can be underlined by relating it to culturally familiar concepts, such as the rite of initiation, community identity formation and transformation, community solidarity and friendship, awareness of spiritual forces in African cosmology, communal unity, and togetherness.

In many African communities, initiation rites mark a transition from one stage of life to another (childhood, adulthood, marriage, eldership, and death), bringing the individual into a new social or religious status and granting the individual full membership into a group or community. In most cases, water, blood, or sacrifices can be used in the celebration of initiation as a symbol of cleansing or purification. In addition, most rites are performed in the presence of the community to bear witness that the rite has been performed and that the individual is now a full member of the community. Different traditional rites, whether into adulthood, women's council (*umu ada*), eldership ceremonies, masquerade cult, or into ancestral worship, are all geared toward involvement in community affairs, community

25. Thomas F. Best, *Baptism Today: Understanding, Practice, Ecumenical Implications* (Liturgical Press, 2008), viii.

26. Michael Root and Risto Saarinen, *Baptism and the Unity of the Church* (Eerdmans, 1998), 68.

27. Thomas F. Best, *Baptism Today: Understanding, Practice, Ecumenical Implications* (Liturgical Press, 2008), 195.

28. John W. Jack Carter, "The Subjects of Baptism: A History of Controversy," *The American Journal of Biblical Theology* 13, no. 5 (2012): 1–10.

unity, and identity formation, not excluding spiritual transformation. Underscoring the importance of youth initiation rituals, Mbiti notes that they are

> a symbolic experience of the process of dying, living in the spirit world and being reborn (resurrected). The rebirth, that is the act of rejoining their families, emphasizes and dramatizes that the young people are now new, they have new personalities, they have lost their childhood, and in some societies, they even receive completely new names.[29]

Both baptism and African initiation rites function as identity formators, linking individuals with the age groups, tribe, community, or ancestry, and teaching the individual the values and responsibilities of belonging to either a religious or social family/group.[30] Thus, as with baptism, by virtue of membership in any traditional group, she/he shares equal rights and responsibilities with other members.

Although performing certain African initiation rites, such as naming or marriage ceremonies, has no serious implications for an African Christian, there are other initiation rites that, while they capture the beliefs, values, and identity of the African, remain a challenge for authentic Christian faith. Some rites of passage, such as initiation into adulthood, eldership ceremonies, masquerade cults, ancestral worship, and veneration can contain a very rigid set of rules, practices that involve the use of spiritual powers and divination, oath taking, blood sacrifices, or physical mutilation, which for some Christian Africans could put their allegiance to Christianity on trial. And the avoidance of these initiation rites can bring about suffering for the individual at best, and societal disorder at worst. Thus, for some the marrying of cultural identity and Christian faith can be a sensitive and complex issue. From these highlighted concerns, the question is, can baptism replace African traditional values? If the answer is in the negative, how can our Christian baptism as an identity marker accommodate cultural identity markers?

We have experienced situations where Christian preachers advise their congregation to desist from attending or participating in traditional rites, believing that a Christian has nothing to do with grassroots African traditions and culture. Granted, there are certain initiation rites that may lead to human sacrifices, but there are also initiation rites that promote human dignity, equality, harmony of the cosmic order, and the good of the community. It is during initiation rites that a young boy or girl could be taught essential life skills, social responsibilities, moral values, cultural norms, and the sense of belonging. These rites are meant to ensure that cultural continuity is maintained and that the individual is fully integrated into the social fabric of the community. African initiation rites serve several purposes that Christian baptism may not replace. While baptism as a spiritual sacrament/

29. John S. Mbiti, *African Religions and Philosophy* (Heinemann International, 1990), 118.

30. Rachel T. Lebese, Tebogo M. Mothiba, Mercy T. Mulaudzi, Ntsieni S. Mashau, and Lufuno Makhado, "Rite of Passage: An African Indigenous Knowledge Perspective," in *Working with Indigenous Knowledge: Strategies for Health Professionals*, ed. F. M. Mulaudzi and R. T. Lebese (AOSIS Books, 2022), 51–68.

practice holds significant spiritual meaning, African initiation rites are embedded with religious and social values that are indispensable for social and cultural transformation and for the good of the society.

In addition, the notion of social or religious groups fosters harmony, communalism, shared values, shared beliefs, shared responsibilities, and interconnectedness.[31] The mere thought of belonging to a group or community presupposes submission to a certain level of good behavior or responsibility toward the group and the interests of the community. This fostering of identity strengthens communal bonds, motivates cooperative behavior, and inspires collective action toward common goals.

There is no doubt that African traditions have enormously contributed to the positive shaping of Africans in their social and religious behaviors. And for many Africans, the adjustments to Western civilization have led to issues of identity crisis, which in turn may be part of the reason behind the tensions and concerns about the reception of baptismal theology. One could suggest that a better way to positively engage Christian Africans in creative theological dialogue, understanding, and implementation of the dynamics of baptism is by using traditional African religious epistemologies and cultures that can drive home the sense of baptism as a source of unity, identity formation, spiritual transformation, and Christian responsibility toward one another. As already pointed out earlier, Christianity does not require believers to abandon their cultural heritage and identity, provided that such heritage does not conflict with biblical injunctions. This means that there is room for constructive appreciation and positive integration of African cultural identity with Christian initiation, but careful discernment is needed.

Understanding the Manifestations of the Spirit in Galatians as an African

It is not by accident that Paul's letter to the Galatians begins and ends its larger unit with discussions on the Spirit.[32] Corresponding to the different references to the Spirit in Galatians, it is as though the theme of Galatians is life in the Spirit theology. The Spirit theology is so important in Galatians that Paul will constantly return to it in a variety of ways: In Galatians 3:1–5, Paul rebuked the Galatians because they had once begun a life in the Spirit but were now turning back to a life in the flesh. In Galatians 3:14 Paul identifies the promise of Abraham as the promise of the Spirit obtained through faith. In Galatians 5:24–25, Paul exhorts the Galatians to live a Spirt-filled life, comprising of love, joy, peace, patience, kindness,

31. Bukunmi Deborah Ajitoni, "Ubuntu and the Philosophy of Community in African Thought: An Exploration of Collective Identity and Social Harmony," *Journal of African Studies and Sustainable Development* 7, no. 3 (2024): 1–15.

32. Gal 3:1–5 is the introduction as well as the beginning of the larger unit of chapters 3–5. This observation may not be out of place as some scholars have suggested that what is in Galatians is the issue of the Spirit; who possesses the Sprit and what kind of evidentiary value has the Spirit in Galatians. See Charles H. Cosgrove, *The Cross and the Spirit: A Study in the Argument and Theology of Galatians* (Mercer University Press, 1988); David John Lull, *The Spirit in Galatia: Paul's Interpretation of Pneuma as Divine Power*, SBLDS 49 (Scholars Press, 1980); Sam K. Williams, "Justification and the Spirit in Galatians," *Journal for the Study of the New Testament* 29 (1987): 91–100.

generosity, faithfulness, gentleness, and self-control. And in Galatians 4:3–6, Paul refers to the act of living under elemental spirits as enslavement as against living under the Spirit of Jesus, which brings freedom. In sum, the Spirit's influence and presence in Galatians clearly serves to accentuate four key points: (1) indispensability of the Spirit in the formation of Christian identity; (2) in framing the Christian life as a life of virtue; (3) as the basis of the Abrahamic promise; and (4) as the source of Christian freedom.

An African reader of Galatians may attempt to understand Paul's vision about the manifestations and roles of the Spirit given that Africans nurture strong belief in the powerful presence and extraordinary powers of spiritual beings.[33] In African cosmology, spiritual beings possess powers that can bless, heal, liberate, but also harm. Issues of community identity, communitarian life, formation, and moral aspirations are also tied to the roles of spiritual beings. For instance, in Igbo religious experience, Elochukwu Uzukwu and A. Ogbannaya claim that the relationship which exists between the Almighty (Chukwu), the Sun-God (the eye of Chukwu), and Idemili (daughter of Chukwu and Ala) underlines the African communitarian spirit, as well as their mode of being, seeing, and acting.[34] Apart from the spirit deities, there are also minor or lesser spiritual beings that act as emissaries or messengers of the supreme God, as well as capricious spirits that can bring about harm or evil.

The rise and phenomenal growth of Pentecostal and charismatic movements in Africa can also attest to why and how Africans engage with spirit traditions. On the one hand, one can argue that the African understanding about the spiritual world attests to the groundbreaking reception and widespread witnessing to charismatic movements as a new religious movement in Africa. It is possible that the African traditional understanding of the role of the spirits in African cosmology prepared the ground for the Pentecostal and charismatic movements. According to Dena Freeman, the new Pentecostal and charismatic churches "offer a form of Christianity that fits well with African sensibilities, and which acknowledges the validity of traditional African beliefs—in witches, spirits, ancestors—while at the same time providing a way to break from them."[35]

Though Africans' sacred constructs about the spiritual world have some similarities with Christian pneumatology, such as their emphasis on supernatural power, healing, and protection, the foundational beliefs and theologies of these two traditions differ significantly. The way that some Africans (for example, Nigerians and Ghanaians) would pray to the Spirit

33. See Ikechukwu Anthony Kanu, "The Dimensions of African Cosmology," *Filosofia Theoretica: Journal of African Philosophy, Culture and Religion* 2 (2013): 533–555; John Mwangi and Loizer W. Mwakio, "The African Traditional Religious Ontology of God, Divinities, and Spirits," in *Advances in Religious and Cultural Studies*, ed. Essien D. Essien (IGI Global, 2021), 44–64.

34. A. Ogbannaya, *On Communitarian Divinity: An African Interpretation of the Trinity* (Paragon House, 1994), 1; Elochukwu E. Uzukwu, "Distance-Nearness, Absence-Presence: Reevaluating the Relational Triune God Through the Lens of Igbo (and West African) Health-Focused Religion," in *Interface Between Igbo Theology and Christianity*, ed. Akuma-Kalu Njoku and Elochukwu Uzukwu (Cambridge Scholars, 2014), 102.

35. Dena Freeman, "The Pentecostal Ethic and the Spirit of Development," in *Pentecostalism and Development: Churches, NGOs and Social Change in Africa. Non-Governmental Public Action*, ed. Dena Freeman (Palgrave Macmillan, 2012), 10.

during charismatic prayer sessions attests to the ongoing process of the appropriation of Christianity in Africa. However, there is excessive focus on the Spirit performing miracles and signs as a true manifestation of his presence. It is this kind of radical theology of the Spirit that has given rise to theatrical and manipulative tales about deliverance services. There is also the emphasis on the prosperity gospel, with its notion of the Holy Spirit as the source of or means to wealth, wholeness, and success. In some contexts, it is as though the Christian Spirit has replaced the African spirits, embodying their roles and attributes.

Some of these aberrations, while not reflective of all that is to be known about African Pentecostal and charismatic movements, highlight areas where the Pentecostal or charismatic devotion to the Spirit differ from orthodox Christian pneumatology. Although African spirit traditions may have influenced charismatic movements in Africa, providing a religio-cultural terrain to embrace the new Christian religious movement, there are fundamental differences that cannot be overlooked.[36] A reading of Paul's teaching on the Spirit in Galatians can help enrich our understanding of some of the discourses about the manifestations of the Spirit in Christian tradition.

One of the central roles of the Spirit in Paul's letter to the Galatians is indeed the formation of Christian identity. Paul's idea about the indispensability of the Spirit in the formation of Christian identity places strong emphasis on the fact that it is Christ's spirit that unites people together as believers in Christ (3:14, 28; 4:6–7). More so, it is through the Spirit of Christ that believers are confirmed as "adopted children of God," and by the Spirit they can cry out "Abba, Father" (Gal 4:6–7). Of special importance here is that the Spirit plays a transformative role in forming and transforming believers to see one another as children of God, irrespective of their racial, ethnic, gender, or class identities.

I have earlier discussed the controversies surrounding identity formation in African religious and social communities and provided a helpful critique and suggestions for improvement in areas of unity and oneness among believers. As suggested earlier, we can create a more thoughtful and concrete approach to how Christianity can engage and dialogue with African religious traditions. Such dialogue, through a better understanding of the role of the Spirit, can foster a more inclusive, respectful, and transformative Christian community that values the spiritual heritage of African cultures while maintaining fidelity to the gospel.

Aside from the issue of identity formation, the Spirit also functions to bring about the promise. In Galatians, Paul identified the Abrahamic promise as the "Spirit of Christ." In the closing verses of Galatians 3:1–14, Paul redefined the relationship between Abraham and Isaac by identifying and redefining Christ as the seed of Abraham and the means through which the blessings of Abraham have come to the gentiles. Here, Paul spiritualized the role of Abraham and the content of the promise, from a physical to a spiritual fatherhood, and from a presumed physical inheritance to a spiritual one. Of course, the spiritualization of the promise as the "the Spirit of Christ" narrows down the question of the evidentiary importance of the Spirit in Galatians.

---

36. Birgit Meyer, "Christianity in Africa: From African Independent to Pentecostal-Charismatic Churches," *Annual Review of Anthropology* 33 (2004): 447–474.

The spiritualization of the promise, of Abraham, of the seed is a radical theology that challenges and uproots not only the mainline tradition that Paul reacted against in Galatia, but also spiritualities and religious traditions that have embraced Christianity while their teachings differ from the gospel of Christ preached by Paul. In African spirituality, contextual realities are emphasized as part of the function of deities/gods (wealth, power, health, progress, prosperity, fertility, abundance of food, etc.). Thus, Paul's "spiritualization of the promise" theology is particularly challenging for an African man/woman whose system is riddled with actual social crises like poverty, sickness, failure in businesses, family curse, spiritual attacks, discrimination, oppression, political violence, and abuse. Little wonder the prosperity gospel is booming in Africa, and remains a vestige of the African's "search for abundant life through the Christian faith."[37]

Spiritualizing the content of the promise not only challenges the African cosmological understanding of the role of spiritual beings/deities, but effectively addresses the abuse and misuse of Christian faith in African communities and churches. In the face of poverty, diseases, sicknesses, human suffering, injustice, and abuses, many preachers of Christ's message have taken to propagating the prosperity gospel as part of the promised inheritance. This type of theology remains problematic for an African audience because it fails to channel societal ills—lack of social development, the problem of evil, poverty, violence—to the proper agencies that should address them. This has resulted in erroneous notions of religion and religiosity.

The above discussion brings us to another role of the Spirit in Galatians, namely, framing the Christian life as a life of virtue. From speaking of Christ's Spirit as fulfillment of the promise, Paul reinforces his understanding of the promise as "living a life in the spirit" (Gal 5:16–6:10). Beyond being identified as a Christian, Paul admonishes the Galatians to live a life in the Spirit, and when one is under the control of the Spirit, their character and behavior bear witness to the life of love, joy, peace, patience, kindness, generosity, faith, gentleness, and self-control (Gal 5:24). According to Paul, these human qualities are the fruit of the Spirit.

That the Spirit can empower a person to live a life of good human conduct and positively impact social values is also a common experience in African spirituality. Beyond the belief that there exist malevolent spirits that can bring about disasters or bodily harm, there are other spiritual beings that are "able to transform into human features to befriend, train or empower human being to provide healing, counseling and other human services."[38] It is also part of African cosmology that good conduct and goodness to one another attracts divine blessing, just as bad conduct or evil deeds bring about calamities or bad consequences upon individuals and the community as a whole. As Paul would say in Galatians 6:8, a life in the Spirit brings eternal life, the promised inheritance.

37. Stan Chu Ilo, "Introduction: The Search for Abundant Life in African Christian Religion. Historical Reinterpretation of Christian Mission in Africa," in *Wealth, Health, and Hope in African Christian Religion*, ed. Stan Chu Ilo (Lexington Books, 2017), 19.

38. Daniel Darko, *Against Principalities and Powers: Spiritual Being in Relation to Communal Identity and the Moral Discourse of Ephesians* (HippoBooks, 2020), 181.

The role of the Spirit in living a good life is undoubtedly a manifestation of Christ's Spirit in the life of a believer. The Spirit of Christ enables the believer to live a life of love, joy, peace, patience, kindness, generosity, faith, gentleness, and self-control. The Spirit does not only promote individual peace, but also harmonious coexistence, and it sustains loving relationships that overlook differences, such that it harnesses Paul's theology of oneness in Christ. Where the Spirit of Christ dwells, he fosters the kind of Christian communal identity that Galatians emphasizes.

Conclusion

Paul's letter to the Galatians is remarkable in its emphasis on living an authentic Christian life and being true to the gospel of Christ. Authentic Christianity is not about conforming to a specific culture or tradition but remaining authentic to one's cultural identity while living out one's faith in Christ (that is, living the true essence of Christian religion). At its core, the Christian gospel transcends cultural, ethnic, gender, and national boundaries. Its message is intended for all people, regardless of their background. In his discussion against accepting circumcision, Paul has underscored the place of the Christian faith in its interaction with the worldviews and traditions of the gentile world, which translates to the other peoples of the world with whom the gospel of Christ has come in touch.

From the concern highlighted above, this chapter addressed a range of issues and concerns of the African world in dialogue with the Christian message of Galatians. The work adopted a contextual-based approach to allow an African audience to read and understand the words of Paul through the eyes of an African, connecting with African experiences, needs, symbols, and worldviews, and where possible seeking cross-cultural and religious points of contact that can awaken an African to the universality of Paul's message to the Galatians. Galatians emerges as Paul's response to crucial theological issues, such as: (1) circumcision and the question of authentic Christianity; (2) Christology—understanding Christ as an African; (3) reading Galatians 3:26–29 in the context of ethnic, gender, and social differences among Christian Africans (4) baptism and the African identity phenomenon; and (5) understanding the manifestations of the Spirit in Galatians as an African.

Engaging Galatians in a way that speaks to the different sociocultural and religious dynamics of the African world shows how Christian theology can be at home with the African peoples, speak to the African, and transform the African. It is by underlining these points of contact that an African can be truly African, and truly Christian, a theological negotiation that can create a lasting impact for Christianity in Africa.

Further Reading

Chitakure, John. *African Traditional Religion Encounters Christianity: The Resilience of a Demonized Religion*. Pickwick Publications, 2017.

Éla, Jean-Marc. *My Faith as an African*. Orbis, 2009.

Mbuvi, Andrew. *African Biblical Studies: Unmasking Embedded Racism and Colonialism in Biblical Studies*. Bloomsbury T&T Clark, 2023.

Michael, Matthew. *Christian Theology and African Traditions*. Wipf & Stock, 2013.

Nabofa, M. Y. "Blood Symbolism in African Religion." *Religious Studies* 21, no. 3 (1985): 389–405.

Ngewa, Samuel. *Galatians*. Africa Bible Commentary Series. HippoBooks, 2010.

Ngewa, Samuel. "Galatians." In *Africa Bible Commentary: A One-Volume Commentary Written by 70 African Scholars*, edited by Tokunboh Adeyemo. WordAlive Publishers; Zondervan, 2006.

Nyang, Sulayman. "Reflections on Traditional African Cosmology." *New Directions* 8, no. 1 (1980): 28–32.

Uzukwu, Elochukwu E. "Distance-Nearness, Absence-Presence: Reevaluating the Relational Triune God Through the Lens of Igbo (and West African) Health-Focused Religion." In *Interface Between Igbo Theology and Christianity*, edited by Akuma-Kalu Njoku and Elochukwu Uzukwu. Cambridge Scholars Publishing, 2014.

Uzukwu. Gesila N. "Crisis of Faith: Today's African Christians and Mami-Wata (Mother-Water) Spirituality." *Journal of Ecumenical Studies* 59, no. 2 (Spring 2024): 157–173.

Uzukwu, Gesila. "Religion and Religiosity of Women in the Scripture and Africa: A Study of a Living Paradox." *Abuja Journal of Philosophy and Theology* 4 (2014): 19–36.

Uzukwu, Gesila. *The Unity of Male and Female in Christ: An Exegetical Study of Galatians 3.28c in Light of Paul's Theology of Promise*. LNTS 531. Bloomsbury T&T Clark, 2015.

Wa Gatumu, Kabiro. "Authentic Biblical Christian Community: Paul's Perspective on Ethnicity and Gender Relations vis-à-vis the African Church." *Sapientia Logos* 5, no. 2 (2013): 32–76.

CHAPTER TWELVE

The Letter to the Ephesians

Caroline Nkoberanyi
The Catholic University of Eastern Africa
Kenya

Introduction

The letter to the Ephesians has a universal appeal and application among Christians. It clarifies Paul's message of God's gracious offer of salvation and the believers' appropriate response. It helps one understand God's purpose and one's position in creation and in Christ Jesus. Even so, it presents the reader with many puzzles about its authorship, date, addressees, and literary genre. Hence, before examining its theological themes and their inferences for Christian Africans I will briefly examine the disputed aspects.

Authorship and Date

Traditionally, the letter to the Ephesians has been attributed to Paul. The author begins in the usual Pauline fashion, "Paul, an apostle of Christ Jesus by the will of God" (Eph 1:1), similar to 1 Corinthians 1:1, 2 Corinthians 1:1, and Galatians 1:1. He again mentions his name in 3:1 as in 2 Corinthians 10:1, Galatians 5:2, 1 Thessalonians 2:18, and Philemon 1:19. External evidence likewise indicates that it was recorded in Marcion's canon in the New Testament as a letter addressed to the "Laodiceans" and was acknowledged in the Muratorian canon (180 CE) as the work of Paul. This view was accepted by early church fathers like Irenaeus, Tertullian, and Clement of Alexandria.[1] Today, not all scholars are in agreement that the letter was written by Paul. Among other reasons, they argue that it is unlikely that Paul could write that he had just heard of the faith of the Ephesians (Eph 1:15). In addition, he closes the letter with no extended greetings, in spite of the fact that, according to the book of Acts, he spent more than two years in Ephesus.

Regarding the style, Paul typically writes in short sentences, but those in Ephesians are long and composite, such as 1:3–14 and 3:1–7.[2] Also, the literary resemblance of Ephesians with Colossians, which is likewise considered Deutero-Pauline, is a reason used to doubt Paul's authorship. The two letters share vocabularies and themes, as the following examples show:

1. Arthur G. Patzia, *Ephesians, Colossians, Philemon*, NIBCS (Hendrickson Publishers, 1990), 121.

2. In his comment on long sentences, John Muddiman states that in the English translations "Ephesians does not read like an expanded or edited text. Its intolerably long sentences have been broken up, missing verbs supplied, ambiguities in the positioning of adverbial phrases and participles have been resolved, and irregularities smoothed over." See John Muddiman, *The Letter to the Ephesians*, BNTC (Continuum, 2001), 22.

the household codes (Eph 5:21–6:9; Col 3:18–4:1), the mention of Tychicus (Eph 6:21–22; Col 4:7–8), and of the Gospel of Paul as a mystery that was revealed to him (Eph 3:1–13; Col 1:24–29).[3] Nonetheless, it can equally be argued that if Paul wrote the two letters, it is easy to account for the similarities, for the author likely used Colossians in writing his letter to the Ephesians. This introduction maintains that the letter contains a legitimate development of Paul's thought and that he is its author.

The date is dependent on the issue of authorship. If the author is Paul, it was written while he was in prison in Rome (62 CE). This implies that Ephesians was written around the named date. Conversely, some critical scholars who question Paul's authorship propose a date between 80 and 90 CE.[4] On the basis of the acknowledgment in this introduction that Paul is the author, 62 CE is taken to be the date of writing.

Recipients

The actual recipients of the letter are doubted. If the author is Paul, it is difficult to understand why he had only "heard" of their faith and love if he knew them well (1:15). A somewhat similar expression in the letter to the Colossians infers that the readers had not met Paul face to face (Col 1:4; 2:1). Again, it is problematic for Paul, who had lived with the Ephesians (Acts 19:8, 10; 20:31), to presume that his readers had only heard (presumably from other sources) about his God-given responsibility to preach to the gentiles (Eph 3:2).[5] It is hence likely that the letter was not designated for just one church but for several of them in Ephesus. This is so because the words "in Ephesus" are lacking in the earliest manuscripts,[6] implying that they may be a later addition to the original composition. It is possible that the document was intended to be a circular letter to many churches within the region of Asia Minor[7] and the church at Ephesus was one of them. While the arguments have some persuasive elements, for lack of other specific recipients named, the traditional title "Ephesians" as indicated in the New Testament canon is retained in the rest of the chapter.

Historical Setting

Ephesus was the dominant city of the Ionian league and the capital of the Roman province of Asia Minor. The political status of Ephesus and the harbor, the largest of its kind in Asia

3. Margaret Y. McDonald, "Ephesians," in *The International Biblical Commentary: A Catholic and Ecumenical Commentary for the Twenty-First Century*, ed. William R. Farmer (The Liturgical Press, 1998), 1672.

4. Bart D. Ehrman, *The New Testament: A Historical Introduction to the Early Christian Writings* (Oxford University Press, 2004), 381–384; Markus Barth, *Ephesians: Introduction, Translation, and Commentary on Chapters 1–3*, AB 34 (Doubleday, 1974), 50–51.

5. Harold W. Hoehner, *Ephesians: An Exegetical Commentary* (Baker Academic, 2002), 6–7.

6. The manuscripts include P^{46} (3rd century), Sinaiticus, and Vaticanus (4th century). The words "in Ephesus" appear in the latter two as a fifth-century addition. Without the words "in Ephesus," the Greek could be rendered "to the holy ones and faithful brothers in Christ" as in Col 1:2. Cf. Ralph P. Martin, *Ephesians, Colossians, and Philemon*, Interpretation: A Bible Commentary for Teaching and Preaching (John Knox Press, 1991), 5.

7. Martin, *Ephesians, Colossians, and Philemon*, 5.

Minor, facilitated the economic growth of the city. In New Testament times, many trade routes of Asia joined in Ephesus and the Romans used it as the point of departure when measuring distances from Asia. It was easy to access Ephesus by both land and sea because it had an artificial harbor that could be reached even by the largest ships. Due to its strategic location, political, commercial, and religious developments flourished and it was beneficial for missionary activities.[8] Toward the end of his second missionary journey, Paul visited Ephesus with Priscilla and Aquila while on his way from Corinth to Jerusalem (Acts 18:19–21). He preached in the synagogue for some time and promised to return (Acts 18:18f). The city also had a splendid temple devoted to Artemis, the fertility goddess also known as Diana, one of the marvels of the ancient world.[9] The centrality of the city in the province of Asia Minor and Paul's previous association with the Christian community there could have motivated him to write to the believers in Ephesus in order to strengthen them in their faith.

Occasion and Purpose

Ephesians is one of the "Prison Letters" that Paul wrote while in prison in Rome (others include Philippians, Colossians, and Philemon). Paul himself states that he was in prison at the time of writing (3:1; 4:1). Unlike Paul's other letters, such as Galatians and 1 and 2 Corinthians, Ephesians lacks mention of specific problems facing the audience for which he intended to provide solutions. It is not a polemic nor an apologetic for Paul's life or mission.[10] What can be inferred from the letter itself is that it was written to reinforce the recipients' Christian identity and encourage them to live in accordance with their calling in the midst of unbelievers (Eph 4–6). Paul's emphasis on the church as the body of Christ in which both Jews and gentiles are one, implies that he wished to promote unity amongst them (2:11–22; 4:1–16).

Literary Genre

The structure of Ephesians generally resembles Paul's other letters that are introduced with a greeting followed by thanksgiving (1 Cor 1:4; Phil 1:3; Col 1:3). In Ephesians this is extended into a eulogy placed between the greeting (1:1–2) and the thanksgiving (1:15–23). The body, however, varies from the Pauline corpus, for it consists of instructions (1:3–3:21), exhortations (4:1–6:20), and a recommendation (6:21–22). As to the conclusion, Ephesians (6:23–24) lacks Paul's customary farewell and well-wishes.[11] Accordingly, Ephesians is more like a baptismal liturgy than a letter, for liturgical forms are noticeable in the opening blessing (1:3–14) and there is a prayer offered on behalf of the recipients (1:15–23).[12] In view of these, Ephesians can be regarded as a letter with liturgical components.

8. Clinton E. Arnold, *Ephesians: Power and Magic* (Cambridge University Press, 1989), 13.

9. Arnold, *Ephesians: Power and Magic*, 20.

10. Roy R. Jeal, "Rhetorical Argumentation in the Letter to the Ephesians," in *Rhetorical Argumentation in Biblical Texts*, ed. Anders Eriksson, Thomas H. Olbricht, and Walter Übelacker (Trinity Press International, 2002), 311.

11. Muddiman, *The Letter to the Ephesians*, 6.

12. David A. deSilva, *New Cambridge Bible Commentary* (Cambridge University Press, 2022), 30.

Outline

Ephesians can be divided into two main parts: (1) theological (1:1–3:21) and (2) ethical (4:1–6:20). The first part deals with what God's people in Christ ought to understand, and the second invites believers to live in the world as God's chosen people. The divisions are a modification of Raymond Brown's structure which is based on content.[13]

- Greetings (1:1–2)
- Theological section (1:3–3:21)
  - Praising God (1:3–14)
  - Intercessory prayer (1:15–23)
  - Unity of believers (2:1–3:13)
  - Prayer and doxology (3:14–21)
- Ethical section (4:1–6:20)
  - Unity and walking in the light (4:1–5:21)
  - Household code (5:22–6:9)
  - Mission to Tychius (6:21–24)
- Blessing (6:23–24)

Theological Themes

In order to understand how the letter to the Ephesians could be understood in the African traditional and/or contemporary contexts, significant related thematic concepts will be identified, analyzed, and brought into dialogue. The interaction discloses how theological concepts in Ephesians could enrich and challenge Africans toward meaningful Christian living, and how some African realities could enhance the perception of the biblical message. Subsequently, the enduring significance of this hermeneutic is to show that although the principles drawn from a careful study of Ephesians transcend time and space, they have contextual relevance for Africans today. The related theological concepts in Ephesians and African society include supremacy of God, prayer, fellow citizens, wife–husband relationship, and spiritual battle.

Supremacy of God

Throughout the letter to the Ephesians, God is depicted as the main character around whom everything revolves. Paul refers to himself as an apostle by the will of God (1:1) and in his farewell message he wishes believers the peace that comes from God (6:23–24). God is portrayed as one but in three divine persons that is, Father, Son (Jesus Christ), and Holy Spirit. In some texts, each divine person has a specific role, but in others they work together. In Paul's prayer of blessing (1:3–4) it was God the Father who planned our salvation (1:3–6), God the Son who

13. The stated main and subdivisions below are a modification of Raymond E. Brown's structure. Cf. Raymond E. Brown, *An Introduction to the New Testament* (Doubleday, 1997), 621.

brought about our salvation (1:7–12), and God the Spirit who sealed it (1:13–14). Paul invokes the three divine persons together when he prays that through Jesus's sacrificial death on the cross Jews and gentiles "have access in one Spirit to the Father" (2:18). He also exhorts Christians to be filled with the Spirit and give thanks to God the Father through Jesus Christ (5:18–20).

Africans likewise believe in the existence of God, an idea that they derived from their reflection on the universe. The order, beauty, and continuity of created beings, forces of nature displayed through storms, thunder, moon and stars, night and day, as well in the changing seasons, led them to posit that there must be a Supreme Being. This notion is expressed in songs, proverbs, short statements, names, prayers, myths, and religious ceremonies.[14] Focusing on the names, the Zulu of South Africa refer to God as *Unkulunkulu*, meaning "the Great-Great-One"; the Ewe people of Ghana name him Mawu, acknowledging his sovereignty as creator, sustainer, and provider.[15] The Yoruba of Nigeria refer to God as the *Oludumare*, implying his supremacy or mightiness,[16] and the Igbo of Nigeria name him *Chukwu*, the one who orders the theocratic universe. Other divine beings simply collaborate but don't compete or struggle with him.[17] The supremacy of God is also revealed in tribal names for kings, rulers, governors, chiefs, and judges. When the Ganda people of Uganda, for instance, refer to God as *Kabaka*, meaning the king, they imply that he is the ruler of the universe, similar to the way kings govern their tribes.[18] The highlighted names and many others are used by African Christians today in their prayers, songs, and biblical translations into local languages. By so doing, they acknowledge that the God whom they worship is not different from the one worshipped by their predecessors (although one must be cautious not to equate them given that the character and nature of the Christian God is unique).

In Ephesians, God is equally portrayed as supernatural, exceedingly powerful, all-knowing, the originator and ruler of the universe. The aim of this depiction was to encourage believers who were overly concerned about power and their seeming lack of it. The fact that there were countless powerful magical and spiritual adversaries made them feel vulnerable and fearful. For, as Clinton E. Arnold explains, in the first century CE the people of the Hellenistic world had a strong interest in supernatural powers and demonic forces. This was manifested in the various magical beliefs and practices in Western Asia Minor in which Ephesus was located.[19] Paul thus counteracts this paralyzing fear by stressing the matchlessly superior divine force which is available to them due to their faith in Jesus Christ.

This exceedingly powerful God enables believers to overcome spiritual battles, live new lives, and unite together as one body regardless of their differences. The attribute of power is first mentioned in 1:19–23. In 1:19 Paul prays for believers to experience the "immeasurable

14. John S. Mbiti, *African Religions and Philosophy* (Heinemann, 1969), xiii.

15. Edwin Anaegboka Udoye, *Resolving the Prevailing Conflicts Between Christianity and African (Igbo) Traditional Religion Through Inculturation* (Lit Verlag, 2011), 26.

16. Anaegboka Udoye, *Resolving the Prevailing Conflicts*, 35.

17. Aloysius Eberechukwu Ndiukwu, *Authenticity of Belief in African (Igbo) Traditional Religion: A Critical Appraisal in the Light of Christian Faith* (Peter Lang, 2012), 166.

18. John S. Mbiti, *Introduction to African Religion*, 2nd ed. (Waveland Press, 2015), 52.

19. Clinton E. Arnold, *Power and Magic: The Concept of Power in Ephesians* (Wipf & Stock, 1997), 5.

greatness of his power" that is at "work in Christ when he raised him from the dead and seated him at his right hand" (1:20). Consequent to these events, God conferred on Jesus a place of honor at his own right hand (1:20) "far above all rule, authority, power and dominion" (1:21) and "put all things under his feet" (1:22). Paul also talks of "rulers and authorities" and "cosmic powers" residing "in the heavenly places" (3:10; 6:12), referring to forces opposed to God. The phrase "heavenly places," according to Daniel K. Darko, is the territory for spiritual beings and it is here that Christ was enthroned, and from where he exercises lordship over all beings (1:22).[20] Since people who converted to Christianity continued to be impacted by belief in evil forces,[21] Paul's assertions were intended to persuade them not to be enticed by such inferior powers. Instead, they needed to trust in Jesus Christ, who possesses ultimate power and controls all potentates.

Like in Ephesians, spiritual beings in the traditional African worldviews are apprehended and graded in a hierarchical order. The Supreme Being who is the greatest and highest is followed by lesser beings like divinities and spirits that occupy a higher rank than human beings. Below humans are animals, plants, and several inanimate beings. Authority, power, influence, and significance are determined by each being's position within the hierarchy.[22] While Africans acknowledge the Supreme Being as the highest and utmost powerful being, some people believe that he simply created but does not participate directly in the maintenance of the world, but leaves this role to the lesser deities.[23] In spite of this, the Supreme Being remains significant in their lives as the mastermind of fate and causality. Other beings can intervene, but they do not determine the outcome.[24] The notion of God in Africa as creator and above all things is in accord with that in Ephesians, with the exception of the latter's apparent remoteness from his creatures. The faith of Africans is thus enhanced by their acceptance of the lordship of Jesus Christ, who is accessible.

The belief in the supremacy of God is attested by the fact that almost all cultures in Africa have local names for God that portray his nature. When names like "creator" and "king" are refined of their anthropomorphic features, they can enrich the notion of God and enable the truth of the gospel to become meaningful to Christian Africans. Anthropomorphic terms are not bad in themselves, for even in the Old Testament they are used to refer to the activities of an invisible God (cf. Gen 2–3). Refining requires Africans to go beyond the physical features ascribed to God in space and time and think of him as a spiritual and eternal being. Also, the practice of accessing God in Africa through intermediaries is not out of place, for there is a sense in which Jesus himself is a mediator of the new covenant (Heb 9:15). Nonetheless, Christian Africans ought to remember that all other intermediaries apart from Jesus have been superseded. Jesus is the ultimate mediator between God and human beings. He is "Emmanuel,"

20. Daniel K. Darko, *Against Principalities and Powers: Spiritual Beings in Relation to Communal Identity and the Moral Discourse of Ephesians* (Hippo Books, 2020), 89–90.

21. Arnold, *Power and Magic*, 41.

22. Jacob K. Olupona, *African Religions: A Very Short Introduction* (Oxford University Press, 2014), 21.

23. Mbiti, *African Religions and Philosophy*, 68.

24. Olupona, *African Religions*, 21–22.

meaning "God is with us" (Matt 1:23), and thus easily accessible. The understanding in Ephesians of an exceedingly great God ought to rule out idolatrous and syncretistic practices that are prevalent among Christian Africans.

Praise and Prayer

The letter to the Ephesians consists of praise and prayer as the main forms of worship. Praise refers to the expression of gratitude or to a declaration of who holds higher power. It is "to offer thanks and honor God—to glorify him, especially in songs and with dancing."[25] On the other hand, prayer is a means of asking for help, privilege, or to link with a superior power. It is "an acknowledgment that there is a superior realm that affects the physical and visible world."[26] These significant realities are equally central to the lives of African peoples, both in the traditional and contemporary society. They are considered to be a means of direct communication with God and thus an essential part of religion.[27] They point to the reality that one is not in control of his or her destiny but needs a higher being to direct it. God is viewed not simply as the creator but also the sustainer of all created beings.[28] This belief in the creator negates "fatalism," the belief that considers the whole universe to be a deterministic system under which everything is subjugated.

In Ephesians 1:3–14 Paul praises the triune God for blessing the believers in various ways. Praise is related to the notion of blessing, for when a person blesses God, it shows that they acknowledge him as the source of their contentment.[29] In 1:3–14, praise is directed to the Triune God—Father, Son and the Holy Spirit. In each of the verses ending the subsections of the three persons in the Trinity (1:5–6; 1:10–12; 1:13–14), there is a doxology that praises God's glory (1:6, 12, 14). God the Father is the main character and he acts through Jesus Christ.[30] In the first place, praise is addressed to God the Father, who "destined us for adoption as his children through Jesus Christ" (1:3–6). Paul refers to God as the "Father of our Lord Jesus Christ" (1:3), and thereby underlines the special relationship that exists between the two. Second, praise is directed to the Son, for "in Christ we have also obtained an inheritance" (1:11–12). The death of Jesus created the opportunity for human beings to live in peace with

25. Tokunboh Adeyemo, "Worship and Praise," in *Africa Bible Commentary: A One-Volume Commentary Written by 70 African Scholars*, ed. Tokunboh Adeyemo (WordAlive Publishers; Zondervan, 2006), 251.

26. Bonifes Adoyo, "Prayer," in *Africa Bible Commentary: A One-Volume Commentary Written by 70 African Scholars*, ed. Tokunboh Adeyemo (WordAlive Publishers; Zondervan, 2006), 1212.

27. Ibigbolade S. Aderibigbe, "Origin, Nature, and Structure of Beliefs System," in *The Palgrave Handbook of African Traditional Religion*, ed. Ibigbolade S. Aderibigbe and Toyin Falola (Palgrave Macmillan, 2022), 42.

28. Aderibigbe, "Origin, Nature, and Structure of Beliefs System," 43.

29. Harold W. Hoehner, *Ephesians: An Exegetical Commentary* (Baker Academic, 2002), 162–163.

30. Prayers of blessings were common in the Jewish tradition and the "Benedictus" of Zechariah (Luke 1:68) is a typical example in the New Testament. Usually, in the proper sense, it is only God who can "bless" since it is him who is the source of goodness and can give what is good. Nevertheless, in the Bible we have examples of people like Isaac who blessed Jacob (Gen 27:27–29). In this act Jacob invoked God's blessing upon his son. In Psalm 96:2 we have an example of a man blessing God when the Psalmist says, "Sing to the Lord, bless his name; tell of his salvation from day to day."

God. Third, praise is addressed to the Holy Spirit: "In him you also . . . were marked with the seal of the promised Holy Spirit" (1:13–14). Anyone who hears and believes the message of Christ is saved and marked as God's possession by the Holy Spirit.[31] In this Trinitarian hymn Paul highlights the focus of all Christian prayers.

Paul praises God for: choosing believers long before the creation of the world (1:4); adopting them as God's children (1:5); pouring out his grace (1:6); redemption and forgiveness of sins by the blood of Christ (1:7); and revelation of his ultimate purpose (1:9–10). Further, Paul praises God for bestowing the Holy Spirit on the believers as a seal and guarantee of their inheritance and confidence in future redemption (1:13–14). He explains that since Christians have been chosen by God, their purpose should be to "live for the praise of his glory" (1:12), a phrase which also occurs in 1:14. In all these Paul, indicates that God has sealed his readers with the promised Holy Spirit for two reasons: to provide them with a kind of "down payment" of what they are to inherit in future and an assurance that the believers would be saved from God's wrath on the final day for the praise of his glory.[32] The Holy Spirit began the work of redemption and keeps believers safe from the wrath of God which is to come.

Praise is also evident in 3:20–21, whereby Paul, after hearing about the faith of the Ephesians, glorifies God for the power he bestows upon them for the accomplishment of his work. Thus Bruce rightly says, "the contemplation of God's eternal purpose and its fulfilment in the gospel calls forth a doxology."[33] In these verses Paul reiterates what he had stated earlier in 1:3–14—that he acknowledges God's supreme influence in the lives of the believers. Again, in 3:20 he acknowledges that God acts mightily and the doxology is used as a reminder of the great power which is accessible to believers through God. Accordingly, Paul states that "to him be glory in the church and in Christ Jesus" (3:21). It is through Jesus Christ that Jews and gentiles have been unified through the grace of God. And through the glory the Church accords to him, the wisdom of God is revealed to the spiritual forces in the heavenly realms.[34] Praise acknowledges the eternal plan of God for salvation which Christ mediates in the lives of the believers.

Prayer in Ephesians takes the forms of thanksgiving, intercession, and petition. It was common in Hellenistic culture to begin letters by thanking the gods on behalf of the recipient or by recommending the person to the gods. In his prayers Paul follows the Jewish pattern that often began by thanking God and continued with petition and intercession.[35] In 1:15–16 he writes, "I have heard of your faith in the Lord Jesus . . . and for this reason I do not cease to give thanks for you as I remember you in my prayers." In this prayer Paul acknowledges the faith the Ephesians had in Christ and the love they exhibited for the saints. He feels it necessary therefore to thank God for the spiritual growth of the believers.

---

31. Yusufu Turaki, "Ephesians," in *Africa Bible Commentary: A One-Volume Commentary Written by 70 African Scholars*, ed. Tokunboh Adeyemo (WordAlive Publishers; Zondervan, 2006), 1453–1454.

32. Frank Thielman, *Ephesians*, BECNT (Baker Academic, 2010), 83; see also F. F. Bruce, *The Epistles to the Colossians, to Philemon, and to the Ephesians* (Eerdmans, 1984), 330.

33. Thielman, *Ephesians*, 84.

34. Bruce, *The Epistles to the Colossians*, 331.

35. Peter S. Williamson and Mary Healy, *Ephesians* (Baker Academic, 2009), 46.

In the consequent texts there are prayers of petition and intercession. Paul prays that the believers would receive the following spiritual benefits: (1) reception of the Spirit of wisdom in order to comprehend the hope to which they had been called (1:17–19); (2) strengthening with power so as to comprehend the love of Christ that exceeds all knowledge (3:16–19); and (3) becoming what they had already received in Christ, that is, "the fullness of him who fills all in all" (1:23; see also 3:19). Again, in 6:18–20 we have a prayer of petition which is in two sections. In the first part (6:18a) Paul exhorts the believers to dedicate themselves to prayer. In part two (6:18b–20) he designates the object of the believers' prayers. He urges them to pray for everybody, including himself. Frank Thielman justifies the reason for Paul's need of prayers by relating it to his imprisonment. He says that in view of the tension Paul was undergoing as a prisoner, he needed the strength to continue proclaiming the mystery of the gospel.[36] Intercessory prayers underline the believers' responsibility to pray for the well-being of others, including their leaders.

In Africa, praise and prayer are facts of life and essential parts of religion. They are expressed in words, symbolic actions, dances, and rituals. Praise and prayer are not usually distinguished from each other, and this is why when John Mbiti enumerates the various forms of prayer he mentions "praise, thanksgiving, a declaration of the state of affairs in which the prayers are offered, and requests."[37] Mbiti elsewhere indicates that "joy, praise and thanksgiving belong together and express another dimension of African spirituality."[38] In the same vein, for Aylward Shorter, the different kinds of prayer include "petition, intercession, thanksgiving, praise, confession, contrition and amendment, purification from defilement, blessing, cursing, lament, forgiveness, vows or promises, divination and commemoration."[39] The overriding purpose of prayer could include any of the aforementioned aspects. Focusing on the concept of praise in particular, Mbiti explains that when God provides his people with good things, they sing and beat musical instruments in order to praise him. Below is an example of how Africans praise God:

I shall sing a song of praise to God
Strike the chords upon the drum.
God who gives us all good things
Strike the chords upon the drum.
Wives, and wealth, and wisdom
Strike the chords upon the drum.[40]

---

36. Thielman, *Ephesians*, 432.

37. John S. Mbiti, *African Religions and Philosophy* (Heinemann African Writers Series, 1969), 55.

38. John S. Mbiti, *Introduction to African Religion*, 2nd ed. (Waveland Press, 2015), 146.

39. Aylward Shorter, *Prayer in the Religious Traditions of Africa* (Oxford University Press, 1975), 15.

40. John S. Mbiti, *The Prayers of African Religion* (SPCK, 1975), 148.

In most cases when Africans communicate with God directly, they refer to him as the creator who masterminded the cyclical phenomena of nature. This is exemplified by the hymn to Mwari, the Great Spirit of the Shona people of Zimbabwe:

> *Great Spirit,*
> *Piler up of rocks into towering mountains!*
> *When thou stampest on the stone,*
> *The dust rises and fills the land.*
> *Hardness of the precipice;*
> *Waters of the pool that turn*
> *Into misty rain when stirred.*
> *Vessel overflowing with oil!*[41]

Prayers are said during occasions of childbirth, rites of passage, weddings, epidemics and sickness, death, old age, planting, war, drought, and reconciliation.[42] They are done individually or in a community and people use them in all situations of life. Individually people request things like guidance, healing, success, prosperity, protection from danger, preservation of life, peace, and safety when traveling. Communally people may pray for peace, rain, cessation of epidemics, success in raids or war, fertility of crops, animals, and people.[43] It is the appropriate outlook of those who are in communion with God.

The prayers used are generally short, spontaneous, and directly state the intention. Shorter underscores the petitionary nature of African prayers when he cites how the Meru people of Kenya implore God's providence and blessings:

> Kirinyaga, owner of all things, I pray thee, give me what I need, Because I am suffering, And also my children (are suffering) And all things that are in this country of mine. I beg thee for life, The good one, with things, Healthy people with no disease, May they bear healthy children. And also to women who suffer because they are barren, Open the way by which they may see children. (Give) goats, cattle, food, honey. And also the troubles of the other lands That I do not know, remove.[44]

The cited prayer of the Meru people demonstrates the common trend in African traditional prayers. They are spontaneous and display the trust of the petitioner that his/her desires will be granted. They focus more on material than spiritual needs and thus differ from those in Ephesians that pray for wisdom, blessings, knowledge, and enlightenment (Eph 1:17–18).

---

41. Shorter, *Prayer in the Religious Traditions of Africa*, 41.

42. Shorter, *Prayer in the Religious Traditions of Africa*, 15.

43. Mbiti, *Introduction to African Religion*, 61–62; Aderibigbe, "Origin, Nature, and Structure of Beliefs System," 42.

44. Shorter, *Prayer in the Religious Traditions of Africa*, 45.

The recipient of prayer in Ephesians is the Triune God (2:18). In Africa, scholars are divided on whether the Supreme Being receives prayers directly or they are addressed to him through intermediaries. On the one hand, some contend that prayers are usually directed to the Supreme Being in crises of life, such as when there is childlessness in marriage, a difficult birth, intrusion of horrific diseases and epidemics, and wars.[45] Otherwise, in most cases prayers are addressed to God through the mediation of divinities and ancestral spirits, who then translate them into a language understandable to the Supreme Being.[46] Other scholars however, argue that people experience themselves as living in a network of relationships that connects them with God and nature, and the notion of an aloof God is not tenable. Mbiti explains that the addressees of African prayers are many. He states that primarily prayers are addressed to God, who is normally mentioned by his personal name or attribute and sometimes by implication. A few, about 10 percent, are directed to divinities, spirits, the living dead, and personifications of nature (trees, rivers, earth).[47] Bénézet Bujo concurs with Mbiti when he writes that "much of what has been written about Africa's 'absent God' must be considered mistaken. God is not far from the African world. All relationships, between person and person, living and dead, and between persons and nature, are rooted in God and point towards God and towards the end of all things in him."[48] Mbiti and Bujo's assertions are true to some extent, although there is also a prevalence of praying through divinities and ancestral spirits in Africa whom people consider to be more accessible. Ancestors are particularly perceived to be concerned with the welfare of their descendants and they have power to either bless or harm them. Below is an example of an ancestral prayer said by a traditional healer:

> Our grand ancestors—[names] and all the others who are with you, hear us. Listen to our cries. The medicines are yours. The healing is yours too. Oh—answer us positively and provide your strength to the healing of this sufferer. We plead with you in good spirits. Come! Destroy the satanic spirits that have attacked our patient. Direct us to the right herbs to give. Please present our prayers to God the creator, the provider of health and complete healing, and the owner of all herbs.[49]

Prayer involves the use of gestures like kneeling, as mentioned in 3:14. In the Old Testament, kneeling expresses a humble cognizance of being an inferior, dependent on an exalted lord. In the book of Esther, the King ordered his officials to demonstrate their respect for Haman by kneeling (Esth 3:2) and when Mordecai refused to kneel Haman was furious and decided

45. Paul O. Gaggawala, *Fully Christian . . . Fully Human: A Model for the New Evangelization* (Jeremiah Press, 1999), 62.

46. Aderibigbe, "Origin, Nature, and Structure of Beliefs System," 42.

47. Mbiti, *The Prayers of African Religion*, 3.

48. Bénézet Bujo, *African Theology in Its Social Context*, trans. John O'Donohue (St. Paul Publications–Africa, 1992), 32.

49. George Odiko, "Prayers Through Ancestors: The Force Behind Traditional Healing Among the Giriama People," *African Cultures and Religion* 1, no. 3 (1999): 59.

to punish him (Esth 3:5–6). The same attitude is reflected in the story of an officer and the fifty men who were sent by the King to plead with Elijah to spare their lives (2 Kgs 1:13). Kneeling before God also signifies a confession of faith as in Isaiah 45:23. This is why the Israelites were prohibited to kneel before any god other than Yahweh their true God (1 Kgs 1:18). Kneeling before Yahweh is a confession of faith, as the Psalmist says, "O come, let us worship and bow down, let us kneel before the LORD, our Maker!" (Ps 95:6). As a penitential ritual, at the time of sacrifice Ezra knelt and made a confession of sin (Ezra 9:4ff.). Moreover, in 1 Kings 8:54 the author writes that "when Solomon finished offering all this prayer and this plea to the LORD, he arose from facing the altar of the LORD, where he had knelt with hands outstretched toward heaven."

In the New Testament, especially in the Gospels, standing rather than kneeling seems to be the suitable posture of prayer (Matt 6:5; Mark 11:25; Luke 18:9–14). For instance, Mark writes that Jesus directed his followers thus, "Whenever you stand praying, forgive, if you have anything against anyone" (Mark 11:25). Nonetheless, in the Gospels kneeling is noticeable when Jesus kneels during his agony on the Mount of Olives (Luke 22:41), and when Peter knelt down to pray for Tabitha, who had died (Acts 9:40). These examples indicate that the gesture of kneeling that Paul mentions in Ephesians 3:14, although not common in the New Testament, was used in some circumstances in the Bible.

By analogy, the gesture of kneeling is practiced by some Christian Africans in some denominations. Roman Catholics, for instance, have moments of standing, sitting, and kneeling in their liturgical celebrations. Among the African Instituted Churches like Zionists and Kimbanguists, the common position while praying is kneeling. People kneel with hands placed on their chests and with their eyes closed.[50] There is need therefore to adopt or rediscover the gesture of kneeling during prayers wherever it is lacking or neglected. Besides kneeling, Africans sing, dance, and clap their hands during communal prayerful festivities. These gestures, when well utilized, make prayer an enjoyable and enriching spiritual experience.

Praise and prayer are means of worship through which believers express their commitment to God by acknowledging and appreciating his benevolence, and petitioning him for individual and communal needs. The similarities that exist in Ephesians and African forms of prayer make it easy for Christian Africans to appropriate those highlighted in Ephesians in their own spirituality. Again, while some Africans address their prayers directly to God, others believe in the intercessory role of their ancestors. Ancestral veneration is not equated with the questionable practice of asking diviners to consult spirits on one's behalf. Similarly, some Christians, such as Roman Catholics and Orthodox Christians, ask for the intercession of Mary and the saints in their prayers. The practice is not viewed in any way as rivalry to the unique mediatory role of Jesus. One of the significant distinctions between saints and ancestors is that, whereas the ancestors in Africa are biological predecessors in their families and are basically men, the saints

50. J. K. N. Mugambi, "The Ecumenical Movement and Future of the Church in Africa," in *The Church in African Christianity: Innovative Essays in Christology*, ed. J. K. N. Mugambi and Laurenti Magesa (Initiatives Publishers, 1990), 48.

(for Roman Catholics), however, can mediate for everybody irrespective of their geographical boundaries, and they consist of both men and women.[51] Mugambi rightly argues that one of the reasons for the rise of African Indigenous churches is the failure of mainline churches to appreciate the African religious and cultural heritage of ancestral veneration.[52] Given the importance accorded to the ancestors in Africa, it is necessary to assess their role in people's lives in order to determine whether giving honor to ancestors can be integrated into Christianity without compromising the belief in the oneness of God. However, it is doubtful that there is any way that ancestor veneration can be practiced without it being syncretistic.

Fellow Citizens

The church is made up of people from different cultural, racial, and tribal backgrounds. These differences can either be used to build up the church or to destroy it. As in his other letters (Rom 9–11; Gal 3), Paul in Ephesians is concerned with the relationship between the gentiles and the Jews in the church and in God's plan of salvation. In some of his other letters, Paul describes the unity of gentiles and Jews into one new creation as a future event, but in Ephesians he portrays that unity as an already achieved reality (Eph 2:13). Gentiles and Jews had disparities in their cultural and religious practices that led them to harbor prejudices against one another.[53] In the church one group viewed themselves as those in the center and the others as being at the periphery. The way Christians relate amongst themselves in Africa is almost similar to that of the Jews and gentiles who, despite their union in Christ, engage in discriminatory practices based on tribal and religious differences. The invitation to gentiles to view themselves as "citizens with the saints" (Eph 2:19), irrespective of their differences, is also a plea to Africans to strive toward unity.

In simple terms the word "gentile" refers to any non-Jewish person. In Ephesians, gentiles are portrayed as outsiders who lacked the key element of the Jewish community that God gave them through Abraham (Gen 17:10–13). This element was circumcision, a mark that sealed God's covenant with Abraham as the father of nations. Circumcision distinguished the Jews from the people of other nations and bestowed upon them rights to partake in God's covenant promises (Acts 7:8). It further symbolized their incorporation into the commonwealth of Israel, an aspect that unfortunately caused them to potentially nurture the attitude of spiritual preeminence among other people.[54] The Law itself instructed the Jews to uphold strict separation from the gentiles in matters of religion, politics, and marriage (Exod 23:28–33; Josh 23:4–13). It is no wonder therefore that Paul himself was almost killed for supposedly taking Trophimus the Ephesian, and thereby a gentile, to the temple premises (Acts 21:27–31).

51. J. K. N. Mugambi, *African Heritage and Contemporary Christianity* (Longman Kenya, 1989), 68.

52. Mugambi, *African Heritage and Contemporary Christianity*, 68.

53. Thielman, *Ephesians*, 159.

54. Craig S. Keener, *The IVP Bible Background Commentary: New Testament*, 2nd ed. (InterVarsity Press, 2014), 546.

Paul mentions the disadvantages the gentiles had as unbelievers: separation from Christ, alienation from the citizenship of Israel, strangers to the covenants of promise, living without hope and without God (Eph 2:12). In 2:14 he uses the imagery of a dividing wall to demonstrate the hostility that existed between Jews and gentiles.[55] This is an allusion to the wall in the temple at Jerusalem that separated the court of the Israelites from the court of the gentiles. The wall kept gentiles from accessing the inner parts in the Jerusalem temple.[56] The physical barrier, in addition to the gentiles not being people of the covenantal promise, drew them far apart from the Jews. The dividing wall was destroyed by Jesus through his death on the cross.

However, because Jesus had broken the barriers through his sacrificial death, Paul confidently tells the gentiles thus, "But now in Christ Jesus you who once were far off have been brought near by the blood of Christ" (2:13). This is so because all human differences, barriers, and hostilities based on race, tribe, and religion are resolved. The means used to resolve the conflict differs greatly from those used in the Old Testament, whereby animal sacrifices were the means of reconciling people with God (Lev 16:2; Heb 9:7). In the New Testament, it is Jesus's own blood which is the means by which sinners are drawn near to God. Paul explains the transformation that the gentiles achieved in Christ when he says, "So then you are no longer strangers and aliens, but you are citizens with the saints and also members of the household of God" (Eph 2:19). This implies that all who believe in Jesus, regardless of their disparities, are citizens in the kingdom of God. Christ did not make gentiles citizens of the nation of Israel, but of the kingdom of heaven. It is this kingdom that Paul refers to when he states that "There is no longer Jew or Greek, there is no longer slave or free, there is no longer male and female; for all of you are one in Christ Jesus" (Gal 3:28).[57] The text cited here implies that, like the Jews, gentiles are not strangers or second-class citizens in the kingdom of God.

The relationship between gentiles and Jews in Ephesus resonates with the African experience. In African society, each ethnic group traces its origins to a particular hero and is united around certain beliefs and practices that distinguish it from other tribes. Relationships generally depend on family ties, the use of the same language, or living in the same geographical region. This kind of unity is suspect since anyone beyond these boundaries is regarded as an outsider, or worse still, an enemy.[58] Ideally, various tribes in a nation or church setting enhance the social, economic, and spiritual well-being of the community based on their unique qualities.

Nonetheless, due to the struggle for survival and maintenance of the tribal group's own standards, the inclination toward negative ethnicity is great. Unfortunately, discriminations based on ethnic differences exists even in churches. Some commentators like Rubin Pohor

55. However, Hoehner, *Ephesians*, 369, argues against this view, as the reference to the wall in Jerusalem is lacking in the passage, and that the wall "was still standing when Paul wrote this letter." See also Stephen E. Fowl, *Ephesians*, NTL (Westminster John Knox, 2012), 90–91; John Stott, *The Message of Ephesians*, BST (InterVarsity Press, 1989), 99; Lynn H. Cohick, *Ephesians*, NCCS (Cascade Books, 2010), 76.

56. Turaki, "Ephesians," 1456.

57. Adrienne Von Speyr, *The Letter to the Ephesians* (Ignatius Press, 1996), 110.

58. Kuzuli Kosse, "Unity of Believers," in *Africa Bible Commentary: A One-Volume Commentary Written by 70 African Scholars*, ed. Tokunboh Adeyemo (WordAlive Publishers; Zondervan, 2006), 1314.

attribute this to the fact that many missionary organizations tended to work with particular ethnic groups. This focus led to the composition of churches that were constituted by one majority ethnic group. According to Pohor, the features of mostly "African Protestantism, in conjunction with the linguistic realities of the continent, have reinforced the differences between groups, whether these are institutional, doctrinal or organizational, and whether they appear in terms of our pastoral ministry, our academic emphasis, charitable work or our social action."[59] What Pohor says is true, for discriminations are manifest in churches in the form of selective sharing of resources, use of native languages in mixed congregations, discriminatory employment opportunities, and unwarranted transfer of church leadership.

A puzzling and horrific manifestation of negative ethnicity in Africa was experienced in the Rwanda genocide which took place in 1994. Emmanuel Katongole explains that "within a period of less than one hundred days, more than 800,000 Rwandans were killed by fellow Rwandans."[60] The underlying cause of the genocide was mainly negative ethnicity, since it was Hutus and Tutsis killing one another. What makes this genocide particularly challenging is the fact that Rwanda is one of the most Christianized nations in Africa and at that time, an estimated 90 percent of the population was Christian. What is still more saddening is the fact that many of the killings took place around or within churches and involved Christians killing one another. Commenting on this tragedy, Timothy Longman writes, "Not only were the vast majority of those who participated in the killings Christians, but the church buildings also served as Rwanda's primary killing fields."[61] A common slogan related to this event, that "blood is thicker than water," indicates that racial, ethnic, and tribal allegiance and affinity take priority over the teachings of Christianity.

Subsequently, Paul's exhortation to gentiles and Jews to view themselves as fellow citizens is a challenge to Christian Africans, who continue to struggle against hostilities and discriminations based on religious and ethnic grounds. They need to be reminded that although there are differences that separate them from other believers, Jesus's sacrificial death brought forgiveness and salvation to all people. Henceforth, there are no more distinctions between them. They ought to regard each other as fellow citizens in the Christian community by avoiding and opposing discriminatory practices. Varieties of ethnic groups and Christian traditions need to be viewed as assets that enrich individuals, churches, nations, and society at large.

Wife–Husband Relationship

Marriage is an essential institution in society and its success or failure depends on how wives and husbands relate to one another. In Africa, marriage is the place where members of the community meet; that is, the living, the departed, and those yet to be born. It is not only the

59. Rubin Pohor, "Tribalism, Ethnicity and Race," in *Africa Bible Commentary: A One-Volume Commentary Written by 70 African Scholars*, ed. Tokunboh Adeyemo (WordAlive Publishers; Zondervan, 2006), 316.

60. Emmanuel Katongole, "Christianity, Tribalism, and the Rwandan Genocide: A Catholic Reassessment of Christian 'Social Responsibility,'" *Logos: A Journal of Catholic Thought and Culture* 8, no. 3 (June 2005): 67–93.

61. Timothy Longman, *Christianity and Genocide in Rwanda* (Cambridge University Press, 2010), 4.

concern of husbands and wives, but also the coming together of two extended families. To facilitate credible marriage relationships among Christians, Paul directs in Ephesians 5:22–33 that wives should be subject to their husbands, and that husbands should love their wives, just as Christ loved the church. Understood literally, for a wife to submit to her husband would be regarded as an endorsement of the Greco-Roman and African patriarchal structures in which authority is exerted by the husband and the wife's role is simply to obey. On the other hand, judging by today's standards, Paul's message could be viewed as outdated, since for some wives to submit implies acceptance of male dominance and oppression. What is less stressed in the text is the exhortation to husbands to love their wives as Christ loves the church, an aspect which makes the teaching of Paul appropriate and liberating for many Christian Africans. What is more, submission is the responsibility of all Christians and not only for those who are inferior. Hence, Paul writes, "Be subject to one another out of reverence for Christ" (Eph 5:21). A truly happy marriage would be the one in which husbands and wives submit to one another.

The text that deals with the wife–husband relationship is a subsection of 5:22–6:9 which reflects the household code in Greco-Roman society. In this cultural setting, there was differentiation of power between husband and wife, parent and children, and master and slave.[62] For Aristotle, it is these three basic relationships that form a household. What concerns the wives is found in 5:22–24; for husbands it is in 5:25–32; and a synopsis of the directives for both is in the concluding section (5:33).[63] This household code is a continuation of the ethical directives Paul gives to gentile believers. Before they became Christians, they lived according to the desires of the "flesh" (2:3), they were "without Christ" (2:12), and were darkened in their understanding (4:18). In the household code, Paul advises them on how to live in accordance with gospel values. Thus, whereas the framework for Paul's advice is from the Greco-Roman setting in which the gentile believers lived, it is also infused with the message found in the first three chapters of the letter.[64] These chapters explain the spiritual benefits the Ephesian Christians have attained through their faith in Jesus Christ.

In Greco-Roman society the lines of subservience and authority were plainly drawn. The husband had authority over the wife in a strong social hierarchy. Ephesians 5:22–33 harmonizes with the code in Colossians 3:18–4:1 where wives are instructed to be subject to their husbands, the husbands to love their wives, children to obey their parents, and slaves to obey their masters. The consequent verses (Eph 5:23–24) advance the idea of submission in 5:22 required of wives. The reason why the wife should submit to her husband is because he is the head, in the same way as Christ is the head of the church (5:23). The imagery of the head is used also in 1 Corinthians 11:3, thus, "But I want you to understand that Christ is the head of every man, and the husband is the head of his wife, and God is the head of Christ." Christ relates to the church not in a domineering way but as its Savior. Paul's statement is therefore a reversal of the traditional status quo in Greco-Roman society.

62. David A. deSilva, *Ephesians*, NCBC (Cambridge University Press, 2022), 275.

63. Charles Talbert, *Ephesians and Colossians*, Paideia (Zondervan Academic, 2007), 139.

64. Thielman, *Ephesians*, 392.

Paul's instruction to wives resonates with the African patriarchal system whereby wives are obliged to be submissive to their husbands. This practice has its basis in the socialization process for boys as compared to that for girls. Boys are groomed to view themselves as heads of households and breadwinners, while girls are taught to be submissive housekeepers. Within marriage itself, there are many cultural practices that promote women's subordination. One of them is the requirement to pay bride price in order to authenticate the marriage. In spite of its value as a gesture of appreciation to the woman's family, it is abused when it is considered to be bride price. This leads to the perception and treatment of wives as purchased property that can be treated in any way the husbands choose. The practice of paying bride price is equally oppressive to men, especially the poor ones, for it makes it hard for them to pay for the women they truly love.[65] In order to fulfill this obligation, some borrow money or pay it in installments. It is no surprise then that some men eventually treat their wives as commodities. Additionally, the practice of female genital circumcision, which some women undergo, is intended mostly to compel them to be faithful wives to their husbands. This ritual deprives women of their sexual sensitivity, leads to health complications, and above all deprives women of their human dignity.[66] For these reasons, the practice is contested today, though it continues secretly in some cultures.

For their part, some women in Africa resist the command to obey their husbands. This is generally instigated by the feminist movement for gender equality. Positively, the movement has helped to improve the status of women, especially in educational, economic, political, and some ecclesial spheres. Radical feminists consider patriarchy to be a social and cultural system in which men acquire all substantial roles and keep women in subsidiary positions. This kind of feminism poses challenges to the manner in which wives relate to their husbands, especially those that are less affluent or educated than themselves. Paul's instruction challenges such women to reconsider their practices, for a home cannot function properly with two people competing for headship. It would be easy for a wife to submit to her husband if he fulfills his responsibilities as the head, but the biblical teaching is not dependent on the nature of the husband one has, it is modeled on the submission of the church to Christ (5:22–24). Nonetheless, this does not imply that the wife should not think for herself or use her gifts and abilities for the well-being of her family and society. Submission should also not be used to force women to stay in marriage relationships that are injurious to their lives.

After his exhortation to wives, Paul tells husbands to love their wives. He writes, "Husbands, love your wives, just as Christ loved the church and gave himself up for her" (5:25). The verb "to love" is repeated in verses 28 and 33 to underline its significance. In 5:25 Paul explains how husbands should love their wives. He compares it to the manner in which "Christ loved the church" when he gave up his life for her. Accordingly, Paul postulates that Christian husbands exercise their headship as Christ did by sacrificing themselves for their wives' well-being. Here Paul upholds the ancient Greco-Roman ideal for wives to submit to their husbands but qualifies it by instructing husbands to love their

65. Khofi Arthur Phiri, *African Christian Marriage: A Christian Theological Appraisal* (Paulines Publications Africa, 2011), 92.

66. Bénézet Bujo, *Plea for Change of Models for Marriage* (Paulines Publications Africa, 2009), 52–53.

wives as Christ loved the church.[67] Moreover, husbands should love their wives "as their own bodies" (5:28). As it is natural for a man to love, cherish, and protect himself, he should likewise do so for his wife.

In Africa, the primary purpose of marriage is not love but procreation. This makes it difficult for a man to love a childless wife. While child-bearing is valued in Christian marriages as well, Paul prioritizes love and compares it to Christ's sacrificial love for the church. Surprisingly, in Africa some husbands who genuinely love their wives are viewed with suspicion. Ester Rutoro, writing from the Shona context of Zimbabwe, states that usually when a man loves his wife, people accuse the wife of giving him a love potion. This is a magical drink intended to make the person who takes it fall in love with the giver. The same is said when the husband spends much time at home with his wife.[68] The attribution of a man's love to supernatural powers weakens the virtue of love in married life. The love husbands should have toward their wives is willed by God. Thus, Paul compares it to the relationship between Christ and the church and refers to it as a great mystery that can hardly be understood on human terms.

In Ephesians 5:22–33 Paul upholds the ancient ideal for wives to submit to their husbands, but qualifies it by instructing them to love their wives as Christ loved the church, by voluntarily sacrificing himself for it. Contrasted to the absolute authority of husbands, Paul compares the husbands' role to Christ's headship over the church. This understanding rejects the domineering attitude of some husbands that leads them to mistreat their wives. On the part of African Christian women, their submissive cultural attitude makes it easier for them to appropriate Paul's teaching in marriage. It frees them from negative feminism that advocates for gender equivalence rather than equity. Proper submission should not be forced and if a wife refuses to comply, the Christian husband should endeavor to win her over by his loving behavior. The challenge of the wife–husband relationship is expressed thus by John S. Mbiti: "Marriage can be an area of the greatest extremes. It is in marriage that you can experience the most profound experience of love, or expression of hatred. It is in marriage that you can be extremely courteous or extremely rude to each other. In is in marriage that you can live in heaven of joy and happiness or in the very hell of misery and wretchedness."[69] In order to reap the positive aspects of marriage, it is suitable for a wife to submit to the legitimate directives of her husband and for the husband to sacrificially love his wife by considering her as a partner with whom he can deliberate on matters pertaining to the welfare of their family.

Spiritual Battle

The African cosmos comprises visible and invisible beings. Besides God, who is above all things, there are human beings and spirits. Since the spirits are nonbodied in nature, they are

67. Keener, *The IVP Bible Background Commentary*, 552.

68. Ester Rutoro, "'Your Desire Shall Be for Your Husband and He Shall Rule Over You!' Desire and Rule in Traditional Shona Understandings of Marriage," in *Living with Dignity: African Perspectives on Gender Equality*, ed. Elna Mouton, Gertrude Kapama, Len Hansen, and Thomas Togom (Sun Media, 2015), 312.

69. John S. Mbiti, *Love and Marriage in Africa* (Longman, 1977), 98.

believed to take their abode in trees, water, forests, rocks, mountains, caves, animals, and even human beings.[70] Spirits are usually considered to be neutral; they could be beneficent as well as malicious. People seek what they consider to be benevolent spirits to assist them to have children, succeed in business, acquire property, power, or have protection for their lives and property.[71] On the other hand, the spirits could harm humans and property, inflict illnesses, death, disability, incapacitation, destruction, and create natural disasters. When the spirits enter the life of human beings, they cause them to behave in abnormal ways.

Generally, when Africans face misfortunes, they immediately think that these are caused by evil spirits.[72] The spirits are feared for they are believed to be more powerful than human beings, and it is nearly impossible to resist their influence. Richard J. Gehman notes that in Africa there are some people who ignore the spirits and do not fear them. He cites the example of the Murle people of southern Sudan who neither fear nor seek help or blessings from spirits. When someone dies, they believe that he/she descends into a hole and lives in the shadowy world in the ground and does not return to trouble the living. The Murle people thus have no words for spirit possession and those who claim to be possessed are believed to have mental problems.[73] This example is an exception rather than the norm, for many people believe in spirits and try to guard and deliver themselves and others from those they believe to be malevolent.

Paul's message on spiritual warfare is contextualized in the city of Ephesus. The city had a reputation for a profusion of magical practices. Magic was mainly concerned with getting hold of supernatural powers and the handling of the spirit world in the interests of their users. In Ephesus, magic charms or spells were sold and used all over the Roman Empire.[74] Artemis of Ephesus was the chief divinity of Asia Minor and was widely worshipped more than other deities. This goddess was perceived to be the mother of fertility and to possess astrological authority. She controlled the religious, cultural, and economic life of the people of Ephesus.[75] It is no surprise therefore that it was in Ephesus that Paul encountered the seven sons of Sceva who failed to exorcize a demon-possessed man. The fear which engrossed the city consequent to this event (Acts 19:17) and the burning of large volumes of magical papyri confirms the prevalence of sorcery and magical practices in Ephesus. Moreover, the violent response of the silversmiths at the loss of their business underscores the involvement of evil forces in business, culture, and religion (Acts 19:27).

There is an intimation that evil powers do not have the right to oppress believers except those who sin, but they always threaten to resurface and resume their operations in the lives of those who have accepted Jesus Christ (4:26–27). They cause believers to fall; this is why Paul

70. Mbiti, *African Religion and Philosophy*, 80.

71. Mbiti, *Introduction to African Religion*, 70.

72. J. K. N. Mugambi, *African Heritage and Contemporary Christianity* (Longman Kenya, 1989), 64.

73. Richard J. Gehman, *African Traditional Religion in Biblical Perspective* (East African Educational Publishers, 2005), 214.

74. Arnold, *Power and Magic*, 20.

75. Margaret Y. MacDonald, *Colossians and Ephesians*, SP 17 (Liturgical Press, 2000), 343–344.

uses the term "the wiles of the devil" (6:1) and also states that they attack believers through "flaming arrows" (6:16). Paul also equates the work of false teachers to that of evil powers. He states that these use "people's trickery, by their craftiness in deceitful scheming" (4:14) to undermine the faith of immature believers (4:14). He shows that the devil motivates all deceitful scheming activities (6:11). In all these examples the emphasis is on the deceitful nature of the enemy, who often uses indiscernible strategies to mislead the believers.

To counteract the impact of evil powers, Paul directs that Christians should use the "armor of God." Armor refers to military tools used for protection, defense, covering, and shielding from attacks. The imagery of the "armor" is derived from what the Roman soldiers used to ready themselves with for battle. Hence, it easy for Paul's readers to understand and relate his message to their spiritual combat against the demonic forces.[76] Since the battle is not physical, the means Paul exhorts his readers to use are of a spiritual nature. They include the following: standing up, fastening the belt of truth, putting on the breastplate of righteousness, putting on shoes on one's feet, and taking the shield of faith (6:14–16). In all these, the Christian warrior is defensive, trying to protect him/herself.[77] The believer also has to "take the shield of faith, with which you will be able to quench all the flaming arrows of the evil one" (6:16).[78] The burning arrows signify all types of assault planned by the evil one, including persecution, false teaching, and despair. Faith empowers the believer and enables him/her to resist and prevail over the devil's attacks.[79] Finally, the spiritual warrior ought to "Take the helmet of salvation, and the sword of the Spirit, which is the word of God" (6:17). When soldiers dressed up for battle, the last piece they put on was the helmet. It was necessary for survival, for it protected the head, a vital part of the body.[80] As for the sword, for the believer this is the word of God. While the other aforementioned aspects are defensive, the "sword" is offensive for its purpose is to attack and destroy the enemy.

Correspondingly, malicious powers in Africa lead people to use various ways to rid themselves of evil spirits. Generally, recourse to witchcraft and sorcery[81] mirror in African spiritual

---

76. Keener, *The IVP Bible Background Commentary*, 554.

77. Raymond F. Collins, "Ephesians," in *The Paulist Biblical Commentary*, ed. José Enrique Aguilar Chiu, Richard J. Clifford, Carol J. Dempsey, Eileen M. Schuller, Thomas D. Stegman, and Ronald D. Witherup (Paulist Press, 2018), 1417.

78. Keener explains that "Roman soldiers were most commonly equipped with large rectangular wooden shields, four feet high, the fronts of which were made of leather. Before battles in which flaming arrows might be fired, the leather would be wetted to quench any fiery darts launched against them. After Roman legionaries closed ranks, the front row holding shields forward and those behind them holding shields above them, they were deemed virtually invulnerable to any attack from flaming arrows." Cf. Keener, *The IVP Bible Background Commentary*, 554–555.

79. Andrew T. Lincoln, *Ephesians*, WBC 42 (Thomas Nelson, 1990), 449.

80. Collins, "Ephesians," 1417.

81. Africans consider witchcraft to be the power people have to harm others by supernatural means. Witchcraft powers are inherited but could also be acquired or bought. A sorcerer on the other hand could use rituals, incantations, and various substances intended to harm others. These two practices were not tolerated in African society and those convicted of them faced serious consequences. Some were speared, killed, stoned, beaten to death or strangled, burnt alive, or banished. Cf. Mbiti, *African Religions and Philosophy*, 201; Laurenti Magesa, *African Religion: The Moral Traditions of Abundant Life* (Paulines Publications Africa, 1997), 172. In some cultures, people believe that

battles. Also, some people drink the blood of animals, others tie the gall bladder of animals on their heads, while others put medicine around their wrists.[82] Some healers recommend water for stomach complaints, for they believe that there is power embedded in water to counteract evil powers that cause illnesses. The patient could vomit the stuff which is thought to be the cause of sickness.[83] For stomach ulcers, patients drink lukewarm water mixed with salt. When water is mixed with salt it is believed to dispel evil forces. At times people beat drums to drive away witches when doing exorcisms. Others use amulets as charms to protect themselves and their children against probable attackers.[84] In communities that believe in spirit possession, there is recourse to spirit mediumship. The diviner enters into an intimate relationship with a possessed person through ecstatic experiences in order to drive out the spirit.[85] These practices are done both privately and publicly, depending on the nature of the problem.

Many Pentecostals, African Initiated churches, and charismatic religious movements use prayers and scriptural passages for exorcising demons from their oppressed members. In addition, some employ annointing oil and water for deliverance and protection. To succeed in their mission, some church members and preachers volunteer to act as "prayer warriors" to intercede for those affected and the exorcists. They deal with problems like sicknesses, barrenness, marriage breakdown, loneliness, and joblessness that are often attributed to evil magic, witchcraft, and sorcery. The reluctance of some leaders from the mainline churches, such as Roman Catholics, Anglicans, Methodists, and Presbyterians, to address the challenges of evil powers in society have led many of their adherents to join the new religious movements that help them solve their problems. As for the people who choose not to join these movements, they often at least attend their healing or deliverance services.

In sum, the belief in the existence of evil powers and the means used to combat them are widely known in Africa. Discourses concerning spiritual battles against evil forces, whether traditional or Christian, usually blame external spiritual agents like witchcraft and evil spirits. Sometimes people overstress the existence and influence of evil spirits, especially by attributing bad practices like greed, incompetency, corruption, poverty, and every type of sickness to them. There is therefore a need to critically assess how spiritual forces operate in order to look for relevant solutions. It is important to remember that the battle is not against human enemies but the spirits of evil in the heavenly places (6:12). Even though we have a terrifying enemy, we are protected by the power of God. Hence, there is no reason to tremble at his threats. Our victory in Christ is assured. The growth of Pentecostalism and the African Initiated Church is partly attributed to their involvement in exorcism.

---

the practice of witchcraft is a means to fight malicious spirits. They use rituals, incantations, and charms to protect and deliver themselves and their societies from seeming evil forces.

82. A. G. Khathide, *Hidden Powers: Spirits in the First-Century Jewish World, Luke-Acts and in the African Context* (Achad SA Publishing, 2007), 368.

83. S. I. Maboea, *The Influence of Numinous Power in the African Traditional Religion and the Zionist Churches in Soweto: A Comparative Study* (University of Durban-Westville, 1999), 69.

84. Paul Hiebert, R. Daniel Shaw, and Tite Tiénou, *Understanding Folk Religion: A Christian Response to Popular Beliefs and Practices* (Baker Books, 1999), 144.

85. Mugambi, *African Heritage and Contemporary Christianity*, 64.

Christians need to avoid some African practices of guarding against and fighting evil powers, for they diminish the dignity of human beings and others are devilish. This is so because they are linked with invoking demonic beings, cursing people, making pacts with the devil, using animal and human sacrifices in the course of rituals, using black magic to manipulate others, and involvement in sexual rituals with demonic beings in order to cause suffering to others. The teaching on the armor of God (6:13–17) challenges Africans to discard the use of charms and ritual sacrifices to deal with evil spirits. For, as Paul teaches, Christians have superior powers at their disposal to fight against evil forces (6:12). Accordingly, since the spiritual weapons mentioned in Ephesians are already familiar to Christian Africans, they need to utilize them for their spiritual well-being. If they do so, they will definitely win the battle because God through Jesus Christ has already won the victory for the believer.

Conclusion

A consideration of the nature of God in traditional African religions has shown that in both there is a belief in an eternal, self-existent being who is greater, powerful, and the originator of all created things. In Ephesians God is revealed as one but manifests himself in three divine persons, that is, Father, Son, and Holy Spirit. This belief in the Trinity is uniquely Christian and includes the belief in Jesus Christ as the sole mediator between God and human beings. On the other hand, the African worldview comprises a Supreme Being who is worshipped alongside other lesser beings such as the divinities and ancestors that lack absolute existence by themselves. In this case, while there are similarities between the Ephesian and African understanding of a God who is one and supreme, these two do not have similar theological meaning. Clarifying this distinction is essential for a proper appropriation of the Christian message in the African context.

Paul teaches in Ephesians that God in Christ reconciled everything to himself by his grace. This graciousness of God is what moved Paul at the very beginning to praise, thank, and bless him for all that he has bestowed on the church (1:3–14). This reconciliation is universal for it incorporates the entire cosmos. In Christ, God reconciled humanity with himself and also united varied nations into one body, the church. Unity achieved through Christ is manifest throughout the letter, especially in the new relationship he offered the Jews and gentiles when he broke down the barriers between them in order to create a new community of believers. This unity surpasses ethnic, cultural, and social boundaries, and emphasizes the believers' common identity in Christ.

Praise and prayer as shown in the letter to the Ephesians are well established also in traditional African practices. While there are some differences in what is prayed for and the addressees, there is a general feeling for all of dependence on a God who is great, powerful, and able to respond to their needs in all circumstances. Africans who embrace Christianity bring with them a valuable tradition that enriches the prayer practice highlighted in the letter and also allow themselves to be enriched by the biblical teaching on prayer.

In the letter, Paul also addresses the relationships between wives and husbands. He directs that women should submit to and respect their husbands. This submission is not an expression of women's inferiority but rather an acknowledgment of the Lordship of Jesus Christ. The role of the husbands is to love their wives. They should do this sacrificially, in the same way as Christ loved the church and gave up his life for her. The love of husbands needs to be selfless, looking toward the welfare of their wives. Once Christian Africans and others elsewhere adhere to these principles, conflict in marriage will be resolved and unity preserved. The prevalent battle among the sexes will give way to peace and harmony.

Moreover, in Ephesians there is a clear message that the essential struggle of Christians is not against other people but against malevolent spiritual forces (6:10–18). Even though we should guard against thinking that all difficulties in the world are directly related to the influence of Satan, Ephesians makes it clear that evil forces are real and that there is the need to stand against them. This reality sadly leads some around the world, including Africans, and even including some Christian Africans, to engage in forms of witchcraft that lead to more complications like hopelessness, depression, and financial bankruptcy. Moreover, recourse to magic, witchcraft, or anything besides Christ for protection is futile and sinful. Accordingly, Christians ought to utilize the spiritual weapons suggested to fight against Satan. These weapons should inspire a feeling of confidence in a God who is exalted above all powers and principalities.

Finally, this chapter has dealt with the theological themes of the supremacy of God, prayer, and praise, the wife–husband relationship, believers as fellow citizens, and how to engage in spiritual battle against evil forces. These themes as viewed in Ephesians and from an African religious viewpoint have revealed a number of similarities as well as differences. Today there is the challenge of integrating African beliefs and practices into Christianity without falling into the danger of syncretism. It is true that there are some incongruent beliefs between African religions and Christianity, such as idol worship, gender inequality, and recourse to magic and witchcraft to wage spiritual warfare, but there are also good values that are worth adopting to live in an authentically African Christian church. Moreover, in the early church, there was a need to discern what should be regarded as authentic Christian practices from those that were not so. Thus, although the gentile Christians were declared free from practicing the Mosaic Law, including the issue of circumcision, the Jews themselves were not required to abandon it. The church in Africa ought to let itself be challenged by the Christian message whenever necessary, but also needs to identify the different aspects of its religious and cultural practices that could enrich its Christian faith as long as the supremacy and finality of Jesus Christ is upheld.

Further Reading

Arnold, Clinton E. *Ephesians: Power and Magic*. Cambridge University Press, 1989.

Arnold, Clinton E. *Power and Magic: The Concept of Power in Ephesians*. Wipf & Stock, 1997.

Barth, Markus. *Ephesians: Introduction, Translation, and Commentary on Chapters 1–3*. AB 34. Doubleday, 1974.

Bujo, Bénézet. *African Theology in Its Social Context*. Translated by John O'Donohue. St. Paul Publications-Africa, 1992.

Bujo, Bénézet. *Plea for Change of Models for Marriage*. Paulines Publications Africa, 2009.

Cohick, Lynn H. *Ephesians*. NCCS. Cascade Books, 2010.

Darko, Daniel K. *Against Principalities and Powers: Spiritual Beings in Relation to Communal Identity and the Moral Discourse of Ephesians*. Hippo Books, 2020.

deSilva, David A. *Ephesians*. NCBC. Cambridge University Press, 2022.

Gehman, Richard J. *African Traditional Religion in Biblical Perspective*. East African Educational Publishers, 2005.

Hoehner, Harold W. *Ephesians: An Exegetical Commentary*. Baker Academic, 2002.

Katongole, Emmanuel. "Christianity, Tribalism, and the Rwandan Genocide: A Catholic Reassessment of Christian 'Social Responsibility.'" *Logos: A Journal of Catholic Thought and Culture* 8, no. 3 (June 2005): 67–93.

Khofi, Arthur. *African Christian Marriage: A Christian Theological Appraisal*. Paulines Publications Africa, 2011.

Longman, Timothy. *Christianity and Genocide in Rwanda*. Cambridge University Press, 2010.

Maboea, S. I. *The Influence of Numinous Power in the African Traditional Religion and the Zionist Churches in Soweto: A Comparative Study*. University of Durban-Westville, 1999.

Magesa, Laurenti. *African Religion: The Moral Traditions of Abundant Life*. Paulines Publications Africa, 1997.

Mbiti, John S. *African Religions and Philosophy*. Heinemann, 1969.

Mbiti, John S. *Love and Marriage in Africa*. Longman, 1977.

Mbiti, John S. *The Prayers of African Religion*. SPCK, 1975.

Mugambi, J. K. N. *African Heritage and Contemporary Christianity*. Longman Kenya, 1989.

Mugambi, J. K. N. "The Ecumenical Movement and Future of the Church in Africa." In *The Church in African Christianity. Innovative Essays in Christology*, edited by J. K. N. Mugambi and Laurenti Magesa. Initiatives Publishers, 1990.

Ndiukwu, Aloysius Eberechukwu. *Authenticity of Belief in African (Igbo)Traditional Religion: A Critical Appraisal in the Light of Christian Faith*. Peter Lang, 2012.

Phiri, Khofi Arthur. *African Christian Marriage: A Christian Theological Appraisal*. Paulines Publications Africa, 2011.

Rutoro, Esther. "Your Desire Shall Be for Your Husband and He Shall Rule Over You!" Desire and Rule in Traditional Shona Understandings of Marriage." In *Living with Dignity: African Perspectives on Gender Equality*, edited by Elna Mouton and Gertrude Kapuma. Sun Media, 2015.

Shorter, Aylward. *Prayer in the Religious Traditions of Africa*. Oxford University Press, 1975.

Thielman, Frank. *Ephesians*. BECNT. Baker Academic, 2010.

Turaki, Yusufu. "Ephesians." In *Africa Bible Commentary: A One-Volume Commentary Written by 70 African Scholars*, edited by Tokunboh Adeyemo. WordAlive Publishers; Zondervan, 2006.

Udoye, Anaegboka Edwin. *Resolving the Prevailing Conflicts Between Christianity and African (Igbo) Traditional Religion Through Inculturation*. Lit Verlag, 2011.

CHAPTER THIRTEEN

The Letter to the Philippians

Alice Matilda Nsiah
University of Cape Coast
Ghana

Introduction

MANY INTRODUCTIONS ON Paul's letter to the Philippians have been written; this chapter does not intend to repeat what others have done but moves in a different direction, anticipating African readership. It highlights some elements in Ghanaian everyday life experiences that find expression in the Philippian texts and invites Ghanaians and Africans of all nationalities to be challenged by and apply them. This chapter presents the letter as a rhetorical speech and identifies the different rhetorical roles in its structure, with a clearly identifiable beginning, middle, and closing. It employs the African hermeneutic theory of Gerald O. West that includes text, context, and appropriation.[1] The elements in the Ghanaian context are discussed under these three steps. The letter is considered a personal one that also serves as a public document to be read aloud in a worship setting, and it is to be kept for future reference.

Introductory Matters

The City of Philippi

The letter to the Philippians takes its name from the Christian community at Philippi. Paul had a long and happy relationship with the primary recipients. During his second missionary journey, Paul was directed in a vision to go to Macedonia (Acts 16:6–10). Philippi was a small Roman colony, probably established by Philip of Macedon, the father of Alexander the Great, who named the city after himself.[2] The city was important due to the discovery of gold on one of its mountains and the fact that the city might have been given for the settlement of

1. Gerald O. West, "Biblical Hermeneutics in Africa," a paper presented at the Ujamaa Centre (University of KwaZulu-Natal, 2008), 1–14.

2. Dennis Hamm, *Philippians, Colossians, Philemon*, CCSS (Baker Academic, 2013), 62; Richard R. Melick Jr., *Philippians, Colossians, Philemon*, NAC 32 (B&H, 1991), 22–24; Andreas J. Köstenberger, L. Scott Kellum, and Charles L. Quarles, *The Cradle, the Cross and the Crown: An Introduction to the New Testament*, 2nd ed. (B&H, 2016), 645.

ex-military personnel.[3] This may explain the profound use of military terminology. Added to these is the Via Egnatia (the Egnatian Way), the road that linked the city to other important commercial centers. The church was doubtless mixed in ethnic and social character, and was likely founded around 50 CE (Acts 16:9–12). This might have been the first church planted on European soil during the second missionary journey.[4] When Paul arrived in the city, he was probably with Silas and Timothy, and they met Luke, who was probably a native of the city.[5] They discovered there was no synagogue, but a few devout women were praying along a river bank outside the city gate (Acts 16:13). This is an indication that there were few Jews, probably not enough to form a synagogue, but there were both Greek and Jewish God-fearers, slave and free citizens, men and women.[6]

Genre

More than any other letter of Paul, Philippians reflects the warm affection of the apostle for his brothers and sisters in Christ. In terms of its epistolary genre, the letter typifies the rhetoric of friendship.[7] Hence, it is generally viewed as a personal and friendship letter from Paul to his converts at Philippi. Paul's affection for them is evident (1:9–11; 2:19; 4:19). Paul is confident that the Philippians have similar affections for him (2:22; 4:10). Such an affection confirms the conception of the people of God as kin to "[provide] them with a legitimate connection to the promises of God."[8] What motivates Christians to share resources is the kinship bond they perceived. This phenomenon is echoed in an Akan proverb: "Some friends relate better than blood relatives, they are always there for you through thick and thin." In light of this, the Philippians appear to be some of the most trustworthy supporters of Paul. They had supported his ministry in Thessalonica and Corinth (2 Cor 11:9; Phil 4:15–16). They also supported him while he was in prison, providing for his needs and giving assistance (1:9, 4:1, 15, 16, 18). They seemed to be the only ones who sent Paul financial support during his difficult situation. Paul was very appreciative of their generosity. As a result, the letter is imbued with friend terminology, "sharing" or "fellowship"; Paul emphasizes his reciprocal relationship with the Philippians;[9] he exudes concern and cares for their well-being; he prays for them (1:3–11) and acknowledges that they pray for him (1:9); he recognizes their affection (1:7) and expresses affection for them (1:8). He also uses intimate addresses which define and solidify relationships. Paul refers to the Philippians as his "beloved" friends whom he

3. Markus Bockmuehl, *A Commentary on the Epistle to the Philippians*, BNTC (A&C Black, 1997), 3.

4. N. T. Wright, *Paul for Everyone: The Prison Letters: Ephesians, Philippians, Colossians and Philemon* (Westminster John Knox Press, 2004), 84.

5. Bockmuehl, *A Commentary on the Epistle to the Philippians*, 12–13.

6. Bockmuehl, *A Commentary on the Epistle to the Philippians*, 9–10.

7. Bockmuehl, *A Commentary on the Epistle to the Philippians*, 34–35; G. Walter Hansen, *The Letter to the Philippians*, PNTC (Eerdmans, 2009), 6–12.

8. David A. deSilva, *Honor Patronage, Kinship & Purity: Unlocking New Testament Culture* (InterVarsity, 2000), 200.

9. Köstenberger, Kellum, and Quarles, *The Cradle, the Cross and the Crown*, 646.

"loves and longs for" (4:1). He also uses kinship terms to describe them as "brothers and sisters" to express the fictive family he shares with them. The letter also conveys the shared life and unity of mind that constitutes friendship.[10] Ben Witherington III[11] is correct that the letter conforms to rhetorical conventions, and many commentators who rely at least in part on rhetorical criticism argue that the epistle bears all the marks of a carefully crafted singular rhetorical argument.[12]

Authorship

Many scholars claim that the early church was unanimous in holding to Pauline authorship;[13] however, some scholars doubt Pauline authorship of Philippians.[14] This difficulty is however believed to be resolved by some statement in the document itself, strong evidence from church fathers, the warm and natural Pauline style of the book, and its historical affiliations with other prison letters of Paul.

Occasion, Purpose, Place of Composition, and Date

There are various suggestions for why Paul wrote this letter. Some submit that the letter is all about partnership or friendship with the Philippians.[15] Others, who identify themes beyond friendship and partnership, point out that the church was dealing with the problem of disunity (2:1–4; 4:4) and false teachers (3:2–4).[16] Paul also intends to appraise them about Epaphroditus's return to Philippi after his health had improved and this also forms part of the situation behind the letter (2:25–30). Paul takes advantage of his journey to keep the Philippians informed about his situation, to express his pleasure that all had turned out well, and to give them encouragement and advice.

The provenance of Philippians is contentious.[17] Paul was in prison when he wrote this letter, but he does not say where exactly. While some suggest that he wrote from prison in Caesarea, others are convinced that he wrote from Rome. However, there have also been strong advocates for Ephesus as the place of writing. Even though there is no explicit statement that Paul was ever imprisoned in that city, N. T. Wright, for example, proposes that the apostle's

---

10. Köstenberger, Kellum, and Quarles, *The Cradle, the Cross and the Crown*, 646.

11. Ben Witherington III, *Paul's Letter to the Philippians: A Socio-Rhetorical Commentary* (Eerdmans, 2011), 11–20.

12. Witherington, *Paul's Letter to the Philippians*, 22–30.

13. Köstenberger, Kellum, and Quarles, *The Cradle, the Cross and the Crown*, 646; Hamm, *Philippians, Colossians, Philemon*, 61; D. A. Carson and Douglas J. Moo, *An Introduction to the New Testament*, 2nd ed. (Zondervan, 2005), 499.

14. F. C. Baur, *Paul, the Apostle of Jesus Christ: His Life and Works, His Epistles and Teachings* (Hendrickson, 2003).

15. Hamm, *Philippians, Colossians, Philemon*, 67.

16. Köstenberger, Kellum, and Quarles, *The Cradle, the Cross and the Crown*, 645–646; Carson and Moo, *An Introduction to the New Testament*, 507–508.

17. See Melick, *Philippians, Colossians, Philemon*, 34–39.

words about his many imprisonments (2 Cor 11:23) and the short proximity between Ephesus and Philippi, among other factors, have convinced many today in favor of an earlier imprisonment of Paul in Ephesus in the mid-50s. News of his imprisonment reached the Christians in Philippi (1:7, 13–14), who sent Epaphroditus to help him with financial assistance during his incarceration (4:14, 18). Unfortunately, Epaphroditus got sick (2:25–27), which was cause for concern. As soon as his health improved, Paul sent him back to Philippi, perhaps with this letter, to reassure the people (2:28–30) and thank them for the gift. Paul also planned to send Timothy to them with more news, and he was expecting to be released soon so that he could visit them personally (2:19–24).[18] However, the traditional view is that Paul wrote from Rome around 59 CE when he was under house arrest (Acts 28:30).[19]

Literary Character/Style

Philippians' literary integrity has been questioned even though there is no manuscript evidence for that. There are ancient references of Paul writing more than one letter to the church at Philippi.[20] The double letter theorists suggest that Philippians is a composite of two or more letters: 4:10–20 forms letter 1; 1:1–3:1a, 4:4–7, 21–23 forms letter 2; and 3:1b–4:3, 8–9 forms letter 3.[21] Based on some of its distinctive vocabulary, themes, and several endings, the Philippians we have today seems to reflect an editorial combination of two or more letters from Paul to the church. For instance, there is a sharp shift in mood and tone between 1:1–3:1a and 3:1b-4:3. While 3:1a speaks of rejoicing and Paul's pastoral care, 3:2 opens a new subject with a polemical attack. Then again, the letter appears to have more than one conclusion (3:1a; 4:8) and also double benedictions (4:4–7; 4:9b; 4:23). Again, it is plausible that chapter 4:10–20 is an interpolation from an earlier "appreciation" letter Paul wrote to the Philippian church after he had received their gift from Epaphroditus. Whereas 4:9 seems to be winding down to the end of the letter and should be smoothly followed by 4:21–23, suddenly 4:10–20 seems inserted. This passage expresses Paul's gratitude to the Philippians for their gift, but the gift has already been already alluded to (1:3–11; 2:25–30). The fact that the "thank you" of 4:10–20 comes so late in the letter increases the likelihood that it was originally a separate letter or part of an earlier letter sent to Philippi.[22]

The single-letter theorists, however, argue that Philippians is a coherent whole as it stands today and that the arguments put forward by the double-letter theorists are not

---

18. Wright, *Paul for Everyone*, 84.

19. Raymond Brown, *An Introduction to the New Testament* (Doubleday, 1997), 484; Köstenberger, Kellum, and Quarles, *The Cradle, the Cross and the Crown*, 638, 641–642.

20. Hansen, *The Letter to the Philippians*, 16–19.

21. Mark Avery Jennings, "'Make My Joy Complete': The Price of Partnership in the Letter of Paul to the Philippians" (PhD diss., Marquette University, 2015), 12–14; Hansen, *The Letter to the Philippians*, 16; Valentine Umoh, "The Rhetoric of Joy in Paul's Letter to the Philippians," in *That They May Have Life: A Festschrift in Honour of Most Rev. Dr Camillus Raymond Umoh*, ed. Idara Otu and Valentine Umoh (Paulines Publications Africa, 2021), 159–160.

22. Jennings, "Make My Joy Complete," 12.

insurmountable. They explain that the shift in mood and tone do not necessarily imply that a redactor has combined two or more originally separate letters. Paul Ricoeur argues that all background information on ancient letters is mere conjecture, since there are no structures and systems put in place to help determine exactly what happened. Knowing the author's background is helpful but it is not the only way to determine the authenticity or otherwise of ancient documents.[23] I therefore accept the unity and integrity of the letter as it is presented today by the single-letter theorists.

Structure of Philippians

Many different structures have been offered by scholars, depending on their perspective on the epistle and whether they consider if the letter conforms to some rhetorical conventions or not.[24] Some scholars accept the epistle as speech and agree that it conforms to many elements of rhetorical convention, while Jean-Noel Alleti suggests that the letter is cast against the elements of epideictic rhetoric.[25] Yet others suggest that the purpose of the letter is more deliberative speech since Paul is persuading the church to stay in conformity to his gospel mission.[26] Consequently, the epistle is studied with rhetorical criticism, dissecting some rhetorical elements from the letter. However, others suggest that Paul is very adaptive and does not restrict himself to one particular rhetorical element but combines various elements that suit his purpose. It is therefore not right to put the straightjacket of one particular species on the letter since rhetorical practice was more flexible. Modern scholars therefore do not use any Greco-Roman conventions but rather use modern rhetoric that puts emphasis on argumentation or a text-centered approach to rhetorical exegesis.

After the epistolary greeting (1:1–2) and thanksgiving (1:3–11), Paul lays out the situational context of the letter (1:12–26) and exhorts the community to unity (1:27–4:3) with the sacrifice demonstrated by Christ (2:5–11), Timothy and Epaphroditus (2:19–30), and Paul himself (3:4–14) as exemplary paradigms of self-giving for the good of the whole. The letter ends with Paul's profound gratitude for their recent gift (4:10–20) and practical exhortations (4:21–23). The structure and outline here are not definite but a guide for efficient study of the epistle is adapted from Duane F. Watson:[27]

23. Paul Ricoeur, *Interpretation Theory: Discourse and the Surplus of Meaning* (The Texas Christian University Press, 1976), 43–44, 75–79.

24. See Hansen, *The Letter to the Philippians*, 12–15.

25. Jean-Noël Aletti, "Rhetorical Approach to the Periautology of Philippians 3:2–16," *Religions* 15, no. 2 (2024): 164, https://doi.org/10.3390/rel15020164.

26. See Hansen, *The Letter to the Philippians*, 12–13; Emil Pretorius, "Role Models for a Model Church: Typifying Paul's Letter to the Philippians," *Neotestamentica* 32, no. 2 (1998): 547–571.

27. Duane F. Watson, "A Rhetorical Analysis of Philippians and Its Implications for the Unity Question," *Novum Testamentum* 30, no. 1 (1988): 57–88.

Rhetorical Structure of the Letter

Exordium	1:3–26
Narratio	1:27–30
Probatio	2:1–3:21
Argument 1	2:1–11
Argument 2	2:12–18
Argument 3	3:1–21
Peroratio	4:1–20
Postscript	4:21–23

Theological Themes

The content of Philippians is conditioned by practical matters. However, the central emphasis is on strengthening the commitment and faith of the Philippian Christians. Paul expresses his present suffering (1:12–26) but also develops the theme of joy and hope amidst such suffering and uncertain future (1:4, 18, 25; 2:2, 17–18, 28; 4:4, 10). Paul adapts what seems to be an early Christian hymn that celebrates the self-emptying of Christ even to death (2:5–11) as a prime example to explain why the Philippians should also be willing to empty themselves of their own opinions.[28] Paul reinforces his argument for unity with his own example and self-surrender in the face of suffering and death to exhort Euodia and Syntyche (4:2–3).

Prison Experience

Paul's Context

There is enough evidence to suggest that in 57 CE Paul traveled to Jerusalem and was arrested (Acts 21). He was transferred to Caesarea for his own safety, where he came under the custody of Felix for two years (Acts 23–24). Felix could have released Paul, but he was hoping to get something from him. Festus replaced Felix as governor, and Paul appeared before Festus and Agrippa (Acts 25–27). Paul appealed to Caesar and was transferred to Rome (Acts 28:30–31) where he was under house arrest for two years. Yet, he was allowed to receive visitors, to teach and preach.[29] Wright suggests that prisoners of that nature were not catered for in terms of food and other basic necessities and that they had to rely on friends, family, and benefactors. Paul relied on the benevolence of the Philippians and others for his sustenance "since he could not carry out his tent-making business in prison."[30]

28. Gregory P. Fewster, "The Philippians 'Christ Hymn': Trends in Critical Scholarship," *Currents in Biblical Research* 13, no. 2 (2015): 191–206.

29. Hansen, *The Letter to the Philippians*, 22. But note here that Hansen advocates for Ephesus as the provenance for Philippians.

30. Wright, *Paul for Everyone*, 84.

There are certain statements that indicate Paul was in custody: he mentions the praetorium (1:13), which gives some hint that Paul was guarded by a palace guard, probably in Rome in Caesar's house. There seems to be discussion that Paul was in the company of those who were part of Caesar's household (4:22). This suggests that Paul was jailed in Rome.[31] The use of certain language seems to suggest that Paul was contemplating his impending death and going home to meet Christ (1:20–21). Rome was his last resort; if Caesar condemned him, there was no reverse, so death weighed heavily on the apostle's mind in Rome rather than elsewhere. In Philippians 1:17, Paul echoes the thought expressed in Acts 23:11 which contains compelling evidence that the letter was written in Rome. This indicates that Paul would not die in Caesarea but would live to travel to Rome, so contemplating an imminent death was possible. The bold preaching in 1:14 also fits a Roman context better.

Paul was a prisoner for the cause of Christ (1:7–14). He persevered in prison by finding reasons to be joyful in suffering and he took time to explain and defend this joy to encourage the Philippian church (1:12–26). Paul is joyful because his present ministry is successful even if he is in prison, so that he has not labored in vain (1:12–18; 2:16–17). He counts everything as loss for the sake of knowing Christ Jesus (3:7–11). Paul is joyful in the hope of his deliverance (1:18–21) and in anticipation of the future ministry (1:22–26). He rejoices in the selfless financial and emotional support he receives from the Philippians and he rejoices in the partnership he shares with them, especially through Epaphroditus, Timothy, and others (2:19, 23, 25; 4:10–20). Although he has learned to live with little, the church had not abandoned him in prison (4:8–10). The joy of the Lord encouraged the spirit of Paul in prison.

The prison experience may have contributed to the rhetorical effectiveness of the letter. It probably contributed to the increased concern and support the church demonstrated to Paul. It perhaps worked on their emotions and inspired them to do more for their leader and for one another. This may explain why Paul was very confident and happy with the members of the church. The attitude of the church members may have inspired Paul to stay stronger throughout his incarceration.

The Ghanaian Context

There are forty-six prison facilities in Ghana that are supposed to house a maximum of eight thousand inmates, but which, according to Dasmani Laary, have been known to house over fifteen thousand prisoners. The state of the prisons puts many inmates' health at risk. Skin diseases are rampant, and tuberculosis, malaria, hepatitis, pneumonia and other diseases are prevalent.[32] The prisons are so overcrowded that inmates are packed tightly together when they are sleeping, creating lack of privacy that harms the mental health of inmates, leading

31. Acts 28:16; Eusebius, *Hist. eccl.* 2.25.

32. Amnesty International, "'Prisoners Are Bottom of the Pile': The Human Rights of Inmates in Ghana," April 25, 2012, https://www.amnesty.org/en/documents/AFR28/002/2012/en.

to increasing rates of violence, self-harm, and even suicide.[33] Added to this are the budgetary constraints, insufficient resources and personnel, and lack of staff development for officers. This is exacerbated by a lack of education and vocational skills for inmates and even a procedure for how to integrate them back into society when they are finally released. Food and medical care are inadequate, to the extent that inmates rely on family members, friends, benefactors, and other organizations for help and support.

Article 15 (5) of the constitution of the second Republic of Ghana states that "anybody who is unlawfully arrested, restricted or detained by any person shall be entitled to compensation."[34] Yet false arrests and imprisonment are common. A number of cases concern alleged theft of private or company properties by employees and disputes surrounding family lands and other family properties where a very strong element of local politics is involved, as well as domestic issues. People are arrested on false charges and detained for hours, weeks, months, or even years. Sometimes unscrupulous persons use the machinery of criminal law to satisfy their own private grievances. The high incidence of false charges leading to the wrongful detention of innocent citizens is clearly worrying.[35] Ransford Aninagyei-Bonsu filed a suit against Vodaphone Ghana on July 19, 2023, for his unlawful arrest and detention on October 11, 2022.[36] At the time of publication this case is still in court. The law states in Act 13 (30), that if a person is arrested, he/she should be brought to court within forty-eight hours of the arrest, restriction, or detention, even on the weekend, during public holidays, and during strike action. Many people in Ghana are arrested and detained pending trial, and they could be in detention and be forgotten for years.[37] This is especially the case for the poor and the uneducated. In most cases, no compensation is paid to them when they are acquitted. Justice delayed is justice denied.

I visited the Ankaful Prison Annex on January 6, 2024, with the Society of St. Vincent de Paul of our Lady Seat of Wisdom Catholic Church at the University of Cape Coast. We went with two final-year medical students, three nurses, fifteen members of the society, the chaplain, the church president, and myself. We met twenty-three inmates in the one section of the male quarters of the prison. We were allowed to interact with eleven of them, although all were allowed to be screened, clothed, and fed.

The prisoners we were allowed to interact with were: three convicted prisoners, five prisoners on remand, and three prisoners awaiting trial. I interviewed only those on remand. The names here are pseudonyms to ensure anonymity.

---

33. Dasmani Laary, "Decongesting Prisons in Ghana," Development and Cooperation, July 24, 2023, https://www.dandc.eu/en/article/ghanas-prisons-are-extremely-overcrowded-tackle-problem-human-rights-activists-call-more.

34. 1992 Constitution of the Republic of Ghana, Article 15 (#5).

35. Gilbert Kodiliny, "False Imprisonment Through Ministerial Officers: The Commonwealth Experience," *The International and Comparative Law Quarterly* 28, no. 4 (1979): 766–774.

36. Ransford Aninagyei-Bonsu Vrs Vodafone Ghana and 2 Others (2023) GHAHC 98, July 19, 2023, https://ghalii.org/akn/gh/judgment/ghahc/2023/98/eng@2023-07-19.

37. Amnesty International, "Ghana: What Is Happening in the Prisons?," May 2008, https://www.amnesty.org/en/wp-content/uploads/2021/07/afr280022008eng.pdf.

1. Issa is a forty-one-year-old surface miner who was working with a Chinese company. He and his colleagues were arrested as illegal miners by government security forces and the company abandoned him. He has been on remand for nine months and no one says anything to him. He is not an illegal miner, but the company has used and dumped him. His relatives visit and support him, but his bank account has been confiscated, and that is what is making him even more miserable.
2. John Kumah is a thirty-five-year-old commercial driver who had an accident on the Accra–Cape Coast Highway when a tipper truck ran into his Sprinter passenger bus, killing two people on the spot and injuring ten others. He was arrested with the tipper truck driver who was released the following day on bail, but John has been kept here for four weeks now. The owner of the bus he was driving and who he worked for did not bother to help him. His family and friends are supporting him. The trial of the case has been postponed several times while he remains in remand.
3. Kofi Adams is a forty-year-old fisherman who was accused of stealing premix fuel belonging to the Assembly.[38] When confronted, he beat the assembly member for the area who reported the case to the police. He was arrested and put on remand without trial two months ago. He thinks that the Assembly member is a politician so he is using his authority to influence the case. Only his wife and children visit him with some food items and medicine.
4. Selorm is a fifty-one-year-old carpenter who joined with others to apply for a loan, but has been unable to access his money in GN Bank, a private commercial bank in Ghana whose license has been revoked by the central bank of Ghana because they were unable to meet debt obligations. Customers are still battling for their money and the cases are still in court. "How can I be arrested over money I did not even use?" he said. But his debtors fear he will run away if released on bail. He has been there for two weeks. He cannot afford a lawyer.
5. Mr. Awotwi is a forty-eight-year-old trader who beat his wife until she miscarried. He was subsequently arrested and remanded for five months now; he has not heard from anybody.

These stories confirm that the prison situation in Ghana needs some reform, and the government of Ghana is introducing noncustodial sentences to parliament for consideration to reduce the prison population. If this is passed into law, offenders will carry out community service instead of being jailed.

Appropriation

There appears to be some connection between the text and the Ghanaian context. People who are arrested may remain in custody for a long time without trial. This is especially the case

38. This is an authority in the municipality that performs legislative and executive functions of government.

for the poor, who do not have the money to influence and speed up the justice system. Just as Paul was unjustly arrested due to the machination of some unscrupulous Jews, so also many Ghanaians are arrested and forgotten. Even if they commit a crime, the law says they are to go to court within forty-eight hours, but this does not happen.

In the same way Paul depended on the benevolence of others, similarly many prisoners in Ghana depend on others for their sustenance and survival. In spite of all the difficulties, Paul was joyful and confident in the Lord. He did not allow anything to discourage him. He was sure God was going to use the difficult situation for something good. Paul's imprisonment even encouraged the brothers to speak the word with boldness and Paul's own boldness and courage was an inspiration to the brothers.

Partnership (koinōnia)

Paul's Context

The Greek word κοινωνία (*koinōnia*) is usually translated as fellowship. N. T. Wright proposes that fellowship does not convey all the nuances of *koinōnia*, and this is because the Christian understanding of fellowship includes the delighted sharing of worship, prayer, friendship, and mutual support. But *koinōnia* for Paul also meant business partnership. In this connection, partners do not only share the work involved in that partnership but also financial responsibilities.[39] John Brug confirms that *koinōnia* connotes a close relationship or association that involves the tendency to give or to receive something and the particular contextual situation determines whether one is giving or receiving. Brug continues that, in its secular usage, the word may mean friendship, marriage, or business partnership. He opines that in the New Testament the word also suggests a living bond by which Christians unite themselves with God and in fellowship with one another. It is this kind of bond that motivates any giving or offering.[40]

In Philippians, the word is translated as partnership, participation, or sharing. Jennings suggests that in this letter Paul demonstrates his partnership with the Philippians and intends to persuade the church to maintain this partnership with him and his gospel mission (3:16; 4:1, 14–20). Consequently, references to mutuality and reciprocity are found at several places in the epistle. Paul is certain such partnership does not only benefit partners in this life, but also provides security for partners in the life to come. In fact, Jennings perceives that Paul suggests that it is advantageous to church members to remain in the partnership and a disadvantage, in the life to come, for any member that separates from the partnership (3:1, 7–11, 12–20).[41] With such a rhetorical argument, Paul thus persuades the church to be committed to the covenant family beyond friendship, thus offering an explanation why it is for the security of the church within the family of God to remain faithful to the partnership (2:2–11; 4:1). The

39. Wright, *Paul for Everyone*, 84.

40. John F. Brug, "The Principles of Financial Stewardship in Paul's Letter to the Philippians," *Wisconsin Lutheran Quarterly* (Spring 1989): 1.

41. Jennings, "Make My Joy Complete," 6.

Philippians were partners with Paul in sharing the good news about Jesus Christ (1:3, 5, 7). They were partners in their financial support and their prayers for him since true *koinōnia* means praying for one another and serving God together (4:10–20; 1:19). They share his vision in proclaiming the good news of Christ (1:3). He mentions some of the partners as Timothy and Epaphroditus, whom he considered as fellow workers, for they shared his vision and had often risked their life to help Paul spread the good news (2:19ff.; 3:10). Paul was sure that the good work that God had begun in them would come to a glorious end (1:6). The imprisonment of Paul is a way of sharing in the sufferings of Christ. It also means sharing in God's grace (participation) and trusting in God's sovereignty (3:10–11).

The Ghanaian Context

Although Ghana is a secular state, her constitution recognizes all religious organizations as relevant institutions that need representation in specific constitutional bodies and state institutions as partners. The Christian groups in Ghana include the Roman Catholic, Presbyterian, Methodist, Anglican, Lutheran, Mennonite, Seventh-Day Adventist, Pentecostal, charismatic, African Instituted churches, and so on. There is no governmental body that regulates religious affairs; all registered religious bodies are independent institutions. The government does not provide financial support for any religious organization, but acknowledges some partnership with them and offers tax exemptions to all registered religious bodies for non-profit ecclesiastical, charitable, and educational activities. The ministry of education includes religious and moral education in its national educational curriculum.[42]

Christianity in Ghana has been able to transcend ethnic and regional boundaries, forging a united sense of community and shared values that partners with the government. It is acting as a moral compass to instill honesty, compassion, and respect which are vital for peaceful coexistence in order to act with one voice in the interest of the common good. Christian organizations have been instrumental in education and health-care delivery in Ghana to complement the efforts of government. In the past there were more Christian schools than those established by the government. It is the dream of every parent to have their ward in mission schools where priests and nuns are involved in the running of the school. This is because these schools were traditionally the hallmark of discipline and they ensured character formation and discipline. Missionary schools and hospitals play pivotal roles in providing quality educational and medical services, especially to remote and deprived areas where government services are absent. Again, Christian schools are better able to reach out to orphans and other children with special educational needs than the government education systems. These institutions also generate employment opportunities to empower individuals and enhance the well-being of Ghanaians to complement the efforts of the government.[43] The government decided to

42. Kofi Quashigah, "Religion and the Secular State in Ghana," in *Religion and the Secular State* (Servicio de Publicaciones de la Facultad de Derecho de la Universidad Complutense de Madrid, 2015), 331–340.

43. Charles Kojo Vandyck, "Opinion: Christianity in Ghana: Overcoming Challenges, Unleashing Potential for Nation Building," Development Report, July 30, 2023, https://developmentreport.online/

improve on the partnership by absorbing all Christian schools into government schools in order to provide salaries and infrastructure to improve quality of educational delivery in Ghana. In so doing, most Christian schools have been taken over by the government which now dictates the curriculum.[44]

The churches in Ghana are able to come together to partner with the government on other national issues such as illegal and surface mining and other environmental challenges. When the government campaigned for "green Ghana," most religious bodies participated actively with their time and resources and also educated the people, even during church services.[45] The church in Ghana is also faced with religious fundamentalism, extremism, and exploitative practices within certain Christian circles that sometimes lead to violence, intolerance, division, and lack of trust in the churches. Some churches focus all their attention on personal wealth rather than community development projects aligning with their faith. What is very disturbing is the "breakthrough culture" by which churches place excessive emphasis on instant success and miracles, which has the tendency to diminish the value placed on hard work and perseverance.

Appropriation

The churches in Ghana have partnered very well with the government in the provision of essential services, especially in rural areas. They have also reached out in various ways to orphans and those with special needs. Religious bodies in Ghana also partner with the government to respond to national crises. However, sometimes the partnership is challenged with the over-domination of government machinery against the financial and other services of the church. Again, the African Instituted churches that are not supervised by any organized body pose a challenged to the partnership in terms of accountability and should develop a balanced approach to prophetic utterances to diminish over-reliance on prophecies. Accountability and transparency in financial management are critical for maintaining public trust.

Joy in the Lord

According to Valentine Umoh, the letter opens and closes with grace (χάρις), a related terminology for joy (χαρά) (1:2; 4:23). Umoh further argues that there might be a relationship or a linkage between grace and joy in Philippians, which is why the body of the text contains various forms of joy enclosed by grace. Joy is the state of being happy regardless of one's circumstances

christianity-in-ghana-overcoming-challenges-unleashing-potential-for-nation-building.

44. Nicholas Nibetol Aazine, "Growing Disunion Between Government and Mission Schools" Citi News Room (CNR), March 7, 2022, https://citinewsroom.com/2022/03/growing-disunion-between-government-and-mission-schools-article.

45. "Rev. Dr. Cyril G.K. Fayose leads CCG to Plant Trees in Accra to Mark Green Ghana Day," Christian Council of Ghana, June 11, 2021, https://www.christiancouncilofghana.org/NewsPages/Rev-Dr-Cyril-G-K-Fayose-leads-CCG-to-plant-trees-in-Accra-to-mark-Green-Ghana-Day.php.

(4:1, 4), and joy is seen by Umoh as the unifying theme of the letter.[46] The letter expresses the kind of joy a Christian ought to have.

The Joy of a Christian in Paul's Context

Joy is listed as one of the characteristics of a true Christian in this difficult and challenging world. The Christian is to be joyful always in the Lord, and illuminate the world with the life of Christ (4:4). They are to rejoice in prayer and thanksgiving as they recall their faith in the gospel (4:6). Paul, for example, is joyful whenever he prays for the church (1:3–4). The Christian should rejoice in the hope of victory in trial and suffering (1:6–7). Joy is the experience of gladness or the state of being happy (4:1, 4).[47] Joy is the response of one who brings salvation (God or his representative), so joy and faith appear to run parallel (1:25; cf. 2:1–2; Cor 1:24), since "joy is the way in which faith is present."[48] Umoh also perceives that "*joy* is linked to hope, a virtue that is also manifested in the *prayer* of petition and thanksgiving to God (4:6), and in the peace that God brings to our hearts and thoughts (1:2; 4:7, 9)."[49] The Philippians are a source of joy for Paul in accepting the gospel and bearing fruit on that account, in being humble and being united to form one mind and heart. They are also a source of joy in the hope of the eschaton (3:21).[50]

Umoh suggests that the letter manifests joy as the true attitude of an apostle and teacher of faith. He continues that the concept of joy in the letter consists "in the reality that souls are converted" for Christ.[51] There is joy in the proclamation of the good news irrespective of the preacher (1:8), there is joy in the fact that others have accepted the good news and have started bearing fruit. In this case, the Philippians are encouraged to do everything with one mind and heart in order to complete Paul's joy (2:2). They are to be united in their decisions and actions. This implies dialogue and discussions that will empower individual members to own their collective decisions. Jesus prayed for unity for his followers (John 17:20–21). Suffering, persecution, and even death will not take away the joy that Paul shares with the saints (Phil 2:17–18). His presence (life) or absence (death) from them will not take away his joyful relationship with them. Joy unites Paul and his audience in advancing the gospel of Christ despite the challenges and difficulties involved. They will fill up Paul's joy by being of one mind (2:2). Paul is with them for their advancement in the faith; even while he is in prison, he prays to God on their behalf. Rejoicing with them compliments their mutual suffering. The followers of Paul are his joy and crown—symbols of victory—on account of which the apostle will be rewarded. His followers are his scorecard, the fruits of his labor, his sweat, and his sacrifices. Their perseverance will bear witness that he did not labor in vain (2:16). The

46. Umoh, "The Rhetoric of Joy in Paul's Letter to the Philippians," 163, 169.

47. Umoh, "The Rhetoric of Joy in Paul's Letter to the Philippians," 169.

48. Umoh, "The Rhetoric of Joy in Paul's Letter to the Philippians," 170.

49. Umoh, "The Rhetoric of Joy in Paul's Letter to the Philippians," 171, emphasis in original.

50. Umoh, "The Rhetoric of Joy in Paul's Letter to the Philippians," 176.

51. Umoh, "The Rhetoric of Joy in Paul's Letter to the Philippians," 158.

fact that they partner with him in the work of the gospel gives him joy (1:5–6). Joint activities of believers are the basis for joy and not competition and litigation (1:6–7, 29–30; 2:12–13, 16); it is an occasion of thanksgiving (1:3–11). The joy of a Christian is his partnership and mutual collaboration with others in the work of Christ (4:10). It is remarkable to note that such a joyful exhortation is coming from one in prison.

The Ghanaian Context

According to the 2021 population and housing census in Ghana, 71.3 percent of her 32.4 million people claim to be Christians. This is an increase over the 2000 census that recorded 68.8 percent as Christians. The various censuses recorded the breakdown as follows: Pentecostal/charismatic, from 24.1 percent in 2000, to 28.3 percent in 2010, to 31.6 percent in 2021; other Protestants, from 18.6 percent in 2000, to 18.4 percent in 2010, to 17.4 percent in 2021; Catholic, from 15.1 percent in 2000, to 13.1 percent in 2010, to 10.0 percent in 2021. This is a demonstration that the Pentecostal/charismatic churches are the fastest-growing churches in Ghana with a membership of about 9.7 million people nationwide.[52] Some pastors in Ghana share the joy of Paul and claim that they are happy for sharing the good news with others. A pastor submits that a person's faith is transformed as he shares what he has acquired in Christ with others. He adds that it costs money, time, family, and even one's life, but that is what Christ also risked for humanity and so he finds joy in sharing in Christ's mission. But Keren Lauterbach thinks that many young people are aspiring to be pastors in Ghana as a way of ascending to higher social status especially in the Pentecostal/charismatic churches. She attributes this partly to socioeconomic problems and political instabilities of the 1980s that contributed to propel the growth of neo-Pentecostalism in Ghana. Young people are taking advantage of the opportunity to become pastors since it appears to be a lucrative area in which to become rich quickly without much education and effort. With fewer public sector jobs available and a high level of unemployment in the civil service, it is a way of securing income and higher status by becoming an officeholder who engages with important people. Being a pastor is associated with spiritual power and the ability to make things happen so that one can command respect and esteem from people. She contends that members of neo-Pentecostal churches are usually people with aspirations for material wealth and economic success and so the personal appearance and grandeur of the pastor is important for the status of the church. In her opinion, these pastors act as mediators between God and the world and they invoke a spiritual power to provide success and protection against evil forces. She concludes that neo-prophets are a reappropriation and reinvention of African prophetism in which the centrality of the prophet is very important.[53] With such a background, emphasis is put on the pastor, not salvation of souls or the Lordship of Christ.

52. Doris Dokua Sasu, "Religious Affiliation in Ghana as of 2010–2021," Statista, January 20, 2023, https://www.statista.com/statistics/1172414/religious-affiliation-in-ghana.

53. See Karen Lauterbach, "Becoming a Pastor: Youth and Social Aspirations in Ghana," *Young: Nordic Journal of Youth Research* 18, no. 3 (2010): 259–278.

James Quansah confirms the above reflection when he writes that, with almost 80 percent of the population in Ghana claiming to be Christians, the demand for ministers of the gospel continues to rise. Consequently, Quansah submits that many sorcerers, necromancers, magicians, fetish priests, diviners, and traditional healers have cleverly modified and turned their operations into what looks like Christianity to exploit ignorant believers. False ministers who are enemies of Christ and servants of the devil are preaching the gospel they do not believe. They twist messages to draw people to them.

Dei and Nsiah contend that the pursuit of fame has taken on a significant role in determining ministerial progression in Ghana. This is often heightened by the theology of wealth or prosperity preaching, where money and fame are viewed as indicators of God's blessings on his loved ones. Some pastors showcase a lifestyle of wealth to their congregation to present an image of a blessed life. To sustain and maintain such a lifestyle, pastors sell holy water, anointing oil, wrist bands, handkerchiefs, bath soap, and car stickers to church members to help them ward off alleged evil spirits. Sometimes members must "sow seeds," make donations, and pay for other consultation fees to bring deliverance and God's blessings on individuals. People with fertility problems, those who are unemployed, and applicants for visas often seek spiritual assistance from their pastors. This often diverts attention from modest living to a focus on acquiring wealth and recognition that may potentially undermine genuine faith in God. There is also the risk of commodifying the gospel and commercializing religious items as if they determine one's relationship with God.[54] Girish Daswani accuses some charismatic pastors of focusing on money and fame without caring for the people they serve.[55] Unlike Paul, who is joyful in the Lord, some pastors in Ghana are unfortunately joyful in fame and money.

Appropriation

The job of a minister is to fear God, give him reverence at all times, and obey the commandment with joy, quickly repenting when they make mistakes so that they will not give opportunity to unbelievers to profane the name of God. This is what some pastors in Ghana need to do. The work of the minister is not to acquire wealth and social status and claim to own the churches they shepherd but to consider themselves as stewards, God's coworkers, and Christ's ambassadors. Good ministers do their work willingly and not under compulsion, they are not domineering over those under their charge, and their single focus is the salvation of souls.[56] A balance between material and spiritual prosperity is crucial in pastoral ministry in Ghana.

54. Daniel Dei and Alice M. Nsiah, "Money, Fame and Pastoral Ministry in Acts 8:18–24: Implications for Ghanaian Pastors," *Pan-African Journal of Theology* 2, no. 1 (2023): 46–62.

55. Girish Daswani, "A Prophet But Not for Prophet: Ethical Value and Character in Ghanaian Pentecostalism," *The Journal of the Royal Anthropological Institute* 22, no. 1 (March 2016): 108–126, esp. 109.

56. James Quansah, "Good and Faithful Pastors," DailyGuideNetwork, August 10, 2019, https://dailyguidenetwork.com/good-and-faithful-pastors.

Financial Stewardship and Generosity

Paul's Context

John Battle opines that one of the greatest supports that the church in Philippi offered to Paul was the offerings they sent to support the mission of Paul. They did this twice when he was in Thessalonica and once when he was in Corinth (2 Cor 11:9; Phil 4:15–16). They gave sacrificially for Paul's offering for the Jerusalem church in spite of their own poverty and persecution. While Paul was imprisoned, they sent money to him through Epaphroditus.

John Brug suggests that this letter is the second most important, after 2 Corinthians (8 and 9), in terms of outlining principles of financial stewardship. He confirms that the generosity of the Philippian church to Paul cannot be underestimated and that this letter is written to acknowledge the support and the generosity of the church. In this connection, Brug considers the Philippian church to be a model congregation of generosity.[57]

The Ghanaian Context

Luterbach observes that Ghanaian pastors put emphasis on the principle of giving and receiving in their congregations, stressing the fact that all that one has is a gift from God. When church members give back to God what he has given to them, it comes back to them multiplied. The principle stresses that whatever is given to the church and the pastor is given to God. Luterbach submits that there is no mutuality here, since the pastor directs the receiver to God and diverts the responsibility of the pastor in accountability and expression of contentment for what is received.[58] Church members are encouraged not only to give money, but houses, cars, building materials, land, and other properties, as well as time, talents, and other gifts to God for the service of the church. A pastor who is able to move people to give is credited as a powerful preacher who is able to invoke the power of the word to make people pay and this helps to build up his reputation. There seems to be a relationship in people's minds between spiritual richness and material wealth. In other words, many Ghanaians are very generous to their pastors, but the motivation for giving may be problematic, and pastors are capitalizing on what may be the ignorance of some members.

In this connection, Shaibu Adam observes that managing church funds gathered from the offertory has become a problem in many churches in Ghana, and there is the "challenge of embezzlement of offering."[59] When monies are not strictly accounted for, some ushers also steal some money "from the offertory bowl" when counting the money.[60] In many cases, monies and other valuables collected for the poor do not get to the poor. Some independent churches

57. Brug, "The Principles of Financial Stewardship in Paul's Letter to the Philippians," 1.

58. See Lauterbach, "Becoming a Pastor."

59. Iddrisu Adam Shaibu, "Towards an Effective Financial Management of Funds Generated from Offertory in the Church: A Study of Some Selected Classical Pentecostal Churches in the Ashanti Region of Ghana," *Research on Humanities and Social Sciences* 3, no. 2 (2013): 218.

60. Shaibu, "Towards an Effective Financial Management of Funds," 218.

which are not under any mother-body umbrella are not using appropriate professional methods in the area of finances. Ministers are supposed to be custodians of morality and ethics, but their poor handling of church funds is a serious blow to the integrity of Christian leadership.

Appropriation

One of the greatest supports of the Philippian church was the regular financial help they willingly and freely gave to support the gospel mission of Paul. This giving in faith and love made them partners with Paul in Christ. It is important to note that Paul did not force any idea on them. They gave willingly because they trusted Paul and held him in high esteem. Similarly, Ghanaian pastors must consider their church members as partners in Christ for the gospel mission. They should appreciate their generosity and account transparently for the use of church funds to the greater honor and glory of God.

Unity and Disunity

Paul's Context

Paul mentions unity/disunity several times in the letter, such that some scholars suggest that this was one of the main problems in the church. Some suggest that, among other things, the letter talks about disunity in the church (1:27; 2:1–5; 3:15; 4:2, 8).[61] There seem to be disputes between Euodia and Syntyche (4:2–3), the cause of which is not clear, but some scholars argue that their quarrel is the cause of disunity in the church. Others think that the call for unity is an attempt to encourage the church to remain corporate in fellowship with Paul and that he does not consider the conflict between Euodia and Syntyche to be of significant influence on the church.[62]

Regardless of the conjecture surrounding the conflict, what we could infer from the letter is that unity is paramount for the church. Any kind of conflict should be resolved quickly. Eshetu Abate is on point when he writes, "Disagreement weakens the power of the people of God to influence the world around them."[63]

The Ghanaian Context

The religious bodies in Ghana are comprised of the Ghana Catholic Bishops' Conference, the Christian Council of Ghana (for the Protestant churches), Ghana Pentecostal and Charismatic Churches, and the National Association of Charismatic and Christian Churches. All these bodies come together to ensure national interest as a strong and formidable voice for the

61. Hansen, *The Letter to the Philippians*, 25.

62. On the various proposals regarding the dispute, see Hansen, *The Letter to the Philippians*, 25–26; Melick, *Philippians, Colossians, Philemon*, 146–148.

63. Eshetu Abate, "Philippians," in *Africa Bible Commentary: A One-Volume Commentary Written by 70 African Scholars*, ed. Tokunboh Adeyemo (HippoBooks; WordAlive Publishers; Zondervan, 2006), 1473.

voiceless in the country. On May7, 2021, the Catholic Bishops' conference and the Christian Council of Ghana came together in Accra to worship and pray for the nation. Among other issues, they prayed for the president and his ministers, and for God's intervention in the affairs of the nation amid the fear and uncertainty of the COVID-19 era.[64] The national security minister, the honorable Albert Ken Dapaah, is quoted as saying that the joint religious bodies in Ghana are powerful enough to safeguard national security since they can touch minds and hearts in a way that no one else can.[65] Similarly, Kwabena Opuni-Frimpong, the secretary general of the Christian Council of Ghana, urged politicians to use their campaign platforms to unite Ghana rather than to bring ethnic division.[66] These are signs that, when these bodies are united, they wield significant religious and political power and they collaborate very well on serious national issues for the good of the nation. However, at the grassroots level, there is little unity.

Nsiah observes that there is growing competition among the different Christian denominations on the media, where churches use television, radio, audio cassettes, pamphlets, and brochures as a means of evangelization. The competition seems to suggest that the more the church is broadcast on the media, the better that church is as compared to its alternative. Hence churches have multiple TV stations where they broadcast all their activities live, especially healing and deliverance services, without considering the privacy and confidentiality of church members and some of the adverse effects of such broadcasts.[67] This diverts the attention of ministry from Christ to the minister, whose job appears to center on personal fame.[68] It is important to note that, while the competition aspect of this is negative, this broadcasting allows for more people to participate in the Christian faith and to hear the gospel.

There appears to be more collaboration between the Protestant and the Pentecostal/charismatic churches than between any of these churches and the Catholics.[69] The Pentecostal churches pride themselves on being able to respond to the needs of the people in Ghana. As the fastest-growing denomination they accuse the Catholic Church of being bookish and dwelling on the recitation of the rosary and some traditions that are not biblical and that do not respond to the needs of Ghanaian Christian. Many Catholics, on the other hand, pride themselves on belonging to the church founded by Jesus himself, and hence the true church.

64. Christian Council of Ghana and Ghana Catholic Bishop's Conference, "2021 Joint Communique of CCG and GCB," May 5, 2021, https://www.cbcgha.org/1709; Charles Prempeh, "Religion and the State in an Episodic Moment of Covid-19 in Ghana," *Social Sciences & Humanities* 4, no. 1 (2021): 1–8.

65. Edghougui, "Ghana Has Enhanced Its Reputation Globally for Effective COVID-19 Management-Veep," Atlantic Federation of African Press Agencies, September 19, 2020, https://gna.org.gh/2020/09/ghana-has-enhanced-its-reputation-globally-for-effective-covid-19-management-veep.

66. Bervelyn Longdon, "Expedite Prosecution of Persons Responsible for Election 2020 Deaths–Opuni Frimpong," CitiNewsRoom, August 21, 2024, https://citinewsroom.com/2024/08/expedite-prosecution-of-persons-responsible-for-election-2020-deaths-opuni-frimpong.

67. Alice M. Nsiah, "Breaking the Ethnic Barrier in Mark 7:24–30: Implication for the Ghanaian Context," *E-Journal of Humanities, Arts and Social Sciences (EHASS)* 2, no. 10 (October 2021): 166–167.

68. Dei and Nsiah, "Money, Fame and Pastoral Ministry in Acts 8:18–24," 48, 53.

69. For further on the competition between various religion in Ghana, see Nsiah, "Breaking the Ethnic Barrier in Mark 7:24–30," 166–167.

Consequently, they do not want to belong to any young church that has come to reap a copious harvest where they have not sowed. Similar exchanges make it difficult to consider other members of different denominations as potential friends. These exchanges make it difficult to see Christ as the center, and if we truly have fellowship with Christ then it follows that we, as a Christian obligation, ought to have fellowship with one another in the Lord.

Appropriation

Ghanaian Christians are yet to come to terms with the fourfold formula for unity proposed in Philippians. Interdenominational relations are officially very coordinated among the church leadership for the good of the Christian faithful, but this is very porous at the grassroots level, indicating an overall superficial approach that is theologically ill-equipped and unhealthy. It is important that Christian leaders ensure that the collaboration experienced at the top is disseminated to the bottom to defuse all denominational rivalry and eliminate all potential opposition so that Christ can reign supreme in the hearts of all.

Conclusion

It is observed that Ghanaians will find much relevance to their own context in the letter to the Philippians: the experiences of unjust incarceration and high judicial officials looking for a bribe (Acts 24:26–27). Felix was hoping to receive something from Paul, an inmate having to depend on family and friends for maintenance, among others. Similarly, there are various partnerships that are beneficial to the church and to the nation at large, the collaboration between the various churches and government for the provision of schools and hospitals being among them. There is also the Christian joy that is derived from sharing in the mission of Christ that is sometimes overshadowed by material acquisition and fame. The pastor and church members are partners in financial stewardship, and must be accountable to one another and to the Lord. Finally, united with one heart and mind is the way to remain in the partnership and participate in the future or eschatological joy to come.

Further Reading

Abate, Eshetu. "Philippians." In *Africa Bible Commentary: A One-Volume Commentary Written by 70 African Scholars*, edited by Tokunboh Adeyemo. HippoBooks; WordAlive Publishers; Zondervan, 2006.

Bockmuehl, Markus. *A Commentary on the Epistle to the Philippians*. A&C Black, 1997.

Brown, Raymond. *An Introduction to the New Testament*. Doubleday, 1997.

Dei, Daniel, and Alice M. Nsiah. "Money, Fame and Pastoral Ministry in Acts 8:18–24. Implications for Ghanaian Pastors." *Pan-African Journal of Theology* 2, no. 1 (2023): 46–62.

Fewster, Gregory P. "The Philippians 'Christ Hymn': Trends in Critical Scholarship." *Currents in Biblical Research* 13, no. 2 (2015): 191–206.

Hamm, Dennis. *Philippians, Colossians, Philemon*. CCSS. Baker Academic, 2013.

Hansen, G. Walter. *The Letter to the Philippians*. PNTC. Eerdmans, 2009.

Jennings, Mark Avery. "'Make My Joy Complete': The Price of Partnership in the Letter of Paul to the Philippians." PhD diss., Marquette University, 2015.

Melick, Richard R., Jr. *Philippians, Colossians, Philemon*. NAC 32. B&H, 1991.

Nsiah, Alice M. "Breaking the Ethnic Barrier in Mark 7:24–30: Implication for the Ghanaian Context." *E-Journal of Humanities, Arts and Social Sciences (EHASS)* 2, no. 10 (October, 2021): 159–169.

Umoh, Valentine. "The Rhetoric of Joy in Paul's Letter to the Philippians." In *That They May Have Life: A Festschrift in Honour of Most Rev. Dr Camillus Raymond Umoh*, edited by Idara Otu, and Valentine Umoh. Paulines Publications Africa, 2021.

Wright, N. T. *Paul for Everyone The Prison Letters: Ephesians, Philippians, Colossians and Philemon*. Westminster John Knox Press, 2004.

CHAPTER FOURTEEN

The Letter to the Colossians

Elkanah K. Cheboi
Kabarak University
Kenya

Introductory Matters

The proclamation of the gospel in the first century by Christ's witnesses led to the founding of the church in Colossae, a city in Asia Minor (modern-day Turkey). As the gospel crossed cultural frontiers, the converts needed spiritual guidance to address contextual challenges, deceptive philosophies, heretical teachings, and practical concerns about Christian living. The church needed doctrinal clarity in confronting opposing beliefs and practices. The letter to the Colossians responds to pressing issues for the nascent church.

Other than the typical epistolary introductory structure (featuring the author and recipients, and greetings) and conclusion sections (greetings and benediction), the body section of Colossians addresses the following themes: the spread of the gospel, the supremacy of Jesus Christ over all things, reconciliation through the work of Christ on the cross, warning against heretical beliefs and practices, false philosophies, believer's union with Christ, practical aspects of the Christian life, and Christian duties at home, work, and in the public space.

Since the letter addresses contextual issues that the Colossian believers wrestled with in their own time and space, a faithful interpretation and application of the letter requires closely examining the first-century context and the biblical text. Studies have shown that Colossian Christians struggled with how to handle the apostolic teachings, given their local pagan and Jewish folk beliefs.[1] The potential fallback to syncretistic practices would re-enslave believers and expose them to oppressive spiritual powers and empty philosophies.

This chapter traces the major themes of the letter and shows how the message resonates with Christians in the African context. This is achieved by examining the text within its context to determine its message for modern readers. For a meaningful application of the message of the letter, the interpreter should listen to and take seriously the questions raised by the contemporary readers of the text and seek to answer those questions. The hermeneutical process should consider how the message answers the reader's questions.

1. Clinton E. Arnold, *The Colossian Syncretism: The Interface Between Christianity and Folk Beliefs at Colossae* (Baker Books, 1996), 5.

Author

Internal evidence (1:1) indicates that, with Timothy, Paul wrote the epistle. Notable scholars subscribe to this traditional view that Paul wrote the epistle.[2] However, some critics believe that a Paulinist (a follower of Paul after his death) wrote the letter in Paul's name.[3] This second view is, however, relatively recent. Pauline authorship of the whole or any part of Colossians remained undisputed until the nineteenth century when the rise in historical criticism led to challenges to traditionally held views on Scripture.[4] In addition, the letter faced no objection during canonization.[5] Therefore, there are credible grounds to believe that the apostle Paul wrote the epistle. Paul introduces himself as an apostle of Jesus Christ. Although he was not among the twelve, he met Christ on his way to Damascus and was commissioned by God to proclaim the gospel to the gentiles.

Based on the letter (2:1), Paul did not plant the church at Colossae and had not personally met the believers there. It is most likely that Epaphras, presumably a convert of Paul in Ephesus, was the founder of the church at Colossae (1:7–8; 4:12–13; 4:12). According to Acts 19, apostle Paul ministered in the larger area of Ephesus during the third missionary journey and thus had acquaintances in Colossae. Epaphras had visited Paul in prison to get help dealing with emerging heresies in this church; thus, Paul responded by writing them an epistle.

Audience and Place

The addressees in Colossae are referred to as "the saints and faithful brothers and sisters in Christ" (1:2). The work of Christ on the cross and the proclamation of the gospel at Colossae resulted in a community of saints in Christ, members of God's household. The church was a mixed congregation comprising Jews (2:11, 16, 17) and gentile believers (1:12, 27; 2:13) who had come to believe in Christ. Philo made a general observation that Jews were in every city in Asia (*Leg.* 245). Likewise, Josephus mentions that in the late third century BCE, Antiochus

2. Donald Guthrie, *New Testament Introduction*, 4th ed. (InterVarsity Press, 1990), 572–577; F. F. Bruce, *The Epistles to the Colossians, to Philemon, and to the Ephesians*, NICNT (Eerdmans, 1984), 28–33; N. T. Wright, *The Epistles of Paul to the Colossians and to Philemon*, TNTC (InterVarsity Press, 1986), 31–34; Douglas J. Moo, *The Letters to the Colossians and to Philemon*, PNTC (Eerdmans, 2008), 45–50.

3. Scholars who contest Pauline authorship include: Mark Kiley, *Colossians as Pseudepigraphy*, The Biblical Seminar (JSOT Press, 1986); Andrew T. Lincoln, "The Letter to the Colossians," in *The New Interpreter's Bible* (Abingdon, 2000), 577–583; Margaret Y. MacDonald, *Colossians and Ephesians*, SP 17 (Liturgical Press, 2000), 6–9; R. McL. Wilson, *A Critical and Exegetical Commentary on Colossians and Philemon*, ICC (T&T Clark, 2005), 9–35. Scholars who cast aspersions on Pauline authorship opine that the writing style, Greek vocabulary, and the theology in the letter are different from undisputed Pauline letters. Some of the textual issues cited are that in this letter some synonyms have been merged like "wisdom" and "understanding" (1:9), also, "teaching and admonishing" (3:16). Another objection is that the letter has several hapax legomena; while this is true, it is not a unique aspect in undisputed Pauline Epistles. The vocabulary depends on one's subject matter, and the nature of the issues/groups addressed. See D. A. Carson and Douglas J. Moo, *An Introduction to the New Testament* (Zondervan, 2005), 518.

4. Guthrie, *New Testament Introduction*, 576.

5. Moo, *The Letters to the Colossians and to Philemon*, 48, 50.

the Great settled two thousand Jewish families in Lydia and Phrygia (*Ant.* 12.147–153) and reports that a large Jewish population existed in this region (*Ant.* 14.185–265; 16.160–178). Further, extant grave inscriptions found at nearby Hierapolis confirm the involvement of Jews in the broader Asian culture.[6]

In Paul's day, Colossae was in the Lycus River valley of west-central Asia Minor. The city was in the Phrygian region, part of the Roman province of Asia, and was strategically located at the crossroads of two major highways: one that ran east and west, connecting the coastal cities of Ephesus (about 193 km to the west) and Sardis with the interior east, while another ran north and south.[7] It was a small city compared with Laodicea (about 19 km west) or Hierapolis (about 24 km northwest).

Date

The internal evidence indicates that Paul was in prison when he wrote the letter (4:3, 18). The book of Acts records three imprisonments of Paul: overnight in Philippi (Acts 16:19–34), two years in Caesarea (Acts 23:23–26:32; 24:27), and two years in Rome (Acts 28:11–31), but also, Paul claims to have been imprisoned more frequently (2 Cor 11:23). It is likely that Paul must have written the prison epistles during his house arrest in Rome between 60 and 62 CE.[8]

Purpose of the Letter

Paul writes the letter to address rising heretical beliefs and philosophies in Colossae characterized by asceticism and syncretism of Jewish and Hellenistic teachings. He further redirects their focus to the supremacy of Christ and his work which should inform Christian conduct at home, at work, and in the public sphere.

Overview of the Letter

The introductory section of the letter (1:1–2) states the authorship of the letter, audience, and greetings. Although Paul presents himself as an apostle, he relates to the Colossians as "brothers and sisters in Christ." This personal address sets the tone on which Paul will base his instructions. In this letter, Paul does not address them in a top-down model, although he was an apostle, but as a coequal in Christ.

The succeeding section, 1:3–14, features a thanksgiving and prayer section. Paul confirms the work of God among the Colossians that resulted from the proclamation of the gospel. He praises God that the gospel has brought forth fruit among the Colossians just as it is "bearing fruit and growing" in the whole world (1:6). He commends their love for God and saints and

---

6. Charles H. Talbert, *Ephesians and Colossians*, Paideia (Baker Academic, 2007), 179. See also Craig S. Keener, *The IVP Bible Background Commentary: New Testament* (InterVarsity Press, 2003), 569.

7. Moo, *The Letters to the Colossians and to Philemon*, 44.

8. This is a view supported by Moo, *The Letters to the Colossians and to Philemon*, 59.

their faith and hope in Christ. He reveals his heart's desire and constant prayer for the spiritual formation of the Colossians. He enumerates some of the spiritual blessings believers enjoy in Christ: God the Father has enabled them to share in the inheritance of the saints, rescued them from the power of darkness, and brought them into the kingdom of his beloved Son. In Christ, believers have redemption and forgiveness of sins.

In Colossians 1:15–23, Paul instructs on the supremacy of Christ. Christ is supreme and Lord over all. He highlights the identity and what the work of Christ on the cross achieved. In 1:24–2:5, he presents himself as a participant in God's agenda. Paul regards himself as a servant and as one entrusted with the revealed mystery of God, namely Christ.

In Colossians 2:6–23, the believer's freedom and union with Christ is given attention. Believers in Christ have died and are now free to live for God. They are exhorted not to fall captive through philosophy and empty deceit hinged on human traditions and elemental spirits of the universe. Instead, they are to depend on Christ, the wisdom of God. Based on this background, he admonishes believers to stand firm in their faith. In this section, he uses circumcision and baptism imagery to illustrate putting off the sinful nature and embracing the new life in Christ.

Colossians 3:1–17 puts forth the motivation for Christians to live their identity in Christ. Due to the new identity in Christ, believers have a role to play. They are to "put to death" whatever is earthly and all that characterized their former lives. Changed lives should be the evidence of their union with Christ. They are to clothe themselves with the new self, which brings forth values such as compassion, kindness, humility, meekness, and patience (3:12). Paul shows that in this new self, external modes of differentiation become inconsequential; all that matters is a person being "in Christ."

The closing section (3:18–4:6) deals with Christian conduct and duties in the context of family, work, and public life. The household codes stipulate the responsibilities of each member of a Christian Roman household that, if followed, can make the Christian home and workplace a context where Christian witness is evidenced. Paul concludes with greetings and commendation of faithful servants of the gospel known to the Colossians (4:7–18).

Outline

Introduction (1:1–2)
God the Father and the Spirit at Work (1:3–14)
God the Son: Identity and work (1:15–23)
Participating in God's agenda (1:24–2:5)
Implications of believers' freedom and union with Christ (2:6–23)
Living authentic Christian life (3:1–17)
Christian conduct and duties (3:18—4:6)
Greetings and conclusion (4:7–18)

Points of Contact with African Realities

A faithful reading and interpretation of the letter to the Colossians highlights critical themes that the first-century audience faced, thus prompting Paul to write the epistle. Since the author and the original audience lived in the same historical time, geographical space, and cultural context, they easily interpreted the message with minimal difficulties. However, the modern reader of the letter needs to bridge the temporal, historical, geographical, and cultural divide to grasp the intended meaning and correctly apply the message.

On the one hand, the modern African audience faces issues that sometimes parallel practices in the Bible world. On the other hand, the issues addressed in the Bible must be rearticulated in ways relevant to the modern audience. The contextualization process of the biblical message should ensure that the authorial intent within its historical context is faithfully conveyed in the context of the reader, with sensitivities to time, space, and cultural distance.

The end goal of reading and interpreting the Bible should lead to applying the meaning of the text. The interpreter should highlight possible areas of contact and relevance. For the gospel to be rooted, strengthened, and bear meaningful fruit among African believers, there is a need to relate the teachings of the Bible to the realities people face.

The section below highlights Paul's message and the corresponding reflection points for the contemporary African audience. It confirms that, despite the historical distance, the letter speaks clearly to issues critical to the African worldview. It discusses seven African realities that emerge from Colossians as ways in which the message of Colossians can be effectively communicated today. The seven realities surveyed are certainly not meant to be exhaustive but illustrate the modern-day relevance of the letter.

Christ's Power Over the Visible and Invisible Worlds

Having discussed the salvific work of God the Father and the Spirit that has brought fruit in Colossae and the whole world in 1:3–14, Paul, in 1:15–20, highlights the supremacy and lordship of Christ. The hymnic material highlights Christ's redemptive work and cosmic significance over visible and invisible powers in heaven and on earth, both now and in the new creation. The "invisible" creations of God include the angels in heaven.

Christ is presented as "the image of the invisible God" (1:15; also see Heb 1:3), the first-born "of all creation" (1:15), the creator of all things, the one through whom all things hold together (1:17). He is the one through whom God has reconciled all things (1:20), the head of every spiritual power and authority (2:10, 15). In him, all the fullness of God dwells (1:19; 2:9). He is the sustaining power of the universe, holding the center together.

Paul discusses the sufficiency of Christ against a backdrop of heretical teachings in Colossae. Douglas Moo argues that the cosmological Christology of Colossians addresses the false teachers' allegation that Christ was insufficient to protect believers from all the "powers" rampant in the world.[9] According to this view, Paul is seen as making counterarguments

9. Moo, *The Letters to the Colossians and to Philemon*, 88.

against heretical teachings; this view is also strengthened by the affirmations that God in Christ has "disarmed the rulers and authorities" (2:15).

On the reality of invisible powers in the New Testament, it is noted that

> Mortals sought some understanding of and access to the supernatural powers that controlled their lives, often via intermediary or daemonic beings or through mystical experiences. This would involve discovering some sort of effectual meaning for appeasing, worshipping, or manipulating these powers in order to obtain a degree of protection or in order to escape the corrupted, terrestrial world, either in this life or the next.[10]

Concerning the ultimate control of the universe, ancient Judaism believed that God created both the visible and invisible realities and that wisdom existed before all things, and through it, God created the world. The Greco-Roman philosophers believed that all things emanated from, were sustained by, and would return to the logos, nature, or the primeval fire.[11] They thought that all things were held together by Zeus or by the logos, divine reason.

An insightful study by Clinton E. Arnold that examined angel inscriptions, magical texts, and archaeological evidence from Asia Minor indicated that the believers in Colossae may have sought to combine the teachings of Christ with local pagan and Jewish folklore beliefs. This syncretistic practice kept them captive to the fear of evil spirits and oppressive powers of the underworld, thus making them rely on the power of magic and amulets, intermediary spirits, or angels for protection. They also engaged in rituals of power and other ascetic practices believed to be much sought-after protection from hostile powers.[12]

In this context, Paul presents a Christology that emphasizes the cosmic role of Christ and his powers over the visible and invisible realities in this present age and the age to come. Those who have been united with Christ have come under the mighty power of Christ, and thus, they need not live in fear or be under any form of oppressive power. Christ's power rescued them from the dominion of darkness and transferred them to the kingdom of God (1:13). The redemptive power of Christ is projected as the great power over all conceivable powers in this age or in the age to come, whether visible or invisible (2:15).

In many parts of the world, including Africa, belief in spiritual beings and realities remains strong. Spiritual powers over human affairs are recognized and feared.[13] In African cosmology, it is believed that the visible and invisible realities coexist and are in constant contact. The

---

10. W. T. Wilson, *The Hope of Glory: Education and Exhortation in the Epistle to the Colossians*, NovTSup 88 (Brill, 1997), 3–4.

11. Keener, *The IVP Bible Background Commentary*, 572.

12. Arnold, *The Colossian Syncretism*, 246, 310.

13. Elkanah K. Cheboi, *Crucified and Cursed Christ: An Analysis of Galatians 3:1–14 in the Context of Curses in Biblical Times and Its Relevance to Marakwet Culture* (Langham, 2023), 159.

visible world permanently faces the transcendent, whether impersonal (material) or personal (a soul, a spirit, or a god). The supreme being(s) is or are considered the cause of everything; the lesser gods are constantly involved in human affairs.[14] This holistic view of life and reality differs from the dualistic approach of Western philosophy.

In the African worldview, the world is filled with divinities and spirits that can positively or negatively affect every aspect of life. Those alive have to be conscious of the implications of their actions on the spiritual world comprising spirits and ancestors. When the actions of the living are not in tandem with the stipulated traditions, the deities would be provoked to anger. It is observed that the Yoruba people of Nigeria have at least 1,700 deities; these spirits comprise the invisible world and control the physical world.[15] Evil spirits are deemed to cause injury, accidents, or suffering; therefore, many daily occurrences in the physical world are interpreted in light of spiritual influence. People with this worldview live in fear of the dire consequences of the invisible world, which involve curses, binding spells, diseases, demonic powers, and witchcraft.[16]

Christ's preeminence over all things (visible and invisible realities) is thus significant and meaningful in such a context. The spirits (whether evil or good) or deities are not omnipotent or omnipresent but are limited and subordinate to Christ. Satan, demons, and the powers of the dark world are not the ultimate; Christ is. Witchcraft and all forms of demonic activities have been conquered and rendered powerless by Christ through his death and resurrection. They have no power over believers in Christ. Therefore, believers should not fear the powers of the physical or spiritual world. They should not resort to syncretistic practices of combining African traditional beliefs about the spiritual world and Christ's teachings. Christ's power encompasses the physical and spiritual spheres, the present time, and the time to come. Thus, believers should not live in the deception of these pseudo-powers, for Christ has rendered them powerless at the cross. Amidst syncretistic practices in Africa today, the sufficiency of Christ and his work should be proclaimed (2:6–15). Christian apologetics in Africa should articulate the biblical truth that Christ is enough in all things.

In Christ, nothing is lacking in his identity and work that human beings or systems should supply. His work on the cross is complete, sufficient, and final. Paul's message about the crucified and the risen Lord of all is quite liberating: "All the forces of the universe are subject to him, not only the benign ones but the hostile ones as well. They are all subject to the one through whom they were created; the hostile forces are also subject to the one by whom they were conquered."[17] Therefore, to be united with Christ is to be liberated from these invisible (and visible) powers and to enjoy freedom in Christ. Paul further develops this thought of union with Christ and freedom in Christ in Colossians 2–3.

---

14. Aloysius M. Lugira, *World Religions: African Traditional Religion*, 3rd ed. (Chelsea House, 2009), 16, 48.

15. Samuel Waje Kunhiyop, *African Christian Ethics* (Hippo Books, 2008), 18.

16. Kunhiyop, *African Christian Ethics*, 53.

17. Bruce, *The Epistles to the Colossians, to Philemon, and to the Ephesians*, 112–113.

The Value of Authentic Tradition

In his letter to Colossians, Paul underscores the value of the biblical tradition by distinguishing two natures of tradition: divine and human (2:8). Human tradition through philosophy and empty deception is patterned according to "the tradition of men" and according to "the elemental spirits of the universe" and not according to Christ (2:8, 22). The false teachers in Colossae presented a false reality hinged on human traditions (2:8–23) at face value, but beneath it was a deeply spiritual reality. Arnold clarifies, "On the human level, the source of 'the philosophy' is in tradition, but on the supernatural/personal level, it has its source in evil spiritual powers (the *stoicheia*) and not Christ."[18] It was created and passed down by humans but influenced by demonic spirits, the powers of the present evil age. Paul warns believers against being taken captive by them or judged by people (2:8, 16), noting that Christ had already rescued and redeemed them from these powers. In Galatians 4:3, 9, Paul feared that the Galatian believers were returning to be enslaved to the "elemental spirits of the world" from which they had been delivered. Believers' identification with the death, burial, and resurrection of Christ brings deliverance from this captivity for Christ is the center and finality of God's redemption. The nature of the philosophy at Colossae was based on empty deception and externals like the observance of certain food and drink, festivals, new moons, or sabbath (2:16), and not on the fullness of Christ. These false teachers focused on angels (1:16, 20; 2:10, 15, 18) and practiced ascetic disciplines (2:18, 23). Moo remarks, "The false teachers were appealing to spiritual beings, visions, and rules to find security in this uncertain universe. In doing so, they were questioning the sufficiency of Christ."[19] Human tradition and empty philosophies were not the only heritage the Colossians received.

When the Colossians heard the gospel, they received the tradition of Christ through faithful ministers like Epaphras (1:5). The faithful "tradition" or apostolic heritage that the Colossians received can be summed up as "Christ Jesus as Lord" (2:6). In his gospel account, Luke (1:2) underscores that he passes on the tradition "as they were handed on to us by those who from the beginning were eyewitnesses and servants of the word." In 1 Corinthians 2:2, Paul's kerygma focused on Christ and the cross. Again, the church in Thessalonica is admonished to stand firm and hold fast to the apostolic tradition (2 Thess 2:15). The tradition that the apostles received and passed down revered the Scriptures and highly regarded the atoning work of Christ, his death, and resurrection (1 Cor 15:1–4).

The Colossians needed to uphold the true gospel they had heard without deviating from it (1:23). Paul is convinced that the Colossians had received the true message of the gospel; they only needed to live in Christ, be rooted, and built up in him (2:6–7). According to Paul, there was already a firm and trustworthy tradition of the true gospel that false teachers sought to destabilize. Therefore, believers were to stand firm (2:5). The apostles were conscious and deliberate in handing over the apostolic tradition based on what they saw and heard from

18. Arnold, *The Colossian Syncretism*, 188–189.

19. Moo, *The Letters to the Colossians and to Philemon*, 75.

Christ (1 Cor 11:23; 2 Tim 2:2; 1 John 1:3). It was supposed to be handed down to reliable persons who would, in turn, entrust it to others (2 Tim 2:2).

The concept of tradition was common in Judaism. It referred to the handing down of oral and written law and its interpretation from generation to generation. The unwritten tradition was "the tradition of the elders," also referred to as "the custom of our fathers" or "the law of our fathers" (Acts 6:14; 15:1; 21:21; 22:3; 26:3; 28:17; Gal 1:14). In the Old Testament, parents were instructed to teach their children concerning God's words and deeds (Gen 18:19; Deut 4:9; Ps 78:3–7). The focus was on the posterity of the traditions which were a reference point for their identity.

Disciples of particular sects or movements perpetuated their traditions to the subsequent generation. These traditions were preserved and defended. The Jewish tradition recorded how "Moses received the Torah from Sinai, and he delivered it to Joshua, and Joshua to the elders, and the elders to the prophets, and the prophets delivered it to the men of the great synagogue."[20] The Zealots in the Jewish community passionately defended the traditional values (both religious and material) enshrined in the covenant of the people.

Jesus quoted the Old Testament Scriptures as authoritative and reinterpreted them to give the original meaning. He did not come to abolish but to fulfill the law and the prophets (Luke 4:16–21). Conversely, Jesus denounced the practices of those who handed over "the tradition of the elders" because the traditions were no longer God-centered but human-centered. The traditions opposed the very law they were supposed to safeguard: "You abandon the commandment of God and hold to human tradition" (Mark 7:8). When the Pharisees and the teachers of the Law came to Jesus and asked him why the disciple had broken the tradition of the elders by not washing their hands before eating, Jesus questioned them back, "And why do you break the commandment of God for the sake of your tradition?" (Matt 15:3). The human practices that had influenced their traditions negatively affected their interpretation of Scripture. Judaism highly regarded tradition as authoritative, sometimes even over Scripture.

Tradition is a crucial element in African cosmology. It is what orders individual and public values, convictions, aspirations, and life in the community. Positively, traditions preserve beliefs, values, wisdom, practices, and cultural identity. Indigenous traditions and thoughts were passed orally from one generation to another through myths, stories, customs, songs, and proverbs. These traditions were human-centered; using the language of the Preacher (Eccl 1:9), they focused on life "under the sun."

Traditions also convey people's identity and history. The question of what happens to one's cultural identity when one becomes a believer in Christ is a critical theological and missiological concern. It touches on whether (or to what extent) one's past continues or discontinues after salvation. The interaction between cultural and Christian identities needs to be examined critically. In the recent past, Christian theologians in Africa have attempted to conceptualize how Africa's rich past religious and cultural traditions can be integrated with the Christian faith. Kwame Bediako, in his insightful study, observed that, during the colonial period, the

20. Bruce, *The Epistles to the Colossians, to Philemon, and to the Ephesians*, 93.

Western missionaries dismissed Africans' rich pre-Christian religious heritage as evil, pagan, and superstitious, unworthy of serious theological reflection. Consequently, Africans had to abandon their former heritage to accept the gospel wrapped in Western culture, thus impairing their identity as a people.[21]

Bediako evaluated how the second-century Christians in the Greco-Roman culture related to their traditional backgrounds. He investigated whether Christianity destroys/discontinues or affirms/continues one's past background. He analyses the continuity and discontinuity views in second-century Greco-Roman and twentieth-century African contexts. In a balanced approach, he recommends a critical look at past traditions to determine positive aspects to be retained and negative ones to be abandoned. He emphatically rejects any attempt to minimize African heritage and identity.[22]

After the salvation experience, Christian Africans should not continue their cultural and religious traditions blindly or uncritically. Rather, they should discern the powers at work within some of those traditions and embrace traditions that do not contradict God's word. In line with Paul's message to the Colossians, they should recognize truths and falsehoods in traditions. Traditions can sometimes promote idolatry in the name of traditional deities or (ancestral) heritages; Christians should discern these landmines and avoid them. Two examples of the tension between Christianity and traditions should suffice. First, traditional burial rites involve rituals and observances that contradict Christian practices. Sometimes, pastors conducting funeral services are asked to come early or at the very end after the traditional rites are completed. Depending on the culture, these traditional burial rites stipulate the burial site, the direction the dead should face at the grave, and the send-off rituals to be performed depending on the age and moral standing of the deceased, or the manner in which the person died. A minister of the gospel should be prepared to handle these deep-held convictions with care and wisdom to avoid syncretism or hindering the family from uncontested burial rites and rituals. Second, the payment of bride price in many African cultures is required and determined by the family of the bride. In a context that is becoming extremely materialistic, many misinterpret the spirit of this tradition by placing suffocating demands on the groom's family. Christians who find themselves in this mix cite the age-long traditions but fail to recognize their own transformative role and calling as the light of the world (Matt 5:14).

Thus, on the question of tradition, there should be a meaningful dialogue between the un-Christian past and the present Christian identities, and the Bible should guide what should be continued or discontinued. In the church community, theologians, pastors, and church leaders in Africa must establish Christocentric, biblical, and culture-sensitive faith traditions that can be passed on to future generations. These should be traditions rooted in salvation by grace through faith and the authority of God's word in matters of faith and practice. In addition, they should be traditions that highly regard the salvific work of Christ on the cross.

21. Kwame Bediako, *Theology and Identity: The Impact of Culture Upon Christian Thought in the Second Century and Modern Africa* (Regnum Books, 1992).

22. Bediako, *Theology and Identity*, 31–33, 67, 71, 76, 175–197.

Holding fast to such a tradition involves the rejection of all traditions that are contrary to the gospel.

Making Peace Through Blood

In Colossians 1:19–22, Christ is portrayed as the reconciler of all things, bringing peace through his blood. Through the cross of Christ, reconciliation for believers was achieved, and the Colossian believers were beneficiaries of this reconciliation work. It is through the blood of Christ that peace is made. Christ restored peace between God and human beings; a relationship that had been distorted because of the sinfulness of human beings was restored. The blood of Christ atoned for the sins of humankind and restored peace with God. The peace achieved through the sacrifice of Christ ended the hostility. The universal scope of Christ's reconciliation and peacemaking is "to restore the harmony of the original creation, to bring into renewed oneness and wholeness."[23]

In the Old Testament, blood signifies life, which is regarded as sacred (Gen 9:4–6; Lev 17:11; Deut 12:23). Shedding innocent blood is prohibited, and God demands accountability and respect for human life. In the Passover, the angel of death would pass over the house with blood on its doorpost (Exod 12:13). The blood of the substitutionary lamb spared the Israelites from judgment. In the Sinaitic covenant (Exod 24:6–8), blood was used to unite parties to a covenant. The Levitical priesthood system required the sacrifice of an unblemished animal to be offered for human sin (Lev 1:10; 16:14, 15). The sacrifice restored the relationship between God and humanity, which had been distorted by sin.

The significance of shedding blood for the atonement of sins is a theme that is also prominently featured in the New Testament. Upon seeing Jesus, John the Baptist exclaimed, "Here is the lamb of God who takes away the sin of the world" (John 1:29). He predicted the substitutionary role Jesus would play as an atonement sacrifice, reconciling humanity to God. In Hebrews 9:11–28, the blood of Jesus also seals the new covenant and achieves what the blood of goats and bulls could not. Hebrews 9:22 emphasizes the necessity of blood in forgiving sins: "Indeed, under the law, almost everything is purified with blood, and without the shedding of blood, there is no forgiveness of sins." The celebration of the ordinance of the Lord's Supper includes partaking of the cup, signifying the shed blood of Christ (1 Cor 11:25, 26).

The concept of blood is not abstract in traditional African religions. Blood was used in many traditional African ceremonies, worship, and rituals to validate covenants.[24] It was associated with life. Bringing reconciliation or restoration of a relationship in the African worldview required the shedding of blood, mainly of animals. Sacrifices were also performed to nullify curses and their effects.[25] Blood, rituals, and sacrifices are key elements in divination.

23. James D. G. Dunn, *The Epistles to the Colossians and to Philemon: A Commentary on the Greek Text*, NIGTC (Eerdmans, 1996), 104.

24. Victor B. Cole, "Blood," in *Africa Bible Commentary: A One-Volume Commentary Written by 70 African Scholars*, ed. Tokunboh Adeyemo (WordAlive Publishers; Zondervan, 2006), 139.

25. Cheboi, *Crucified and Cursed Christ*, 170.

As a result, from such a background, many Christian Africans find the theme of the shedding of Christ's blood significantly relevant. The power in the blood of Christ assures believers of a greater power beyond animal blood, as required in traditional altars.

The blood of Christ shed on the cross is sufficient to remove all sin, once and for all, thus restoring the relationship with God. The blood of Jesus purifies believers from all sin (1 John 1:7) and brings forgiveness, redemption, and justification (Rom 3:24–25; 4:7; 5:9). The traditional understanding of blood and sacrifice can provide the relevant categories through which the message of the Bible can be applied. The inculturation process of the biblical message should guide Christians to interrogate African traditional beliefs regarding blood and sacrifices and relevantly articulate biblical affirmation of the sufficiency of Christ's work on the cross. Believers tempted to use traditional means of sacrifice to deal with past issues or experiences (like curses) should be reminded that Jesus is the ultimate sacrifice and answer.

Having been reconciled with God through Christ, believers in Christ have been given a message of reconciliation of people, families, communities, and nations to God (2 Cor 5:18–20). The cost of reconciliation and peace has been paid through the work of Jesus on the cross. Through him, he reconciled to himself all things—the hostility between the Creator and the creation is now restored; "Just as things in the heavens and the earth were created in him, so now are all things in the same realms reconciled to God through the blood of the cross."[26] In this reconciliation, the offended party took the initiative to reconcile humanity with himself. This demonstrates that reconciliation does not have to rely on the initiative of the offending party; rather, the offended individual and community can initiate the reconciliation process, following the example of Christ. Therefore, in Christ, there is the cessation of enmity, exclusion, hostility, and rejection. The message of reconciliation through the work of Christ is a message of transforming hope and healing in a context of incessant conflicts and wars.

The Locus of a Person's Identity

Like Romans 6, believers' union with Christ is given much attention in Paul's letter to the Colossians, just like in Romans 6. *In* Christ, believers live (2:6) and were circumcised (2:11); *with* Christ, believers died and were buried in baptism (2:12, 20), raised (2:12; 3:1), and are now alive with Christ (2:13), their lives hidden with Christ in God (3:2). Christ is "all and in all" (3:11). Believers are members of one body, Christ's peace rules the hearts of believers (3:15) and his message should dwell among believers (3:16). Whatever believers do, in word or deed, should be done "in the name of the Lord Jesus" (3:17) and household relationships should be conducted *in/for* the Lord (3:18, 20, 22–24, 4:1). The ministers of the gospel serve *in the Lord* (4:7, 17).

Using the metaphor of baptism, Paul writes that believers share in Christ's death, burial, and resurrection (the same imagery is used in Rom 6:4). Bruce notes, "Those who have been raised with Christ have been raised through faith in the divine power which brought him back from the dead, and from now on that power energizes them and maintains the new

26. Michael F. Bird, *Colossians and Philemon*, NCCS (The Lutterworth Press, 2011), 57.

life within them—the new life which is nothing less than Christ's resurrection life flowing through all the members of his body."[27] The contrast between the "old person" and the "new person" probably alludes to Adam, and is used in the light of Jewish concepts of communal identity. Believers in Christ have their identity first in relation to Christ and then to the faith community. The relationship with Christ makes one a new creation and a member of God's household. In the Christian community, all believers should first identify with Christ through rebirth and then be part of the faith community.

The question of identity encompasses both individual and communal aspects. An individual's identity also includes their communal and social identities and their participation in various social groups.[28] In the African worldview, individuals closely identify with the community (extended family, clan, or tribe). This kind of communal solidarity is summarized in the expression, "I am because we are, and since we are, therefore I am."[29] While community identity was important in the traditional African setting, individual responsibility was not denied. Individuals were to be responsible members of the community. Therefore, the individual and communal identity were defined in relation to each other. Mbiti argues,

> In traditional life, the individual does not and cannot exist alone except corporately. He owes his existence to other people, including those of past generations and his contemporaries. He is simply part of the whole. The community must, therefore, make, create, or produce the individual, for the individual depends on the corporate group.[30]

Ethnic identity is a critical aspect of African communal life. People within an ethnic group easily relate to or support each other as compared to those from different ethnic groups. The idea of community can be positive because it can lead to caring, helping, and sharing concern for one another. It can also be negative because it can lead to tribalism, nepotism, ethnicity, and prejudice toward others if used as a reference point for exclusion.[31] Therefore, Christians from contexts where ethnic identity is the prime identity should be challenged to embrace their identity in Christ, which encompasses the other. Those who are the same as well as those who are different from "us" have been made one person in Christ. It is no longer about the "me" versus "you" and "us" versus "them" distinction; all have become one people in Christ.

When pioneer missionaries came to African countries, they demarcated the vast regions into blocks and allotted various mission agencies their respective jurisdictions of operation. One of the reasons was to reduce potential conflicts in the mission field. These multiple blocks, by default or design, were based on ethnic groups. Hence, from the beginning, many churches

27. Bruce, *The Epistles to the Colossians, to Philemon, and to the Ephesians*, 105.

28. Stephanie Lowery, *Identity and Ecclesiology: Their Relationship Among Select African Theologians* (Pickwick, 2017), 4.

29. John S. Mbiti, *Introduction to African Religion* (Praeger, 1975), 175.

30. John Mbiti, *African Religion and Philosophy*, 2nd ed. (Heinemann, 1990), 108.

31. Wilbur O'Donovan, *Biblical Christianity in Modern Africa* (Paternoster Press, 2000), 11.

were planted alongside tribal lines. This reality of ethnic majority in many missionary-established churches has persisted long after the missionary era. While ethnic unity or churches planted along ethnic lines are not necessarily evil, the definition of the church as a multiethnic community should still be pursued. The church should be a community that embraces people from diverse ethnic or racial backgrounds and where every believer is recognized and valued. In a context where politics of exclusion is rampant, the church should be the model community demonstrating that diversity or difference is not a threat but a God-given value for a healthy society. The new transformative identity in Christ should bring unity beyond ethnicities. The new "supra-ethnic community"[32] should be open to other believers in Christ.

Christianity promotes the concept of community: "Christianity is communal faith—it creates a community—and as such it affirms African values of relationships shaping a person's identity."[33] The Christian community is not defined by human blood relations or ethnic or racial distinctions but by the saving blood of Jesus on the cross. A personal relationship with Christ brings one into a new community of faith: "In that renewal there is no longer Greek and Jew, circumcised and uncircumcised, barbarians, and Scythian, slave and free; but Christ is all in all!" (Col 3:11). The church in cosmopolitan Colossae became the melting pot of these differentiations because of their higher identity achieved through their union with Christ. The church community should cultivate virtues that promote the focus on the other, for instance, hospitality, generosity, care of others, being mindful of others, and thoughtfulness.[34] For Christianity to make a meaningful impact, "The Christian identity must be both distinctive and culturally relatable. Christian identity must be inculturated in Africa if it is to redeem African identities for Christ."[35]

Major Turning Points of Life

While encouraging Christians to live according to the gospel they have received, Paul presents the concept of the new man or new self through the imagery of circumcision. In the Old Testament, circumcision was the seal of God's covenant with the family of Abraham. It was a sign of membership in the Mosaic covenant. The Hebrew circumcision of an infant of eight days old (Luke 2:21) is contrasted with spiritual circumcision through Christ. The believer puts off the former self and its passions and embraces the new life in God through Christ. The "circumcision of the heart," as opposed to the circumcision made with hands (external), is emphasized (Deut 1:16; 10:16; 30:6; Jer 4:4; Ezek 44:7). The circumcision of the heart, referring to inward purification, comes through the work of Christ on the cross and by the regenerating work of the Holy Spirit in the believer. In 2:11–13, Paul reframes the Old

32. Titre Ande, *Leadership and Authority: Bula Matari and Life-Community Ecclesiology in Congo*, Regnum Studies in Mission (Regnum, 2010), 144, 155.

33. Lowery, *Identity and Ecclesiology*, 25.

34. Joe M. Kapolyo, *The Human Condition: Christian Perspectives Through African Eyes*, Christian Doctrine in Global Perspectives (InterVarsity Press, 2005), 39.

35. Lowery, *Identity and Ecclesiology*, 33.

Testament idea of circumcision. He provides a spiritual meaning of the imagery as "putting off the body of the flesh in the circumcision of Christ" (v. 11).

After their union with Christ, believers should "put to death" that which is earthly in them (3:5). The former way of life (as an unbeliever) should cease after coming to Christ. Paul lists actions/practices, thoughts, words, and emotions in 3:5, 8, that a believer needs to put to death. Those in Christ should no longer live in sin; Paul reminds them: "You have stripped off the old self with its practices and have clothed yourselves with the new self, which is being renewed in knowledge according to the image of its creator" (Col 3:9b–10).

In 3:1–4, he outlines the motivations for a new life. Believers have been raised with Christ; therefore, they should "put to death" whatever is earthly (3:5) and focus on the things above. In addition, they have died, and their lives have been hidden with Christ in God, protected from evil. What is regarded as "earthly" includes "fornication, impurity, passion, evil desire, and greed (which is idolatry)" (3:5). This should lead to believers "clothing" themselves with "compassion, kindness, humility, meekness and patience" (3:12). The new self "is being renewed in knowledge according to the image of its creator" (3:10). In his thought, Paul draws a contrast between Adam (the "old man") and Christ (the "new man").

In the African worldview, life consists of many transitions or instances where one is expected to be a "new person." One such transition is the rite of passage from being a boy to a man or a girl to a woman and so becoming a full member of society.[36] Such transitions are observed differently depending on the community. In some communities, circumcision and the accompanying rites become the turning point of boyhood to manhood. The initiates are taught the cultural wisdom and ways of life of an initiated man/woman, as well as about work, sex, marriage, family, and community life.[37] They are expected to put off their old self, characterized by immaturity, and put on a new self that reflects the ideal person. These initiation rites and events aim to produce a person who conforms to the cultural definition. The new life is expected to be seen in the initiates' thinking, speech, behavior, and ability to lead.

Care should be exercised in this endeavor because many of these rites of passage, like female genital mutilation (FGM), are harmful. The main point here is that there are rites of passage that mark significant transitions in life that can be harnessed to apply the biblical message appropriately without compromising both the integrity of the passage and of the biblical teaching. Further, care should be exercised to determine the cultural understanding of a mature man or woman; some definitions oppose the biblical understanding of a man and woman being made in the image and likeness of God. However, alternative ways of rearticulating rites of passage from a Christian perspective can be explored in cases where the cultural element is rich.

For a human being to be a new person, there must be an encounter with Christ and the regenerating work of the Holy Spirit so that new thinking and living patterns are consistent with biblical teachings. Christians should identify and interrogate these relevant

36. Solomon Andria, "Colossians," in *Africa Bible Commentary: A One-Volume Commentary Written by 70 African Scholars*, ed. Tokunboh Adeyemo (WordAlive Publishers; Zondervan, 2006), 1453.

37. Wilbur O'Donovan, *Biblical Christianity in African Perspective*, 2nd ed. (Paternoster Press, 1997), 232.

cultural elements to apply the gospel to the local culture and people without compromising biblical truths.

Church and Extended Family Systems

In 3:18–4:1, Paul issued rules for Christian households (similar to Eph 5:22–6:9, where he states some domestic responsibilities). The broader relationships within the extended family setup test one's faith and love for God and neighbor. The pericope deals with the relationships of husband and wife, parents, and children.

The complementary duties between the husband and wife are governed by the statement "as is fitting in the Lord" (Col 3:18). The woman is to submit, and the husband is to love "as is fitting in the Lord." Children are to obey their parents in everything because this is an "acceptable duty in the Lord" (3:20); "In such a situation, the law of Christ would have to take precedence even over parental orders, but in a spirit of love, not of defiance, since the law of Christ is the law of love."[38] Children and parents are bound together "in the Lord." The reference point of submission, love, and obedience is Christ, who modeled love and humility "and became obedient to the point of death—even death on a cross" (Phil 2:8). Christ fulfilled the expectations of each of the stated groups, hence is a model for all who follow him.

Likewise, Christian slaves were required to obey their masters in everything, seeking to please the Lord, who would reward their labor (3:22–24). They were to do everything primarily for the Lord and not for their masters. Christian servants, because of their faith in Christ, were no longer mere slaves but brothers and sisters in Christ serving God in their vocations. This instruction gives meaning to the different marketplace vocations as these can be done to the Lord and for the magnification of his name. It also acknowledges the expansive scope of Christ's rule over various kinds of work, gifts, and talents. Christian masters were required to treat their servants justly and fairly (4:1). They are reminded that they, too, have a master in heaven to whom they are accountable. There is no room for passive, dictatorial, or autocratic rule, as it is not in line with the example of Christ, who offered himself to serve. The way the Lord relates to them should be how they relate to their servants. Using the parable of Jesus, they should not be like the unmerciful servant who was forgiven a massive debt but could not exercise the same forgiveness to another servant who owed him a relatively small debt (Matt 18:21–35).

The Roman household (*familia*) was more expansive than a nuclear family. It comprised a father, mother, children, grandparents, slaves, freedmen, and clients. The male head of the household (*paterfamilias*) had power over the family members. In the New Testament, there are examples of women who are heads of households like Lydia (Acts 16:15), Chloe (1 Cor 1:11), and Nympha (Col 4:15). This is also a period where church worship services were hosted not in church buildings but in believers' houses. The Hellenistic family (*oikos*) was a multi-generational unit that included members of the family by blood and marriage, as well as

38. Bruce, *The Epistles to the Colossians, to Philemon, and to the Ephesians*, 165.

property "movables" (slaves, animals) and "immovables" (house, land, tools).[39] Jewish households consisted of two to three generations of kin by blood and marriage; most Jewish families did not own slaves. Christians who originally came from Jewish and pagan families needed clear guidelines on acceptable household codes for Christian families. Jeffers opines that Jewish and Christian families would have constituted "weakened patriarchies."[40] The household codes were reworked; hence, there were areas of continuity and discontinuity because Christians were supposed to live out their faith in this context.

Moo observes that these "household codes" are controversial, but notes that they "warn us that our common life in Christ does not erase our responsibilities toward one another within family and society. They are set on a new footing and given a new motivation: reference to 'the Lord' permeates this passage."[41] The obligations of these identities are to be done in relation to Christ: Husbands had the lead role in the family, women were to manage the home, and children were obligated to obey their parents.

Traditionally, the African understanding of a family was based on its composition and function. The definition of a family is not just a nucleus (father, mother, and children). It comprises parents, children, grandchildren, close family members such as uncles, aunts, grandparents, the departed (living dead), and the unborn. Modern trends like urbanization have not significantly impacted the family system as understood traditionally. Parental obligation and communal role in creating a safe environment is still central; as is commonly said, "it takes a village to raise a child."

Extended family systems provide social support, security, and common life between individuals, families, clans, and entire communities.[42] However, due to technological advancement and urbanization in Africa, extended families have lost their primary place and role as the principal organizing factor in society and have been replaced by smaller family units. It is also noted that "the shift from a communitarian to an individualist framework of societal organization is not yet complete, and individualism has no inbuilt support system."[43] Extended family systems and the concept of community are still prominent in Africa.

In traditional society, the need for economic, emotional, and psychological support is generally addressed among biological and extended family members. As it is commonly put, "blood is thicker than water." Many families come together during times of crisis or need to address issues related to conflict, sickness, death, weddings, and education, among other things. Now with the spread of Christianity, the church has in many instances become an alternative support community in times of crisis, making the connection through the blood of Christ "thicker" than the biological bond.

39. James S. Jeffers, *The Greco-Roman World of the New Testament Era: Exploring the Background of Early Christianity* (InterVarsity Press, 1999), 239.

40. Jeffers, *The Greco-Roman World of the New Testament Era*, 240.

41. Moo, *The Letters to the Colossians and to Philemon*, 87.

42. Daniel Bitrus, *The Extended Family: An African Christian Perspective* (CLMC, 2000), 1.

43. Elizabeth Mburu, *African Hermeneutics* (HippoBooks, 2019), 41.

The depiction of the church as family is found in the Bible (Gal 6:10; Eph 2:19–20; 1 John 3:1). The family imagery is also at play in Acts 2:42, where believers were together and ate together in their homes. God's church is diverse but one. It brings together people from different walks of life into one community. Interdependence, relationality, solidarity, respect for diversity, and equality should characterize this family.[44] The church must be a life-giving community where the life-giving Spirit reigns. As a family, the church ought to create a nurturing environment where each person contributes to the community and where values such as respect, care, and concern for each other are realized.[45] In a context facing urbanization and globalization, and where family and communal support systems are disintegrating, the church should live up to its identity as a true family of God that embraces all.

Final Greetings as Last But Not Least

Salutations were a customary feature in ancient letters. Paul starts his letters with greetings[46] and ends with greetings. At the beginning of his letters, he replaces the regular Greek χαίρειν *chairein* (greeting) by combining the Greek greeting χάρις *charis* (grace or favor) and the Jewish standard greeting εἰρήνη *eirēnē* (peace; Hebrew: *Shālôm*). Grace refers to God's unconditional favor toward his people, while *shalom* expresses wholeness, multidimensional well-being, and harmonious relationships with God and others. The unmerited favor and shalom spring from a relationship with God through which one can enjoy every spiritual blessing.

Equally, the closing sections of Paul's letters usually have *a* peace and grace benediction, a hortatory section, greetings, and an autograph. These often neglected sections are not appendices to the letter but are carefully constructed units that summarize the teachings and highlight the central concerns and themes.[47] In these sections, Paul portrays an existing relationship with his audience, thus establishing the spirit of oneness that is critical in reading, interpreting, and applying the message of the letter.

The closing section of the letter (4:7–18) lists the names of specific ministry partners and their role in advancing the gospel. Tychicus is referred to as "a beloved brother, a faithful minister, and a fellow servant in the Lord"; Onesimus is described as "the faithful and beloved brother"; Aristarchus, "my fellow prisoner." Epaphras is described as "a servant of Christ Jesus" who is "always wrestling in prayer" on behalf of the Colossians. Other coworkers mentioned are Mark, Jesus (Justus), and Luke. Paul was not a lone ranger in prison or in ministry; he was with the army of the Lord which gave him the requisite physical, moral, and spiritual support. He understood that one gifted person could not do the whole of God's work. He thus acknowledged the need for many hands in God's work and the need to develop other

44. Elochukwu Uzukwu, *A Listening Church: Autonomy and Communion in African Churches* (Wipf & Stock, 2006), 14.

45. Lowery, *Identity and Ecclesiology*, 137–138.

46. Other examples: Rom 1:7; 1 Cor 1:3; 2 Cor 1:2; Gal 1:3; Eph 1:2; Phil 1:2; 1 Thess 1:1.

47. Jeffrey A. Weima, "The Pauline Letter Closings: Analysis and Hermeneutical Significance," *Bulletin for Biblical Research* 5, no. 1 (1995): 177.

ministry workers. Diversity is needed in the body of Christ. There is enough work for every servant and every opportunity for service for every Spirit-given gift. In Romans 16:1–16, Paul mentions twenty-six people by name and refers to many others in a church he had not visited (16:5, 10–11, 13–15). He sends them greetings and commends their partnership in the ministry. Irrespective of the tone used in the letter, the closing greetings always give an assurance of love, interdependence, togetherness, and community. The church should become a caring and thriving community that demonstrates to Africa how variety and diversity can become a blessing and not a curse.[48]

Africans typically engage in extensive daily greetings whenever people meet. From firm handshakes and hugs, to frequent phone calls to find out how one is faring, all of these demonstrate the high value placed on greetings and relationships. Greetings are not just for starting a conversation but also express concern for others and their well-being. The sending and receiving of greetings from different individuals and churches is standard in many churches. Often, greetings and visits are complementary. Even in the ministry of Paul, greetings were sent to those he had visited or intended to visit. Sending letters that featured greetings was a way Paul maintained contact with his hearers and ministry coworkers. Swahili speakers will be familiar with the phrase radio callers use when sending greetings to their loved ones in distant places: *salamu ni nusu ya kuonana* (lit. "sending of greetings is a halfway form of seeing each other").

Commonly, when there is no time for visitors to speak in churches, they are told to "wave to the congregation and sit" as a sign of greeting and an acknowledgment of their presence. What could be said with words can be summarized in a simple nonverbal greeting, which in itself is a sign of love and togetherness. In some churches in rural parts of Africa, the members of a congregation shake hands with one another outside the church building before saying the grace benediction. The practice of shaking hands had to be modified rather than done away with during the COVID-19 period. Sending greetings provides an opportunity to share and extend an existing relationship: "It feels that a person cannot presume upon the relationship of yesterday or last month to care for the relationship needs of today. Hence, a relationship must be renewed each day even when a good relationship already exists."[49] Since relationships are elaborate, it takes time to build and sustain them. The general welfare of others is vital in the African worldview; hence, a reunion is a time of reflection and reestablishing the relationship. The growing individualism is a threat to this positive aspect of culture. The role of greetings and concern for the well-being of others in the contemporary context is sadly often minimized and seen as a waste of time in a fast-moving world. Perhaps social media partly contributes to a culture where casual greetings like "hi," "hello," or waving emojis are considered sufficient. This fails to consider that greeting is an expression of love, connection, attention, and a hand of fellowship.

48. Mercy Amba Oduyoye, "The Church of the Future, Its Mission and Theology: A View from Africa," *Theology Today* 52, no. 4 (1996): 498.

49. O'Donovan, *Biblical Christianity in Modern Africa*, 8.

In this greeting section, Paul models what a Christian community should be. The body of Christ is both local and global. He has in view the broader body of Christ that is united in the Spirit. The union of the church, the spiritual community, is not limited by any geographical distance.

Further, the greeting section validates the ministries of every believer in Christ, even those who serve at the margins. Paul did not work alone as an apostle; he worked with coworkers God had raised and strategically utilized their gifts for ministry. The church community should accept all persons as equals and encourage participation and interdependence.[50]

Conclusion

Paul's message to the Colossians is still relevant to the modern African context. The task of every diligent interpreter is to identify contact points between the message and the readers' context. In writing Colossians, Paul addressed contextual issues in Colossae, showing his deep understanding of the issues involved.

The letter revealed Christ's power over the visible and invisible world. Believers in Colossae struggled with spiritual powers at work in their context, but Paul articulates the preeminence of Christ and his work on the cross as the solution to the problems they faced. Believers, therefore, should not fear the powers of the spiritual world but understand that Jesus is over all these powers. Colossians 2 looked at the topic of divine and human tradition. Human traditions can have a positive heritage but can be corrupted by those who hand it down. In matters related to belief and practice, believers should be guided by the apostolic tradition preserved in the Scriptures. Any good tradition elevates the work of Christ on the cross. One of the things Christ's work on the cross achieves for believers is making peace through his blood. He restores the human relationship with God, which had been characterized by enmity and separation. Believers now enjoy this blessing of coming near to God. The letter to the Colossians also builds an understanding of Christian identity. Believers' union with Christ and the consequent participation in his death, burial, and resurrection accords believers blessings of life and victory. The believer's identity is hidden in Christ and cannot be threatened by their past or present powers. Paul further discusses the putting to death "the old person" and the present reality of the "new person" in Christ. Those in Christ should reflect this newness that evidences God's work in a person's life.

Family systems in the Greco-Roman world were more of extended family; Christians were required to live out their identity in this context. The working of God should be seen in these relationships and household codes. Finally, the letter highlights the value of greetings and relationships. Like his other letters, Paul mentions several ministry partners and coworkers, showing that God's work is done individually and collectively. He recognizes the diverse ministries of those who served with him.

These point-of-contact topics were not exhaustive but present a paradigm in which Paul's message can be applied to contemporary African realities. For the gospel to take root, be strengthened, and bear much fruit in Africa, it must answer African questions. It must take

50. Lowery, *Identity and Ecclesiology*, 43.

people's concerns in a particular location and time seriously. A faith that is rooted provides true transformation of lives and thought systems. The inculturation process should ensure that the gospel is expressed in culturally relevant forms, allowing Christians to grasp God's truth in their own language and concepts.

Further Reading

Ande, Titre. *Leadership and Authority: Bula Matari and Life-Community Ecclesiology in Congo*. Regnum Studies in Mission. Regnum, 2010.

Andria, Solomon. "Colossians." In *Africa Bible Commentary: A One-Volume Commentary Written by 70 African Scholars*, edited by Tokunboh Adeyemo. WordAlive Publishers; Zondervan, 2006.

Arnold, Clinton E. *The Colossian Syncretism: The Interface Between Christianity and Folk Beliefs at Colossae*. Baker Books, 1996.

Bediako, Kwame. *Theology and Identity: The Impact of Second Century Fathers on Christian Thought*. Regnum Books, 1992.

Bird, Michael F. *Colossians and Philemon*. NCCS. The Lutterworth Press, 2011.

Bruce, F. F. *The Epistles to the Colossians, to Philemon, and to the Ephesians*. NICNT. Eerdmans, 2008.

Cheboi, Elkanah K. *Crucified and Cursed Christ: An Analysis of Galatians 3: 1–14 in the Context of Curses in Biblical Times and Its Relevance to Marakwet Culture*. Langham, 2023.

Cole, Victor B. "Blood." In *Africa Bible Commentary: A One-Volume Commentary Written by 70 African Scholars*, edited by Tokunboh Adeyemo. WordAlive Publishers; Zondervan, 2006.

Dunn, James D. G. *The Epistles to the Colossians and to Philemon: A Commentary on the Greek Text*. NIGTC. Eerdmans, 1996.

Kapolyo, Joe M. *The Human Condition: Christian Perspectives Through African Eyes*. Christian Doctrine in Global Perspectives. InterVarsity, 2005.

Kunhiyop, Samuel Waje. *African Christian Ethics*. Hippo Books, 2008.

Kunhiyop, Samuel Waje. *African Christian Theology*. Zondervan; HippoBooks, 2012.

Lowery, Stephanie. *Identity and Ecclesiology: Their Relationship Among Select African Theologians*. Pickwick, 2017.

Lugira, Aloysius M. *World Religions: African Traditional Religion*. 3rd ed. Chelsea House, 2009.

Mbiti, John. *African Religion and Philosophy*. 2nd ed. Heinemann, 1990.

Mburu, Elizabeth W. *African Hermeneutics*. HippoBooks, 2019.

Moo, Douglas J. *The Letters to the Colossians and to Philemon*. PNTC. Eerdmans, 2008.

O'Donovan, Wilbur. *Biblical Christianity in African Perspective*. 2nd ed. Carlisle: Paternoster Press, 1997.

O'Donovan, Wilbur. *Biblical Christianity in Modern Africa*. Paternoster Press, 2000.

Oduyoye, Mercy Amba. "The Church of the Future, Its Mission and Theology: A View from Africa." *Theology Today* 52 (1996): 494–505.

Uzukwu, Elochukwu. *A Listening Church: Autonomy and Communion in African Churches*. Wipf & Stock, 2006.

Weima, Jeffrey A. "The Pauline Letter Closings: Analysis and Hermeneutical Significance." *Bulletin for Biblical Research* 5, no. 4 (1995): 177–198.

Wright, N. T. *The Epistles of Paul to the Colossians and to Philemon*. TNTC. InterVarsity, 1986.

CHAPTER FIFTEEN

The Letters to the Thessalonians

Gift Mtukwa
Africa Nazarene University
Nairobi, Kenya

Introduction

THE TWO LETTERS to the Thessalonians are arguably the earliest in the New Testament corpus.[1] Regardless of the view someone takes on Paul's timeline, they still form part of the early Christian writings. If one is to know the issues that were of concern to the earliest Christians, these letters provide a sneak preview of their world. For those of us in Africa, these documents are relevant in that they relate to the experiences of those struggling to embrace the new Christian faith in light of their former faith. This chapter will look at the historical issues surrounding the two letters and then consider fictive kinship, holiness, work and community, and eschatology as thematic issues that are of concern to Paul and the African church. We assume here that Paul penned the two letters to the Thessalonians. We shall demonstrate our theory of authorship to show why we believe Paul wrote the two letters. It is also assumed here that the two letters have no substantial difference in their concern for work and community building and eschatological views.[2]

Introductory Matters

Authorship

It is a fact that Paul adopted a strategy used in his time when he wrote letters to his churches.[3] Steven J. Friesen has surmised that the letters functioned as a "substitute for his presence within the community." As such, "the letter offered a scripted

1. Some of the ideas in this chapter were shaped in the writing of this book: Gift Mtukwa, *Work and Community in the Thessalonian Correspondence: An African Communal Reading of Paul's Work Exhortations* (Langham Creative Projects, 2021).

2. Gift Mtukwa, "An African Reading of Paul's Work Exhortations in the Thessalonian Correspondence" (PhD diss., University of Manchester, 2020).

3. Mtukwa, "An African Reading," 38.

performance—Paul's words delivered orally by someone else who read what Paul's scribe had written."[4] These missives should be seen as part of an ongoing conversation between Paul and his fledgling churches.[5] Most scholars accept the traditional designation of 1 Thessalonians to Paul.[6] Its vocabulary, grammatical constructions, and style reflect Pauline authorship.[7] However, not every passage in the letter is considered Pauline—some passages have been considered interpolations, the most significant of which is 1 Thessalonians 2:13–16.[8] It is claimed that the ideas espoused in this passage are incompatible with Paul's ideas in other undisputed Pauline letters.[9] Upon scrutiny, even the passages considered interpolations are actually seen to be Pauline as well. However, space does not allow us to engage this issue.

Some scholars consider 2 Thessalonians to be pseudo-Pauline. They argue that its vocabulary, literary style, tone, and theology are different from those of Pauline letters.[10] For instance, John A. Bailey writes "the tone of II Thessalonians is official and formal; instead of the 'we give thanks' of 1 Thess. i. 2, ii. 13, there is the 'we are bound to give thanks' of II Thess. i. 3, ii. 13."[11] Even M. J. J. Menken, who denies Pauline authorship, concedes that "The difference in tone *per se* is not sufficient reason to deny Pauline authorship to 2 Thessalonians."[12] As many writers are capable of doing, Paul was able to adapt his language to the situation at hand.[13] Weima is right to note that "Paul was willing and ready to adapt his tone to fit better the specific historical context that he is addressing."[14]

Menken reads 2 Thessalonians 2:2 as referring to a forged letter, which is taken to be 1 Thessalonians.[15] One then wonders, if the forger is trying to imitate Paul, why would he bring into question the authentic letter of Paul? If he is trying to legitimize his letter, he would need to do it without disputing the real Letters of Paul.[16] This is surprising considering that Menken

4. J. Steven Friesen, "Second Thessalonians, the Ideology of Epistles, and the Construction of Authority: Our Debt to the Forger," in *From Roman to Early Christian Thessalonikē: Studies in Religion and Archaeology*, ed. Laura Salah Nasrallah, Charalambos Bakirtzēs, and Steven J. Friesen (Harvard Theological Studies, Harvard Divinity School, 2010), 190–191.

5. Willi Marxsen, *Der erste Brief an die Thessalonicher* (Theologischer Verlag, 1979), 9–11.

6. Jewett, *The Thessalonian Correspondence: Pauline Rhetoric and Millenarian Piety*, Foundations and Facets (Fortress Press, 1986), 3.

7. Jeffrey A. D. Weima, *1–2 Thessalonians* (Baker Academic, 2014), 40; Werner Georg Kümmel, *Introduction to the New Testament* (SCM Press, 1987), 185.

8. Weima, *1–2 Thessalonians*, 41.

9. Weima, *1–2 Thessalonians*, 42.

10. Edgar Krentz, "2 Thessalonians," in *The Blackwell Companion to the New Testament*, ed. David E. Aune (Wiley Blackwell, 2010), 520.

11. John A. Bailey, "Who Wrote II Thessalonians?," *New Testament Studies* 25, no. 2 (1979): 137.

12. M. J. J. Menken, *2 Thessalonians*, New Testament Readings (Routledge, 1994), 31.

13. Krentz, "2 Thessalonians," 520.

14. Weima, *1–2 Thessalonians*, 49.

15. Menken, *2 Thessalonians*, 33–34.

16. Abraham J. Malherbe, *The Letters to the Thessalonians: A New Translation with Introduction and Commentary* (Doubleday, 2000), 371.

himself considers 2 Thessalonians "an authentic reinterpretation of 1 Thessalonians."[17] Such views are essentially based on an improper understanding of pseudonymous letters. Critics must realize that the goal of pseudonymous letters was not "so much to grab apostolic power as it was a device with which writers could apply what they considered apostolic teaching to a new context."[18]

The signature in 2 Thessalonians 3:17 has also been advanced as a reason to doubt Pauline authorship. Since Paul says, "I, Paul, write this greeting with my own hand. This is the mark in every letter of mine; it is the way I write." It is claimed Paul does not use such a signature in the letters we have, including 1 Thessalonians, and as a result, what we have is a forger trying to present his work as authentic.[19] If 2 Thessalonians was written later than most Letters of Paul, as advanced by those who doubt its authenticity, 2 Thessalonians 3:17 would be false since Paul does not usually sign in his own handwriting.[20] D. L. Mealand, through the use of numerical and statistical analysis of the stylistic variation of the text, has demonstrated that 2 Thessalonians is closer to other Pauline letters when compared to 1 Thessalonians, which most critics have no problem ascribing to Paul. He concludes that "when 2 Thessalonians was specifically subjected to discriminant analysis as a doubtful sample it was decisively classed with Paul."[21] Similarly, Paul Foster concludes that "the epistle [2 Thessalonians] shows closer stylistic coherence with the *Hauptbriefe* that 1 Thessalonians, a letter whose authenticity is widely accepted."[22]

It is apparent that in this community, circumstances have changed rapidly and therefore a different response is required.[23] Given how situational Paul's letters are, this certainly affects the manner, style, and content of what they contain.[24] We can conclude then that the arguments advanced for pseudonymity are at best inconclusive, and the label "cumulative evidence" is justified.[25] We can then safely conclude that both 1 and 2 Thessalonians were written by Paul. No reason that has been advanced is able to stand the scrutiny of the evidence available. Let us now consider the audience.

Audience

Some scholars have suggested that the Thessalonian letters have different recipients. First Thessalonians is seen to be addressed to a group of gentiles, and 2 Thessalonians is seen as

17. Menken, *2 Thessalonians*, 43.

18. Malherbe, *The Letters to the Thessalonians*, 371.

19. Earl J. Richard, *First and Second Thessalonians*, Sacra Pagina (Liturgical Press, 1995), 394.

20. Paul Foster, "Who Wrote 2 Thessalonians? A Fresh Look at an Old Problem," *Journal for the Study of the New Testament* 35, no. 2 (2012): 166, https://doi.org/10.1177/0142064X12462654.

21. D. L. Mealand, "The Extent of the Pauline Corpus: A Multivariate Approach," *Journal for the Study of the New Testament* 18, no. 59 (2016): 86.

22. Foster, "Who Wrote 2 Thessalonians?," 168.

23. G. K. Beale, *1–2 Thessalonians* (InterVarsity Press, 2003), 30.

24. Charles A. Wanamaker, *The Epistle to the Thessalonians*, The New International Greek Testament Commentary (Eerdmans, 1990), 25; Malherbe, *The Letters to the Thessalonians*, 368.

25. Malherbe, *The Letters to the Thessalonians*, 369.

addressed to a Jewish Christian group.[26] The tone between the two letters is seen as the reason for this view. This, as noted by Jewett, is unlikely as it would have enhanced the issue of factionalism, which Paul fought against elsewhere. In the Thessalonian letters, we do not get the impression that Paul is addressing factionalism.[27] Other scholars like E. Earle Ellis, have noted that 1 Thessalonians is written to an entire church, whereas 2 Thessalonians is written to the leaders.[28] It is also unlikely that Paul would have done something like that.

It is unlikely that the problem of laziness described in 2 Thessalonians 3 would be a problem of the Jewish believers; it seems to be me to be a problem likely to be espoused by the gentile believers.[29] Foster is right to note that "despite what this theory possesses in intellectual imagination and creativity, it lacks in solid evidentiary support. There is no archaeological or textual evidence on which to postulate the existence of two ethnically segregated communities of believers in Jesus at Thessalonica in the first or second centuries (or beyond)."[30] We can conclude that the two letters were written to the church at Thessalonica rather than to a faction of the church. The church comprised Jews and gentiles (who were the majority).[31]

Date of Writing

The question of date of writing is closely linked with the authorship question.[32] It is commonly accepted that Paul wrote 1 Thessalonians in 50 CE from the metropolis of Corinth.[33] There is no consensus, however, as to when and where 2 Thessalonians was written. Scholars not only question its authorship but its dating as well. This has resulted in two camps—those who date it close to the writing of 1 Thessalonians (who accept Pauline authorship) and those who date it around 70 CE (those who doubt Pauline authorship).[34] Bailey represents those who accept a late date when he says "the last decade of the last century."[35] However, one wonders why a forger would write a letter with the same contents to the same community which received a genuine letter from Paul. How the Thessalonians received such a letter ought to be queried.[36]

26. Adolf von Harnack, "Das Problem des zweiten Thessalonicherbriefs," in *Sitzungsberichte der Königlich-Preussischen Akademie der Wissenschaften* (Berlin, 1910), 560–578.

27. Mtukwa, "An African Reading," 46.

28. E. Earle Ellis, "Paul and His Co-Workers: For the Very Rev. Professor James S. Stewart on His Seventy-Fifth Birthday," *New Testament Studies* 17, no. 4 (1971): 437.

29. Mtukwa, *Work and Community in the Thessalonian Correspondence*, 25.

30. Foster, "Who Wrote 2 Thessalonians?," 161.

31. Mtukwa, *Work and Community in the Thessalonian Correspondence*, 25.

32. Mtukwa, *Work and Community in the Thessalonian Correspondence*, 25–26.

33. Ben Witherington III, *1 and 2 Thessalonians: A Socio-Rhetorical Commentary* (Eerdmans, 2006), 10; Beale, *1–2 Thessalonians*, 14; I. Howard Marshall, *1 and 2 Thessalonians: A Commentary* (Regent College Publishing, 2002), 20–23; Victor Paul Furnish, *1 & 2 Thessalonians*, Abingdon New Testament Commentaries (Abingdon Press, 2007), 30; Weima, *1–2 Thessalonians*, 38–39.

34. Mtukwa, *Work and Community in the Thessalonian Correspondence*, 25–26.

35. Bailey, "Who Wrote II Thessalonians?," 143.

36. Mtukwa, *Work and Community in the Thessalonian Correspondence*, 25–26.

Byron's question deserves a response: "How would they react to a previously unknown letter from Paul that suddenly surfaced after a significant delivery delay?"[37]

The question that has to be asked relates to *Sitz im Leben* (situation in life) addressed by 2 Thessalonians. One has to wonder how a letter written much later (30–40 years) after 1 Thessalonians addresses the same issues (persecution, eschatology, and idle church members) as those of the first letter.[38] The evidence available suggests that 2 Thessalonians was written a few months after the first, and the date would be between late 50 CE to the spring of 51 CE. This would mean that Corinth is the place of origin.[39]

Occasion and Purpose

We noted above that Paul wrote these letters to a predominantly gentile congregation based in Thessalonica. What is left now to consider is what occasioned these two letters and what Paul intended to accomplish by writing them. New Testament writings are generally occasional writings, more so the Pauline letters. What occasioned these letters is critical to our understanding of these two letters to the Thessalonians. This is primarily because Paul is addressing specific issues in the community which have the potential to threaten the very fabric of the churches he has founded.[40]

Scholars like Walter Schmithals and W. Marxsen are of the opinion that Paul was dealing with some of early form of Gnosticism.[41] Schmithals surmised that Paul's opponents in Galatia, Corinth, Philippi, and Thessalonica were gnostic missionaries. Paul's defense concerning charges of not speaking with power (1 Thess 1:2–2:2) and exhortations on abstaining from sexual immorality (1 Thess. 4:3–8) are aimed at gnostic permissiveness. He interprets those who are not respecting church leaders in 1 Thess 5:12 as pneumatics who are drunk on the Spirit.[42] The problem with this view is that it has not been demonstrated beyond reasonable doubt that Gnosticism was in existence early in the mid-first century. Leon Morris states that "until it can be shown that Gnosticism preceded the Christian movement it is difficult to take seriously the idea that the basic Christian writings depend on and express or oppose Gnostic concepts."[43] The distinctive features of Gnosticism, such as dualism, christological speculation, and libertinistic behavior, cannot be found in Thessalonica.[44]

Marxsen understood the unruly to be "enthusiasts who because of the nearness of the *parousia* are no longer taking seriously the things of everyday life."[45] These people through

37. John Byron, *1 and 2 Thessalonians* (Zondervan, 2014), 215–216.

38. Mtukwa, *Work and Community in the Thessalonian Correspondence*, 25–26.

39. Mtukwa, *Work and Community in the Thessalonian Correspondence*, 26.

40. Mtukwa, *Work and Community in the Thessalonian Correspondence*, 24.

41. Walter Schmithals, *Paul & the Gnostics*, trans. John E. Steely (Abingdon Press, 1972), 129–218.

42. Schmithals, *Paul & the Gnostics*, 129–218.

43. Leon Morris, *The Epistles of Paul to the Thessalonians: An Introduction and Commentary*, rev. ed., Tyndale New Testament Commentaries (InterVarsity Press, 1984), 10–11.

44. Jewett, *The Thessalonian Correspondence*, 149.

45. Marxsen, *Der erste Brief an die Thessalonicher*, 71.

their actions bought into disrepute the reputation of the house churches by violating proper social standards.[46] The unruly are seen as related to those who fail to recognize congregational authority in 1 Thessalonians 5:22. The issue with the unruly is not laziness per se, as demonstrated by the fact that Paul offers his example of self-reliant work.[47]

Lutgert Wilhelm proposed that the problem of the ἄτακτοι was as a result of spiritual enthusiasm.[48] Similarly, Bruce sees them as "an over-enthusiastic expectation of the imminent advent of Christ," which came about as a result of improperly digesting Paul's teaching.[49] Robert Jewett follows this lead when he interprets the Thessalonians letters in light of what he terms the millenarian model or millenarian radicalism.[50] Jewett's millenarian model has its basis in the work of Yonina Talmon and one of its characteristics is often "cessation of economic activity."[51] This characteristic seems to fit the problem of the ἄτακτοι in Thessalonica.[52] Work was perceived as a symbol of the old order which is fallen and as such must be replaced with innocent play at the coming of the new age. Jewett sees this at play among the Taborites in Hussite Bohemia, who not only neglected their work but turned their property into communal property.[53] The threat of apocalyptic certainty was then the reason Paul wrote the letter of 1 Thessalonians. The house church was unsettled by the persecution and death of its members since they had misunderstood Paul's message. They thought that salvation, as preached by Paul, eliminated any earthly afflictions.[54] For Jewett, these people had "refused to prepare for a future παρουσία of Christ because in principle they were experiencing and embodying it already in their ecstatic activities."[55]

In summary, it is in such a scenario that Paul puts pen to paper. Paul seeks to correct and encourage the Thessalonians in their faith, encourage them to put their hope in Christ who resurrected even as some die and others face persecution, correct their eschatological views, and demonstrate the importance of work in community life. The issues of persecution, eschatology, and unruliness are picked up in the second letter; the evidence from the letters shows that these issues have escalated since the first letter. Paul is attempting to nurture the community he had founded through these letters.[56]

---

46. Marxsen, *Der erste Brief an die Thessalonicher*, 62, 72.

47. Marxsen, *Der erste Brief an die Thessalonicher*, 105.

48. Lutgert Wilhelm, "Die Volkommenen im Philipperbrief und die Enthusiasten in Thessalonich," *Beiträge zur Förderung Christlicher Theologie* 13 (1909): 628.

49. F. F. Bruce, "St Paul in Macedonia: 2. The Thessalonian Correspondence," *Bulletin of the John Rylands Library* 61 (1980): 337–354, 333; Jewett, *The Thessalonian Correspondence*, 145.

50. Jewett, *The Thessalonian Correspondence*, 133–157.

51. Yonina Talmon, "Millenarian Movements," *European Journal of Sociology/Archives Européennes de Sociologie* 7, no. 2 (1966): 159–200.

52. Jewett, *The Thessalonian Correspondence*, 173.

53. Jewett, *The Thessalonian Correspondence*, 173.

54. Jewett, *The Thessalonian Correspondence*, 171.

55. Jewett, *The Thessalonian Correspondence*, 176.

56. Mtukwa, *Work and Community in the Thessalonian Correspondence*, 26.

In conclusion, Paul wrote the Thessalonian letters to a church he founded in the leading city of Macedonia, the capital of Thessalonica. These letters were written sometime between 50 and 51 CE. The recipients of these letters were a predominantly gentile congregation and not a group of leaders, as has been suggested by some scholars.[57] We shall look at four themes and demonstrate their relevance for the African context. These themes are kinship, holiness, eschatology, and work and community.

Outlines

1 Thessalonians

I. Greeting and thanksgiving (1 Thess 1:1–10)
II. The missionaries' ministry and conduct (1 Thess 2:1–12)
III. Strengthening the community in persecution (1 Thess 2:13–16)
IV. Paul's yearning to visit (1 Thess 2:17–3:13)
V. Living a life of holiness and love (1 Thess 4:1–12)
VI. Comfort in grief and eschatological hope (1 Thess 4:13–18)
VII. Preparing for the day of the Lord (1 Thess 5:1–11)
VIII. Encouragements for community life (1 Thess 5:12–22)
IX. Final blessing and conclusion (1 Thess 5:23–28)

2 Thessalonians

I. Greeting and thanksgiving (2 Thess 1:1–12)
II. The coming day of the Lord (2 Thess 2:1–12)
III. Established in the faith (2 Thess 2:13–17)
IV. The problem of indolence and the example of the apostles (2 Thess 3:1–15)
V. Discipline and restoration (2 Thess 3:13–15)
VI. Final greetings and benediction (2 Thess 3:16–18)

Theological Themes

This section will look at the theological themes that we find in the Thessalonian correspondence. These include but are not limited to kinship, holiness, eschatology, and work and community. We shall attempt to interpret these within the African worldview demonstrating their significance, particularly for the church in Africa. Yet these themes are not limited to one geographical area; they have timeless principles that can shape any community anywhere.

57. Mtukwa, *Work and Community in the Thessalonian Correspondence*, 26.

Kinship

The concept of kinship in 1 Thessalonians resonates with the African communal worldview. Scholars have noted that Paul uses various familial metaphors as he adopts a fictive kinship in this letter. Trevor J. Burke has rightly noted how Paul reflects family ideals where family members had obligations to the *oikos* and were required to contribute to its welfare.[58] Paul's use of familial metaphors is unparalleled in this letter, and there are about nineteen references to family metaphors in his Thessalonian correspondence.[59] Plutarch, in his essay "On Brotherly Love," laments that "brotherly love is as rare in our day as brotherly hatred was among the men of old,"[60] and then further states that brothers, like twins, should "more readily co-operate with one another."[61]

Plutarch grounds his understanding of brotherly love on the fact that brothers come from the same parents. He asks a poignant question: "What deed or favour or disposition, which children may show toward their parents, can give more pleasure than steadfast goodwill and friendship toward a brother?"[62] As such, for Plutarch, brotherly love is an expression of parental love. Paul's audience would have been familiar with what was required in Greco-Roman society for those who were related by blood. Now, Paul is calling them to extend the same affection to those with whom they were not related by blood. As Plutarch notes, "For no father is so fond of oratory or of honour or of riches as he is of his children; therefore, fathers do not find such pleasure in seeing their sons gaining a reputation as orators, acquiring wealth, or holding office as in seeing that they love one another."[63]

The noun αδελφός appears twenty-one times in both 1 and 2 Thessalonians, fourteen of which are in 1 Thessalonians and the remaining seven in 2 Thessalonians. This is the highest concentration, considering that Paul uses this word sixty-nine times in all the Pauline letters. This usage represents 30 percent of Paul's usage of this word. Paul, as suggested by Burke, is primarily concerned about relations between ἀδελφοί (5:12a, 14a).[64] In 1 Thessalonians, αδελφός is used three times as a form of address; some of the usages are certainly more pronounced than others.[65] Paul certainly saw the Thessalonians as his brothers and sisters, and he expected them to relate to each other as such.

Other familial metaphors that Paul uses are found in 1 Thessalonians 2. Here Paul has child (1 Thess 2:7), mother (1 Thess 2:7), and father (1 Thess 2:11). In 1 Thessalonians 2:7 we have a textual issue which scholars have wrestled with. The word νήπιοι can be translated as "gentle," but, without the ν, it reads ἤπιοι, which translates as "child." The most difficult

58. Trevor J. Burke, *Family Matters: A Socio-Historical Study of Kinship Metaphors in 1 Thessalonians* (T&T Clark International, 2003), 218.

59. Trevor J. Burke, "Paul's 'New Family in Thessalonica," *Novum Testamentum* 54, no. 3 (2012): 270–271.

60. Plutarch, *On Brotherly Love*, trans. W. C. Helmbold, LCL (Harvard University Press, 1939), 249.

61. Plutarch, *Mor.* VI.251.

62. Plutarch, *Mor.* VI.257.

63. Plutarch, *Mor.* VI.259.

64. Burke, *Family Matters*, 227.

65. Burke, *Family Matters*, 279.

reading is νήπιοι; since Paul calls himself a child, this reading is to be preferred over gentle, which is the easier reading. This is a classic case of dittography, where an editor puts a letter from the previous word into the following word.

In the same verse, Paul uses the word τριφός, which is translated as "nursing mother," as a way to compare himself with the role of a nursing mother. The Thessalonians had become so dear to Paul that he cared for them the same way a nursing mother cares for a child or children who are not her own. A few verses later, Paul mentions that he, as a πατήρ "father," encouraged and comforted the Thessalonians (1 Thess 2:11). Scholars have noted that it was the duty of the father to teach his children about the direction they should take and also to discipline them should they stray. Paul similarly functions the same way, providing instruction and encouraging the Thessalonians in the way of the gospel. His role is versatile; he can be a child, a mother, and a father at different times so as to mold the Thessalonians in the way of Christ.

Based on the familial metaphors, Trevor Burke has argued that Pauline communities were hierarchical. The paternal metaphor engrosses him and he totally disregards the fact that Paul calls himself an infant. He mistakes structure for hierarchy; it is possible to have structure in a community and still be egalitarian.[66] Burke even suggests that we have "ordinary/led brothers"; in other words, a "hierarchy of brothers."[67] His conclusion is that "rather than thinking that such communities were initially 'egalitarian' in structure and became more rigid or hierarchical through time, on the strength of the evidence which we have presented, and in what is regarded by most scholars as the earliest extant letter written by Paul, some degree of structure was in existence from their earliest inception."[68] Burke has allowed the ancient sources he was reading to define what Paul was saying rather than allowing Paul to speak on his own. Burke seems keener to show the parallels between early Christian communities and the household structure than allowing the texts to speak freely.[69]

The communities Paul founded then cannot be said to be "hierarchical in structure"; authority was not vested in one individual.[70] Banks considers Paul's communities "theocratic in structure."[71] All are to participate in communal activities using gifts distributed by the Spirit, who dispenses them unequally; some are required to contribute more than others.[72] This is why those mentioned can provide warning to the rest of the community.[73] Paul's desire is that the Thessalonians "respect and acknowledge their authority, leadership and work."[74]

Paul's kinship language points to the fact that Paul is more concerned about building a community that is fashioned after the household. As Abraham Malherbe has observed, "These

66. Burke, "Paul's 'New Family in Thessalonica,'" 234.

67. Burke, *Family Matters*, 248.

68. Burke, "Paul's 'New Family in Thessalonica,'" 287

69. Burke, *Family Matters*, 248.

70. Robert J. Banks, *Paul's Idea of Community: The Early House Churches in Their Cultural Setting* (Baker Academic, 2012), 148.

71. Banks, *Paul's Idea of Community*, 148.

72. Banks, *Paul's Idea of Community*, 148.

73. Wanamaker, *The Epistle to the Thessalonians*, 193.

74. Witherington, *1 and 2 Thessalonians*, 160.

passages show . . . the God of creation as calling the Gentiles into a new relationship with himself in which he would be their father and they his beloved children . . . [this is] . . . God's new family in Thessalonica."[75] The African idea of Ubuntu, which is encapsulated in the saying "I am because we are and since we are therefore I am," is similar to what Paul is trying to do with the community at Thessalonica. Even though the people are not related by blood, they have now become related because of the blood of Jesus Christ. Within the African setting, Ubuntu relates to those who are from the same clan—they are not close family members; however, they are related since they share a clan, and in some cases that is evidenced by a totem. As such, they are to treat each other the same way family members treat each other. Let us now discuss the concept of holiness.

Holiness

In African society holiness is often associated with places, times, and people. There are places where one cannot graze cattle since such places are holy, and the same is true of holy times—you cannot do certain activities during holy days or seasons. For instance, among the Shona people of Zimbabwe, November is a holy month, and no one is supposed to marry during that month. We also have holy people like the rainmakers, those who are able to connect to the divine in ways ordinary men and women cannot. In 1 Thessalonians, holiness is required for all people and not a few. However, in Africa, morality was required of all people. Individuals had to live by the ethical code to which the community subscribes. When an individual repeatedly acts contrary to this code they may be ostracized by the community.

Andy Johnson has spoken of holiness as "the sanctification of imagination" in the Thessalonian letters.[76] This is an appropriate articulation of the idea of holiness. When one considers the background of the Thessalonians as pagans (1 Thess 1:9–10), their need for sanctification is even more critical since sanctification entails a total reimagination of life. These people who were steeped in paganism are now "God's elect people in a covenant relationship with Yahweh."[77] The Thessalonians would have had to give up honoring patron gods or goddesses associated with their trade guild, and this would have come with serious economic ramifications.[78] They would have risked losing customers and even suppliers. Citing Abraham Malherbe, Johnson asserts, "if the patriarch of the extended household was not a member of the *ekklesia*, refusing to honor one's household gods would cause domestic tensions in the household."[79]

The result of holiness in the Thessalonian community would have been visible to anyone. Holiness would have resulted in a particular ethical code that affected their relationships

75. Abraham J. Malherbe, "God's New Family in Thessalonica," in *The Social World of the First Christians: Essays in Honor of Wayne A. Meeks*, ed. Michael L. White and O. Larry Yarbrough (Fortress Press, 1995), 116.

76. Andy Johnson, "The Sanctification of the Imagination in 1 Thessalonians," in *Holiness and Ecclesiology in the New Testament*, ed. Kent E. Brower and Andy Johnson (Eerdmans, 2007), 275.

77. Johnson, "The Sanctification of the Imagination in 1 Thessalonians," 277.

78. Johnson, "The Sanctification of the Imagination in 1 Thessalonians," 280.

79. Johnson, "The Sanctification of the Imagination in 1 Thessalonians," 280.

with each other. Holiness was not something the Thessalonians achieved on their own, it was "grace-enabled, embodied practices that require a network of communal relations. Paul depicts his audience as *one* eschatological instantiation of Israel reconfigured around a crucified Lord."[80] Johnson says of the holy community, "it would be permeated with God's own character/holiness as definitively revealed in the faithfulness of Jesus. It would be a 'colony of cruciformity,' an eschatological instantiation of the holiness of God."[81]

For Michael J. Gorman, "God's primary aim is to create alternative, sanctified, social bodies in which God's cruciform character is visibly embodied."[82] Holiness is not just something that has to do with our relationship with God alone but with our fellow neighbors, it entails πίστις (our relationship with God), ὁσίως (holy), δικαίως (righteous), αμέμπτως (blameless).[83] The process of making holy αγιασμός (sanctification) is something not peripheral to our salvation, it is rather the θέλημά του θεού (the will of God) (1 Thess 4:3). In this passage, it is connected specifically with the idea of πορνείας (sexual immorality), even though it has to do with all of the life of the people of God.

Douglas Harink has captured the full breadth and depth of holiness in the Thessalonian letters when he says that, "participation in God's gracious work through Christ and the Spirit is . . . depicted as spread over the whole range of human life, active and passive, attitudinal and bodily, inner and outer, personal, social, and political."[84] It is for that reason that such a small group of Christ followers would have been seen as a threat to the alternative narrative of the empire. This has relevance for the African church; the gospel should be proclaimed fully, and such proclamation should include holiness/sanctification. The evils that often characterize the African church should not be accepted as normal. The people of God must be like the God who calls them, such a God is holy and so should they be. Holiness should not be just a trademark of a few holiness churches but all the church of Jesus Christ. The church cannot experience all that God desires of it until it has experienced the holiness of God.

The concept of holiness is not absent in the African traditional setting. The aspect of the numinous is present—there are places where animals could not graze since such places were considered holy; this relates to the holiness of space. We also evidence the holiness of time as, some cultures, such as the Shona, identify days on which one is not supposed to work since such days are considered holy. In the same culture, people are not supposed to get married in November as that is considered a holy month. The holiness of persons is also attested as certain people are considered holy since they mediate the holy presence of God to the people. The concept of holiness is therefore not foreign to African peoples coming out of traditional society. This, however, does not mean holiness is exactly the same; the Christian understanding has the aspect of cleansing from sin which is absent from the African setting. Let us now discuss the theme of eschatology.

80. Johnson, "The Sanctification of the Imagination in 1 Thessalonians," 275–276, emphasis in original.

81. Johnson, "The Sanctification of the Imagination in 1 Thessalonians," 285.

82. Michael J. Gorman, *Cruciformity: Paul Narrative Spirituality of the Cross* (Eerdmans, 2001), 439.

83. Johnson, "The Sanctification of the Imagination in 1 Thessalonians," 284.

84. Douglas Harink, *Paul Among the Postliberal* (Brazos, 2003), 35.

Eschatology

One of the major themes of the Thessalonian letters is the issue of the end times, commonly referred to as the doctrine of eschatology. It should be observed that Paul does not engage in an abstract discussion of the eschaton, but always does so in "service of the exhortation he is giving to his converts in Thessalonike."[85] As such he is not engaging in a philosophical discussion of the end times. Paul's eschatology is eclectic in that it borrows the concept of "peace and security" from Jewish, Christian, and imperial language as well as royal language, which speaks of dignitaries visiting a city and being greeted by the residents.[86]

The question that arises is whether there are African resources that can help African people make sense of Christian eschatology. Kenyan theologian John Mbiti's work *New Testament Eschatology in African Background* remains definitive. In this work, Mbiti's thesis is that African time is two-dimensional—that is, a "long past" and "a dynamic present." As such, "The 'future' as we know it is in the linear conception of Time is virtually non-existent."[87] Even though Mbiti's study was conducted primarily among the Akamba tribe of Kenya, he sees the same understanding of time across African tribes. He writes that "the future is virtually absent because events which lie in the future have not been realized and cannot, therefore, constitute Time which otherwise must be experienced."[88] The problem Mbiti saw with the teaching of eschatology by the African Inland Church was that it was purely futuristic and therefore incapable of being understood by Africans, who understand time in two modes—past and present.

The question that arises is whether Mbiti's assessment is correct. Scholars have challenged Mbiti's generalization of his study to other African groups. For instance, Chammah J. Kaunda and Mutale Kaunda have questioned Mbiti's assessment through their study of Bemba eschatology. For them, "the Bemba people understand that they are becoming more and more a radically relationally balanced community in which *Lesa* will be fully expressed in human daily interaction."[89] This view is augmented by Janet Martin Soskice when she says, "what we will be is not separable from what we were made to be and what we now are."[90] Even though living life more abundantly is seen as the climax of African eschatological thought, we need not forget the fact that beyond this life there is another life which is qualitatively different from what the very best of life can be on this side of destiny. Even Kaunda and Kaunda acknowledge that "this does not in any way negate the notion of the Second Return of Christ because the

85. Witherington, *1 and 2 Thessalonians*, 125.

86. Witherington, *1 and 2 Thessalonians*, 126.

87. John S. Mbiti, *New Testament Eschatology in an African Background: A Study of the Encounter Between New Testament Theology and African Traditional Concepts* (Oxford University Press, 1971), 25. Mbiti also says "The significant point for our purpose here is that there are no myths about the future, as far as I have been able to gather from all the available sources that record African myths and stories." Mbiti, *New Testament Eschatology in an African Background*, 25–26.

88. Mbiti, *New Testament Eschatology in an African Background*, 25.

89. Chammah J. Kaunda and Mutale Mulenga-Kaunda, "In Search of Decolonial Eschatology: Engaging Christian Eschatology with Bemba Futurism," *Theology Today* 75, no. 4 (2019): 477.

90. Janet Martin Soskice, *The Kindness of God: Metaphor, Gender and Religion* (Oxford University Press, 2007).

return itself points to the fullness of justice and radical relational mutuality and balance of all things."[91] What Mbiti found among the Akamba is applicable to most African tribal groups. As Mbiti has noted, "Time as a separate reality does not 'move'; only events come and go, often in a rhythmic succession."[92] Personally I know this to be true in my own tribal community, the Shona people of Zimbabwe. Even the critics of Mbiti's thesis, if they are sincere, can attest that their own cultures also focus on events rather than time as a separate reality.

The Greco-Roman world did not have actual cases of people rising from the dead. Even though they did many things to prepare people for the afterlife, there was no real afterlife that included bodily resurrection.[93] Theocritus captures this when he says "hopes are for the living, but the ones who die are without hope" (*Id.* 4.42).[94] Similarly Catullus (5:4–6) says "The sun can set and rise again / But once our brief light sets / There is one unending night to be slept through" (cf. Homer, *Il.* 11.241).[95] In the African setting the dead don't necessarily resurrect; however, they become ancestors or the living dead. This attitude makes sense for the Thessalonians, who are concerned for those who have died before the resurrection—their concern is that they might miss out on the resurrection. Witherington states that "Paul's focus is on the current state of the dead and the significance of the future for the present behavior of the living."[96] F. F Bruce also notes that "the hope which believing Jews and Christians had in the face of death was the hope of resurrection; for Christians this hope was grounded in the resurrection of Christ."[97]

The fact that Paul left town (Thessaloniki) before he was ready to do so has been cited as a reason why problems arose in relation to the departed.[98] Through this letter and the emissaries Paul sent, he teaches the Thessalonians basic eschatology. For Paul, "those who have existed εν Χριστώ in mortal life remain εν Χριστώ after death."[99] Bruce further states that "the added adverb πρώτον being caught up by the immediately following ἔπειτα . . . indicate[s] that, far from suffering any disadvantage at the Parousia, the faithful departed would actually have precedence over those still alive."[100]

Mbiti laments the fact that many Kamba Christians are disoriented (the same way Thessalonians were) upon seeing some among them dying off without seeing Christ's return, since Christian eschatology has been presented primarily in futuristic terms. He states "sorrows continue to bombard them, but Jesus does not return immediately to 'rapture' them from this world. Heaven which they now have discovered as a future place for them, does not snatch

91. Kaunda and Mulenga-Kaunda, "In Search of Decolonial Eschatology," 477.

92. Mbiti, *New Testament Eschatology in an African Background*, 25.

93. Witherington, *1 and 2 Thessalonians*, 128.

94. Witherington, *1 and 2 Thessalonians*, 129.

95. Witherington, *1 and 2 Thessalonians*, 129.

96. Witherington, *1 and 2 Thessalonians*, 125.

97. F. F. Bruce, *1 & 2 Thessalonians*, Word Biblical Commentary (Word, 1982), 96.

98. Witherington, *1 and 2 Thessalonians*, 130.

99. Bruce, *1 & 2 Thessalonians*, 101.

100. Bruce, *1 & 2 Thessalonians*, 101.

them away quickly and give them the riches, comfort and bliss they miss here on earth."[101] Paul's teaching on resurrection is a necessary antidote to this kind of disillusionment.

In 1 Thessalonians, Paul seeks to correct the Thessalonians' understanding of his eschatological teachings. It is probable that they also needed to understand some of his teachings in this letter, and 2 Thessalonians is written to address a situation created by a misinterpretation of 1 Thessalonians. From this perspective, it cannot be said that we have two different eschatologies in the Thessalonian correspondence. Paul is responding to issues as he assesses the situation, and each situation is different, and therefore needs a nuanced response.

There is a relationship between the theme of eschatology and holiness. Paul sees a connection between hope and the holiness of the Thessalonians. If they have hope, they will behave in a manner that is consistent with the hope they have.[102] In fact, "Paul's pastoral concern was to guide the way the Thessalonians were living, not provide them with eschatological gnosis. This is not a passage about the parousia but a passage about grieving for the dead."[103] The ethical teachings in African society were connected to how people live their earthly lives. One had to conduct oneself in a proper way so as to become an ancestor upon death. It becomes easier to teach the connection between holiness and eschatology in Africa with such a background.

When Paul speaks of the coming back of Jesus Christ, he uses imperial language: his use of the word παρουσία, which referred to the official visit of a dignitary to a city, and the word ἀπάντησις, which referred to the escorting of the dignitary back to the city.[104] In actual fact he is challenging Roman imperial propaganda. For Paul, real παρουςία is that of Jesus Christ and not Caesar Augustus. Another challenge to Roman ideology is seen in the way Paul challenges the slogan "peace and security." Those who proclaim such cheap propaganda will be the ones that "destruction will come" upon.[105] As Ben Witherington has noted, "it is the imperial propaganda and prophecies that Paul is offering a rebuttal to here."[106]

A discussion of eschatology in Thessalonians would not be complete without discussing ἁρπάζειν, which is often translated as "rapture" from the Latin (*rapere*). This view has been understood as the snatching away of believers at the end of time.[107] This understanding of ἁρπάζειν has led to the perception of end time where believers are taken away from the evil world to a place where they are safe. The infinitive ἁρπάζειν has to with "violent action, sometimes indeed to the benefit of its object."[108] Nothing here says anything about snatching away. What Paul is saying is that God will act on behalf of his people and his judgment will be meted out to the unbelievers. As Mbiti has shown among the Kambas, this perspective does not exist in the African worldview. He writes, "the Akamba have no conception that this universe will

101. Mbiti, *New Testament Eschatology in an African Background*, 57.

102. Witherington, *1 and 2 Thessalonians*, 132.

103. D. Michael Martin, *1, 2 Thessalonians*, The New American Commentary 33 (Broadman & Holman, 1995), 143.

104. Bruce, *1 & 2 Thessalonians*, 45.

105. Witherington, *1 and 2 Thessalonians*, 147.

106. Witherington, *1 and 2 Thessalonians*, 147.

107. Bruce, *1 & 2 Thessalonians*, 102.

108. Bruce, *1 & 2 Thessalonians*, 102.

ever change radically or come to an end, and the same seems to be the case with other Africa peoples."[109] Mbiti further comments, "man looks back whence he came, and man is certain that nothing will bring this world to a conclusion. The universe is endless. There is nothing to suggest that the rhythm of days, months, seasons and years will ever come to a halt, just as there is no end to the rhythm of birth, marriage, procreation, and death."[110] However, the fact that this concept does not exist in African thinking does not mean we should give up hope and abandon an important part of Christian eschatology, as Mbiti seems to suggest. The Thessalonian correspondence cautions us from doing so; we need to find contextualized ways of teaching the fact that Christ is coming.

There is much that the African church can learn about eschatology from Paul. Our preoccupation with the dead should be informed by what Paul says about the hope we have in Christ. The fact that there exist ancestors, what Mbiti refers to as "the living dead," is important in that it helps us articulate the fact that death is not the end of life as we know it. Mbiti has this to say about the living dead: "the departed of up to four or five generations are best described as the 'living-dead' for they are dead in body, but alive in spirit and in the memories of their surviving relatives."[111] In African thinking the dead continue to live, albeit in a different realm from the living, and they are considered part of the community. There is life after death, and we must not mourn as those without hope (1 Thess 4:13–18). We should not buy into the language of our political systems that proclaim "peace and security" when there is no such thing. The gospel challenges the false hopes that people cling to. We do not have saviors in the political sphere; the real savior is Jesus Christ, and it is he who is coming. We must be ready to meet him when he comes; and we must then be God's holy people.

In summary, we have discussed Paul's eschatology in light of the African view of time. We have confirmed that Mbiti's assessment is correct and we need not present eschatology in purely futuristic terms. There are points of contact between the African setting and the biblical text that should be emphasized as we teach eschatology. Even in the biblical perspective of time, the past and present are important and should be emphasized. However, there are also aspects that are different between the African and Christian views. The radical move from the present realm to another realm is not there within the African paradigm due to the cyclical understanding of time. The Thessalonian correspondence has much to offer us in our understanding of the doctrine of eschatology in Africa. Let us now discuss work and community.

Work and Community

Another significant theme in the Thessalonian correspondence is the issue of work and its relationship to community. In traditional African society, work was not approached from an individualistic perspective. Work was communal, as is evidenced by work parties or what

109. Mbiti, *New Testament Eschatology in an African Background*, 25.

110. Mbiti, *New Testament Eschatology in an African Background*, 25.

111. Mbiti, *New Testament Eschatology in an African Background*, 29.

the Shona refer to as *nhimbe* (communal work), which was done to accomplish various tasks in the homestead, such as building a house or harvesting. The person or people who wanted work to be done had only to provide food and traditional beverages, and the people who came did the work free of charge.

Work parties are also seen in various tribes among a particular age set which the Kikuyus call *riika* (age set). People who were born at the same time (or men who were circumcised around the same time) would help each other with work. Again, one would have to announce that he or she was building a house, and his or her age set would come to assist. These age sets "act as one body in all tribal matters and have a very strong bond of brotherhood and sisterhood among themselves."[112] This illustrates that work in Africa was a communal event rather than an individual task that one does by oneself. The alienating aspect of work is reduced when it is shared. Often, people would sing while working, as work was viewed as something to celebrate rather than drudgery.

In Africa, there is a sense of duty to the family and community that one carries wherever one goes. It is in this regard that everyone ought to work and contribute their fair share to the group. As Gelfand has noted concerning the Shona of Zimbabwe: "Every member of the village will do all he can for his community, provided he is working for the good of all and thereby contributing to the universal harmony."[113] Proverbs also convey what is required of the African in relation to work; for instance, the Swahili people say *Mgeni siku mbili, ya tatu mpe jembe*, which literally translates as "a guest for two days, the third day give him/her a hoe." This proverb helped the community regulate visitors' conduct: one was not to be a visitor perpetually; at some point, you cease being a guest and start working for the good of the household you have joined.[114]

We contend that this African worldview can assist us in reading Paul's work exhortations in the Thessalonian correspondence. When Paul visited Thessalonica, he did not wait to be given a hoe; he rather joined the community as a worker. He did not take advantage of his position as an apostle or philosopher, he became one with the Thessalonians and shared life with them (1 Thess 2:8). Sharing of life is followed by Paul's reference to his labors in 1 Thessalonians 2:9.[115] Scholars[116] have rightly noted that Paul came from a higher social class, which did not engage in manual labor; as such, Paul's engagement in manual labor was an act of selflessness. Paul reveals the reason for his manual labor when he says "that we might not burden (μὴ ἐπιβαρῆσαί) any of you" (1 Thess 2:9). It is evident here that Paul's motivation is the well-being of the community. Paul's understanding of κοινονία would not allow him to take advantage of his brothers and sisters.[117]

---

112. Jomo Kenyatta, *Facing Mount Kenya*, school ed. (Heinemann Kenya, 2011), 1, 72–73.

113. Michael Gelfand, *The Genuine Shona* (Mambo Press, 1973), 80.

114. Mtukwa, "An African Reading," 138.

115. Mtukwa, "An African Reading," 13–39.

116. Witherington, *1 and 2 Thessalonians*, 54; Jon A. Weatherly says "Paul took a voluntary step down the social ladder by engaging in such work." Jon A. Weatherly, *1 & 2 Thessalonians* (College Press, 1996), 71.

117. Mtukwa, "An African Reading," 138.

In 1 Thessalonians 4:11 Paul speaks about "working with his hands" in the context of Φιλαδέλφειας. As we have already noted Φιλαδέλφειας was known among blood relatives and Paul adopts it for people who are not blood relatives but have come together because of Jesus Christ. We can truly say that "the identity of Christians as ἀδελφός is the reason they can practice φιλάδελφος."[118] They are to express their love not only through work but also "to live quietly, tending to one's affairs." We need not lose the communal context of these exhortations, as Bridges has noted: "The artisans worship together. They are dependent upon one another for their income. One person's work influences another person's work. If one person becomes lazy, the entire community suffers. If one person becomes less productive, interfering in the affairs of another's work and forgetting his own job, then chaos results."[119]

In 1 Thessalonians 5:12–14a Paul admonishes the community to "recognize" those who labor, manage communal affairs, and admonish those who do not work.[120] Those who are to be recognized are to be given this recognition "because of their work," which is done on behalf of the community. I have stated elsewhere that "Paul understands that there cannot be a community without those who give of themselves to serve the community in various ways—within the African setting everyone is meant to contribute to the well-being of the community."[121] Paul understands that for communal life to thrive, everyone must contribute their fair share for the good of the community.

In the African setting it is often those who are not working for the good of the community who bring problems to the community. Such individuals are often censored for their wrong behavior. The same is true of the group of people Paul calls τοὺς ἀτάκτους—the idlers. These people are not only failing to work to contribute to the well-being of the community, but they are also busy disrupting the community through the things they are doing that they are not supposed to do. The τοὺς ἀτάκτους are "disorderly," "unruly," and "insubordinate."[122] This reveals that failure to engage in meaningful work can result in people doing things that are either destructive to themselves or to the community.

The last passage which addresses work is 2 Thessalonians 3:6–15, and it is clear that Paul is addressing an intra-community issue since he uses the word αδελφοί. The censorship of the ἀτάκτως is something the community should take seriously. As such, "it is the plural αδελφοί who are to 'keep away' from singular ἀδελφοῦ."[123] Paul sets himself as a paradigm that the Thessalonians are to imitate, the same way elders in the African context present themselves as models. The way Paul and the missionary team lived is contrary to the way the ἀτάκτως are living. Paul contrasts his way of life when he uses the perfect tense οὐκ ἠτακτήσαμεν (we were not idle). Paul and the missionary team were not out of line but worked to earn their keep.

118. Mtukwa, "An African Reading," 152.
119. Linda McKinnish Bridges, *1 & 2 Thessalonians* (Smyth & Helwys, 2008), 107.
120. Mtukwa, "An African Reading," 152.
121. Mtukwa, "An African Reading," 152.
122. BDAG, 148.
123. Mtukwa, "An African Reading," 152.

Paul's example is also seen in the sense that he and his colleagues δωρεὰν ἄρτον ἐφάγομεν παρά τινος (did not eat anyone's bread without paying for it). Literally, Paul is saying that he did not consider his bread a δωρεάν (gift) but had to work earn it. Paul indeed must have accepted hospitality while at Thessalonica; however, he did not live off the generosity of others as a lifestyle.[124] The fact that Paul did not use his ἐξουσίαν (right, authority, power) is a challenge in the African context. This act of self-giving does not exist in the African context; this is something the gospel challenges the African person to do beyond what culture expects. F. F. Bruce has rightly noted that "if those who were entitled to be supported by others chose rather to support themselves, how much more should those who had no such entitlement earn their own living!"[125] Paul's actions are patterned after Christ's story in which he emptied himself (Phil 2:6–8).

Second Thessalonians 3:10 is the hermeneutical key for 1 Thessalonians 3:6–15. Paul states that "even when we were with you, we gave you this command: Anyone unwilling to work should not eat" (1 Thess 3:10). This passage has to be interpreted with the communal worldview in mind. The African communal worldview is closer to the Greco-Roman communal setting in which this passage was written. In this community, it likely had "prerogatives over the frequent daily meals of its members."[126] It is from this perspective that a maxim like μηδὲ ἐσθιέτω (let him not eat) can make sense. What is at stake here is not the "independent self-support of individuals and families" but "a communal or familial system."[127] The irresponsible misconduct of the disorderly threatens the social fabric of the community since they are only consumers and not producers.

The fact that food brings people together and cements social relationships is an accepted truth.[128] One knows that he or she is accepted in a community when they can share a meal. As Mary Douglas explains "If food is treated as a social code, the message it encodes will be found in the pattern of social relations being expressed. The message is about different degrees of hierarchy, inclusion and exclusion, boundaries and transactions across the boundaries."[129] The Shona people have a proverb which illustrates the importance of food in social relationships: *hukama igasva hunozadzikiswa nekudya* (relations are incomplete unless people have eaten together). Even economic and political connections require food to cement them. Those who eat alone were often shunned in African society. Consequently "If one did not meet the obligations of eating together prior to the meal, then he or she was excluded from the meal. As such Paul's dictum makes sense to African people steeped in communal worldviews."[130] We can see here that the connection between work and community is undeniable. Food is a result of work, and if one does not work, one cannot participate in eating the food.

124. Mtukwa, "An African Reading," 152.

125. Bruce, *1 & 2 Thessalonians*, 206; Weima, *1–2 Thessalonians*, 612.

126. Mtukwa, "An African Reading," 152.

127. Robert Jewett, "Tenement Churches and Communal Meals in the Early Church: The Implications of a Form-Critical Analysis of 2 Thessalonians 3:10" (n.d.): 38; Bridges, *1 & 2 Thessalonians*, 10.

128. Mtukwa, "An African Reading," 152.

129. Mary Douglas, "Deciphering a Meal," *Daedalus* 101, no. 1 (1972): 61; Shirin Edwin, "Subverting Social Customs: The Representation of Food in Three West African Francophone Novels," *Research in African Literatures* 39, no. 3 (2008): 41.

130. Mtukwa, "An African Reading," 152.

In verse 13 Paul turns to those who are not busybodies and addresses them. He encourages them to continue doing what is καλοποιέω (good/right). The temptation is for those who are doing the right thing to become tired. They are to "take note" of those who fail to obey what Paul is saying and μὴ συναναμίγνυσθαι (have nothing to do with them). Yet this is to be done without treating these people as enemies but as brothers (μὴ ὡς ἐχθρὸν ἡγεῖσθε ἀλλὰ νουθετεῖτε ὡς ἀδελφόν). The focus of this text is the restoration of the erring brother.

The African perspective on work is that it is not supposed to isolate people. Work is meant to bring people together; it is not supposed to be something boring but exciting. The so-called "work parties" in Africa were joyous events to which people came to sing and dance while they worked. The results of work are also supposed to be shared rather than enjoyed individually. Just as people share work, they should also share its results. The African perspective is helpful in letting the modern person see the communal perspective of work in the biblical texts. The problem is not that the Bible is individualistic but that our hermeneutic is often flawed; we need to learn to read Scripture with the original context in mind.

In summary, Paul's work exhortations are aimed at community building. Paul is concerned about the social fabric of the community and addressing issues that he sees as having the potential to tear that fabric. The disorderly have already undercut themselves from the community, and the community is to have nothing to do with such an individual. The practice of not associating was meant to bring shame on the individual and in turn bring that individual back to the community. It is true that "work is an important part of communal life which warrants discipline when one fails to do it as a member of the Christian community."[131]

Conclusion

In summary, the two Thessalonian letters were written by the apostle Paul. They are the earliest Christian writings we have on record. Paul wrote them within a few months of each other. Paul addresses various issues in the letters, which include the disorderly (those not working), kinship language (he conceives the Christian community as a family) eschatology (he provides comfort to the believers who have lost their loved ones through death), and last but not least, work and community (he highlights principles about work that result in building and reinforcing community). These letters have much to teach the African church since the audience are pagans who struggled with the same issues that we are struggling with in the twenty-first century.

Further Reading

Beale, G. K. *1–2 Thessalonians.* InterVarsity Press, 2003.

Burke, Trevor J. *Family Matters: A Socio-Historical Study of Kinship Metaphors in 1 Thessalonians.* T&T Clark, 2003.

Burke, Trevor J. "Paul's 'New Family in Thessalonica.'" *Novum Testamentum* 54, no. 3 (2012): 269–287.

131. Mtukwa, "An African Reading," 152.

Edwin, Shirin. "Subverting Social Customs: The Representation of Food in Three West African Francophone Novels." *Research in African Literatures* 39, no. 3 (2008): 39–50.

Foster, Paul. "Who Wrote 2 Thessalonians? A Fresh Look at an Old Problem." *Journal for the Study of the New Testament* 35, no. 2 (2012): 150–175.

Gelfand, Michael. *The Genuine Shona*. Mambo Press, 1973.

Johnson, Andy. "The Sanctification of the Imagination in 1 Thessalonians." In *Holiness and Ecclesiology in the New Testament*, edited by Kent E. Brower Johnson and Andy Johnson. Eerdmans, 2007.

Kaunda, Chammah J., and Mutale Mulenga-Kaunda. "In Search of Decolonial Eschatology: Engaging Christian Eschatology with Bemba Futurism." *Theology Today* 75, no. 4 (2019): 469–481.

Koudougueret, Rosalie. "1 Thessalonians." In *Africa Bible Commentary: A One-Volume Commentary Written by 70 African Scholars*, edited by Tokunboh Adeyemo. WordAlive Publishers, 2006.

Koudougueret, Rosalie. "2 Thessalonians." In *Africa Bible Commentary: A One-Volume Commentary Written by 70 African Scholars*, edited by Tokunboh Adeyemo. WordAlive Publishers, 2006.

Malherbe, Abraham J. "God's New Family in Thessalonica." In *The Social World of the First Christians: Essays in Honor of Wayne A. Meeks*, edited by Michael L. White and O. Larry Yarbrough. Fortress Press, 1995.

Mbiti, John S. *New Testament Eschatology in an African Background: A Study of the Encounter Between New Testament Theology and African Traditional Concepts*. Oxford University Press, 1971.

Mtukwa, Gift. "An African Reading of Paul's Work Exhortations in the Thessalonian Correspondence." PhD diss., University of Manchester, 2020.

Mtukwa, Gift. *Work and Community in the Thessalonian Correspondence: An African Communal Reading of Paul's Work Exhortations*. Langham Publishing, 2021.

Witherington, Ben III. *1 and 2 Thessalonians: A Socio-Rhetorical Commentary*. Eerdmans, 2006.

CHAPTER SIXTEEN

The Letters to Timothy

Ferdinand I. Okorie
Catholic Theological Union
Chicago

Introductory Remarks

THE PASTORAL LETTERS of the New Testament, including 1 and 2 Timothy, are often called the best-kept secret of the Christian scriptural tradition because they are seldom read at Sunday worship across denominations, and they rarely feature in Bible study programs. Be that as it may, the pastoral letters are the source of the conception and formation of the ecclesial structures of bishop, presbyter, and deacon that continue to define church leadership organization across Christian denominations. Also, the use of these titles for the ministries of the church today is informed and supported by the pastoral letters. Furthermore, the understanding of the separation of ecclesial roles, duties, and responsibilities among men and women are supported by the pastoral letters. This chapter interprets 1 and 2 Timothy from an African perspective by drawing readers, particularly African readers, into an intentional engagement of their cultural context and lived experiences with the New Testament.

Authorship

Generally, there is very little debate in scholarship about the single authorship of 1 and 2 Timothy. However, after a closer examination some scholars are persuaded that 2 Timothy was mostly likely written by Paul. At the very least, the majority opinion is that these letters are written by a single author, but what remains to be addressed in scholarship concerns the identity of the author of the pastoral letters. Since these letters have been added to the Christian canon, Paul has been identified as their author. After all, there are ten other letters attributed to Paul, he was prolific in sending letters to the communities he founded, and the two addressees of the pastoral letters are his reliable companions. As they stand in the New Testament canon, some of these letters are indisputably accepted to be written by Paul; others, however, are disputed and vaguely attributed to Paul. Irenaeus is one of the church fathers who cited each of the pastoral letters and reached the conclusion that they were written by Paul. There is very little or no evidence to support the claim of Irenaeus, and it is disputed whether he was in a position to know that Paul wrote these letters.

In the modern period of critical biblical scholarship, the majority of New Testament scholars are increasingly convinced of the authorial differences between the undisputed Letters of Paul and 1 and 2 Timothy, thereby placing the latter among the disputed Letters of Paul. Because of apparent stylistic and lexical differences, and theological and biographical dissimilarities, most scholars conclude that Paul did not write 1 and 2 Timothy. They believe they were written in the late first century by a follower of Paul, who is drawing from Paul's apostolic authority. Another group of scholars is adamant that 1 and 2 Timothy are pseudonymous, but argues that they were written in the second century with very little connection to the apostle Paul and his followers. Broadly speaking, 1 and 2 Timothy were written by someone we will never know. Benjamin Fiore's comments are very instructive when he observes that, although the author of 1 and 2 Timothy was not Paul, yet the author decidedly placed the letters "within the Pauline tradition, albeit with alterations that make accommodations to the situation of a more developed church structure and a more complex relationship with the larger society."[1] This is the scholarly opinion I find particularly insightful in the effort to situate 1 and 2 Timothy within the milieu of the early church.

Date and Recipients

The scholarly debates on the authorship of 1 and 2 Timothy have profound implications in dating the letters. Indeed, if Paul wrote these letters, as suggested by Irenaeus and others who rely on Irenaeus's proposition, then the letters will be dated during the life and ministry of the apostle, and certainly prior to his death during the reign of Emperor Nero (54–68 CE). But, as I outlined in the previous section, critical scholarship has discounted the assumption that, as they stand in the canon of the Christian Scripture, 1 and 2 Timothy were written by Paul. Internal evidence places the letters at a period far removed from the time of Paul's life and ministry. In fact, the guidelines and recommendations for selection of offices in the church, and the qualifications and responsibilities of leadership in the church, suggest a time in the history of the early church during the post-apostolic generation of church leadership. With the introduction of the ritual of the imposition of hands as necessary for the assumption of responsibility in the church, as recommended in 1 and 2 Timothy (1 Tim 4:14; 2 Tim 1:6), most scholars place the writing of 1 and 2 Timothy during the end of the first century. The choice of this period for the publication of 1 and 2 Timothy takes into account the contents of the letter and not the historical figure, Timothy, who is a companion of Paul and purportedly the addressee of the letters. These letters are not intended to be a private missive. Rather they are "intended to be read to the church as a whole and, therefore, to function as manuals of discipline for the benefit of whole congregation."[2]

1. Benjamin Fiore, SJ, *The Pastoral Epistles: First Timothy, Second Timothy, Titus*, Sacra Pagina (Liturgical Press, 2007), 16.

2. James D. G. Dunn, "The First and Second Letters to Timothy and the Letter to Titus," in *The New Testament Survey*, ed. Leander E. Keck, NIB (Abingdon Press, 2005), 277.

We know that the community who shared these epistles with Timothy, the supposed addressee, included men and women who were educated in the faith and in the Christian life. They had taken up the responsibilities of teaching others the Christian faith in which they had been called. Some of them were later branded as false teachers by the author of 1 and 2 Timothy and their membership in the community rescinded. Slaves were also members of this community; while some acted in autonomy, making the decision to become Christians, others joined the community together with their Christian slaveowners. There were widows in the community, who were actively involved in the life of the church. There were also wealthy independent women in the community, whose fame is attributed to the opportunities for commerce and aristocratic lifestyle in Ephesus, the capital city of the province of Achaia. Probably, there were some unmarried men, who might have been in leadership positions in the church long before they could start a family and manage a household, but lost their positions due to the new regulations and policies that only married men can hold church offices.

Structures of 1 and 2 Timothy

The modern interpretations of 1 and 2 Timothy have suggested various structures for the letters, each of which supports the modern author's interpretative goals. The structures that I have suggested for both letters pay attention to the overarching themes that run through them. The structure of 1 Timothy reveals the contours of a personal letter (having a semi-public function) written by a minister to a fellow minister. After the opening section (1:1–2), the main section of the letter opens with an invitation to Timothy to oppose false teachings (1:3–20); the other major section in the body of the letter engages communal order and regulations (2:1–3:16), and this section is followed by another invitation to Timothy to oppose false teachers and their views (4:1–11). Then the author of 1 Timothy provides instruction on leadership in the church (4:12–6:2a). The letter also includes directives on the proper use of wealth in the household of God (6:2b–19), and, finally, the author of 1 Timothy concludes with the customary closing section (6:20–21). Similarly, the structure of 2 Timothy begins with an opening section (1:1–5), followed by the main body of the letter (1:6–4:18), which contains a series of rhetorical tropes presented as an invitation to Timothy to eschew a model of leadership that sets him apart in the presence of false teachers. A series of exhortatory statements are separated by statements about faith and false teaching, and ordinances on the organizational life and structures in the household of God. Between the exhortations (2:22–4:18) are teachings on eschatology, a farewell discourse, and a request to the addressee made in the closing section of the letter. The table below is provided in order to guide a reader's appreciation of the structures of the letters. Nevertheless, this chapter interprets 1 and 2 Timothy by examining themes that are common in both letters, and engages them from the context of African Christian biblical hermeneutics. Readers of this chapter, therefore, should keep in mind that these themes are drawn from each section of the structures of the letters. Table 16.1 provides a helpful structure for 1 and 2 Timothy on the themes that I discerned to be critical to the interpretation of the letters that I will explore in this chapter.

Table 16.1. Structures of 1 and 2 Timothy.

1 Timothy	2 Timothy
Opening section 1:1–2	Opening section 1:1–5
Opposition to false teaching 1:3–20	Exhortation 1:6–18
Ecclesial community 2:1–3:16	Exhortation and belief 2:1–13
Opposition to false teachings 4:1–11	Opposition to false teachings 2:14–21
Instructions on leadership in the community 4:12–6:2a	Exhortation and eschatology 2:22–3:9
Directives on the use of wealth 6:2b–19	Exhortation and farewell 3:10–4:8
Closing section 6:20–21	Closing section and request 4:9–18

Genre and History of Interpretation

1 and 2 Timothy are identified in scholarship as letters of encouragement and instruction. They are purportedly personal letters, and 2 Timothy is more personal in content than 1 Timothy and Titus. The author encourages Timothy in his capacity as a leader in the community, and also outlines the duties and responsibilities specific to Timothy as a leader of the community in Ephesus, which is already fraught with false teachers and doctrines, together with the author's perceived understanding of proper conduct in the ecclesial community. The letters employ well-known Hellenistic ethical values that Timothy is enjoined to promote in his teachings on the truth of Christian faith. The author's encouragement to Timothy to be a strong leader and teacher of Christian faith includes admonitions and warnings (see 1 Tim 6:11–14, 20–21). Timothy must defend and guard the apostolic message handed down to him (2 Tim 13, 14); he ought to be guided by the truth of the gospel and by Scripture (2 Tim 3:10–17); and he must be ready to suffer for teaching the truth of the gospel message of God's gift of grace to humankind through Christ. The structure of this chapter does not follow the structures of 1 and 2 Timothy that I have examined in this section. Rather it follows a thematic structure that the reader will notice runs through the letters.

Similarities with the pastoral letters and 1 Clement—dated about 96 CE—have been established in scholarship. Several passages in the pastoral letters are indistinguishable from the Letters of Ignatius, which are dated to about 110 CE. Furthermore, scholars have established strong evidence to show that Polycarp (117 CE) and Justin Martyr (140 CE) used the pastoral letters. In his letter to the Philippians, Polycarp made several references to the pastoral letters. Marcion rejected the pastoral letters, an indication that he knows these letters, as Tertullian recounted in his *Adversus Marcionem* (5.21). In the second century, when books of the New Testament were linked with a single author, Irenaeus knew the pastoral letters to be written by Paul. Clement of Alexandria (150 CE) cited the pastoral letters. In addition, the pastoral letters are included in the Muratorian canon because they received wide acceptance in the second century.[3] Modern scholars have engaged with 1 and 2 Timothy recently in the form of postcolonial scholarship from Asia, and Latin and Central America, and through the work of feminist scholars. Each engage in a methodic appeal to lived experiences and their contexts in the interpretation of Scripture. In a similar approach, this chapter engages the African context and lived experiences in the interpretation of 1 and 2 Timothy.

Reading from an African Perspective

The African perspective involves a conscious engagement of cultures and the experiences of the peoples of Africa with the narrative of Christian Scripture. Such interaction is aimed at naming the existential impact of their faith in God's presence in the world through Jesus Christ. Since inculturation is the incarnation of the life, death, and resurrection of Jesus Christ in the context of the lives of believers in Africa, then whatever is life-giving in the cultures of the peoples of Africa is affirmed, and whatever is not is dismantled. This is because the cultural imagination of the Christian experiences of the peoples of Africa is a conscious act of uniting a community and/or an individual with Christ's life in a sociocultural context. For this reason, in interpreting 1 and 2 Timothy from an African perspective, my goal is to show the contours of affirmation and transformation in the interaction between the African contexts and the letters; and the invitation for rejection and change in the interaction between the African context and the letters. I have organized my interpretation of the letters into themes about theology and Christology, family life and social relationships, gender and church leaderships, and finally, false and true teachers and ministers in the church.

The Identity of God and Jesus Christ

Africans are immersed in the consciousness of the presence of the one supreme God. This consciousness is central to African cosmology, albeit with little or no substantive pious activities honoring the one supreme God. For example, in Chinua Achebe's *Things Fall Apart*, Mazi Akunna explained to the European missionary, Mr. Brown, the fundamental reason behind the nonexistence of any concrete ritual activities honoring the one supreme God in most African religions. This is because the other gods and/or deities who are the messengers of the one supreme God are present to the people on behalf of the one supreme God. The people of Umuofia, for instance, approach the one supreme God through his messengers (see Rom 8:5–6). Mazi Akunna explains, "We make sacrifices to the little gods, but when they fail and there is no one else to turn to then we go to Chukwu," the one supreme God. "We appear to pay greater attention to the little god but that is not so, we worry them more because we are afraid to worry their Master." Mazi Akunna explained that the fear of the one supreme God is based on humanity's inability to fulfill and do the will of the one supreme God.[4]

3. See George W. Knight III, *The Pastoral Letters: A Commentary on the Greek Text* (Eerdmans, 1992), 13–14.
4. Chinua Achebe, *Things Fall Apart* (Anchor Books, 1994), 180–181.

When African cultures speak of the mystery and immensity of the universe, it is a reflection, therefore, that leads to the identity of the creator. E. Bolaji Idowu observes that belief in the supreme God, who is identified as "father, creator, eternal, completely beneficent, ethically holy, and creatively omnipotent" is present among cultures with genuine monotheistic tendencies.[5] The belief in the creation of the world inexorably leads to the belief in the sole creator of the world. The immensity of the created world strengthens the presence of God among African cultures and religious traditions.

The various descriptive identities for the one supreme God in Africa bespeak God's divine nature, activities in creation, and attributes. For instance, in *Things Fall Apart*, Mazi Akunna revealed to Mr. Brown that the people of Umuofia believe in the one supreme God, who they call Chukwu because he created "the world and the other gods." Mazi Akunna further discloses to Mr. Brown that "our fathers knew that *Chukwu* was the Overload and that is why many of them gave their children the name *Chukwuka—Chukwu* is Supreme."[6] The supreme God is also known as Chineke, the creator God, whose ongoing creative power and activity are present in the world. Similarly, among the Yoruba of the western part of Nigeria, God is called Orișẹ, which means the source of being, the creator. Additionally, the Akan of southern Ghana call the one supreme God *Odomankoma*, recognizing God as the creator who creates out of divine fullness. Differently said, the one supreme God, who is the creator of the world, has the sole responsibility of sustaining and saving the world. Similarly to what is written in 1 and 2 Timothy, Africans believe that the one supreme God is also the savior of the world. It is on basis of this belief that the Igbo people call God Osebuluwa, the sustaining and supporting deity of the earth. Lesser deities and humankind have delegatory roles in this sustaining and saving plan of the one supreme God.

The consciousness of the one supreme God in the African religious imagination is supported by the awe-inspiring forces of nature. Day and night, storm, thunder, wind, lightning, sky, and so on, inspire awe, drawing the people of Africa deeper into the nature and identity of the one supreme God. The dependance on the light from the sun and moon, on the rain that waters the earth, and so on, strengthen the conceptual belief in the supreme powers and activities of the one supreme God. Liturgical music across the religious traditions of African people, particularly in contemporary charismatic and Pentecostal movements, ritualizes the powers of God, which are manifested in natural phenomena. The very vastness of the sky, which serves as the source of the natural forces that they experience on earth, leads African people to entertain the belief in the heavens as the abode of the supreme God, unlike the other deities known to the African people, who have earthly habitation. Therefore, Africans believe that the rain, light, cool air, warmth, and so on, are the works of the one supreme God, who sustains creation out of divine benevolence, thereby providing humankind with the natural things they enjoy that come from the sky and/or heavens. On this note, the existence of the one supreme God is not foreign to Africa, and the consciousness of the supreme deity in the

5. E. Bolaji Idowu, "God," in *Biblical Revelation and African Beliefs*, ed. Kwesi Dickson and Paul Ellingworth (Orbis, 1969), 18.

6. Achebe, *Things Fall Apart*, 179–180.

African religious imagination certainly predates the European Christian missionary enterprise in the continent. The credibility of this point of view is supported by the observation of the Belgian Franciscan missionary in the Congo, Placide Tempels. Tempels observes that the one supreme God is the "great *Muntu*" in the conceptual framework of Congolese and African religious imaginations, who is evidently similar to the Christian God.[7]

Turning to the pastoral letters, the fundamental belief in the one supreme God in 1 Timothy and throughout the New Testament (1 Cor 8:4; 12:5–6; Rom 3:30; Eph 4:5–6) is influenced by Judaism. Judaism foregrounds the belief in the oneness of God in the creation story in the book of Genesis. The belief in the oneness of God received a contractual agreement on Mount Sinai, where God declared that he alone is God and there is no other to whom the children of Israel should acquiesce (see Exod 20:1–11; Deut 6:4). The reaffirmation of the oneness of God in the Synoptic tradition continues to deepen the monotheistic connection between Judaism and Christianity. Jesus quotes Scripture, which the Markan community reads as a fundamental feature of their faith in the one true God (Mark 12:29; ὁ θεὸς ἡμῶν κύριος εἷς ἐστίν). Correspondingly, the affirmation of the oneness of God reinforces the belief in the humanity of Jesus Christ, who is a mediator between God and humanity. Regarding the religious tradition of the people of Umuofia in *Things Fall Apart*, Mr. Akunne explains to Mr. Brown that Jesu Kristi is one of the messengers of the one supreme God through whom the community approaches God. In the opening section of 1 and 2 Timothy, both letters are consistent with naming the fatherhood of God (1 Thess 1:1; Gal 1:1), and the lordship of Jesus Christ. God's fatherhood and the lordship of Jesus Christ are titles of divine and imperial dimensions in the Greco-Roman world.

In the Greco-Roman world, Zeus (Homer, *Od.* 4.341) is addressed in extant literature as father (Ζεὺς πατὴρ). Homer (*Od.* 1.45) called Zeus "father of us all and higher about all lords" (πάτερ ἡμετερε. ὕπατε κρειόντων). It is in this context that God assumes the identity of father (θεοῦ πατρὸς). For his part, when writing about the fatherhood of God, Paul describes God's relationship with believers as adoption. By adoption believers are made children of God's household, with the rights and privileges to call God "Abba Father" (Gal 4:6; Rom 8:15). Notice that God's identity as a father emerges from the context of the ancient family value system with the male as the head of the household, the *patria potestas*. Keep in mind that the fatherhood of God emerged in traditional societies that are firmly established on patriarchal values, just as in Africa. In this context, fatherhood is readily linked with power, leadership, and authority. For this reason, God is a father in the African context and in the pastoral letters because God is a supreme authority with the sole power and leadership of the world. It is important to note that God exercises the authority of fatherhood with a supreme disposition for the welfare of humanity, loving and caring for humanity with compassionate authority. The evidence for this point of view is the divine sending of Jesus Christ into the world to bring to completion God's divine leadership of saving the world from sin, death, and eternal perdition, as one reads in the narrative of Christian Scripture. That said, patriarchal imagery

7. See Janheinz Jahn, *Muntu: An Outline of the New African Culture*, trans. Marjorie Grene (Grove Press, 1961), 104–105.

and structures, such as the idea of fatherhood in the African context, that deny the dignity and equality of women must be deconstructed and dismantled.

The author of 1 Timothy has an unusual identity for God, namely God is "our savior" (1 Tim 1:1). Consistent early Christian soteriology links the salvation of the world with the activities of Jesus Christ, whom God sent into the world as savior. Be that as it may, the identity of God (1 Tim 1:1; 2:3; 4:10; 2 Tim 1:9; see Titus 1:3; 2:10; 3:4), alongside Jesus (2 Tim 2:10; Titus 1:4; 2:13; 3:6) as savior in the pastoral letters, merits attention. It is not particularly clear to the reader whether the author of the pastoral letters introduces two salvific activities, one by God and the other by Jesus Christ, or whether he speaks of one saving act by both God and Jesus Christ, or whether he has chosen to name the central message of Christian understanding of the salvation history in which Jesus Christ is the agent of the saving plan of God. In the Old Testament, for instance, God is identified as a savior (Deut 32:15). The psalmist calls God "my savior," insisting that God's saving presence dispels fear (Ps 27:1, 9). Ultimately, God is revealed to the Israelites as savior and God of justice (Isa 45:15, 21). Needless to say, in the history and quest for national identity, God is revealed to the children of Israel as a savior. Differently said, the exodus story is ubiquitous in the consciousness of the children of Israel's understanding of God's activity in their history as a savior. Be that as it may, the evidence does not support the point of view that the author of the pastoral letters is drawing from the Old Testament tradition of God's saving activity

The early church conception of God's saving plan in human history reaches its fulfillment in the life and death of Jesus Christ. It is plausible, therefore, that the author of the pastoral letters conceives the activity of God's saving plan in history to reach its consummation in Jesus Christ. The author's profession of faith in one God is supported with cultic worship (2 Tim 1:3). More so, the author identifies a connection between the oneness of God and the creative activity of God (1 Tim 4:3–5; 6:13). God gives life to all things, and 1 Timothy correspondingly affirms the goodness of creation (1 Tim 4:4). It is reasonable, therefore, for the author of the pastoral letters to employ fatherhood, kingship, or imperial language to God. As the one supreme God, and creator, God governs the universe as its sole king (1 Tim 1:17; 6:15–16; 2 Tim 1:8). In God's capacity as the king of the universe, it is then God's sole duty to distribute the wealth of the world to humankind, by richly providing humanity "with everything for our enjoyment" (1 Tim 6:17), and gratuitously imbues humankind with the spirit of power, love, and self-control (2 Tim 1:7).

Unlike the identity of the one supreme God, whose divine attributes in African religious imagination are felt in the immensity of the created world and in the activities of lesser deities, the person of Jesus Christ in the African religious imagination presents some conceptual and identity challenges, as evident in the advent of Christianity among the people of Umuofia as recounted in *Things Fall Apart*. When the European missionary, Mr. Brown, arrived in Umuofia, speaking through an interpreter, he included the introduction of the Son of God, whom he called Jesu Kristi, in his catechetical and Bible study enterprise. As the most vocal elder of the community in the audience, Mazi Okonkwo interjected, "You told us with your own mouth that there was only one god. Now you talk about his son.

He must have a wife, then." The crowd vociferously agreed with the observation of Mazi Okonkwo.[8] At the very least, African belief in the one supreme God is completely devoid of any corresponding belief in a divine household that includes a wife and a son. For this reason, African belief in the one supreme God is closer to Judaism in its strictest sense of a monotheistic belief system. The lack of an African name or identity for Jesu Kristi is a testament to the absence of an African Christology. Nevertheless, the name and identity of Jesu Kristi has become central to African Christianity, and the conceptual framework of faith in Jesus Christ among Christian Africans has grown. In 1991, in an effort to collate the various identities of Jesus Christ in African Christianity in a systematic christological belief, Robert J. Schreiter edited an anthology that presented the many faces of Jesus in Africa.[9] Trying to identify the role of Jesus Christ in the saving and sustaining work of the one supreme God in the world, African Christianity proposes the following descriptive identities for Jesus Christ: Christ is an ancestor, diviner, healer, chief, warrior, life giver, family member, elder, brother, liberator, Black messiah, miracle worker, chief, ruler, king, and so on.

From these christological identities, two distinct but related approaches emerged from the African christological enterprise. The first approach draws from the biblical narratives about the life and teachings of Jesus Christ, and then find a corresponding identity in African culture. The second approach begins from the African context, and then proceeds in search of similarities with the biblical narratives about Jesus Christ. Broadly speaking, there is a strong connection and belief in the humanity of Jesus in African Christianity. The incipient perception of the sonship of Jesus Christ among the people of Umuofia in *Things Fall Apart* suggests a nativity story and a human nature for God's only son (see 1 Tim 1:16; Luke 1:31–32; John 1:14). In fact, the two distinctive approaches to Christology in the Africa context draw extensively from the humanity of Jesus Christ, which shares affinity with the pastoral letters' christological statements against gnostic ideas about Jesus Christ. The first approach received a thorough and detailed investigation by the Guinean theologian, Cécé Kolié. Kolié surveys the healing activities of Jesus in the Gospels by itemizing them into "specific and catechetical cures, resurrection and social integration."[10] He further examined the complex experiences of sickness and healing in Africa. The results of his investigation led Kolié to identify Jesus Christ as a healer in Africa.[11] In the second approach, Congolese theologian François Kabasélé identified Jesus Christ as an ancestor, elder brother,[12] and as a chief.[13] Kabasélé began by examining the traditional and cultural images of a chief, ancestor, and an elder brother in an African context. On the basis of his investigations, he applied the images and characteristics of a chief, ancestor, and elder brother to the Christ of the Gospels. It is not unusual, therefore, to experience in African liturgy and music the ritualization of the belief in the humanity of Jesus

8. Achebe, *Things Fall Apart*, 146–147.

9. Robert J. Schreiter, ed., *Faces of Jesus in Africa* (Orbis, 1991).

10. Cécé Kolié, "Jesus as Healer?," in *Faces of Jesus in Africa*, ed. Robert J. Schreiter (Orbis, 1991), 130.

11. Kolié, "Jesus as Healer?," 128–150.

12. François Kabasélé, "Christ as Ancestor and Elder Brother," in *Faces of Jesus in Africa*, ed. Robert J. Schreiter (Orbis, 1991), 116–127.

13. François Kabasélé, "Christ as Chief," in *Faces of Jesus in Africa*, ed. Robert J. Schreiter (Orbis, 1991), 103–115.

Christ. In theological discourses and in rituals, the consciousness of Christ as a proto-figure and/or archetype of the various identities assigned him in African Christianity reveal that Christ is not just a human figure, but one whose life, death, and resurrection manifested his divine attributes. This led to him becoming, therefore, a source of faith for Christian Africans' hope for life with God, just as he became a source of faith for their counterparts in Ephesus, led by Timothy. It goes without saying that, from the first missionary activities of European Christians in Africa in places like Umuofia, African faith in Jesus Christ has moved from ambivalence to resolute certainty, faith, and piety.

The Christology of 1 and 2 Timothy underlines the nativity story of Jesus by speaking about Jesus's birth as being revealed in the flesh (1 Tim 1:16), which validates Jesus's humanity. The author continues in the so-called Christ-hymn to affirm Jesus's humanity by specifically mentioning the nativity story (1 Tim 3:16). Like most epistles, the death of Jesus on the cross stands out in the Christology of 1 and 2 Timothy. Jesus Christ successfully testified before Pilate (1 Tim 6:13), and Jesus's vindication by the Spirit (1 Tim 1:16; 2 Tim 2:8)—evidence of the resurrection (1 Tim 1:16)—confirmed Jesus's divinity. The event of Jesus's passion and death validates his saving identity. He is the savior of the world with the divine mandate to save sinners (1 Tim 1:15), and he did so by giving himself as a ransom for sinners (1 Tim 1:6). Jesus's saving actions continue to benefit believers (2 Tim 3:11). In 2 Timothy 4:17–18, the author is even more descriptive of his experience of Jesus's saving presence in his own life. The parousia is a key christological statement of 1 and 2 Timothy, as Jesus's return heralds the judgment of the world (2 Tim 4:1). Those who keep the commandment (1 Tim 6:14) will inherit the heavenly kingdom (2 Tim 4:18). Notice that in the pastoral letters the Christian faith is based on the acceptance of the humanity of Jesus together with his divine nature made evident in the story of his passion, death, and resurrection. This central belief system in the pastoral letters impinges on the teaching of gnostic Christians about the nature of Jesus Christ and the Christian faith.

Family, Society, and Church and Systems of Relationship

In Africa, emphasis is placed on family, social identity, and belongingness, and less on individual autonomy and freedom. In this context, the values of solidarity, communion, and unity are more important and therefore promoted more than personal agency, individual autonomy, and free will. The family is the primary origin of an African claim to status, and the basic locus of the consciousness of one's self-identity. The family is central to the identity of individual members to the extent that no member of the family thinks of themselves outside of family identity, and no one acts in a manner that undermines family cohesion, honor, and identity. In other words, family life is the source and foundation of social relationships for an integral personhood. It is impossible to conceive of self without first considering the primacy of individual belongingness in a community. This is the basis of the social identity theory in Africa as articulated by John Mbiti: "I am, because we are; and since we are, therefore I am."[14]

14. John Mbiti, *African Religions and Philosophy* (Doubleday, 1970), 172.

Community and social life in the African context is a bond between the families and relatives of a young man and woman in a marriage contract. Through marriage rituals and traditions, families bind themselves together in an extended family system that certainly establish a union of relationships that extend their presence in the community. Since family is the basic and essential unit of society, then the church in Africa is commonly identified as the family of God.

In postcolonial times, the people of Tanzania conceived of *ujamaa* as an encapsulation of their understanding and appreciation of their social life and identity. The Roman Catholic Association of Members of the Episcopal Conference of Eastern Africa (AMECEA) began to articulate their understanding of the Christian life from the social philosophy of *ujamaa*. It embodies the spirit of cooperation, sharing, and support that defines the notion of family life in the African context. In this way, the African church is a love-centered and spirited communion toward the growth and flourishing of every member. To truly reflect the image of God's people in communion with one another, and to realize the presence of the kingdom of God, then the African church must be stripped of the characteristic features of patriarchy and cultural dominance that stymie the equality of men and women so that the church can promote the rise of the latter to leadership and authority. It is clear that the family image of the church in Africa embraces some significant characteristics of the traditional understanding of the family unit among African cultures. At the same time, however, the image of the church in Africa as a family of God presents some salient challenges to the African church to unmask and dismantle cultural modes of living in the African family system that continue to subjugate and oppress women from reaching their full potential as children of God in the church and society. Like the Mediterranean world, the traditional African family system bears similar characteristics, with the male as the head of the household and women being assigned limited roles and limited rights of ownership. The bearing and raising of children are an important component of the African household, and are part of the basic duties and responsibilities of women.

The pastoral letters disclose the important place family life occupied in the formation of Christian identity in the early church. The complex character of family relationships that existed in the Greco-Roman world is pervasively rehearsed in the pastoral letters. The letters appeal to the values of family life in the Greco-Roman world, and at the same time invite the Christian community to reject the vices that destroy family bonds. First and second Timothy reveal how Greco-Roman social institutions serve as models of understanding the church as a community of believers. They should shun the vices that undermine a family life worthy of the children of God, which is a common exhortation in the epistolary tradition of the New Testament. In the affirmative, the author singles out some family for praise and recognition. The family of Onesiphorus is singled out for praise (2 Tim 1:16; 4:19). The author invokes the mercy of God upon this household and sends greetings to this same family alongside Prisca and Aquila. The families that are named in the epistles often serve as benefactors to the author of the letters and to the community. It is most likely that, like Philemon, Onesiphorus made his home available for community gatherings. Prisca and Aquila, who are mentioned in the closing section of 2 Timothy, are among the famous companions of Paul from their first meeting in Corinth (see Acts 19:18). The family experiences of Timothy under the guidance of this grandmother and his mother, Lois, are presented in 2 Timothy 1:5 as an example of a family life where faith is nurtured (see Acts 16:1–5). Lois and her mother created a home where Timothy grew up into a man of "sincere faith" (2 Tim 1:5). Therefore, Timothy was raised in a well-managed household, and as a child he was "submissive and respectful in every way" (1 Tim 3:4). The public recognition of Timothy's leadership and managerial skills is a testament to the household values nurtured by his mother and grandmother.

Being raised in a household based on virtuous lifestyle and being able to exercise leadership as the head of a household (1 Tim 3:4) are important features of the identity of the early church. A mandatory credential for qualification to hold the office of deacon in the early church is a proven record of being a good head of a household, a *paterfamilias*, who has legal authority over the household (*patria potestas*). The early church operated from the maxim that to be a good leader of the church demands that one has an experience in leading one's household, where the wife exudes the virtues of a model wife, the children are respectful, and the slaves are submissive and obedient (see 1 Tim 3:5; 6:1). This is because, in the ancient world, the man is husband, father, and master, exercising authority over his wife, children, and slaves, as seen in Aristotle's description of the characteristics of household management in the *Politics*.[15] It is the duty of the male leader of the household to protect his family from injury, shame, and dishonorable behavior and also to support the weak. Women are expected to preserve family honor in the public sphere through sexual purity. The separation of the space of women from that of the men means that women are to be protected, controlled, and guarded. Public spaces and leadership belong to men, while private and domestic spaces belong to women (*materfamilias domina*), who are under the legal guardianship of a male relative. In the *Moralia*, Plutarch insists that a virtuous woman should be visible only in the company of her husband, and she should remain at home, away from the public eye when her husband is away.[16] It is important to note that class and status often determine social roles for women. Women of the elite and aristocratic class enjoy more social freedom than women of lower status. Seneca insists that the responsibilities and duties assigned to a man as a *paterfamilias* do not make the duties and responsibilities of his wife as the *materfamilias* any less important. Rather the division of obligation and the service each renders to the other builds up a harmonious family life that creates a stable social relation.[17]

The pastoral letters portray an ideal family out of which social order and harmony are established in the empire. In 1 Timothy 1:9–10, the lawless and disobedient are those who undermine family values and are disobedient to the *paterfamilias*. Some have no religious identity and practices, rather they engage in unholy acts with the result that some murder their parents and engage in acts of sexual immorality. They are slave traders who undermine the teachings of God (see also 2 Tim 3:1-5). They are homewreckers, lacking in values and earthbound in their outlook on life, and they destroy family relationships (2 Tim 3:6). The

15. Aristotle, *Pol.* 1.2 (1252a, 25–32), 1.13 (1260a, 9–14).

16. See Plutarch, *Mor.* 138A–146A.

17. Seneca the Younger, *Ben.* 18.1–2.

author of 2 Timothy represented the wider perception of women in the Greco-Roman world as morally weak, hence the author uses a socially derogatory term (γυναικάριον) to describe women in the community. Furthermore, the author adds a religious sentiment to his perception of women, including those who are believers. They are overcome with sinning, always being led (ἀγόμεθα) by desire (ἐπιθυμίαις), they are devoid of free will and reason with the result that the instructions they receive never bring them to the knowledge of the truth (1 Tim 3:6b–7). Also, the author of the pastoral letters considers a different dress code for men and women as important for social decorum and church life (1 Tim 2:8–9) in order to control the dress code of wealthy and free women in the community. The author further mandates that women should remain silent in the ecclesial community, exercising no ministry in the church (1 Tim 2:11–12). The author uses the Adam and Eve story to argue for modesty from women in the household and in the ecclesial community. He invites Timothy to model the best form of respect in the ecclesial family in his interaction with older men, and model a good character in the community to younger men and women (1 Tim 5:1–2). In the Greco-Roman world, married women who survived the birth of their children and who survived their husbands, faced the heartbreaking and socially challenging experience of widowhood. The appearance of widows in the pastoral letters reveals their active presence in the community. Caring and showing compassion toward the vulnerable members of our family is central to the ecclesial identity of the community of the pastoral letters (1 Tim 5:3–7).

The Greco-Roman period of early Christianity was a society of class and status. Slaves were the lowest cadre, and they obviously had no status or recognition of their humanity, notwithstanding the fact that slave labor was the bedrock of commerce and social development of the polis. It is important to keep in mind that the Greco-Roman manumission policy still kept a slave dependent and loyal to their former master.[18] It is in this social context that the author of the pastoral letters admonishes slaves to honor their masters, which 1 Timothy inexorably linked with divine piety (1 Tim 6:1). In spite of the social experiences of inequalities, class, and social strata of Greco-Roman imperial society, these early Christians believed that their experience of freedom in Christ united them as brothers and sisters in Christ. This social formation of the early Christian community is one that is countercultural and obviously disruptive of the social relationships between a slave and a master. But the message of 1 and 2 Timothy reveals the possibility that the Christian communal framework would potentially create family disharmony. To prevent such situations in the home, slaves are admonished to be all the more loyal and obedient and carry on with their duties with greater zeal (1 Tim 6:2). This is an example of the campaign of the pastoral letters to model church life according to the values of family life in the Greco-Roman world, which some interpreters regard as the author's policy of eliminating the central message of Christian identity as a family of God in communion and equality (see Gal 3:28).

Exhortation on the proper use of wealth is demanded from the wealthy members of the community. The wealthy class of the Greco-Roman world were essentially the patrons of individuals, groups, associations, the community, and the nation. As I observed elsewhere,

18. See Ferdinand Okorie, "Mapping Paul's Rhetorical Discourse About God in Philemon," in *God in Paul's Letters*, ed. Timothy Milinovich, Normand Bonneau, and Robert F. O'Toole (Cascade, 2023), 120.

"they are the owners of lands and slaves, and they are the socioeconomic and political elites."[19] Their disposition to be generous with their wealth invariably earned them honor and praise from the recipients of their benefaction. Among early Christians, Paul was a recipient of the benefaction of wealthy Christians, and he encourages benefaction among members of the community, and indeed, wealthy Christians such as Philemon were benefactors of the community that apparently met in his house (Phlm 2). The admonition in 1 Timothy 6:17 is based on the tendency for wealthy elites to become unconcerned and thoughtless in their relationship with the poor, especially slaves. But the invitation "to do good, to be rich in good works, generous and ready to share" (1 Tim 6:18) is based on the reminder that God is the source of wealth (1 Tim 6:17). Therefore, the wealthy members of the community should do good (v. 18a; ἀγαθοεργεῖν) and be rich in doing noble deeds (v. 18b; πλουτεῖν ἐν ἔργοις καλοῖς), becoming benefactors of the community just as God is the benefactor of their wealth. Their activities of benefaction bring about reciprocity, rewards, and honorific acclamations. First Timothy 6:19b exhorts wealthy members of the community to aim beyond the earthly reward benefactors in the Greco-Roman world would typically receive, but rather they should aim to receive the reward of "life that really is life" (NRSV), which only God grants.[20]

Gender and Leadership in the Church

The identity of the church in Africa as the family of God promotes the distribution of roles across gender and age. Customarily, women and men are socialized into normatively approved appropriate roles and duties, and are subsequently admonished to avoid inappropriate roles and duties, either in private (family) or public (society) spaces. Motherhood empowers women in the family unit as much as it remains a burden of limitation against the autonomy and public leadership of women in the society. Also, motherhood is important to the African family, but the family setting of the African context does not significantly improve the public life of women in society. The narrative of 1 and 2 Timothy fosters the kind of subjugation and oppression of women in public life that is prevalent in the African context. The letters limit women in the household and assign them limited duties in the Christian community. Mercy Amba Oduyoye identifies the twin forces of culture and religion as standing against the empowerment of women. In fact, the brand of Christian community promoted in 1 and 2 Timothy is against the self-actualization of women as children of God alongside their male counterpart. Critical observation of the presence of Christianity in Africa reveals that religion has done little to challenge gender disparity in the church and in society, notwithstanding the statistical fact that more women than men participate in weekly religious worship and activities. Patriarchal ideology and structures in society and in the church label women as

19. Ferdinand Okorie, "Greco-Roman καλοκαγαθός in the Pauline and Pastoral Letters," in *Forget Not God's Benefits (Psalm 103:2): A Festschrift in Honor of Leslie J. Hoppe, OFM*, ed. Barbara E. Reid (The Catholic Biblical Association of America, 2022), 242.

20. Okorie, "Greco-Roman καλοκαγαθός," 242.

inferior, thereby perpetuating the forces of marginalization and oppression against women. In Oduyoye's words, Christianity in Africa "reinforces the cultural conditioning of compliance and submission and leads to the depersonalization of women."[21] In fact, the capitulation of 1 and 2 Timothy to the dominant Greco-Roman cultural values of male authority and leadership in public life is commonplace in the church in Africa.

However, as much as Christianity in Africa upholds the division of roles across gender, similar to the situation in the Christian community in Ephesus under the leadership of Timothy, women across Christian denominations in Africa maintain steady and significant roles in pastoring and leading churches. In the Pentecostal tradition in Africa, women assume and share in the leadership of their churches as pastors and ministers alongside their male counterparts. In the prophetic, revivalist, and charismatic movements of the African Instituted churches, African women are taking on leadership roles, and exercising ecclesial and ministerial freedom as leaders and founders of churches. These apparent ministerial roles women exercise in some Christian communities in Africa by no means address the indignation around the absence of women on the public stage of African culture and Christianity in the same and similar roles as their male counterparts. Even in instances in the life of the community where women share in decision making with their male counterparts, such as in politics, commerce, and industry, the disparity in representation is palpable. Differently said, gender-based duties and responsibilities are strictly adhered to in both social and religious settings across Africa, thereby keeping women out of sharing in the divine invitation of discipleship of the faithful. In the Roman Catholic tradition in Africa, vibrant pious societies have leadership across genders, which obviously does not replace the reality of male-dominated ministry in the Catholic Church, just as in the church led by Timothy in Ephesus.

When we review the leadership structures of African Instituted churches, for instance, one will recognize a more visible presence of women in important roles in the church community than would be accorded to women in the cultural or mainline Christian denominations. In the edited volume by Victor E. W. Hayward, *African Independent Church Movements*, it is demonstrated that women find the opportunity to be visibly active in leadership and ministry of the church.[22] There is evidence that in traditional African religious systems, women were diviners, prophetesses, medicine aficionados, herbalists, and priestesses. African Instituted churches provide a platform for African women to lead and find legitimacy in the life of the church. In the Aladura churches for instance, women occupy leadership positions. Keep in mind that the Sacred Eternal Order of the Cherubim and Seraphim was founded by Christianah Abiodun Akinsowon in collaboration with Moses Orimolade. Christianah was reported to have fallen into a trance for days in June 1925 after attending a Corpus Christi Procession in the Roman Catholic Church. She woke from the trance to discover that her family had reached out to Moses Orimolade, a known healer in town, to pray for her. Christianah is known as the founder of the Cherubim and Seraphim Movement in Nigeria. Likewise, in

21. Mary Amba Oduyoye, *Daughters of Anowa: African Women and Patriarchy* (Orbis, 1995), 9.

22. Victor E. W. Hayward, *African Independent Church Movements* (Edinburgh House Press, 1963).

Kenya, Gaudencia Aoko founded the Legio Maria Church of Africa in 1963.[23] Be that as it may, it is important to point out that while some of the African Instituted churches elect women to positions of power, others have maintained and foster the traditional views of gender roles which is conspicuous in African cultures, and in the Christian community of Ephesus under Timothy's leadership.

As the early church moved on from the era of apostolic leadership to the period of local leadership and ecclesial organization, the church began to look a lot more like the leadership structures of the Greco-Roman world. In fact, the early church organized itself based on the same family and social values that undergirded the leadership structures of the Greco-Roman world. The Ephesian church community added the office of bishop to the office of deacon that had been in place since the apostolic period. The office of bishop is a noble position for those who desire to serve as bishops (1 Tim 3:1; καλοῦ ἔργου ἐπιθυμεῖ). A candidate's managerial skills as a *paterfamilias*, running his household well, teaching his children to be obedient and respectful, and being married once were the requirements for the office (1 Tim 3:2, 4). The candidate must have modeled the qualities in the polis that made him an exemplary *paterfamilias* and avoid the vices that would impede his ability to lead his household (1 Tim 3:2–3). A new convert was disqualified from the position because of lack of depth and experience as a believer. The author of 1 Timothy knows that an honorable *paterfamilias* must also have a public presence and recognition. For this reason, a candidate for the office of bishop in the church must also have had a public honor just as he exercised honorable leadership in his household (1 Tim 3:7).

Similarly, the candidates for the office of deacon must have been married once, and must have exhibited the capacity to manage a household well (1 Tim 3:12), just as for those who aspired to the office of bishop. In other words, such a candidate must be a capable *paterfamilias* to his household. The one elected for the office of deacon must be grounded in the faith (1 Tim 3:9). On the basis of this recommendation, the deaconate was not open to a new convert or to anyone who did not hold to the sound teachings that Timothy is strongly encouraged to uphold and teach. The service of deacons ought to be anchored on confidence in their faith in Christ. It is important to note that by itemizing the requirements for women in the section where the author discusses the leadership role of deacons, the author is indicating that women could continue to serve as deacons in the early church just as they did during the times of the apostles (see Rom 16). Wealthy Ephesian women who were members of the church served in leadership capacities and they were the target of comments about modesty and church decorum by the author. In the second century, Pliny the Younger's letter to Emperor Trajan supported the fact that women were deacons in the early church and in the Ephesian church. Pliny the Younger wrote that he interrogated "two slave-women, whom they [namely, the Christians] called deaconesses."[24] Above all, women deacons are exhorted to be faithful in

23. For more examples of female leaders in African Independent churches, see Philomena Njeri Mwaura, "Gender and Power in African Christianity: African Instituted Churches and Pentecostal Churches," in *African Christianity: An African Story*, ed. Ogbu U. Kalu (African World Press, 2007), 368–384.

24. Pliny the Younger, *Ep.* 10.96–97.

their service on behalf of Christ (1 Tim 3:11). The argument buttressing the presence and ministry of female deacons in the early church has received detailed exposition in the works of feminist scholars, who insist that the author of 1 Timothy has decided to restrict the ministerial role women played in the early church. By applying the hermeneutic of suspicion to their interpretation of 1 Timothy 5:1–16, feminist scholars insist that the author of 1 Timothy redefines the ministerial office of independent women. The author's recognition of their good works and leadership is a testament of their ministerial leadership in the church (1 Tim 5:10).[25]

The office of elders, or presbyters was added to church organizational leadership in Ephesus. Presbyters exercise the responsibility of preaching and teaching (1 Tim 5:17). In the early church, the teaching office of the church, namely, those who exercise the duties of teaching the faith to new members just like the apostles did in Act 2:42; 6:2, is vital to the growth of the church because of the opportunity for growth as new members join the community. Because the role of elder was an exclusive and important office in the early church, an accusation against an elder, who is a teacher of the faith, would lack merit except when evidence was provided by two or three witnesses. An elder of the church enjoyed such honor because of his status as a teacher of the faith, just as did the apostles of Christ.

False Teachers and True Leaders

It is important to mention from the outset that African Christianity is completely devoid of the debate in 1 and 2 Timothy about the nature of Jesus Christ that bedeviled the church in Ephesus. As I mentioned earlier in this chapter when I engaged with the encounter between the people of Umuofia and Mr. Brown, the European missionary, we learned from that encounter that the problem of African Christology has little to do with the nature of Jesus Christ; rather, it has more to do with the belief that the one supreme God has a biological child. Therefore, the imagination of the people of Umuofia as the missionary speaks about the sonship of Jesus Christ does not diminish Jesus's divine nature as child of the one supreme God, rather their imagination seeks to understand the family configuration of the one supreme God. One notices that the African christological framework has both biblical and contextual frameworks as their faith in Christ progressed through the various contextual identities of Christ that speaks to their lived experiences. The incipient gnostic idea disavowed by the author of 1 and 2 Timothy is never the preoccupation of African Christianity.

Rather African Christianity has witnessed a growing band of alleged anointed and spirit-filled ministers, whose christological propositions are completely removed from the central belief system of Christianity in the message of God's gift of salvation to humanity through the passion, death, and resurrection of Jesus Christ. These allegedly spirit-filled ministers make a mockery of the authentic and genuine workings of the Holy Spirit in the life of the

25. See Elisabeth Schüssler Fiorenza, *In Memory of Her: A Feminist Theological Reconstruction of Christian Origins* (Crossroad, 1983) xiv, xvi; Joanna Dewey, "1 Timothy," in *Women's Bible Commentary*, 3rd ed., twentieth anniv. ed., ed. Carol Newsom, Sharon H. Ringe, and Jacqueline E. Lipsley (Westminster John Knox, 2012), 595–601; Linda M. Maloney, "The Pastoral Epistles," in *Searching the Scriptures*, vol. 2, *A Feminist Commentary*, ed. Elisabeth Schüssler Fiorenza (Crossroad, 1997), 361–380.

leadership of the church and the community in Africa. There is no discounting the fact that church leaders in Africa face similar dilemmas in order to walk the fine line between the right teachings of faith and moral uprightness. Pneumatological possessions and the hunger for miraculous deeds have become the coveted gifts and preoccupation of church leaders over and above the teaching and proclamation of the gospel of God's gift of life to humanity through the death and resurrection of Christ as the basis of Christian faith. Just as for the church in Ephesus under the leadership of Timothy, likewise the church in Africa faces the challenge of the absolutization of an ideological perception and inclination toward a single Christian belief over objective doctrinal teaching about how God has chosen to be involved in the world through the story of Jesus Christ. We are living through an era in church leadership in Africa that is immersed in a brand of pastoral theology that is weakened by apparent self-justification, flamboyant displays of material possessions, and self-glorification masked as God's mouthpiece, who is the sole recipient of modern divine prophecy.[26]

Across Africa are the allegedly spirit-filled and growing miracle-driven church leaders who are swindling god-fearing believers apparently hungry for divine presence in the everydayness of their lived experiences. The flamboyant and theatrical display of perceived spirit-filled evangelism evidently supports the impoverishment of millions of Africans, as church leaders accumulate wealth and engage in a brazen display of materialist lifestyles. In return for monetary compensation they promise to turn misery into prosperity and they instill awe and fear into gullible divine-wonder-seeking worshippers, often by organizing false witnesses to validate their pretenses of divine power and charisma. They sell fake religious items purported to have been blessed with spiritual powers to turn misery into joy and bring physical and spiritual healing. These sham church leaders or pastors conjure up and perform fake miracles and coach willing followers to witness to their awe-inspiring deeds. They recommend excessive fasting, asceticism, and abstinence from food which becomes detrimental to the health of their followers; in short, they are acting like the false teachers in Ephesus (see 1 Tim 4:1–3). Alas, this is just fleeting religious showmanship of a degrading magnitude and spiritually shambolic acts. It is important to note that the rise in fake and sham ministers and church leaders in Africa has been hastened by socioeconomic challenges across the continent, which are exacerbated by poor and inept political leadership and increasing environmental degradation. Poverty and nonexistent economic opportunities in the continent drive millions of people in Africa into the predatory hands of fake church leaders, whose promises to end poverty and misery result in nought. Be that as it may, this is not the entire story of African Christianity today.

The growth in Christianity in Africa, the continent predicted to be the most populace Christian continent in the world, is buoyed by good leadership and sound doctrinal catechesis, similar to the authorial exhortation to Timothy to embrace good leadership. This growth has been brought about by the vernacular translation of the Bible, the proclamation of the good news of God's presence in the world through Jesus Christ, the personal witness

26. More work has been done on pastoral ministry in Africa that could offer more insights into the context of ministry and leadership in the African church. See Esther E. Acolaste, *For Freedom or Bondage? A Critique of African Pastoral Practices* (Eerdmans, 2014).

of church leaders, the community of faith, and the manifestations of the gifts of the Holy Spirit in the lives of believers. African ministers and church leaders draw their communities closer into the presence of the one supreme God and the saving work of Jesus Christ, thereby diminishing the fear and the potency of witchcraft, diabolical medicine, and the forces that cause cosmological disruptions in society. Scholars acknowledge the efforts of the pastoral letters to establish an organized church identity by both drawing from the cultural values of the Greco-Roman world, and that of the Christian faith. By doing so, a community of the children of God emerges that is uniquely different from the civic and religious associations of the Greco-Roman world.

Turning to the African context, church leaders and ministers have promoted significant transformation in the lives of the people of Africa. Their charismatic leadership in proclaiming the gospel message has drawn African peoples into an encounter with the one supreme God, previously distant to the people of Africa. As a result, African cultures have seen transformation in their relationships with one another and across genders. The experiences of transformation under the good and strong church leadership of African ministers and pastors have led to empowerment of men and women in Africa. African Christianity discerns the ministry of Jesus Christ and the apostles as one of empowerment of humanity against forces of evil that diminish their dignity as children of God. Needless to say that in the mainline Christian denominations, the Pentecostal movements, and the African Instituted churches, both men and women have been empowered to be vanguards of social change in the continent. The signs of transformation and empowerment in the continent are undergirded by an authentic practice of healing and deliverance ministry. The testimonies and experiences of wellness/good health, success, and prosperity are attributed to the ministry and leadership of African pastors and ministers who genuinely nudge believers into encounters with and experiences of God's gift of grace through faith in the power of Jesus's passion and resurrection.

The overarching concern of the author of the pastoral letters is the growing number of false teachers, their heretical teachings, and how this impacts the faith of the community. The apparent desire to organize church leadership and to engage in the proper vetting of candidates for church leadership as outlined in 1 and 2 Timothy betrays the intention of the author to sabotage the ministry of the so-called false teachers in the community. These false teachers are labeled as engaging in teachings contrary to standard doctrine (1 Tim 1:3; ἑτεροδιδασκαλέω). They engage in myths and endless genealogies about the law that are devoid of faith (1 Tim 1:4–8). They promote celibacy and teachings against marriage, and encourage asceticism together with abstinence from food (1 Tim 4:3).

The author of 1 and 2 Timothy called some of the false teachers by name, perhaps to expose them to the wider community and to publicly disclose his denunciation of their teachings. Alexander the coppersmith in Ephesus was called out for causing great harm and evil to the author (2 Tim 4:14). Timothy is warned about Alexander the coppersmith's strong opposition to the ministry of the proclamation of Christ to the gentiles. This summation is based on a similar opposition Paul experienced in Ephesus, as recounted in the Acts of the Apostles. The riot of the silversmiths led by Demetrius in Ephesus resulted in Paul's departure from the city, thereby bringing the ministry of Paul in the city to a premature end (Acts 19:23–20:1). Hymenaeus and Alexander are accused of blasphemy (1 Tim 1:20). They are accused of undermining Christian belief about God, Jesus Christ, and the essence of the Christian faith. A detailed examination of Hymenaeus and Philetus is presented in 2 Timothy 2:16–18 as they are accused of profane chatter that leads to impiety. They are also accused of upsetting the faith of many by claiming that the resurrection has already happened, which the author identifies as a fundamental eschatological error and a heretical position.

The author couches his invitation to Timothy to rise above the doctrinal errors of the false teachers with the language of affection and intimacy, by calling Timothy "my child" (1 Tim 1:18), and "my true child in faith" (1 Tim 1:2). Paul uses the same affectionate expression in his description of his relationship with Timothy in some of the letters identified by scholars as written by Paul. Timothy is a beloved and faithful child (1 Cor 4:17), and he has served Paul like a son to a father (Phil 2:22). The author presents himself as a role model who embodies the true qualities of a teacher of faith. The teacher-and-servant relationship Timothy has established with the author of the pastoral letters is the basis of the invitation to Timothy to practice what he observed about the author (2 Tim 3:10–11). What he has observed and learned from his teacher, then he certainly must practice (2 Tim 3:14). The belief in Jesus Christ will lead to persecution (2 Tim 3:12; 2 Tim 4:5), a point of view that supports the idea that the christological propositions of the early church have generated controversy, dispute, division, and violence in the community led by the false teachers (2 Tim 4:3), and in the society as Christians are persecuted for their anti-imperial beliefs.

Appealing to Timothy on the basis of the bond between him and the author of 1 and 2 Timothy strengthens the invitation to him to become a better leader in the community and fight the good fight of faith (1 Tim 1:18). The good leadership that Timothy is encouraged to cultivate manifests in good conduct, love, faith, and purity of the leader (1 Tim 4:12). The public reading of Scripture, which was the centerpiece of the liturgical life of the early church, is key to Timothy's leadership, which counters the false teachings in the community that is perhaps not grounded on Scripture. Timothy is called "man of God" (1 Tim 6:11), prophets confirmed his divine calling, and Timothy was installed as a leader of the church in Ephesus with the laying on of hands by a council of elders (1 Tim 4:14). Reemphasizing the exhortation to Timothy to "fight the good fight of faith" (1 Tim 6:12) reveals what is at stake in the leadership of the church in Ephesus, namely the essence of the community's faith in the teachings about God and Jesus Christ over and above the impious teachings of the false leaders.

Conclusion

Reading 1 and 2 Timothy from an African perspective, as I have attempted in this chapter, gives prominence to the experience and the faith of Africans in their relationship with God, Jesus Christ, and one another as believers in the ecclesial community. In the effort to contextualize their faith, Christian Africans search Scripture and read 1 and 2 Timothy for a message of hope and growth, and to engage in proper transformation of their social relationships for the flourishment of the human family. On this note, African readers of 1 and 2 Timothy ought to engage the text for liberation and the invitation for change from the status quo of family, social, and ecclesial structures that undermine the humanity of the children of God in the continent. It is an exercise in unmasking cultural imbalances in society so that 1 and 2 Timothy become the tools to promote resistance against the use of Scripture such as 1 and 2 Timothy as a means of oppression and subjugation of men and women. It is worthy of note that Christianity impacts the lives of millions of Africans by determining their outlook on life. For this reason, Christianity is a force for transformation under the leadership of good and faithful ministers who are imbued with the mandate of Christ-like discipleship to lead others into embracing their own invitation to follow Christ to promote equality, dignity, and a just socioeconomic and political life in society.

Further Reading

Acolaste, Esther E. *For Freedom or Bondage? A Critique of African Pastoral Practices*. Eerdmans, 2014.
Collins, F. Raymond. *1 & 2 Timothy: A Commentary*. Westminster John Knox Press, 2002.
Dickson, Kwesi, and Paul Ellingworth, eds. *Biblical Revelation and African Beliefs*. Orbis, 1969.
Fiore, Benjamin. *The Pastoral Epistles: First Timothy, Second Timothy, Titus*. SP 12. Liturgical Press, 2007.
Hayward, E. W. Victor. *African Independent Church Movements*. Edinburgh House Press, 1963.
Huigenza, Bourland Annette. *1–2 Timothy: Wisdom Commentary*. Liturgical Press, 2016.
Joshua, Nathan Nzyoka. *Benefaction and Patronage in Leadership: A Socio-Historical Exegesis of the Pastoral Epistles*. Langham, 2018.
Kalu, Ogbu U., ed. *African Christianity: An African Story*. African World Press, 2007.
Katongole, Emmanuel. *Born from Lament: The Theology and Politics of Hope in Africa*. Eerdmans, 2017.
Mbiti, John. *African Religions and Philosophy*. Doubleday, 1970.
Oduyoye, Amba Mary. *Daughters of Anowa: African Women and Patriarchy*. Orbis, 1995.
Okorie, Ferdinand, and Mark Enemali, eds. *Bible, Interpretation and Context: Reading Meaning from an African Perspective*. Lexington Books/Fortress Academic, 2023.
Orobator, E. Agbonkhiameghe. *Theology Brewed in an African Pot*. Orbis, 2008.
Schreiter, J. Robert, ed. *Faces of Jesus in Africa*. Orbis, 1991.

CHAPTER SEVENTEEN

The Letter to Titus

Dogara Ishaya Manomi
Theological College of Northern Nigeria
Nigeria

Devison Telen Banda
Justo Mwale University
Zambia

Introduction

MANY PREVIOUS AND recent studies have succinctly argued and demonstrated that the letter to Titus is primarily an ethical letter—a letter on ethics, of ethics, and for ethics.[1] This means that the letter to Titus is primarily more concerned with the behavior of Christians[2] on the island of Crete than with developing or expounding theological issues, even though Pauline theology grounds the ethical concerns and message of the text. Beyond recognizing the letter to Titus as an ethical text, a recent study[3] has adequately described the specific nature of the ethics of the letter to Titus as character or virtue ethics, meaning it is primarily concerned with acquisition and expression of good character in all aspects of life rather than with rules and regulations or dos and don'ts. In other words, the letter to Titus is more concerned with moral *being* than *doing*. Martin Luther had previously realized the ethical and theological value of the letter to Titus, which is why he referred to it as "a short epistle, but a model of Christian doctrine, in which is comprehended in a masterful way all that is necessary for a Christian to *know* and to *live*."[4] In this African introduction to the letter to Titus, we will reflect on its content and appropriate it as a theologically grounded Christian ethical resource

1. See Dogara Ishaya Manomi, *Virtue Ethics in the Letter to Titus: An Interdisciplinary Study*, Contexts and Norms of New Testament Ethics XII, WUNT II/560 (Mohr Siebeck, 2021).

2. To avoid inconsistency in how followers of Jesus Christ are referred to in the early church period and in contemporary Africa, the term "Christians" will be used throughout this chapter to refer to believers in or followers of Jesus Christ across all centuries and locations.

3. Manomi, *Virtue Ethics in the Letter to Titus*.

4. Martin Luther, "Preface to the Epistle of St. Paul to Titus," in *Word and Sacrament I*, ed. E. T. Bachmann, *Luther's Works*, vol. 35 (Fortress Press, 1960), 389, emphasis added.

that helps us as Christian Africans to *know* and to *live* our Christian life in light of our African contexts and realities.

After a brief overview of the historical background of the letter to Titus, we will pay attention to general ethical issues, character ethics, and specific ethical virtues in the letter to Titus, and bring these into dialogue with African contexts. In these various sections, we will identify and discuss specific aspects of the letter to Titus that resonate with African realities, pointing out specific implications such ethical issues have for Christians in Africa today. The understanding of the letter to Titus as an ethical text (and more specifically concerned with character ethics) forms the basis for most of our discussions.

Historical Background of the Letter to Titus

Just as knowing a person's background helps you understand and relate meaningfully with the person, so also understanding the historical background of the letter to Titus as it pertains to its authorship, date and place of writing, audience, genre, and purpose helps us understand and relate its content and message to the African contexts meaningfully.

Titus Among the Pastoral Epistles

The letter to Titus is one of the three New Testament books that are commonly referred to as the Pastoral Epistles (PE) or pastoral letters. Even though we commonly call them Pastoral Epistles today, this nomenclature developed in stages over a long period of time. Thomas Aquinas first called 1 Timothy "a rule, so to speak, for pastors." D. N. Berdot later called Titus a "Pastoral Epistle" in 1703, and P. Anthon of Halle later referred to the letters in a series of lectures as "Pastoral Epistles," and the nomenclature has remained to this day.[5] In recent years, however, some scholars have suggested alternative names like "Mentoring Epistles"[6] and "Letters to Paul's Delegates,"[7] while others have suggested that we say farewell to the unifying term Pastoral Epistles or *Corpus Pastorale* (collection of pastoral writings) because it restrains their individuality and makes scholars treat them as a corpus rather than as individual texts with distinctive voices, despite their overlap.[8]

Even though scholars are greatly divided as to whether these letters are authentically Paul's letters or not, as we will see below, scholars generally agree that the three letters belong to the Pauline tradition, commonly called *Corpus Paulinum* (collection of writings from the Pauline tradition). Some scholars hold the opinion that the PE were written to supplement Acts of the Apostles in the way that they provide a guide on congregational leadership and church well-being, which had started to develop in Acts ostles.

5. Andreas J. Köstenberger, *Commentary on 1–2 Timothy and Titus*, BTCP (Holman, 2017), 5.

6. N. T. Wright and Michael F. Bird, *The New Testament in Its World: An Introduction to the History, Literature, and Theology of the First Christians* (HarperCollins, 2019), 528.

7. Luke T. Johnson, *Letter to Paul's Delegates: 1 Timothy, 2 Timothy, Titus*, NTC (Trinity Press, 1996), 91–97.

8. Jens Herzer, *Die Pastoralbriefe und das Vermächtnis des Paulus: Studien zu den Briefen an Timotheus und Titus*, WUNT 476, ed. Jens Quenstedt (Mohr Siebeck, 2022), 3.

Due to its smaller size compared to 1 and 2 Timothy and the fact that most of its contents are more elaborately treated in 1 and 2 Timothy, the letter to Titus has trailed way behind the shadows of 1 and 2 Timothy in both academia and ecclesia (scholarship and church). The inadequate attention given to the letter to Titus is not only seen in Western scholarship and the church but in Africa as well. In a recent bibliographic entry of scholarly works on the Pastoral Epistles in Africa[9] one sees clearly that only a few works are based on Titus as the main text.

Outside academic contexts, the letter to Titus is often only referred to in African churches and society during election(s) and installation of church leaders or during campaigns for leadership positions. For instance, within the faith community of Justo Mwale University (Zambia), which has weekly worship services (such as mid-week services and Holy Communion services), hardly does one hear a sermon on the letter to Titus, despite several references to biblical texts during the many weekly spiritual activities. In the past three years, one of the authors of this chapter has observed, as an insider, that in all the various worship services in Justo Mwale University, less than ten people preached from the Pastoral Epistles, and none of them preached specifically from Titus as the main text. This shows that even though the PE are highly neglected compared to other Pauline letters, Titus is even more neglected compared to 1 and 2 Timothy.

Interestingly, in the wider Zambian society, it was during the political campaigns of the tripartite elections of 2011 that some small Christian groups appropriated the list of qualifications of an elder (leader) in 1 Timothy (3:1–13) and Titus (1:6–9) in composing an inventory of what they called "qualifications of a presidential candidate" who can rule Zambia as a Christian nation. Qualifications of integrity, being a husband of one wife, being soberminded, and the like, were listed. The hypocrisy of such a list, however, was evident in the way that the group did not include the expected good behavior of children among the qualifications of the Zambian presidential candidates because the two top contenders for the presidency had at least one child who was alleged to be problematic. Consequently, the general public reacted

9. The bibliography may be accessed via Chuck Bumgardner's (the compiler) Academia page, https://www.academia.edu/101525080/A_Bibliography_of_the_Letters_to_Timothy_and_Titus_in_Africa_2023_revision_. Here are a few examples of some works on the Pastoral Epistles by African scholars: E. Ola Adeogun, "Exploring Pauline Teaching on Piety, Wealth and Economic Management in I Timothy 6:6–10 from the Contemporary African Context," in *Biblical Studies and Economic Management in Africa: Refereed Conference Proceedings of the 30th Annual Conference of the Nigerian Association for Biblical Studies Held at Benue State University, Makurdi, Benue State, Nigeria, 4th–7th July 2017*, ed. O. Dada Adekunle, N. Toryough Godwin, Hope E. Amolo, and O. Berekiah Olugbemiro (The Nigerian Association for Biblical Studies, 2019), 1–16; Samuel Olugbenga Akintola, "Teaching for Life-Transformation in Titus 2:1-15 as Core Duty of Pastoral Ministry and Its Implications for the Contemporary Church in Nigeria," *Asia-Africa Journal of Mission & Ministry* 16 (2017): 19–37, https://doi.org/10.21806/aamm.2017.16.02; Olubiyi Adeniyi Adewale, "Living in the Perilous Times: An African Reading of 2 Timothy 3:1–5," *UBS Journal* 8.2–9.1 (2012): 38–60; Isabel Apawo Phiri, "The 'Proper' Place of Women (Genesis 1, 1 Timothy 2): A Biblical Exegetical Study from a Malawian Chewa Presbyterian Perspective," in *"Walk, My Sister": The Ordination of Women: Reformed Perspectives*, ed. Ursel Rosenhäger and Sarah Stephens (WARC, 1993), 24–33; Oyeleke Oluwafemi Babawale, "Godly Training in Titus 2:1–15 as Antidote to Corruption in African Churches," *Practical Theology* 11 (2018): 137–148; Mathias Teepa Bumie, "A Critical Analysis of Pastoral and Bishopric Appointment and Self-Appointment in the African Pentecostal Church in Ndola Zambia Based on 1 Timothy 3:1–7" (master's thesis, University of Pretoria, 2018), https://africantheses.org/abstracts/2037-103668.

negatively to that list of leadership qualifications, tagging the group that composed that list as sympathizers of the then ruling party.

It appears, thus, that Titus is one of the most neglected, or even silenced, writings of Paul, having lost its distinctive voice to 1 and 2 Timothy and often appropriated selectively. Hence, the extent to which Titus is neglected in both Western and African scholarship and church is all the more reason why this chapter is important, as it gives the letter to Titus its distinctive voice rather than reading and appropriating it as an addendum to 1 and 2 Timothy.

Authorship of Titus

Pseudonymity Versus Authenticity Arguments

Recognizing that the authenticity versus pseudonymity debates have significantly defined and shaped the scholarly study of the PE, it is helpful to summarize the arguments of both sides here. From the early church period up to the Reformation it was generally accepted that apostle Paul wrote these letters. This was until Edward Evanson (between 1731 and 1805) questioned the authenticity of Titus and later of 1 Timothy, followed by J. E. C. Schmidt (1804) and F. D. Ernst Schleiermacher (1807), who questioned the authenticity of all the three letters.[10] From that point on, the pseudonymity argument kept gaining more ground, such that a significant number of scholars now regard the PE as written by a pseudonymous author or at least as one of the disputed Letters of Paul.

Six different opinions regarding the authorship of the PE can be identified: first, those who hold the opinion that they are Paul's authentic letters; second, those who argue that they are Paul's letters but were written by his secretary (e.g., Luke or Tychichus); third, those who hold the opinion that someone took pieces of Paul's letters and redacted or significantly edited them by way of addition and subtraction, to their present form (the Fragmentary Hypothesis view); fourth, those who regard the letters as "transparent fiction," meaning a later author with good intentions, who regarded pseudonymity as merely a literary style rather than deception, wrote them to advance Paul's legacy; fifth, those who regard the letters as outright forgeries, arguing that a later author forged the documents in Paul's name with an intention to deceive; and sixth, those who hold to the allonymity or allepigraphy view, regarding the letters as written by a faithful disciple of Paul, without a deceptive intent, but just "under another name," incorporating Paul's original notes and thoughts.[11]

With specific reference to Titus, those who regard Paul as the author do so partly because of the close association between Paul and Titus and the format of Titus that takes the form of Pauline letters with an author (1:1–3), recipient (1:4), greetings (1:4), then the body of the letter. Generally, the arguments against Paul's authorship of the letter to Titus do not seem more convincing than the arguments in favor of Paul's authorship. Therefore, in this African introduction to the letter to Titus, we take the letter to Titus on its own terms, as a letter

10. Jermo van Nes, "The Origin of the Pastorals' Authenticity Criticism: A 'New Perspective,'" *New Testament Studies* 62 (2016): 315–320.

11. See Philip Towner, *The Letters to Timothy and Titus*, NICNT (Eerdmans, 2006), 23–25.

written by apostle Paul to Titus, his dear son in the faith (1:1–4), aligning with the traditional authorship view from the early church up to the Reformation, and agreeing with a significantly large number of contemporary scholars who also find the arguments against Paul's authorship inadequate or unconvincing enough to dislodge the historical view.

Date, Destination, and Recipient(s) of the Letter to Titus

Dating the letter to Titus depends largely on the authorship question. Those who hold the opinion that Paul wrote the letter date it between 63 and 65 CE, while those who hold that a pseudonymous author wrote it date it between 90 and 100 CE.[12]

Titus, a disciple or mentee of Paul whom Paul calls "my loyal child in the faith we share" (1:4) is the primary recipient of the letter, but the letter was intended to be read in or among Christians in the island of Crete, the destination of the letter (1:5). The island of Crete was known for extreme moral decadence, which may explain the letter's strong focus on ethics rather than theology. Polybius, an ancient Greek historian, said it was almost "impossible to find . . . personal conduct more treacherous or public policy more unjust than in Crete,"[13] adding that "so much in fact do sordid love of gain and lust for wealth prevail among them that the Cretans are the only people in the world in whose eyes no gain is disgraceful."[14] Cicero, an ancient Greek poet, philosopher, and historian, also said "moral principles are so divergent that the Cretans . . . consider highway robbery honorable."[15] These nonbiblical descriptions of the level of moral decadence in Crete resonate with Titus 1:12, which affirms one of the Cretan prophet's description of Cretans: "Cretans are always liars, vicious brutes, lazy gluttons."

Unlike many of Paul's companions, Titus is not mentioned in Acts of the Apostles. However, the Titus referred to in the letter is most likely the Titus whose name appears in other Pauline letters with various descriptions, such as "brother" (Gal 2:1, 3; 2 Cor 2:13); "partner and co-worker" (7:6, 13, 14; 8:6, 13, 16, 23); and other references in 2 Corinthians 12:18 and 2 Timothy 4:10. Titus was a Greek or gentile disciple of Jesus Christ and a mentee of Paul (Gal 2:3).

Purpose of the Letter to Titus

Two primary purposes of the letter to Titus can be identified in the text. First, it was written to instruct Titus to "put in order what remained to be done" and second, to "appoint elders in every town" (1:5). The opponents that were misleading the Cretan believers, therefore contributing to the need to write the letter and instruct Titus on what to do, are described as

12. For detailed discussions of the authorship debate from all sides, see, among many others, Lewis R. Donelson, *Pseudepigraphy and Ethical Argument in the Pastoral Epistles* (Mohr Siebeck, 1986); Philip H. Towner, *The Letters to Timothy and Titus*, NICNT (Eerdmans, 2006), 23–25.

13. Ray van Neste, "The Message of Titus: An Overview," *The Southern Baptist Journal of Theology* 7, no. 3 (Fall 2003): 18–30.

14. Van Neste, "The Message of Titus," 18–30.

15. Van Neste, "The Message of Titus," 18–30.

"those of the circumcision group" (1:10; cf. Acts 10:45; 11:2; Gal 2:12; Col 4:11), most likely referring to Christian Jews who insisted on following some of the Jewish traditions, customs, and purity regulations as necessary for Christians.

Genre and Subgenre of the Letter to Titus

As a genre or type of literature, Titus follows the typical pattern of Hellenistic letters. Due to its contents, it is commonly regarded as an "ecclesial paraenesis" (practical instructions for the church) that contains the opening (1:1–4), body (1:5–3:11), and closing (3:12–15).[16] However, within the broad genre of a letter, we find the following subgenres in the text: polemical statements and proverbs (1:12); virtue lists (1:8; 2:2, 3, 5, 7, 12; 3:2); vice lists (1:6–7, 10; 2:12; 3:3); household codes (2:2–10); creedal formulas (2:11–14; 3:4–7); and baptismal hymn (3:4–7).

Structure and Message of Titus

As noted above, the letter to Titus has the threefold simple structure of a Hellenistic letter, comprising the opening (1:1–4), which is the lengthiest opening statement among the Pastoral Letters, body (1:5–3:11), and closing (3:12–15). However, beyond the simple structure mentioned above, we can structure the letter to Titus in terms of the specific ethical tasks assigned to him under the broad task of "putting in order what remained to be done" (1:5). Each of the three chapters contains a specific ethical task, thereby giving a good structure that hinges on the three tasks. The first task is for Titus to appoint elders who have good character (1:1–16). The second task is for him to shape the moral character of all believers in the "household" (older men, older women, young men, young women, and slaves) through rigorous teaching (2:1–15). The "household" here literally refers to the family unit but also metaphorically to the church in Crete as a "household." And the third task is for Titus to train the believers for life in society through rigorous teaching (3:1–15).

Task-Oriented Structure of Titus

We can further elaborate our task-oriented structure of the letter to Titus as follows:

Task 1: Appointing elders with good character (1:1–16)

1. Moral qualities of the elders (1:6): without reproach, a husband of one wife, having faithful/believing children, not accused of debauchery and not rebellious.
2. Moral qualities of the bishop (1:7–8): without reproach, not self-pleasing, not quick-tempered, not addicted to wine, not a bully, not greedy; but hospitable, loving good, self-controlled, just/righteous, holy, disciplined.

16. Philip H. Towner, *The Goal of Our Instruction: The Structure of Theology and Ethics in the Pastoral Epistles*, JSNTSup 34 (Sheffield Academic Press, 1989), 108.

3. Theological (nonmoral) qualities of the leaders (1:9): devotion or passion for healthy doctrine; ability to teach healthy doctrine; and ability to confront those who teach false doctrine.
4. Reason for such leaders (1:10–16): presence of false teachers (1:10–11) and moral decadence of Cretans (1:12–14).
5. Theological and ethical statement regarding the false teachings and moral condition (1:15–16): "To the pure, all things are pure."

Task 2: Training all Christians to have good moral character (3:1–15)

1. Older men (2:2): temperate, honorable, self-controlled, healthy in the faith, in love, and in perseverance.
2. Older women (2:3): reverent in behavior, not slanderers or slaves to alcohol, they are to teach what is good, so that they can exhort the young women.
3. Younger women (2:4–5): love their husbands and children, self-controlled, chaste, devoted to domestic works, good, submissive to their own husbands.
4. Young men (2:6): sensible or self-controlled.
5. Titus himself (2:7–8): standard of good works; standard of integrity and dignity in teaching; healthy speech beyond reproach.
6. Slaves (2:9–10): submissive to their own masters, pleasing, not speaking against their masters, not hiding back anything for themselves; demonstrating perfect trust.
7. Christian "cardinal virtues" (2:11–12): self-control; justice/righteousness, and godliness/piety.
8. Theological and ethical basis of the second task (2:11–12): "For the grace of God has appeared, bringing salvation to all, training us to renounce impiety and worldly passions and in the present age to live lives that are self-controlled, upright, and godly."
9. Eschatological basis of the second task/ethical argumentation or motivation (2:13): "while we wait for the blessed hope and the manifestation of the glory of our great God and Savior, Jesus Christ."
10. Theological basis of the second task (2:14): "Christ gave himself for us that he might redeem us from all iniquity and purify for himself a people of his own who are zealous for good deeds."
11. Reaffirming the second task (2:15): "declare these things; exhort and reprove with all authority."

Task 3: Training believers for responsible life in society (3:1–15)

1. Christians and state authorities/all people (3:1–2): submissive and obedient to authorities; ready for every good work; to blaspheme no one; peaceable; gentle; and humble toward all people.

2. Reason for such attitudes? The pre-conversion condition of believers (3:3): formerly foolish, disobedient, being led astray, serving various lusts and pleasures, living in malice and envy, being hateful, hating one another.
3. Theological basis and motivation of the third task (3:4–7): "But when the goodness and loving kindness of God our Savior appeared, he saved us, not because of any works of righteousness that we had done, but according to his mercy, through the water of rebirth and renewal by the Holy Spirit. This Spirit he poured out on us richly through Jesus Christ our Savior, so that, having been justified by his grace, we might become heirs according to the hope of eternal life."
4. Reaffirming the third task (3:8–11): Speak confidently; avoid foolish genealogies, strife and conflicts concerning the law; avoid a divisive person after the first and second admonition.
5. Final instructions and concluding remarks (3:12–15).

Having introduced the historical background and the theological and ethical structure of the letter to Titus above, we now turn to discussing the contents, paying attention to some ethical issues and how they relate to African realities. We will do this under three major headings: broader ethical issues in Titus and in African contexts; character in the ethical perspectives of the letter to Titus and in African contexts; and specific moral virtues in Titus and in African ethics.

Broader Ethical Issues in Titus and in African Contexts

In this section, we will discuss some general ethical issues in Titus and how they relate to our African contexts, noting the similarities and dissimilarities between the two perspectives. Such general ethical issues include leadership ethics, holistic ethics, and moral exemplars.

Leadership Ethics in Titus and in African Contexts

Leadership ethics in Titus is framed in such a way that it emphasizes a leader's "honorable character in domestic, interpersonal, and ecclesiastical settings."[17] This is evident in the way that all the list of the virtues required of the bishop are more of personal moral qualities than administrative or intellectual competences. *Character* is the main focus, though giftedness is also mentioned at least once. "Emphasis on selection is maturity in character, not riches, position, or ability."[18] However, the male dominance of leadership positions in Titus, though

17. David D. Jones, "Titus," in *The New Testament and Ethics: A Book-By-Book Survey*, ed. Joel B. Green (Baker Academic, 2013), 75.

18. J. Robert Clinton, *Titus: Apostolic Leadership*, Clinton's Biblical Leadership Commentary Series (Barnabas Publishers, 2001), 10–11. Clinton notes that "character, not giftedness, is the foundation of leadership" (10).

similar to leadership positions in many African churches, provides a hermeneutical challenge to today's gender-sensitive culture. Male dominance in most leadership positions in Africa today is increasingly being challenged by the wider culture of our time.

Since the reason for appointing only male leaders in Titus's Crete was to "relate positively to the hierarchical and status-conscious larger society, to maintain their own power and privilege,"[19] it is hermeneutically plausible for us to suggest that African church leadership at all levels today should also include women, in order to relate positively to the gender-sensitive and equality-conscious culture of the twenty-first century, in agreement with other Pauline letters where we find mention of female leaders (e.g., Rom 16:1-16; Col. 4:15). In this case, the male-specific leadership ethics (e.g., a husband of one wife) can be appropriated in its female-specific context too (e.g., a wife of one husband). Applying it in this way makes the leadership ethics of Titus relevant to our twenty-first-century African contexts without compromising its core message of appointing believers (whether male or female) with high moral qualities into church leadership. It is noteworthy that the primary message and concern of the letter to Titus is not the gender of church leaders but the need to have leaders, whether male or female, who maintain the highest level of good character and integrity in their personal, professional, social, and general life.

Holistic Ethics (Perfectionism) in Titus and in African Contexts

The ethical perspective of the letter to Titus is holistic or, to use a technical term in character (virtue) ethics, perfectionist, in two ways: First, in showing that ethics concerns every aspect of a Christian's life. For example, Titus is instructed to show himself as an example "in all things" (2:7); slaves[20] are instructed to demonstrate trust "in all things" (2:10), and the believers are instructed to demonstrate humility "in all things" and toward "everyone/all people" (3:2). Second, it is holistic in the sense that it lists virtues that are expected to be applied in everyday life, without giving a concrete ethos for actions. For instance, virtues like self-control, godliness, hospitality, humility, and being blameless (Titus 2:2–6, 12) are "open-ended" and apply in every aspect of life. Self-control, for instance, could apply in aspects of sexual chastity, control of anger, avoiding excessive drinking or drunkenness, and the like.

Similarly, ethics in African contexts is holistic in that religion and ethics permeate the entirety of life, and commonplace, everyday actions are considered ethically relevant and used in assessing one's morality. For example, how one greets elders properly; squatting down in the Zaar culture of Nigeria and in the Chewa culture of Zambia or prostrating in the Yoruba culture of Nigeria are considered morally relevant to the extent that they are used to determine whether a young person has a good character or not. Similarly, how one respects elders by not

19. Russell Pregeant, *Knowing Truth, Doing Good: Engaging New Testament Ethics* (Fortress Press, 2008), 280.

20. Knowing the sad history of transatlantic slavery, intertribal slavery, and neocolonialism that Africans have been subjected to, this instruction to slaves to demonstrate trust to their masters "in all things" is problematic to Africans. Hence, in appropriating this verse in African contexts, we can talk about it in terms of employer–employee relationships rather than slavery.

addressing them by their names is used to judge if one has a humble character or not. A child who calls his parents or elders by their names is considered disrespectful or arrogant in the Zaar culture of Nigeria and many other African cultures. These two examples of everyday morality in Africa may not be considered as an ethical issue in the Western world, but, as we have seen, it is a significant ethical issue in Africa, agreeing with the letter to Titus in its concern with everyday and commonplace morality rather than dilemmatic morality that concerns itself only with major ethical issues and dilemmas such as abortion, war, euthanasia, and the like.

Moral Exemplar in Titus and in African Contexts

A moral exemplar is a person who is considered a model, prototype, or good example of the kind of right behavior that others should emulate. Both the ethical perspectives of the letter to Titus and that of African ethics have the concept of a moral exemplar, and more specifically, a gendered concept of moral exemplar. In this gendered moral exemplar, older women are to teach younger women how to behave in terms of self-control and other virtues (2:3–5), just as, in most African cultures, it is primarily the role of the older women to teach younger women not only how to behave virtuously but how to do general domestic work.

However, one minor difference needs to be noted. The author of the letter to Titus does not ask older men to teach younger men; instead, he asks Titus (who is presumably also a young man) to teach the younger men the virtue of self-control. This is not common in the African traditional view of a moral exemplar. Moral exemplarity in African cultures is normally based on gender and age in the sense that older women teach younger women while older men teach younger men through the different rites of passage and other activities aimed at character development. In African cultures, both boys and girls have different rites of passage (e.g., puberty rites and marriage rites), which are organized and supervised by older members of the different genders as a means of inculcating good character among children and youth.

Nevertheless, there are exceptions as to who qualifies as a moral exemplar in many African cultures. For example, in Zaar culture, a young person who has a track record of living a morally responsible life or has a position of leadership that places him in a higher societal status than his age-mates, may be considered a moral exemplar to them. This is the sense in which we can still find similarities between Titus being a moral exemplar of self-control to the younger men in the Cretan churches and the concept of a young moral exemplar in African cultures.

Appropriating the concept and practice of moral exemplar in the letter to Titus in African contexts is simple, due to their close similarity. Older women in African Christian communities and churches are to be encouraged to continue teaching younger women good behavior as encouraged also in 2:3–5. Likewise, older men and younger men in leadership positions who have proven to be of good moral character should be encouraged to continue teaching younger men all the virtues that they need to develop good character, in similar ways to the initiation rites in traditional African religions and cultures. However, while the content of the instructions or training curricula changes in Christian materials, the different stages of the rites of passage, such as puberty rites and marriage rites (where the bride and groom are prepared for marriage by the elderly members of both sexes), are to be maintained.

Initiation as a rite of passage in African cultures marks an important point in one's life. Through initiation rites, children graduate from childhood to adulthood. Through rites of passage, many of the virtues needed for personal and social life are imparted and acquired. Michael Jackson rightly says that, in many African cultures, "creation of moral persons"[21] is not left to chance but achieved through initiation rites. By means of the initiation rites, a person acquires new perspectives to life and becomes a "new person."[22] The moral effect of the Christ-event, as described in Titus (e.g., 2:11–14) resonates with initiation rites in African cultures. Just like the Christ-event imparts the right virtues for Christian living, such as self-control, justice, and godliness (Titus 2:11–14), initiation rites in African Christianity can impart appropriate virtues for responsible Christian living in African communities.

Having discussed three general ethical issues of leadership, wholistic living, and moral exemplar in Titus and how they relate to African realities, we now turn our attention to the issue of character as (re)presented in the letter to Titus and in African worldviews, contexts, and realities.

Character (Virtue) in the Ethical Perspectives of Titus and in African Ethics

As noted above, the letter to Titus is primarily an ethical letter, and the nature of its ethics is specifically character or virtue ethics. Character or virtue ethics is also present in many African cultures, but with some significant distinctives from the kind of character ethics we find in the letter to Titus and in neo-Aristotelian virtue ethics which are prevalent in the Western world. In this section, we will discuss selected issues pertaining to character in the letter to Titus and in African ethics, noting their similarities and dissimilarities and appropriating the two perspectives in African Christian contexts. We will discuss selected issues such as the sources of character, moral agency, cardinal virtues, and the tension between individual-oriented and community-oriented views of character in the letter to Titus and in African contexts, respectively.

Sources of Character in Titus and in African Cultures

Differences exist between the letter to Titus and traditional African ethics when it comes to the source of a person's character. In African ethics, three sources of character or virtue are

21. Michael Jackson, *Allegories of the Wilderness: Ethics and Ambiguity in Kuranko Narratives* (Indiana University Press, 1982), 24.

22. Jackson's term; see Jackson, *Allegories of the Wilderness*, 24.

identified: divine source (God, gods), biological heredity, and community. The notion of an inherited character explains why, in many African traditions, an entire family, clan, or ethnic group could be associated with a certain virtue or vice, which forms the basis of how other people relate to them.[23] For example, a certain tribe could be regarded as generally having hot tempers, indicating that they have inherited such a character or that they have acquired such a character through habituation in their family or community. As a result of such notions of inheriting bad character, some parents in Africa would reject the idea of their children marrying people from certain tribes that are associated with certain characters.

However, in the letter to Titus, the Christ-event is the source of character of the believers. The Christ-event is described as bringing about a new life, identity, and character of the believer, which makes it possible to live a life of good character (2:11–14). Moreover, the description of who "we were" but now who "we are" in 3:3–7 also indicates a conception of the Christ-event as the decisive source of the believers' character. It shows a clear demarcation between pre-conversion and post-conversion morality. The emphasis on teaching sound doctrine is, therefore, to enable the believers to grow in their new identity and to develop the character and specific virtues that this new identity has accomplished in them.

Moral Agency in Titus and in African Cultures

The concept of moral agency in African ethics is different from that of Titus. African ethics does not have a sense of divine moral agency or co-agency, even though divine or spiritual entities are always in view. Spiritual entities such as gods and the living dead sanction, reward, or punish moral acts, but do not give special moral capacity or enablement. However, in 2:11–14, the Christ-event effects a new life, identity, and character in the believer, and "the grace"—referring to the moral transformative effect of the Christ-event—continues teaching (with an implicit nuance of empowering) the believer to deny worldly vices and live a self-controlled, righteous (just), and godly life. Such a continuous divine moral enablement is absent in African ethics. Hence, African Christian ethics can learn to explicate the role that our new life in Christ plays in enabling us to live responsible Christian lives, since such a concept is a "blind spot" in African ethics.

Some of the virtues which are taken seriously in African ethics, such as hospitality, kindness, truthfulness, and the like, are also present among the virtues in Titus (cf. 1:7–8). However, the difference lies in the moral agents of the virtues. Titus's list of such virtues often appears as requirements associated with specific leadership or gender roles (cf. 1:6–9; 2:2–6), while in African ethics it is a requirement for everyone in the community, including children.[24] Mbiti notes that professionals in African Traditional Religion, for example, priests and medicine-men, are also expected to be morally upright, trustworthy, and friendly like

23. Manomi, *Virtue Ethics in the Letter to Titus*, 269–274.

24. However, it is worth noting that humility in African ethics is expected of different genders and age groups with varying degrees or shapes, as will be discussed below.

everyone else.[25] This means that most of the leadership virtues in Titus are general virtues in African cultures, which every member of the community is expected to imbue and express in everyday life.

Cardinal Virtues in Titus and in African Cultures

Taking a cue from Greek philosophical "cardinal virtues" (referring to the most important character traits that individuals and societies need in order to flourish), Titus 2:12 lists three cardinal virtues as self-control, justice (righteousness), and godliness. Similarly, the following virtues have been identified as "African cardinal virtues": wholesome human relations, respect for elders, community fellow-feeling, a live-and-let-live philosophy, altruism, and hospitality.[26] In other words, African cardinal virtues are, to a large extent, community-oriented virtues. The standard of any virtue in African ethics is the community. This means that any virtue whose social or communal relevance is not readily evident falls below the standards of African ethics. Even the sense of personal purity which exists in African ethics is socially oriented in the sense that the goal of personal purity is to relate well with the gods, ancestors, and deceased relations, and to participate in the life of the community. When one breaks a taboo and by implication commits abomination, he or she is considered impure and cannot relate well with the community and the gods or the "living-dead."[27] Therefore, such a person has to be purified via the prescribed sacrifices, after which one regains his or her purity and social relations are restored.

Nevertheless, the cardinal virtues in the letter to Titus and in African cultures are similar in the sense that, to a large extent, they both present moral virtues compared to physical (e.g., beauty, strength, height) or intellectual virtues (e.g., knowledge and intelligence).[28]

Personal-Based Versus Community-Based Ethics in Titus and in African Cultures

One of the major differences between the ethical orientation of the letter to Titus and that of African cultures is their personal versus communal outlook toward morality, respectively. While ethics in the letter to Titus is not divorced from its communal aspect, it tends to focus more on personal character formation and function (e.g., self-control in Titus 2:1–10 is primarily a personal virtue), while in African ethics, the focus is on communal ethical formation and function. This communal orientation to ethics in Africa, though praiseworthy, is not

25. John S. Mbiti, *African Religions and Philosophy* (Heinemann, 1969), 167.

26. J. A. Sofola, *African Culture and the African Personality: What Makes an African Person African* (African Resources Publishers, 1973), 66–123.

27. See Mbiti, *African Religions and Philosophy*, 46.

28. See Robin W. Lovin, *An Introduction to Christian Ethics: Goals, Duties, and Virtues* (Abingdon Press, 2011), 199–204, for a discussion on the different kinds of virtues such as intellectual, moral, and theological virtues.

without its weaknesses. It has been rightly observed that the primary weakness of the sense of community in African cultures and ethics lies in its discriminatory aspects.[29]

The disadvantage of the community-based ethics in most African cultures is that an entire community could be unjustly and generally stereotyped with certain vices (We also see this in the collective description of Cretans by the Cretan poet in 1:12., which Titus acknowledges is a true saying). As noted above, this affects one's attitude to people from such communities, as exemplified in the cases of parents or families unanimously hindering their children from marrying a spouse from certain families and tribes because they are stereotyped with certain bad character traits. An African Christian ethics, in light of the message of Titus, would concede and accept that even if it were true that the individuals in such stereotyped groups shared in certain acquired bad character traits, the power of the Christ-event defines a new identity, character, and entire life (cf. the "we were . . ." now "we are . . ." rhetoric of 3:3–7; 2:11–14) of individuals and renders such stereotypes invalid and obsolete. Even if bad character is hereditary or one acquires it by being in a certain family or clan, the character of individuals could change positively and keep developing. It is un-Christian, therefore, to perpetuate pre-Christian and in some cases, myth-inspired stereotypes against certain groups of people without making room for the transforming power of the new life in Christ (Titus 3:3–7, cf. 2 Cor 5:17) or at least for a possibility of individual differences. An African Christian ethics would concede this unchristian African tradition and accept that character or virtue is basically an individual and not a community phenomenon, which finds (or should find) expression in the community. In this way, African Christian ethics promotes respect for every person irrespective of their family or tribal background and promotes communal harmony and flourishing.

In this same vein, in light of the ongoing ethno-religious crises and loss of many lives and properties in Nigeria and many other parts of Africa, an African Christian character ethics would redefine its boundaries of what a community is. Christian Africans need to see beyond the local definition of community which restricts itself to one's clan, ethnic group, or family. They are to have a broader view of community that transcends not only the people in their church denomination, ethnic group, or religion, but one that recognizes everyone as part of the human community. In other words, the community fellow-feeling (sense of togetherness) of African ethics should be redefined to include both the faith and human communities, and one's sense of fellow-feeling should include the two broad aspects of immediate and wider human community. This agrees with the two-layered sense of community in Titus: faith community and human community. It is from the two-community perspective that the author encourages the Cretan believers to be subject to authorities, to be ready for "every good work" for everyone (including non-Christians), and to live lives that earn the respect of outsiders (3:1–2).

Moreover, Christian Africans can learn something from the overall goal of the letter to Titus. Scholars almost entirely agree that the letter to Titus and 1 and 2 Timothy were written

29. Paulinus I. Odozor, *Morality Truly Christian, Truly African: Foundational, Methodological, and Theological Considerations* (University of Notre Dame Press, 2014), 244.

to negotiate the place of early Christians in the world due to the delay in an imminent parousia that had characterized Pauline Christianity, but without compromising the central message of their faith in Christ. In this way, the letter to Titus becomes a model for us Christian Africans to continually (re)define our place in Africa, remaining relevant within our immediate faith communities and in the wider African community. To this extent, we will respect the humanity of everyone and relate to everyone in love, peace, and justice. This is what is truly "useful and profitable to everyone" (Titus 3:8).

Jens Herzer applies the message of Titus 3:8 to the issue of communal reconciliation, especially with the former members of the German communist secret service known as the Stasi, after the political reunification of Germany in 1989.[30] Herzer shows that communal reconciliation is what is useful for the common good; in other words, what is truly "useful and profitable to everyone" (Titus 3:8). We could appropriate Herzer's message in Africa in the context of forgiveness and reconciliation between ethnic or religious groups, between which there have been crises and loss of lives and properties. Forgiveness and reconciliation is possible in the light of, or as a result of, the new life, character, and identity we have in Christ as individuals and as African Christian communities. Even though ethnic and religious conflicts in Africa often involve both Christians and non-Christians, a change in attitude and commitment to forgiveness and reconciliation among Christians would be an important step and significant contribution toward reconciliation and peaceful coexistence in Africa. This cross-border[31] or intertribal sense of community fellow-feeling will contribute to a peaceful and egalitarian coexistence with neighboring communities and people of different faiths. In the Middle-Belt and northern parts of Nigeria, which have persistently suffered from ethno-religious conflicts, this understanding will usher in the much-needed reconciliation, healing of relationships and bringing love and peaceful coexistence to the region.

Having discussed the form and function of character or virtue, such as the sources of character, moral agency, cardinal virtues, and the individual versus communal orientations of ethics in the letter to Titus and how they relate to African realities, we now turn to discussing specific moral virtues mentioned in the letter to Titus and their points of connection and departure from African realities.

Specific Moral Virtues in Titus and in African Ethics

In this section, we will take specific ethical virtues in the letter to Titus, such as justice, godliness, self-control, and humility, and discuss them in light of the African realities, noting the similarities, differences, and how to appropriate them in African Christian contexts.

---

30. See Jens Herzer, "'These Things Are Excellent and Profitable to Everyone' (Tit.3:8): The Kindness of God as Paradigm for Ethics," in *Character Ethics and the New Testament: Moral Dimensions of Scripture*, ed. Robert L. Brawley (Westminster John Knox Press, 2007), 134.

31. This term in this context is inspired by a title of an article by Michael Theobald. See Michael Theobald, "'Lauter Milde allen Menschen gegenüber!' (Tit 3,2): Grenzüberschreitendes Ethos in Pastoralbriefen," in *Biblical Ethics and Application*, WUNT 384, ed. Ruben Zimmermann and Stephen Joubert (Mohr Siebeck, 2017), 305.

Justice (Righteousness) in Titus and in African Cultures

Among the four Greek-philosophical cardinal virtues (justice, prudence, temperance, courage), prudence and justice are related to the habits that an individual develops for making right judgments, unlike temperance and courage which are related to controlling various kinds of desires.[32] Justice simply means giving each person his or her due. It also refers to the equal or fair distribution of burdens and benefits among individuals and groups in a community.[33] In contemporary discourse, justice is often associated with politics and political leaders in relation to the distribution of goods and services. However, in virtue ethics, as inspired by its Greco-Roman roots, justice is equally an individual virtue, which individuals are to acquire and express in everyday life.[34]

Justice in the letter to Titus conveys nuances of both the political and individual aspects. For example, the political nuance is expressed in naming justice as a quality required of a leader or bishop (1:8), while the individual nuance is expressed in naming justice among the virtues in which the "grace" teaches believers to live (2:12; cf. 3:3–7). However, considering the fact that the bishop is "to be" just—implying "being" more than "doing" and character more than actions—the individual nuance is more represented in Titus than the political nuance.

In appropriating the concept of justice in Titus in African ethics, both the individual and political nuances of virtue are to be equally emphasized. The individual aspect of justice emphasizes how Africans are to learn to strike a good balance between work and leisure, temperance and courage, and so on.[35] It also teaches Africans how to strike a fine balance between the place of the community and that of the individual, between respect for elders and hypocrisy, between demanding respect from a wife and younger ones and being a burden to them, between age and respectability, between privileges and humility, and similar balances that need to be made.

The political nuance of justice relates to judicial and distributive justice in terms of ensuring that human rights are respected, ensuring gender equality, providing equal access to education, fighting against domestic violence and child labor, and fighting for freedom of expression and association. Political justice in Africa should also include an insistence on the equitable distribution of communal resources, such as land, infrastructure, and political appointments; fighting against ethno-religious discrimination and violence, and similar vices; and the fair distribution of goods and services. Such a just and balanced life at individual and communal levels can lead to both individual and community flourishing in Africa.

Godliness in Titus and in African Cultures

While godliness or piety in the letter to Titus is an inner disposition and attitude that the Christ-event accomplishes in the believer's life, African ethics views piety as an external action

32. Lovin, *An Introduction to Christian Ethics*, 191.
33. Lovin, *An Introduction to Christian Ethics*, 191.
34. Lovin, *An Introduction to Christian Ethics*, 191.
35. Lovin, *An Introduction to Christian Ethics*, 191.

of reverence toward the gods, ancestors and totems in specific consecrated places and times. Piety in African ethics also involves faithfully fulfilling religious rituals. The author of Titus adapts the Greco-Roman concept of piety and widens it to include the nuances of "godliness" as understood in the Christian tradition. He appropriates a concept of godliness which realigns faith, knowledge, and corresponding conduct.[36]

African ethics, however, has a limited concept of piety. It does not include the nuance of an inner disposition that is found in the letter to Titus, neither does it have a concept that aligns faith, knowledge, and conduct simultaneously. Traditional African religions focus more on religious acts such as sacrifices and rituals than on a personal relationship with divine beings, as found in Christianity. Hence, an African Christian account of godliness would adopt the concept of godliness as, first of all, an inner disposition or attitude of respectability, but which shows itself in corresponding external behavior, grounded in the Christ-event.

The prevalence of the rule- or law-based attitude of reverence toward God among Christians in Africa today can be said to be a carryover of African Traditional Religions where people think worshiping the gods or reverence to ancestors is basically obeying their instructions or carrying out some prescribed sacrifices properly. As a result, people think that when they give tithes, offerings, or attend church services, they have paid God his dues for the day or week, after which they are free to live the way they like. But Titus's concept of godliness as an internal virtue of reverence with corresponding conduct in daily life challenges this attitude among some Christian Africans. Unlike their external rule- and sacrifice-based relationship with the God or gods of African Traditional Religions, the Christ-event effects an inner change of character, therefore calling for reverence and conduct that is based on a genuine inner and spiritual relationship with God through Christ. External activities of piety are virtuous only to the extent that they express an inner attitude of genuine reverence to God. In addition, external conduct of respect for elders, religious leaders, and indeed everyone is only virtuous to the extent that it corresponds with an inner attitude of respect. In this case, a person cannot "pay God his dues" unless his or her external actions align with his or her inner character.

Moreover, African religious practices of offering different kinds of material sacrifices to appease the gods, spirits, or ancestors when one breaks their rules differ from the once-and-for-all sacrifice of Christ in and through the Christ-event, as seen in 2:11–4 and 3:3–7. Such practices in African cultures have been carried over into many Christian churches in Africa today, characterized by frequent "sacrifices" in the form of "seed-sowing" to pastors, prophets, and apostles for prayers for forgiveness, breakthrough, and fortune. Christians in Africa can learn from the message of Titus such as in 3:3–7 that, when they sin, they only need to repent, ask God for forgiveness, and trust that they are forgiven without having to do something concrete or give any material sacrifice to any church leader to access or secure forgiveness for their wrong. In certain contexts where restitution is possible it is helpful to restitute as a way of restoring trust and giving assurance of change.

---

36. Towner, *The Goal of Our Instruction*, 152.

Understanding the nature of the God that Jesus Christ reveals will save many Africans from a "fear-full" rather than a "faith-full" relationship with God. The God Jesus reveals is a loving God and Emmanuel who is with us (including when we have done wrong), and not a "vengeful Other."[37] And since God is love, "Christian morality is a responsive ethic. It is a morality of love . . . it is a morality that responds to love," both to God and to others.[38] Hence, Christian Africans need not live in fear of doing wrong and receiving God's vengeful punishment. Instead, they are to live in faith, free from a religious narrative that has tied them down to fear and a restless effort to "win God's favor," into a narrative of a loving, gracious, and forgiving relationship with God, which the Christ-event has made possible (1:1–3; 2:11–14; 3:3–7).

Self-Control in Titus and in African Cultures

The concept of self-control among the Kuranko people of Sierra Leone neatly illustrates how self-control is understood in many African cultures. Through initiation rites, one is taught the virtue of self-control. The person learns to control his/her feelings, thoughts, and actions, thereby achieving "steadiness of mind and body."[39] Unlike Western cultures, where self-control is an individual achievement and a mark of excellence, self-control in African cultures is "always regarded as an aspect of social order, not as a means of self-aggrandizement."[40] In this case, self-control is closely associated with upholding communal values and laws.[41]

The letter to Titus provides a model of how Christians can appropriate the philosophical concept of self-control in specific contexts. The Greco-Roman concept of self-control is appropriated in Titus by "de-selfing" the "self," giving room for both the human and divine cooperation in living a self-controlled life (2:12: "the grace" teaching "us" to say no to ungodliness and to live self-controlled, just, and godly lives). As noted above, African ethics does not have the notion of divine agency in moral agency. Hence, Titus's concept of co-moral agency could be appropriated into African ethics, showing that the Christ-event not only saves but also teaches and enables the believer to continuously live a self-controlled life. In this way, Christian Africans learn to develop the consciousness of divine enablement for everyday morality, thereby not depending on their own efforts alone but always trusting in God to help them live morally responsible lives.

"Good Works" in Titus and in African Cultures

Even though it is called "good works," implying *doing* more than *being*, the understanding of "good works" in the letter to Titus is not really oriented toward *doing* but *being*. African ethics,

37. Odozor, *Morality Truly Christian, Truly African*, 204–205.

38. Odozor, *Morality Truly Christian, Truly African*, 204–205.

39. Jackson, *Allegories of the Wilderness*, 24–25. Jackson's discussions is in the context of the Kuranko people of Sierre Leone, but it is applicable to many African cultures.

40. Jackson, *Allegories of the Wilderness*, 25.

41. Jackson, *Allegories of the Wilderness*, 25.

on the other hand, is strong on doing and less on being, as noted above. Hence, to appropriate Titus's "good works" into African Christian contexts, we need to raise the standard of what is considered a good work from external observable actions only to the ones that correspond with the inner attitudes behind the works. This shows that assessing a good work is not only done by outsiders but also through an individual constantly seeking to develop the right inner attitudes from which their external works flow. In other words, the moral agent strives toward "being," while their "doing" simultaneously expresses and re-affirms their "being." The virtue-ethical concept of "learning to bring out good works" (3:14) in Titus expresses the process of seeking to develop inner virtues and dispositions.

Such a conception of assessing external good works as being good only to the extent that they align with the inner attitude and motivation of the doer poses a significant challenge to many African church and (Christian) political leaders who seem to only do good works "for the cameras" (for public show), as it is commonly said in Nigeria. Many church and Christian political leaders in Africa engage in "good works" in the form of humanitarian services such as distribution of food items to people displaced by wars or natural disasters, sponsoring orphans in schools, and the like. While these acts are good in themselves, if the motive is mainly to win votes, cover up their corruption in the form of financial embezzlement, or to make a name for themselves rather than a genuine concern from their hearts to meet the needs of the people, then it falls below the standard of good works that the letter to Titus teaches.

Moreover, the concept of good works that we encounter in the letter to Titus, as emanating from an inner character, without stating the concrete examples of good works intended by the author, enables us to apply it in a variety of contexts in Africa. For example, we can appropriate this concept of good works in the contexts of social and distributive justice, such as, care for the environment (ecology); hospitality to strangers; engaging in conflict prevention and resolution; volunteering social services; providing for one's family needs; and being faithful to one's spouse.

Humility in Titus (3:2) and in African Cultures

Addressing all believers in Crete (not a specific group as with other virtues in 2:2–10), Titus 3:2 says "in all things to demonstrate humility to all men (people)." However, the virtue of humility in the African context is in most cases only expected from younger people to elderly ones, women to men, wives to their husbands, or subjects to their masters. This is not to say that elders, husbands, and traditional rulers are not expected to show humility; the issue is in the undue level of emphasis and expectation of humility placed on younger persons or females compared to older males or those in authority. Humility in African contexts is normally expected and expressed in traditional ways, such as: wives squatting down to serve their husbands food; younger people helping to carry luggage for elderly persons; not "talking back" to an elder in the form of disagreement or quarreling; not calling an elderly person by name; and not maintaining direct eye contact with an elderly person. Observably, all these forms of expressing humility in African cultures are often expected from the "weaker" to the "stronger" person or from the younger to the older person.

Such a one-sided application of the virtue of humility and respectability has been abused in cases where the older ones (especially males) take advantage of younger people or females. It has also instilled fear in those expected to be humble such that they display hypocritical humility. In such cases, for example, younger persons or wives could hardly ask for relief or seek help from older ones or husbands even when they feel overworked, because asking for such may be misunderstood as pride or disrespect. To give a more specific example, in many African cultures today, both husband and wife go to the farm and return at the same time. However, when they return from the farm in the evening, the husband sits and relaxes or goes to socialize with friends, while the wife goes to the kitchen to prepare a meal for the family. Even if she is very tired, the wife finds it difficult to ask her husband to help her with household chores such as washing dishes or cleaning the house while she cooks. So, her remaining quiet and being overworked while her husband sits idly is regarded as humility and respect for her husband. This view of humility is unhealthy in human relationships and promotes dishonesty, inequality, and injustice.

The letter to Titus, however, teaches us that humility is a virtue for all believers and is to be shown to all people and by all people: believers and nonbelievers, women and men, young and old, slaves and masters. Therefore, the letter to Titus teaches us that elders in African communities should not just expect humility from younger people or husbands from their wives. Instead, they should see humility as a virtue that they also need to acquire and practice in their relationships with all people. In this case, elders and husbands should concede their "special place" of privilege that "entitles" them to respect and humble service from the younger ones and women, and learn to equally reciprocate such humble services. Such Christian humility would be seen in how husbands participate with their wives in domestic chores. If one of the reasons for expecting humility from younger ones and wives is to inculcate virtue in them, as it seems the case in African cultures, then such virtues are more effectively inculcated if elders and husbands also demonstrate the same virtues in "all things" to "all people," thereby serving as moral exemplars.

Conclusion

In providing an African introduction to the letter to Titus, we have, in this chapter, paid particular attention to ethical issues in the text and how they relate to African realities under three main sections. In the first section, we discussed broad ethical issues of common concern to the letter to Titus and African contexts, such as leadership ethics, holistic ethics, and moral exemplars. Both in the letter to Titus and in African cultures, a distinction is not made between a leader's personal, professional, social, and general life. Hence, leadership ethics expects the highest moral standards and integrity of leaders, whether male or female, in their personal, family, professional, and general life. In the letter to Titus and in

African cultures, ethics is viewed holistically, meaning that every aspect of life is considered relevant for ethics. Equally, both the letter to Titus and African cultures place emphasis on moral exemplars in the way that older people are expected to transmit moral qualities to the younger ones.

In the second section, we paid attention to the topic of character in the letter to Titus and in African contexts. While in many African cultures, character is viewed as a communal phenomenon, regarded as hereditary, acquired in the family or community, or imparted by divine entities, the letter to Titus shows how character is primarily a personal rather than a communal phenomenon (even though the communal aspect is not absent), and how the power of rebirth and new life of believers in Christ transforms their character such that they live a responsible life in the family, church, and society at large. This understanding challenges the African traditional practice of stereotyping families, clans, and ethnic groups with certain bad character, giving room for individual differences and the power of the new life in Christ to change people's characters.

In the third section, the chapter focuses on specific moral virtues like justice (righteousness), self-control, godliness (piety), "good works," and humility in the letter to Titus and in African contexts. In addition to showing the personal and communal functions of these moral virtues, the chapter shows how godliness and "good works" in contemporary African cultures are largely viewed or done externally as if to "pay God his dues," then we move on with our own lives in our own ways. Hence, Christian Africans learn from the letter to Titus the need to show piety and good works that correspond with our inner dispositions and attitudes, thereby meeting the Christian standards of piety and good works, as well as genuinely meeting the many humanitarian needs in African communities.

In these ways, the letter to Titus teaches Christians in Africa all that they need to *know* and *live* their Christian lives in ways that are faithful to the Bible and relevant to their personal, communal, and societal contexts and realities in Africa.

Further Reading

Akintola, Samuel Olugbenga. "Teaching for Life-Transformation in Titus 2:1-15 as Core Duty of Pastoral Ministry and Its Implications for the Contemporary Church in Nigeria." *Asia-Africa Journal of Mission & Ministry* 16 (2017): 19–37.

Babawale, Oyeleke Oluwafemi. "Godly Training in Titus 2:1–15 as Antidote to Corruption in African Churches." *Practical Theology* 11 (2018): 137–148.

Bonnah, George Kwame Agyei. "The Responsibilities of Titus on the Island of Crete: A Replica for the Leadership of the Church in the Contemporary West African Society." In *Ein Meisterschüler: Titus und sein Brief. Michael Theobald zum 60. Gerburtstag*, edited by Hans-Ulrich Weidemann and Wilfried Eisele. Stuttgarter Bibelstudien 214. Katholisches Bibelwerk, 2008.

Bray, Gerald. *The Pastoral Epistles*. International Theological Commentary. Bloomsbury T&T Clark, 2019.

Fiore, Benjamin. *The Pastoral Epistles: First Timothy, Second Timothy, Titus*. Sacra Pagina. Liturgical Press, 2016.

Genade, Aldred A. "A Text-Centered Rhetorical Analysis of Paul's Letter to Titus." PhD diss., University of Free State, 2007.

Joshua, Nathan Nzyoka. *Benefaction and Patronage in Leadership: A Socio-Historical Exegesis of the Pastoral Epistles*. Langham, 2018.

Köstenberger, Andreas J. *Commentary on 1–2 Timothy & Titus*. BTCP. Holman, 2017.

Manomi, Dogara Ishaya. *Virtue Ethics in the Letter to Titus: An Interdisciplinary Study*. Contexts and Norms of New Testament Ethics XII. WUNT II/560. Mohr Siebeck, 2021.

Ngewa, Samuel M. *1 and 2 Timothy and Titus*. Africa Bible Commentary Series. Zondervan, 2009.

Oderinde, Olatundun Abosede. "The Church and the Development of Christian Youths: A Contextual Analysis of Titus 2:6–8." *African Journal of Biblical Studies* 27m, no. 1 (2009): 54–63.

Sewakpo, Honore. "An African's Perspective on Leadership in the Book of Titus." *Ilorin Journal of Religious Studies* 5, no. 2 (2015): 1-22.

Towner, Philip. *The Letters to Timothy and Titus*. NICNT. Eerdmans, 2006.

Yarbrough, Robert W. *The Letters to Timothy and Titus*. Eerdmans, 2018.

Zimmermann, Ruben, and Dogara Ishaya Manomi, eds. *"Ready for Every Good Work" (Titus 3:1): Implicit Ethics in the Letter to Titus*. Contexts and Norms of New Testament Ethics XIII. WUNT I/484. Mohr Siebeck, 2022.

CHAPTER EIGHTEEN

The Letter to Philemon

Endale Sebsebe Mekonnen
Shiloh International Theological Seminary
Ethiopia

Introduction

SEVERAL COMMENTARIES AND New Testament introductions have devoted adequate coverage to the introduction to the letter to Philemon. Scholars attempt to deal with the letter in terms of different perspectives and facets.[1] This chapter does not reiterate every aspect of these introductions; rather, it focuses only on those areas that are crucial for understanding the letter. The major purpose of chapter work is to contextualize the message of the letter for African realities and to provide an example of how an African reader can apply the text to convey the message of the gospel in an African context. However, I will address only one key theme of the letter, as its brevity limits the number of themes one can extract from it. Although forgiveness, reconciliation, participation, and identity reflect the theology of the letter this can be subsumed under reconciliation. Therefore, I am convinced that the letter's message can be grasped through one key theme—reconciliation—and can be contextualized for an African reader.

Introductory Matters

In this section, I will briefly discuss introductory matters, that is, authorship, audience, place and date of composition, and occasion of the letter.

Authorship and Audience

The letter to Philemon is the shortest letter in the Pauline corpus, composed of only 335 Greek words. Scholars generally agree that Paul wrote the letter (v.19), with the exception of Ferdinand Christian Baur, who first questioned the letter's apostolic origin.[2] However, some think that Timothy was also a cowriter, whereas others believe that Paul included him simply as a companion or courtesy.[3] As to the recipient, while the majority of scholars conclude that the primary addressee is Philemon, who hosted the church in his house, John Knox argues for

1. D. Francois Tolmie, ed., *Philemon in Perspective: Interpreting a Pauline Letter* (De Gruyter, 2010).

2. Ferdinand Christian Baur, *Paul, the Apostle of Jesus Christ: His Life and Work, His Epistles and Teachings* (Hendrickson Publishing, 2003), 80–81.

3. Douglas J. Moo, *The Letters to the Colossians and to Philemon* (Eerdmans, 2008), 323.

Archippus as the primary addressee of the letter.[4] The former view depends on the pattern of letter writing in the Greco-Roman world, arguing that the first person mentioned in a letter that includes more than one name in the greeting section is the addressee. The latter view argues that Archippus, whose name is the closest antecedent to the phrase "your house," should be the primary addressee (v. 2). Further, Knox contends that Philemon was not a resident of Colossae but of Laodicea, and a leader of all the Lycus valley churches; therefore, he was only instrumental in handing over the letter to Archippus, who was the owner of Onesimus and the house where the church was gathering. Although Knox's reconstruction is possible, some scholars reject his reconstruction, primarily based on Paul's contemporary letter-writing pattern, which places the primary addressee in the first line if the letter contains lists of names in the greeting section.

Despite admitting Philemon as a primary addressee, there is still an unresolved question regarding the roles of Apphia and Archippus, who are mentioned in Paul's greeting. There are some speculations around them. Some believe Apphia was Philemon's wife and Archippus their child, while others think she was a wealthy benefactor who supported the church in Philemon's household. It is uncertain whether these individuals listed in the letter can be definitively identified, as there is a lack of concrete external evidence to determine their identity and role. The only information available is that Paul briefly stated their names. It is likely that Archippus, like Timothy, served as a colleague in spreading the gospel; and that Apphia served much like Phoebe. This conjecture is plausible, because if Apphia were the wife and Archippus the child, Paul would have employed the second-person plural "your house" as he did when referring to the married couple Priscilla and Aquila in his writings in Romans 16:3–5 and 1 Corinthians 16:19. What, then, is the reason for their inclusion in the greetings? They are most likely the secondary recipients, whereas the church is the broader recipient. Therefore, even though the letter is primarily directed toward Philemon, making it "private," it appears to have a community or semi-public function. This is evident from the greetings, which address more than one individual, and the closing, which includes specific names of those who should receive Paul's greetings and intentions.

Place and Date of Composition

There is disagreement over the date and place of the writing, although Paul indisputably authored the letter during his period of imprisonment. Undoubtedly, Paul encountered multiple imprisonments during his ministry. Therefore, there are many alternatives available: Acts 28:11–31 makes reference to Rome during the 60s, but the distance between Rome and Colossae, the intended destination of the message, was about two thousand kilometers, making it very difficult to travel.[5] Another alternative is found in Romans 16:7, 1 Corinthians 15:3, 16:8–9, and 2 Corinthians 1:8, which record that Paul's imprisonment occurred in Ephesus

4. John Knox, *Philemon Among the Letters of Paul: A New View of Its Place and Importance*, rev. ed. (Abingdon Press, 1959), 57.

5. Batanayi I. Manyika, "Philemon: A Transformation of Social Orders" (PhD diss., South African Theological Seminary, 2019), 124.

in the mid-50s. However, Acts 19:21–41 does not make any reference to imprisonment. According to Acts 23:31–35, there is a reference to Paul's imprisonment in Caesarea, which is around 800 kilometers away from Colossae, in the late 50s. The issue is further complicated as there is a lack of consensus regarding the recurrence of imprisonments of Paul in Rome. It is believed that there were two occasions, one in the early and the other in late 60s, whereas others think that it occurred only on one occasion in the early 60s. With all these uncertainties, Rome, Ephesus, and Caesarea are alternative places of writing, but Ephesus and Rome are the two main competitors.[6] Unless one intends to outline the life and ministry of Paul, any decision does not seriously impact the theme of the letter.

Occasion of the Letter and Interpretation Issues

Although one of the key determinants for the interpretation of the letter is its occasion, it remains challenging to identify. Some clues in the text suggest, however, that Onesimus is Philemon's slave (v. 16) who had wronged him (vv. 18–19) and separated from him (v. 15), and was once deemed useless (v. 11). But converted by Paul, Onesimus became valuable to Paul (vv. 10–11), which prompted Paul to request Philemon to receive him as a brother (v. 16). Despite these clues about the occasion of the letter, scholars have proposed several theories about the relationship of Onesimus and Philemon, and Paul's intention of writing the letter.[7] The dominant view postulates that Onesimus was a runaway slave who stole from Philemon but at some point encountered Paul and was converted.[8] Many scholars, including Ambrosiaster and John Chrysostom, posit this theory, but such speculation was criticized for lack of explicit evidence.[9]

The second theory suggests that Onesimus sought Paul's help to mediate a dispute with Philemon rather than fleeing, but this hypothesis, proposed by Roman Law, is unconvincing, as slaves were generally viewed as property and unlikely to seek mediation.[10] The third conjecture claims that Onesimus was Philemon's biological brother and that they were involved in a dispute; but this theory has not gained widespread acceptance because of insufficient textual support. The fourth hypothesis suggests that Onesimus was sent by Archippus to deliver a gift to Paul, and that this gave occasion for Paul's request to Philemon to forgive and reinstate Onesimus.[11] None of these theories have achieved unanimous agreement among scholars, highlighting a need for further investigation. This introduction, based on the above-mentioned

6. James W. Thompson and Bruce Longenecker, *Philippians and Philemon*, Paideia (Baker Academic, 2016), 61–62.

7. D. F. Tolmie, "How Onesimus Was Heard—Eventually: Some Insights from the History of Interpretation of Paul's Letter to Philemon," *Acta Theologica* 39 (2019): 101–112.

8. Moo, *The Letters to the Colossians and to Philemon*, 367.

9. Tolmie, "How Onesimus Was Heard," 101–105.

10. See J. A. Harrill, "Using the Roman Jurists to Interpret Philemon: A Response to Peter Lampe," *Zeitschrift für die Neutestamentliche Wissenschaft und die Kunde der Älteren Kirche* 90 (1999): 135–138.

11. Knox, *Philemon Among the Letters of Paul*, 17.

textual clues, cautiously suggests that Onesimus was likely a slave in dispute with Philemon, while remaining open to new evidence that could alter this interpretation.

Structure

There are various alternatives for structuring Philemon, but we follow the general structure:

Opening: Greeting and thanksgiving (vv. 1–7)
Body: Appeal to Philemon to reconcile with Onesimus (vv. 8–22)
Closing: Closing greeting and request (vv. 23–25)

The Overarching Theological Theme of Philemon

Reconciliation

As stated above, although some specific themes can be gleaned from the letter, they can be encapsulated within the overarching theme of reconciliation. This theme will be discussed in detail in the following section. First, I will establish the core theme of the letter; thereafter, subthemes such as greetings, redefined identity, embodying sacrificial love, influence of age, participation, identification, and restitution will be discussed as the means by which Paul worked to process the reconciliation between Philemon and Onesimus.

Establishing the Core Theme

There is almost consensus among scholars that the major theme of the letter is conflicted relationships.[12] Alex Hon Ho Ip's socio-rhetorical analysis of Philemon argues that "the letter was deliberatively rhetorical in form, with a clear inclination toward the reconciliation of Onesimus and Philemon in a relationship based on Paul's idea of love."[13]

The words "appeal" (v. 9), "separation" (v. 15), and "receiving back" (v. 15) indicate that there was a negative relationship between Onesimus and Philemon. However, Paul's appeal to Philemon does not identify the reason for this separation. Therefore, determining whether Onesimus ran away, stole something, or received a gift from Philemon is merely a matter of scholarly conjecture. Paul's statement, "receive him back," probably refers to "be paid back in full or to receive in full what is due." If we adopt this interpretation, then it suggests that the separation might have cost Philemon something significant, which is bolstered by Paul's willingness to reimburse Philemon for Onesimus. In addition, Paul's statement about Onesimus, if he "wronged you in any way or owes you anything" (vv. 18–19), implies that there is a probability that such a condition occurred, although Paul was not sure.

12. Alex Hon Ho Ip, *A Socio-Rhetorical Interpretation of the Letter to Philemon in Light of the New Institutional Economics: An Exhortation to Transform a Master–Slave Economic Relationship into a Brotherly Loving Relationship*, WUNT II/444 (Mohr Siebeck, 2017), 24.

13. Ip, *A Socio-Rhetorical Interpretation*, 220.

Thus, we can make two assumptions regarding exegetical and hermeneutical approaches to, and decisions about, the letter. First, the letter concerns the broken relationship between Onesimus and Philemon, which has caused a "separation." Such a separation cost Philemon something he should have been paid for in full. However, the cause of the separation is unknown. We cannot definitively state any scenario. Therefore, the focus will be on how Paul mediated between the parties to heal this separation. Second, Onesimus and Philemon's social status was a slave–master relationship, as Paul explicitly stated in his appeal to "receive him back as no longer a slave, more than a slave, a beloved brother" (v. 16). Such an appeal indicates that a separation occurred in a state of power or status difference between the two, and Paul is attempting to transform the relationship from unequal status to equal status. Therefore, we get as the crux of the letter this statement of Paul's:

> I [Paul] would rather appeal to you on the basis of love . . . [v. 9] . . . for . . . my child, Onesimus, [v. 10] . . . I am sending him . . . back to you [v. 12] . . . for, he was separated from you for a while so that you might have him back forever, no longer as a slave, more than a slave, a beloved brother [vv. 15–16] . . . So, . . ., welcome [receive] him as you would welcome [receive] me [v. 17].

If this is the crux of the matter, then Paul used all of the other information in the letter to persuade Philemon to agree to his core proposal. As the extract indicates, Paul's fundamental concern is the relationship between Philemon and Onesimus. The key words Paul employed in the extracted section convey the meaning of positive and negative relationships. The word "appeal" (παρακαλέω) means to entreat. However, the word is fluid, carrying different meanings depending on the context. BDAG provides five submeanings: "1. to ask to come and be present where the speaker is, *call to one's side*; 2. to urge strongly, *appeal to, urge, exhort, encourage*; 3. to make a strong request for something, *request, implore, entreat*; 4. to instill someone with courage or cheer, *comfort, encourage, cheer up*; 5. to treat someone in an inviting or congenial manner . . . invite in, conciliate, be friendly to, or speak to in a friendly manner."[14] Philemon verse 9 is categorized under the third meaning: to make a substantial *"request for something, request, implore, or entreat."*[15] Paul used this word in many places to encourage, urge, or comfort the Christ-believing group; he has also applied it in the context of conflict as an appeal to reconciliation (1 Cor 1:10, 4:13; Phil 4:2). Although the word carries apostolic authority in many instances, Paul made it clear in Philemon that he does not want to use apostolic authority but presents his appeal on the basis of love (vv. 8–9). Therefore, the word in this context is relational rather than authoritative.

Similarly, Paul uses the word χωρίζω (separate) in contexts where a relationship is in crisis, connoting a negative relationship, whether it is about a relationship with a nonhuman entity or a human relationship, such as separation from Jesus (Rom 8:35, 39), separation from marriage (1 Cor 7:10–11, 15; similarly Matt 19:6; Mark 10:9). Likewise, the author of Hebrews uses it to

14. BDAG, 764.

15. BDAG, 764, emphasis in original.

express separation from sin (Heb 7:26). However, the verb is also used for physical departure from one place to another (Acts 18:1–2).

The word ἀπέχω is a commercial word meaning "to receive in full what is due, to be paid in full, to receive in full."[16] Philemon verse 15 conveys this meaning according to BDAG. However, it is notoriously complicated for scholars to grasp its meaning in this context, and translators generally prefer the meaning to "have him back." Douglas Moo suggests that the sense is commercial: "provide a receipt for a sum paid in full," as used in Matthew 6:2, 5, 16. But he confesses that the word is in an unusual construction; therefore, he prefers the meaning "receive back."[17] James D. G. Dunn also argues that the sense is commercial, but he thinks that it is unclear what "Philemon will receive back: a better slave or a loyal freedman (having been freed by Philemon) and client."[18] Therefore, even though Paul's proposal of compensation in verses 17–19 supports the commercial connotation, Dunn is unable to determine its meaning in this context. David W. Pao acknowledges that this word refers to business transactions in the sense of "receiving full payment" in Philemon, but concludes that it refers to "the full and willing reception of Onesimus."[19]

However, rejecting the commercial interpretation is unfounded, given Paul's use of the term in the context of a transaction in Philippians 4:18. Other New Testament texts also use it in this way, such as Matthew 6:2, 5, 16, and Luke 6:24, as well as statements like "the account is closed" in Mark 14:41.[20] Although the meaning is not as straightforward as scholars would wish, one thing is clear: according to Paul, the purpose of separation is connected to ἀπέχω by ἵνα. The object of the verb ἀπέχω is Onesimus, and therefore, the transaction is happening between Paul and Philemon. Paul is sending Onesimus to rejoin Philemon after a temporary separation, which Paul probably believes that God used to bring Onesimus to salvation. If this is the case, Paul is now passing Onesimus to Philemon as part of a new transaction between God and Philemon, in which God fully compensates Philemon for his loss (commercial sense) by converting Onesimus for salvation and making him his brother forever. In this sense, time and new relationships are the full payment. It is most probable that what Philemon lost was property (Onesimus himself), time, and services (in the commercial sense). However, the transaction was not in terms of services, as Philemon would receive him not as a slave, which signifies service and ownership, but in the value of a higher relationship that is a beloved brother, symbolizing equality, intimacy, and inseparability as a family for eternity, with Philemon losing his ownership as the father of the household in the spiritual sense.

The fourth key concept is προσλαμβάνω. BDAG categorizes the use of this word in Philemon verse 12 as "to extend a welcome, *receive into one's home, or circle of acquaintances.*"[21] In his other epistles, Paul uses the word to refer to Christians receiving others (Rom 14:1;

16. BDAG, 102.

17. Moo, *The Letters to the Colossians and to Philemon*, 420.

18. Dunn, *The Epistles to the Colossians and to Philemon*, 334.

19. David W. Pao, *Colossians and Philemon*, ZECNT (Zondervan Academic, 2016).

20. BDAG, 102.

21. BDAG, 883, italics in original.

15:7a), God and Christ accepting believers (Rom 14:3; 15:7b), and showing kindness to another person (Acts 28:2). The term appears in Philemon in two places: verse 12 and verse 17. In the latter, Paul requests that Philemon treat Onesimus as he treats him because Onesimus is now the child of Paul and Philemon's brother, both of them were born into the family of God through Paul's ministry. Therefore, Onesimus deserves respectful treatment and honor as a family member. In this sense, Paul is making a radical claim to Philemon, saying that Onesimus deserves equal honor not just as a brother, but as a beloved brother. In doing so, Paul transforms the relationship to a higher level and reveals the true meaning of reconciliation.

Therefore, the core theme of the letter of Philemon is reconciliation, though the word is not explicitly stated. Suffice it to concur with Max Turner's conclusion: "Philemon is 'all about' human reconciliation; indeed, probably the most detailed discussion in the New Testament."[22] Hence, there are four key concepts: separation, love, reception, and transformed relationships. Although Paul does not explicitly state the cause of the separation, it could be a divine arrangement for Onesimus's salvation. Indeed, some scholars suggest that the passive construction is due to the presence of a divine subject, in which case Paul's intervention is necessary to bring Onesimus and Philemon back together. Had the word "separation" not implied an undesired relationship, Paul would not have appealed to Philemon to receive Onesimus. Therefore, the separation stems from a conflict, the cause of which readers of today cannot discern; instead, they can only appreciate Paul's efforts to resolve the issue. It is also difficult for the reader to know whether the reunion went as planned or not, except to assume that it did on the basis of Paul's love relationship, confidence, and his portrayal of Philemon (v. 21). However, Paul's persuasive argument to Philemon enlightens the reader about the process of reconciling the two parties. Therefore, for African readers, it is possible to read Philemon in the context of Africa, as conflict, separation, and reconciliation are part of our day-to-day experiences. The next section discusses reconciliation in the African context, based on Paul's reconciliation theme in Philemon.

Reconciliation

The Role of Greetings in Philemon in the African Context (vv. 1–7)

Exchanging greetings is a common practice in all human communities, and each society educates its people on the appropriate manner of greeting others.[23] According to Beata Wójtowicz, the Austin Speech Act Theory categorizes greetings as illocutionary acts and suggests that they should not be interpreted literally, as they are merely expressions of courtesy.[24] This theoretical category represents the common portrayal of Western societies, where greetings are

---

22. Max Turner, "Human Reconciliation in the New Testament with Special Reference to Philemon, Colossians and Ephesians," *European Journal of Theology* 16, no. 1 (2007): 38–39.

23. Ulrich Schiefer, Ana Catarina Carvalho, and Alexandre Costa Nascimento, "Greetings in Africa—Beyond the Handshake: An Essay on Greeting and Leave-Taking Rituals as Communication Practice in Sub-Saharan African Agrarian Societies," *Kwanissa: Revista de Estudos Africanos e Afro-Brasileiros* 4, no. 11 (2021): 90.

24. Beata Wójtowicz, "Cultural Norms of Greetings in the African Context," *Roczniki Humanistyczne* 69, no. 6 (2021): 173.

primarily used to create an atmosphere through phatic communication (i.e., social interaction that serves a functional purpose rather than conveying information or idea). However, in African contexts, greetings, being deeply embedded in our cultures,[25] serve as more than just a courteous gesture or phatic communication; they are a means of conveying ideas.[26] They convey a message of peace, express acceptance and reconciliation, foster fellowship, demonstrate care and consideration for others, provide a means of obtaining relevant information about the community, and show appreciation for others, which we will elaborate on in the next section.

Africans value greetings, for they provide an occasion to discuss matters dearly valued by both parties, that is, the greeter and the greeted. This is time invested for reflecting core values by acquiring information about the state of health and welfare of family, loved ones, or household of the greeted, neighbors, wider community, livestock, and farms. It is the time for expressing sympathy and sharing burdens if the greeted one is facing challenges. If possible, it is an occasion to collaboratively discover solutions for challenges. For example, in rural Ethiopian communities, greetings differ during the rainy season, which is a challenging period characterized by natural calamities and crop scarcity.[27] The occasion of greeting someone includes discussions not only on familial affairs, but also on specific information regarding livestock, farming, neighbors, and the wider community. However, the nature of such greetings varies based on the kind of ethnic group, with each group having a distinct focus. For example, in Amhara and Oromo cultures, the primary emphasis is placed on a person's well-being, family, agriculture, livestock, and community. On the other hand, Wolayita and Nuer greetings specifically highlight the importance of peace.[28]

Likewise, Paul's greeting is not just mechanical courtesy; rather it is specifically dedicated for important matters valued by himself and his addressee's context. Through his greetings, he expresses his specific concern and values related to individuals, the believing community, and his main topic. In Philemon, his greeting is both at the personal and community levels. At the personal level, he uses relational expressions: Timothy as "our brother," Philemon as "our beloved," and "coworker" (v. 1), Apphia as "our sister" and Archippus as a "our co-soldier" (v. 2), and the church (v. 1–2). A similar concept is found in the conceptual extension of the greeting section into the body, such as "brother" (v. 7), "old man" (v. 9), "my child" (v. 10), "to you and to me" (v. 11), "my own heart" (v. 12), and "beloved brother" (vv. 16, 20). Paul also informs the community of his current personal challenges that is, as "a prisoner for Christ Jesus" (v. 1). These phrases convey critical values such as familial relationships (our brother, our sister, my child), love (beloved), teamwork (coworker and co-solder), community (the church). In so doing, Paul emphasizes interpersonal connections, particularly the core value of love (vv. 1, 5, 7, 9); and at a community level, he expresses concern for the well-being of the believing community (vv. 1–2).

25. E. Y. Egblewogbe, "Social and Psychological Aspects of Greeting Among the Ewes of West Africa," *Research in Review* 6, no. 2 (1990): 9.

26. Wójtowicz, "Cultural Norms of Greetings in the African Context," 175.

27. Baye Yimam, "The Programmatics of Greetings, Felicitation and Condolence Expressions in Four Ethiopian Languages," *African Languages and Cultures* 10, no. 2 (1997): 118.

28. Yimam, "The Programmatics of Greetings," 106.

Both African greetings and Paul's greeting overlap in their purpose in that it is time and space dedicated to reflect on matters that are dear to both the greeter and the greeted.

African greetings encompass not only verbal communication but also physical gestures that show respect and appropriate conduct. According to Yoruba culture, it is customary for younger persons to begin the greeting when they encounter older people, and it is anticipated that women will greet men before men greet them. Physical gestures are also important. In Ethiopia, showing respect and good manners, regardless of gender, involves joining the left hand with the right hand during a handshake and bending one's head. According to Beata Wójtowicz, in West Africa, women display respect for males by squatting when they greet them, whereas younger persons demonstrate respect for their elders by avoiding direct eye contact.[29] Therefore, for Africans, greeting is respect for the Other and public acknowledgement of the worthiness of the Other in the community. Thus, physical posture is a language conveying an important message both to the greeted person and to the community in which the greeted person is residing.

Although Paul's physical posture is not described while writing this section of greeting to Philemon, Paul publicly acknowledges the worthiness of Philemon as the letter was intended to be read for the community in public. Paul concedes that Philemon is a leader of the church in his house, respected in his character, especially about his love and faith, which refreshed all the saints or the members of the church in his house (vv. 4–7). Paul publicly shows respect and love for Philemon, not only in the introductory section of the letter but also in the greeting proper, publicly declaring that Philemon is "our beloved fellow worker" (v. 1). This is not just to boost Philemon's ego through rhetoric but is an honest expression of his respect and an acknowledgement of the worthiness of Philemon to himself and the church. Such public respect and acknowledgment of the Other within the community through greeting is common in the African context, although it is also expressed in physical language. Hence, for Africans and Paul greetings send a message to the greeted and to the community about the worthiness and position of the one receiving the greeting.

Greetings in Africa also build new relationships and restore broken ones. Africans offer greetings irrespective of whether the person they are greeting is known or unknown to them. For example, the Ngoni of Tanzania, Akan of Ghana, Baatombu of Benin, and the Ewe of West Africa exchange greetings with one another regardless of familiarity.[30] This is not just the experience of these particular African peoples; rather it is the experience of peoples in the majority of African countries. They greet the Other not only to maintain existing relationships but also to build new ones by filling the gap and fostering depth in the subsequent conversations, encounters, and relationships.[31] In this letter to Philemon, Paul is not just expressing appreciation of his relationship with his ministry colleagues in his greeting; rather he is going beyond the ingrained social status to bulwark the creation of a new level of relationship among his addressees; in particular, a new level of relationship between Philemon and Onesimus.

29. Wójtowicz, "Cultural Norms of Greetings in the African Context," 174.

30. Wójtowicz, "Cultural Norms of Greetings in the African Context," 180.

31. Humphrey Mwangi Waweru, "The Power of Greetings in African Christianity," *Athens Journal of Humanities and Arts* 7, no. 4 (2020): 348.

Paul's appreciation of Philemon regarding his love and reputation among the members of the church in his house is an intentional rhetoric that aims at inviting him to a new level of relationship with Onesimus. This unfolds as he goes on to discuss the issue between Philemon and Onesimus. At the outset, Paul is creating a foundation through his greeting to fill the gap of relationship. African readers of Paul discern that the greeting is a call to Philemon to a new level of relationship.

Africans use greetings as a sign of peace and good relationships, as well as a tool for restoring and reconciling broken relationships. For instance, declining to greet a friend signals a strained relationship and is usually interpreted by the community as the existence of animosity, pride, or rudeness. In Ethiopian culture, the act of withdrawing greetings from friends, neighbors, or colleagues carries significant meaning. Observers interpret it as discord or offense between friends, even without additional context, whereas resuming it signifies reconciliation. Paul's greeting, as discussed above, is filled with a relational and communal word, "our," which is repeated four times in relation to individuals (vv. 1–2), referring to the church "your house." This is immediately followed by a benediction of grace and peace from God upon Philemon. Although Paul does not include Onesimus's greeting to Philemon, he uses greetings as a door for reconciliation and peace by emphasizing relationship rather than explicit doctrines to highlight relationship issues in the ensuing part of his letter.

As Wójtowicz rightly observes, African greetings are thought of as a door to every conversation, not just something to set an atmosphere.[32] Wójtowicz provides Yoruba and Egblewogbe as an example, but this is the normal daily exercise of the majority of Africans, using greetings as a door to every crucial conversation, especially with regard to the issue of reconciliation and restoration. Greetings are not only used at the beginning of conversations of reconciliation; every occasion for reconciliation and restoration of relationships is also concluded with greetings as a symbolic expression of that reconciliation. For instance, in Ethiopia, reconciliation is normally concluded with the reconciled indivuduals greeting one another and the intermediaries as the practical sign of the reconciliation that has taken place. Paul uses greetings not only at the beginning of his letter but also at the end as the conclusion of his message to Philemon, although we do not see Onesimus greeting Philemon. For African readers, this greeting smoothly resonates in their cultures since they use greetings as the conclusion to an intense conversation of reconciliation.

Everyday verbal and nonverbal greetings in Africa convey messages that foster communal togetherness, harmony, reconciliation, and healthy relationships. Therefore, greetings have a substantial impact on fostering mutual coexistence with high regard for the Other, despite gender, status, and the otherness of the Other. Essentially, African greetings go beyond mere phatic communication to embody relationships that entail respect, care, and affirmation of the Other on a daily basis. Similarly, Paul's greetings go beyond phatic communication to initiate reconciliation, show respect, acknowledge the other in public, and foster a new level of relationship. Next, we will analyze reconciliation through redefined identity, embodying sacrificial love, age influence, participation, and identification. But first we will discuss identity, prototypes, and identity descriptors in Philemon.

32. Wójtowicz, "Cultural Norms of Greetings in the African Context," 175.

Reconciliation
The Role of Identity in Philemon in the African Context

This section aims to establish a connection between Paul's reconciliation in Philemon and African reconciliation through identity. Batanayi I. Manyika thoroughly discussed the role of identity in Philemon, especially focusing on nested social identity.[33] His work focuses on South African domestic workers; however, identity in this introduction is analyzed as a tool for reconciliation for all Africans. First, we will define the concept and theory employed for the analysis.

Defining the Meaning of Identity in the Context of Philemon

Paul uses several identity and relational descriptors in the letter to Philemon. But defining the term "identity" is crucial before applying the concept, given its ambiguity and slippery nature. After studying the current meanings of identity, James D. Fearson concludes that it refers to either: "(a) a social category, defined by membership rules and (alleged) characteristic attributes or expected behavior, or (b) socially distinguished features that a person takes a special pride in or views as unchangeable but socially consequential or (a) and (b) at once."[34] Identity is all about self-definition and perception, either at the personal or social level. Generally, it is "the set of *meanings* that define who one is when one is a member of a particular group (social identity), when one is an occupant of a particular role in society (role identity), or when one claims particular characteristics that identify the person as a unique person (personal identity)."[35] In this introduction, the focus lies on the social identity that shapes an individual's self-definition or self-concept based on their affiliation with a specific group.

Social identity theory (SIT), which was developed by social psychologists Henri Tajfel and John Turner, assists in understanding identity with regard to social groups, especially a *depersonalized* identity based on group membership and a self-concept that is derived from membership in a given group.[36] Michael Wenzel, Amelie Mummendey, and Sven Waldzus have indicated that group members create prototypes, defined as "the ideal-type member of a category that best represents its identity in a given context and frame of reference."[37] Some scholars state that "shared membership in a social category justifies entitlement to equal treatment to the extent that it implies psychological equivalence of those included; it suggests, on the other hand, dimensions and standards (in terms of its prototype) for a differentiation of its members or subgroups and their entitlements."[38] Therefore, a prototype is "a positive

33. Manyika, "Philemon," 202–312.

34. James D. Fearson, "What Is Identity (as We Now Use the Word)?" (unpublished paper, Stanford University, 1999), 1.

35. Fearson, "What Is Identity (as We Now Use the Word)?," 1, italics in original.

36. John C. Turner, *Rediscovering the Social Group: A Self-Categorization Theory* (Basil Blackwell, 1987); Henry Tajfel and John C. Turner, "An Integrative Theory of Intergroup Conflict," in *The Social Psychology of Intergroup Relations*, ed. William G. Austin and Stephen Worchel (Brooks/Cole, 1979), 33–47.

37. Michael Wenzel, Amélie Mummendey, and Sven Waldzus, "Superordinate Identities and Intergroup Conflict: The Ingroup Projection Model," *European Review of Social Psychology* 18, no. 1 (2007): 335.

38. Wenzel, Mummendey, and Waldzus, "Superordinate Identities and Intergroup Conflict," 336.

reference standard,"[39] which dictates, "describes and prescribes who one is and how one should behave."[40] Hence, a prototype is a fuzzy set of attributes such as perceptions, beliefs, attitudes, and behavior that define and distinguish a group from other groups in a specific context.[41] The attributes are often ideal and sometimes extreme.[42]

Each group member is seen through the lens of prototypes; therefore, each member is not seen as a unique individual but is depersonalized to be one in the group,[43] in that a fellow group member agrees with group perceptions, beliefs, and behaviors. A prototypical leader is perceived by followers to embody the attributes of the group; therefore, the leader is the personification of the group identity.[44]

Philip F. Esler used social identity theory (SIT) to interpret the letter to the Romans. Instead of using the term "norms," which SIT uses to describe how groups inculcate their unique identity in individual members, he employed the term "identity descriptor."[45] This includes defining acceptable and unacceptable attitudes, values, and behaviors, as well as instructing group members on how to behave in order to belong to the group and share its identity. This section does not aim to analyze how Paul constructed identity in the letter to Philemon. Instead, it focuses on how Paul used identity to bring about reconciliation, particularly by emphasizing self-categorization as an intragroup based on the defined prototype.

Identity Descriptors and Prototypes in Philemon

In the letter, Paul describes individuals he mentions. The descriptions include those of Paul himself, Timothy, Philemon, Apphia, Archippus, the church (saints), God, Jesus, Epaphras, Mark, Aristarchus, Demas, and Luke (vv. 23–24). Paul is the prisoner of Christ (vv. 1, 9), an old man (v. 9), and Philemon's partner (v. 17). He offers prayers for Philemon (vv. 4, 6), expresses gratitude to God for Philemon's good deeds (v. 4), finds encouragement in Philemon's love (v. 7), asserts his authority in Christ to command Philemon (v. 8), makes appeals based on love (vv. 9–10), fathers Onesimus (v. 10), sends Onesimus (v. 12), seeks for Philemon's concession on the matter (v. 14), is prepared to repay Philemon for whatever Onesimus has done to wrong him (v. 19), and concludes the letter with prayers (v. 25).

Timothy, "our brother" (v. 1), is probably the co-sender of the letter to Philemon (v. 1). Apphia is "our sister" (v. 2), Archippus is "our fellow soldier," and "church" refers to the saints who assemble in Philemon's house (v. 2), but no description is ascribed to these persons except that they are the receptors of Paul's greetings. Epaphras is Paul's "fellow prisoner in Christ

39. Wenzel, Mummendey, and Waldzus, "Superordinate Identities and Intergroup Conflict," 335.

40. Michael A. Hogg and Amber M. Gaffney, "Prototype-Based Social Comparison within Groups: Constructing Social Identity to Reduce Self-Uncertainty," in *Communal Functions of Social Comparison*, ed. Zlatan Krizan and Frederick X. Gibbons (Cambridge University Press, 2014), 152.

41. Hogg and Gaffney, "Prototype-Based Social Comparison within Groups," 155.

42. Hogg and Gaffney, "Prototype-Based Social Comparison within Groups," 155.

43. Hogg and Gaffney, "Prototype-Based Social Comparison within Groups," 155.

44. Hogg and Gaffney, "Prototype-Based Social Comparison within Groups," 160.

45. Philip F. Esler, *Conflict and Identity in Romans: The Social Setting of Paul's Letter* (Fortress Press, 2003), 20–21.

Jesus" (v. 23), and Mark, Aristarchus, Demas, and Luke are Paul's "fellow workers" (vv. 23–24); likewise, no descriptions are ascribed to them.

Philemon is "our beloved and co-worker" (v. 1), he is Paul's brother (vv. 7, 20), expected to do the proper thing (v. 8), has love for all the saints and faith toward the Lord Jesus Christ (v. 5), refreshed the hearts of the saints (v. 7), loves the saints (v. 5), has faith toward the Lord Jesus, became an instrument in refreshing the hearts of the saints (v. 7), his love and faith works created joy, and comfort for Paul (v. 7), considers Paul as partner (v. 17), was requested to receive Onesimus as he would receive Paul to refresh Paul's heart (v. 17), and won Paul's confidence in him (v. 21), receives guests, and is expected to offer prayers (v. 22). Onesimus, the key person in the letter, is the heart of Paul (v. 12), Paul would love to keep him to serve him on behalf of Philemon; he was separated from Philemon (v. 15), he was a slave of Philemon, and he should be accepted as a beloved brother (v. 15).

God, who is both the Father of the community and Paul himself, and Jesus Christ, who is the Lord of the community and Paul himself, are both sources of peace and grace (v. 3). God receives prayers and thanksgiving (v. 4); Christ Jesus is an object of faith (v. 5); Christ Jesus unites the members (v. 6); he is the source of authority (v. 8) and the one for whom Paul suffers (v. 9); and he defines the sphere of relationship (v. 16).

Thus, what are Paul's prototypes for persuading or requesting that Philemon do what he wants him to do? The prototypes or positive reference standards are found in relationships and community descriptors: our father, our Lord, our brother, our sister, our fellow soldier, our beloved and co-worker, my fellow workers, my fellow prisoner in Christ, old man, my brother, my partner, my child, and my beloved brother. These relational words are descriptors of intragroup member self-perception, conveying group cohesion. The second group of prototypes are the actions of the people Paul mentions: prayers, good deeds, encouraging others, consensus, restitution, doing the right thing, love, faith, refreshing hearts, and hospitality. As I will demonstrate below, these two facets of the attributes of the group function as the model and foundation for reconciliation.

Reconciliation Through Redefined Identity, Status, and Role

Conflict is a universal experience, and it is ubiquitous in Africa in all its forms: national, local, within communities, within families, systems, states, and individuals.

But Philemon is not a letter written to solve a large-scale problem or local conflict as it focuses on issues between individuals in the believing community; therefore, no claim can be made based on a one-to-one correspondence with the African church's experience of conflict within the believing community. However, we can draw certain useful connections or principles between Paul's context-specific reconciliation methods in Philemon and African traditional reconciliation practices that help African readers. Zartman contends that African traditional reconciliation practices are still alive and practiced today.[46] A practice becomes a tradition if it continues for an extended period of time, evolving within a society.

46. I. William Zartman, "African Traditional Conflict 'Medicine,'" in *Traditional Cures for Modern Conflicts: African Conflict "Medicine,"* ed. I. William Zartman (Lynne Rienner, 2000), 7.

The first most important concept of identity with respect to reconciliation in Africa is the concept of family. African tradition uses family to refer not only to close kinship terms such as brother, sister, mother, and father in order to ascertain sharing common descent, but also to those not necessarily closely related or in physical or geographical proximity; rather it is simply sharing common descent in some way and is used to establish harmony, ensure protection, and foster unity.[47] The modern concept of family in the Western world, which refers only to husband, wife, and children, does not fit into Paul's world nor into an African worldview. In the Roman world, family was a large household in both legal and social terms, which included parents, children, and other relatives, slaves, dependents, freedmen, or clients.[48] In other words, a family encompassed all individuals who are under the authority of their father, whether through natural inheritance or legal decrees. Although the African concept of family does not encompass such a wide community as in the Roman conception, it does refer to a group much wider than the nuclear family (husband, wife, and children). In Ethiopia, *beteseb* (family) can even refer to close friends and neighbors.

In Roman law, the name father was applied to "the ascendant male (usually the father or grandfather) within a family in the exercise of his 'power' . . . over his descendants and property."[49] The father, in this context, was the ultimate source of power and authority. Even Roman emperors were father figures, often referred to as "fathers of the fatherland."[50] In Roman family life, the father's power included the right to punish slaves at will, the power of life and death over newborn children, and the power to discipline even adult children. His responsibility was to provide food and care for all household members while maintaining family dignity. The father served as the family's patron. The father's power and symbolism bound together the family's lineage, integrity, authority, and honor.[51] Family members were expected to demonstrate loyalty to the father and vice versa.[52] However, for Paul, it is about a new family that does not neatly conform to either the prevailing modern Western or traditional African concepts of family, or to his own contemporary norms. Paul's concept of the new family challenges the stereotypical status and role of each member in all of these systems. This challenge holds relevance for all people, since family is a key identity marker and concept in any culture.

The relational descriptors in Philemon can be grouped into two categories: familial and responsibility-related (roles in the group). The former category includes our father, our Lord, our/my brother, our sister, our beloved, my child, and old man, whereas the latter are our fellow soldiers, workers, prisoner in Christ, and partners. All of the descriptions state shared responsibility and intimacy within the family. However, the notion that God is "our father"

47. Kathryn Coe, Craig T. Palmer, and Khadijah elShabazz, "The Resolution of Conflict: Traditional African Ancestors, Kinship, and Rituals of Reconciliation," *African Conflict and Peacebuilding Review* 3, no. 2 (2013): 117.

48. L. Michael White, "Paul and *Pater Familias*," in *Paul in the Greco-Roman World: Handbook*, ed. J. Paul Sampley, vol. 2 (Bloomsbury T&T Clark, 2003), 172.

49. White, "Paul and *Pater Familias*," 171.

50. White, "Paul and *Pater Familias*," 172.

51. White, "Paul and *Pater Familias*," 172.

52. White, "Paul and *Pater Familias*," 172.

does not imply equality, but rather ownership and the family's source. Jesus's Lordship, on the other hand, refers to his leadership as the center of family bonding and unity, the source of authority and responsibility, the reason for sacrificial obedience, and the object of faith. However, among all the other descriptors, "a slave" is anomalous, as it does not speak of equality, shared responsibility, intimacy, or family, although a slave could be part of the household in Paul's contemporary world context.

The letter to Philemon emphasizes the role of a father figure as well as lordship: God, as the Father, and Jesus, as the Lord. These serve as the ultimate prototype leaders, residing as the head of the family and embodying peace, grace, and love for all believing group members (v. 3). However, Paul also claims a spiritual fatherhood position in relation to Onesimus within the family, birthing him into the family of Father God and the Lordship of Jesus Christ (v. 10). Philemon also serves as a patron, hosting the church in his home and welcoming Paul, fathering his own household, in which Onesimus is not a member as a child or an extended close relative but rather as a slave. It is likely that Paul claims spiritual fatherhood over Philemon, despite the lack of an explicit declaration. Therefore, the responsibilities of fatherhood are held by God, Paul, and Philemon himself, who owns a house and is responsible for the church within it. If the assumption holds true that Apphia is Philemon's wife and Archippus is their son, then Philemon assumes the role of a biological father as well. However, Jesus, as the center of unity, establishes a distinct bond within the family system, not by biological kinship or status but because of their unique bond with him and thus with one another.

Therefore, God, the father figure and Jesus the Lord are the ultimate prototype leaders, modeled through the acts of Paul and fellow coworkers, including Philemon. Despite attributing the father role to Paul and Philemon, their membership status transitioned to that of brothers and fellow workers. Thus, as children of God and brothers, they are expected to be obedient to the ultimate prototype leader who has embodied the expected behavior. A tension arises between the household authority, in this case Philemon, and the new family under the authority of the Lord Jesus. Paul is challenging Philemon's identity and role due to the new family perception, where hierarchy gives way to equality. He specifically requests that Philemon accept Onesimus as a brother rather than a slave.[53] Furthermore, Christ's Lordship, as both the Lord of the slave and the master, challenges Philemon's legal authority. The new community challenges not only Philemon's authority but also the "existing social norms within the church,"[54] welcoming slaves and offering them a new status as brothers under one Lordship; thus, Paul is calling Philemon to embody the responsibility of the new community's prototype.

In the African context, a family extends beyond husbands, wives, and children; it also includes other relatives under the leadership of a family head (a father), and it has an important role in the process of reconciliation. One of the ways to resolve intrafamily, intraclan, and interethnic conflicts is through claims of common familial identity. In Igbo, Nigeria, if the

53. Margaret Y. MacDonald, "Kinship and Family in the New Testament World," in *Understanding the Social World of the New Testament*, ed. Dietmar Neufeld and Richard E. Demaris (Routledge, 2010), 40.

54. MacDonald, "Kinship and Family," 40.

conflict is within the family, the community and village should not be informed.[55] According to Ernest E. Uwazie, the majority of the Igbo community prefer to resolve family matters based on family values, especially because exposing family issues to outsiders compromises the privacy of the disputants' association or intimacy.[56] The family ensures that the dispute does not disrupt family unity and solidarity. For instance, the Buems community on the Ghana–Togo border has a saying—"*ortorkeme li temi*"—which translates to "house matter must not allow outsiders to hear,"[57] that is, outsiders should not be privy to household matters. Even a fight between two Buems is a fight between blood relations.[58] Within the family conflict, outsiders are perceived as "enemies," as they could use this opportunity to undermine family security and honor. The family is "us," and those outside the family, whether they are neighbors, villagers, or communities, are "them." Reconciliation among family members is crucial because it does not only maintain peace among family members but also maintains the family's identity, honor, dignity, and unity within the community. In this case, identity plays a crucial role in bringing about reconciliation. This type of identity-based reconciliation applies not only to close family or relatives but also to intra- and interethnic conflict. The weakness of this approach is that it ostracizes the "Other," or "them," who are not considered family, part of a clan, or an ethnic group because it secretly considers them as "enemies."

However, the African Christian reader of Philemon can leverage its positive aspects, as Paul employs familial language such as "brother," "sister," "my child," "my brother and saints," and references to a common Father, God, and a common Lord, Jesus Christ. African churches can uphold the extended family identity concept to embrace the Christian community as the new familial identity. Therefore, the existing African value of family as an identity can easily be redefined in light of Philemon as being children of God under God as the head of the family, who brings reconciliation within the larger family of God for all who believe in Jesus Christ despite their differing family, ethnic, and political backgrounds. This definition allows for its application, but it also challenges the headship of Christian African fathers to redefine the position of their fatherhood as members of the church.

The language of siblingship, particularly when applied equally to both the master, Philemon, and a slave, Onesimus, is a deliberate claim of identity in preparation for the reconciliation Paul is planning. Paul demands that if Philemon remains a member of the group, he should respect the intragroup member prototype. Philemon must also reimagine his position within the church, recognizing God, the Father and Jesus the Lord as the model leaders and head of the family, deserving respect and authority to decide on relationship matters within the Christ-believing community, particularly at the spiritual level. Being a family of spiritual siblings is one of the prototypical attributes of a Christ-believing community that

55. Ernest E. Uwazie, "Social Relations and Peacekeeping Among the Igbo," in *Traditional Cures for Modern Conflicts: African Conflict "Medicine"* (Lynne Rienner, 2000), 17.

56. Uwazie, "Social Relations and Peacekeeping," 20.

57. Ben K. Fred-Mensah, "Bases of Traditional Conflict Management Among the Buems of the Ghana-Togo Border," in *Traditional Cures for Modern Conflicts: African Conflict "Medicine"* (Lynne Rienner, 2000), 34.

58. Fred-Mensah, "Bases of Traditional Conflict Management," 34.

provides equal status to anyone, including slaves, spiritually born into the family by God the Father through the Lordship of Jesus Christ. In contrast to Roman society's prevailing norms, Philemon should embrace the new family membership norms and forgo his exclusive status within the church. This should also manifest in his personal household as a way of life. Although such a perspective is a challenge for an African family head as well, an African kinship-based social system, as Coe, Palmer, and elShabaz indicate, is a "relinquishing of power," as in such a system headship is not ultimately about power but about carrying out duties.[59] Hence, the concept of duty rather than power in African familial headship is probably closer to Paul's concept of fatherhood than that of the Romans, which was more about power and position.

For Paul, reconciliation is not just a matter of resolving the cause of the conflict between Philemon and Onesimus; it is about the transformation of Philemon's values and perception with regard to the Christ-believing community he joined. The change of perception and values about each member of the Christ-believing family also provides the opportunity for the members to elevate each other to equal status so that every member of the family can play an honored role within the new family. The reconciliation between Onesimus and Philemon is not solely about them reuniting to continue their usual relationship, which is common in African traditional reconciliation; rather, it is primarily about the quality of their reunion, which is based on their redefined identities, their new experiences in Christ Jesus, and their new equal status in the house of God, the Father. This challenges an African reader who is ingrained in the African traditional reconciliation system that aims to deal with the cause of the conflict and resume the usual relationship rather than potentially transforming the quality of relationship.

Reconciliation
Through Embodying Sacrificial Love

The concept of sacrifice is integrated in the process of reconciliation in the African context. The sacrifices are substances offered (food, drink, different animals depending on the specific cultural demands of the specific African community) as a gift, and it is a form of communication to ameliorate the relationship.[60] Usually such an offering is made by the offender, for example in the culture of Igbo, Hausa, Zulu, Ganda, Nibwidi, Dagon, Akan, and others it is made to appease the ancestral god or as a token of reconciliation to the offended party.[61] Interestingly, Paul is willing to compensate Philemon for the way he was wronged by Onesimus, which can be perceived as sacrifice from Paul's side (v. 18). Paul's sacrifice in Philemon in the context of reconciliation goes beyond compensation and appeasement of God. African mediators of reconciliation may sacrifice their time, energy, and emotions in the process of mediating reconciliation, which is an expression of love and duty as leaders. The offender might

59. Coe, Palmer, and elShabazz, "The Resolution of Conflict," 17.

60. Coe, Palmer, and elShabazz, "The Resolution of Conflict," 119–120.

61. Coe, Palmer, and elShabazz, "The Resolution of Conflict," 119–121.

sacrifice social status by publicly admitting wrongdoing and the offended by dining with the offender. However, such sacrifice from the offender or the offended is minimal as compared to Paul's request to Philemon to embody sacrificial love.

Paul's first key value and ethos is love, which he addresses both explicitly and implicitly. The first implicit reference to love occurs when Paul describes himself as "a prisoner of Christ Jesus." The word δέσμιος could be read as a descriptive noun, as in Paul, who is in prison. Paul does not use his usual description of himself—the apostle of Jesus Christ. Some scholars reason that Paul was writing to Philemon simply as a friend, while others believe he was requesting a favor.[62] Others assume that Paul is implying that the sacrifice he is requesting from Philemon is not as great as his own imprisonment for the sake of Christ.[63] Still others believe that Paul is describing his commitment, giving a reminder of his sacrifices for the gospel, to compel Philemon to waive his rights; he is aligning himself with the weak, an implicit theme of the letter which can be understood as "the reconfiguration of relationships in terms of the gospel."[64] Many of these possible readings have some contributions to understanding why Paul preferred prisoner over apostle in this letter.[65]

With reasonable certainty, I think that Paul is connecting his own description as a prisoner to the purpose of the letter: to remind Philemon to what extent love for the lost and commitment to the mission of Christ are required from Christ-believing group members who are God's family, particularly from those who are in the leadership. As a result, he is setting an example of sacrifice and commitment, as well as what it means to demonstrate love for the saints and faith in Christ from the outset in his own life and experience. In this instance, Paul serves as a tangible and visible role model, embodying the qualities of love and dedication for the Christ-believing group to follow. He represents God the Father and Jesus Christ, who made a complete sacrifice for humanity's salvation. Paul mentions Timothy, a brother who is likely sending greetings, if not writing the letter, and is aware of the situation with Philemon and Onesimus. In other epistles, Timothy is known for his sacrifices for the sake of the gospel, even to the point of death, and is among the prominent members of the group who stand as prototype leaders among the Christ-believing members, embodying what it means to live according to the values of God the Father and the Lord Jesus Christ (Phil 2:19–24).

Similarly, the portrayal of Archippus as a soldier among the members implies that he faced opposition from enemies and fought for the gospel. Likewise, Paul closes the letter by reminding Philemon that there are other team members who have the same experience of love, and commitment, such as Mark, Aristarchus, Demas, and Luke, who are fellow workers (vv. 23–24). Particularly, Paul mentions Epaphras (v. 23), a fellow prisoner in Christ Jesus, as an *inclusio* (i.e., specific theme idea or phrase is repeated) in the letter, serving as a reminder to Philemon of fellow leaders' commitment and willingness to sacrifice their rights for the sake of the gospel, following their prototype leaders, namely: God the Father and Lord Jesus

62. F. F. Bruce, *The Epistles to the Colossians, to Philemon, and to the Ephesians* (Eerdmans, 1984), 205.

63. Robert H. Gundry, *Commentary on Colossians and Philemon* (Baker Academic, 2010).

64. Moo, *The Letters to the Colossians and to Philemon*, 380.

65. Handley C. G. Moule, *Colossian and Philemon Studies: Lessons in Faith and Holiness* (Fleming H. Revell, 1861).

Christ. Therefore, they are equally prototype leaders, embodying the gospel of Jesus Christ in their own right, just like Paul in his own role as a missionary (vv. 23–24). Among these leaders, Paul describes Philemon as beloved and our fellow worker (v. 1). The word "our" (ἡμῶν) expresses a relationship within the same group. In order to uphold his status as a fellow worker and prototype leader within this deeply devoted team, Philemon must demonstrate his faith, love, and commitment by going above and beyond his cultural context and values. This meant letting go of his traditional mindset and value system, which was the master–slave relationship prevalent in his contemporary cultural, political, economic, and social milieu. Additionally, he must depersonalize his social status in the new community. This includes not only reconciling with Onesimus, but also embracing him as a brother and offering him a new status and level of relationship within his household.

Paul's narration of Philemon's past experience and the testimony from the Christ-believing members further substantiate this line of thought. From verses 5–7, Paul speaks about Philemon's character: his love and faith toward the Lord Jesus and all the saints. Paul repeatedly heard about the love and faith of Philemon, as the verb ἀκούω indicates that it is the habit of Philemon or his ethos, which is also expected from all members of the new family. Therefore, the manifestation of Philemon's prototypical attributes serves as the basis for Paul's thanksgiving to God. Paul explicitly states, "your love," emphasizing that Philemon's love originates from his own heart and is manifested in his actions. The phrase σου . . . τὴν πίστιν (your faith/faithfulness) is also an attribute that Philemon demonstrated in the community. Scholars, however, disagree on the appropriate translation of these phrases, proposing various options: (1) Philemon's love and faith are both directed to the Lord and all the saints, and (2) while Philemon's love is directed to the Lord's people, his faith is directed toward the Lord Jesus only. Pauline usage demonstrates love for God and for God's people, but it is uncommon for Paul to express faith in all saints. Therefore, some scholars opt to interpret it as faithfulness rather than faith, expressing relationships with all the saints. However, Pauline usage does not support this interpretation, that is, "faith in all saints"; hence, for the sake of clarity, "faith in the Lord Jesus is superior to the other option.[66]

In any case, the two prototypical attributes of Philemon were demonstrated, especially love for "all the saints." Paul's use of "all the saints" is intentional because Philemon's love was not discriminatory or prejudiced. Verse 7 reiterates the impact of Philemon's love on Paul and the saints' hearts. Philemon refreshed the hearts of the saints through his manifested love, and hearing about it brought joy and encouragement to Paul himself. The heart represents the innermost and most profound aspect of a person, serving as the seat of emotions. However, in Philemon, it encompasses not only the emotions but also the saints' deepest thoughts. To refresh the saints' heart is to put it at rest,[67] or at peace and confidence in Philemon's true personality and leadership. Therefore, Paul abrogates his authority or right in Christ and instead appeals on the basis of love, a prototypical attribute of the Christ-believing community.

---

66. Moo, *The Letters to the Colossians and to Philemon*, 387–389.

67. Johannes P. Louw and Eugene Albert Nida, "Ἀναπαύω," in *Greek–English Lexicon of the New Testament: Based on Semantic Domains*, 2nd ed. (United Bible Societies, 1996), 1:260.

In doing so, Paul prioritized ethos (character) above authority. Philemon has to do that which is required, ἀνήκω (v. 8). According to Louw-Nida, the word ἀνήκω implies moral judgment, that is, the right thing to do.[68] Paul implies that he can command Philemon to do the right thing, but he prefers him to do the right thing out of love. So, love for Paul means doing what is right willingly or manifesting one's good deeds without any external compulsion (v. 14). The right thing to do is to receive Onesimus "no longer as a slave but more than a slave, a beloved brother" or to "receive him," as Philemon "would receive" Paul (vv. 15–18). This is the crux of the letter. The adverb οὐκέτι ("no longer") refers to "extension of time up to a point but not beyond";[69] it means never again or no more. The right thing Paul is requesting Philemon to do is to abrogate his legal authority over Onesimus, as Paul did his apostolic authority in Christ over Philemon, and to treat Onesimus as a beloved brother on the basis of love.

The word ὑπέρ is translated as "more than" or "over, beyond" and refers to "a degree beyond that of a compared scale of extent in the sense of excelling, surpassing,"[70] but Paul did not say "more than as a slave," which is a comparison, but "more than a slave."[71] Robert H. Gundry argues that Onesimus is no longer Philemon's slave in the Lord even now.[72] Ben Witherington III writes, "It does not mean "not only as" or "not merely as," but it means "no longer," emphasizing "that the former condition is to stop and the latter condition exceeds and supersedes it."[73] In the same vein, Gundry argues that "a beloved brother" defines the meaning of "more than a slave" and provides Onesimus with a status in relation to Philemon that is on par with that of Philemon to Paul and Timothy."[74] Only in Philemon verse 16 is a slave explicitly and directly referred to as a brother. Onesimus has now become a brother, a new status, both in the flesh and in the Lord. In the flesh, it refers to his physical, social, and geographical condition, while in the spiritual sphere, it is his union with Christ.[75] Therefore, not only in the spiritual sense but also in day-to-day life, Onesimus should be viewed, accepted, and honored as an actual brother in his social location within Philemon's home and church; just like Philemon himself, a beloved brother (v. 1), and Paul, a brother, and just like Timothy, a brother, this term now applies to Onesimus, a beloved brother.

Onesimus should be treated equally with prominent figures like Philemon, Paul, Timothy, Epaphras, Mark, Aristarchus, Demas, Luke, Apphia, and Archippus (vv. 23–24). To accept this new group ethos and values, Philemon should relinquish his social honor, status, and economic benefits, which is a sacrifice for him. In order to embody the prototypical leadership

---

68. Johannes P. Louw and Eugene Albert Nida, "Ἀνήκω," in *Greek–English Lexicon of the New Testament: Based on Semantic Domains*, 2nd ed. (United Bible Societies, 1996), 1:626.

69. William Arndt, Frederick W. Danker, and Walter Bauer, "Οὐκέτι," in BDAG, 736.

70. William Arndt, Frederick W. Danker, and Walter Bauer, ""Ὑπέρ," in BDAG, 1031.

71. Gundry, *Commentary on Colossians and Philemon*, 55.

72. Gundry, *Commentary on Colossians and Philemon*, 47–50.

73. Ben Witherington III, *The Letters to Philemon, the Colossians, and the Ephesians: A Socio-Rhetorical Commentary on the Captivity Epistles* (Eerdmans, 2007), 75–78.

74. Witherington, *The Letters to Philemon*, 45.

75. Witherington, *The Letters to Philemon*, 78.

attributes of the new group in both his home and church, Philemon should not only reconcile with his slave but also receive him not as a slave but as a beloved brother. This necessitates embodying sacrificial love that results in a transformation of perception and perspectives about others in the Lord, living beyond social norms, and receiving others without prejudice or discrimination. Hence, reconciliation is more than merely making peace between two parties; rather, it is a transformative process that reshapes one's perception and perspective about those involved, avoiding prejudice and discrimination. It entails accepting and embracing a new relationship and identity that embody equality, ensuring the relationship's longevity. Paul expects Philemon to make a sacrifice by transforming and depersonalizing his identity and status, not only to reconcile but also to embody the values of the new identity and embrace the other.

Although the African traditional mechanism of reconciliation restores the existing relationship through ritual sacrifices and offerings through the dedication of a mediator who sacrifices time and energy, Paul's concept of reconciliation is not to maintain the existing status of relationship or to restore the traditional harmonious coexistence. It is a call to embrace a new status that is culturally and conceptually at a different level from the tradition which demands those who were traditionally higher to embody the sacrifice of the past and embrace the new status within the new community of faith. Reading Philemon with this concept of reconciliation in mind serves as social critique for African reconciliation which mainly focuses on restoring the status quo rather than transforming the relationship into a new level of lasting cooperation.

Reconciliation
Through Age, Influence, Partnership, and Identification

One of the common elements of African reconciliation is the key role of age and eldership. Whether there is conflict within the family, community, village, or ethnic group, eldership plays a major role in peace-building. Studies conducted in Nigeria, Ghana-Togo, and Ethiopia,[76] and studies on all of Africa,[77] and also by Yimer specifically on Ethiopia[78] show that elders are highly respected in Africa because they embody wisdom, ancestral values, and tradition, and reputable character at the community or national level. In most African countries, disobedience to elders' decisions results in exclusion from the community; therefore, they exert tremendous influence in reconciliation. For instance, the Boro-Shinash in the Benishangul-Gumuz region in Ethiopia have a conflict resolution tradition called *Enasha*, which is a process of resolving conflict through *Eneshas* (community elders) which

76. I. William Zartman, ed., *Traditional Cures for Modern Conflicts: African Conflict "Medicine"* (Lynne Rienner Publishers, 2000), 20, 34, 69, 79.

77. Rasaki Lawal and Ganiyu Ibikunle, "Resolving Conflict in African Traditional Society: An Imperative of Indigenous African System," *Euro Afro Studies International Journal* 4 (June 30, 2020): 46.

78. Benyam Lake Yimer, "Abegar Indigenous Conflict Resolution System-Community Based Reconciliation," *Conflict Studies Quarterly* 36 (2021): 55.

refers to old age, though it can also be used for a younger adult person elected to be part of *Enasha*.[79] *Enasha* also involves the blood father lineage of kings, highly respected and revered by the community. Rejecting eldership decisions results in ostracism or stigmatization of the defiant from the community and the loss of the benefit of being part of the community. So, eldership includes bearing the responsibility of reconciliation on behalf of the community.

Paul bases his appeal not only on love but also on age (v. 9), partnership (v. 17), and identification (vv. 17, 18–19). Paul referred to himself as πρεσβύτης, which LN[80] defines as "an adult man advanced in years." Similarly, BDAG defines it simply as "old man, aged man"[81] which includes a reference to Philemon 9. Some scholars contend that it must be translated as "ambassador" in the context of Philemon, a view that the RSV also reflects. Such a translation is reasoned based on two arguments: textual emendation and context. In the former case, it is argued that the word "ambassador" differs from *presbytes* only in one vowel, reading *presbeutēs*; therefore, the former replaced the latter unintentionally,[82] whereas in the latter case, it is argued that it parallels Ephesians 6:19a–20, and it fits because Paul is comparing "ambassador" with "prisoner" in the context of Philemon 9. However, Moo and Witherington[83] argue convincingly that the evidence for "ambassador" is very weak,[84] and the reference to verse 1 is not appropriate as the construction is different; it does not fit the context because "ambassador" connotes authority, on which Paul did not want to base his appeal. Paul referring to himself as an old man fits his rhetoric perfectly, as he is appealing on the basis of the prototypical attributes of the Christ-believing group. Moo and Witherington understand that Paul's purpose in mentioning age is to initiate Philemon's sympathy, as the letter is emotive. This is a possible scenario given that "old age in Greco-Roman society was often associated with helplessness and the consequent need for family members to provide for their elders."[85]

However, Paul is emphasizing the value of aging and experience in the Lord as the basis for his appeal to effect reconciliation. Studies in the Greek and Roman worlds about aging reveal the existence of both positive and negative perspectives on old age, just like in our modern time. "Old man" in the Greco-Roman world referred to "someone between fifty and fifty-six years of age."[86] Therefore, there is a possibility that Paul is claiming seniority over Philemon on a cultural and ethical basis rather than weakness and helplessness. He still travels to carry on his mission (v. 22). He turns to others for support, not because of his age and inability to

79. Million Esho Dezo, "Traditional Conflict Resolution Mechanisms in Ethiopia: The Case in Afar and Oromiya," *Lakhomi Journal Scientific Journal of Culture* January 1 (2021): 39–42.

80. Johannes P. Louw and Eugene Albert Nida, "Πρεσβύτης," in *Greek–English Lexicon of the New Testament: Based on Semantic Domains*, 2nd ed. (United Bible Societies, 1969), 1:107.

81. BDAG, 863.

82. Moo, *The Letters to the Colossians and to Philemon*, 404.

83. Witherington, *The Letters to Philemon, the Colossians, and the Ephesians*, 67.

84. Moo, *The Letters to the Colossians and to Philemon*, 405.

85. Moo, *The Letters to the Colossians and to Philemon*, 405.

86. Dennis Hamm, *Philippians, Colossians, Philemon*, CCSS (Baker Academic, 2013), 45.

sustain himself, but because of his imprisonment and lack of freedom to travel. What fits in this context is not weakness and helplessness due to age; instead, according to the ancient Greeks and Romans, "the old, or at least the older, are always in the commanding position, as fathers, teachers, judges, senators, and censors."[87] Additionally, it conveys "ethical qualities and values—strength and weakness, wisdom and foolishness, autonomy and dependence" in a metaphorical and symbolic manner.[88] Thus, Paul's reference to himself as an old man is to instill respect for his leadership as a father who relies on relationships, wisdom, and experience rather than for his apostolic authority. Paul's use of "my child, Onesimus, whose father I have become in my imprisonment" (v. 10) further supports this reading. Paul is a spiritual father, not only to Onesimus but also probably to Philemon himself. In other words, Paul is also claiming ownership of Onesimus on the basis of fatherhood, just as Philemon is claiming legal ownership of him. Therefore, the trust he had built, his commitment, and his leadership experience warrant him being given a hearing and respect.

Paul refers to himself as an "old man" in reference to his leadership, wisdom, experience, and role as a father to the church in Philemon's house, which serves as the foundation for his appeal to Philemon to accept Onesimus as a brother rather than a slave. When African readers encounter the term "old man," it evokes an image based on their own cultural perceptions, which hold the elderly in high esteem. In Ethiopia, elders are referred to in the Amharic language as *shimagile* (singular) or *shimagileowch* (plural), but they are not just old men; they are also called "fathers," not biological, but in terms of caring for the community. African societies prefer eldership-based reconciliation over going to court. Paul's definition of fatherhood, which does not necessarily imply biological or blood ties but rather refers to someone who cares for the community, is simple for an African reader to comprehend in their context. The church in Africa can leverage such foundational and common traditions and values to enhance its reconciliation ministry within and outside the church.

Several studies have demonstrated that African traditional reconciliation is participatory and communal. In Igbo society, for instance, all family members gather under the leadership of the family head during intrafamily conflict, and the disputant receives an equal opportunity to present their case, irrespective of their gender and status.[89] Participants pose questions, the disputants respond, and the elders, who moderate the reconciliation, reach a consensus through group decisions. The disputants may decline to give their consent, particularly in situations where the communal decision compromises their values, which they cannot relinquish for the benefit of the community. Therefore, in most cases, reconciliation is based on consensus and the free will of the disputants, not forced, but influenced.

Paul repeatedly uses the concept of Philemon's fellowship or participation in the ministry of the gospel, which is primarily about reconciling sinners with God. The value of participation in African traditional reconciliation easily connects to participation in Paul's

87. M. I. Finley, "The Elderly in Classical Antiquity," in *Old Age in Greek and Latin Literature*, ed. Thomas M. Falkner and Judith deLuce (State University of New York, 1989), 9.

88. Finley, "The Elderly in Classical Antiquity," xi.

89. Uwazie, "Social Relations and Peacekeeping Among the Igbo," 16–17.

letter to Philemon. Community for Africans means participation, playing one's role, and responsibility.

Further, Paul's appeal is based on the concept of partnership, which is defined as "one who participates with another in some enterprise or matter of joint concern."[90] The relationship between Paul and Philemon is likely a ministry partnership.[91] In his prayer, Paul mentions partnership, or κοινωνία "an association involving close mutual relations and involvement" or "sharing one's possession, with the implication of some kind of joint participation and mutual interest."[92] N. T. Wright defines κοινωνία in the context of Philemon (v. 6) as "Christians not only belong to one another but actually become mutually identified, truly rejoicing with the happy and genuinely weeping with the sad . . . [it] is part of the truth about the body of Christ. All are bound together in a mutual bond that makes our much-prized individualism look shallow and petty."[93] Adopting these definitions, Christ-believing group members prioritize community over individualism, a concept that social identity theory characterizes as the depersonalization of individuals. Paul appeals to Philemon both in terms of his identity as a ministry partner and his status within the faith community, particularly his faith in Christ, who embodies the ultimate or ideal prototype leader and who receives and welcomes all.

Paul explicitly conveys this idea to Philemon based on identification: receiving Onesimus is receiving Paul; rejecting Onesimus as a beloved brother is rejecting Paul, the partner, the elder, the brother, the one who has authority in Christ, and the prisoner because of the ministry of the gospel (v. 17). Paul even says that Onesimus is his "very heart" (v. 12). This is not just mechanical identification with the Other, but it involves both emotional and vicarious responsibility, as Paul is willing to take responsibility in the place of Onesimus; "if he has wronged [Philemon] at all or owes [Philemon] anything," it is to be charged to Paul's account (v. 20). Boldly, Paul said, "I will repay it" (v. 19). Vicarious identification is the key attribute of the ideal prototype leader of the community, Jesus Christ; and it is reincarnated in the life of Paul, who challenges Philemon to do the same: reconcile and receive Onesimus with equal status as himself. In so doing, Paul introduces the notion of restitution, emphasizing that genuine reconciliation necessitates the application of justice and fairness.

The African conflict resolution process also entails identification with the nuclear family, head of the family, and the community as a whole. It is more about being part of a family or community rather than just resolving individual issues. In other words, it is identifying oneself with the community, family, and its values over pursuing one's own individual desires. For such a cause, sacrifice in the process of depersonalizing is inevitably required from both parties involved in the reconciliation.

---

90. Johannes P. Louw and Eugene Albert Nida, "Κοινωνία," in *Greek–English Lexicon of the New Testament: Based on Semantic Domains*, 2nd ed. (United Bible Societies, 1996), 1:445–446.

91. Witherington, *The Letters to Philemon, the Colossians, and the Ephesians*, 83.

92. L&N 34.5, 57.98.

93. N. T. Wright, *Colossians and Philemon: An Introduction and Commentary* (InterVarsity Press, 2015), 171.

Conclusion

The letter to Philemon is all about restoring and transforming relationships. Scholars generally agree that the primary focus is the restoration of relationships or reconciliation, despite the extensive conjecture surrounding the event, the cause of Onesimus and Philemon's separation, and the lack of a clear resolution. This introduction has demonstrated that Paul primarily approaches the reconciliation process on the basis of redefined identity as a result of a unique relationship with the head of the Christ-believing community, specifically God, the Father, and Christ Jesus, the Lord. This identity compels Philemon to accept Onesimus as a brother, treating him equally based on the new prototype beliefs and values. This approach depersonalizes Philemon's unique status, which he derived from his contemporary milieu.

Paul also challenges Philemon to embrace the role of representative prototype leadership, embodying sacrificial love, to break the slave–master relationship ingrained in the Greco-Roman culture, even if it costs him his social status and economic benefits in the society in which he lives. In doing so, Philemon participates as a coworker and partner in the Pauline team, whose marks are sacrificial ministry for the sake of the mission of the kingdom of God. Paul not only presented his case for reconciliation with a redefined identity and sacrificial love; he also leveraged his influence as an elderly, mature, wise, and experienced leader in the house of God. He identified himself as a father to Onesimus, even going so far as to make up for any losses Philemon suffered due to their conflict. Therefore, reconciliation is not just resuming the former level of relationship one has before the conflict occurs, but also transforming the perceptions of the parties about one another and entering into a higher level of relationship that lasts a long time.

The letter to Philemon easily finds a home in an African context, although the image of the slave and master relationship reminds readers of the worst experiences that African society had in its history, especially during times of colonization. Despite the negative memories the letter evokes, African readers can easily immerse themselves in the letter. This is especially true when it comes to the role of greetings and the principles of reconciliation, as demonstrated in this chapter. These elements are common in the day-to-day lives and traditional reconciliation practices of most African countries. For Africans, greetings convey a message of sound relationships, care, and building bridges; they involve investing time to understand and support each other, signaling to observers that the relationship is sound and healthy. In Africa, people highly value greetings as they foster healthy relationships among friends, neighbors, and community members. Paul's reconciliation principles easily find connections with African traditional reconciliation, while also challenging it on some fronts. The principles that Paul uses for reconciliation and fostering brotherhood within the church work very well for the church in the African context: redefined identity, embodying sacrificial love, and influence through exemplary life among the Christ-believing group.

Further Reading

Bruce, F. F. *The Epistles to the Colossians, to Philemon, and to the Ephesians*. Eerdmans, 1994.

Dunn, James D. G. *The Epistles to the Colossians and to Philemon*. Eerdmans, 1996.

Ip, Alex Hon Ho. *A Socio-Rhetorical Interpretation of the Letter to Philemon in Light of the New Institutional Economics: An Exhortation to Transform a Master–Slave Economic Relationship into a Brotherly Loving Relationship*. Mohr Siebeck, 2017.

Knox, John. *Philemon Among the Letters of Paul: A New View of Its Place and Importance*. Rev. ed. Abingdon Press, 1959.

Manyika, Batanayi I. "Philemon: A Transformation of Social Orders." PhD diss., South African Theological Seminary, 2019.

Moo, Douglas J. *The Letters to the Colossians and to Philemon*. Eerdmans, 2008.

Pao, David W. *Colossians and Philemon*. ZECNT. Zondervan Academic, 2016.

Soungalo, Soro. "Philemon." In *Africa Bible Commentary: A One-Volume Commentary Written by 70 African Scholars*, edited by Tokunboh Adeyemo. WordAlive Publishers; Zondervan, 2006.

Thompson, James W., and Bruce Longenecker. *Philippians and Philemon*. Paideia. Baker Academic, 2016.

Tolmie, D. F. "How Onesimus Was Heard—Eventually: Some Insights from the History of Interpretation of Paul's Letter to Philemon." *Acta Theologica* 39 (2019): 101–117.

Tolmie, D. Francois, ed. *Philemon in Perspective: Interpreting a Pauline Letter*. De Gruyter, 2010.

Turner, Max. "Human Reconciliation in the New Testament with Special Reference to Philemon, Colossians and Ephesians." *European Journal of Theology* 16, no. 1 (2007): 37–47.

Witherington, Ben III. *The Letters to Philemon, the Colossians, and the Ephesians: A Socio-Rhetorical Commentary on the Captivity Epistles*. Eerdmans, 2007.

Wright, N. T. *Colossians and Philemon: An Introduction and Commentary*. InterVarsity Press, 2015.

CHAPTER NINETEEN

The Letter to the Hebrews

Abeneazer G. Urga
Evangelical Theological College
Ethiopian Graduate School of Theology
Addis Ababa, Ethiopia

Introductory Questions[1]

THE LETTER TO the Hebrews is dubbed the "Epistle to African Christians" because of its "deep relevance" to the numerous questions Africans raise.[2] Most importantly, many Africans find Hebrews relevant because the epistle zeroes in on "sacrifice, priestly mediation, and ancestral function."[3] This chapter aims to highlight some of the "deep relevance" of Hebrews to African readers/hearers and cement the notion that God still speaks to Africans by his own Son. As such, the chapter explicates some theological themes that resonate with Christian Africans, particularly Ethiopians. These themes include the priesthood of Christ, sacrifice, and the motifs of perseverance and Christian hospitality.

Hebrews is described as "a riddle"[4] and "an enigma"[5] because it does not answer a number of questions asked by the modern inquirer. For example, the author is not mentioned. The date, place of composition, destination, and the addressees appear to be elusive. Therefore, in attempting to answer the introductory questions pertaining to the epistle, interpreters have ended up with varying conclusions. After an overview of these multiple answers, the positions assumed in this study will be noted before delving into the discussion of the theological themes.

1. Most of the introductory section originally appeared in Abeneazer G. Urga, *Intercession of Jesus in Hebrews: The Background and Nature of Jesus' Heavenly Intercession in the Epistle to the Hebrews*, WUNT 2/585 (Mohr Siebeck, 2023). Used by permission from Mohr Siebeck Tübingen.

2. Kwame Bediako, "Christian Faith and African Culture: An Exposition of the Epistle to the Hebrews," *Journal of African Christian Thought* 13, no. 1 (June 2010): 46.

3. Kwame Bediako, *Jesus and the Gospel in Africa: History and Experience* (Orbis Books, 2004), 28.

4. Harold W. Attridge, *The Epistle to the Hebrews*, Hermeneia (Fortress Press, 1989), 13; Jeremy Punt, "Hebrews, Thought-Patterns and Context: Aspects of the Background of Hebrews," *Neotestamentica* 31, no. 1 (1997): 119–158, here 119.

5. T. W. Manson, *The Epistle to the Hebrews* (Hodder & Stoughton, 1951), 1.

Authorship

Throughout the centuries, interpreters of Hebrews have proposed several candidates as to who could have authored Hebrews: Paul,[6] Luke,[7] Apollos,[8] Barnabas,[9] Clement of Rome,[10] and Priscilla[11] are the prominent ones. Other candidates considered include: Philip, Peter, Mary, Epaphras, Silas, Judas, Aristion, and Mark.[12] Nonetheless, most scholars postulate that no one can know the author of Hebrews; as such, they echo Origen's oft-quoted statement: "But who wrote the epistle only God knows."[13]

In a recent article, however, Matthew J. Thomas contends that Origen's statement regarding Paul's authorship of Hebrews is misunderstood and misused by scholars.[14] He asserts that Origen believes Paul wrote Hebrews, but that Origen "suspects its composition to involve more than Paul alone."[15]

In Thomas's estimation and interpretation of Origen's statement, the epistle's content comes from Paul, while an amanuensis is responsible for the epistle's literary style and form.[16] The author is a highly educated Hellenistic-Jewish Christian who is also well-versed in the Scriptures. He also cared for his audience (Heb 13:22).[17] Regardless of the real identity of

6. William Leonard, *The Authorship of the Epistle to the Hebrews* (Burns, Oates & Washbourne, 1939); David A. Black, *The Authorship of Hebrews: The Case for Paul* (Energion, 2013); David A. Black, "Who Wrote Hebrews? The Internal and External Evidence Re-Examined," *Faith and Mission* 18 (2002): 57–69.

7. David L. Allen, *The Lukan Authorship of Hebrews*, NACSBT (B&H, 2010).

8. Martin Luther, *Luther's Works*, vol. 35 (Fortress Press, 1960), 395–396; H. W. Montefiore, *A Commentary on the Epistle to the Hebrews*, BNTC (A&C Black, 1964), 9–16; George H. Guthrie, "The Case for Apollos as the Author of Hebrews," *Faith and Mission* 18, no. 2 (2001): 41–56.

9. Tertullian, *Pud.* 20.2 (*ANF* 4:97); Ceslas Spicq, *L'Épître aux Hébreux: I. Commentaire* (Gabalda, 1952), 199–202; T. W. Manson, "The Problem of the Epistle to the Hebrews," *Bulletin of the John Rylands Library* 32, no. 1 (1949): 1–17; most recently, Herbert W. Bateman IV and Steven W. Smith, *Hebrews: A Commentary for Biblical Preaching and Teaching* (Kregel, 2021).

10. Eusebius, *Hist. eccl.* 6.25.

11. Ruth Hoppins, *Priscilla's Letter: Finding the Author of the Epistle to the Hebrews* (Lost Coast Press, 2009); Ruth Hoppins, "Priscilla and Plausibility: Responding to Questions About Priscilla as Author of Hebrews," *Priscilla Papers* 25 (2011): 26–28; Adolf Harnack, "Probabilia über die Adresse und den Verfasser des Hebräerbriefs," *Zeitshrift für die Neutestamentliche Wissenschaft und die Kunde der aelteren Kirche* 1 (1900): 16–41.

12. J. C. McCullough, "Some Recent Developments in Research on the Epistle to the Hebrews," *Irish Biblical Studies* 2 (1980): 141; Paul Ellingworth, *The Epistle to the Hebrews*, NIGTC (Eerdmans, 1993), 15–20.

13. Origen quoted in Eusebius, *Hist. eccl.* 6.25; cf. Dana M. Harris, *Hebrews*, EGGNT (B&H, 2019), 4; Patrick Gray and Amy Peeler, *Hebrews: An Introduction and Study Guide*, T&T Clark's Study Guides to the New Testament (T&T Clark, 2020), 2–4; Mary Healy, *Hebrews*, CCSS (Baker Academic, 2016), 19; F. F. Bruce, *The Epistle to the Hebrews* (Eerdmans, 1990), 20; George H. Guthrie, *Hebrews*, NIVAC 15 (Zondervan, 1998), 27; David A. deSilva, *Perseverance in Gratitude: A Socio-Rhetorical Commentary on the Epistle "to the Hebrews"* (Eerdmans, 2000), 24–25; Punt, "Hebrews, Thought-Patterns and Context," 120.

14. Matthew J. Thomas, "Origen on Paul's Authorship of Hebrews," *New Testament Studies* 65 (2019): 598–609; for a similar argument, see Black, *The Authorship of Hebrews*; Black, "Who Wrote Hebrews?"

15. Thomas, "Origen on Paul's Authorship of Hebrews," 600.

16. Thomas, "Origen on Paul's Authorship of Hebrews," 607–608.

17. For the pastoral nature of the epistle, see Peter R. Jones, "The Figure of Moses as a Heuristic Device for Understanding the Pastoral Intent of Hebrews," *Review & Expositor* 76, no. 1 (1979): 95–107; also Gray and Peeler, *Hebrews*,

the author, Hebrews indicates that the author is a second-generation male (διηγούμενον) Christian.[18]

Contrary to the consensus of modern scholarship on the authorship of Hebrews, the *Andemta* Commentary (AC) tradition of the Ethiopian Orthodox *Tewahido* Church (EOTC) asserts that Paul is the author of Hebrews. According to this tradition, Paul authored fourteen epistles.[19] The commentators assert that, Paul wrote Hebrews to encourage the audience to hold onto the gospel and not give in to the pressure from some of the Jewish Christians to embrace the Law. He also wanted to comfort the congregation that was under persecution so that they could persevere. Paul urged the audience to live out their Christian faith by showing hospitality and love to those who were disadvantaged and suffering for the sake of the faith.

Unlike his other epistles, Paul wanted to be anonymous when he wrote Hebrews so that the Jewish Christians would not reject him outright because he had lost credibility among them. The *Andemta* Commentary addresses the apparent discrepancy between Hebrews 2:3, where the author states that he is a second-generation Christian, and Galatians 1:12, where Paul claims that he received the gospel through direct revelation. The AC tradition considers the "we" language in Hebrews 2:3 to be an "inclusive 'we'" where Paul identifies himself with the audience out of humility:[20]

> If they say, "Did not he say in his book to the Galatians 'For I did not receive it from man, nor was I taught it, but it came through a revelation of Jesus Christ'?" he is showing solidarity with the Hebrews out of humility.

Date and Provenance

There is also a lack of consensus concerning both the date of Hebrews and its provenance. The proposed date for Hebrews ranges between 60 and 96 CE.[21] Gareth L. Cockerill helpfully classifies scholars' dating of Hebrews into three categories:[22] those who believe it was written pre-70 CE, shortly after 70 CE, and post-70 CE.[23] In this study, the traditional position that

4–5; J. C. McCullough, "Hebrews in Recent Scholarship," *Irish Biblical Studies* 16 (1994): 69; Harris, *Hebrews*, 3; William L. Lane, *Hebrews 1–8*, WBC 47A (Zondervan, 1991), xlix–li.

18. This is because the masculine singular participle term διηγούμενον is used in Hebrews 11:32. On the author being a second-generation Christian, see Hebrews 2:3.

19. For more on this, see Abeneazer G. Urga, "Why Did Paul Write Hebrews? Reasons for the Composition of Hebrews in the Ethiopian Orthodox Tewahido Church's *Andemta* Commentary Tradition," in *Reading Hebrews and 1 Peter from Majority World Perspectives*, ed. Sofanit T. Abebe, Elizabeth W. Mburu, and Abeneazer G. Urga, LNTS 700 (Bloomsbury T&T Clark, 2024), 8–18.

20. See also Urga, "Why Did Paul Write Hebrews?," 16n21–22.

21. Craig R. Koester, *Hebrews: A New Translation with Introduction and Commentary*, AB 36 (Doubleday, 2001), 50; McCullough, "Some Recent Developments," 151–152; Thomas R. Schreiner, *A Commentary on Hebrews*, BTCP (B&H, 2015), 5–6; Attridge, *Hebrews*, 6–9; Bruce, *The Epistle to the Hebrews*, 20–22.

22. Gareth L. Cockerill, *Hebrews*, NICNT (Eerdmans, 2012), 35.

23. Jason A. Whitlark, *Resisting Empire: Rethinking the Purpose of the Letter to the Hebrews*, LNTS 484 (T&T Clark, 2014), 8; Ellen Bradshaw Aitken, "Portraying the Temple in Stone and Text: The Arch of Titus and the Epistle

Hebrews was composed pre-70 CE is adopted.[24] The reason for this is that Hebrews does not mention the destruction of the temple, which could have been used to strengthen the author's argument of the ephemeral nature of the earthly temple with its Levitical priestly order.[25] Another plausible reason scholars suggest for the pre-70 CE composition of Hebrews is the author's reference to the tabernacle in the present tense (7:8; 8:4; 9:6–7, 9, 13; 13:10). However, some scholars consider the argument from the present tense to be tenuous.[26]

Scholars' proposals for the destination of Hebrews also vary: Jerusalem, Rome, Alexandria, Cyprus, Caesarea, Antioch, Ephesus, Colossae, Galatia, Palestine, and Samaria.[27] Regardless of the proposals proffered by scholars, it is worth noting Philip Hughes's conclusion on the provenance and destination of Hebrews: "Speculations concerning the places from which and to which the Epistle to the Hebrews was written have been no less varied and inventive."[28] F. F. Bruce also asserts that it is impossible to pinpoint Hebrews' destination, yet "fortunately its exegesis is for the most part independent of this question."[29]

The Identity and Situation of the Recipients of Hebrews

What is pertinent to this study is the audience's identity and the situation that prompted the epistle's composition. Cockerill highlights the importance of identifying who the addressees were when he states: "One can understand Hebrews without identifying either the name of the author or the location of the recipients. One cannot, however, interpret Hebrews without taking a position as to whether the recipients were Jewish or Gentile believers."[30] So who were the recipients? Again, potential answers to this question abound.

The title "To the Hebrews" (ΠΡΟΣ ΕΒΡΑΙΟΥΣ) is one of the proofs that many scholars offer for their conclusion that the recipients of Hebrews were Jewish Christians. The designation appears in 𝔓[46] ℵ A B C.[31] The title, however, is a later scribal addition in the second

to the Hebrews," in *Hebrews: Contemporary Methods, New Insights*, ed. Gabriella Gelardini, SBL 75 (Brill, 2005), 131–148, here 133–136.

24. Cockerill, *Hebrews*, 36–37; Schreiner, *A Commentary on Hebrews*, 6; Attridge, *Hebrews*, 8; David M. Hay, *Glory at the Right Hand: Psalm 110 in Early Christianity*, SBLMS 18 (SBL, 1989), 20.

25. Brooke F. Westcott, *The Epistle to the Hebrews: The Greek Text with Notes and Essays* (Eerdmans, 1984), xlii; Philip E. Hughes, *A Commentary on Hebrews* (Eerdmans, 1977), 30–31; David L. Allen, *Hebrews*, NAC 35 (B&H, 2010), 75; Luke Timothy Johnson, *Hebrews: A Commentary*, NTL (John Knox Press, 2006), 38–40; Healy, *Hebrews*, 23.

26. Koester, *Hebrews*, 53; Schreiner, *A Commentary on Hebrews*, 5–6.

27. Healy, *Hebrews*, 20; Hughes, *Hebrews*, 17–18; Bruce, *The Epistle to the Hebrews*, 10–14; Simon C. Mimouni, "Le 'grand prêtre' Jésus 'à la Manière de Melchisédech' dans l'Épître aux Hébreux," *Annali Di Storia Dell'Esegesi* 33, no. 1 (2016): 79–105, here 87.

28. Hughes, *Hebrews*, 15.

29. Bruce, *The Epistle to the Hebrews*, 14.

30. Cockerill, *Hebrews*, 19.

31. Westcott, *Hebrews*, xxvii; Bruce, *The Epistle to the Hebrews*, 3; Christian Rose, *Der Hebräerbrief*, BNT (Vandenhoeck & Ruprecht, 2019), 15.

century.[32] The frequent citation of Old Testament passages and the stress that Jesus is better than the antecedent revelation, institutions, and mediators are additional reasons for the claim that the recipients were Jewish Christians.[33]

Although this traditional view—that the recipients were Jewish Christians—has been dominant,[34] other alternatives have also been suggested. A few scholars contend that the epistle was intended for a predominantly gentile audience, with E. M. Roeth being the first to postulate this view.[35] A recent proponent of the primarily gentile audience is Jason A. Whitlark. In his *Resisting Empire*, Whitlark contends that the audience was steeped in idolatry but turned toward God in response to the gospel (Heb 6:1–2).[36] Two decades ago, Paul Ellingworth anticipated Whitlark's argument, particularly the phrase "dead works," addressing and convincingly countering it. Scholars who argue for a gentile audience employ two pieces of evidence: the exhortation not to fall away and the expression "dead works." In the first piece of evidence, they assert that Jews who renounce Christianity remain monotheistic; thus, the exhortation is geared toward gentiles. Second, the phrase "dead works"—which Whitlark takes to mean idolatry—is thought to indicate a non-Jewish audience. Ellingworth, however, contends that these two expressions should not be confined to gentile recipients, as they are "general statements."[37] In this study, the recipients are considered to be predominantly Jewish Christians with possible gentile converts in their midst.

Although scholars debate the specific ethnicity of the addressees, most of them concede that the recipients of Hebrews are Christians.[38] But why was Hebrews composed? The text of Hebrews provides both the occasion for and the purpose of its composition. Hebrews is composed as a "word of exhortation" (τοῦ λόγου τῆς παρακλήσεως) (Heb 13:22) to the

---

32. Rose, *Der Hebräerbrief*, 15; Bruce, *The Epistle to the Hebrews*, 4; Ellingworth, *The Epistle to the Hebrews*, 21.

33. James W. Thompson, *Hebrews*, Paideia (Baker Academic, 2008), 7; Ellingworth, *The Epistle to the Hebrews*, 22–24.

34. Francesco Lo Bue, "The Historical Background of the Epistle to the Hebrews," *Journal of Biblical Literature* 75, no. 1 (1956): 52–57, here 54.

35. Sheila Griffith, "The Epistle to the Hebrews in Modern Interpretation," *Review & Expositor* 102 (2005): 235–254, here 241; Ellingworth, *The Epistle to the Hebrews*, 22; Marie E. Isaacs, *Sacred Space: An Approach to the Theology of the Epistle to the Hebrews*, JSNTSup 73 (JSOT Press, 1992), 23n4; Erich Grässer, *An die Hebräer (Hebr 1–6)*, EKK XVII/1 (Benziger/Neukirchener, 1990), 23–25; Herbert Braun, *An die Hebräer*, HNT 14 (Mohr, 1984), 2.

36. Whitlark, *Resisting Empire*, 12–16, 49–76; Kenneth Schenck, *A New Perspective on Hebrews: Rethinking the Parting of the Ways* (Lexington Books; Fortress Academic, 2019), 31–58.

37. Ellingworth, *The Epistle to the Hebrews*, 24–25. Others have argued that Hebrews was composed to former Essenes to counter some theological themes found in their community or to convert the Essenes to Christianity. See Yigael Yadin, "The Dead Sea Scrolls and the Epistle to the Hebrews," *Scripta Hierosolymitana* 4 (1958): 36–55; Hans Kosmala, *Hebräer–Essener–Christen: Studien zur Vorgeschichte der frühchristlichen Verkündigung*, StPB 1 (Brill, 1959); Ceslas Spicq, " L'Épître aux Hébreux, Apollos, Jean-Baptiste, les Hellénistes et Qumrân," *Revue de Qumrân* 1, no. 3.3 (1959): 365–390; Hurst, *The Epistle to the Hebrews*, 43–85; McCullough, "Some Recent Developments," 145–148. F. F. Bruce, "'To the Hebrews' or 'To the Essenes'?" *New Testament Studies* 9, no. 3 (1963): 217–232, here 232, contends that "it would be outstripping the evidence to call them Essenes or spiritual brethren to the men of Qumran."

38. D. A. Carson and Douglas J. Moo, *An Introduction to the New Testament*, 2nd ed. (Zondervan, 2005), 609; Whitlark, *Resisting Empire*, 49.

Jewish Christians who are facing shame, persecution, and suffering that could lead them to leave the believing community and ultimately become apostate (Heb 2:1–4; 3:6, 12; 4:1; 6:4–6; 10:24–39; 12:3, 12–17). These recipients also appear to struggle with inhospitality, sexual immorality, greed, insubordination within their congregation, and false teachings (Heb 13:1–17).

Temptation, suffering, persecution, and sin are threatening the spiritual and physical well-being of the recipients. In response, the author of Hebrews highlights the better mediatorship of Jesus as encouragement but also warns them of the danger of relapsing into the ways of the former days. The warnings of the author delineate the seriousness of the recipients' situation, but at the same time, they encapsulate encouragement to the recipients so that they may persevere (see esp. Heb 12).[39]

When issuing the call to persevere in the face of the danger of drifting away, succumbing to sin, rebellion, dullness, but mainly apostasy, the author underlines Jesus's past and present (high) priestly mediation for the believers. The anonymous author especially points out Jesus's perpetual intercession in heaven for his followers, who are beleaguered by every sort of temptation to leave the fold and renounce the faith.

Outline

Introduction (1:1–4)
The Son is superior to the angels, and the incarnate God (1:5–2:18)
Jesus is a faithful apostle and a better Great High Priest (3:1–5:10)
Christian maturity and God's promise (5:11–6:20)
Jesus, the high priest in the order of Melchizedek (7:1–28)
Jesus, the high priest of a better covenant (8:1–10:18)
Perseverance in the face of persecution (10:19–12:29)
Guidelines for practicing the Christian life (13:1–19)
Benediction and greetings (13:20–25)

Theological Themes

This section explores a few theological themes that resonate with Christian Africans, particularly Ethiopians. These themes are the priesthood of Christ, the better sacrifice of Christ, the motif of perseverance in the face of persecution, and Christian hospitality.

39. The extent of the verses of the warning passages vary. Some suggest Heb 2:1–4; 3:7–4:13; 5:11–6:20; 10:19–39; 12:3–29; others propose Heb 2:1–4; 3:7–4:13; 5:11–6:12; 10:19–39; 12:14–29; still others locate the warnings in Heb 2:1–4; 4:12–13; 6:4–8; 10:26–31; 12:25–29. A few still identify the warnings in Heb 2:1–4; 3:7–19; 6:4–8; 10:26–31, and 12:25–29. See Harris, *Hebrews*; Herbert W. Bateman, "Introducing the Warning Passages in Hebrews: A Contextual Orientation," in *Four Views on the Warning Passages in Hebrews*, ed. Herbert W. Bateman (Kregel, 2007), 23–85; Adrio König, *Christ Above All: The Book of Hebrews* (Lexham Press, 2019); George H. Guthrie, *The Structure of Hebrews: A Text-Linguistic Analysis* (Baker Books, 1994).

The Priesthood of Christ

The priesthood of Christ is an important element in the Ethiopian theological landscape. One of the theological contentions between Ethiopian Protestants and the EOTC is the priesthood or mediation of Christ vis-à-vis other intermediaries like angels, saints, and Mary the mother of Jesus. The EOTC contends that Christ has finished his mediatorial task on earth and currently reigns as the divine one and judge at the right hand of God. EOTC's high Christology as such drives the church to conclude that Christ's high priestly, mediatorial function has ceased.[40] Instead, angels, saints, and Mary assume the task of mediation on behalf of God's people. These human and angelic mediators are known as *amalajoch* (intercessors).[41]

In response, Ethiopian Protestants highlight the mediation of Christ by emphasizing his current role, not only as a reigning king, but also as an active high priest who intercedes for and represents God's people before God. Ethiopian grassroots theologians have produced numerous songs that reflect the priesthood of Christ both to appreciate the current ministry of Christ in heaven and to defend his invaluable mediation. Azeb Hailu, for instance, in her song "My Priest," highlights Christ's priestly ministry in heaven:

> *Not deposed by death, nor prevented by death,*
> *The priesthood of the Lord continues in heaven.*
> *The others were prevented so they did not live;*
> *From the Aaronic priesthood, Jesus's is better.*
> *My priest, in the order of Melchizedek, you are appointed forever*
> *My priest, for the salvation of my life, my priest you are the reason.*
> *My priest, by the indestructible priesthood, my priest that death can't depose*
> *My priest, who intercedes for me, my priest by standing before Abba.*
>
> *My priest, the one at the right hand of the Father*
> *My priest, who is the advocate for my soul*
> *My priest, so that my suffering stops*
> *My priest, so that my sorrow ends*
> *My priest, you broke down,*
> *My priest, the wall of hostility*
> *My priest, you shed your blood*
> *My priest, as a sacrifice for my guilt.*

40. See further Abeneazer G. Urga, "Christ Intercedes or Judges? An Examination of the Ethiopian Orthodox *Tewahido* Church's Rendering and Interpretation of *Entynchanō* in Hebrews 7:25," in *The New Testament Around the World: Exploring Key Texts from Different Contexts*, ed. Mariam Kamell Kovalishyn (Baker Academic, 2025), 231–232.

41. Urga, "Christ Intercedes," 232–233; see also Nebeyou A. Terefe, "Ἐντυγχάνειν in Hebrews 7.25 and Its Translation in the Millennium Amharic Bible," in *Reading Hebrews and 1 Peter from Majority World Perspectives*, ed. Sofanit T. Abebe, Elizabeth W. Mburu, and Abeneazer G. Urga, LNTS 700 (Bloomsbury T&T Clark, 2024), 71–87.

One cannot help but realize that this song is replete with quotations from and allusions to Hebrews. Azeb Hailu and others have heavily appealed to Hebrews to contend—through their songs—that Jesus Christ is the unrivaled mediator and high priest on behalf of believers.

Alexander Nairne aptly titled his commentary on Hebrews *The Epistle of Priesthood*.[42] Hebrews, more than any other New Testament book, underscores the high/priesthood of Christ. In fact, while other books of the New Testament allude to or explain the priesthood of Christ, it is only in Hebrews that Christ is explicitly identified, not just as a priest, but as a high priest (Heb 2:17; 3:1; 4:14, 15; 5:5, 10; 6:20; 7:26; 8:1; 9:11).

Jesus's high priesthood in heaven is a continuation of his priesthood on earth (cf. John 17). As a high priest on earth, Jesus offered a sacrifice on the altar of the cross to deal with the issue of sin (Heb 1:3; 2:17). Jesus, both as the Son of God and the sinless mediator, is a superior high priest because he "has passed through the heavens" (διεληλυθότα τοὺς οὐρανούς) (4:14) which the Levitical high priests were unable to do.[43] Here the expression "pass through" (διέρχομαι) connotes the fact that, as a high priest, "Jesus stands out as a unique great high priest."[44]

The author of Hebrews also highlights that the sympathizing high priest Jesus is χωρὶς ἁμαρτίας ("without sin") (Heb 4:15; cf. 7:26–27). This essential fact gives Jesus a superior position over that of other mediators, particularly over the Levitical priestly order.[45] Jesus had to become a human being to serve as a high priest because "every high priest is chosen from among men" (Heb 5:1). The incarnation enabled Jesus to be a high priest on earth and in heaven. As a faithful high priest (Heb 3:1–2), Jesus offered a prayer on behalf of God's people "in the days of his flesh" (Heb 5:7).[46] Jesus's high priestly task in heaven is explicitly mentioned in Hebrews 7:25 and 9:24. These two vital passages, particularly relevant to the Ethiopian context, underscore that Jesus is actively and verbally praying for the in-between people of God.

Jesus's perpetual priestly ministry in heaven is captured with the terms ἐντυγχάνω in 7:25 and ἐμφανίζω in 9:24. God's people receive mercy and grace when they approach God's throne through his Son and priest (Heb 4:14–16) because the Son is actively interceding on their behalf (Heb 7:25). He represents God's people in the heavenly tabernacle (Heb 8:1–2) by appearing (ἐμφανίζω) before the Father (Heb 9:24). He constantly speaks on behalf of God's people.[47]

Jesus carried out his priestly ministry in two ways: by offering sacrifice on the cross and by praying for God's people. Whereas his priestly sacrifice is concluded on earth, his priestly prayers continue in the heavenly tabernacle (Heb 1:3; 7:25; 9:24).

42. Alexander Nairne, *The Epistle of Priesthood: Studies in the Epistle to the Hebrews* (T&T Clark, 1913).

43. See Urga, *Intercession of Jesus in Hebrews*, 178.

44. Urga, *Intercession of Jesus in Hebrews*, 179.

45. Urga, *Intercession of Jesus in Hebrews*, 180–181.

46. For an extensive discussion of Jesus's priestly prayers on earth, see Urga, *Intercession of Jesus in Hebrews*, 118–135, 184–195.

47. Urga, *Intercession of Jesus in Hebrews*, 220.

In light of the priestly Christology of Hebrews, we can surmise that Ethiopian Protestants are accurate in stating that Christ is the faithful high priest who represents them before God. As such, angelic, human, or Marian mediation is unnecessary. Christ's superior priesthood is more than enough to bring us closer to the throne of grace. No other mediator has achieved what Christ has achieved through his priestly ministry as both the offering and the offerant. Ethiopian grassroots and oral theologians are correct to repeatedly remind their fellow believers and others that Jesus is actively carrying out his priestly task in heaven, and this fact does not denigrate Christ's divinity.[48]

It is vital to remember that the audience to whom Hebrews was written faced a similar challenge. The congregation was tempted to fix their eyes on the prophets, angels, Moses, Joshua, Aaron, and other mediators. However, the author reminds his audience that Jesus, and what he has accomplished, is better. The angels are God's servants; the prophets are God's messengers with partial revelation, Moses is an honored servant in the house of God, the Levitical priests were beset by sin and weakness. Nonetheless, Jesus is the unique Son of God who is without sin, and he was not deterred by the power of death. Similarly, those believers who are tempted to latch onto the lesser mediators and deemphasize the priestly task of the Son of God need to pay attention to the better high priest who offered a better sacrifice and is now serving in a better tabernacle in heaven.

The Better Sacrifice of Christ

The two main tasks of the high priest are the offering of sacrifices and prayers. Christ's sacrificial ministry is mentioned from the outset of the epistle. Hebrews 1:3 denotes that Christ was seated at the Father's side "after making purification for sins" (καθαρισμὸν τῶν ἁμαρτιῶν ποιησάμενος). Here the operative word that signifies Christ's sacrificial work both as the offerant and the offering is καθαρισμός ("purification"). The term καθαρισμός accentuates Christ's sacrificial death on the cross.[49] The session of Christ in heaven was preceded by his sacrificial offering on earth. Such sacrifice was necessitated by the sins of God's people that required purification.

The language of sacrifice is also expressed in Hebrews 2:14 whereby the author declares that "through [his] death" (διὰ τοῦ θανάτου) Jesus "was able to disable the devil and conquer death."[50] The better high priest "tasted death" (γεύσηται θανάτου) as a mediator between God and the sinful people. His ultimate sacrifice on the cross would disempower the devil and free those enslaved by the fear of death.

In Hebrews 2:11, the author presents Jesus as the one who sanctifies (ὅ ἁγιάζων) and his siblings as those who need sanctification by him (οἱ ἁγιαζόμενοι). But this sanctification cannot happen without the element of blood shed through death (διὰ τοῦ θανάτου, 2:14).

48. See Urga, "Christ Intercedes," 231–233.

49. Urga, *Intercession of Jesus in Hebrews*, 160–161.

50. Abeneazer G. Urga, "The Victorious High Priest in Africa: Christ and the Logic of Atonement in Hebrews 2:14–18," *Stellenbosch Theological Journal* 10, no. 1 (2024): 1–24, here 15.

This is precisely what Hebrews 2:17 makes clear. Jesus became incarnate so that he could become a high priest "in order to make a sacrifice of atonement for the sins of the people" (εἰς τὸ ἱλάσκεσθαι τὰς ἁμαρτίας τοῦ λαοῦ). The lexeme ἱλάσκομαι ("to atone") indicates what Christ's sacrifice on the cross has achieved: he propitiated and expiated the sins of God's people.[51]

Hebrews 7:27 declares the uniqueness of Christ's sacrifice. First, the sacrifice was not "for his own sins." He offered sacrifice for the people. In the Levitical order, the high priests needed to offer sacrifices both for their own sins and the people they represented. Second, the sacrifice Christ offered was not repetitive. It was done once-for-all. Third, the sacrifice he offered was nothing other than himself. These three elements make Christ's priesthood and his sacrifice better than the Aaronic priesthood and their animal sacrifices.

The argumentation of Christ's better sacrifice vis-à-vis the Levitical sacrifices ensues in 9:11–15. In these passages, the author stresses that, unlike the Aaronic high priests who entered into the holy of holies every year to offer animal sacrifices, Christ entered into the heavenly tabernacle "because *or* after he obtained an eternal redemption."[52] Christ perpetually prays for God's people in the heavenly tabernacle and offers his assistance to those in need because he offered his own blood on the cross and secured redemption for his people (Heb 9:12).[53] Hebrews 10:1–18 reiterates the fact that Christ offered a single and superior sacrifice that procured definitive redemption. Hebrews 10:12 in particular states: "But when Christ had offered for all time a single sacrifice for sins, 'he sat down at the right hand of God.'"

The altar whereby Christ offered the ultimate sacrifice is explicitly mentioned in Hebrews 12:2. Jesus "endured the cross" (ὑπέμεινεν σταυρὸν). The cross (σταυρός) is only mentioned here to signify that Jesus's sacrificial and superior death was shameful. The audience is called to imitate Jesus's endurance and perseverance in the face of death because he paid the ultimate price by "[tasting] death" on their behalf (Heb 2:9; 12:3). The purpose of the death of Christ on the cross is "to sanctify the people by his own blood." Sanctification requires the shedding of blood through sacrificial death (cf. Heb 9:22).

The constant iteration of Christ's sacrifice in Hebrews at the heart of his high priestly ministry is still relevant in many African cultures. For instance, Kwame Bediako observes the ritual and importance of sacrifice in his context when he writes: "Sacrifice as a way of ensuring a harmonious relationship between the human community and the realm of divine and mystical power, is a regular event in Ghanaian society."[54]

Blood sacrifices—whether animal or human—are common practices in Africa. According to Cornelius Olowola, these practices have two major purposes. First, blood sacrifices unify those "who participate in the rite." Second, "blood revitalises the ones to whom the offering

51. Urga, "The Victorious High Priest in the African Context," 19–20.

52. Urga, *Intercession of Jesus in Hebrews*, 217.

53. Urga, *Intercession of Jesus in Hebrews*, 217–218.

54. Bediako, *Jesus and the Gospel in Africa*, 28.

is made."[55] Both the offerers and the recipients of blood sacrifices are revived by the element of blood. However, "Biblical sacrifices were never a means of revitalising God or man."[56]

Several Ethiopian traditional religions still practice blood sacrifices by slaughtering sheep, oxen, or cows. These blood sacrifices are offered to a specific god or goddess to prevent destruction, calamity, plagues, sickness, theft, and barrenness. Blood sacrifices are also considered instrumental in restoring broken relationships because of violence. Many consider that blood sacrifices can assuage the indignation and wrath of the spirits who appear to be capricious.

On the contrary, the author of Hebrews stresses the fact that the blood of animals "cannot perfect the conscience of the worshipper" (Heb 9:9). The blood of goats and bulls provides only outward cleansing (Heb 9:9–10). Nonetheless, Christ's sacrificial blood definitively deals with the perfection of the conscience of the believer. In Hebrews 9:13–14, the author puts the role of the blood of animals in relation to the worshipper to rest when he declares: "For if the blood of goats and bulls, with the sprinkling of the ashes of a heifer, sanctifies those who have been defiled so that their flesh is purified, how much more will the blood of Christ, who through the eternal Spirit offered himself without blemish to God, purify our conscience from dead works to worship the living God!"

The author employs a typical Jewish argument, from the lesser to the greater, to make his case that Christ's blood supersedes any kind of animals' sacrificial blood. Christ's mediatorial death and high priestly ministry are for the definitive redemption of sinners, which the blood of animals could not deliver (Heb 9:15; 10:1–4). As such, the blood sacrifice rituals in Ethiopian traditional religions should be rejected for the better sacrificial blood of Christ. Christ's single sacrifice has displaced any form of blood sacrifice done in the African context or elsewhere.[57] Selam Desta, in her song, "His Blood," asserts this theological fact when she sings:

The blood of Jesus cleanses from all sins
His Son's, Jesus's blood justifies from all transgression
The blood of Jesus cleanses from all sins
His Son's, Jesus's blood justifies from all transgression
Amen! It cleanses; it justifies.

It's not according to the priesthood of the sons of Aaron
nor according to the order of the tribe of Levi
My dear one's [his priesthood] is not like that
My dear one's [his priesthood] is not like that
to justify me He did not enter [into the holy of holies]
with the blood of bulls and pigeons

55. Cornelius Olowola, "Sacrifice in African Tradition and in Biblical Perspective," *Africa Journal of Evangelical Theology* 10, no. 1 (1991): 3–9, here 4.

56. Olowola, "Sacrifice in African Tradition," 4.

57. See Samuel Ngewa, "The Place of Traditional Sacrifices," in *Africa Bible Commentary: A One-Volume Commentary Written by 70 African Scholars*, ed. Tokunboh Adeyemo (WordAlive Publishers; Zondervan, 2006), 1528–1529, here 1529.

He offered his body once and was beautiful forever
His blood was shed and my sin was forgiven
He died at Calvary, and I was born again
I called the Father my Father, and I was told that I was his daughter.[58]

Gleaning from Hebrews, Selam Desta denotes that the blood of Christ is what made her clean, just, and a daughter of God, not the blood of animals that is too weak to deal with sin, transgression, and broken relationships with the divine. In this regard, Cornelius Olowola aptly captures the difference between blood sacrifice in African Traditional Religions and the blood of Christ when he writes: "African sacrifices might be able to remove ceremonial pollution, like the breaking of taboos, but they are unable to remove the guilt of sin. They cannot provide inward cleansing. But according to the Bible, the blood of Christ powerfully atones for sin."[59]

Perseverance in the Face of Persecution

The repeated warnings (Heb 2:1–4; 3:7–4:13; 5:11–6:12; 10:19–39; 12:14–29) and the frequent reminders about the great high priest "we have" (ἔχομεν) (Heb 4:14, 15; 8:1) who is faithful, co-suffering and merciful (Heb 2:17; 3:2; 4:15), indicates the existential danger the congregation is facing.

As I note elsewhere, "Temptation, suffering, persecution and sin are threatening the spiritual and physical well-being of the recipients."[60] As such, the author firmly but also pastorally calls the audience to stand firm in their faith so that they do not fall into faithlessness, rebellion, and hardened hearts.[61]

In this section, I would like to focus on a few lexemes that convey the idea of endurance, that are used to call the audience to persevere: κρατέω ("hold fast"), κατέχω ("hold"/"hold fast"), ὑπομένω ("to endure"), and ὑπομονή ("endurance").[62] The focus on these four terms does not mean the notion of endurance is absent when these terms do not appear. In fact, the motif of endurance is interspersed throughout the epistle, albeit usually without the explicit term "endurance" or "to endure" (Heb 3:6, 12, 14; 4:1, 11; 6:11–12, 18; 10:23, 37–39; 12:12–14).

Endurance is not a foreign concept for East Africans. Long-distance runners—whether from Kenya or Ethiopia—often remind us what endurance is and the result of enduring to

58. Selam Desta, ደሙ::/"His Blood." Translation from Amharic to English is mine.

59. Olowola, "Sacrifice in African Tradition," 5; cf. Tesfaye Kassa, "Hebrews," in *Africa Bible Commentary: A One-Volume Commentary Written by 70 African Scholars*, ed. Tokunboh Adeyemo (WordAlive Publishers; Zondervan, 2006), 1526–1527.

60. Urga, *Intercession of Jesus in Hebrews*, 159.

61. Urga, *Intercession of Jesus in Hebrews*, 159–160.

62. For more on persecution and suffering in Hebrews and the African church, see Abeneazer G. Urga, "Persecution, Perseverance and the Mission of the Church in Hebrews: Implications for the Church in Africa," paper presented at the Africa Society of Evangelical Theology (ASET) at Pan African Christian University in Nairobi, Kenya, March 8, 2024.

the end. A recent *Selamta* magazine (from Ethiopian Airlines) featured the Dibabas—five Ethiopian sisters who are known as "the fastest siblings in the world."[63] The feature article inquires whether these siblings win medals because of their "heritage" or "hard work," or, if I may, their endurance. For instance, Tirunesh Dibaba won two gold medals—in 5,000-meter and 10,000-meter races—at the Beijing Olympics in 2008.[64] The reality is that heritage alone does not help someone get to the finish line. The author of this feature article acknowledges that Tirunesh Dibaba, for example, trains daily for several hours.[65] This "hard work" coupled with "determination" is what helps athletes like Tirunesh Dibaba shine on world stages and win gold, silver, or bronze medals. These athletes persevere through the arduous training every single day and during the competitive races in which they participate.

The term κρατέω appears twice in Hebrews (4:14; 6:18). In both places it means to hold fast or remain faithful to the superior high priest and Son of God. Hebrews 4:14–16 comes right after the discourse on the wilderness generation, whereby the author paints a grim picture of God's people in the desert. They were rebellious; they had evil and hardened hearts that ignored the voice of the Spirit (Heb 3:7–4:13). The wilderness generation did not persevere, and, as such, they perished in the wilderness. They were unable to hold fast to their faith in God. On the contrary, they questioned and tested God (cf. Exod 17:7).

The consequence of their disobedience and lack of commitment to the Lord was that their "bodies fell in the wilderness" (Heb 3:17). The narration of the story of the wilderness generation serves to warn the congregation not to repeat the same fatal error. The author is urging them—heuristically—that lack of commitment, faithlessness, and spiritual apathy lead to divine punishment.[66] The identity and work of Christ—both the great high priest and God's Son—is used as a motivation for the congregation to hold fast to the better high priest. John W. Kleinig rightly notes that κρατέω is "a technical term for the retention of what has been handed on to the congregation and received by it in catechetical instruction."[67] Striving "to hold fast the hope set before us" (ESV) is a healthy sign of perseverance, our commitment to the better high priest and Son of God.

Another term that conveys a similar idea as that of κρατέω is κατέχω. The expression appears in three instances (Heb 3:6, 14; 10:23). In 3:6, it states that if the congregation holds fast their confidence (παρρησία) in the faithful Son of God rather than the lesser mediators and messengers of God, they will continue to be God's house or dwelling. Again in 3:14 the conditional language is used to solicit perseverance: "For we have become partners in Christ, if only we hold our first confidence firm to the end."

Much like Tirunesh Dibaba and her siblings, the audience needs to persevere to receive the gold medal (here being "partners of Christ"). They have to run all the way to the end and cross the finish line if they intend to maintain their partnerships with Christ.

63. Victoria Beardwood, "Running in the Family," *Selamta* (July–August 2024): 036–043, here 036.

64. Beardwood, "Running in the Family," 039.

65. Beardwood, "Running in the Family," 043.

66. See Urga, *Intercession of Jesus in Hebrews*, 176–177.

67. John W. Kleinig, *Hebrews*, Concordia Commentary (Concordia Publishing House, 2017), 225.

Finally, Hebrews 10:23 states: "Let us hold fast to the confession of our hope without wavering, for he who has promised is faithful." This passage reiterates what the author has already asserted in 4:14. Here the author adds ἀκλινής ("without wavering") to modify κατέχω. The manner in which they need to hold on to the confession and show their perseverance in the face of every sort of danger and uncertainty is "without wavering."

The discourse on endurance continues using the explicit terms ὑπομένω ("to endure") and ὑπομονή ("endurance") in chapters 10 and 12. However, the entire passage of Hebrews 10:19–12:29 deals with perseverance and faith extensively. In fact, two of the five warnings appear in this section. It is also in this section where we find the verbal and noun forms of endurance mentioned (10:32, 36; 12:1, 2, 3, 7). The exhortation to persevere now and in the future is by appealing to their past commendable perseverance under the threat of persecution. Hebrews 10:32–39 details their faithfulness: they "endured a hard struggle with sufferings" (πολλὴν ἄθλησιν ὑπεμείνατε παθημάτων); they received "abuse and persecution" (ὀνειδισμοῖς τε καὶ θλίψεσιν), they "cheerfully accepted the plundering of [their] possessions" (τὴν ἁρπαγὴν τῶν ὑπαρχόντων ὑμῶν μετὰ χαρᾶς προσεδέξασθε) (Heb 10:32–34). This exemplary past perseverance must continue in their current faith journey. By holding on to their "confidence" (παρρησία), they display their commitment to the Son of God.

Hebrews 10:36 makes clear that the congregation is probably wavering in their faith and abandoning their confidence in the superior and great high priest. The author asserts: "For you need endurance (ὑπομονῆς), so that when you have done the will of God, you may receive what was promised." The author then proceeds to list faithful believers in God who persevered and completed their faith journey successfully (Heb 11:1–40). The historical narration of God's men and women in Hebrews 11 is utilized to nudge the audience to get their act together and take their confession of the Son of God and the better high priest seriously.

In Hebrews 12:1–3 the author again exhorts the congregation to persevere in the faith. Here he employs athletic imagery. Philip Hughes notes that the congregation has "set out on the race but, after a good start (10:32–34), [is] now slackening in the will to persevere."[68] The sources of their lack of endurance, spiritual apathy, and lack of determination are "weight" (ὄγκος) and "sin" (ἁμαρτία). They need to "lay aside" the weight in order to continue their race and make it to the finish line. The message of the imagery is clear: "For an athlete, extra weight is a hindrance. As such, removing one's clothing ahead of the competition is paramount."[69] After getting rid of the dead weight, the congregation is exhorted to "run with perseverance the race that is set before [them]" (Heb 12:1). An athlete cannot slack off in the middle of a race and expect to be rewarded for their feebleness. To the contrary, determination, perseverance, and making every effort to stay on track will help them receive God's promises. The call for endurance and the language of contest (ἀγών) "all point to the inevitable suffering and pain the Christian journey entails."[70]

---

68. Hughes, *Hebrews*, 520.
69. Urga, *Intercession of Jesus in Hebrews*, 233.
70. Urga, *Intercession of Jesus in Hebrews*, 233.

The perfect example to persevere in the face of persecution is Jesus himself. Jesus persevered to the end. The author of Hebrews states: he "endured the cross" (ὑπέμεινεν σταυρὸν) (Heb 12:2). The weight, sin, and other mediators have distracted them and made them take their eyes off Jesus. But "looking to Jesus" (ἀφορῶντες εἰς τὸν Ἰησοῦν) will help them endure to the end. Jesus faced utter humiliation and suffering, but he stayed on track; he ran his race with endurance and completed his mission as the sent Son and high priest. He was not distracted by the shame associated with the degrading cross. Rather, he "[disregarded] its shame" and as a result is now seated at the right hand of his Father (Heb 12:2). His exaltation is because he "endured (ὑπομεμενηκότα) from sinners such hostility against himself." Jesus was determined and committed to finish his task despite the hostility (ἀντιλογία) he faced.

Therefore, the congregation should also follow in his footsteps and endure any and every kind of hostility that may come their way. However, they can only persevere if they consider (ἀναλογίσασθε) Jesus, who "endured the cross" for their sake.

Tamrat Haile, an Ethiopian singer, aptly captures the idea of endurance particularly found in Hebrews 10:37–39:

> *"The righteous one lives by faith*
> *The righteous one lives by faith*
> *If he shrinks back, he will be hated by me*
> *My soul has no pleasure in him"*
> *Jesus said.*
>
> *Wait for him patiently in silence*
> *The Lord will lean forward*
> *Do not be fooled, my friend, for the time is done*
> *You are about to complete the long journey*
> *A little is left for you to hear the trumpet*
> *To enter and rest in the beautiful city.*[71]

Tamrat Haile urges his listeners—Ethiopian Christians—to persevere to the end. The end is so near and the conclusion of the journey is so close, that the believer should not give up when he or she is almost there. For Tamrat Haile, it is foolishness to give up when what is left is "a quarter of an hour." Rather, the believer is to be patient, silent, and hopeful.

The message of perseverance in Hebrews and its echo in Tamrat Haile's song needs to reverberate in Africa, particularly in Ethiopia where prosperity gospel preachers assure the people that there is no pain, suffering, and difficulty in life. The denial of pain and suffering does not make pain and suffering go away. What will help the church in Ethiopia and beyond is to acknowledge that the Christian life is never without pain and suffering, recognizing gratefully that the book of Hebrews has given us a few pointers on how to respond to pain, suffering, and hostility.

---

71. Tamrat Haile, በእምነት ይኖራል ጻድቅ ("The just lives by faith"). My translation from Amharic to English.

First and foremost, the church needs to "look to" (ἀφοράω) Jesus. Sigurd Grindheim is on point when he comments: "To fix one's gaze, it is necessary to ignore everything else."[72] The congregation in the book of Hebrews is distracted by inferior mediators, temptation, sin, suffering, and persecution. The solution is not denial but rather gluing their eyes on the mediator of the better covenant. Second, they need to "consider" (ἀναλογίζομαι) Jesus. Comparing and contrasting their situation with Jesus and then realizing that they have not yet experienced hostility to the extent that he did (cf. Heb 12:4) but that he endured severe persecution will help them endure pain, suffering, and persecution themselves.

Ethiopian Christians should not be fooled by false promises propagated by prosperity gospel preachers. They should strive to enter God's rest and inherit God's promises despite the pain and suffering they are facing. As Tamrat Haile reminds us, we have only "a quarter of an hour" left in our faith journey. Hence waiting for God "patiently in silence" while fixing our eyes on Jesus and what he endured will enable us to finish the race and receive our gold medal—like Tirunesh Dibaba—at the finish line.

Christian Hospitality

Hospitality is considered one of the cultural hallmarks of Africans. Ethiopians pride themselves on being very hospitable. One Ethiopian, for instance, reflects the notion that being an Ethiopian and showing hospitality are one and the same:

> I grew up with the understanding that Ethiopia was a hospitable country. This was communicated through media, the government communicated this, there was just this idea that Ethiopians are hospitable people, we love to welcome strangers, we are kind, we always have our arms open to outsiders. It was almost like a synonym for Ethiopia—hospitality.[73]

Emily J. Choge is correct that "in most African languages the same word is used for both 'stranger' and 'guest.'"[74] For instance, in Ethiopia both a stranger and a guest are called *engida*. The *engida* could be a total stranger that one does not know, a friend who comes to one's home as a guest, or an unknown honored guest that is invited to one's home.

Guests and strangers are usually welcomed in the name of God. They are considered or received—especially in rural areas—as *ye'egziher engida* ("God's guests" or "strangers sent by God"). The host of God's guests provides food, drink, and lodging. Jessica A. Udall records a conversation with one Ethiopian who narrates his childhood memory of his grandma's hospitality to strangers. Udall writes:

72. Sigurd Grindheim, *The Letter to the Hebrews*, PNTC (Eerdmans, 2023), 614.

73. Jessica A. Udall, *Building Community Through Hospitality: Insights from Ethiopia for America's Loneliness Epidemic*, EMSMS 21 (Pickwick Publications, 2024), 88.

74. Emily J. Choge, "Hospitality in Africa," in *Africa Bible Commentary: A One-Volume Commentary Written by 70 African Scholars*, ed. Tokunboh Adeyemo (WordAlive Publishers; Zondervan, 2006), 390.

> The ancient hospitality rituals of Ethiopia have intensely spiritual undertones and remind Christian observers of biblical stories and commands. [An Ethiopian interviewee] describes his childhood home as situated in a hub for foot travel in an area that did not have roads that could accommodate cars. Very often, a traveler would stop by their house and say the expected phrase: "I am God's guest, can you host me?" His grandma would reply warmly, "Well, this is God's house. Welcome!" She would wash their feet, feed them, give them a bed for the night, make them breakfast, and pack them a lunch for the road. "There was no wondering, 'Who are they? Where are they coming from?'" he reminisces.[75]

However, such a beautiful practice of hospitality has become a thing of the past. The prosperity gospel, individualism, political and economic factors, and tribalism have become obstacles to Christian hospitality in Ethiopia.[76] In addition to this, a robust theological underpinning for the practice of hospitality in Ethiopia is wanting. When the practice of hospitality is purely built on the foundation of culture with an unarticulated spiritual element, it cannot withstand whatever erosion comes its way.

The author of Hebrews exhorts his audience to keep practicing hospitality. It appears that a once vibrant and hospitable congregation has become apathetic and inhospitable. Hence the author commands his audience: "Do not neglect to show hospitality to strangers, for by doing that some have entertained angels without knowing it" (Heb 13:2).

In Hebrews 13, the author concludes his sermonic letter with a string of exhortations (esp. 13:1–6)[77] and reminds his audience that they need to showcase their faith in the superior high priest and Son of God by practicing Christian virtues. Among the prescribed practices is hospitality to others. Indeed, "The practice of hospitality is not a uniquely Christian virtue."[78] The practice of hospitality by Christians is one area where Christians and their Greco-Roman and Jewish cultures agree. Hence, according to Andrew Arterbury, "early Christian hospitality was in continuity with the broader Mediterranean social convention of hospitality."[79]

The reasons for the exhortation "not to neglect to show hospitality to others" could be to assist those believers who "are ostracized, forced to migrate or lost their possessions and wealth for the sake of their faith."[80] It could also be because of the indifference of the audience toward their fellow worshippers and other strangers, which stems from their inattentiveness

75. Udall, *Building Community Through Hospitality*, 51.

76. See Choge, "Hospitality in Africa," 390; Kassa, "Hebrews," 1532–1533; Abeneazer G. Urga, "Possessions, Greed and the Christian Community: Interrogating Prosperity Gospel in Africa in Light of Hebrews 13:1–6," in *Healthy and Wealthy? A Biblical-Theological Response to the Prosperity Gospel*, ed. Rob Plummer (Fontes Press, 2022), 143, 145.

77. Schreiner, *A Commentary on Hebrews*, 409.

78. Urga, "Possessions," 142.

79. Andrew Arterbury, *Entertaining Angels: Early Christian Hospitality in its Mediterranean Setting*, NTM 8 (Sheffield Phoenix Press, 2005), 94; see also Bruce, *The Epistle to the Hebrews*, 370.

80. Urga, "Possessions," 142.

to the word they heard from the Lord's messengers (cf. Heb 2:1). Hence, the author urges his audience "not to neglect" the practice of hospitality.

Whatever the reason for the exhortation, the audience needs to practice the virtue of hospitality. The exhortation in Hebrews 13:2 stands out for two reasons. First, the term "hospitality" (φιλοξενία) is fronted for emphasis.[81] Second, as Amy Peeler rightly denotes, the focus is not "what they should do" but what they should not do: "Don't forget!"[82]

The root word for the term φιλοξενία is ξεν- —which conveys the idea of being "strange," "foreign," "alien," or "guest."[83] When ξένος is combined with φίλος, we get "hospitality," "the love of hospitality," or "love of strangers or guests" (cf. Rom 12:13). The audience is urged to "not neglect to love hospitality or love strangers." The negative imperatival expression, μὴ ἐπιλανθάνεσθε, urges the congregation to be attentive to, care for, and be hospitable to strangers. Doing so will be rewarding in the eyes of God (cf. Heb 6:10; 13:16).[84]

Some contend that the command to show hospitality is confined to fellow Christians who were experiencing persecution and those who were itinerant teachers, prophets, evangelists, and apostles.[85] Nonetheless, the exhortation to practice hospitality is not limited to fellow Christians; it also extends to non-Christians.[86] The early church was able to assist fellow believers during severe persecution and forced displacement by providing food, shelter, and protection. The church was also able to spread the gospel message through Christian hospitality.[87]

Why should the congregation practice hospitality, and love the stranger? The motivation for being mindful to show hospitality to fellow Christians and non-Christians alike is introduced by the subordinate conjunction γάρ ("for"): "for through this some received angels as guests without knowing it" (Heb 13:2, my literal translation). The motivation alludes to Abraham's and Lot's extension of hospitality to strangers (Gen 18–19). Abraham received the three men and offered them food, a place to rest and to wash their feet (Gen 18:2–16). Lot also welcomed two angels and offered them food, lodging, and to wash their feet (Gen 19:1–3).

Abraham and Lot were the ideal exemplars who did not neglect hospitality. They accepted strangers sent by God. The patriarch and his nephew Lot did not know (ἔλαθόν) that the strangers were angels, but they welcomed them anyway. They offered the guests food, lodging, protection, and washing of their feet.

---

81. Cockerill, *Hebrews*, 679.

82. Amy Peeler, *Hebrews*, CCF (Eerdmans, 2004), 403.

83. Stählin, "ξένος κτλ.," 1–2; cf. Arterbury, *Entertaining Angels*, 97.

84. Peeler, *Hebrews*, 403; see also Kleinig, *Hebrews*, 676.

85. Ellingworth, *The Epistle to the Hebrews*, 694.

86. Urga, "Possessions," 142; cf. Amos Yong, *Hospitality and the Other: Pentecost, Christian Practices and the Neighbor* (Orbis Books, 2008), 115.

87. On the missional aspect of hospitality, see Edward L. Smither, *Mission as Hospitality: Imitating the Hospitable God in Mission* (Cascade Books, 2021).

The author of Hebrews nudges the congregation to show hospitality because they might be welcoming "a divine messenger in disguise."[88] The idea that strangers or guests are *ye'egiziher engida* is not unique to Ethiopia. In antiquity the notion of "theoxenic hospitality" already existed. People in antiquity believed "that the gods or their representatives often visited humans in the form of beggars or strangers."[89] As such, "many hosts were subsequently motivated to treat all strangers with kindness."[90] Such a welcoming posture is considered a service to the divine. In other words, hospitality is grounded in theological assumptions: it is welcoming and pleasing the divine being.[91]

A few Ethiopian singers have reflected on the idea of *theoxenia* (offering hospitality to God). For instance, one of Tamrat Haile's well-known songs, "Alegn Ketero" ("I have an appointment"), indicates the idea of entertaining Jesus the Lord:

> *I have an appointment with a guest called Jesus*
> *Let me rise up and prepare my home.*
>
> *His hour is not known, his coming is like a thief*
> *His footsteps are not heard when he goes in and out*
> *His voice doesn't disrupt anyone, his cry doesn't bother*
> *The coming of Jesus will be sudden.*
>
> *After inviting a guest why [am I] sleeping?*
> *Let me make lunch for the day and dinner for the night*
> *Let me stay awake and wait for the Lord of my life*
> *Let me gird my loins and say "Maranatha"!*[92]

Tamrat Haile considers Jesus the eschatological guest who needs to be entertained. The honor that a guest deserves is scripted in the song. Preparing the home includes cleaning it and making it presentable, as well as preparing a meal for the guest so that he feels welcomed. Once a guest is invited there is no rest or slacking off because the unprepared host will lose face and the guest will be dishonored.

Tamrat Haile should be commended for this creative utilization of culture to nudge his audience to be ready for the eschaton because Jesus will come back. The church needs to be ready to welcome him, getting busy with sharing the gospel in the meantime. However, the Ethiopian church should also consider showing hospitality to the Lord by entertaining and

88. Koester, *Hebrews*, 558.

89. Arterbury, *Entertaining Angels*, 95.

90. Arterbury, *Entertaining Angels*, 95.

91. For other motives on why people in the Greco-Roman society practiced hospitality, see Arterbury, *Entertaining Angels*, 95–97.

92. Tamrat Haile, አለኝ ፡ ቀጠሮ/ "I have an Appointment." Translation from Amharic to English is mine.

welcoming the poor, the vulnerable, and their fellow believers and unbelievers alike. The eschatological should be coupled with the present.

The fact that welcoming strangers who need food, lodging, cleansing, and comfort is welcoming God and his messengers should nudge us "not to neglect to show hospitality to strangers." There are several faithful ministers of God and his gospel who are languishing because of persecution or lack of money and food. Instead of scattering the possessions God has given us to the swindling prosperity gospel preachers and teachers, it is more fitting to entertain those who are in need by providing food, clothing, shelter, tuition fees for their children, and so on.

Instead of inviting the "haves" so that we can get invited back to their mansions, it is worthy to invite those who cannot invite us back. Welcoming them as *ye'egizeher engida*, as God's messengers or those in need to encounter God as their host is more profitable and in line with Hebrews 13:2. Doing so is doing it unto God himself (cf. Matt 25:40).

Conclusion

Bediako is correct in giving Hebrews the epithet, the "Epistle to African Christians," because of the strong resonance of the theological themes found in the sermonic letter. The four main themes discussed in this chapter are the priesthood of Christ, the sacrifice of Christ, perseverance in the face of persecution, and Christian hospitality. These theological motifs resonate with African cultural and theological landscapes by confirming the consciousness of Africans, in this case, Ethiopians, in their articulation and practices of these themes. However, the themes also simultaneously challenge Africans where they fall short in understanding and putting into practice the explored themes.

The confirmation and challenge Hebrews brings to the table of theological discussion of the African church provides an important theological fact: God still speaks to Africans by his Son. Hebrews nudges Christian Africans to confess the unique Son of God, who is the better high priest who offered a better sacrifice, and live out their confession in practical ways: by being hospitable to others and being courageous in the face of inevitable persecution.

Further Reading

Asumang, Annang. *Unlocking the Book of Hebrew: A Spatial Analysis of the Epistle to the Hebrews*. Wipf & Stock, 2008.

Bediako, Kwame. "Christian Faith and African Culture: An Exposition of the Epistle to the Hebrews." *Journal of African Christian Thought* 13, no. 1 (June 2010): 45–57.

Bediako, Kwame. *Jesus and the Gospel in Africa: History and Experience*. Orbis Books, 2004.

deSilva, David A. *Despising Shame: Honor Discourse and Community Maintenance in the Epistle to the Hebrews*. Rev. ed. SBL, 2008.

deSilva, David A. *Perseverance in Gratitude: A Socio-Rhetorical Commentary on the Epistle "to the Hebrews."* Eerdmans, 2000.

Ekem, John D. K. *Priesthood in Context: A Study of Priesthood in Some Christian and Primal Communities of Ghana and Its Relevance for Mother-Tongue Biblical Interpretation*. SonLife Press, 2009.

Gause, R. Hollis. *Hebrews*. PCS. Brill, 2022.
Grindheim, Sigurd. *The Letter to the Hebrews*. PNTC. Eerdmans, 2023.
Hughes, Philip E. *A Commentary on Hebrews*. Eerdmans, 1977.
Kalengyo, Edison Muhindo. *Sacrifice in Hebrews and the Pauline Epistles*. Acton Publishers, 2015.
Kassa, Tesfaye "Hebrews." In *Africa Bible Commentary: A One-Volume Commentary Written by 70 African Scholars*, edited by Tokunboh Adeyemo. WordAlive Publishers; Zondervan, 2006.
Nyende, Peter. "Hebrews' Christology and Its Contemporary Apprehension in Africa." *Neotestamentica* 41, no. 2 (2007): 361–381.
Nyende, Peter. "Why Bother with Hebrews? An African Perspective." *Heythrop Journal* 46 (2005): 512–524.
Olowola, Cornelius. "Sacrifice in African Tradition and in Biblical Perspective." *Africa Journal of Evangelical Theology* 10, no. 1 (1991): 3–9.
Punt, Jeremy. "Hebrews, Thought-Patterns and Context: Aspects of the Background of Hebrews." *Neotestamentica* 31, no. 1 (1997): 119–158.
Schreiter, Robert J., ed. *Faces of Jesus in Africa*. Orbis Books, 1991.
Stinton, Diane B. *Jesus of Africa: Voices of Contemporary African Christology*. Orbis Books, 2004.
Terefe, Nebeyou A. "Εντυγχάνειν in Hebrews 7.25 and Its Translation in the Millennium Amharic Bible." In *Reading Hebrews and 1 Peter from Majority World Perspectives*, edited by Sofanit T. Abebe, Elizabeth W. Mburu, and Abeneazer G. Urga. LNTS 700. Bloomsbury T&T Clark, 2024.
Urga, Abeneazer G. "Christ Intercedes or Judges? An Examination of the Ethiopian Orthodox *Tewahido* Church's Rendering and Interpretation of *Entynchanō* in Hebrews 7:25." In *The New Testament Around the World: Exploring Key Texts from Different Contexts*, edited by Mariam Kamell Kovalishyn. Baker Academic, 2025.
Urga, Abeneazer G. "Evangelism in Hebrews." In *Reading Hebrews Missiologically*, edited by Abeneazer G. Urga, Edward L. Smither, and Linda P. Saunders. William Carey Publishing, 2023.
Urga, Abeneazer G. *Intercession of Jesus in Hebrews: The Background and Nature of Jesus' Heavenly Intercession in the Epistle to the Hebrews*. WUNT 2/585. Mohr Siebeck, 2023.
Urga, Abeneazer G. "Persecution, Perseverance and the Mission of the Church in Hebrews: Implications for the Church in Africa." Paper presented at the Africa Society of Evangelical Theology (ASET) at Pan African Christian University in Nairobi, Kenya, March 8, 2024.
Urga, Abeneazer G. "Possessions, Greed and the Christian Community: Interrogating Prosperity Gospel in Africa in Light of Hebrews 13:1–6." In *Healthy and Wealthy? A Biblical-Theological Response to the Prosperity Gospel*, edited by Rob Plummer. Fontes Press, 2022.
Urga, Abeneazer G. "The Victorious High Priest in Africa: Christ and the Logic of Atonement in Hebrews 2:14–18." *Stellenbosch Theological Journal* vol. 10, no. 1 (2024): 1–24.
Urga, Abeneazer G. "Why Did Paul Write Hebrews? Reasons for the Composition of Hebrews in the Ethiopian Orthodox Tewahido Church's Andemta Commentary Tradition." In *Reading Hebrews and 1 Peter from Majority World Perspectives*, edited by Sofanit T. Abebe, Elizabeth W. Mburu, and Abeneazer G. Urga. LNTS 700. Bloomsbury T&T Clark, 2024.
Young, Norman H. "Suffering: A Key to the Epistle to the Hebrews." *Australian Biblical Review* 51 (2003): 47–59.

CHAPTER TWENTY

The Letter of James

Axolile N. M. Qina
New College, University of Edinburgh
United Kingdom

Introduction

THE EPISTLE OF James's five chapters provocatively challenge Christians to exercise restraint regarding what comes out of their mouths because the tongue can praise God and curse humans made in the image of God (cf. Jas 3:6–9), and to refrain from boasting about what tomorrow may bring but receive tomorrow as something given to humans in accordance with the will of God (cf. Jas 4:14–15). James also challenges Christians to show no partiality to people regardless of their socioeconomic standing but rather to treat all with mercy that triumphs over judgment (cf. Jas 2:8–13). If such instructions are not adhered to, at least in the literary world of James, Christians are described as follows: (1) sinners that are transgressors of the law—to show partiality breaches God's commandment to love your neighbor as you love yourself (cf. Jas 2:8–11; Lev 19:8); (2) arrogant—as boasting about tomorrow is grounded in a persons' own arrogance and they commit sin (cf. Jas 4:16–17; Prov 27:1–2); and (3) those who defile their whole body—because the tongue is a fire that can make the human body impure and if it is not monitored can result in destruction and condemnation (cf. Jas 3:2–8, Ps 34:13; Prov 18:21). These assertions may seem foreign and archaic to us in our capitalist technological era, where the accumulation of wealth is precipitated with prestige, peoples' speech can be written and verbally transmitted through social media platforms, and determining our future is to be applauded as a human virtue that ultimately allows humans to discern their destiny.

How then should we read and interpret James for Christians living on the African continent? And what parallels can we draw between the "world of the text" and the context of Christian Africans? The Epistle of James does have significant parallels to Christian African contexts. For example, in James 1:3–4, trials are not only a test of faith, but also produce an endurance that develops a maturity within the life of a Christian. This maturity ensures that a Christian is complete, whole, and lacking in nothing (cf. Jas 1:3). The Greek word for "whole" (ὁλόκληροι) is an adjective in the nominative plural form of "sound, whole, and complete" (ὁλόκληρος).[1] In African Traditional Religions, wholeness is measured through

1. Cf. Barclay M. Newman, *A Concise Greek–English Dictionary of the New Testament*, rev. ed. (United Bible Societies, 2010), s.v., ὁλόκληρος; BDAG, 703–704.

a human person's right-standing with their ancestors, who are understood to reside in the unseen spiritual realms. Among Xhosas in South Africa, ancestors, referred to as *izinyanya*, are deceased relatives who operate as mediators between humans and the Supreme High god (or "the Supreme Being"). Human relationships between ancestors are maintained through the observation of ritual traditions that include animal sacrifices and beer offerings after the birth of a new child, following male rites of passage and female stages of maturation, at the time of marriage, during funerals, and at the conclusion of mourning periods with regards to familial relatives' death.[2] Similarly to other ethnic Indigenous groups on the African continent, if a person is not in good standing with their ancestors, they can experience disharmony in their everyday life. Such a disconnection leaves them vulnerable to forces residing in the unseen spiritual realms, like evil spirits, personal and impersonal forces, and other divinities.[3] However, continual observance of these traditional rituals avoids disunification, since Africans' adherence to their Indigenous customs ensures fortune, good luck, and favor from the ancestors that reside in the spiritual realms before the Supreme Being.

Humans' disharmony with their ancestors can manifest itself physically in the form of illness, misfortune, and even sudden death. Though some may consider these beliefs as mere superstition, they are a lived reality in Xhosa and other African Indigenous belief systems. To rectify this disunity with the spiritual realm, in Xhosa Indigenous religion it is necessary to consult a "priest-diviner" (*iGqira*) or a "spiritual doctor" (*iSangoma*) to understand how to restore their relationship with their ancestors. Justin K. Ukpong contends that offerings to deliver a person from spiritual disharmony ought to be directed to the actual spirit that is responsible for carrying out the punishment.[4] However, among the Xhosa, ancestors are the guardians of the home and are ultimately responsible for protecting or allowing punishment toward their human relatives, regardless of the spiritual source responsible for the production of negative effects. James's call for Christians to endure suffering, trials, and tribulations counterculturally challenges African Indigenous belief systems in which difficult situations are considered of no benefit and ought to be avoided at all costs. Thus, in some African contexts, James 1:3–4 requires converts to change their relationship with the unseen realm in light of their faith in Jesus Christ.

To this end, I first clarify the parallels between the literary "world of the text" (James) and the contextual "world in front of the text" Christian Africans particularly Africans' religious beliefs prevalent in their Indigenous and ritual traditions. After exploring this

2. See also John H. Soga, *Ama-Xosa: Life and Customs* (Lovedale Press, 1932), 145–182; Sithembele Sipuka, "The Sacrifice of the Mass and the Concept of Sacrifice Among the Xhosa: Towards an Inculturated Understanding of the Eucharist" (PhD diss., University of South Africa, 2000), 133–175.

3. For more information: Jacob K. Olupona, *African Religions: A Very Short Introduction* (Oxford University Press, 2014), 1–37; Ogbu U. Kalu, "Ancestral Spirituality and Society in Africa," in *African Spirituality: Forms, Meanings, and Expressions*, ed. Jacob K. Olupona, World Spirituality: An Encyclopaedic History of the Religious Quest 3 (The Crossroad Publishing Company, 2011), 54–58; Mercy A. Oduyoye, "Women and Ritual," in *The Will to Arise: Women, Tradition, and the Church in Africa*, ed. Mercy A. Oduyoye and Rachel A. Kanyoro (Orbis Books, 1992), 20–22.

4. Cf. Justin K. Ukpong, "Sacrificial Worship in Ibiobio Traditional Religion," *Journal of Religion in Africa* 13 (1982): 184.

"pre-understanding" of what the text of James says in relation to Christian Africans' contexts, "the world of the text" is examined within its historical context ("the world behind the text"). In doing so, connections that were made between James and Christian Africans' Indigenous context are comprehended in James's original setting before they can be applied to the African context. The third and final section of this chapter provides a theological interpretation that applies the findings from "the world behind the text" to the initial points of contact between "the world in front of the text" and "the world of the text" so a transformed rereading and interpretation can be articulated in "the world of the text" for Christian Africans today. In what follows, I examine the textual world of James in connection with the cultural and religious context of African Indigenous beliefs.

Bridging the Horizons
Situating James in the African Context

African religious practices are covenantal ritual traditions between humans and their ancestors, who expect sacrifices, offerings, libations, and observation of customs in exchange for their favorable mediation and protection. James 5:13–20 challenges this and offers alternative spiritual practices for Christian converts to adhere to until the parousia. This includes: praying "in the name of the Lord" (5:13–15), Christian church elders anointing the sick with oil (5:14–15), singing songs of praise to God (5:13), confession of sins to Christians in the church community (5:16), and actively participating in God's salvific work to restore humans through faith in the Son of God, Jesus of Nazareth. This restorative work also includes those Christians that have "wandered from the truth" associated with Jesus (cf. Jas 5:19–20).

Such an ingroup focus and concern in James does not prevent evangelism of non-Christian peoples. For instance, "true religion" that is "pure" and "undefiled" before God the Father cares for the poor, orphans, and widows who are in distress (cf. Jas 1:27). These characteristics align with the two types of "wisdoms" articulated in James, namely: (1) the wisdom from God that is "pure" and "full of mercy," and produces the fruit of righteousness (3:17–18); and (2) the wisdom that is of this world, which is not "from above" (3:13, 17), and categorized to be earthly, unspiritual, and devilish (3:15). These two types of wisdoms from God or the literary textual world in James have intertextual resonance with relevant Old Testament and New Testament texts. For example, in Old Testament wisdom literature, it is "the fear of the Lord that is the beginning of wisdom/knowledge" (cf. Prov 1:7; 2:5; 9:10; Job 28:28; Ps 111:10). The New Testament, on the other hand, presents the righteousness of Christian converts before God, which can be received through their "faith in Jesus Christ" (cf. Rom 3:22–23; Phil 3:8–9; Gal 5:5).

James contests the New Testament argument of righteousness through faith alone. For instance, in Galatians 3:1–9 (compare with Jas 2:19–26), Paul admonishes the Galatian Christian community and uses Abraham as an example of faith (cf. Jas 2:20–26; Gal 3:6–9). However, in both texts, James 2:23 and Galatians 3:6, Genesis 15:6 is cited to emphasize the faithfulness of Abraham to God. For James, though, faith and works are synonymous (cf.

Jas 2:24), while Paul argues that faith alone obtains righteousness (cf. Gal 3:9, 11; see also Rom 3:22–24; Phil 3:8–9). Paul focuses on how the faith of Abraham relates to God's future promise to him, which entails receiving all nations as descendants (cf. Gal 3:7–9; Gen 15:5). James primarily focuses on the willingness of Abraham to sacrifice his son, Isaac, to God (cf. 2:21–22; Gen 22), as supporting evidence that faith which is not expressed through works/deeds is flawed (cf. 2:21–24).

There is evidence of James blending traditional Jewish wisdom ideas and Jesus's teachings as found in the Gospels. For instance, James 1:10–11 retorts that "rich people" will be humbled and wither away like a flower that is scorched by the heat. The poor, however, are "rich in faith" and will become exalted in the future as "heirs of the kingdom" of God (cf. Jas 2:5). Significantly, the *syncrisis* between rich and poor is also a prominent theme in the wisdom text of Proverbs, which are literary figures juxtaposed continuously against each other throughout the text. For example, Proverbs 15:16 reads "Better is a little with the fear of the Lord than great treasure and trouble with it." In the next chapter, "Better is a little with righteousness than large income with injustice." (cf. Prov 16:8). More to the point, the ethic of God favoring the poor is a theme employed in the Synoptic Gospels, and is evident in the case of the rich man being instructed by Jesus to first sell all his wealth before he can follow him and become his disciple (cf. Matt 19:16–23; Mark 10:17–23; Luke 18:18–25).

Thus, James's pragmatic view concerning non-Jewish converts obtaining God's righteousness provides Christian Africans with some practical guidelines on how to live out their faith in their cultural contexts. James achieves this view by merging Old Testament wisdom ideas and early the Christians' New Testament teachings within a Jewish Christian framework that reinterprets ancient Israelites covenant beliefs, and the Torah/Law revelation attributed to Jesus Christ. This is significant for Christian Africans for two reasons: (1) the prosperity gospel's insistence on accumulating wealth as evidence of faith in God; and (2) the ways Christian Africans continue to use spiritual means to cure their health and improve their precarious life situations.

Prosperity gospel churches on the African continent reverse God's priority for the poor and even exploit Christians from lower socioeconomic backgrounds to give the little they have as an offering of faith to allegedly ensure a blessing from God. Other African churches commercialize Christian spiritual practices of healing that are present in James, financially exploiting Christian Africans in their church communities. Additionally, exploitation can take different forms and includes the denial of women's rights to live and freely enjoy the benefits associated with post-apartheid South Africa. For example, in a recent case, young girls were prohibited from receiving an education in school and forced to live on a rural church property as sex slaves, since education was interpreted to be from the devil.

The pioneer of this church demonized any active participation in the democratic vision of South Africa, claiming it to be the work of the antichrist.[5] In other cases, Christian African

5. See also "South Africa Busts Evil Angels Church with Sex Slaves," Vanguard News, February 25, 2018, https://www.vanguardngr.com/2018/02/south-africa-busts-evil-angels-church-100-sex-slaves; "South Africa's 'Prophet of Doom' condemned," BBC News: Africa, November 21, 2016, https://tinyurl.com/mrynxwus; News24, "Angels

leaders claim to be able to imbue water with the power to produce spiritual and physical healing and to cure severe illnesses and diseases like cancer and HIV/Aids. Similarly, they claim that substances like Doom insect spray have healing properties, and regard even their own sexual organs as tools to make followers "holy," with the male pastor insisting that his semen is "holy juice."[6] These disturbing, exploitative, and criminal approaches, unfortunately present in some African churches, need to be urgently addressed to ensure that all Christian Africans can identify non-Christian spiritual healing methods falsely presented as such.

Now that the parallels between "the world of the text" (James) and "the world in front of the text" (contemporary context of Christian Africans) have been considered, I will proceed to examine the "world behind the text" (historical context). This analysis assists in situating the literary text of James ("world of the text") in its historical context so Christian Africans can comprehend what the letter's language would mean for early Christian readers and hearers within the ancient Mediterranean world. I explore this in the next section, which has two objectives: first, it considers James within its historical context, and second, it aims to discuss grammatical elements of genre, textual structure, themes, key words, and various rhetorical techniques employed by the author.

I then synthesize the historical findings and literary analysis by delineating the "purpose and issues" of the Epistle of James. The section "Purpose and Issues" helps to provide a bridge that considers the language of James contextually for first readers in antiquity, which then in turn prepares the ground for the final section of this chapter, "Theological Themes," that attempts to interculturally apply the findings for Christian Africans' discernment and consideration. However, as a brief introduction to "the world behind the text," I begin by distinguishing between time in the New Testament and African Traditional Religions to not only show the physical distance of time and space between James and Christian Africans' contexts, but also to highlight their cultural and religious contextual differences.

Issues of Context

The Greek word "complete" (ὁλόκληρος) occurs in James 1:4 and 1 Thessalonians 5:23. While James uses it in an ethical sense, Thessalonians specifically refers to Christians keeping their spirits, so that they are complete when Jesus returns (cf. 1 Thess 5:23). James 5:7–8 talks about the "coming of the Lord," an expression which in other New Testament texts refers to the second coming of Jesus on earth, the parousia. This is the moment of final judgment for all humanity, the establishment of a new creation, and God's final triumphant victory over human sin and its forces of evil (i.e., the devil and other fallen angels) (cf. Mark 13:24–27;

of Death: A News24 Documentary," YouTube Video, March 15, 2018, https://www.youtube.com/watch?v=oAx-KZOTV_3s, 00:00–29:09.

6. For more information: Collium Banda, "Not Anointing, But Justice? A Critical Reflection on the Anointing of Pentecostal Prophets in a Context of Economic Injustice," *Verbum Ecclesia* 39 (2018): e2–3, https://doi.org/10.4102/ve.v39i1.1870; Mookgo S. Kgatle, "Healing Practices in the Epistle of James Applied to New Prophetic Churches in South Africa," *Neotestamentica* 55 (2021): 114–119; Maria Frahim-Arp, "Pentecostalism, Politics and Prosperity in South Africa," *Religions* 9 (2018): e2–e6, https://doi.org/10.3390/rel9100298.

Matt 24:26–31; Luke 21:25–28; 1 Thess 4:13–18; 5:1–11; 2 Thess 1:5–12; 2 Pet 3:1–13; Rev 20). The present time, until Jesus returns, is a temporary period determined and known by God the Father alone (cf. Mark 13:32; Matt 24:36; Acts 1:7; Luke 12:35–48).

This is seemingly different to how time operates in an African Traditional religious (ATR) context. For instance, John S. Mbiti broadly divides time in African religion as *Sasa* and *Zamani*.[7] *Sasa* refers to the present time in which we live, the now moment that is short lived and in which individuals are fully conscious. *Zamani* is a "macro" view of time, as it is the ultimate reality that all things are destined to be and will eventually absorb reality to completion. In Mbiti's study on New Testament eschatology and time among Kenyan Akamba beliefs, he explains that there is no future like in linear conceptions of time since time moves back and forth through the observation of events grounded in the past.[8] Instead, as Mbiti puts it

> History does not move towards any goal yet in the future: rather, it points to the roots of their existence, such as the origin of the world, the creation of ***humans***, the formation of their customs and traditions, and the coming into being of their whole structure of society. The "present" must conform to the "past" in the sense that it is the "past," rather than any distant future, by means of which people orientate their living and thinking.[9]

Mbiti's point of view is valid even for Xhosa Indigenous beliefs, where humanity derives from *uhlanga*, the source and origin of creation in Xhosa cosmogony.[10] According to Mbiti, the Akamba organize human life in accordance with their past as the universe is an endless reality that will never cease, and "the rhythm of days, months, seasons and years will ever come to a halt, just as there is no end to the rhythm of birth, marriage, procreation and death."[11] However, Xhosa South Africans organized society around their agricultural cycle derived from the stars and which was connected to the changing of seasons and related to observation of ritual traditions. For instance, Janet Hodgson's previous work on the origins of the Xhosas' Supreme Being further highlights this:

> *Isilimela* comes from *ukulima*, which means: "to hoe in seed, dig, plough, and cultivate." *Ukulima* coincides with the cultivation season, where the first appearance of the Pleaides that arises at eastern horizon dawn of each year, is the time when

7. Cf. John S. Mbiti, *African Religions & Philosophy*, 2nd ed. (Heinemann Education Botswana Publishers, 1990), 21–24.

8. Cf. John S. Mbiti, *New Testament Eschatology in an African Background: A Study of the Encounter Between New Testament Theology and African Traditional Concepts* (Oxford University Press, 1971), 24–61.

9. Mbiti, *New Testament Eschatology*, 25, italics mine!

10. See also Janet Hodgson, *The God of the Xhosa: A Study of the Origins and Development of the Traditional Concepts of the Supreme Being* (Oxford University Press, 1982), 18; Jeffrey B. Peires, *The Dead Will Arise: Nongqawuse and the Great Xhosa Cattle Killing Movement of 1856–7 CE* (Raven Press, 1989), 231–232.

11. Mbiti, *New Testament Eschatology*, 25.

> farmers (males herded cattle and women were responsible for the crops) begin their cultivation. This symbolized the new year, called *eyesilimela*, and it occurs in the month of June. The symbolic link with the earth by way of the cultivation period, also symbolized new life in a newly circumcised Xhosa male. Thus, *isimela* symbolized the beginning of a new life in man, as it coincided with coming out ceremony of *abakwetha* (initiate) which was determined by the appearance of this constellation.[12]

Similarly, the Akamba adopt this constant rhythm of life that does "not point to either a teleology or end of the world."[13] Though James admittedly has little eschatology for Mbiti, it still highlights "the coming of the Lord," where Christians are encouraged in the interim to be patient and exercise true religion as form of obedience (cf. Jas 1:22, 27; 2:8; 5.7).[14] This futuristic hope in the New Testament presents challenges for Christian Africans. For instance, afterlife in an African context is a common belief, as ancestors, who continuously live among humans, experience life in the unseen spiritual realm like humans do in this seen realm but without its earthly limitations. Hence, death is not the end of a human's existence but is a transition of a person to existence in the life hereafter. Moreover, African Indigenous ritual traditions are covenantal acts that preserve human relations with the ancestors, who have powers to protect human relatives from evil spirits, misfortune, and illness, and provide descendants with blessings, favor, and prosperity.

Therefore, Africans who convert to Christianity and believe in the second coming of Jesus in the future are faced with the question: How are they to live out their faith convictions within the context of the various cultic demands coming from their Indigenous religious belief systems? What kind of Christian spiritual practices of healing can we find in James that can help Christian African converts deal with misfortune in their independent postcolonial African societies today and ensure a whole spiritual life? To answer these questions, we first need to understand why James was written and how this early Christian text would have been understood in the ancient Mediterranean world.

Authorship and Date

The authorship of James is contingent on the date of this New Testament epistle. For instance, if authorship is attributed to an unknown early Christian named James, or a disciple/editor that compiled the document after the destruction of the Second Jewish Temple in 70 CE, a later date around 90 CE is plausible. This later date is generally accepted because church

12. Hodgson, *The God of the Xhosa*, 53.

13. Mbiti, *New Testament Eschatology*, 48.

14. Cf. Mbiti, *New Testament Eschatology*, 48. See also Todd C. Penner, *The Epistle of James and Eschatology: Re-Reading an Ancient Christian Letter*, JSNTSup 141 (Sheffield Academic Press, 1996).

fathers in the late first century and early second century CE were already using James (cf. 1 Clem 10.1; 11.2; 12.1; Herm. Sim. 9.17.1; 5.4.3; Herm. Mand. 11.8).[15]

A pre–70 CE temple destruction date leads some scholars to following options suggest the following options for authorship: (1) James, the brother of the Lord (known also as: "James, the Just"), (2) James, the Less, (3) James, the Son of Alpheus, (4) James, an unknown early Christian, and (5) James, the son of Zebedee.[16] Options (2), (3), and (4) are difficult to accept, however, since an exhortatory text like James required the writer to have some form of known authority, and to not need to assert clearly the validity of their authorship in the greeting (1:1) (e.g., Rom 1:1–7; 1 Cor 1:1; 2 Cor 1:1; Gal 1:1–2). James (1) and (5), on the other hand, did have this unique authority but both died as martyrs in 62 and 44 CE, respectively. James (5) cannot be ruled out either, even if his early death would seem to suggest an insufficient time to have written a letter for wider circulation among early Christian church communities in the diaspora. Thus, James (1) and (5) are the most likely options, though potentially circulated by their followers.

Nevertheless, the case for an early date and authorship attributed to James the brother of Jesus has textual evidence present in the letter. For example, Luke T. Johnson and Douglas J. Moo, who are proponents of this position, list the following as evidence: the lack of ecclesial structure, instances that characterize opponents, generic usage of "synagogue" (συναγωγή) and "assembly" (ἐκκλησία) as spaces of worship for this Christian church community, and "the elders of the assembly" (τοὺς πρεσβυτέρους τῆς ἐκκλησίας) as a reference to age rather than an established ecclesial position (cf. 2:2; 5:14).[17] In addition to this, James's resonance with the sayings of Jesus (cf. Jas 1:5, 9, 12; 2:5, 8; 5:9, 12), practical approaches of caring for the sick, poor, orphans, and widows (cf. Jas 1.27; 2:14–17), and emphasis on the anticipated "coming" (παρουσία) judgment of the Lord (cf. Jas 2:12–13; 3:1; 4:11–12; 5:7–9) also allude to an earlier dating. To determine the validity of this position, I examine the audience below and consider if authorship should be attributed to James, Jesus's brother, or James, the son of Zebedee, though it will become clear that the former is preferred because of the latter's early death by martyrdom.

Audience

The attribution of authorship to James, the brother of Jesus, or James, the son of Zebedee, posits an initial pre-70 CE Second Jewish Temple date. Commentators agree that the readers and hearers of this epistle were Jewish Christians. Some even highlight how the epistle expresses a schism between Jewish Christians and the gentile Christian mission of Paul. Textual evidence is provided to support this position, particularly in the debate about whether humans can obtain the righteousness of God by "works and faith" or "through faith alone" (cf. Jas 2:20–26;

15. See Ben Witherington III, *Letters and Homilies for Jewish Christians: A Socio-Rhetorical Commentary on Hebrews, James and Jude* (Intervarsity Press, 2007), 397–398.

16. See Scot McKnight, *The Letter of James*, NICNT (Eerdmans, 2011), 13–38; Douglas J. Moo, *The Letter of James*, PNTC (Eerdmans, 2000), 9–27.

17. Cf. Luke Timothy Johnson, *Brother of Jesus, Friend of God: Studies in the Letter of James* (Eerdmans, 2004), 105–108.

Rom 3:22–23; Phil 3:8–9; Gal 5:5). However, Johnson correctly argues that prioritization of Paul in relation to James squarely posits early Christianity being dependent on Paul alone, without consideration of other early Christian writers prevalent in these periods.[18] There are also no cultic issues of gentile Christians having to become circumcised in the letter, nor debates regarding the correct observation of the Law/Torah in a Jewish religious sense for non-Jews that become followers of this new Messianic Jewish movement.

Historically, James, the Lord's brother, was head of the Jewish Christian church in Jerusalem between 44 and 62 CE.[19] The connection of James's overseeing the church in Jerusalem is portrayed positively in both the writings of Luke and Paul, particularly in Acts 15:12–21 during the Council, and when Paul reports who he saw when he visited Jerusalem to confirm his mission to the gentiles (cf. Gal 1:15–20; Acts 21:18; see also 1 Cor 15:7). Moreover, the Christian community of James meets in an "synagogue" (cf. Jas 2:2), and within the "assembly" (cf. Jas 5:14; see also 1 Cor 11:18, 14:19, 34–35) that suggests a formal structure akin to the Pastoral Epistles (e.g., 1 Tim 2–5; Titus 1:5–2:15) is nonexistent. In addition, the Law/Torah is the guiding ethical foundation that recipients universally accept and adheres to the Jewish Shema belief, "God is One" (cf. Jas 1:25–27; 2:19; Deut 6:4). James emphasizes the supremacy of God's Law and advances two Jewish Torah instructions: to love the Lord your God with all your heart and soul, and to love your neighbor as one loves themselves (cf. Jas 1:26–27; Deut 5:6; Lev 19:18). Both instructions constitute the two "greatest commandments" from Jesus in the Synoptic Gospels (cf. Mark 12:29–31; Matt 22:37–40).

In either case, the recipients of James's letter are described as "the twelve tribes in the dispersion" (ταῖς δώδεκα φυλαῖς ταῖς ἐν τῇ διασπορᾷ) (cf. Jas 1:1). Moo argues that "dispersion" refers to the Jewish groups that were exiled following the Assyrian and Babylonian invasions.[20] However, Moo offers socioeconomic conditions to further support an earlier date, locating it around the middle of 40 CE, when there was a severe famine in Judea in 46 CE.[21] If we accept the assertions of Jacob Neusner, Lester Grabbe, E. P. Saunders, Adele Reinhartz, and others who argue that, before the destruction of the Second Jewish Temple, ancient Judaism had various sects (i.e., Zealots, Sadducees, Christians, Sicarii, Essenes, Pharisaic, and Apocalyptic),[22] why were these groups not mentioned in this letter? Johnson cautions interpreters from inferring that "zeal" (ζηλόω) in James 4:1–2 is alluding to the Zealots' activities in the

18. Cf. Johnson, *Brother of Jesus*, 111–116.

19. Cf. Gerald Bray and Thomas Oden, eds., *James, 1–2 Peter, 1–3 John, Jude*, ACCS 11 (Intervarsity Press, 2000), 1–3; Timothy B. Cargal, "The Letter of James," in *The New Oxford Annotated Bible: NRSV with the Apocrypha, An Ecumenical Study*, ed. Michael Coogan, Marc Brettler, Carol Newsom, and Pheme Perkins, 5th rev. ed. (Oxford University Press, 2018), 2165–2166.

20. Cf. Moo, *The Letter of James*, 23–24.

21. Cf. Moo, *The Letter of James*, 26–27.

22. See also Jacob Neusner, "Judaism in a Time of Crisis: Four Responses to the Destruction of the Second Temple," *Judaism* 21 (1972): 313–327; Lester L. Grabbe, *An Introduction to Second Temple Judaism: History and Religion of the Jews in the Time of Nehemiah, the Maccabees, Hillel and Jesus* (T&T Clark, 2010), 76; E. P. Saunders, *Jesus and Judaism* (SCM Press, 1985); Adele Reinhartz, "How Christianity Parted from Judaism," in *Early Judaism: New Insights and Scholarship*, ed. Frederick E. Greenspahn (New York University Press, 2018), 97–120; Magdelane Knopko and Mariusz Rosik, *Church and Synagogue (30–313 AD): Parting of the Ways* (Peter Lang, 2018), 11–44.

first century CE. Rather, as Johnson explains, James utilizes various *topoi* from Hellenistic moral philosophy teachings.[23] Though this does allude to the genre of "the world of the text," which is discussed next, Moo's indication of the socioeconomic circumstances of a famine in Judea rules out James, the son of Zebedee, since he had already died in 44 CE.

I contend that the primacy of the Jewish Torah within the early Christian teachings of Jesus and Paul presents a diasporic Jewish Christian audience. The word diaspora here is important, as Moo also highlights, because it could be alluding to the dispersed covenant people of God. This is further supported by James, the brother of Jesus, becoming appointed as head of the church in Jerusalem in Acts 15. In the retelling of James's martyrdom in 62 CE, Eusebius affirms that the Lord's brother was indeed appointed by the apostles to be the leader in Jerusalem, and his unjust death at the hands of some Jewish leaders set in motion the Judean wars with Rome in 66–70 CE (cf. *Hist. eccl.* 2.23).[24] Whether Eusebius's account is valid or not, his characterization of James "the Just" as righteous and attributing to him the writing of one of the first catholic epistles is relevant for this chapter. Eusebius highlights seven "so-called Catholic epistles" that include Jude and explains that these letters were all read together publicly within most of the churches. With this in view, I argue that this early Christian group is still articulating their convictions of Jesus's messiahship in a Jewish religious setting.

I agree with commentators that a Jewish Christian audience does not make the letter polemic toward gentile Christian inclusion. Instead, the recipients of the letter are the "twelve tribes in the diaspora" (cf. Jas 1:1) and this highlights a wider scope of recipients that include not only Christians of Jewish descent, but also Christians of non-Jewish origin, who have become followers of Jesus through the preaching of the Christian gospel message. Thus, I propose that the author was James, the brother of Jesus, and later, as Eusebius explains, the letter was circulated in Christian communities, following his martyrdom death by stoning,[25] and it was read publicly beyond Jerusalem to the dispersed early Jewish Christian groups spread across the Roman Empire.

Outline

Greetings (1:1)
Prologue (1:2–27): main topics (*topoi*) introduced thematically (*Exordium*)
Topos on wisdom and faith (2:1–3:18) (*Probatio/Refutatio*)
  Partiality contradicts Christian faith witness (2:1–13) (diatribe)
  Speech and actions relationship to authentic faith (2:14–26)
  The corruptible nature of humans' tongues and teaching (3:1–12)
  What true faith born of wisdom looks like (3:13–18) (*Peroratio*)

23. Cf. Johnson, *Brother of Jesus*, 109–110.

24. Cf. Eusebius Pamphil, *Ecclesiastical History: Books 1–5*, trans. Roy J. Deferrari, The Fathers of the Church: A New Translation 19 (Catholic University of American Press, 2005), 124–130.

25. Cf. Eusebius Pamphil, *Ecclesiastical History*, 130; Ralph P. Martin, *James*, Word Biblical Commentary (Thomas Nelson, 1988), lxiv–lxvii; Josephus, *J.W.* 4.305–317; Josephus, *Ant.* 20.180–181.

Topos on conflicts in community and covetousness (4:1–18) (*Probatio/Refutatio*)
Topos on a humble and godly life of faith until parousia (5:1–20) (*Peroratio*)

Purpose and Issues

In James, "rich people" (5:1–3, 4–6) are described as hoarding wealth (5:2–3) at the expense of their employees, who in turn suffer from exploitation through receiving poor wages/salaries (5:4). Already in James 1:10–11, the rich are introduced as those that will be humbled and eventually wither away. The poor are already humble due to their lower socioeconomic status but have a higher spiritual position compared to the rich (cf. Jas 1:9). However, the rhetorical techniques of creating "imaginary dialogue" partners to support their argument and widespread reading of this sermon among the diasporic Christians from both Jewish and non-Jewish descent makes it difficult to envision or suggest that there were rich people present in the congregations. Margaret Aymer assists in directing how this interpretative tension of "the world behind the text" can be addressed, namely:

> James structures his encyclical according to the rules of ancient rhetoric: *exordium, propositio, probation, peroration*. This "letter" was meant to be heard; and we must, therefore, try to "listen" to James and "hear" the points that James makes at his speech as he tries to convince those he calls the "twelve tribes" to live according to "the religion from above" (1:1; 3:17).[26]

In the above literary structure, I have attempted to follow these rhetoric elements so the letter can be heard by readers today. Witherington suggests that once the rhetorical discourses have been identified, interpreters must determine whether they are forensic or judicial, deliberative, or epideictic rhetoric, which are defined as follows:

- forensic rhetoric is a rhetoric of law court and attack that focused on passed things done; deliberative rhetoric, a rhetoric of trying to convince someone to change their course of action or affirm a policy or vote; and an epideictic rhetoric, is rhetoric of display and seeks to not only change beliefs, behaviours, opinions, or attitudes but rather reinforces existing ones.[27]

I propose that James primarily utilizes an epideictic rhetoric but is coupled with deliberative and forensic instances in the letter that can be delineated through a comprehension of the historical context. For example, Ingeborg Mongstad-Kvammen argues that the story of the

26. Margaret Aymer, *James: Diaspora Rhetoric of a Friend of God* (T&T Clark, 2017), 19.

27. Ben Witherington III, *New Testament Rhetoric: An Introduction Guide to the Art of Persuasion in and of the New* (Wipf & Stock, 2008), 7. See also Clifton C. Black, "Rhetorical Criticism," in *Hearing the New Testament: Strategies for Interpretation*, ed. Joel E. Green (William B. Eerdmans, 2010), 256–277.

beggar and the rich person entering the synagogue in James 2:2–4 reflects a Roman cultural etiquette of organizing seating according to rank.[28]

Mongstad-Kvammen connects this to the "golden ring" and "fine clothing" (cf. Jas 2:2–3), where this behavior of allocating seating favorably to the affluent individual over the beggar presents the "rich person" as "a Roman equestrian running for political office."[29] The equestrian class in the Roman political system was comprised of individuals that operated primarily in the army, financial administration, imperial fleets, and as prefects/praetorian guards in smaller Roman provinces.[30] Since diasporic communities were located away from the capital of Rome and regions overseen by prefects/praetorian guards, James's diatribe and imaginary characters of "rich and poor" (cf. Jas 2:2–3) can arguably be considered as epideictic rhetoric addressing a cultural behavior prevalent among these Christians communities. The appeal is evident in his rebuke to the unlawfulness of partiality and how it is prohibited in the Law/Torah (cf. Jas 2.4–11; Lev 19:15; Deut 1:17, 16:19; Prov 24:23). Thus, congregations that adhere to this societal cultural norm go against the ethos associated with their religious heritage and demonstrate the cultural challenges of hybridity prevalent among Jewish Christians living within diasporic imperial subjugation.[31] Following Mongstad-Kvammen, I argue that James attempts to provide these early Christian communities with ethical guidelines to navigate some of these social pressures and cultural expectations that contradicted the commands given to them by God.

Alicia J. Batten's argument that pushes against the scholarly rejection of connecting James 4:4 to Q 16:13[32] further assists this hypothesis. For instance, though the Q 16:13 text reflects the saying of Jesus that expresses a servant's inability to serve two masters, God and Mammon (i.e., money) (cf. Matt 6:24; Luke 16:13), Batten contends that James's omission of mammon points to his appeal to hearers to adopt friendship with God, which was not a foreign concept for the Jewish people but propagated more commonly among Greco-Roman philosophers.[33] James is clearly aware of this when he mentions that Abraham is a "friend of God" earlier in the letter (cf. Jas 2:23; see also Isa 41:8; 2 Chr 20:7). In terms of Greco-Roman philosophies, Batten indicates that Stoics considered good human beings to be friends of the gods.[34] At least for Batten, friendship with the world versus friendship with God (cf. Jas 4:4) merges both Judaic and Greco-Roman perspectives to emphasize hearers' moral behavior as a means of improving the human soul. I agree with Batten but would emphasize that James is also using this friendship language to ensure fidelity to God. This is evident in the marriage covenantal language of labeling the duplicity of affiliation to both God and the world as adulterous

28. Cf. Ingeborg Mongstad-Kvammen, *Toward a Postcolonial Reading of the Epistle of James: James 2:1–13 in Its Roman Imperial Context*, BibInt 119 (Brill, 2013), 10.

29. Cf. Mongstad-Kvammen, *Towards a Postcolonial Reading*, xiv, 10.

30. See also Axolile N. M. Qina, "Reading John's Gospel Within Its Socio-Political Context: A Rhetorical Analysis of John 8:12–59" (master's thesis, University of Stellenbosch, 2019), 86–88; and, *DNTB*, 996–997, 1000–1002.

31. Cf. Mongstad-Kvammen, *Towards a Postcolonial Reading*, 10–11.

32. Cf. Alicia J. Batten, "The Urbanization of the Jesus Tradition in James," in *James, 1 & 2 Peter, and Early Jesus Traditions*, ed. Alicia J. Batten and John S. Kloppenborg (T&T Clark, 2014), 90.

33. Cf. Batten, "The Urbanization of the Jesus Tradition," 91–92.

34. Cf. Batten, "The Urbanization of the Jesus Tradition," 91.

(cf. Jas 4:4–5). In the Old Testament, God's covenant relationship with the Israelites is also a marriage, whereby their disobedient acts of worshipping other foreign gods is considered adultery against God (cf. Hos 3:1; Jer 2:2; 3:20; Ezek 16:32, 23:30; Isa 1:21).

Therefore, I propose that James wants early Christians to remain faithful to God in both speech and action, where they adhere to moral behaviors in accordance with "royal law" (cf. Jas 2:8). In doing so, diasporic Jewish and non-Jewish Christ-followers keep themselves "unstained by the world" (cf. Jas 1:27), which in turn purifies their hearts because they will be drawn nearer to God (cf. Jas 4:8). These moral behaviors include caring for the poor, widows, and orphans (cf. Jas 1:27); not showing partiality toward fellow humans (cf. Jas 2:1–9; 3:17); and avoiding conflicts in the life of the Christian communities since conflict breeds sinful behaviors of covetousness, judgmentalism, and arrogance (cf. Jas 4:1–2; 4:11–17). Such ethical principles and behaviors, as we will see in what follows, continue to challenge Christian Africans' witnessing their faith in the modern world. Though written in the time of the ancient Jews' subjugation to Roman imperial rule, James's moral teachings still speak to Christians today, calling them to listen and remain loyal to God above all else.

Theological Themes

A recent survey on the "African Christian Theology" Facebook group indicated that the books Christian Africans predominately read on the continent are authored by North American pastors and focus on human providence and socioeconomic individual advancement. These figures, which include the likes of Joel Osteen, Joyce Meyer, T. D. Jakes, and the late Myles Munroe, for example, emphasize that Christians should actively seek God through faith and he will ultimately provide them with a purpose-filled life of material success. While James challenges this "Christian" approach, characteristically resembling "worldly" wisdom, the findings of this survey posit two concerns for African Christian theologians and scholars: first, American authors are preferred over African writers that theologize the Christian message and texts for Christian Africans on the continent; and second, some of the said American authors articulate a "worldly wisdom" that appropriates teachings from the Bible. For instance, in his book, *In Pursuit of Purpose*, Munroe utilized Proverbs 16:1 to argue that humans have the mandate to plan for their purpose on this earth.[35] Munroe ignores the subsequent verses of 16:2 and 16:9 which indicate that God is ultimately responsible for ordering the steps and plans of humans, not the other way round. James 4:14–16 critiques this behavior, calling it evil. Instead, Christians, according to James should be humble, strive to do what is right, and submit their life to God (cf. 4:7, 10, 15, 17).

In what follows, I provide a biblical-theological approach to James 1–5 that thematically develops "discernment principles" to adequately interpret this New Testament letter for contemporary Christian Africans' daily lives until the parousia. I utilize what Alison Sharrock defines as intratextuality, which investigates the relationship of a specific text to other parts of the same text and considers how these parts fit together in the whole (of the

35. See Myles Munroe, *In Pursuit of Purpose* (Destiny Image Publishers Incorporated, 1993).

specified text).[36] This intratextuality of James, however, also employs intertextuality—which refers to the relationship of a specific text to other different texts in order to determine if there are relevant parallels or transformations.[37]

In doing so, the other literary traditions that the author uses are considered in order to further articulate their teaching to Christian readers. The exegesis is interculturally situated in an African Indigenous religious and ancient Mediterranean context, to ensure that Christian Africans are equipped with the necessary parameters to differentiate between Christian theological instructions that resemble "worldly wisdom" and those which are drawn from the wisdom of God from above. Relevant African religious beliefs, principles, theologies, hymns, poetry, and proverbs are also used to elucidate James to Christian Africans. To this end, I have suggested three discernment principles that are addressed in turn below as follows: "the wisdom of God as reverence and faith that obeys the Torah/Law's greatest commandments," "a self-less liberative Christian ethic for Christ followers in the world until parousia," and "biblical spiritual practices and methods of healing for African Christian communities."

Discernment Principle 1
The Wisdom of God as Reverence and Faith That Obeys the Torah/Law's Greatest Commandments

James utilizes the ancient Jewish wisdom tradition. In some Old Testament texts, wisdom, referred to as "Sophia" (σοφία) in the Septuagint (henceforth LXX), is personified in wisdom literature (e.g., Prov 8), and articulated as an act of faith that is represented ethically through one's religious devotion (e.g., Prov 9:10; 1:7; Ps 111:10; Job 28:28). James 3:13–18, however, differentiates between the wisdom of God and the wisdom of the World, which are seemingly opposed.

In James 1:5, Christians can receive "wisdom" (σοφία) by asking God. However, they must ask God in faith and should not have any doubt, for the doubting person is unstable, double-minded, and cannot expect to receive anything from the Lord (cf. Jas 1:6–8). Solomon Andria is correct to assert that wisdom is not something humans can simply understand, but it must be learned.[38] Leo G. Perdue takes a broader view in terms of Old Testament theology, and argues that wisdom is connected to the ancient Israelites' covenant with God, who maintain a relationship with Yahweh through observing the Torah, the source of wisdom.[39] Perdue proposes three focal points on exactly what wisdom is: (1) a body of knowledge concerned

36. Cf. Alison Sharrock, "Intratextuality: Texts, Parts, and (W)holes in Theory," in *Intratextuality: Greek and Roman Textual Relations*, ed. Alison Sharrock and Helen Morales (Oxford University Press, 2000), 1–39.

37. Cf. Chris Baldick, "Intertextuality," in *The Oxford Dictionary of Literary Terms*, 4th ed. (Oxford University Press, 2015), 128.

38. Cf. Solomon Andria, "James," in *Africa Bible Commentary: A One-Volume Commentary Written by 70 African Scholars*, ed. Tokunboh Adeyemo (WordAlive Publishers; Zondervan, 2006), 1536.

39. Cf. Leo G. Perdue, *Wisdom Literature: A Theological History* (Westminster John Knox, 2007), 31–35.

with understanding God, the world, nature, humanity, and human society; (2) discipline that produces character and virtue; and (3) a moral discourse of righteousness that is legitimately constructed behaviors with cosmological emphasis.[40]

Perdue argues that ancient Jewish sages were influenced by Egyptian philosophical ideas of *ma'at*.[41] *Ma'at* was the personification of ancient Egyptian concepts of truth, balance, order, harmony, law, morality, and justice. It also represented the ethical and moral principles that Egyptian people were expected to follow and observe throughout their daily lives. Similarly, a starting point in learning wisdom in the Old Testament Proverbs is to "Fear the Lord" (1:7). The main operative word "fear" or "terror" (φόβος/ יִרְאָה), here refers to "reverence" or "deep respect" toward God. In James 1:5 such wisdom is given to those who ask God, who gives freely and generously to those that request it genuinely before him (cf. 1:5–8).[42] William R. Baker has also previously made this connection and highlighted that James's usage of wisdom with speech ethics is akin to Hebrew wisdom texts (i.e., Proverbs, Ecclesiastes, Wisdom of Solomon, and Sirach) and Babylonian and Egyptian wisdom literature.[43]

The link cannot be ignored when James 3:13 compares those that are "born of wisdom" with those who show their understanding of the faith through their actions and conduct. Baker would agree and argues that James's wisdom is not an ideological construct but rather very practical and predicated on the actions of individuals that should reflect godly behavior.[44] If we consider "wisdom" and the speech ethics' relatedness to human actions, it is significant that Proverbs 16:23 considers the heart of a wise person to be determined through the "prudence of their mouth" and "teachings from their lips." Sirach 1:20 connects the practicality of wisdom to the fear of the Lord, which is the root of wisdom. Later Sirach delineates what hypocrisy is, and that it should be avoided by persons keeping watch over their lips as wisdom is made known by speech and education through the ways of words from a person's tongue (cf. Sir 1:29; 4.24). In a similar vein, within a Xhosa Indigenous religious context, reverence is also bequeathed to the Xhosa Supreme Being, *Qamatha*.[45] So much so, in pre-Christian times, Xhosas would not point to the sky lest they cause an offence to the deity, who resides far above the skies. Also, if persons or cattle were killed by lightning strikes, their sudden deaths would be interpreted as being on account of the Supreme Being, and the intention of the animal sacrifices that would accompany the deceased at their funeral was to offer it as a burnt offering so it could be received by *Qamatha* alone. This is different from animal offerings

40. Cf. Perdue, *Wisdom Literature*, 29–30.

41. Cf. Perdue, *Wisdom Literature*, 332.

42. See also William R. Baker, *Personal Speech-Ethics in the Epistle of James*, WUNT 2/68 (Mohr Siebeck, 1995); Robert J. Foster, *The Significance of Exemplars for the Interpretation of the Letter of James*, WUNT 2/376 (Mohr Siebeck, 2014).

43. Cf. Baker, *Personal Speech-Ethics*, 7–8.

44. Cf. Baker, *Personal Speech-Ethics*, 10–12.

45. Cf. Hodgson, *The God of the Xhosa*, 49–52. See also Garvey Nonki, "The Traditional Prose Literature of the Ngqika" (master's thesis, University of South Africa, 1968), 28, 50; and Charles Brownlee, "A Fragment on Xhosa Religious Beliefs," *African Studies* 14 (1955): 37–38.

directed to the ancestors, where sacrificed animals were eaten by human offerants in a feast that included the entire community.

The emphasis on speech and action differs from Christian Africans' Indigenous beliefs in observing customs inherited from their ancestors as way to ensure favor, prosperity, and spiritual protection. For instance, Jacob K. Olupona rightly attests that the elevated status of ancestors, who occupy a higher state of existence after death, imbues them with the power to bless and curse members of their living human relatives.[46] In a Xhosa religious setting, "ancestors" (*izinyanya*) can communicate with relatives through dreams, omens, visions, and visitations. If *izinyanya* are unhappy in any manner, animal sacrifices and beer offerings are officiated to appease them and restore their relationship.[47] This may seemingly relate to *ma'at* and Jewish reverence for deities and adherence to certain principles and laws/Torah to guarantee divine providence. However, at least for Xhosas and other African Indigenous converts, adherence to and preservation of ritual traditions and customs of animal sacrifices and beer offerings to the ancestors ensure divine fortuity. Even so, ancestors' spiritual powers after their death does not make them gods. Kwame Bediako also attests to this when he describes ancestors as the human equivalent in the African spirit world.[48] Bediako even asserts that African deities and divine agents can often disappear and be forgotten by Indigenous groups, but the ancestors never do. How then should Christian Africans negotiate their faith in relation to the continual presence of their ancestors? To answer this question, I have divided what follows into two brief subsections, "Ubuntu, Ancestors, and God" and "James's Love Action Ethic," followed by a short analysis of their significance. I propose that James's practical wisdom and speech ethics point to an adoption of life which aims for Jesus Christ's followers to ultimately adhere to the two greatest commandments of the Law/Torah, namely to "love God" and "love your neighbor as you love yourself." Such an interpretation, I contend, can be articulated in accordance with the African concept of Ubuntu, since it is a type of African wisdom principle that resonates with Indigenous beliefs and other ethical practices toward fellow humans, nature, and the spirit world.

Ubuntu, Ancestors, and God

In some African contexts, humans' relationship to the ancestors is morally bound to the concept of *ubuntu*—an ethical framework for people to adhere to within their societies. For instance, the Shona of Zimbabwe refer to *ubuntu* as an ideological principle that centers around shared humanity, and call it *unhu*, which means: "a person is a person because of

46. Cf. Olupona, *African Religions*, 28.

47. For more information: Bertholow A. Pauw, *Christianity and Xhosa Tradition: Belief and Ritual Among Xhosa Speaking Christians* (Oxford University Press, 1975), 152–153; Patrick McAllister, "Ritual and Social Practice in the Transkei," in *Culture and the Commonplace: Anthropological Essays in Honour of David Hammond-Tooke*, ed. Patrick McAllister (Wits University Press, 1997), 279–309; and Jeffrey B. Peires, *The House of Phalo: A History of the Xhosa People in the Days of Their Independence* (University of California, 1982), 6.

48. Cf. Kwame Bediako, *Christianity in Africa: The Renewal of a Non-Western Religion* (Edinburgh University Press, 1995), 217–218.

other persons" (*munhu munhu nekuda kwevanhu*). Symphorien Ntibagirirwa also categorizes *ubuntu* as the manner in which humans act and behave, but aligns it to the aim of producing unity and societal harmony within the universe that surrounds them.[49] Ntibagirirwa then connects this to Bantu Africans' connection to human community that consists of "human beings actually living (the present generation), human beings who are dead (the past generation) and human beings who are not yet born (the future generations)."[50] Vincent Mulago would agree and argues that *ubuntu* is bound to the individual members of a community actively participating in the cultural religious life of their tribe, clan, familial household, and the dead, who are an invisible element of these families.[51] It is apt to mention the popularized African proverb: "the child who is not accepted by their village will burn it down until they feel its warmth." If we then consider "village" in connection to the above mentioned *ubuntu* relationality, this proverb can be expressed as the child being denied their collective relationships to which they are bound and that forms part of their intrinsic humanity that does not exist without their kinship groups.

In South African Xhosa and Zulu language, *ubuntu* is expressed like Shona's *unhu* "a person is a person through other persons" (*umntu ngumtu ngabantu*). Zilibele Mtumane argues that "person" (*umtu*) is a combination of a prefix "a" or "the" (*um*) and "human" (*ntu*).[52] Mulago, on the other hand, proposes that "*ntu* is a synthesis of the ancestors and a living expression of the Supreme Being, along with its divine munificence."[53] In terms of the Supreme Being, some scholars suggest that "*ubuntu* is a metaphysical oneness with *uMdaliwabantu* ('the Creator of humanity')."[54] Nevertheless, the relationality between humans, ancestors, and God assists in comprehending the observation of Indigenous customs and ritual traditions as part of Africans' spirituality. This is also evident in the symbiotic relationships that allude to Africans' understanding of humanity and how it is connected to divinities that reside in unseen spiritual realms. Africans consider their humanity to be interconnected with spiritual entities, such as ancestors, by way of adherence to rituals and living in continual reverence of the Creator God. This reverence for God and adherence to traditional rituals toward the

49. Cf. Symphorien Ntibagirirwa, "Cultural Values, Economic Growth and Development," *Journal of Business Ethics* 84 (2006): 306. See also Christian B. Gade, "What Is *Ubuntu*? Different Interpretations Among South Africans of African Descent," *South African Journal of Philosophy* 31 (2012): 484–503; and Zilibele Mntumane, "The Practice of *Ubuntu* with Regard to *AmaMfengu* Among *AmaXhosa* as Depicted in S. E. K. Mqhayi's *Ityala lamawele*," *International Journal of African Renaissance* 12 (2017): 69–80.

50. Ntibagirirwa, "Cultural Values," 306.

51. Cf. Vincent Mulago, "Traditional African Religion and Christianity," in *African Traditional Religions in Contemporary Religions in Contemporary Society*, ed. Jacob K. Olupona (Paragon House, 1991), 120–121.

52. Cf. Mntumane, "The Practice of *Ubuntu*," 69.

53. Mulago, "Traditional African Religion," 122.

54. Mark Malisa and Michelle McAnuff-Gumbs, "*Ubuntu* Is Utopia: The Individual and the Community Work in the Work of Nelson Mandela," in *The Individual and Utopia: A Multidisciplinary Study of Humanity and Perfection*, ed. Clint Jones and Cameron Ellis (Routledge, 2015), 301–302. See also Mokoko P. Sebola, "Refugees and Immigrants in Africa: Where Is an African *Ubuntu*?," *Africa's Public Service Delivery and Performance Review* 7 (2019): 1–7; Axolile N. M. Qina, "The *ubuntu* We Need: Post Covid-19 and Beyond," *Young African Magazine*, January 22, 2021, 24–28, https://www.mandelarhodes.org/news-impact/yam/the-ubuntu-we-need-post-covid-19-and-beyond.

ancestors does have resonance with Jewish beliefs of the "fear of the Lord" and keeping of the Torah commandments, though Jewish responses are directed solely to God, since worship is attributed to God alone and no other divine entities. I suggest that James has this in view but draws from Leviticus 19 to emphasize how this practical wisdom proposed in the letter must be grounded in the Law/Torah of God.

James's Love Action Ethic

Johnson rightly asserts that James 2:8 quotes the Greek translation of Leviticus 19:18b (LXX) word for word, which states: "You shall love your neighbor as yourself" (NRSV).[55] However, Johnson further proposes six other possible allusions to Leviticus 19:12–18 (except 19:14) in James 5:12 (cf. Lev 19;12), 5:4 (cf. Lev 19:13), 2:1 and 2:9 (cf. Lev 19:15), 4:11 (cf. Lev 19;16), 5:20 (cf. Lev 19:17b), and 5:9 (cf. Lev 19:18a).[56] Though Johnson does indicate that James 5:9 and 5:20 are "the least likely allusions,"[57] I disagree that Leviticus 19:17b is at all in view in James 5:20 because the Levitical passage that is inferred prohibits the reproval of one's neighbor lest they incur guilt upon themselves (cf. Lev 19:17b). James 5:20, on the other hand, explains that the effects of assisting in the redemption of a sinner's soul back to God "covers a multitude of sins." James 5:9 is at least thematically plausible, since Leviticus 19:18a prohibits holding a grudge against fellow covenant people of God, and James 5:9a warns hearers of grumbling against each other within their Christian groups, which in part addresses a behavior that should be avoided, albeit the prohibited conducts in both these texts are different.

It is my contention that James merges some of the prohibitions in Leviticus 19:12–18 alongside Jesus's sayings and Jewish beliefs in relationship of "the fear of the Lord" and wisdom. For instance, as alluded to above, "the fear of the Lord is the beginning of wisdom" (cf. Prov 9:10; Job 28:28; Ps 111:10). In other texts, this "fear of the Lord" is also related to the start of acquiring the "knowledge" of God (cf. Prov 1:7, 2:5, 9:10), which adherents then practically do through turning away from evil by keeping God's commandments (cf. Job 28:28; Eccl 12:13; Prov 8:13). Moreover, God is described in Proverbs 8:13 as hating pride, arrogance, the way of evil, and perverted speech. James 3:13 begins with a rhetorical question to introduce the issue of "wisdom," and provides characteristics of wisdom discerned as originating from God or from the world. Already in the prologue, religious practice accepted by God the Father is caring for the poor, orphans, and widows, and for Christians "to keep themselves unstained by the world" (cf. Jas 1:27). The practical approach to care is analogous to Leviticus 19:13 and 19:15, which prohibit defrauding one's neighbor, keeping wages from one's employed workers, and not becoming partial to the poor or deferring to the rich. All the prohibitions of Leviticus 19:13 and 19:15 are elaborated in James 5:3, 5; 5:4; 1:9–10, and 2:1–7, respectively. James's letter then offers a moral behavior that is "born of wisdom" (3:13), not hypocrisy (3:17), which pragmatically works to live a good life (3:3) instead of showing partiality toward others

55. Cf. Johnson, *Brother of Jesus*, 123–124.

56. Cf. Johnson, *Brother of Jesus*, 126–132.

57. Johnson, *Brother of Jesus*, 132.

(3:17); produces the fruit of righteousness (3:17–18) rather than selfish ambition (3;14, 16); acts mercifully to neighbors (3:17) not with arrogance (3:14); and pursues gentleness (3:13, 17), peace (3:17–18), purity (3:17) over bitter envy (3:14, 16), lies (3;14), and disorder and wickedness (3:16). For James, these acceptable moral behaviors are godly because they are "from above" (3:15, 17), while the opposite actions that are to be avoided are characterized as "earthly, unspiritual, and devilish" (3:15).

The organizing ethical principle or command that binds this "wisdom characterization" together is Leviticus 19:18b, "to love your neighbor as you love yourself" (cf. Jas 2:8). For example, in the Jesus tradition, to love God includes loving your neighbor; these are the greatest commandments (cf. Mark 12:28–31; Matt 22:35–40; Lev 19:18; Deut 6:5).[58] This is significant since Leviticus 19:15 LXX prohibits showing partiality by favoring a high official and rejecting a poor person (cf. Jas 2:2–3). In relation to God, however, the Old Testament connects "to love God" as an active pursuit of the holiness of God through observance of God's decrees (cf. Lev 19:1, 19, 19:17; Deut 6:5). In a similar vein, fearing God is synonymous with keeping the commandments, along with walking in the ways of the Lord with all one's heart (cf. Eccl 12:13; Deut 10:12; 1 Sam 12:24).[59] For contemporary Christian Africans church leaders and communities "born of wisdom" have great respect for the living God that can be practically confirmed through their gentle attitude to others (cf. Jas 3:13, 17), showing mercy to those in need (cf. Jas 2:13; 3:17), and striving to live in a manner acceptable to the Lord (cf. Jas 1:27; 3:13). Christian Africans should also be wary of churches that are guided by aspirations to expand internationally ("reach all the nations") but are uninterested in assisting the poor, widowed, and sick locally (cf. Jas 1:27; 3:14–16). Such a neglect of the command to love their neighbors in their workplaces, residences, families, and wider communities presents a hypocrisy that breeds partiality (cf. Jas 2:1–4, 2:9–11; 3:17). The global mission Christian outreach message preached in some churches is justified by the great commission of Jesus to preach the gospel to the four corners of the earth (cf. Matt 28:18–20; Mark 16:15–18), but ignores participating in addressing the inequalities and injustices prevalent in the countries where Christians are residing. Focusing on global outreach that ignores the local community is a fabrication of the truth of God into a false witness (cf. Jas 2:14–16; 3:14). It denies Christian Africans the opportunity to articulate their faith journey from an *ubuntu* wisdom that reveres the Lord God in heaven, making them implicit transgressors of the Law/Torah through their sin of showing partiality (cf. Jas 2:9–11; 3:17), and unable to claim allegiance to having genuine faith in Jesus Christ (cf. Jas 2:1; 3:14–16). Christian Africans can assess this through the speech ethic propagated by

58. See also Johnson, *Brother of Jesus*, 123–135; Moo, *The Letter of James*, 110–112; Martin, *James*, 67–68; Dale C. Allison, *James: A Critical and Exegetical Commentary*, ICC (T&T Clark, 2013), 401–408; Andria, "James," 1538.

59. See also Matt A. Jackson-McCabe, *Logos and Law in the Letter of James: The Law of Nature, the Law of Moses, and the Law of Freedom*, NovTSup 100 (Brill, 2001); David H. Edgar, *Has God Not Chosen the Poor? The Social Setting of the Epistle of James*, JSNTSup 206 (Sheffield Academic Press, 2001); and Darian Lockett, "'Unstained by the World': Purity and Pollution as an Indicator of Cultural Interaction in the Letter of James," in *Reading James with New Eyes: Methodological Reassessments of the Letter of James*, ed. Robert L. Webb and John S. Kloppenborg, LNTS 342 (T&T Clark, 2007), 49–74.

some Christian denominations and traditions to see whether the concerns are truly guided by love for our human neighbor, involved in the care of the marginalized in society, and rooted in a deep reverence for the Creator God.

Discernment Principle 2
A Self-Less Liberative Christian Ethic for Christ-Followers in the World Until Parousia

James 4:1 begins with two rhetorical questions and clarifies why those who doubt are double-minded when asking God through prayer (cf. 1:6–8; 4:2–4). James 4:4 classifies doubters as "adulterers." Such a designation, however, is not based on unfaithfulness to a human marital spouse. Instead, it refers to, as Scot McKnight also attests, covenantal infidelity toward God.[60] For example, the Greek word for "adulterers" (μοιχαλίδος) is also found in Ezekiel 16:38 LXX, referring to the unfaithfulness of Israel to Yahweh for worshipping the gods of foreign nations (cf. 16:23–29), sacrificing their own children to the gods of these foreign nations (cf. 16:20–24), and giving foreign rulers treasures and sacred foods that were dedicated and reserved as offerings to the Lord (cf. 16:15–19). James 4:4 has this in view, particularly considering the statement that "friendship with the world" makes one an enemy of God. However, in James, if Christians choose to humble themselves before God (cf. 4:10), purify and cleanse their hearts (cf. 4:8), submit their life unto the Lord and do what is right as doers of the Law/Torah (cf. 4:7–8, 15, 17), and draw near to the Lord God (4:11), they will be exalted by God, who in turn draws near to them (cf. 4:8, 4:10).

As alluded to previously, James's omission of choosing between God or Mammon reflects not only his proposal for allegiance to God over the allure of worldly prestige but also calls those listeners to have fidelity to God above all else. Alicia Batten is again helpful here, when describing that the hearers in the Roman provincial cities were predominantly "monetized," unlike in the village, which had few money transactions.[61] Darian Lockett develops Batten's friendship proposal and argues that in the Greco-Roman world "friendship meant above all to share, that is, to have the same mindset, the same outlook, the same view of reality."[62] Lockett further adds that "world" is not just an analogous characterization of opposites, rather, "it is an entire cultural value system or world order which is hostile toward what James frames as the divine value system."[63] In essence, James, according to Lockett, develops a worldview that frames a symbolic universe between God and "the world" where the former is preferred and to be adopted, while the latter is to be avoided and abandoned at all costs.[64] I agree with Lockett here, especially if we consider that the two wisdom tables above do not, strictly speaking, indicate a clear juxtaposition of behaviors that are opposite to each other. Instead,

60. Cf. McKnight, *The Letter of James*, 331–332.

61. Cf. Batten, "The Urbanization of the Jesus Tradition," 90–91.

62. Lockett, "Unstained by the World," 58.

63. Lockett, "Unstained by the World," 58.

64. Cf. Lockett, "Unstained by the World," 58–59.

following Lockett, they delineate characteristics akin to the worldview that James creates to assist hearers align with the moral order and value system of God.

The different affiliation to God and not the world challenges African prosperity gospel theology among some Christian Africans. Maria Frahim-Arp defines African prosperity theology as follows:

> (1) an attitude of hope in a positive future; (2) an entrepreneurial attitude of "winning ways," which in Africa usually means making a break with the past and the wider claims of extended families and culture; (3) the use of life improvement strategies that might include an ethic of hard work or how to cope with life through "strong prayers"; (4) consistent tithing or employing various means to sow the "seed offering by giving money to the church"; and (5) preacher-prophets gifted with special powers to speak against and fight the "spirit of poverty."[65]

James advocates for Christians to be patient and have hope in the eschatological promises associated with "the coming of the Lord" (cf. 5:7–8). The hoarding of wealth in these last days until Jesus's return will be condemned (cf. Jas 5:3–5). Furthermore, those that boast in tomorrow are arrogantly in pursuit of their own selfish ambition, which James characterizes as being constituted of wisdom from the world (cf. 3:14–16; 4:13–17). Instead, Christians should remove all "moral filth" (or "defilement") (ῥυπαρία) and wicked "superfluity" (περισσεία) and receive the "implanted word" (ἔμφυτον λόγον) that can save their souls (cf. Jas 1:21). Superfluity (περισσεία) is a better translation here than "rank growth." There are two reasons for this: first, the rich are also condemned for living in opulence at the expense of not paying the laborers their wages (cf. Jas 5:1–5); and, second, James is not necessarily interested in persons elevating their political status, but rather in making a judgment regarding the hypocrisy that excessive wealth can create within a Christian community (cf. 2:1–4). For instance, the golden ring in James 2:2 was an insignia of the equestrian upper class, the second level of Roman aristocracy.[66] In treating the official more favorably than the poor (2:2–3), the Christians in this community are not only guilty of the sin of partiality, but also break the Law/Torah through their judgment toward human neighbors according to their socioeconomic class status.

In the honor-shame culture of the ancient Mediterranean, where the rich people were highly esteemed and considered superior to lower classes, Ingebord Mongstad-Kvammen is correct to argue that such an expected cultural act in a Roman world contradicted the precepts of their Jewish Christian religious beliefs. Again, Leviticus 19:15 (MT), attributes such an act of judgment to fellow humans based on classism, as "rendering an unjust judgement." James reworks this and morally argues that judgment is reserved for God alone, who is also the lawgiver of rules humans should adhere to and obey (cf. 2:4, 2:12–13; 4:11–12). Christians, at least for James, are accountable to the whole law (cf. 2:10–11), and faith is predicated on actions that reflect it (cf. 2:12–26). Connecting this to Darian Lockett's worldview proposal,

65. Frahim-Arp, "Pentecostalism," e3 of 16.

66. Cf. Mongstad-Kvammen, *Towards a Postcolonial Reading*, 65, 67; Moo, *The Letter of James*, 103.

he rightly contests that "uncontrolled speech" is "worthless" (μάταιος) piety.[67] Lockett indicates that "worthless" here is also used in the LXX of Jeremiah 2:15 and 10:3 to express the futility of idol worship. This link confirms how such speech can stain, which makes those who practice it impure before God (cf. Jas 1:26; 4:4).

Nevertheless, the prosperity gospel's insistence of pastors' self-proclaimed abilities of speaking away poverty and encouraging followers to have a winning attitude to accumulate wealth apart from their familial households, contradicts James's practical strategy in accordance with God's worldview to adhere to actions that care for orphans and widows in distress (cf. Jas 1.27). In addition, faith without works is dead (cf. Jas 2:17; 2:26), since telling others to take care of themselves when they do not have the means to do so (cf. Jas 2:14–16) is not good, and denies the poor provision, while those that accumulate wealth live in luxury only to condemn themselves and fall subject to the Lord's judgment (cf. Jas 1:10–11; 5:3–6). Instead, the poor are chosen by God (cf. Jas 2:5), to which Locket suggests that the dative of "the world" (τῷ κόσμῳ) should be viewed as a "dative of advantage" and translated as "poor in the eyes of the world."[68] When considered from this perspective, Black liberation and other liberation theologies of God favoring the poor and marginalized in society find agreement with James, who introduces himself as a "slave" or "servant" (δοῦλος) of Jesus Christ (cf. Jas 1:1).

In terms of African kinship relationality embodied in *ubuntu*, the separation from familial relations destroys the biblical and African institutions of family. The prioritization of material success and positive hope for the future does not, at least according to James, guarantee salvation in this interim period until the parousia. Unfortunately, the Bible is used to develop incorrect interpretations that are inconsistent with the Christian gospel message. This same Bible was used as an instrument of colonialism, as is best captured in the following sub-Saharan African saying: "when the white people came, they had the Bible, and we had the land; then they said, 'let us pray' and when we opened our eyes, they had the land, and we had the Bible."[69] However, Christian Africans did have agency with this Bible book in the midst of colonial imperialism in African territories. For example, as an early Xhosa Christian convert, Ntsikana encouraged his disciples to observe morning and evening prayer, weekly worship services and the singing of hymns, and study of the word of God,[70] so much so that when British Cape Colonial troops were encroaching into their Ngqika Xhosa lands in 1815–1816, Ntsikana and his disciples emphasized prayer as a means of overcoming the imperial threat instead of launching a military campaign.

Sadly, the Ngqika-Xhosas lost, but blame was put on the "praying people" of Ntsikana, forcing them to leave the area due to persecution. Ntsikana would later die on the road to the mission station where they intended to find refuge. Nevertheless, he encouraged his disciples

67. Cf. Lockett, "Unstained by the World," 55–56.

68. Lockett, "Unstained by the World," 58.

69. Jomo Kenyatta is said to be the originator of this saying.

70. For more information: Janet Hodgson, "The 'Great Hymn' of the Prophet, Ntsikana: An African Expression of Christianity, 1815–1821," *Religion Journal of Southern Africa* 1 (1980): 33–58; Vuyani Booi, "Ntsikana," in *African Intellectuals in the 19th Century and Early 20th Century South Africa*, ed. Mcebisi Ndletyana (HRSC Press, 2008), 7–15; John K. Bokwe, *Ntsikana: The Story of an African Convert* (Lovedale Mission Press, 1914).

to remain united. Moreover, the unwavering faith of Ntsikana is also expressed in his "Great Hymn," indicating that Jesus is the shield who can protect (cf. stanza 2). The Xhosa word for "shield" Ntsikana uses is *iKaka* and referred to the "oxhide shields" Xhosa warriors used for protection in battle. Considering Ntsikana and James, I contend that Christian Africans should put their faith in Jesus, where strong prayers are directed to him and hard work attributed to knowing God through the Word. The church ought to work together amid ongoing socioeconomic inequality and use tithe money to assist members in the congregation. Such a selfless approach can truly break the cycle of poverty and liberate the poor, so the church not only "says" it is a Christian community but "acts" as the covenant family of God through deeds of charity. Individuals have the responsibility to test the Christian community's speech ethics, which in this case can be against the worldview of James, in order to discern whether their faith community is consistent with that of God or that of the world.

Discernment Principle 3
Biblical Spiritual Practices and Methods of Healing for African Christian Communities

In James, the power of healing comes from God, who administers human spiritual restoration by way of prayer and anointing through elders of the assembly (cf. 5:13–14). If Christian converts "suffer misfortune" (κακοπαθέω), they must pray (5:13); if they are "cheerful," they must sing songs of praise (5:13); when sick, they must call the elders to pray over them and anoint them with oil (5:14). In Xhosa Indigenous religions, misfortune and illness can be attributed to the neglect of ancestors, incurring pollution on account of not officiating traditional rituals, or other malevolent forces in the unseen spiritual realms. However, this can be averted by preserving covenant relations with ancestors that are maintained through rituals involving animal sacrifice and beer offerings during moments of liminality like the birth of a child, rites of passages, marriage, and death.[71] These rites are maintained to avoid misfortune, with some Xhosa Christians continuing to practice them on account of respect and honor for their parents (cf. Deut 5:16; Exod 20:12; Lev 19:2). Converts that decide to abandon these practices can be negatively labeled as "deserters of the home" (*amatsipha*).[72] The Xhosa Indigenous belief system is often characterized as superstitious, consisting of magic, witchcraft,

71. For more information: William D. Hammond-Tooke, "Do the Southern-Eastern Bantu Worship Their Ancestors?," in *Social System and Tradition in Southern Africa: Essays in Honour of Eileen Krige*, ed. John Argyle and Eleanor Preston-Whyte (Oxford University Press, 1978), 142–147; Andrew Ainslie, "Harnessing the Ancestors: Mutuality, Uncertainty and Ritual Practice in the Eastern Cape Province, South Africa," *Africa* 84 (2014): 544–546; McAllister, "Ritual and Social Practice," 282; Monica Wilson, "Co-Operation and Conflict: The Eastern Cape Frontier," in *The Oxford History of South Africa*, vol. 1, *South Africa to 1870*, ed. Monica Wilson and Leonard Thompson (Clarendon Press 1969), 233–271.

72. Cf. G. C. Oosthuizen, "The Interaction Between Christianity and Traditional Religion," in *The Bantu Homeland: A General Survey* (Fort Hare University Press, 1971), 114; Pauw, *Christianity and Xhosa Tradition*, 111–113; Ainslie, "Harnessing the Ancestors," 546–547.

ritual, manipulation, custom, and taboo.[73] For example, when a Xhosa wants to show gratitude to their ancestors for good fortune, a "thanksgiving" (*umbulelo*) animal sacrifice and beer offering ritual is hosted.

The libation and animal offering are not a propitiation to the ancestors but are rather a rite that honors them (and incidentally provides food for the community, which joins in the celebrations). However, mainline/mission churches (MC) forbid converts from participating in such Indigenous ritual traditions, considered to be linked to demon/idol worship. Yet, many Christians from MC churches are syncretistic and often still participate in their African Indigenous customs but do so in secret, away from their official church context. African Instituted Churches (AIC's), on the other hand, continue to observe some aspects of African Traditional Religions openly in the context of the church, but assign, and emphasize, spiritual healing powers to the pastor or prophetic figure in authority.[74] I argue that James challenges both positions of MC and AIC Christian methods, as the epistle instructs Christians to keep themselves "unstained" or "undefiled" (ἄσπιλος) from the world (cf. 1:27). This can be achieved through a speech ethic that strives toward "controlled speech" (cf. Jas 3:2), and an adherence to a piety that is acceptable in the sight of God.[75] Darian Lockett assists again here when highlighting that "undefiled" (ἄσπιλος) does not occur in the LXX but is present four times in the New Testament: this occurence in James, two in contexts that refer to Christ as an "unblemished lamb" (cf. 1 Pet 1:19; 2 Pet 3:14) and one in a charge to Christians to preserve themselves until Jesus's return (cf. 1 Tim 6:14).

In a Xhosa religious setting, becoming stained or defiled occurs when in situations of proximity with a corpse or contaminable blood, drinking of milk during a mourning period, and having sexual intercourse when a mother is still breastfeeding a child. Strategies employed to diminish the risk of getting "stained," which are even found among Xhosa Christians, include: In the case of deaths, water is placed in the area outside the graveyard for attendees to purify themselves after attending a funeral with relatives of the deceased and avoiding milk altogether until after the funeral rite. In the case of sexual contact after a birth, the welcoming ceremony of a newborn child symbolically marks the end of the breastfeeding period with the animal sacrifice of a goat symbolizing the beginning of weaning and formally allowing the child's parents to sleep in the same bed again after observing a period of postpartum seclusion. These prevention methods resonate with James, as Mookgo S. Kgatle also attests, arguing that sickness and sin are connected. Sickness is a symptom of an angry spirit that humans

73. Cf. Pauw, *Christianity and Xhosa Tradition*, 11–16; Nelson R. Mandela, *A Long Walk to Freedom: The Autobiography of Nelson Mandela* (Little Brown, 1994), 11; and Audrey Elliot, *The Magic World of the Xhosa* (Collins, 1970), 104–106.

74. Cf. Luvuyo Ntombana, "The Trajectories of Christianity and African Ritual Practices: The Public Silence and the Dilemma of Mainline or Mission Churches," *Acta Theologica* 35 (2015): 105–113; Wallace G. Mills, "Missionaries, Xhosa Clergy & the Suppression of Traditional Customs," in *Mission and Christianity in South African History*, ed. Henry Bredekamp and Robert Ross (Wits University Press, 1996), 157–164; and Bengt G. Sundkler, *Bantu Prophets in South Africa*, Lutterworth Library 32: Missionary Research Series 14 (Lutterworth Press, 1948), 38–43.

75. Cf. Lockett, "Unstained by the World," 56–57.

must resolve through observation of rituals directed to God.[76] For example, if a Christian is sick, it is the prayer of faith and confession of their sins that can heal them (cf. Jas 5:15–16). However, this is not to say that one becomes sick on account of sin. Instead, sickness, like sin, can also be treated in a spiritual way in the Christian community. In James, the elders of the church community can facilitate this through prayer and anointing the sick "in the name of the Lord" (cf. Jas 5:13–14). It is as if James is trying to tell us that if our faith resembles the speech and actions that God deems true, actions of prayer, anointing, and confession of sin can be additional measures that can heal sickness.

In either case, some neo-prophetic churches in South Africa commercialize these Christian spiritual practices. Kgatle highlights two major problems with the neo-prophetic movement: (1) centrality of healing mediated only by the prophetic figure; (2) commercialization of healing products such as oil and water.[77] Kgatle highlights that James 5:13–16 indicates that God alone is the sole source of healing. It is God who is responsible for facilitating healing through human prayers and confessions of sins, not one single individual "anointed" with the ability. There are three types of prayers Christians can adopt in James: (1) "prayer of faith" (5:14–15)—saves the sick and guarantees that God will raise them; (2) prayers of intercession for other Christians in the community (5:16); and (3) "prayer of the righteous" (5:16–17)—morally exemplified through the Jewish prophet, Elijah, who prayed fervently to stop the rain and again for it to return (cf. 5:17–18; 1 Kgs 17:1; 18:1–2). Similarly, Elijah achieves this through the word of the Lord, and it is indeed the Christian converts' "humble" acceptance of the "implanted" (ἔμφυτος) word that can save their souls (cf. Jas 1:21). Lastly, God (cf. Jas 5:15) forgives human sins, but Christian converts can participate in his wholeness-restoration agenda by individual confession of sins to fellow Christians in the church community (5:16) and by actively getting involved in bringing Christians that have wandered away from the covenant community back to faith in God (5:19–20).

Conclusion

In this chapter, I have attempted to provide an interpretation of James that is sensitive to Christian Africans' Indigenous beliefs and the cultural context of early Christians living in the diaspora under Roman imperial rule. First, after broadly introducing this New Testament letter, I provided parallels of James to African Indigenous religions. This was a hermeneutical strategy of initially exploring the "world of the text" (James) and "the world in front of the text" (Christian Africans' context) which is informed by the African Bible interpretative approach of readers/interpreters acknowledgment of their social location and points of contact between the text and their contemporary settings. Second, these points of convergence were clarified with the "world behind the text" (historical background). However, the examination has a twofold process between the text of James and its historical context. To this end, comprehending who and when James was written (authorship and date), the nature of its

76. Cf. Kgatle, "Healing Practices," 117–119.

77. Cf. Kgatle, "Healing Practices," 119–121.

composition (genre), literary structure, and purpose and issues were explored. Lastly, I provided three discernment principles for Christian Africans to consider in the last section (theological themes). Before synthesizing them systematically, the strategy here was to reconfigure what was discovered in James's historical context cross-culturally for Christians living on the African continent. The initial parallels required either confirmation or abandonment, so a new rereading could be considered for Christian Africans today.

In conclusion, the diasporic letter of James offers Christian Africans an array of spiritual practices of healing that include prayer, confession of sins, and actively restoring Christians that have fallen away into the covenant church community of the Lord. This corrects South African neo-prophetic movements that commercialize healing in the name of the Lord. James also challenges Christian Africans to put their faith in Jesus and to start to become consciously aware of the speech ethics present in their verbal and written communication, both individually and in the context of the Christian Church. In addition, Christian communities must instigate communal financial measures, where tithing does not enrich a church leader but rather assists those of lower socioeconomic status. Such a change in thinking would demonstrate the Christian faith of the converts, since righteousness in James is not an abstract notion that is devoid of practical action. Instead, it is practical and construed in a worldview that aims to care for the marginalized in society and to be more concerned with the work of God rather than that of the world. Such an interpretation of James challenges all modern Christians within our capitalist globalized economy, since James's letter counter-culturally dissuades Christ-followers from seeking material success in this interim period until Jesus returns. The selfish ambition of accumulating wealth in these last days is the wisdom of the world that does not fear God, exploits workers for the sake of self-aggrandizement, and will then ultimately lead to judgment. If our desire for economic liberation and true independence on the African continent and beyond is not born of true wisdom coming from God, and if it is unconcerned with producing the fruits of righteousness, including the eradication of poverty, violence, exploitation, and inequality, and the prioritization of education and ethical economies, we should repent and ask God for his wisdom, living faithfully according to correct interpretations of the Word that produces fruit both in and through our lives.

Further Reading

Adewuya, Ayodeji J. *An African Commentary on the Letter of James: Global Readings*. Cascade Books, 2023.

Andria, Solomon. "James." In *Africa Bible Commentary: A One-Volume Commentary Written by 70 African Scholars*, edited by Tokunboh Adeyemo. WordAlive Publishers; Zondervan, 2006.

Banda, Collium. "Not Anointing, But Justice? A Critical Reflection on the Anointing of Pentecostal Prophets in a Context of Economic Injustice." *Verbum Ecclesia* 39 (2018): 1–11.

Cheung, Luke L. *The Genre, Composition and Hermeneutics of the Epistle of James*. Paternoster Biblical and Theological Monographs. Paternoster Press, 2003.

Hodgson, Janet. "A Battle for Sacred Power: Christian Beginning Among the Xhosa." In *Christianity in South Africa: A Political, Social and Cultural History*, edited by Richard Elphick and Rodney Davenport. University of California Press, 1997.

Kgatle, Mookgo S. "Healing Practices in the Epistle of James Applied to New Prophetic Churches in South Africa." *Neot* 55 (2021): 111–123.

Kobe, Sandiswa L. "Steve Biko's Black Theology of Liberation from the Perspective of Ubuntu." *The Ecumenical Review* 74 (2022): 589–599.

Lockett, Darian. *Purity and Worldview in the Epistle of James*. LNTS 366. T&T Clark, 2008.

Mason, Eric F., and Darian F. Lockett, eds. *Reading the Epistle of James: A Resource for Students*. RBS 94. SBL Press, 2019.

Mbiti, John S. *New Testament Eschatology in an African Background: A Study of the Encounter Between New Testament Theology and African Traditional Concepts*. Oxford University Press, 1971.

Mongstad-Kvammen, Ingeborg. *Toward a Postcolonial Reading of the Epistle of James: James 2:1–13 in Its Roman Imperial Context*. BibInt 119. Brill, 2013.

Moo, Douglas J. *The Letter of James*. PNTC. Eerdmans, 2000.

Njeri, Philomena. "Spiritual Warfare and Healing in Kenyan Pentecostalism." In *Pentecostalism, Catholicism, and the Spirit in the World*, edited by Stan Chu. Studies in World Catholicism 8. Wipf & Stock, 2019.

Pauw, Bertholow A. *Christianity and Xhosa Tradition: Belief and Ritual Among Xhosa-Speaking Christians*. Oxford University Press, 1975.

Peires, Jeffrey B. *The House of Phalo: A History of the Xhosa in the Days of Their Independence*. Perspectives on Southern Africa 32. University of California Press, 1982.

Soga, John H. *The Ama-Xosa: Life and Customs*. Lovedale Press, 1932.

Ukpong, Justin S. "Rereading the Bible with African Eyes: Inculturation and Hermeneutics." *Journal of Theology for Southern Africa* 91 (1995): 3–14.

Wafawanaka, Robert. "The Bible, Power and Wealth in Africa: A Critique of the Prosperity Gospel in Sub-Saharan Africa." In *Navigating African Biblical Hermeneutics: Trends and Themes from Our Pots and Our Calabashes*, edited by Madipoane J. Masenya, and Kenneth N. Ngwa. Cambridge Scholars Publishing, 2018.

CHAPTER TWENTY-ONE

The Letters of Peter

Sofanit T. Abebe
Trinity College Bristol
United Kingdom

Introduction

CATEGORIZED IN THE collection of the Catholic Epistles, the epistles of First and Second Peter encompass a wide range of topics and theological themes. Each of these letters deals with the contexts of their respective readers. Although both epistles are ascribed to Simon Peter, the letters address different audiences and exhibit different theological views, with a marked difference in style and language.[1] This has led critical scholars to envisage two different authors behind 1 and 2 Peter, with some arguing for a common Petrine "school"[2] in Rome responsible for authoring the letters in the 80s or 90s CE. Others reject this proposal, arguing that there is nothing specifically Petrine in 1 and 2 Peter.[3] However, as Gene Green notes, "we simply do not possess a large enough corpus of Petrine literature to determine what Peter could or could not have written."[4] Regardless of details of authorship and provenance, it is clear that the figure of Peter serves a theological and literary purpose in both letters. Both letters are written from the perspective of Peter, one of Jesus's disciples and a prominent leader in the Christ-believing community. In both epistles, Peter admonishes allegiance and fidelity to the true gospel of Christ in the face of hostilities.

Through a recalling of Israel's past, Peter helps persecuted Christians in Asia Minor view their present predicament in light of the life, death, resurrection, and enthronement of

1. Richard Bauckham, *Jude, 2 Peter*, WBC 50 (Word Books, 1983), 135–138.

2. Patrick C. Counet, "Pseudepigraphy and the Petrine School Spirit and Tradition in 1 and 2 Peter and Jude," *HTS Teologiese Studies/Theological Studies* 62 (2006): 408–419; Otto Knoch, "Gab es eine Petrusschule in Rom? Überlegungen zu einer bedeutsamen Frage," *SNTSU* 16 (1991): 105–126; Bauckham, *Jude, 2 Peter*, 146–161; see also David G. Horrell, *The Epistles of Peter and Jude* (Epworth, 1998), 7–8.

3. David Horrell considers 1 Peter to be "the product of a consolidating Roman Christianity rather than of a specifically Petrine circle or school" since it is difficult to get a distinctly Petrine view from Acts, John, apocryphal writings in the name of Peter, or 1–2 Peter; cf. David Horrell, "The Product of a Petrine Circle? A Reassessment of the Origin and Character of 1 Peter," *Journal for the Study of the New Testament* 24, no. 4 (2002), 29–60.

4. Gene Green, *Jude and 2 Peter*, BECNT (Baker Academic, 2008), 145; for a more in-depth defense of the traditional position on authorship in 2 Peter, see Michael J. Kruger, "The Authenticity of 2 Peter," *Journal of the Evangelical Theological Society* 42, no. 4 (1999): 645–671.

Christ. Peter encourages the readers to cope with suffering by framing their ordeals within the new spatio-temporal reality Christ has inaugurated and which they have entered by faith through the resurrection (1 Pet 1:5, 20–21). Although 1 Peter addresses the issue of how to respond to persecution, the letter goes further and encompasses a message of encouragement and comfort. This is achieved through a view of reality that underpins what it means to follow Christ, irrespective of how Christians fit within broader society.

In 2 Peter, hostilities the readers face arise from within the believing community. Through false teachers, they were confronted with theological heresies that had serious moral ramifications (2 Pet 2:1). These teachings posed a significant risk to the stability of the community. The eschatology espoused by the false teachers is identified as being skeptical of what the apostles have taught. The form of their teaching has to do with their erroneous understanding that God has failed to intervene to remove evil from the world (cf. 2 Pet 2:4–10). Since divine intervention is precluded and Christ's second coming has not materialized, the false teachers must have concluded that belief in God's intervention is wrong. In response, Peter addresses the threat with a sense of urgency (1:5, 10, 15). Peter also provides a basis for their wrong teaching of freedom from the moral boundaries of sexual ethics (2 Pet 2:2). What is at threat is the very foundation of the community and in this regard 2 Peter can be seen as addressing hostilities that arose from within the community of believers. In this regard, in both 1 and 2 Peter, proper conduct and the related notion of obedience are important aspects in responding to hostilities.

In what follows, the Letters of Peter will be analyzed to demonstrate both an Ethiopian reading and response to these texts. A focus on Ethiopia will provide an important window into the rest of Africa as Ethiopia is the second largest African nation and one of the oldest nations in the world, where the Bible has been read and interpreted continuously since the fourth century. To this end, I will offer an Ethiopian reading of the letters that engages contemporary Ethiopian culture and a contextual and theological reading rooted in the traditional *Andəmta*[5] commentaries on 1 and 2 Peter.

The Historical Context of 1 Peter

Authorship, Date, and Audience

The letter identifies its author as "Peter, an apostle of Jesus Christ" in 1:1. An additional characterization occurs at 5:1 in which he identifies himself as "a fellow elder and a witness to the sufferings of Christ." However, the author's high fluency in Greek, and the letter's similarity to Pauline language and theology, as well as the lack of evidence that shows the author's specific

5. Denotes the Amharic Ethiopian Commentary tradition; the term designates a vast corpus which contains traditional interpretations of religious texts. The term *Andəmta* from Amharic word *andəm* ("or"), is a key technical term which introduces each layer of interpretation for a given concept. Its chief objective seems to be getting to the heart of the texts under analysis by drawing out both the plain sense of the texts and a canonical and spiritualized interpretation inspired by life in rural Ethiopia. As Abraha notes, "time and again they state that their aim is to discover the "mystery" contained, or indeed hidden, in the depths of the texts. . . . the *Andemta* bears the marks of a composite body, in which the merging of different exegetical interests and orientations is easily recognizable." Tedros Abraha, "Andəmta," in *Encyclopaedia Aethiopica*, ed. Siegbert Uhlig (Harrassowitz, 2003), 258.

and intimate familiarity with the teachings of Jesus has led the majority of Petrine scholars to reject the letter as being penned by Peter the apostle. It has also been stated that since the author appears inclined to evangelize non-Jews, which is unlikely of Peter as known from other New Testament passages (cf. Gal 2:7–9), Peter cannot be behind the text. Noting the order in the names of the provinces in 1:1, Elliott notes that beginning with Pontus might indicate the author's awareness of Vespasian's reorganization of the eastern provinces in the year 72 CE.[6] Though inconclusive, this might point to a date for 1 Peter late in the first century, especially in view of (1) the reference to Rome as "Babylon" (5:13), which only occurred after the fall of Jerusalem in 70 CE,[7] and (2) wide dissemination of Christianity in Asia Minor and therefore a date after Peter the apostle's death in 65–67 CE.[8]

However, it must be noted that such objections to Peter's authorship are not definitive or conclusive. The advocates of Petrine origin have argued that, in several instances, the letter seems to preserve the impression of an eyewitness. The author appears to preserve the words of Jesus (e.g., 1 Pet 2:22–25; 5:4). The secretary hypothesis, in which a secretary might play a role of being not only an amanuensis but also an editor or composer, warrants further consideration.[9] Moreover, in the absence of any conclusive reasons explaining the mention of Peter's name in 1:1, and the disputed nature of the evidence rejecting Petrine authorship, one must resist a hasty conclusion against an apostolic origin. If so, it may be possible to maintain the traditional view that Peter wrote it. If one takes 1 Peter to be composed by Peter, then the date before which it had to have been written *terminus ad quem* is ca. 65–67 CE (the date of Peter's death). If it is considered pseudonymous, this date might be extended from anywhere between 80 and 92 CE.[10]

The geographical location of the addressees is described in 1:1 as being in "Pontus, Galatia, Cappadocia, Asia, and Bithynia." Elliott notes that these five locations "refer to five areas of Anatolia which, in the process of Roman eastward military expansion and conquest, since 133/31 BCE onward, had gradually come under Roman control."[11] The address points to a setting in Asia Minor which was composed of an ethnically mixed population of Jews and gentiles. Corresponding to this, the ethnic composition of the addressees can be understood as being mixed.[12]

6. John Elliott, *A Home for the Homeless: A Sociological Exegesis of 1 Peter, Its Situation and Strategy* (Fortress Press, 1981), 60.

7. "Babylon" as a cryptogram for Rome is employed in Revelation (Rev 4:8; 16:19; 17:5; 18:2, 10, 21) and was common in post-70 apocalyptic Jewish writings (e.g., 2 Baruch 11:1–2; 67:7; 2 Esdras 3:12, 28; Sibylline Oracles 5.143).

8. Paul Achtemeier, *1 Peter: A Commentary on First Peter*, Hermeneia (Fortress Press, 1996), 23–27.

9. See the discussion in, for e.g., Green, *Jude and 2 Peter*, 146–147; Karen H. Jobes, *1 Peter*, BECNT (Baker Academic, 2005), 14–19.

10. M. Eugene Boring, *1 Peter*, Abingdon New Testament Commentaries (Abingdon Press, 1999), 35–37, notes that pseudonymity should not be understood as deliberate falsification or forgery. For a discussion of the theological significance of pseudepigraphy in the Bible and an analysis of the process in antiquity, see Brevard S. Childs, *The New Testament as Canon: An Introduction* (Fortress Press, 1984), 376–386.

11. Elliott, *Home for the Homeless*, 59.

12. Elliott, *Home for the Homeless*, 65.

The addressees of 1 Peter are identified as the elect strangers of the diaspora[13] (1:1) who are socially maligned and abused. They make up the Christian "brotherhood" (2:17) that is experiencing suffering "throughout the world" (5:9). The addressees are further characterized as the elect and holy people of God (2:4–10) who belong to the household of God (1:3–2:10; 4:17). While their situation as sojourners and foreigners entailed social marginalization and socioeconomic discrimination, their faith in Christ is associated with the suffering they were subjected to by the society (cf. 1:6; 2:12, 19–23; 3:14–18; 4:1, 12, 19; 5:9–10).

Occasion and Purpose

The major event around which 1 Peter revolves is suffering and persecution.[14] Peter directs his attention to the hostility his readers are facing and the significance of suffering, formulating a response that is specifically aimed at discussing their Christian identity in the face of opposition.

Because of their new life in Christ and consequent abstention from cultic practices that dominated the public sphere, they were slandered and ostracized from society.[15] Rather than being a state-sponsored official persecution, their persecution was "private and local, originating in the hostility of the surrounding population . . . as minority groups living in an environment charged with dislike, misrepresentation and positive hostility, probably with sporadic explosions of violence."[16]

The epistle roots its consolation in the eschatological hope of 1:3–5 to encourage the persecuted readers who are apt to despair (cf. 1:6; 4:13; 5:10).[17] Peter also formulates a response to suffering that he invites his readers to adopt. How he does this has been a point of debate. Scholarly interpretations of Peter's response to the readers' suffering range from a thoroughly conformist attitude to Roman values (David L. Balch)[18] to full resistance against Greco-Roman social norms (Elliott).[19] Beyond the famous "Balch–Elliott debate," there lies a middle

13. For a discussion of this term, see Sofanit T. Abebe, *Apocalyptic Spatiality in 1 Peter and Selected 1 Enoch Literature*, WUNT II/613 (Mohr Siebeck, 2024), 21–23, 90–95. There I argue that, though "diaspora" is a geographic term, it is also a lived space associated with renewal, divine visitation, and restoration. In light of Peter's depiction of the Christian life unfolding in the realm of God, life in the "diaspora" indicates a "this-worldly" space of belonging.

14. Leonhard Goppelt, *A Commentary on 1 Peter*, ed. Ferdinand Hahn, trans. John E. Alsup (Eerdmans, 1993), 18–19. Goppelt notes the two-fold nature of this theme: "Christian existence in the midst of non-Christian society, and Christians' conquering by means of their readiness to endure repression or, in the words of 1 Peter, 'to suffer'"; S. R. Bechtler, *Following in His Steps: Suffering, Community and Christology in 1 Peter*, SBLDS 162 (Scholars Press, 1998), 7.

15. Achtemeier, *First Peter*, 34–35; Elliott, *Home for the Homeless*, 112.

16. J. N. D. Kelly, *A Commentary on the Epistles of Peter and of Jude* (Black, 1969), 10.

17. Eduard Lohse, "Parenesis and Kerygma in 1 Peter," in *Perspectives on First Peter*, ed. Charles H. Talbert (Mercer University Press, 1986), 42.

18. David L. Balch, *Let Wives Be Submissive: The Domestic Code in 1 Peter*, SBLMS 26 (Scholars Press, 1981); David L. Balch, "Hellenization/Acculturation in 1 Peter," in *Perspectives on First Peter*, ed. Charles H. Talbert (Mercer University Press, 1986), 79–101.

19. Elliott, *A Home for the Homeless*; John H. Elliott, *1 Peter*, AB (Yale University Press, 2001), 504–510.

ground occupied by, for instance, Warren Carter[20] and David G. Horrell[21] who see Peter as advocating *both* conformity *and* resistance. More recently, and drawing from James C. Scott[22] and his notion of resistance from below, Wei H. Wan and Horrell have presented a reading of 1 Peter that sees the text as an ideological critique and an overall presentation of reality aimed at dismantling the imperial cult.[23] This sees 1 Peter engaging in subtle double-meanings and other covert forms of resistance hidden in its public (i.e., "on-stage") conversation to avoid being overheard.[24] This reading presupposes a conscious, albeit "polite," resistance against Rome's imperial domination. However, such a political critique is problematic, not least because it fails to explain the *theological* approach Peter takes to craft his response to the readers' persecution.

Problematizing assumptions made in such readings, my analysis of 1 Peter places the text within a Christocentric apocalyptic thought-world and sees the author engaging in a richer and more coherent symbolic depiction of election, otherness, and belongingness in the space of God that makes an ideological resistance against Roman hegemony obsolete.[25]

Peter's purpose is to provide his readers with a fuller picture of life in Christ in terms of not only a new temporal reality but also, and crucially, a spatial and therefore an ideological reorientation that has occurred through their faith in Christ. The readers' space on earth is marked in a new way through the presence of God. Furthermore, a consideration of the apocalyptic framework of 1 Peter 3:19, 22 and 5:8–11 lends further support to the idea that, in the epistle's symbolic world, the readers are the eschatological people of God who exist in a spatial realm that is marked with cosmic realities even in the midst of their earthly dwelling.[26]

Thus, Peter writes to provide comfort and encouragement to the readers by redrawing the structure of the cosmos along the axis of the will of God. In so doing he places the Christ-believing community in the space of God which stands in contrast with the opposing sphere

20. Warren Carter, "Going All the Way? Honoring the Emperor and Sacrificing Wives and Slaves in 1 Peter 2:13–3:6," in *A Feminist Companion to the Catholic Epistles*, ed. Amy-Jill Levine and Maria Mayo Robbins (T&T Clark, 2004), 28, 14–33. Despite Carter's emphasis on the repertoire of practices to honor the emperor, there is no evidence in 1 Peter that the emperor is due any special honor other than what is owed to everyone (cf. 1 Pet 2:17).

21. David G. Horrell, "Between Conformity and Resistance: Beyond the Balch–Elliott Debate Towards a Post-colonial Reading of First Peter," in *Reading First Peter with New Eyes: Methodological Reassessments of the Letter of First Peter*, ed. Robert L. Webb and Betsy Bauman-Martin (T&T Clark, 2007), 41. Horrell sees 1 Peter condoning "measured but conscious resistance to imperial demands" which entails a "polite resistance" aimed at subtly subverting Roman norms; cf. Horrell, "Between Conformity and Resistance," 41.

22. James M. Scott, *Domination and the Arts of Resistance: Hidden Transcript* (Yale University Press, 1990).

23. Wei Hsien Wan, "Repairing Social Vertigo: Spatial Production and Belonging in 1 Peter," in *The Urban World and the First Christians*, ed. Steve Walton, Paul R. Trebilco, and David W. J. Gill (Eerdmans, 2017), 287–303; David G. Horrell, "Re-Placing 1 Peter: From Place of Origin to Constructions of Space," in *The Urban World and the First Christians*, ed. Steve Walton, Paul R. Trebilco, and David W. J. Gill (Eerdmans, 2017), 271–286.

24. John M. G. Barclay, *Pauline Churches and Diaspora Jews* (Mohr Siebeck, 2011), 380–381; cf. 363–387 in reference to Paul's letters.

25. Abebe, *Apocalyptic Spatiality*, 65–125, 169–173.

26. On the topic of overcoming cosmic evil beings in African religiosity and an overview of a Kenyan cosmology, see Andrew M. Mbuvi, "Christology and Cultus in 1 Peter: An African (Kenyan) Appraisal," in *Jesus Without Borders: Christology in the Majority World*, ed. Gene L. Green, Stephen T. Pardue, and K. K. Yeo (Eerdmans, 2014), 141–161.

of the space of the disobedient. Belonging in a divinely ordained and christologically ordered space does not mean an otherworldly existence for the believers, but rather one that is located and provides a sense of rootedness in the cosmic wide space of God. In addition to providing a positive evaluation of his readers' suffering as aligning with God and Christ, what Peter does is identify a spatial practice of obedience and allegiance to God through abstaining from all that hinders one's imitation of God and of Christ.

An Outline of 1 Peter

- Opening greeting (1:1–2)
- Praise to God for salvation through Christ (1:3–12)
- Body of the letter (1:13–5:11)
  - Response to God's salvation (1:13–2:10)
  - How to live with non-Christians (2:11–3:12)
  - Response to suffering (3:13–5:11)
- Final greeting (5:12–14)

Major Theological Themes in 1 Peter

In the world of 1 Peter, categories of otherness abound. Addressing his letter to communities that are being socially maligned and alienated for their faith, Peter tells them that they are God's elect παρεπιδήμοις (sojourners) and πάροικοις (foreigners) living in the diaspora (1:1; 2:11). He concludes his letter by passing on greetings from the church in "Babylon"—another diasporic space from where he writes (5:13). Peter also cites a host of malevolent otherworldly beings (3:19, 22), inlcuding one identified as the devil (5:8), which belong to the hostile nonhuman "other" about whom he warns his readers. The devil is the ultimate Other. Christ's victory in 3:18–22 is declared to be against evil otherworldly beings and evil itself, which awaits complete eradication at the revealing of Christ at the end of ages. In all this, Peter wants to encourage his readers to persevere in faith while "doing good" (1:13–2:3; 3:8–17). Toward this end, Peter highlights the presence of God, which now marks the life of his readers. As a response to this, he encourages them to adopt the posture of allegiance to Christ, obedience to the will of God, and separation from the world, even as they are persecuted for their faith in Christ.

Persecution and the Space of God

At key points in the epistle, Peter employs Christ's innocent suffering, death, and subsequent glory as the interpretative framework for his readers' situation (cf. 2:19–25; 3:18–22; 4:1–2, 12–19; 5:8–11). He provides a christological grounding for their suffering, often drawing on the template provided by Christ to state that future vindication and glory await the suffering addressees. This is evident in the letter's three christological sections, which occur at 1:18–21, 2:22–25, and 3:18–22. All three passages cite Christ's atoning death and its significance for the readers' here and now. First Peter 1:18–21 states that the readers are ransomed with the blood of Christ (v. 19) and 2:22–25 likewise attributes the removal of sin to Christ's death (v. 24). At 3:18 as well, Peter's starting point is the atoning effect of Christ's sinless suffering, which gained access to God for believers. To the threat brought on their status by persecution, Peter points to their honored inclusion in the now-glorified Christ and the blessings that await them at his revelation at the eschaton.[27]

In employing honor/shame language, Peter demonstrates his concern for the status of his readers (see, e.g., 1:7; 2:6–10; 3:6, 7). Although alienated by society, the letter's recipients are the eschatological people of God whose identity is linked to the new birth they received through the death and resurrection of Christ (1:1–12; 2:5–10). Their kinship, as well as the fact of their belonging in the household of God, is to be demonstrated through the antithesis between life before and after conversion, and specifically in holy living and deep love for one another (1:13–2:10, 13–17). Further elucidating 1 Peter's response to suffering, we find, in 4:15 for example, the call for the audience to suffer not "as a murderer or a thief or an evildoer or as a meddler."

In addressing the issue of suffering, Peter transforms the experience of being persecuted by speaking into the spatial aspect of reality. In 1 Peter, the audience's location is transformed from being a place of persecution and suffering in Asia Minor to the exclusive space of God's presence. This transformation has occurred through the readers' divine election, rebirth, and consecration by the Spirit (1:3–5, 23; 2:4–10, 24). Peter then goes on to tell his readers that this transformation was accomplished through Christ "in order to bring you to God" (3:18). Thus, having been empowered to enter the space of God through election and Christ's atoning sacrifice, the readers are to lead holy lives with realigned priorities in order to maintain the space they have entered in Christ (1:13–2:3).

In doing this, Peter essentially draws a new map of the Anatolian Peninsula where the Roman space and the experience of persecution that comes with it simply becomes subsumed under the spatial ideals of the space of God. This is reflected in the missional (i.e., evangelistic) engagement the readers are to have in the world. In 1 Peter the Roman space is also presented in contrast and opposition to the ordered theocentric and christological space of God that the addressees presently occupy as Christians.

Furthermore, Peter elucidates the readers' new life in the transformed space of God by restructuring the cosmos into ordered and disordered space along the axis of the will of God. Their former life was in the space of darkness from which they have been called out into a life in the light (2:9). It was life in a realm from which they had to be ransomed (1:18). In 4:3, Peter identifies that as a realm that runs in accordance with the "will of the nations" (τὸ βούλημα τῶν ἐθνῶν, NRSV: "what the gentiles like to do") and where disorderly conduct marks the life of its inhabitants (4:3–4). It is marked by disobedience to the gospel of God (4:17; cf. 2:8). In contrast, the space of God is where the will of God unfolds: It runs on God's directive activity (1:6–7, 10–12) even when it does not seem like it, given the readers' suffering

27. John H. Elliott, *What Is Social-Scientific Criticism?* (Fortress Press, 1993), 77–78.

(2:15; 3:17; 4:19). Christ, the model sufferer whom the readers are to imitate, is depicted in a manner that highlights his obedient disposition to the will of God (2:20).

By offering this alternative view of reality through the reordering of space and time, Peter offers a response to suffering and a strategy of resistance against cosmic evil—which, in 1 Peter, is the only hostile "Other" whose threat is to be taken seriously. The result is a rich depiction of a world where "resistance," "conformity," or a "hidden transcript" as responses to persecution lose significance and simply recede to the background.

Imitating Christ

In 1 Peter, the appropriate response to persecution is the imitation of God and of Christ demonstrated in the prominence given to exhortations in 1 Peter. In all the three sections of the epistle's body, Peter depicts the characteristics of Christ's suffering as features that need to be emulated by the addressees as they too suffer like Christ.[28] Christ was blameless and pure (1:19; 2:22), righteous (3:18), he did not retaliate (2:22, 23), but rather entrusted himself to God who judges justly (2:23) and who foreknew his suffering (1:11). The readers are thus reminded that their suffering is akin to that of Christ. It is in fact a sharing in his sufferings (4:13). They are thus to imitate Christ "by their behaviour [2:21], thinking [4:1], and the reason for suffering [2:20–21; 3:7–18]."[29]

Sojourner Identity

In 1 Peter 5:13 we find the symbolism of Babylon. In a form of inclusio, the way Peter starts his letter parallels this end. The letter is addressed "to the elect sojourners in Pontus, Galatia, Cappadocia, Asia, and Bithynia" (1:1, the NRSV: "to the exiles of the dispersion").[30] Peter alludes here to the Jewish sojourner tradition. In ending the letter, he writes "your sister church in Babylon, chosen together with you, sends you greetings, and so does my son Mark" (5:13).

Although the term διασπορά (diaspora) primarily indicates a genitive of place that is physically located outside of Judea,[31] the metaphoric use of diaspora is still in view since the

---

28. Mark Dubis, *Messianic Woes in First Peter: Suffering and Eschatology in 1 Peter 4:12–19*, SBL 33 (Peter Lang, 2002), 103.

29. Dubis, *Messianic Woes*, 97; Katherine M. Hockey, *The Role of Emotion in 1 Peter*, SNTSMS (Cambridge University Press, 2019), 149.

30. See Elliott, *1 Peter*, 91, 131, where he proposes that the separate mention of Pontus and Bithynia (despite Bithynia-Pontus being a single province), indicates the circular route taken by Sylvanus, who most likely commenced the journey from somewhere in Pontus (such as Sinope), proceeding south to Galatia and Cappadocia, then turning westward toward Asia, and then finally northward to Bithynia (Sardis to Nicomedia). He thus takes 1 Peter as an "encyclical or 'circular'" letter.

31. Achtemeier, *1 Peter*, 83; David G. Horrell, *Becoming Christian: Essays on 1 Peter and the Making of Christian Identity*, LNTS (T&T Clark, 2013), 223. The author's emphasis is not on the readers' heavenly home. Commenting on the anthropology of 1 Peter, Cavin correctly notes that the epistle gives no indication of their heavenly existence or participation in the heavenly realm in the present time. Robert L. Calvin, *New Existence and Righteous Living: Colossians and 1 Peter in Conversation with 4QInstruction and the Hodayot*, BZNW (Walter de Gruyter, 2013), 71–72.

readers are ascribed a diasporic identity by virtue of their faith in Christ (1:3–7). They are not a people who have experienced a historic exile, but they are described as those who are given the identity of otherness in the foreign space of the diaspora (2:11). However, their homeland is not in heaven.[32] As is made clear in 1:4, what is kept for believers in heaven is not a home but an inheritance.[33] Until the unfolding of the spatio-temporal reality of Christ's return, the readers are to be alert and attentive to their life in the present (cf. νήφω in 1:13; 4:7; 5:8).[34] In ending his letter, Peter identifies those in his locale as the elect people of God. Babylon is thus depicted as a counterpart to diaspora.[35] Just as it is true of the metaphoric use of "diaspora," existence in Babylon is a feature of the Christ-believing community's identity that is associated with Christ. Babylon is both a social space that describes a sojourner identity for both the addressees and those who are sending them greetings, and a geographical location from where the letter is sent. It serves as an inference to what Peter's response to persecution is: As dwellers of the space of God, the Christ-believing community is to hold fast in their faith and avoid the temptation of falling back to their former habits of disobeying the will of God. They are to do this by adopting a mode of existence defined by a sojourner identity in the space of God that is constantly and continually under hostile attacks from the disordered space of the nations.

Obedience

Through the language of "desire" (ἐπιθυμία), Peter identifies an internal condition that the readers need to recognize in themselves and intentionally resist if they are to obey God. Illicit desires that threaten to impair their ability to obey God are expressed at 1:14; 2:11, and 4:2. The first of these appears as Peter's appeal to the readers, whom he calls "obedient children." He exhorts the readers not to be conformed to the "desires" of their former ignorance (1:14). While Peter here affirms their capability to obey God, he also identifies an important aspect of being human that will stand in the way of living in obedience to God, identified as "desires of the flesh."

In 1:15–17 Peter provides a remedy. He tells the readers to be holy as God is holy (1:15) and establishes a form of relating with one another that places the notion of obedience on the identity of God as holy (1:16). This indicates that to intentionally resist the moral impairment of fleshly desires, the readers should begin by imitating God. Again, by evoking "the fear of God" Peter indicates the means by which the internal force of illicit "desires" can be resisted on the basis of the identity of God. Put differently, it is through a new set of relationships

32. For the view that the believers' true home lies in heaven, see, for e.g., Kelly, *A Commentary on the Epistles of Peter and of Jude*, 47, 103; Peter H. Davids, *The First Epistle of Peter*, NICNT (Eerdmans, 1990), 46–47.

33. Regarding inheritance as a reference to the Jewish expectation of a new creation, cf. Goppelt, *A Commentary on 1 Peter*, 107; Dubis, *Messianic Woes*, 41.

34. As Elliott notes νήψατε is used with σωφρονήσατε at 4:7 and highlights "the need for a disciplined life focused on the urgencies of the moment." Elliott, *1 Peter*, 748.

35. J. Ramsey Michaels, *1 Peter*, Word Biblical Commentary (Thomas Nelson, 1988), 311.

that are aligned with the newly accessible space of God that the disordered desires that lead the readers astray can be corrected or mitigated.

After articulating the readers' new identity as the household of God and their consecration for temple services at 2:5–9, Peter begins a new section with the exhortation to abstain from fleshly desires (2:11–25). This restates his earlier call to the readers to imitate the holy God by being holy themselves (cf. 1:15–16). He tells the readers to abstain from illicit desires that threaten their new identity and negatively impact the missional task that is stated at 2:9 (see also 4:3). What threatens the readers' allegiance to God is identified as "the desires of the flesh," which Peter says "wage war against the soul" (2:11). In 4:2–3 as well, Peter urges the readers to adhere to the will of God by resisting human desires (4:2), which further clarifies the inherent nature of illicit desires and the need for the readers to continually overcome these desires. At 4:2, living in accordance with sinful desires is contrasted with living in pursuit of the will of God, which is in turn juxtaposed with the desires of the gentiles at 4:3. Here, Peter describes with more clarity his earlier command to abstain from fleshly desires. The readers are told not to engage in "debauchery, passions, drunkenness, revels, carousing, and lawless idolatry" (4:3). This list of vices sums up Peter's command to not emulate pagan society but rather God himself (1:15–17) and Christ (2:18–21).

The way to mitigate disordered desire and overcome the threat to disobey God is to seek to live in obedience to the will of God. The readers are to obey God by recognizing their new mode of existence, which is expressed here at 2:11 in terms of foreignness and a sojourner identity. This indicates that resisting moral impairment is associated with being conscious of the identity the readers have gained when placed in the space of God through Christ. While imitating pagans amplifies fleshly desires and results in disobedience, adhering to the example of Christ helps overcome it. This association with imitating Christ is relayed at 4:1, where Peter expresses imitating Christ in terms of having his mindset or thought: "since Christ suffered in the flesh, arm yourselves also with the same intention (for whoever has suffered in the flesh has finished with sin)."

By imitating Christ in his thoughts and his response to persecution, the readers will be able to overcome the propensity to act upon illicit human desires that threaten to impair the call to obedience internally.[36] Seen in this light Peter's exhortations can be understood as ways of resisting moral impairment by imitating Christ and by being conscious of God and the new identity the audience has received in Christ.

36. Katherine Hockey rightly notes that there are three ways in which the imitation of Christ is expressed in 1 Peter: in terms of the addressees' behavior, their thinking, and the meaning they ascribe to suffering. She adds that "the behavioural aspect is clear in 2:21, where Christ leaves the believers a pattern (ὑπογραμμός) that they might follow in his footsteps. . . . Imitating Christ's thinking occurs in 4:1, where the believers are asked to arm themselves with the same ἔννοια as Christ. Lastly, in 2.20–21 and 3:17–18 where the call to imitate Christ is present, suffering is qualified as suffering for doing good, which infers that the believers are only imitating Christ if they suffer for the right reasons." Hockey, *The Role of Emotion in 1 Peter*, 149. While Hockey is right in identifying the three ways in which the imitation of Christ is conceptualized, she does not associate this with the notion of human responsibility (moral agency). See also, Dubis, *Messianic Woes*, 96–97.

An Ethiopian Reading of 1 Peter

Christian Africans in Muslim-majority areas face situations that are similar to an intensified version of what Peter's addressees were facing. The addressees were persecuted because of their faith in Christ (1 Pet. 1:13–18; 3:1–6; 4:2–4; 5:9). What they faced was (1) social/cultural estrangement (1 Pet 1:1; 2:11; (2) verbal and physical abuse (1 Pet 2:12, 16; 3:12–17; 4:14, 16); and (3) unjust treatment (1 Pet 2:20–21; 3:14, 16; 4:1, 13, 16, 19). This humiliating state of affairs describes the everyday realities Christians face in northern Nigeria, Libya, Somalia, and Muslim-dominated areas in Ethiopia's Oromia region (in Arsi and Bale).[37] In addressing the issue of the readers' persecution, Peter reformulates the situation. Instead of identifying their human persecutors as the irredeemable "hostile other," he draws Christians' attention to a nonhuman malevolent being. He urges the readers to beware of a dangerous cosmic enemy whom he likens to a prowling lion that is on the lookout for someone to devour (5:8–9). Like Christian Africans, Peter takes on a cosmic outlook in addressing the problem of suffering—a situation his readers face along with the Christ-believing community "in all the world" (5:9).

In discouraging a potential response of retaliation against their persecutors, Peter highlights Christ's nonviolent response to persecution. Instead of their human oppressors or imperial systems that facilitated false accusations before courts, what Peter stresses is a cosmic evil being, the devil, as the ultimate Other. In elucidating the cosmic significance of Christ's death in 3:18–22, what Peter highlights is Christ's victory. Having overcome death, Jesus is "at God's right hand—with angels, authorities and powers in submission to him" (v. 22).

When Peter draws on Christ's paradigmatic suffering and subsequent glory in responding to his community's suffering, it mirrors the Christian African analysis of persecution in light of God's word and the Christocentric vision of a better tomorrow. God's vision of the complete eradication of evil has already began, it is not yet here, but it is coming. Meanwhile, Christians are to stand fast in their allegiance to Christ and respond appropriately to persecution by taking him as an example.

Furthermore, when Peter highlights Christ's suffering and atoning sacrifice in all of the letter's christological sections, the Christ–Christian parallel he speaks to the reality of many Africans, both in Africa and the diaspora. The idea of shared pain or the perception that one is not alone in facing social alienation, marginalization, and the experience of real or perceived cultural assault is a powerful tool by which minorities or minoritized individuals mitigate ethnic, gender, or racial othering. Persecution because of one's faith or ethnocultural and racial identity also results in increased cooperation and better interpersonal relationships. Among African diaspora communities living as minorities in the minority world or minoritized groups within Africa, one observes how shared pain brings people together and becomes an essential lifeline.

37. According to the UK parliamentary launch of the World Watch List 2024, an annual report published by Open Doors, one in five Christians were persecuted in Africa in 2023: Timothy Robinson and Philip Loft, "Religious Persecution and the World Watch List 2024," accessed March 14, 2024, https://tinyurl.com/248kevkh.

While 1 Peter is occasioned by the persecution the readers are undergoing the author shifts his gaze from the persecutors to the underlying evil. If persecution and the general state of being a follower of Christ unfolds within the context of battle with cosmic evil, believers have assurance in Christ's victory. Despite their persecutions and the threat from otherworldly beings, the readers can confidently manage evil knowing that they are protected by the power of God (1:5) and that Christ is victorious over evil. Peter draws on the parallel of Christ to address the readers' situation. Christ is victorious over evil and, for this reason, believers can and are enabled to simply "resist" a cosmic evil being. This resonates with Christians persecuted across the continent.

As 1 Peter 3:18–21 signifies, through baptism believers receive protection from cosmic evil and experience the removal of the defiling force of moral impurity, which may be connected in some sense with evil spirits. Contemporary readers of the letter are thus encouraged to see moral corruption and the various indignities they experience today as an outworking of cosmic evil. If the corrupting effect of sin is related to evil spirits in 1 Peter, then the warding off of evil may find its expression in the life of obedience which is in turn articulated in terms of a sojourner mode of existence, the maintenance of holiness, and a nonretaliatory attitude toward aggressors. To the violently othered and those experiencing social alienation and persecution, Peter's words bring hope and an awakening to a redrawn map that places Christians in the space of the victorious Christ who has overcome evil. As an inhabitant of that space, Christians can confidently manage evil without succumbing to retaliation through a life lived in awareness of God's presence.

An important aspect of an African reading of 1 Peter is founded on an understanding of 1 Peter's theme of suffering that extends beyond the specific situation of being persecuted as a religious minority. The majority of Christian Africans do not constitute a religious minority and thus persecution is an aspect of the past—if at all that. In Ethiopia, Africa's second most populous nation, Christianity has been practiced continuously since the fourth century. Although having a sizeable Muslim presence, mostly in central and east Ethiopia, the majority of the nation is Christian, mostly belonging to the Orthodox Tewahdo Church, various Protestant churches, and independent Pentecostal churches. Although evangelical Christians had been persecuted for nearly two decades by a Marxist military regime, that regime was ousted thirty-five years ago.

As evidenced by Ethiopia's traditional *Andəmta* commentaries of the seventeenth century, 1 Peter is read in the country without limiting its relevance to the religiously persecuted.[38] The *Andəmta* commentary draws on Christ's victory to implore its readers to "be victorious like the Lord," while theologically interpreting 1 Peter 2:5 as follows:

> He said, "Endure like a spiritual stone." Be victorious like the Lord. He is a stone. Just as a stone is not changed when assaulted with heat by day and with cold by night,

38. The *Andəmta* commentaries originated in Gondar, Ethiopia's capital from 1635 to 1855. Having a likely origin in oral tradition, these commentaries were first written in the Amharic language by imperial decree in 1681. See Abraha, "Andəmta," 258.

> he too did not change by all his suffering. There is a trusted teaching that says, "like living stones be built as the house of the Holy Spirit."[39]

In calling their audience to "endure like a spiritual stone," the commentators indicate that they are working within the framework of suffering as a lived reality believers face, not just in the form of persecution but as a general facet of life on earth.[40] In the commentary's elucidation of 5:8–9, they write "being steadfast in your faith, be victorious [over the devil]."[41]

When read from a specifically Ethiopian perspective, 1 Peter has much to say about subjugation and alienation in the hands of the powerful and the resulting threat to the honor and dignity of the poor and the lowly, which includes the economically and politically disempowered. Peter's framework of hope is embedded in the promises of God that there will come a time when evil will be no more. In the here and now, hope can be found in the firm belief of divine judgment against oppressors. This undergirds the way Ethiopians have dealt with suffering in the country's long and traumatic history. In both the narrative world of 1 Peter (and life in Anatolia under the Roman Empire) and in present-day Ethiopia, everyday existence is marked by hegemonic power structures and the domination of the powerless by those in positions of power and privilege.

In addition to a grounding in hope, Peter's response to suffering also draws on the theme of God's judgment. Immorality, along with the unjust treatment of Christians, will bring about God's eschatological judgment (4:17–19). This follows from Christ's response of nonretaliation against his persecutors, who, instead "entrusted himself to the one who judges justly" (2:23).

The theme of divine judgment is an important aspect of the Ethiopian worldview. For Ethiopians, the reverence for ህግ (*heg*, "law") and ፍትህ (*fiteh*, "justice") is evident in the notion of በህግ አምላክ (*behig Amlak*, lit. "in the name of the God of the Law"), which Ethiopians often invoke to express the high value they put on the law.[42] The saying, በህግ አምላክ ሲባል እንኳን ሰው ወንዝ ይቆማል (*baheg sibal enquan saw wanz yeqomal*, "when the law is invoked *even* the river stops moving, let alone a human being") shows how deeply felt the primacy of the law is.

One specific way such an effect takes place is expressed with the notion of ግፍ (*gef*, oppression/exploitation). *Gef* is an action that is committed by people in positions of power and privilege or those who find themselves in positions of strength, even momentarily. Those at the receiving end are not confined to human subjects—one can commit *gef* against food, for instance, by throwing away edible food or letting children play with food. Thus *gef* also describes an attitude of self-reliance or extravagance. Committing *gef* (i.e., oppressing or

---

39. My translation of the 1 Peter's *Andəmta* on 1 Pet 2:5: Liqe Liqawənt Mehari, *Metsehafte Hadisat Sostu: Nəbab Kenetərəgwame* (Artistic Printing, 1958), 224.

40. For the Ethiopian Orthodox Tewahədo Church's tradition on the concept of salvation and the significance of suffering in the process of sanctification, see Yimenu A. Belay, "Salvation Through Suffering: An Ethiopic Reading of Selected Texts of 1 Peter," in *Reading Hebrews and 1 Peter from Majority World Perspectives*, ed. Sofanit T. Abebe, Elizabeth W. Mburu, and Abeneazer G. Urga, LNTS 700 (T&T Clark, 2024), 165–178.

41. My translation of the *Andəmta* on 1 Peter 5:8; see Mehari, *Metsehafte Hadisat Sostu*, 251.

42. Teshale Tibebu, "Modernity, Eurocentrism, and Radical Politics in Ethiopia, 1961–1991," *African Identities* 6, no. 4 (2008): 347.

exploiting) is thought to bring down the wrath of God, while administrating justice has salvific significance. Such an attitude downplays the urge to retaliate against persecutors—God will judge persecutors at the eschaton, but the meting out of God's judgment is in instalments that have already began.

A particularly Ethiopian Pentecostal response to the problem posed by the rich and powerful is the conviction that the oppressors and their progeny will languish under the እርግማን (*ergeman*, "ill-omen") their illicit actions bring on. The oppressed righteous are, on the other hand, indwelt by the Holy Spirit and will receive, in their present lives, spiritual recompense and the blessings that were promised to Abraham.

The idea of *gef* and *ergeman* and the notion of punishment entailed for oppressors sustains the symbolic world that is built upon the belief that good will ultimately triumph over evil. Shared evil that befalls all humanity, but to which the poor are particularly susceptible, is thus understood and managed better.

The Historical Context of 2 Peter

Authorship, Date, and Audience

Although 2 Peter's authority was disputed in the early stages of the canonical process, the transmission of traditions associated with Peter helped establish the letter as a Petrine text written soon after 1 Peter.[43] Contemporary scholarship largely takes the letter as pseudepigraphical and arguments against a Petrine authorship are not without merit. However, the issue of authorship is not an item on the list of social and cultural concerns an Ethiopian brings to the reading of 2 Peter. Also, since the text identifies its author as "Simon Peter" and includes the transfiguration narrative at 1:16–18, the Ethiopian reader does not hear from 2 Peter an invitation to engage the question of authorship.[44] In a country where the apocryphal Apocalypse of Peter (ca. 132–135 CE), holds some prominence and is extant in its more complete form in an Ethiopic translation, 2 Peter's authenticity is an established fact. In this regard, the concern is with the world of the text, with its major concern focused on the struggles a network of churches in Asia Minor faced or will soon encounter (2 Pet 3:1; cf. 1 Pet 1:1).

The form of the letter indicates a testamentary genre that includes the two main topics we find in ancient Jewish literature, namely, ethical admonitions and revelations of the future.[45] In light of literary patterns in 1 Enoch 91–104 and 4 Ezra 14:28–36 and the familiarity of farewell speeches to Ethiopians through Orthodox Ethiopia's inclusion of these and related texts in its canon, 2 Peter is read as the last words of Peter the apostle that contain his ethical

---

43. Kelsie G. Rodenbiker, "The Second Peter: Pseudepigraphy as Exemplarity in the Second Canonical Petrine Epistle," *Novum Testamentum* 65 (2023): 109–131. Concerning authorship in 2 Peter, see the summary in Michael J. Gilmour, *The Significance of Parallels Between 2 Peter and Other Early Christian Literature*, Academia Biblica 10 (Society of Biblical Literature, 2002).

44. This is also the case in the Cameroonian context, as confirmed by Dieudonné Tamfu, *2 Peter and Jude*, Africa Bible Commentary Series (Langham Publishing, 2018), 7–10.

45. Bauckham, *Jude, 2 Peter*, 131–132.

teaching and warning about the future (cf. 1:3–11; 1:12–15; 3:4). This situation mirrors and can speak to the danger of false teachers that churches are facing in Ethiopia today and about whose rise Peter is understood to have written in 2:1–3 and 3:1–4 (cf. 3:17).[46]

Occasion and Purpose

Peter writes to warn his readers about the false teachers' immoral way of life. He also refutes the theological objections they raise against apostolic teaching (cf. 1:16–20; 2:1–3; 3:1–4). Their teachings are "destructive opinions" (2:1) which threaten to destabilize the community and lead people astray, both theologically and morally (2:2, 10, 13–21). So Peter writes with a sense of urgency (1:5, 10, 15) to uphold the truth, impart confidence in the apostolic teaching the Christian communities have received, and restore doctrinal and moral order to the community.

An Outline of 2 Peter

Testamentary literature from Jewish and Christian texts in 200 BCE–100 CE exhibit the literary style that delivers its contents in the form of what purports to be the final words of heroes of the faith. This appears in 2 Peter 1:12–15, where Peter expresses the expectation that he will die soon (likely a reference to Jesus's prophecy in John 21:18–19).[47] Again, in 1:3–11, there is a summary of his teachings followed by the revelation that false teachers will come (2:1–3; 3:1–4). This testamentary setting appears in combination with the epistolary genre with a typical letter opening in 1:1–2 where the author is introduced. The letter maybe outlined as follows:

- Greetings (1:1–2)
- Believers' identity in Christ and a call to respond (1:3–11)
- The letter's purpose (1:12–15)
- Apologia: Christ's glory, judgment, and denunciation of false teachers (1:16–2:22)
  - Eyewitness testimony: Christ is king & he will return (1:16–20)
  - Divine judgment against immorality (2:1–22)
- Christ's promised return and true Christian hope (3:1–18)

Major Theological Themes in 2 Peter

The letter describes life in Christ in terms of the "knowledge" (επίγνωσις) of God and of Jesus Christ (1:2, 3, 8; 2:20; 3:18). Knowledge in this context entails spiritual awareness that points to God and a personal acquaintance with the cognitive content of the gospel

46. For a detailed treatment of 2 Peter's date of writing and authorship, see Ben Witherington III, *A Socio-Rhetorical Commentary on 1–2 Peter* (InterVarsity Press, 2007), 260–272.

47. Cf. Bauckham, *Jude, 2 Peter*, 131–135.

preached. This contrasts sharply with the sort of erroneous claims about Christ the readers are exposed to through the false teachers who deny Christ's second coming (the parousia) and the reality of divine judgment. As Richard Bauckham notes, eschatological skepticism and ensuing antinomianism are what the false teachers advocate. Thus, the reason for 2 Peter's emphasis "on the fundamental Christian conversion-knowledge and its ethical implications is the danger of apostasy through ethical libertinism (2:20–21) which its readers faced."[48] Peter emphasizes that it is through the knowledge of God and Christ—maintained through apostolic teaching—that true grace and peace can be experienced (1:1–2). This for Peter entails a recognition of the fate that awaits false teachers. It also warrants an awareness that God is in control. Believers can thus confidently hold on to the truth expressed through apostolic teaching, knowing that they will not fall prey to the insidious nature of false teachers for God "knows how to rescue the godly from trial" (2:9).

God's Deliverance

In 2 Peter, God is presented as the sovereign creator and judge of the world, whose authority encompasses the whole cosmos. He does this through his mention of the angels over whom God passed judgment (2:4), the Noahic flood through which God's first phase of judgment over evil unfolded (2:5), and God's dealings with Sodom and Gomorrah that represented the meting out of divine judgment against sin and rebellion (2:6). Throughout the chapter, Peter draws from the riches of Israel's sacred past to assure his readers that the God who was faithful in delivering his people in the past will do so again (2:7–9a). Just as God has dealt with evil in the past, now also, he will faithfully address the epistemic injustices false teachers commit through their "destructive heresies" (αἵρεσις ἀπωλείας, 2:1, cf. 2:3, 10–22).[49]

When Peter writes about God's judgment against sin in the past (2:4–6) and assures the readers that injustices will not go unanswered, he implicitly encourages the readers through the very prediction he is making. The sovereign Lord forewarns his people and in so doing equips them with what they need to spot false teachers and the falsehood and destructive ideas that will lead to judgment. Peter states that false teachers are recognizable by their denial of the Lord and their immorality, just like the false prophets of the Old Testament. As Bauckham correctly notes, the three prominent characteristics the false teachers share with the Old Testament prophets are: (1) they do not have divine authority to speak (Jer. 14:14; 23:21); (2) instead of the coming divine judgment, their message is of peace and security (Jer. 4:10; 16–18; Ezek. 13:10); (3) they are "condemned to punishment by God" (Jer. 14:15; 23:15; 28:16–17).[50] The readers are to recognize them by their lack of loyalty to Christ ("they will even deny the Master who bought them," 2:1b). This lack of loyalty is expressed through their immorality and disobedience (2:7, 14), as well as their denial of Christ's true gospel and the fact of his second coming.

48. Bauckham, *Jude, 2 Peter*, 170.

49. Epistemic injustice has been defined as "a wrong done to someone specifically in their capacity as a knower." Miranda Fricker, *Epistemic Injustice: Power and the Ethics of Knowing* (Oxford University Press, 2010), 1.

50. Bauckham, *Jude, 2 Peter*, 238.

An Ethiopian Reading of 2 Peter
Heresies, Sin, and Divine Judgment

The heretics' errors are both doctrinal and moral. In defending true doctrine, Peter focuses on their skepticism of Christ's return and divine judgment (3:3–10).[51] Noting that the promised return of Christ has never materialized, they conclude that Christ will not return and final judgment will not occur. In effect they teach that the apostles and the prophets are wrong (3:4, 9; 1:20–21).

The erroneous teachings of the heretics undergird their immoral way of life (2:18–19; 3:3–4). In his defense against the opponents, Peter notes that what they are doing constitutes a denial of the Lord (2:1); in essence, it is "the rejection of his sovereignty over their moral lives (2:10)."[52]

Peter declares that a new future awaits humanity (3:14–18). Just as he has done in the past, God will deal with evil and he will rescue the world from the corruption of greed, lust, and injustice. At 2:14, the letter's vision of hope contrasts sharply with the empty promise of freedom the heretics hold out: "They have eyes full of adultery, insatiable for sin. They entice unsteady souls. They have hearts trained in greed. Accursed children!"

Ethiopian churches have witnessed a recent tide of antinomianism that is fueled by a complex web of heretical doctrines. One form of such teachings emanates from preterism, which places Christ's second coming in the first century (at the time of Jerusalem's destruction in 70 CE). Although it lacks prominence and does not have much of a following, Addis Ababa is the seat of an association for the proponents of various shades of this heresy. More recently, the denial of Christ's coming has been popularized by the itinerant preacher Kassa Keraga. He rose to prominence around fifteen years ago and has preached in mainline churches and published popular issues of a magazine he has established.

Another antinomian heresy disguising itself as a mainline reformed teaching is what has often been called "hyper-grace"—a set of loosely held teachings that argue that moral laws do not apply to Christ-believers. At the expense of the doctrine of sanctification, these teachings highlight the doctrine of justification where obedience, holiness, and the imitation of Christ in the here and now are subsumed by the righteousness believers have received through Christ.

We find yet another heresy that promotes licentiousness and denies divine judgment in what is known as the "prosperity gospel." Based on a heretical doctrine of salvation, its proponents claim that believers are saved in their spirits. They declare that what the body does has no impact on the spirit. Much like the Gnostics of the second century, they assert that it is not the saved who commit sin, only their body. In addition to all this—and perhaps more aligned to Jude than 2 Peter—there are various heresies in Ethiopia that claim prophetic inspiration against their call to abandon holiness and a life of obedience.

---

51. Green, *Jude and 2 Peter*, 151.
52. Green, *Jude and 2 Peter*, 152.

The difference between the situation in 2 Peter and the litany of heresies Ethiopian Protestant churches have faced argues against an anachronistic reading of contemporary heresies back into 2 Peter.[53] Whoever the heretics are or whatever system of thought they followed, Peter is concerned with countering their claim that Christ will not return and that there is no final judgment because these doctrines are what underpin the heretics' claim that believers are free to disregard the pursuit of holiness and godliness. When an Ethiopian reads 2 Peter, what she brings to the text and what she hears the text addressing is the question of "how should I respond"?

Peter calls for a radical reorientation of life in light of the future. If the future is the time for the revelation of Christ's glory and the unfolding of God's final instalment of judgment against all evil, it entails that we live today in a manner that is radically infused with this hope. When Peter speaks of believers as "partakers of the divine nature" (2 Pet 1:4), he has in mind the biblical notion of personal intercommunion—namely, the mutual indwelling—in the Triune God that believers in Christ share (cf., e.g., John 14:20, 23). Our life in Christ and the intercommunion we share in Christ is given to us by the Holy Spirit in, and through, the gift of faith, which is the conviction the Holy Spirit gives to us regarding the truth of Christ's gospel. Believers have union with Christ only on the basis of grace.[54] In imperial Ethiopia's long history of kingly succession, one's progress or the attainment of any form of success was on the basis of one's social class or familial and economic ties. In today's Ethiopia, more often than not, it is mitigated through ethnic favoritism, nepotism, or economic prowess. In stark contrast, regardless of one's socioeconomic background, ethnicity, tribe, or race, believers are recipients of Christ's gifts and participants in the Giver himself by grace through faith. Examining our life through the prism of the hope 2 Peter envisions entails celebrating this.

In addition to heresies and hostilities within Christian communities, the contemporary Ethiopian reader of 2 Peter lives in a context of political turmoil and rumors of a deep state to explain the apparent nonexistence of the rule of law and the weakening of the state's monopoly on the legal use of force in the last three years. Adding to this, there is the desertification of the Sahara and the ensuing cyclical famine engulfing vast regions of the country. Such a reader latches onto 2 Peter 3:10's "But the day of the Lord will come like a thief, and then the heavens will pass away with a loud noise, and the elements will be dissolved with fire, and the earth and everything that is done on it will be disclosed." In this vision of passing away (παρέρχομαι), hope presents itself in the promise that God will expose all evil by unveiling the heavens, which is a metaphor Peter uses from Isaiah 34:4–5. The theme of justice is what steers Peter's conversation here. God will uncover hidden corruption and put an end to evil and the forces of destruction. How then shall we live? Rather than a quietist acceptance of

53. For a discussion of who the opponents of 2 Peter are, see, for e.g., Green, *Jude & 2 Peter*, 152–159.

54. On union with Christ, see Michael Horton, *Pilgrim Theology: Core Doctrines for Christian Disciples* (Zondervan, 2017). The ancient Ethiopian Orthodox *Tewahido* Church identifies the Holy Communion as the means through which the Holy Spirit would continually effect believers' unification with Christ. See the Eucharistic liturgy (*Akuatêta Querbān*) in the Anaphora of Athanasius in Marcos Daoud, trans., *The Liturgy of the Ethiopian Church* (Kegan Paul, 2005) 138–158, esp. 150, 152, 155. For a descriptive analysis of the Anaphora, see Ernst Hammerschmidt, "Jewish Elements in the Cult of the Ethiopian Church," *Journal of Ethiopian Studies* 3, no. 2 (1965): 1–12.

the status quo, 2 Peter's implicit call is to live a life cognizant of divine authority, refusing to abandon hope, laboring for a just society by bearing witness to Christ, and decrying violence and oppression wherever it rears its head.

Conclusion

The first and second Epistles of Peter address the issue of hostility and othering. While the contexts of their respective first readers differ, both letters embody a distinctly Christocentric response to hostilities. In 1 Peter this entails firm allegiance to Christ that precludes retaliating against persecutors or conforming to the wider culture to avoid persecution. Instead Peter urges the readers to take comfort in the presence of the God who dwells in their midst in the here and now. As a response to the holy God present among them, the readers are urged to embody a Christocentric vision of life which calls for a life of obedience and separation from the world while resisting evil and pursuing goodness.

In 2 Peter, we find an implicit call to defend the faith from teachings and conduct that are hostile to the received tradition of the Christian community and the life-affirming Christocentric vision of a world rescued from evil. In this sense both letters impart a vision of hope which invites us to examine our everyday life in light of the God who confronts injustice now and will soon eradicate all evil.

In this regard both letters anchor the life of their contemporary readers in Ethiopia in an awareness of God's presence and the all-encompassing reality of Christ's victory over evil. Such awareness empowers readers to militate against evil in devotion to God, refusing to bow to the dysfunctional ways the world conducts its life and orders its relationships. In a continent that has suffered much and continues to labor under socioeconomic injustices, violent otherings, and the trauma of past and present wars, the belief that evil will be dealt with on a cosmic scale at the end of days, as well as through God's micro acts of judgment in the here and now, helps to mitigate evil and the hopelessness it threatens to unleash on individuals and communities.

Further Reading

Abebe, Sofanit T. *Apocalyptic Spatiality in 1 Peter and Selected 1 Enoch Literature*. WUNT II/613. Mohr Siebeck, 2024.

Abebe, Sofanit T. "Peter and the Patriarch: Eschatological Perspectives from 1 Peter and 1 Enoch." In *Beyond Canon: Early Christianity and the Ethiopic Textual Tradition*, edited by Meron T. Gebreananaye, Logan Williams, and Francis Watson. T&T Clark, 2021.

Abebe, Sofanit T., Elizabeth W. Mburu, and Abeneazer G. Urga, eds. *Reading Hebrews and 1 Peter from Majority World Perspectives*. LNTS 700. T&T Clark, 2024.

Achtemeier, P. J. *1 Peter: A Commentary on First Peter*. HCHCB. Fortress Press, 1996.

Asumang, A. "'Resist Him' (1 Pet 5:9): Holiness and Non-Retaliatory Responses to Unjust Suffering as 'Holy War' in 1 Peter." *Conspectus* 11, no. 3 (2011): 7–46.

Bauckham, Richard. *Jude, 2 Peter*. WBC 50. Word Books, 1983.

Bechtler, S.R. *Following in His Steps: Suffering, Community and Christology in 1 Peter*. SBLDS 162. Scholars Press, 1998.

Davids, Peter H. *The Letters of 2 Peter and Jude*. Pillar New Testament Commentary. Eerdmans, 2006.

De Campos, Mateus. "Second Letter of Peter." In *The New Testament in Color: A Multiethnic Bible Commentary*, edited by Esau McCaulley, Janette H. Ok, Osvaldo Padilla, and Amy Peeler. InterVarsity Press Academic, 2024.

Dubis, M. *Messianic Woes in First Peter: Suffering and Eschatology in 1 Peter 4:12–19*. SBLDS 33. Peter Lang, 2002.

Elliott, John H. *1 Peter: A New Translation with Introduction and Commentary*. ABC 37B. Yale University Press, 2001.

Gilmour, Michael J. *The Significance of Parallels Between 2 Peter and Other Early Christian Literature*. Society of Biblical Literature, 2002.

Green, Gene. *Jude and 2 Peter*. BECNT. Baker Academic, 2008.

Horrell, David G. *The Epistles of Peter and Jude*. Epworth, 1998.

Horrell, David G. "Re-Placing 1 Peter: From Place of Origin to Constructions of Space." In *The Urban World and the First Christians*, edited by Steve Walton, Paul R. Trebilco, and David W. J. Gill. Eerdmans, 2017.

Jobes, Karen H. *1 Peter*. BECNT. Baker Academic, 2005.

Liqe Liqawənt Mehari. *Metsehafte Hadisat Sostu: Nəbab Kenetərəgwame*. Artistic Printing, 1958.

Mbuvi, Andrew M. "Christology and Cultus in 1 Peter: An African (Kenyan) Appraisal." In *Jesus Without Borders: Christology in the Majority World*, edited by Gene L. Green, Stephen T. Pardue, and K. K. Yeo. Eerdmans, 2014.

Mbuvi, Andrew M. *Temple, Exile, and Identity in 1 Peter*. LNTS 345. T&T Clark, 2007.

Moxnes, H. "Because of 'The Name of Christ': Baptism and the Location of Identity in 1 Peter." In *Ablution, Initiation, and Baptism: Late Antiquity, Early Judaism, and Early Christianity*, edited by Øyvind Norderval, Christer Hellholm, Tor Vegge, and David Hellholm. De Gruyter, 2011.

Pierce, Chad T. *Spirits and the Proclamation of Christ: 1 Peter 3:18–22 in Light of Sin and Punishment Traditions in Early Jewish and Christian Literature*. WUNT 305. Mohr Siebeck, 2011.

Schreiner, Thomas R. *1, 2 Peter, Jude*. NAC 37. Broadman & Holman, 2003.

Tamfu, Dieudonné. *2 Peter and Jude*. Africa Bible Commentary Series. HippoBooks, 2018.

Urga, Abeneazer G., Jessica A. Udall, and Edward L. Smither, eds. *Reading 1 Peter Missiologically: The Missionary Motive, Message, and Methods of 1 Peter*. William Carey, 2024.

Wan, Wei H. *The Contest for Time and Space in the Roman Imperial Cults and 1 Peter: Reconfiguring the Universe*. Bloomsbury, 2019.

Witherington, Ben III. *A Socio-Rhetorical Commentary on 1–2 Peter*. InterVarsity Press, 2007.

CHAPTER TWENTY-TWO

The Letters of John

Julius Kithinji
St. Paul's University
Limuru, Kenya

Mphumezi Hombana
The University of South Africa
Pretoria, South Africa

Introduction

FOR MANY CENTURIES, studies in the Letters of John have formed an important element in the New Testament discipline. Many topics have been tackled and one might even ask what new and important information we, as latecomers, bring to the discourse. Without delving into much justification (which many commentaries have already done), the three Epistles of John have been studied for decades under the genre of Johannine literature. This chapter engages in an interpretation of the Letters of John by tracing the key thematic elements that emerge from an interpretive analysis and textual exploration. By so doing, this chapter seeks to illuminate the enduring relevance and applicability of these epistle, not only to the specific sociocultural, religious, and spiritual landscape of the first century, but also to situate its contemporary relevance for Christian African communities. The primary African contexts envisaged are the Kenyan and South African contexts—though the generic African context will also be applicable.

The conventional study of these letters has mainly highlighted theological conflicts subsumed in the letters, given early Christian comprehension of Christology, soteriology, and church governance. Since the New Testament guild has, in recent times, has shifted from solely focusing on the literary-structuralist approach in investigating the Letters of John, there is now more interest in using social investigative tools to examine the social world of the Letters of John. Hence, the focus of this chapter is on reading these letters in light of African experiences. Reading from an African perspective is not meant to present an exclusivist approach, but rather to feed into the study of these letters' views which have been initially submerged and often overlooked in conventional scholarship.

In this chapter, readers will get a glimpse of life and struggles in one area of the early church through the Letters of John. These reflect a problematic period in the lives of the Christian communities, namely, a period of conflict among Christians involving issues of both behavior and theology. Like all other New Testament Epistles, these three epistles are one-sided because they present the conflict from the perspective of the author. We may never know much about the narrated opponents, the antichrist/s, except from his perspective. The Epistles of John discuss disagreements on various issues that seem to be associated with this conflict, with all three engaging significant issues or ideas that address doctrinal and ethical problems. The Epistles contain key Christian doctrines, for instance, the doctrine of Christ, the idea of *koinōnia*, assurance of salvation, and the work of the Holy Spirit amongst believers. Readers who read these letters will gain a deeper understanding of these issues and be able to reflect on them from the contextual perspectives involved in this chapter.

The historical conditions surrounding the writing of the Letters of John have been the focus of many sharp concerns, particularly with the emergence of critical study. For example, questions have been raised concerning the identity of the recipients and how the letters relate to the fourth Gospel and Revelation regarding literature or history. These questions have been addressed by many authors, and suffice it to say that this brief chapter cannot even attempt to harmonize the myriad of views.[1] Nevertheless, we shall delve into a few of these arguments from time to time in the chapter, specifically where they illuminate the interpretation of a particular verse or section. We will begin by considering the relationship between the three epistles.

The Relationship Between 1, 2, and 3 John

The common authorship of the first two letters is self-evident, hence their striking similarities.[2] It is interesting to note the similarity between 1 John and 2 John because both books discuss people who have rejected the incarnation of Jesus Christ and, by so doing, they are to be rejected by the community (1 John 2:19, 22–23; cf. 2 John 7). These dissidents are also called antichrists in both texts (1 John 2:18, 22; cf. 2 John 1:7). Also, both epistles (1 and 2 John) place stress on the fundamental commandment of love, which is received in conjunction with the gospel (1 John 3:11, 23; 4:7, 21; 5:1–4a; cf. 2 John 4–6). In addition, the writer of 1 John, like the elder in 2 John, finds joy in witnessing his followers' fidelity to the truth (1 John 1:3–4; cf. 2 John 4). As for 2 and 3 John, a similarities in language, theme, and stylistic aspects point to a possible joint authorship.[3] Both letters close with similar statements about future correspondence (2 John 12; 3 John 1:13–14a), show gratitude for the recipients' devotion to the truth (2 John 4; 3 John 1:4), and show affection for the addressees "in the truth" (2 John 1; 3 John 1:1). Such connections in all three epistles direct the focus to an individual author of the Johannine Epistles. On the other hand, the difference in literary form has led

1. We recommend John R. W. Stott, *The Letters of John*, rev. ed. TNTC (InterVarsity Press; Eerdmans, 1988), for a deeper engagement on this subject. Stott delves into quite deep analysis, showing nitty-gritty interrelationships between the Epistles themselves and also between them and the Gospel. See also William Loader, *The Johannine Epistles*, Epworth Commentaries (Epworth Press, 1992).

2. Contrary to what Clement of Alexandria termed as great divergences. See Stott, *The Letters of John*, 28.

3. See Stott, *The Letters of John*, 28–30.

some scholars to propose independent authors for each of the Epistles.[4] This chapter takes the traditional view of authorship and upholds the view that assumes that one author wrote all three epistles.

An Overview of the Letters

We begin with an overview of each of the Epistles of John and consider the most prominent themes in these letters. The obvious theological theme that is dominant in 1 John is the assurance of salvation. The theme is important because the author and his community are facing fierce opponents of the gospel who have left the community and are persuading others to follow suit since they aim to mock the salvific efficacy of the Christ event. Assurance of salvation is therefore a prominent theme and is further outlined throughout the letter under various subthemes. This motif is further expressed in various sections of the letter by the same assertion, "we know" (1 John 2:3), and related phrases as well. For example, assertions such as "whoever claims to live in him" (1 John 2:6) and "anyone who claims to be in the light" (1 John 2:9) emphasize the idea of an individual knowledge or comprehension and intimate personal relation with God, as well as the fundamental aspect of true assurance of salvation. Moreover, the motif of "assurance of salvation" is further illustrated via authentic love for the other, as pointed out in 1 John 3:11. John notes that the foundation of true love is the sacrificial love of Jesus (1 John 3:16). Similarly, those who are truly saved are exalted to love one another, and not to love the world and worldly pursuits.

Among other things, 2 John emphasizes the importance of walking in truth, abiding in love, and being wary of false teachings (2 John 2–4). The encouragement is for believers to walk in the truth, love one another, and adhere to Christ's teachings without being hospitable to false teachers. This is so because they ought to safeguard the church's doctrine. At the beginning of 3 John, the reader is introduced to an affectionate relationship between the author and his dear friend Gaius. Furthermore, the writer expresses his joy because of the report from other believers about Gaius's unshakable devotion to the truth (3 John 1). At the same time, Gaius is commended for being hospitable to fellow believers and even those with whom he might not have personal relations (3 John 5). The church community is informed about Gaius's love, and Demetrius's good reputation. It is clear from the text that the central themes of love, truth, and hospitality are being emphasized in these brotherly affections as expressed by the elder to his fellow believer Gaius. Diotrephes, on the other hand, is censured for being a dictatorial leader, even excommunicating those who show hospitality to those sent by the author.

Genre

For many centuries, the genre of these writings has been debated but not settled. In brief, we can note that though we generically refer to the three as "epistles," 1 John does not strictly

4. David A. deSilva, *An Introduction to the New Testament: Contexts, Methods & Ministry Formations*, 2nd ed. (InterVarsity Press Academic, 2018), 391.

follow the Greco-Roman or New Testament epistolary conventions. In this chapter, the genre of each epistle will be handled separately.

A Brief Note on the Theoretical Orientation of This Chapter

In his 2008 work, Warren Carter explores the intersection of culture, politics, and religion in the New Testament, particularly focusing on how early Christian texts interact with Roman imperial ideology. Carter argues that the New Testament writers were not apolitical or disengaged from the sociopolitical realities of their time.[5] Following after Carter, this chapter acknowledges that the Letters of John are embedded within their era's cultural, spiritual, and political ideas. Our focus will be on examining the sociopolitical, cultural, and theological themes of the letters and how they relate to or resonate with the African context. This will be aided by several theoretical tools, including social-scientific approaches and several aspects of decolonial analysis, particularly where issues of gender, center and margins, and retrieval cannot be read otherwise.

The Historical Context of 1 John

Authorship and Date

Strictly speaking, the epistle is anonymous except for the title in many available Bible versions that reads, "The First Letter of John." This title is probably informed by the traditional view that has associated the authorship of this epistle to John the disciple, the son of Zebedee. The traditional view is supported by many contemporary authors, including Craig S. Keener[6] and Donald Guthrie[7] among others. Though this is not the place to line up all internal and external evidence concerning authorship, including other proposed views for authorship, this chapter favors the traditional view that the author is John the son of Zebedee and the disciple of Jesus.

Concerning the date, much has also been written. If we accept the view of John's authorship, then we must also accept that it was written within John's lifetime. This would also require us to answer the question of which came first—the Gospel of John or 1 John. Some have rightly argued that 1 John was written at a later stage in John's life.[8] Given this, and the fact that John's probable purpose is to counter Docetism and an early form of Gnosticism which arose toward the close of the first century CE, then it seems warranted to date 1 John around 90 CE.[9]

---

5. Warren Carter, *The Roman Empire and the New Testament: An Essential Guide* (Abingdon Press, 2008), 44–52.

6. Craig S. Keener, *The IVP Bible Background Commentary: New Testament* (InterVarsity Press Academic, 2014), 706.

7. Donald Guthrie, *New Testament Theology* (InterVarsity Press, 1981), 243–246.

8. D. Moody Smith, *First, Second, and Third John*, Interpretation (John Knox Press, 1991), 8.

9. Stephen Smalley, *1, 2, 3 John*, WBC (Thomas Nelson, 2007), xxix. Note that scholars are not in agreement regarding the particular heresy.

Genre

First John lacks almost all the generic qualifiers that mark a letter—it has no greeting formula and no opening health wish or thanksgiving; it contains no direct requests; and it includes no messages to or from third parties. This has led many scholars to categorize it in other genres, such as sermons or homilies. However, it is important to note that 1 John fails the test of description for many conventional genres. Such labels also ignore the repeated references to this as a written document and to this writing as being intentional and not a secondary inconsequential stage. Nevertheless, the verb "to write" (γράφειν) is used thirteen times in the epistle (probably to help us categorize it as a writing) and is followed on three occasions by ἵνα and on seven by ὅτι, both expressing purpose (1 John 1:4; 2:1, 11–14, 21 [26]; 5:13).[10] Since the early readers accepted it is a letter, we shall dwell on this convenient labeling and treat it as such in this chapter.

Occasion

The letter implicitly seems determined to win back members who have left and to deter further exit, occasioned by a doctrinal and probably a supremacy secession. Therefore, it seems that the secessionists had been given some time and had even established communities. The main problem is proper acknowledgment of Jesus in relationship to God the Father. The promoters of the view (whether Docetists or proto-Gnostics) that led to a defective Christology have reverted to desperate measures such as the recent secession and false teaching. Moreover, they have downplayed the authority of the elder, contributing to the disintegration of the group—"we." Those who have erred have to be warned and the remaining group protected from any erroneous teaching to do with Christ within the community. The epistle was therefore mainly written to encourage those within the community to remain loyal to that "which was from the beginning" (1 John 1:1) and in so doing responds to the views of opponents who wish to lead the faithful astray.

Conventional Outline

Prologue (1:1–4)
The ethical test (1:5–2:17)
Truth and falsehood (2:18–27)
Children of God and of the evil one (2:28–3:24)
False spirits and the spirit of God (4:1–6)
Our confidence in God's love (4:7–5:12
Epilogue (5:13–21)

10. Judith M. Lieu, "The Audience of the Johannine Epistles," in *Communities in Dispute: Current Scholarship on the Johannine Epistles*, ed. Paul N. Anderson and R. Alan Culpepper (Society of Biblical Literature, 2014), 123–140.

Reading 1 John from African Perspectives

Prologue and Invitation to Fellowship (1 John 1:1–10)

The opening verses of 1 John are often called a prologue (1 John 1:1–4) because they introduce what follows but are not part of the main argument. John Stott, observing the problematic nature of this passage, observes that the first paragraph is written in complex grammar which almost obscures meaning.[11] The similarity of this opening to the prologue of John's Gospel (John 1:1–18) has been a point of much scholarly curiosity and comparison. The similarities in language may arise if we accept the view that both the Gospel and 1 John draw on earlier ideas and formulations that had already begun to take shape within the Johannine school.[12] This pattern of evoking and reworking familiar material is one of the notable characteristics of 1 John and is essential to its persuasive effectiveness. Moreover, the two "prologues" have very different emphases and functions. One key difference is the focus here on the "we" whose experience gives them the authority to proclaim to the "you," who, it is implied, have not had the same direct experience. Although the language of seeing and hearing evokes the idea of an immediate eye- or ear-witness, the grammatical object is not a person but a thing ("that which," v. 1), or, more abstractly, "eternal life" (v. 2). The goal of this proclamation is fellowship between the author (and his colleagues) and the audience. This fellowship is not merely a social community but also a fellowship with God and God's Son, Jesus Christ. It is only with the last verse, verse 4, that what could have been understood as oral proclamation is identified as what is now being written: "We are writing these things so that our joy may be complete."[13] This verse may be treated as the conclusion of this prologue because introducing the "writing" prepares for the chapters that follow.

Enduring Fellowship with God (1 John 1:1–10)

First John 1 focuses on fellowship with God, the embodiment of divine light, and the necessity of walking in that light as a measure of faith. Verses 1–4 emphasize the apostolic testimony of Jesus's incarnation—"what we have heard, seen with our eyes, and touched with our hands" (1 John 1:1). Walking in the light (ἐν τῷ φωτὶ περιπατεῶ) means living in truth, integrity, and confession, while darkness represents sin and deceit.

Lieu observes that the argument in 1 John 4–8 moves into a style of debate and reflection. According to Lieu, the author, instead of making his point by demonstration, spells out the various possibilities and invites his readers to enter into the process of drawing the appropriate conclusions.[14] The issue raised of walking in the light is very important for

11. Stott, *The Letters of John*, 62.

12. The existence of a Johannine school/community is a matter of great scholarly debates, with some accepting it and others rejecting the view altogether. See Wally V. Cirafesi, "The 'Johannine Community' in (More) Current Research: A Critical Appraisal of Recent Methods and Models," *Neot* 48, no. 2 (2014): 341–364.

13. Judith M. Lieu, *I, II, & III John: A Commentary*, NTL (Westminster John Knox Press, 2008), 36.

14. Lieu, *I, II, & III John*, 130.

African Christianity. During the high tides of the East Africa revival movement, "walking in the light" was a key phrase.[15] Walking in the light was more than simply truth-telling; it incorporated all aspects of living the truth. It was a metaphor for being a truthful Christian in all aspects of life and making the truth of one's life evident to the family of believers.

In the South African context, the theological motif of walking in the truth (1 John 1:7) relates deeply with the historical injustices caused by apartheid. It can be argued that the formation of the Truth, Justice, and Reconciliation Commission was built on Johannine foundations of walking in the truth. The call to walk in the truth is a serious call to those who claim to be believers and indeed followers of Christ to take the lead in the nation's bid for justice and reconciliation in their proclamation of Christ. Given that the theme of fellowship of believers dominates 1 John, it should be exemplified by all who profess faith in Jesus in this society that has become so impersonal and full of hatred toward one another. A genuine response to this call is mandatory, not just lip service.

Just as the passage calls believers to reject sin and live in God's truth (1 John 1:9), Christian Africans are challenged to resist the darkness of corruption, patriarchalism, sexism, tribalism, xenophobia, racism, and inequality. This call provides the African church with a very significant moral agenda to attend to regarding all relevant social ills of our times. First John focuses mainly on motifs of truth, heresy, and Christian conduct that are forever relevant to the Christian Church everywhere in the world. Surely, these themes come as a warning to the Christian Church in Africa because of the moral decay and the flood of false teachings in society today. And most importantly, love is key in all these endeavors. However, this love is not without discernment. While Christians are called to live peaceably with others, they must also "test the spirits" (1 John 4:1) and ensure that love is grounded in truth, avoiding the dangers of relativism, where truth is compromised for the sake of inclusivity.

Commitment to Christ as Commitment to Morality (1 John 2:1–11)

In this portion John presents the right view of Christ as resulting in right behavior. While believers are not sinless (1:8–9), they are expected to sin less. And when they do, coming back to Christ for help assures them of perfect forgiveness. Therefore, those who have believed in Christ must consider their behavior so that it is daily aligned to Christ. Here he outrightly contradicts the opponents who taught that so long as one believed, it did not matter how they behaved (1 John 1:10; 2:9). John puts forward love as the test of a perfect moral life. Obedience to the commandment must emanate from love. Keener rightly points out that "the Old Testament and Judaism forbade hatred of brothers and sisters (Lev 19:17); in a Jewish context this language referred to fellow Jews; in a Christian context, it refers to fellow Christians."[16]

15. Johannes J. Knoetze and Robinson K. Mwangi, "A Socio-Historical Background to the Keswick Theology in East African Revival Movement as 'Walking in the Light': Perspectives from Kenya," *Missionalia* 46, no. 3 (2018): 393.

16. Keener, *IVP Bible Background Commentary*, 709.

Right belief must lead to right morals and right practice. Even religious societies often struggle with this aspect. Christians in Africa have certainly struggled with this. In Kenya, for example, it is yet to be explained how a society which is considered 84 percent Christian still remains threatened by corruption, negative ethnicity, killings, murders, and bad governance, to name but a few. Although the religious questions that many Africans grapple with are more existential than metaphysical, it is important to insist on a right understanding of Christ. At the expense of teaching adequate Christology or understanding who Christ is and our relationship to him, many contemporary preachers rush to teach proper ecclesiology. In reality, however, good ecclesiology is rooted in good Christology.

Overcoming the World (1 John 2:12–17)

The section begins with direct exhortations to different characteristically male groups. This has led some scholars to critique the patriarchal nature of these exhortations. Other scholars have felt that these groupings (dear children [vv.12, 14], young men [vv. 13, 14], and fathers [vv. 13, 14]) are generic for both male and female and they represent various stages of progression in the Christian faith.[17] The exhortation not to love the world has many similarities with the teaching in the Gospel (17:13–18). What was said cryptically in the Gospel, "in the world but not of the world" (John 17:14–15), is now clarified in the epistle. They are not to love the world or anything in the world (1 John 2:14–17). Here John is categorical that one cannot love the world and the Father at the same time (Matt 6:24). On this thought the epistle seems to align not only with John's Gospel but also with the Synoptics (see Mark 8:36, Matt 16:26 and Luke 9:25) concerning love of the world.

The notion of the world as a system of belief which is constantly opposed to that which God has instituted is difficult to grasp in contemporary Africa. This is partly influenced by an African worldview where the dichotomy between the sacred and secular is hardly emphasized. Embracing the gospel of Christ in Africa means that we must pay attention to the worldview that John presents and which is prevalent in the New Testament. Contemporary Africans must distance themselves from, as well as confront, worldly systems that continually oppose the Christian message. In Kenya, for example, these include persuasions to accept definitions of family systems that are opposed to those defined in the Bible. Some Kenyans are embracing resurging forms of retrogressive traditional practices that reject the gospel altogether, for example, polygamy, normalizing deliberate single parenthood and resurgent secret families. All these and many others are forms of living that John categorizes as loving the world (1 John 2:16–17).

Worldliness in African Christianity (1 John 2:15–17)

Owing to the demands of globalization in a world that is increasingly becoming a "global village," African Christianity is quickly becoming affected by the secular ethos that accompanies conformities to a global space. Though Africa, south of the Sahara, remains largely

17. This is the view of Keener, *IVP Bible Background Commentary*, 709.

Christian and notoriously religious,[18] its Christian/religious contribution to World Christianity and world morality remains to be seen. Currently, the African religious space remains only a tourist attraction for outsiders—a phenomenon to be observed and, at the same time, a scholarly research arena. First John 2:15–17 warns believers of befriending the world—literally, loving the world (v. 15, Μὴ ἀγαπᾶτε τὸν κόσμον μηδὲ τὰ ἐν τῷ κόσμῳ. ἐάν τις ἀγαπᾷ τὸν κόσμον, οὐκ ἔστιν ἡ ἀγάπη τοῦ πατρὸς ἐν αὐτῷ). The passage provides a framework for particularly addressing the complex issue of worldliness within the context of the church in Africa, which can be witnessed in poor governance, wealth inequalities, killings, and corruption, among other things. Although many African countries boast of populations that are more than 80 percent Christian, many of Africa's societies have increasingly embraced secular values with waning morality, such that 1 John 2:15–17 becomes a relevant text for challenging worldly inclinations. The African church cannot be construed as a dealer in the love of the Father (ἀγάπη τοῦ πατρὸς) if her bishops, clergy, and Christians remain indicted in these corrupt practices.

John warns the church against false teachings and stresses the importance of loving God through obedience and loving one another. The concept of κόσμος (*kosmos*) in 1 John (e.g., 2:15–17; 4:1; 5:4–5) refers not just to the physical world, but also to the system of values and ideologies that are in opposition to God. Thus, John's exhortation against loving the world is a call to reject values that are contrary to the gospel and to maintain purity in devotion to God.[19] Modern-day African churches have embraced the imported prosperity gospel, a movement, or rather teaching, that sees material blessing as a sign of being favored by God. Prosperity preaching has entrenched, in many African churches, a love of the world that may take many generations to correct. Unfortunately, many heralds of this form of teaching exploit Africans' generosity to achieve their ulterior intentions.

The effect of prosperity preaching is that "it dominates our imagination and permeates our conversation."[20] It grips our culture by using the revered platform of the pulpit to form a fertile ground for "loving the world." It normalizes envy and sets the soul on the path of materialism and pursuit of wealth, contrary to Matthew 6:33, where Jesus encourages followers to seek first the kingdom of God.

The pursuit of prosperity as preached predisposes many to corruption, a vice that has crippled many sectors in Africa. The fact that the church is sometimes mentioned in corrupt deals[21] demonstrates a love for worldly power and influence that is incompatible with the gospel. Furthermore, this complicity undermines the church's prophetic voice and its ability to call out injustice and immorality in society. The encouragement for self-sacrifice given in verse 16 is hardly taken up in many African churches. Instead of the love of God being displayed

---

18. John S. Mbiti, *African Religions and Philosophy* (Heinemann, 1969), 1.

19. Gary W. Derickson, *1, 2, & 3 John*, EEC (Lexham Press, 2014), 328.

20. Michael Maura, "True and False Prosperity," in *Prosperity? Seeking the True Gospel*, ed. Ken Mbugua, Michael Maura, John Piper, Wayne Gruden, and Conrad Mbewe (African Christian Textbooks, 2015), 32.

21. For example, in Kenya, some churches were mentioned in the Ndungu report as the recipients of grabbed land, see http://libraryir.parliament.go.ke/handle/123456789/27956.

by meeting the needs of those less fortunate (vv. 17–18), what we often see is the gospel being used as an occasion for greed. It is not uncommon to witness secular hierarchies and mimicry of state power being replicated in the church; this is contrary to the expectations of verse 17. Hence, the notions of self-serving hierarchical structures in many churches mimic worldly power struggles, as pastors and church leaders enjoy promotions and power-oriented ministries, all to the church's detriment. In Africa, which is home to rampant poverty and inequalities, the church should do more than aggravate the situation. Heeding 1 John's message, it can become a place of refuge for the oppressed and a voice for the marginalized, instead of an arena for replicating worldly powers.

Last-Hour Discourse (1 John 2:18–29)

Here John delves into the essence of being a Christian, the culmination of all our efforts. Although Hansjörg Schmid[22] sees the entire worldview of 1 John as highly apocalyptic, it is this section that contains the highest tone of apocalypse with its declaration of the last hour (1 John 1:18). When John the opponents antichrists (2:18; 4:3), false prophets (4:1), and seducers (2:27), this proves that the Apocalypse is on his mind. However, we should also note that the full elements of apocalyptic teaching, for example, gory images of the end times are not present in the epistle. The primary focus of the exhortation here is that, since "it is the last hour" (v. 18), believers should be careful not to exclude themselves from eternal life by being misled by antichrists. John insists that believers have an "anointing" from the Holy Spirit, enabling them to discern truth from falsehood (1 John 2:20–21). Painter points out that the reputation of doctrinal decorum is vital for John, as he argues that disagreeing with the incarnation or messianic role of Jesus leads to trickery.[23] Likewise, in 1 John 4:1–6, followers of Christ are exhorted to "test the spirits" to distinguish between the "spirit of truth" and the "spirit of error." A call to discernment displays the issues of religious dialogue in a pluralistic society where differing doctrinal contentions exist.[24]

A thought that emerges from this "last hour" discourse concerns Christian behavior toward members of other faiths. Although John's religious space involves engagement with leaders of the same religion that arguably has basic doctrinal disagreements,[25] many African religious spaces are increasingly becoming pluralistic societies with fair-minded religious persuasions. In many African countries, for example, constitutional requirements encourage people of different religions to coexist peacefully. Reading 1 John from pluralistic communities may pose some decisional challenges, especially when it comes to cooperation with people who hold different religious persuasions regarding Christianity and Christ. However,

22. Hansjörg Schmid, "How to Read the First Epistle of John Non-Polemically," *Biblica* 85, no. 1 (2004): 24–41.

23. John Painter, *1, 2, and 3 John*, SP 18 (Liturgical Press, 2002), 184.

24. Raymond E. Brown, *The Epistles of John* (Doubleday, 1982), 63.

25. Many commentators agree that the antichrist mentioned here was either a direct reference to early Gnosticism taught by Cerinthus who believed that Christ-Spirit only came to Jesus at baptism and eventually left him and who denied that he was the one and only Christ, or Docetists who believed that Christ was divine but only seemed to be human.

readers ought to appreciate that 1 John was not written with the challenge of modern societies in mind. In such a situation, where John calls believers to disengage with nonbelievers, the modern Christians' option is to engage in religious coexistence without compromising core theological tenets. As Lovemore Togarasei rightly comments, the call to discern truth from error reverberates with the need to navigate religious pluralism while maintaining fidelity to the Christian faith and tolerance with others.[26]

The Features of God's Love (1 John 3:1–3)

Chapter 3 of 1 John introduces the deep theological thought of the nature of the love of God. The love of God as discussed in this chapter contains an eschatological hope that is pegged on ethical demands that are tied to the former theme of abiding.

First John 3:1 begins with a noticeable emphasis on God's love. This description suggests an intimate connection between Christians and God, shown by the love of God toward his children. The family imagery used by John underlines the intensity of God's love and the favored standing of believers as God's children.[27] Keener observes that "no one who agreed with John that Christians were God's children would have disputed his point here."[28]

In many African communities, the idea of unconditional acceptance and transformative love echoes intensely inside both Christian and general cultural circumstances. The perception of being embraced as children of God relates to traditional African beliefs that accentuate communality. In contexts like South Africa, where the country's complex history of racial and social segregation still dominates public discourse, the idea of being embraced as children of God proposes a potent moral of attachment and reconciliation that exceeds social and ethnic boundaries. The idea of communality mentioned above is further buttressed by the eschatological hope introduced in verse 2, where, upon Christ's return, believers will be transformed to be like Christ.

Verse 3 ties the hope of Christ's return with ethical demands for purity in Christian conduct. The expectation of Christ's return is presented as a motivation for Christians to purify themselves, commending them to conduct themselves uprightly.[29] African societies find it difficult to embrace eschatological concepts because the African Traditional religious past does not offer room for thinking about the distant future in the way in which it is presented biblically.[30] Eschatology as presented in the Bible should therefore be taught adequately in African spaces. Much of what is presented is generally only in preaching and is not enough. Eschatological teaching is a great ingredient for faith formation in many African churches. Grasped adequately, the promise of a future life as presented in this chapter gives the Christian message the perfect goal, one that outmatches the Traditional African hope in ancestral lineages.

26. Lovemore Togarasei, "The Prosperity Gospel in African Pentecostalism," *Exchange* 35, no. 1 (2006): 74–76.

27. Brown, *The Epistles of John*, 158.

28. Keener, *The IVP Bible Background Commentary*, 711.

29. Smalley, *1, 2, 3 John*, 140.

30. For more on this, see John S. Mbiti, *New Testament Eschatology in an African Background: A Study of the Encounter Between New Testament Theology and African Traditional Concepts* (Oxford University Press, 1971).

Sin Versus Righteousness (1 John 3:4–10)

Although 1 John deals with the theme of sin in most of its chapters, there is a unique dimension of sin presented in chapter 3. While John writes within an understanding that primarily views sin vertically in other chapters, this chapter presents a more horizontal view of sin as well. In many African conceptions, sin is also more often than not viewed horizontally. In African religions, there is no conception of righteousness before gods which is not primarily anchored on right relationships with people and creation within the arena of *Ubuntu*. In verse 4, John labels sin as lawlessness or disobedience to God's instructions; this should be read as pegged within a moral or horizontal framework. This view aligns with expectations of preaching in Africa where ethical conduct is stressed before dogmatic emphasis.

In verse 5, John introduces the idea of Christ's sacrifice, which is brought forth as the relief from sin. The point is that those who abide in Christ have their sins taken away, for Christ and sin cannot coexist. In an African hearing, Christ becomes the symbol of a perfect elder. Sacrifices were offered by perfect elders, and as such Christ is now not just the elder who is authorized to sacrifice but he has become the perfect sacrifice.

Verse 6 stresses the importance of abiding in Christ as an antidote to a sinful life. Many commentators grapple with the meaning of this verse, for the idea of sinlessness seems to contradict 1 John 1:9 where the claim to be without sin is only made by liars. The point made by Keener is accurate. He states that, "more likely John is turning the claims of false teachers and their followers (1 John 1:8–10) against them: unlike those who err by claiming to be sinless, true believers do not live in sin."[31] Abiding in Christ is presented as essential for spiritual purity and ethical living. This concept of abiding underscores the transformative power of a close relationship with Christ, which leads to a life characterized by righteousness (1 John 3:7) rather than sin.[32] Those who keep sinning not only do not abide in Christ but they are in fact in association with the devil and not with God (1 John 3:8–10). Therefore, the call to abide in Christ as a believer resonates with a broader context of longing for transformation within societies. For the Christian community, unlike other religious expressions, the saving knowledge of Christ is the only hope for transforming communities. Abiding in Christ, therefore, can set Africa on a great path to deepened Christianity, thus countering the indictment that African Christianity is a mile wide but only an inch deep.[33]

African Spirituality and True Christian Spirituality

As noted previously, 1 John frequently emphasizes assurance of salvation (1 John 2:3–6; 2:9–11; 4:7–21) as a standard of belief. For people moving from one system of belief to another, this statement takes on paramount importance. The African belief system has its system of assurance for its adherents. However, viewed in light of the Christian hope that John presents,

31. Keener, *IVP Bible Background Commentary*, 711.

32. Rudolf Schnackenberg, *The Johannine Epistles: A Commentary* (Crossroad, 1992), 74.

33. This widely used and popularized saying does not seem to have a direct attribution.

it would be self-defeating to remain under the hope that has been defined below Christian definitions. For this reason, John presents Christ's hope as the solid hope, whose foundations are rooted in Christ's sacrificial death and eschatological hope. The assurance that Christian hope offers, therefore, is a great ingredient for nurturing faith in Africa, where the fear of losing one's salvation is rampant and often leads to a "works" orientation and transactional dealings with God. It is important to point out that Christian hope is not only eschatologically oriented but it also helps cure much hopelessness that is created by the difficult situations that humanity faces each day.

God's Love (1 John 4:7–5:12)

God's love is the dominant theme in the Letters of John. Chapter 4 seems to be a concentration of love, where the word is repeated several times. Love in 1 John is demonstrated by God sending his Son to be the atonement for humanity's sin. Believers are called upon to reciprocate God's love as the standard of their life in their practical relations with one another, proving that they are beneficiaries, recipients as well as transmitters of this divine love.

For example, the standard set in both the Johannine letters and African *Ubuntu* is largely nonexistent in modern-day South African life, as economic pressure has often led to violent clashes through such vices as xenophobia (the fear of other people, especially foreign nationals), gender-based violence, corruption, and murder, to mention a few. This poses a barrier to the application of the Johannine "love doctrine" in South African Christian communities. First John is a great resource for mitigating against such vices, especially where love, which is manifested as hating what is evil, is emphasized.

Faith and Overcoming the World (1 John 5:4–5)

One of the concrete things that John does is to present faith in Jesus as the solution to overcoming the world (1 John 5:4). As has already been stated, when used in the negative, the world in Johannine literature mostly represents a corrupt system that stands in opposition to God (see 1 John 2:15). He further assures those who believe in Jesus that they are born of God. The writer uses this to derive a comparative lesson between believers (born of God and who know him) who thus overcome the world and the unbelievers who remain clouded with the world's influences and thus are overcome by it. The believers overcome the world not by worldly power but by spiritual resilience through demonstrating faith in Jesus and obedience to God's commandments (1 John 5:5). This overcoming the world, according to John, does not denote financial gain or social status elevation but rather fidelity to Christ, even in the face of suffering and hardships. The repeated birthing analogy utilized to make the point here is quite informative (1 John 2:29; 3:9; 5:1, 4, 18). In Africa and many parts of the world birthing is the mystery of the female gender. Birthing as attributed to God, who is normally presented in the male gender, can be quite a shocking concept in an African worldview. However, to present the gospel in Africa with this imagery means that the recipients are bound as members of the family of God and to Jesus who is the cause of this reality that supersedes birth by natural means. It is faith in this translocation that assures believers that they have the right disposition to overcome the world.

The Testimony of God, Eternal Life, and Love (1 John 5:6–12)

The assurance of eternal life is, according to John, particularized in the person of Jesus due to his unique identity (1 John 5:6–12), which is unparalleled by the false teachers. In order to help correct some syncretistic tendencies often exhibited in African Christianity, the church has to insist that eternal life is obtained through Jesus alone and not any ancestral mediations. This thought can thus act as a liberative alternative for Christian Africans to rely on Jesus alone for salvation.

First John 4:7–5:12 explains the nature of love, which is a central theme in this letter. Love is presented as the assurance of salvation, central to faith in Jesus, and the medium through which fear is overcome. Once fear is dispelled, the community's unity is achieved. The call to love is a sure buttress to the African philosophy of *Ubuntu*. At a time when many African communities are involved in local and cross-border conflicts, the necessity of Christian love becomes more urgent. As Mojola opines, "Ubuntu has to do with the essence of what it means to be human, what really makes humans human."[34] When Ubuntu is buttressed with Christian love, then it remains the strongest ingredient for nurturing peace among communities.

Assurance of Eternal Life (1 John 5:13)

First John 5:13 states, "I write these things to you who believe in the name of the Son of God, so that you may know that you have eternal life." This verse highlights the epistle's purpose: to assure believers of their salvation and eternal life. Brown notes that this assurance is grounded in the believer's faith in Jesus Christ as the Son of God.[35] The assurance of eternal life is a central theme in Johannine literature, emphasizing the intimate relationship between believers and Christ.[36] In African contexts, where many Christians have cherished memories of spiritual assurance offered by traditional religions, this assurance offers profound comfort. At the same time, many Christian Africans experience social and economic instability, which can lead to anxiety about the afterlife. The promise of eternal life in Christ provides an assuring counternarrative to fear and primal religious assurances, thus reinforcing Christian hope amidst life's challenges.[37]

34. Aloo Osotsi Mojola, "Ubuntu in the Christian Theology and Praxis of Archbishop Desmond Tutu and Its Implications for Global Justice and Human Rights," in *Ubuntu and the Reconstitution of Community*, ed. James Ogude (Indiana University Press, 2009), 23.

35. Brown, *The Epistles of John*, 168.

36. Smalley, *1, 2, 3 John*, 276–277.

37. Mbiti, *African Religions and Philosophy*, 68.

The Efficacy of Prayer (1 John 5:14–17)

First John 5:14–15 discusses the confidence believers have in approaching God in prayer. The promise enshrined in these verses reveals the importance of aligning one's prayers with God's will and provides assurance that God responds to such prayers.[38] The habit of prayer is part of the notoriety of African religiosity. In the South African context, for example, the impact of prayer is often emphasized in both Christian and traditional religious expressions. This teaching of 1 John calls for discernment when engaging in prayer. The alignment of prayer with God's will challenges practices that seek to manipulate divine favor for personal gain, which is quite common in some forms of what has been termed the "prosperity gospel."[39] The passage here guarantees believers that prayers in Jesus's name will not escape God's attention. However, the guarantee here should be balanced with other portions of Scripture that warn against sloppy prayers. James 4:3 instructs that unmeasured praying is praying with wrong motives. When John states "whatever" we ask the Father in the name of Jesus, he does not mean that all "prayer" will be answered. His statement should be read within the context of walking in the light, abiding in Christ, love, and discernment. Prayer filtered through these categories should have passed the test.

In both Kenyan and South African church contexts, the efficacy of prayer and the practice of intercessory prayer hold great importance for Christian formation. This is evident across church denominations where prayer often plays a significant role in liturgical practice. According to 1 John 5:14–15, believers are assured that their prayers are heard and answered when they are aligned with God's will. This assurance provides a theological foundation for the robust prayer practices observed in these communities. The emergence of many places of prayer, termed "prayer mountains," and Christian shrines demonstrate the important place of prayer in African Christianity. These prayer mountains have become ecumenical prayer spaces because they are frequented by many pilgrims regardless of their church affiliations or denominations.[40] Prayer in African Christianity receives a lot of emphasis and is a fundamental aspect of Christian worship and spiritual life. Some churches in South Africa and Kenya also regularly prioritize prayer over preaching, giving it more time than other elements in their regular liturgical practices. Many Pentecostal and charismatic churches in these countries regard prayer not as a supplementary activity but as a core element of spiritual discipline. According to Anderson, practices such as mountain prayers, where congregants pray and seek divine encounters in isolated and symbolic locations, all-night vigils, and monthly fasting sessions highlight the centrality of prayer in these churches.[41]

---

38. I. Howard Marshall, *The Epistles of John* (Eerdmans, 1978), 32–33.

39. Vuyani Vellem, "Spirituality of Black Liberation: Moshoeshoe of Basotho and Beyond," *Journal of Theology for Southern Africa* 158 (2017): 105.

40. For example, in Kenya anyone visiting the "Heaven's gate" prayer center in Nakuru or Katoloni Mountain in Machakos and also the Catholic Shrine at Subukia in Nakuru will find Christians from across many denominations visiting these prayer mountains to seek God.

41. Allan Heaton Anderson, *An Introduction to Pentecostalism: Global Charismatic Christianity* (Cambridge University Press, 2000), 151.

Such practices are viewed as essential for bringing God's power and guidance into the lives of believers.

Although Christ has been introduced as an intercessor and advocate with the Father in 2:1, believers are now in 1 John 5:16–17 encouraged to intercede for one another (1 John 5:16–17). The particular injunction here is praying for erring brothers and sisters, where error here may refer to those attracted to the false prophets' ideas (4:1–6). Keener rightly observes that,

> given the use of "life" for eternal life and "death" for its opposite in this epistle, a "sin unto death" (KJV) would seem to be a sin leading one away from eternal life (cf. Gen 2:17; 3:24). The two sins John would likely have prominently in mind would be hating the brothers and sisters (the secessionists' rejection of the Christian community) and failing to believe in Jesus rightly (their false doctrine about his identity as the divine Lord and Christ in the flesh).[42]

In both Kenya and South Africa, Christians should use these verses to discourage tribalism, negative ethnicity, and xenophobia. These harmful traits, which have led to loss of life in both countries, find their condemnation in these verses and are incompatible with the label "children of God," and the hope of eternal life.

In summary, the high value placed on prayer in African Christianity and broader societal contexts highlights the fact that theology results in practice. The teachings of 1 John 5:14–15 and 5:16–17 are important for the continuity of hopeful Christian practices in the context of African Christianity. They are extremely useful for messages that contribute to Christian growth and for curbing contrary practices that undermine the gains of Christianity in Africa.

Knowledge of God and True Belief (1 John 5:18–20)

First John 5:18–20 provides a summary of the epistle's major theological points, with an emphasis on the believer's knowledge of God and the truth of Jesus Christ. John repeats his claim that those born of God cannot keep on sinning. This does not mean that they are sinless; rather it is an exhortation to stay away from deliberate sin. The element of the evil one as a catalyst to sin is introduced in this section, highlighting the possibility of being led astray. Believers are therefore cautioned against abiding elsewhere because any abode outside Christ predisposes them to the influence of the evil one. In Africa especially, where it is not uncommon to hear of believers seeking alternative solutions when Christian solutions are not forthcoming,[43] believers are encouraged that as long as they abide in Christ, the evil one cannot touch them (1 John 5:18).

42. Keener, *IVP Bible Background Commentary*, 715.

43. For example when believers despair of Christian solutions to existential issues like barrenness or convictions of witchcraft and revert to mediums for interventions.

Warning Against Idolatry (1 John 5:21)

The final verse of 1 John, 5:21, offers a direct warning for the dear children to keep themselves from idols. Although idolatry here may not refer exactly to what Paul describes in Romans 1:18–32 as pagan worship, worship of images of the emperor was rampant and sometimes required of all people. Therefore, believers are warned away from anything that leads them astray from an accurate conception of Jesus, which leads to sin such as idolatry and the improper application of love. Although contemporary Africa is no longer home to many of the idols that were prevalent in African religions, idolatry still reigns in many forms. This warning is pertinent in Christian African contexts, as it addresses the temptation to integrate the Christian faith with traditional spiritual practices that may involve idolatry. According to Chammah Kaunda, the challenge of idolatry is not limited to physical objects; it can also include any practices or beliefs that distract from the worship of the one true God.[44]

The Historical Context of 2 John

Introduction

There is little stylistic difference between 1 and 2 John, and it is attributed to the "elder"—probably John the apostle.[45] The epistle, though brief, addresses significant themes that are central to early Christian doctrine and practice. This letter, probably addressing the same secessionists as 1 John addressed, focuses on an inadequate view of Christ. The themes of truth, love, and the dangers of false teaching are brought together to address this christological deficiency and its effects on the Christian community. The letter warns against compromises, adaptations, and adjustments to cultural values that lead away from the truth. The relevance of this letter cannot be overemphasized, for it extends beyond its immediate historical context as it also provides insights into contemporary issues faced by many Christian Africans

Authorship and Date

As has already been mentioned at the beginning of this chapter, many commentators[46] agree that since there are few stylistic differences between 1 and 2 John, the same author may have written the two epistles. Keener refutes any possibility that 2 John could have been forged, for this could have drained its authority for the audience.[47] Dating of this epistle is pegged to Polycarp's letter to the Philippians which was written after Ignatius's martyrdom between 110

44. See Chammah J. Kaunda, "Neo-Prophetism and Re-Branding of *Missio Dei* in African Christianity," in *Africa Bears Witness: Mission Theology and Praxis in the 21st Century*, ed. Harvey Kwiyani (ATNP, 2021), 122–123.

45. Keener, *IVP Bible Background Commentary*, 716.

46. See deSilva, *An Introduction to the New Testament*, 391; also Keener, *IVP Bible Background Commentary*, 716.

47. Keener, *IVP Bible Background Commentary*, 716.

and 117 CE. This would establish 110 CE as the latest date of composition. DeSilva opines that if the Gospel is dated 85–90 CE, then the Epistles would fall between the two dates.[48]

Genre

Second John contains several characteristics of an official letter—the sort that the high priests could have sent to Jewish leaders outside Palestine.[49] Commenting on the length of 2 and 3 John, Keener rightly observes that this could have been occasioned by the single sheet of papyrus on which they were written and, in contrast to most New Testament Epistles, most other ancient letters were of this length.[50]

Occasion

In the opening introduction, it was noted that 2 John probably addresses the same problem as that addressed by 1 John. This is the problem caused by the secessionists, whose inadequate view of Christ was either as a result of bowing to "synagogue pressure" or born out of a desire to tone down their Christology in order to make allowances for pagan compromises (2 John 7). For this reason, they denied the divinity of Christ, a denial which would have helped them accommodate their cultural beliefs, thus deviating from an orthodox Christology. This in turn led to many moral compromises that were not in tandem with love and truth. John writes to warn the church to avoid such people (2 John 8). The mention of "antichrist" is probably intended to mean that the group to be avoided was associated with Cerinthus, although this is by no means certain.

Outline

Address and greetings to the church (vv. 1–3)
Summons to love (vv. 4–6)
Warning against error (vv. 7–11)
Conclusion (vv. 12–13)

Reading 2 John from African Perspectives

The Theme of Truth (2 John 1–5)

Second John begins by emphasizing the importance of truth as heralded by the elder. Elders were highly esteemed in local Jewish communities by virtue of their age. As in African communities, the truth spoken by an elder was perceived to be the perfect truth. The author as an

48. DeSilva, *An Introduction to the New Testament*, 393.
49. See Keener, *IVP Bible Background Commentary*, 716.
50. Keener, *IVP Bible Background Commentary*, 716.

eyewitness (see 1 John 1:1), appeals to truth, and stresses its foundational role in Christian fellowship and conduct.[51] In the context of 1 John, the truth the elder speaks about is Jesus himself, and this truth is buttressed by three christological points: namely Jesus as the Christ, Jesus as the incarnate Son of God, and Jesus's atoning death as the sacrifice for sin.

The elder, having praised his readers for walking in the truth (2 John 4), now emphasizes that walking in the truth is not merely an option for Christian believers but a commandment. The commandment that John mentions here contains modifications of Old Testament expectations and has allusions to Leviticus 19:18 which is probably restated by Jesus in John 13:34–35. "In the context of 1–2 John, 'loving one another' involves cleaving to the Christian community (rather than leaving it, as the secessionists were doing."[52] However, if here John is restating Jesus's command to love one another, then he leaves out the synoptic element of loving even one's enemies (Matt 5:44). Love that loves the enemy involves reaching out to the enemy in order to bring them to Christ. Such love is constantly needed in Africa, which has innumerable historical records of human rights abuses, negative ethnicity, tribal wars, and other forms of dehumanization that have created pockets of enemies all over Africa.

Warning Against False Teachers (2 John 7–11)

Second John 7–9 provides a stern warning against false teachers who do not acknowledge the coming of Jesus Christ in the flesh. Several suggestions have been offered for the identity of the deceivers mentioned here, with some saying that they were probably forerunners of Cerinthus, who distinguished the divine Christ and the human Jesus, or the Docetists, who claimed that Jesus only seemed to be human.[53] Whoever they might have been, John brands them as "antichrists," a term he used in the first epistle not only to highlight their deficient Christology but also to show their arrogance in the resulting behavior. This means that whenever Christ is not fully preached, then the resulting behavior is characterized by moral lapses and the absence of love and truth. The African church must hold firmly to the teaching of Christ (whom they call *muthamaki*, "king" [Kikuyu], *umalusi*, "shepherd" [Zulu], and *mufudzi*, "teacher" [Shona], among other names), in order to overcome the governance and ecclesiastical deficiencies currently being witnessed in the African church.

In verses 10–13, the instruction to deny the "enemy" hospitality seems to go against African values of hospitality, Hebrew tradition (Prov 25:21), Paul's ethic in Romans 12:20, and also Jesus's ethic in the Sermon on the Mount in Matthew 5:44. It is not clear how John overlooks the Scripture to come up with the instruction. Keener observes that, in the Dead Sea Scrolls, "one who provided hospitality to an apostate from the community was considered a sympathizer to the apostate,"[54] and this could probably be the background for such a view. If Keener's observation is correct, then it points to the fact that the Johannine community could

51. Brown, *The Epistles of John*, 179.

52. See Keener, *IVP Bible Background Commentary*, 717.

53. See Keener, *IVP Bible Background Commentary*, 716.

54. Keener, *IVP Bible Background Commentary*, 717.

have been a separatist community, threatened by secession. Those who reject the existence of a Johannine school may not find this point important.

Final Greeting and Farewell

Keener's comment on 2 John 12 notes that "written letters were considered an inferior substitute for personal presence or for a speech, and writers concluded their letters with the promises to discuss matters further face-to-face."[55] In the days of virtual reality and online churches, many churches in South Africa and Kenya grapple with growing numbers of Christians who prefer the online church to the physical church. Many arguments for or against this emerging practice have been made. Nevertheless, there is no distinct divide as to which reality is superior to the other as it was in ancient times. The African value of communality suffers in this new phenomenon and it remains to be seen what the future holds for the church as well as for faith formation in Africa. Second John 13 concludes by mentioning the elect lady mentioned in verse 1. The identity of the elect or chosen lady is not obviously discernible, but it could have been an elderly member of the community,[56] or more probably the personification of a local congregation.[57] The feminine image was occasionally applied to Israel and the church.

The Historical Context of 3 John

Authorship and Date

The same statements can be made about the authorship of this letter as were made for 2 John. For authorship and date, see our introduction on 2 John.

Genre

This is a letter of recommendation for Demetrius who is a traveling missionary (vv. 7–8).[58] Many scholars[59] admit that among the three Epistles of John, 3 John displays many of the features of the ordinary letters surviving from the ancient world. Without delving into much detail, we can note that the letter contains epistolary conventional features, such as a health wish, a thanksgiving, and a sharing of greetings with a third party, before a closing farewell.

55. See Keener, *IVP Bible Background Commentary*, 717.

56. Keener, *IVP Bible Background Commentary*, 717.

57. Stott, *The Letters of John*, 203. If the explanation of personification does not pass the test, then the other possible explanation is like in many patriarchal societies, the elect lady is silenced and her identity submerged through anonymity.

58. Keener, *IVP Bible Background Commentary*, 718.

59. See for example, Lieu, *I, II, & III John*, 265.

Message and Occasion

Despite its brevity as compared to other New Testament books, 3 John's significance lies in its insightful and diplomatic approach to navigating fragile communal relations. This stands in stark contrast to 1 John, which presents a decisive exclusivist approach. The letter is addressed to Gaius, who is otherwise unknown outside the letter. What is known is that he is beloved, one willing to submit to the elder's authority, and a supporter of his mission. The letter also counters the influence of Diotrephes (v. 9). Since congregations met in homes (house churches) for the first three centuries, it is probable that Diotrephes, who is the leader of a house church, was influencing his congregation to reject the elder's apostolic authority, including those sent by the elder.[60]

Outline

Address and greetings to Gaius (vv. 1–2)
Hospitality for mission (vv. 3–8)
Lessons from Diotrephes (vv. 9–11)
Commendation of Demetrius (v. 12)
Conclusion (vv.13–15)

Reading 3 John from African Perspectives

Hospitality for Mission (3 John 1–8)

Hospitality is a central theme in 3 John, underscoring its importance in the early Johannine community. Hospitality that promotes truth is highly encouraged (v. 8). The elder praises Gaius for his generous hospitality because this promotes "walking in the truth" (v. 4). The phrase "walking in the truth" here is used in the same way as it has been used in 1 John 1:6 and 2 John 1:4, with the connotation of abiding in Christ. Walking in the truth is now attached not only to moral conduct but to social responsibility. In verse 5, the practice of hospitality is seen by the author as an extension of the love shown by Christ toward humanity. It can also be seen as an extension of the entire Bible's teaching on generosity. In Africa, hospitality is enshrined in *Ubuntu* and is deeply rooted in cultural practices and community values. Mbiti's view is that many African cultures place a high value on welcoming guests and providing for their needs, as this reflects a broader value of communal responsibility and support.[61] African hospitality aligns closely with Christian teaching on hospitality. In Kenya, for example, children are taught from a very early age to be hospitable. A popular saying among the Meru people of Kenya is that a child born alone does not learn how to share. It can therefore be inferred that

60. See Keener, *IVP Bible Background Commentary*, 718, for this historical insight.
61. Mbiti, *African Religions and Philosophy*, 1.

one of the reasons traditional Meru families, and African communities in general, encourage bearing many children is for the purposes of spreading the values of hospitality and generosity. The epistle's emphasis on hospitality serves as a reminder of the importance of maintaining these practices within Christian communities, and this reinforces the integration of cultural and spiritual values.[62]

The epistle can also be seen as encouraging hospitality for mission purposes. In the Greco-Roman world, itinerant philosophers and professional speakers, including preachers, often made their living from the crowds to whom they spoke, although others received a fee or were supported by wealthy patrons.[63] Whereas this is not exactly the case in contemporary Africa, many missionaries, pastors, and missions are supported by generous Christians. The problem arises when African generosity is exploited for ill motives and sometimes in prosperity preaching. Some African preachers have been accused of exploiting vulnerable congregations and Christians to enrich themselves. While encouraging generosity for furtherance of the gospel, discerning Christians should oppose such persuasions and enlighten their congregations on the dangers of prosperity preaching.

To be fair to Diotrephes, it is not clear whether he was shielding his house church from exploitation or whether he was outrightly rejecting John's authority, which stood behind the missionaries he had backed. It is also not clear what the disagreement was all about; whether doctrinal or ecclesiastical hierarchy. However, we note from Keener that, in the ancient world, to reject a person's representative was to disrespect the person who had written on their behalf.[64] This is all we may know about Diotrephes's fault and it forms the basis for our judgment, particularly when he is compared to Gaius. While not exonerating Diotrephes from bad conduct, it is important to note that it is common in colonial literature to present characters who differ in opinion with normativity in a bad light. The case of Diotrephes and Gaius as presented in 3 John therefore cannot form the basis for treatment of people with different voices and opinions. It is incumbent upon Christian Africans and church leaders to judge each case on its own merit.

Distinction Between True and False Leaders (3 John 9–11)

The above comment notwithstanding, 3 John provides a crucial examination criteria of the character of leaders, not only within the early Christian community but also in contemporary times. The epistle highlights the importance of discerning between true and false leaders. In 3 John 9–11, the letter contrasts the commendable behavior of Gaius with the negative behavior of Diotrephes, who rejects John's authority and is presented as a self-promoter; a distinction that is important for learning which qualities define authentic Christian leadership.

Whereas we may never have the benefit of Diotrephes's defense, in 3 John 9 he is expressly critiqued as a false leader who seeks personal gain and prestige rather than service

62. See Adrian Hastings, *African Christianity: An Essay in Interpretation* (Hurst and Company, 1994), 56.

63. Keener, *IVP Bible Background Commentary*, 719.

64. Keener, *IVP Bible Background Commentary*, 719.

to the community. The author presents Diotrephes's refusal to acknowledge the apostle's authority and his self-promotion in stark contrast to the humility and hospitality displayed by Gaius.[65] Therefore, he becomes an example of leaders that churches should avoid. Keen readers may question the author's presentation of Diotrephes as one-sided propaganda. However, Christians are called to believe that the inclusion of this epistle in the New Testament canon may be an endorsement of the actual historical situation. Therefore, invoking the letter's guidance in the treatment of dissenting leaders may be necessary when the church is presented with similar cases. For all intents and purposes, this section promotes the view that church leadership is not a space for self-seeking individuals who have no mind for Christ. True leaders are characterized by their humility, service to others, adherence to the gospel, and their submission to church hierarchy. True church leaders should not seek personal glory but instead work for the well-being of the community and the advancement of the gospel. This distinction serves as a valuable guide for evaluating leadership within the church and beyond.

Ethical Leadership and Related Challenges in Africa

In many African church contexts, the issue of distinguishing between true leaders who walk in the light and false leaders is particularly pertinent given the diverse and often complex religious landscape. In many African churches, there is a proliferation of churches and church leaders, all of whom claim to be called and true. In such a space, it becomes increasingly difficult to ascertain the claims of each, even from among denominations that seem to command some respect. The instruction by the author to "imitate good" (v. 11) remains relevant even in contemporary African churches.

Ethical leadership therefore, remains a central concern in the African context. Issues of corruption, abuse of power, and self-interest frequently emerge, unfortunately even in church leadership. The challenge of discerning true leaders, who genuinely serve their communities, from those who seek personal gain, is an issue that the church shares in common with the broader African society. The warning against leaders who seek self-promotion rather than to serve the community is particularly relevant in a context where the integrity of the leaders is often in question.[66]

Secular Leadership and Church Leadership in Africa

In addition to evaluating religious leaders, the principles outlined in 3 John can also apply to secular leaders who show great interest in the church. Leaders in the secular scene, for example in politics, and who are pro-church hold significant cultural and social

65. Smalley, *1, 2, 3 John*, 339–340.

66. Lydia Mwaniki, "Practicing Servant Leadership in African Culture," in *The Quest for Biblical Servant Leadership: Insights from the Global Church*, ed. KeumJu Jewel Hyun, Grace Y. May, Philomena Mwaura, and Julius Kithinji (Wipf & Stock, 2023), 93.

influence and are therefore important stakeholders for upholding values of service and integrity. The intersection of political and religious leadership in the African church is important because one cannot be a leader in the church and yet despised in the community. In many African contexts we are experiencing church leadership that is despised and misused by political leaders because of spiritual blunders. Church leadership in Africa should be above board so that it can emphasize the importance of ethical conduct across all forms of leadership.[67] Church leadership, particularly in charismatic and Pentecostal contexts, faces its own set of challenges. There is a danger of overemphasis on personal charisma and miraculous signs, and this can overshadow the fundamental qualities of servant leadership. The lessons from 3 John about avoiding leaders who seek personal glory can guide congregations in developing and preferring commendable leaders—like Demetrius (v. 12)—who are committed to serving others and advancing the mission of the church.

Support for Missionaries (3 John 7–8)

The author commends Gaius for his support of missionaries. Understanding the importance of mission support is a key aspect of Christian discipleship. Spread of the gospel cannot be achieved without mission support. However, it can be counterproductive in Africa if mission support is not encouraged from local communities. In the initial stages of Christianity in Africa, support for churches was mainly sourced from the West. In West Africa, Henry Venn envisaged a church that was self-supporting, self-governing, and self-extending.[68] In Kenya, it was the Presbyterian Church of East Africa that led the clarion call for a moratorium on external aid for mission support.[69] Although there remains a great proportion of the African church that develops as a result of external aid, more than ever before the African church needs to develop its own Gaiuses. The epistle's encouragement to Africans is that they can form support for their missionary activities by providing resources and assistance to those involved in ministry.

Final Greetings (3 John 13–15)

Like most ancient letters, 3 John closes with a final blessing of peace and greeting to "friends." The emphasis on a later face-to-face meeting (v. 14) endorses the view that letters cannot complete the full picture of human interactions. This is probably quite instructive in the African church landscape where virtual and online church services are becoming a common phenomenon.

---

67. Vuyani S. Vellem, "Spirituality of Liberation: A Conversation with African Religiosity," *HTS Teologiese Studies/Theological Studies* 70, no 1 (2014): 6.

68. John Baur, *2000 Years of Christianity in Africa: An African History 62–1992* (Paulines Publications, 1994), 125.

69. Baur, *2000 Years of Christianity in Africa*, 312–313.

Conclusion

The Letters of John were penned by the apostle John to help the churches ground themselves on sound doctrine and live out their faith in their own contexts. Although obvious overlaps have been noted in the letters, including overlaps with the Gospel of John, each letter has been treated on its own merit. The letters have been discussed in this chapter from Kenyan and South African perspectives. Theological motifs like hospitality, true versus false leaders, support for mission, false teachers and their deficient Christology, the significance of prayer, the nature of sin and salvation, worldliness, and God's love have been explored in this chapter. The motifs have been discussed with an African lens in order to bring out the implications for the African church. These epistles promote love, truth, and light, the very essence of Christ, whom they present as our savior. Hence the African church needs to heed the message promulgated in the letters to counter xenophobia, worldly behavior such as self-promotion, greed, and idolatry, false teachings that promote deficient Christology, and unethical leadership.

Further Reading

Brown, Raymond E. *The Epistles of John*. Doubleday, 1982.

Burge, Gary M. *The Letters of John*. Zondervan, 1996.

Derickson, Gary W. *1, 2, & 3 John*. Evangelical Exegetical Commentary. Lexham Press, 2014.

Gade, Christian B. N. "The Historical Development of the Written Discourses on Ubuntu." *South African Journal of Philosophy* 30, no. 3 (2011): 303–329.

Germann, Tim. *The Impact of Christianity on African Traditional Religion: The South African Experience*. University of South Africa Press, 2011.

Hastings, Adrian. *African Christianity: An Essay in Interpretation*. Hurst & Company, 1994.

Jobes, Karen H. *1, 2, and 3 John*. ZECNT. Zondervan, 2014.

Kruse, Colin G. *The Letters of John*. PNTC. InterVarsity Press, 2000.

Kwiyani, Harvey, ed. *Africa Bears Witness: Mission Theology and Praxis in the 21st Century*. ATNP, 2021.

Landau, Loren B. "Xenophobia in South Africa and Problems Related to It." *African Human Mobility Review* 5, no. 2 (2019): 51–73.

Lieu, Judith M. *I, II, & III John: A Commentary*. NTL. Westminster John Knox Press, 2008.

Marshall, I. Howard. *The Epistles of John*. Eerdmans, 1978.

Mbiti, John S. *African Religions and Philosophy*. Heinemann, 1990.

Ngewa, Samuel. "1 John." In *Africa Bible Commentary: A One-Volume Commentary Written by 70 African Scholars*, edited by Tokunboh Adeyemo. WordAlive Publishers; Zondervan, 2006.

Ngewa, Samuel. "2 John." In *Africa Bible Commentary: A One-Volume Commentary Written by 70 African Scholars*, edited by Tokunboh Adeyemo. WordAlive Publishers; Zondervan, 2006.

Ngewa, Samuel. "3 John." In *Africa Bible Commentary: A One-Volume Commentary Written by 70 African Scholars*, edited by Tokunboh Adeyemo. WordAlive Publishers; Zondervan, 2006.

Nyamiti, Charles. *Studies in African Christian Theology*. CUEA Press, 1997.

Painter, John. *1, 2, and 3 John*. SP 18. Liturgical Press, 2002.

Shorter, Aylward. *African Christian Theology: Adaptation or Incarnation?* Geoffrey Chapman, 1977.

Smalley, Stephen S. *1, 2, 3 John*. Rev. ed. WBC 51. Thomas Nelson, 2007.

Stott, John. *The Letters of John*. InterVarsity, 1998.

CHAPTER TWENTY-THREE

The Letter of Jude

Geraldine Chimbuoyim Uzodimma
Veritas University
Abuja, Nigeria

Introduction

The Epistle of Jude is both a polemical tractate and a pastoral letter addressed to a Christian community that was infiltrated by ungodly intruders who invaded the community with antinomian (lawless) and immoral behaviors. The author writes to warn his audience of this development, encouraging them to "contend for the faith that was once for all entrusted to the saints" (v. 3). In spite of its rich theological message, the Epistle of Jude remains one of the least read biblical texts. Its theological, spiritual, and political relevance remain underexplored in contemporary biblical scholarship. Although a marginalized text, Jude remains a very important text for the African church as she navigates through the internal challenges of combating distorted gospels and syncretistic expressions of the Christian faith, as well as growing antagonism toward the church. Its theological themes continue to offer valuable insights that resonate with and enrich the spiritual lives of Africans. This introduction presents an African contextual reading of the Epistle of Jude.

Contextual biblical hermeneutics is a way of reading the Bible that pays particular attention to the context in which the sacred text emerged and the context of the flesh-and-blood reader of the sacred text. This approach is important because, as human beings, we live in a particular social location, and the realities of our social location affect and condition our reading and interpretation of biblical texts. In a contextual hermeneutical approach, the Bible is read against specific concrete human situations, such as poverty, inequality, social injustice, and so on, with the aim of discovering what the sacred text has to say to the reader in their contexts.[1] African contextual hermeneutics (also known as African biblical studies) is a way of reading the Bible from the African perspective.[2] This approach takes into serious consideration the cultural, socioeconomic, religious, and

1. Gerald O. West, "Contextual Bible Study in South Africa: A Resource for Reclaiming and Regaining Land, Dignity and Identity," in *The Bible in Africa: Translations, Trajectories and Trends*, ed. Gerald O. West and Musa W. Dube (Leiden, 2000), 595–596.

2. David Tuesday Adamo, *Explorations in African Biblical Studies* (Wipf & Stock, 2001), 6.

historical contexts of Africans.[3] Using this approach, African biblical scholars engage the Scriptures in ways that resonate with the lived experiences of Africans. More importantly, they consider how African cultural elements and worldviews can be utilized to shed light on biblical passages, thereby fostering a deeper connection between the biblical texts and African readers. African contextual hermeneutics also engages with postcolonial discourse by critically examining the impact of colonialism on biblical interpretation. The goal is to reclaim the muted voices of Africans and to resist colonial narratives that have historically dominated biblical scholarship.[4] It is the above framework that shapes and guides my reading of the Epistle of Jude.

Introductory Matters

Historical Context of the Text

Biblical texts do not emerge in a vacuum, rather they arise out of specific historical contexts. They reflect the circumstances, beliefs, and experiences of the authors and communities in which they emerged. A proper understanding of the historical circumstance surrounding the emergence of a biblical text, such as issues of authorship, audience, circumstance, purpose, and reception history, is crucial for interpreting and applying the text in a meaningful way. By examining the historical background of a text, readers can gain insights into the intentions and concerns of the biblical author, and the sociocultural, political, and theological frameworks within which the text was written, as well as the right of appropriation of the text into a different context.

Authorship

The author gives very simple information about himself: "Jude, a servant of Jesus Christ and a brother of James" (v. 1). There is consensus among scholars that this Jude is not one of the twelve apostles (Luke 6:16; Acts 1:13), but is rather Jude the "brother" of Jesus and James (Matt 13:55; Mark 6:3). Besides disclosing his name, the author also informs us of his status as a "slave" (*doulos*) of Jesus Christ. "A slave of Jesus Christ" is one of the favorite titles of the disciples of Jesus, such as Paul (Rom 1:1; Phil 1:1), Peter (2 Pet 1:1), and James (Jas 1:1). In Jude, the fundamental idea about slavery is that of belonging exclusively to Jesus Christ. In the New Testament period, particularly during the Greco-Roman era, a slave was someone who was completely owned by another person—the master. Although slavery during this era involved various forms of servitude, Greco-Roman slavery allowed for certain rights and social mobility.

While Jude uses "slave" to express his loyalty and devotion to the Lord Jesus, today the word may sound repulsive to many African readers as it brings back the memories of the horrific transatlantic slave trade that saw the selling and dehumanization of millions of

3. Justin S. Ukpong, "Rereading the Bible with African Eyes: Inculturation and Hermeneutics," *Journal of Theology for Southern Africa* 19 (1995): 3–14.

4. Fernando Segovia, "Mapping the Postcolonial Optic in Biblical Criticism: Meaning and Scope," in *Postcolonial Biblical Criticism: Interdisciplinary Intersections*, ed. Stephen Moore and Fernando Segovia (T&T Clark, 2005), 68–69.

Africans across Europe and America. Unlike the Greco-Roman slavery system, the transatlantic slave trade was marked by its racialized nature. It viewed enslaved individuals as property without rights or prospects for emancipation.

The author also identifies himself as a brother of James. Although the term *adelphoi* ("brothers") can refer to males who share one or both parents in common, it can also refer to those who are related by blood but do not share parents. This second sense would be familiar to many African readers, whose idea of family stretches beyond the immediate nuclear setting. For instance, among the Igbos, the word *nwanne* ("brother/sister") refers to a brother or sister by the same parents, as well as extended relatives from either the maternal or paternal side of the family.

When it comes to the authorship of Jude, we are confronted with a critical question: Did Jude the brother of James and Jesus actually write the text? Some have questioned Jude's explicit claim of authorship on the grounds of pseudonymity (fictitious identity). One of the reasons for rejecting Jude's authorship has to do with the excellent Greek style of the letter. The proponents of this theory claim that a relative of Jesus (a Palestinian farmer or craftsman) could not have composed such a sophisticated Greek literary work.[5] In addition, some scholars argue that the way Jude uses "faith" (vv. 3, 20) is indicative of a post-apostolic era when the word "faith" has come to embody specific sets of formal and orthodox doctrines that need to be safeguarded, rather than a dynamic understanding of faith as seen in the Pauline letters. Hence, Jude was tagged as an "early Catholic" text.[6] Likewise, there are those who contend that the call "to remember the predictions of the apostles of our Lord Jesus Christ" (v. 17) is an indication that Jude did not consider himself among the apostles and that the apostolic era had passed by the time the letter was written.[7]

While these objections to Jude's authorship may appear stimulating, they are, however, not compelling enough. First, on the issue of Jude's polished Greek, it would be presumptuous of us to think that Palestinian Jews would not be competent in Greek. Recent studies have shown that during the New Testament period, the Greek language was common in Palestine and many Palestinian Jews possessed a good command of Greek.[8] Moreover, Richard Bauckham has raised the issue of Jude being an itinerant missionary alongside other disciples (cf. Cor 9:5).[9] Therefore, if Jude had traveled as a missionary, there is a possibility that he had acquired greater facility in Greek to enhance his missionary activities. Besides, he may also have deployed the assistance of a secretary, like many other New Testament writers.[10] Second, the tagging of Jude as "early Catholic" and "post-apostolic" based on verses 3 and 17 is misleading.

5. Patrick J. Hartin, *James, First Peter, Jude, Second Peter*, CollBibComm (Liturgical Press, 2005), 1473; Daniel J. Harrington and Donald P. Senior, *1 Peter, Jude and 2 Peter*, SPS 15 (Liturgical Press, 2008), 182.

6. J. N. D. Kelly, *A Commentary on the Epistles of Peter and of Jude* (Black, 1969), 248; Richard Bauckham, *Jude and the Relatives of Jesus in the Early Church* (T&T Clark, 2004), 158–162.

7. Charles Bigg, *A Critical and Exegetical Commentary on the Epistles of St. Peter and St. Jude*, ICC (Charles Scribner's Sons, 1903), 320.

8. David A. deSilva, *The Jewish Teachers of Jesus, James, and Jude: What Earliest Christianity Learned from the Apocrypha and Pseudepigrapha* (Oxford University Press, 2012), 47.

9. Richard Bauckham, *Jude, 2 Peter*, WBC 50 (Word, 1983), 14.

10. Gene L. Green, *Jude and 2 Peter* (Baker Academic, 2008), 8.

Bauckham has shown that the "early Catholic" classification is inconsistent with internal evidence from the letter itself, such as the letter's strong eschatological overtones (vv. 14–15) and the apparent absence of an institutionalized ecclesial structure marked by the presence of authority figures.[11] As we shall see, some early church fathers affirmed Jude's authorship of the letter through explicit statements, as well as by quoting directly or alluding to the letter. In light of the above evidence, I align myself with those who accept the traditional attribution of this epistle to Jude, the brother of James and Jesus.

Audience, Date, and Provenance

Jude uses three phrases to describe his readers: those "who are called," "who are loved by God the Father," and "kept for Christ Jesus" (v. 2). The way Jude identifies his readers is very instructive for African readers. The identity of the audience is theologically construed.[12] What matters for Jude is their relationship with God/Jesus, not their racial/ethnic character. However, among Christian Africans where the water of baptism ought to be thicker than the blood of kinship, it turns out that "the blood of family and tribe was thicker than the water of baptism."[13] Andrew Mbuvi recounts a tragic story of how Christians from a particular ethnic group in Kenya killed fellow Christians (including women and children) from another ethnic group in a church due to an ethnic conflict that had political overtones.[14] The story clearly illustrates how Christian Africans often prioritize family and tribal bonds over their Christian identity. By theologically constructing the identity of both himself and his audience, Jude invites us to prioritize our identity as the people of God and the bond we share through our common faith in Christ.

Many scholars affirm that Jude wrote to a Jewish Christian audience somewhere in Palestine, or to a community with a sizable Jewish population in the diaspora.[15] According to Bauckham, the epistle exhibits "all the marks of a fairly early work of Palestinian Jewish Christian provenance—in its use of the Hebrew Bible . . . its strongly apocalyptic character, its skillful pesher-type exegesis, its imminent eschatological expectation . . . its concern with a controversy about antinomian teaching rather than about doctrine."[16] While the text might have been intended for a Jewish audience, it is possible that there were gentile Christians in the congregation too, reflecting the diversity and inclusive nature of early Christian communities. We do not have any historical clue regarding the dating of Jude. But since the question of dating is directly tied to the question of authorship, scholars who attribute the letter to Jude date the epistle sometime before 70 CE.[17] Those in favor of a pseudonymous text presume a

11. Bauckham, *Jude and the Relatives of Jesus*, 159–162.

12. Fred B. Craddock, *First and Second Peter and Jude*, WBC (Knox, 1995), 134; Andrew M. Mbuvi, *Jude and 2 Peter*, NCCS (Cascade Books, 2015), 29.

13. Jordan Nyenyembe, *Fraternity in Christ: Building the Church as Family* (Paulines Africa, 2005), 90.

14. Mbuvi, *Jude and 2 Peter*, 29.

15. Bauckham, *Jude and the Relatives of Jesus*, 177–178; Green, *Jude and 2 Peter*, 12–13.

16. Bauckham, *Jude and the Relatives of Jesus*, 177.

17. William F. Brosend II, *James and Jude* (Cambridge University Press, 2004), 5–7.

later dating. Having accepted that the author is Jude, "the brother of the Lord," I have implicitly accepted an early dating of the letter.

The Canonicity of Jude

The relationship between the Epistle of Jude and 2 Peter provides interesting insights into the early acceptance and authority of the letter of Jude within the early Christian communities. The fact that 2 Peter used Jude is an indication that the letter was already circulating and considered authoritative and useful in the early church. Similarities in language, themes, and motifs can be observed between 2 Peter 2:1–3:4 and Jude 4–18, suggesting a deliberate engagement with Jude's content and a recontextualization of that material for a new audience.[18] Despite this early reception of Jude, the epistle struggled to make it into the Christian canon. Patristic writers were divided on the canonical authority of Jude. Jude is cited as authoritative by Clement of Alexandria,[19] Origen,[20] and Tertullian.[21] It was included in the Muratorian Canon (200 CE) and attested in the early manuscripts.[22] However, in later times, the canonical status of Jude came to be disputed by certain individuals and groups. Eusebius included Jude in the lists of "disputed" writings.[23] Both Jerome and Bede considered Jude's use of noncanonical sources as a reason for its rejection.[24] Despite these challenges, the Epistle of Jude finally made it into the New Testament canon. Its inclusion within the authoritative Christian canon reflects the recognition of the incalculable theological value of the text for the Christian faith.

Purpose and the Identity of the Opponents/Intruders

Jude clearly defines the purpose of the letter (vv. 3–4). In light of the activities of intruders who had infiltrated the community, promoting ideologies and behavior that deviated from the apostolic traditions that were handed down to the community (vv. 4, 17–19), Jude writes to encourage his audience "to contend for the faith that was once for all entrusted to the saints" (v. 3). The text does not disclose the identity of the intruders. It simply refers to them as *houtoi* ("those people," vv. 8, 10, 12, 16, 19) "who have stolen in among you" (v. 4). Jude devotes much of his letter to describing their actions rather than their identity. He accuses them, among other things, of being "ungodly," "perverting the grace of our God into licentiousness, and denying our only Master and Lord, Jesus Christ" (v. 4). He described them as "sexual perverts" (vv. 4, 7, 8, 10), "those who reject authority" (v. 8), and so on.

---

18. John Painter and David A. deSilva, *James and Jude*, Paideia (Baker Academic, 2012), 188.

19. Clement of Alexandria, *Paed.* 3.8.44; *Strom.* 3.2.11

20. Origen, *Comm. matt.* 10.17, though Origen would later indicate that the Epistle of Jude was not accepted by everyone (cf. Origen, *Comm. Jo.* 19.6).

21. Tertullian, *Cult. fem.* 1.3

22. Jörg Frey, *The Letter of Jude and the Second Letter of Peter: A Theological Commentary*, trans. Kathleen Ess (Baylor University Press, 2018), 6–10.

23. Eusebius, *Hist. eccl.* 3.25.3.

24. Frey, *The Letter of Jude and the Second Letter of Peter*, 9.

The way Jude characterizes his opponents has given room for speculations regarding the identity of these individuals. Early proposals include Gnosticism, an early Christian heretical teaching that placed significant emphasis on esoteric/spiritual "knowledge" (Greek: *gnōsis*), while diminishing the value of the material and physical world.[25] Today, many scholars accept the antinomian proposal. The intruders are those who reject all moral authorities, including that of Christ himself (vv. 4–8), a phenomenon that was common in the early church (cf. Acts 20:30; Rom 6:1; 1 Cor 5:1–11; Gal 5:13; 2 Pet 2:14).[26] There is no hint in the letter as to the reason why they are anti-law, but scholars speculate that this may be due to their wrong perception of the grace of God (v. 4) as freedom from all external moral constraint.[27]

Language and Style of the Letter

The Epistle of Jude is written in the format of a Greco-Roman letter. It begins with the typical epistolary prescript (sender to recipients, and greetings) (vv. 1–2), followed by the body of the letter (vv. 3–23). However, it lacks the conventional farewell greeting found in Greco-Roman letters, and ends with a doxology (vv. 24–25). In terms of genre, Bauckham characterizes Jude as an "epistolary sermon" that combines elements of both a letter and a sermon.[28] The letter format serves as a vehicle for the author to deliver a powerful and exhortative message akin to a sermon to his audience. Duane Watson notes that Jude is "predominantly deliberative rhetoric" (a persuasive speech or writing intended to encourage or discourage an audience from taking a specific course of action), with some elements of epideictic (a discourse that aims at praising or condemning a person, event, or idea).[29] The letter's emphasis on contending for the faith, resisting falsehood, and staying grounded in the true faith aligns more closely with deliberative rhetoric.

The letter is written in "'good' Greek, with some Semitic influence."[30] It is known for its eloquent and forceful style, characterized by vivid imagery and strong language, with a sense of seriousness and urgency. The letter contains a high number of *hapax legomena* (i.e., a word or expression that appears only once). Daniel Harrington lists fourteen words which are not found elsewhere in the New Testament, and three found only in 2 Peter, an indication that 2 Peter took them from Jude.[31] The author is fond of triplets, such as mercy, peace, and love (v. 2), idioms, analogies, metaphors, and epithets, and uses them to convey its message effectively.[32] Jude uses Old Testament references and allusions to make his points, demonstrating a deep knowledge of Jewish Scripture.

---

25. See E. M. Sidebottom, *James, Jude and 2 Peter*, CBC (Nelson, 1967), 75.

26. Bauckham, *Relatives of Jesus*, 162–165.

27. Bauckham, *Jude, 2 Peter*, 11.

28. Bauckham, *Jude, 2 Peter*, 3.

29. Duane F. Watson, "The Letter of Jude," in *The New Interpreter's Bible Volume 12: Hebrews, James, 1 & 2 Peter, 1, 2 & 3 John, Jude, Revelation*, NIB 12 (Abingdon, 1998), 477.

30. Harrington and Senior, *1 Peter, Jude and 2 Peter*, 175.

31. Harrington and Senior, *1 Peter, Jude and 2 Peter*, 176.

32. Harrington and Senior, *1 Peter, Jude and 2 Peter*, 176.

Relationship Between Jude and 2 Peter

One of the major conundrums in reading Jude is how to solve the close textual relationship between Jude and 2 Peter. As we have noted earlier, significant similarity exists between Jude 4–18 and 2 Pet 2:1–3:4. The parallels have been explained in detail by Thomas Schreiner.[33] There are similarities in language, theological themes, and content between the two texts, leading to questions about their possible literary relationship. As Schreiner notes, "three plausible explanations have been offered: (1) Second Peter is dependent on Jude; (2) Jude is dependent on 2 Peter; and (3) they are both dependent on either a written or oral source, or perhaps a combination thereof."[34] One prevailing theory, which seems to have gained a wider acceptance in modern times, is that 2 Peter is dependent on Jude.[35] The use of Jude in 2 Peter highlights the interconnected nature of early Christian writings and the dynamic process of incorporating and adapting existing sources to address new challenges and concerns.

Jude's Use of Apocalyptic Traditions

The Epistle of Jude does not meet the criteria for an apocalypse in terms of genre, but it adopts an apocalyptic worldview and uses apocalyptic themes and imageries.[36] The letter appeals to the authority of two Second Temple Jewish apocalyptic texts: 1 Enoch and The Assumption of Moses, also known as The Testament of Moses (vv. 6, 9, 14). Jude uses 1 Enoch in both explicit citation and in various allusions. The clearest instance is his direct quotation of 1 Enoch 1:9 in verses 14–15.[37] Luke Timothy Johnson notes that Jude's direct citation of 1 Enoch 1:9 is an indication that the author considered "Enoch as an inspired prophet and his work as Scripture."[38] But there are other allusions to 1 Enoch in Jude: In verse 6, the author makes reference to the story of the fallen angels, a narrative event detailed in 1 Enoch 1–19. Also in verse 9, Jude alludes to an obscure story about a dispute between Michael the archangel and Satan over the body of Moses, a narrative that Clement of Alexandria attributes to The Assumption of Moses, a non-extant Jewish apocalyptic book.[39]

Jude did not just appeal to apocalyptic sources; he also incorporated its worldview in his text. For instance, the text endorses apocalyptic epistemology (knowledge through divine revelation) through its appeal to the prophesies of Enoch (vv. 14–15) and that of Jesus's apostles (v. 17–18). According to Jude, what is happening now in the community (the infiltration

33. Thomas R. Schreiner, *1, 2 Peter, Jude*, NAC 37 (Broadman & Holman, 2003), 416–417.

34. Schreiner, *1, 2 Peter, Jude*, 417.

35. Bauckham, *Jude, 2 Peter*, 8.

36. Ruth Anne Reese, *2 Peter & Jude*, THNTC (Eerdmans, 2007), 25.

37. Richard B. Vinson, Richard F. Willson, and Watson E. Mills, *1 & 2 Peter, Jude*, S&HBC (Smyth & Helwys, 2010), 245.

38. Luke Timothy Johnson, *The Writings of the New Testament: An Interpretation* (Fortress Press, 1999), 499.

39. Steve Moyise, *The Later New Testament Writings and Scripture: The Old Testament in Acts, Hebrews, the Catholic Epistles and Revelation* (Baker Academic, 2012), 65.

by the ungodly) was revealed to both Enoch and the apostle of Jesus Christ. They foresaw it (probably through dreams, visions, or by means of an angelic mediation) and spoke about it as a future event. The rhetorical function of this appeal to past predictions is, first, to underscore the sovereignty of God. Jude conveys an apocalyptic outlook in which historical events (even the current situation of the community) are viewed as processes already determined by God.[40] The second reason Jewish apocalyptists appeal to past revelations, according to Adela Yarbro Collins, is so that they can "influence both the understanding and the behavior of the audience by means of divine authority."[41] The shaping of the audience's mindset and ethical behavior by means of divine authority inform both the polemics (strong argument) (vv. 5–16) and paraenesis (ethical or moral exhortations) (vv. 3, 17–23) that we see in Jude.

Besides appealing to divine revelation, Jude also adopts Jewish apocalyptic eschatology which is often articulated in terms of the "two ages" motif. Jude speaks of *zōēn aiōnion* ("eternal life" or "life of the ages") in verse 21. The "life of the ages," which believers are awaiting eagerly, contrasts with the "old age" of sin and evil, which is quickly passing away. Jude describes the current time in which they live as "the last days" (*eschaton*, v. 18). The presence of the intruders is an indication that they are living at "the end of times." Jude believes that the parousia and judgment (vv. 14–16) are imminent. One can sense some urgency in verse 23 where the community is exhorted to save others by snatching them out of the fire. The Epistle of Jude is imbued throughout with this eschatological outlook.

For the African exegete, Jude's appropriation of noncanonical texts and his willingness to break with convention and quote explicitly from otherwise marginal works serves as a legitimate invitation to engage in an inclusive hermeneutics, a hermeneutics that recognizes and incorporates our marginalized contextual perspectives into biblical and theological discourses. It is an invitation to engage in what Edward Said termed "postcolonial contrapuntal reading"—a reading strategy that aims at counterbalancing the singularized and unidimensional view of Western imperial history and culture by means of resistant histories written by the colonized and subordinate groups.

Second, some western scholars' interpretations of Jude's eschatological outlook have contributed to shaping contemporary Western futuristic and linear eschatology with its emphasis on the imminent return of Christ and his kingdom, an event that many believed would bring about a cataclysmic end to our material world. Mbiti has already faulted this kind of extreme "here-after" (future-dominated) eschatology propagated by western missionaries, particularly in the African Inland Mission (AIM) in (Kenya) Africa. He argues that such an eschatological worldview not only encourages "escapism" from the present world, but it is also at odds with African Traditional eschatology which is "this-worldly" in its orientation.[42] Today, other African theologians have noted the tendency of future- and other-worldly-oriented eschatology

40. Brosend, *James and Jude*, 170.

41. Adela Yarbro Collins, "Introduction: Early Christian Apocalypticism," in *Early Christian Apocalypticism: Genre and Social Setting*, ed. Adela Yarbro Collins, Semeia 36 (SBL, 1986), 7.

42. John S. Mbiti, "Christian Eschatology in Relation to Evangelization of Tribal Africa" (PhD diss., Cambridge University, 1963), 130–135.

to encourage laziness and lack of engagement in transformative social praxis and ecological responsibility.[43] Believers often prioritize preparing for the end times and going to heaven over working to bring about social change and caring for the earth. So, there is an urgent need to promote an African eschatology that underscores ethics and active participation in God's created order, as this is clearly seen as important in the broader context of the New Testament.

The Structure and Outline of Jude

Jude is an ancient letter with a simple and straightforward structure. The letter begins with an epistolary prescript where Jude introduces himself and the recipients of the letter (vv. 1–2). Immediately after the introductory remark, Jude discloses the circumstances that informed the writing of the letter, namely the infiltration by the ungodly persons within the community (v. 4). In light of this threat to the character of the community, Jude writes an appeal to his audience to contend for the faith that was once and for all entrusted to the saints (vv. 3–4).

Since the issue with the intruders has to do with their denial of the Lordship of Christ, which is reflected in their ungodly ethical behavior, Jude then provides examples from Jewish and Christian biblical and extrabiblical sources of God's judgment against those who reject God's authority and engage in immoral behavior (vv. 5–16). The purpose is to warn the readers about the consequences of following the teachings and behavior of these intruders. Jude's historical exposition of rebellious and ungodly individuals is followed by some *paraenesis* (vv. 17–23). The text closes with a doxology (vv. 24–25), in which Jude offers praises to God for his ability to keep believers from stumbling. The Epistle of Jude can be structured as follows:

Introduction and salutation (vv. 1–2)
Occasion and purpose of the letter (vv. 3–4)
Warnings from history (vv. 5–16)
Exhortation to believers (vv. 17–23)
Doxology (vv. 24–25)

The Theology of Jude for Contemporary African Readers

God the Father

The Epistle of Jude is theocentric. It conveys a profound theology of the "one God" (v. 25). According to Jörg Frey, "the emphasis on the oneness of God is entirely in line with Jewish and early Christian tradition, but this does not preclude aspects of the divine nature and action from being expressed in reference to Christ."[44] In Jude, the dominant images of God are that of "Father" and "Savior." The letter opens with a reference to God as "God the Father"

43. Elias K. Bongmba, "Eschatology in Africa: Anticipation and Critical Engagement," in *The Routledge Handbook of African Theology*, ed. Elias K. Bongmba (Routledge, 2020), 503.

44. Frey, *The Letter of Jude and the Second Letter of Peter*, 47.

(v. 1) and concludes with a doxology in which God is referred to as "our Savior" (v. 25). The Father not only initiates the believers' call (v. 1), he also preserves their ultimate salvation (vv. 1, 24–25). Jude also portrays God as the supreme judge who will meet the addressees with mercy and love (vv. 17, 20). In light of the inroads of intruders who seek to pollute the faith of the believers, the author seems to underscore the role of God as a Father who loves, protects, and saves the ones he called from the onslaught of the enemies of the faith. Hence, the letter concludes with a doxology underscoring God's ability to preserve the community through their present challenge (v. 25).

Jude's monotheistic view of God is not strange to African readers. This is because Africans share a similar monotheistic understanding of God. Africans believe that God is one. The fact that most African names for God are all in the singular attest to this reality. Many African theologians, such as Mbiti, have excellently defended the African monotheistic concept of God. This is in contrast to the early European writers' ridiculous claims that Africans lacked the rational capacity to posit the existence of a transcendent, single God.[45] In his comparative study of African Traditional Religion and Christianity, Mbiti shows that Africans believe in the existence of "One Supreme Being" who controls the universe and directs everything within it. Mbiti argues that the Supreme Being worshiped by Africans is the same God revealed in Scripture.[46] Africans call him various names; the Igbo call him *Chukwu*, which means the "Great Being." The Akan people call him *Onyame*, which means "God is the one who satisfies." Although monotheistic, Africans believe in the existence of some lesser divinities, spirit beings, and ancestors, who mediate between the Supreme Being and the people. In African ontology, the Supreme Being works with these deputies in a unitary theocratic governance of the universe.

Like in Jude's community, the concept of God as a Father is central in popular African Christianity. The fatherhood of God is beautifully captured in the Mashi expression *Ishe w'abantu n'ebintu*, meaning "God is the father [*Ishe*] of human beings [*abantu*] and things [*ebintu*]." Mbiti affirms that "a number of African people look upon God as a Father and themselves as his children."[47] The imagery here is that of a family where the father plays vital roles as the protector, provider, and keeper of his family. For many Africans, the image of God as a father highlights the relationship between the invaluable roles that a dedicated traditional African father plays within his family and the role of God the Father in relation to his children. While the idea of God as a father resonates with many Africans, there are Africans who find the image of God as father problematic. For them, the image of God as a father only makes sense to a person who has a nice and loving father; however, those with a bullying father find almost nothing exciting in a portrayal of God as a father. In addition

45. Francis O. C. Njoku, *Essay in African Philosophy, Thought and Theology* (Claretian Institute of Philosophy, 2002), 114.

46. John S. Mbiti, *Concepts of God in Africa* (SPCK, 1970), xiii; John S. Mbiti, *Introduction to African Religion* (Heinemann, 1975), 360.

47. Mbiti, *Introduction to African Religion*, 47.

to this, some have pointed out that "the divine fatherhood often creates gender tension for a person that has a loving mother rather than a loving father."[48]

Jesus Christ

Although theocentric, the Epistle of Jude is highly christological. Jude deployed some christological titles to identify Jesus. Jesus is called the "Christ" (vv. 1, 4, 17, 21), "Lord" (vv. 4, 5, 17, 21, 25), and "only master" (v. 4). In the narratives that Jude alludes to, Jesus is portrayed as the "savior" and "judge" (vv. 5–7, 14). He is the one for whom "the called" are kept (v. 1), who spoke to the apostles (v. 17), from whom the beloved awaits his mercy (v. 21). All these christological titles and roles speak to the divine authority of Jesus. Jude has a favorite way of using the title of "Christ." It has been observed that once Jude moves into the main body of the letter, he always combines "Jesus Christ" with "our Lord" (vv. 4, 17, 21, 25).[49] The first reference to Jesus as Lord occurs in an emphatic form: "our only Master" and "Lord," Jesus Christ (v. 4). In the Jewish context of Jude, the title of "Lord" (*Kurios*) refers to Jesus's divinity and preexistence, as seen in verse 5. This title is not merely an honorific, like "Sir" in our context; rather it is a divine and authoritative designation that places Jesus on par with the Father. The Greek word *despotēs* ("master") refers to a slave owner, but it can also refer to a ruler. The title underscores the absolute legal and uncontrolled authority of the master over a slave or the unlimited power of the ruler over his subjects. Therefore, the phrase "our only Master and Lord" underscores the legal, divine, and royal authority of Jesus Christ over the believers because he purchased them with his blood (Acts 20:28; 1 Cor 16:19–20; 1 Pet 1:19).

Some scholars are of the opinion that Jude reasserts an imperial ideology of power through appeals to imperial lordship rhetoric in order to maintain the threatened identity of his community.[50] How should African readers who are familiar with the brutalizing experience of imperial power through colonization and neo-colonization understand Jude's rhetoric of power? Does Jude internalize imperial assumptions about power only to apply it to another marginalized group as has been suggested?[51] I am of the view that Jude, just like the apostle Paul, reflects a subtle anti-imperial stance to the Roman Empire, its lords and gods, ideology and values systems. Wei Wan notes that the "early Christian proclamation of Christ's Lordship, wherever and whenever it was made, constituted an antithesis,

48. Matthew Michael, *Christian Theology and African Traditions* (The Lutterworth Press, 2013), 70. While Africans typically refer to God as Father, there are cultures that depict God as Mother. For example, in the Democratic Republic of the Congo, the Bakongo ethnic group, which practices a matriarchal system, refers to God as "Mother."

49. Rohun Park, "The Letter of Jude," in *A Postcolonial Commentary of the New Testament Writings*, ed. Fernando F. Segovia and R. S. Sugirtharajah, BP 13 (T&T Clark, 2009), 430; Stanly Jones, "The Letter of Jude," in *An Asian Introduction to the New Testament*, ed. Johnson Thomaskutty (Fortress Press, 2022), 530.

50. Betsy Bauman-Martin, "Postcolonial Pollution in the Letter of Jude," in *Reading Jude with New Eyes: Methodological Reassessment of the Letter of Jude*, ed. Robert L. Webb and Peter H. Davis (T&T Clark, 2008), 68.

51. Bauman-Martin, "Postcolonial Pollution in the Letter of Jude," 72.

a challenge, to imperial authority—and, indeed, oppressive forces everywhere."[52] Against the lords of the Roman Empire who dominate and oppress their subjects, Jude proclaims a saving and liberative lordship of God the Father and Christ. In Jude, the Lord is the one "who once for all saved a people out of the land of Egypt" (v. 4), and the Lord is the one who "leads to eternal life" (v. 21).

Many ordinary Christian Africans affirm and relate to the portrait of Jesus that emerges from the Epistle of Jude, such as "Lord," "Christ," "Master," "Judge," and "Savior." They invoke these christological titles in prayers, especially when confronting Satan and his agents. However, these images, with the exception of "Savior," do not resonate with some African theologians. Today, there are African theologians who are constructing unique African Christologies that address who Jesus is for Africans (cf. Mark 8:29). One outstanding christological title in Africa is that of "ancestor" due to Jesus's intercessory and mediatory role, which parallels those of the African ancestors. In his book, *Christ as Our Ancestor*, Charles Nyamiti proposes that Jesus Christ should be seen as a "brother-ancestor." A brother-ancestor in the African context, according to Nyamiti, "is a relative of a person with whom he has a common parent, and of whom he is mediator to God, archetype of behavior and with whom—thanks to his supernatural statues acquired through death—he is entitled to have regular sacred communication."[53] Nyamiti argues that by becoming man, Jesus becomes our true brother in the Father, as well as our Mediator and High Priest. By reason of his divine-human nature, Jesus also becomes the archetype of our supernatural and Christian conduct. Thanks to his divinity and holiness, he had a right to our regular sacred contact with him.[54] Christ however, embodied the African ancestor-ideal in an eminent degree. Given his divine origin as the Son of God, his divine-human nature, and his position as the second person of the Trinity, Jesus's role transcends those of traditional African brother-ancestors; hence, he is seen as "the brother-ancestor par excellence." Ancestor-Christology therefore sheds light on the relationship between Christ and his members who are in Africa. Other images of Jesus that resonate with Christian Africans include Jesus as the Liberator,[55] and Jesus as the Healer (*Nganga*).[56]

Holy Spirit

The Holy Spirit is mentioned only twice in Jude. The first reference to the Holy Spirit occurs in one of his polemics against the intruders: "it is these worldly people (*psychikoi*) devoid of the Spirit, (*Pneuma mē echontes*) who are causing divisions" (v. 19). Since the time of the early church, the possession of the Holy Spirit has been the defining characteristic of believers

52. Wei Hsien Wan, *The Contest for Time and Space in the Roman Imperial Cults and 1 Peter: Reconfiguring the Universe* (Bloomsbury, 2019), 6.

53. Charles Nyamiti, *Christ as Our Ancestor: Christology from an African Perspective* (Mambo, 1984), 23.

54. Nyamiti, *Christ as Our Ancestor*, 35–36.

55. John S. Mbiti, "Some African Concepts of Christology," in *Christ and Younger Churches: Theological Contributions from Asia, Africa and Latin America*, ed. Georg Vicedom (SPCK, 1972), 55.

56. Cécé Kolié, "Jesus as Healer?" in *Faces of Jesus in Africa*, ed. Robert J. Schreiter (Orbis Books, 1991), 128–150.

(Rom 8:9; 1 Cor 6:19; 12:3; 2 Cor 4:13; Gal 5:19–21). Paul uses *pneumatikós* to describe one whose life is guided by the Spirit of God (1 Cor 2:4–15; 1 Cor 10:3–4; Gal 6:1). The *pneumatikós* contrasts with the *psychikos* (unspiritual or worldly person). While the intruders may claim direct spiritual experience (v. 8), in reality, they lack the Spirit (v. 19). They are carnal people who follow their bodily desires (vv. 8, 10, 16, 18), and so cause divisions within the community. Another reference to the Spirit is found in the context of a practical admonition where Jude exhorts his audience to pray in the Holy Spirit (v. 20) as a way of maintaining fidelity to God. Prayer is an important aspect of the Christian's life that is empowered only by the Spirit of God. It is through prayer that believers connect and maintain an intimate relationship with God.

Both African Traditional Religions and Christianity in Africa are characterized by a spirit-infused spirituality. While the term "pneumatology" (study of the Holy Spirit) is generally connected to Christian theology, a closer examination of the spirituality of African Traditional Religions uncovers a rich and complex understanding of spiritual powers and agencies that align with the notion of a pneumatic worldview. However, rather than a singular, unified Holy Spirit, African Traditional Religions have a variety of spiritual beings that interact with human beings. These spiritual forces are not separate from the physical world; rather, they are intricately interwoven with it. Human actions and community life are profoundly shaped by these spiritual influences. In a thought-provoking essay titled "The Flow of African Spirituality into World Christianity: A Case for Pneumatology and Migration," Amuluche-Greg Nnamani investigates how the spirituality of African Traditional Religions has influenced contemporary African Christian practices, especially those in the Pentecostal and charismatic movements. He argues that the strong emphasis on the Holy Spirit in these churches is connected to and shaped by the African traditional worldview on spiritism.[57]

Similar to the community of Jude (Jude 8), there is a significant focus on the tangible or experiential manifestations of the Holy Spirit—such as healing, prophecy, visions, and speaking in tongues, and other gifts of the Holy Spirit—within the African Pentecostal/charismatic churches. Some of their leaders possess a remarkable ability to inspire and connect with the people on both emotional and spiritual levels. But the pneumatological problems Jude addresses are still evident in Africa today. The insurgence of fake preachers, healers, pastors, and prophets, who claim to be highly spiritual but, in reality, engage in practices that do not align with the ethical principles and values of the Christian faith continues to pose a significant challenge to the church in Africa. Many of these so-called men and women of God distort the gospel message of Christ and promote dangerous beliefs and practices. Oftentimes, they use their charisma to manipulate and exploit vulnerable individuals for personal or financial gain. Jude warns us regarding such ungodly people who have infiltrated our churches and are destroying them from within.

57. Amuluche-Greg Nnamani, "The Flow of African Spirituality into World Christianity: A Case for Pneumatology and Migration," *Mission Studies* 32 (2015): 331–352.

Grace

One of the glaring issues that Jude responds to in his letter is the wrong understanding of God's grace by certain people within the community. The first accusation that Jude brought against the intruders is that of perverting the grace of our God into licentiousness (*aselgeia*, v. 4). In Christian theology, grace is a concept that emphasizes God's unmerited favor and unconditional love toward his chosen people. It is possible that the intruders may have misconstrued the grace of God as freedom from the law, including laws around sexuality. They may have misinterpreted God's grace as license to do whatever they want, reflecting the antinomian response to Paul's Gospel of grace (Rom 3:8; 6:1, 15; 1 Cor 6:12–14; Gal 5:13) due to the misunderstanding of Paul's theology of Christian freedom (cf. Rom 4:15, 5:20, 8:1; 1 Cor 6:12).[58] Jude sees the intruders' ideology as a denial of Jesus's right to be obeyed and, implicitly, a denial of his Lordship. For Jude, grace always calls for human response (v. 21). God's saving grace does not denigrate God's moral imperatives; rather, it emboldens us to live a life of obedience and justice. Paul admonishes Christ-believers "not to accept the grace of God in vain" (2 Cor 6:1). Grace enables believers to imitate the character of Jesus Christ, embodying his life of obedience, faithfulness, and justice (Rom 6:1–2, 15–23).

Perversion of God's grace is a reality that was true not only in Jude's time but also in our present time. It takes different forms depending on one's context. In Africa, the exploitation of God's grace can be seen in the form of the present-day prosperity gospel that has now "turned God's grace into an endorsement of unbridled greed."[59] According to the proponents, God's salvation or the evidence of it in this present life is measured by one's financial or material well-being. Poverty is interpreted as the absence of God's favor and in some cases as a curse.[60] The adherents of the prosperity gospel believe that God's salvation effected through the death and resurrection of Jesus Christ has brought liberation from all socioeconomic challenges. Consequently, they advocate an all-round prosperity that excludes any form of suffering. One of the dangers of this ideology is the propensity to relax core aspects of faith and ethics, resulting in a sharp dichotomy between Christian theology and morality.

Mercy and Judgment

Judgment is a prominent theme in the Epistle of Jude. At the heart of the letter is the affirmation of God's judgment on the ungodly who have rebelled against God through their actions (v. 4). The theme of judgment appeareds in the narratives of the fallen angels (v. 6), the battle between Michael and Satan over Moses's body (vv. 9–10), and Enoch's prophecy of God's judgment on the ungodly (vv. 14–15). There are also allusions to judgment in the narratives

58. David R. Nienhuis and Robert W. Wall, *Reading the Epistles of James, Peter, John & Jude as Scripture: The Shaping and Shape of a Canonical Collection* (Eerdmans, 2013), 228.

59. Russell Pregeant, *Converting Christians to the Jesus Ethic* (Cascade Books, 2023), 51.

60. Timothy Barga, "Theological Pitfall of Prosperity Gospel in Nigerian Churches," *Journal of African Studies and Sustainable Development* 1, no. 1 (2018): 209–210.

that highlight divine punishment on the unrighteous. These include: the wilderness generation (v. 5), the fallen angels (v. 6), Sodom and Gomorrah (v. 7), Cain, Korah, and Balaam (v. 11).

In Jude, God is the subject of judgment, and the objects of divine judgment are human and angelic beings, as well as cities that have engaged in rebellious actions against God. Jude sees God as a just judge whose judgments are the expression of his justice and righteousness. Jude's emphasis on divine judgment is very pertinent for the church in Africa, where many "churches are prone to sentimentality, suffer from moral breakdown, and too often fail to pronounce a definitive word of judgment because of an inadequate definition of love. Jude's letter reminds us that errant teaching and dissolute living have dire consequences."[61] The theme of judgment serves as a cautionary message about the seriousness of sin, the certainty of God's judgment and the importance of living in obedience to God.

While the Epistle of Jude may appear harsh and condemnatory, the invectives and judgments are not the last things that Jude offers to his readers. The epistle closes with a sober exhortation to expect divine mercy and to show mercy to fellow believers, even the erring ones (vv. 22–23). Mercy appears together with peace and love in the greeting (v. 2). Divine mercy is among the blessings that Jude wishes in abundance for the community. At the parousia, it is Christ's mercy that will bring the believers into eternal life (v. 21). The theme of mercy in Jude balances the emphasis on divine justice and judgment. It reminds believers of the compassionate nature of God and encourages them to reflect his mercy in their own lives as they navigate the challenges of living out their faith.

Among Africans, the concept of mercy is deeply rooted in cultural and religious traditions that emphasize compassion, forgiveness, and support for those in both spiritual and material need. For instance, the concept of *Ubuntu*, which is prevalent in many African cultures, particularly among South Africans, emphasizes consideration of others and the importance of compassion and empathy.[62] Mercy, within the framework of *ubuntu*, involves recognizing the humanity of others, acknowledging their dignity, and showing kindness and support in times of need. In a time when many African communities continue to experience an accelerating increase in ethnic prejudice, religious intolerance, xenophobic violence, and so on, the *ubuntu* ideal, which finds resonance in Jude's *paraenesis*, challenges Christians to continue to embody mercy and love at all costs.

The "Us" and "Them" Dichotomy

Human beings are diverse by nature. Thus, our identity is fundamentally dialectical. As a result, we often organize ourselves into groups based on shared values, identities, affinities, and goals. Our self-definition typically involves distinguishing ourselves ("us") from others ("them"). The "us" and "them" dichotomy refers to the tendency to categorize people into two opposing groups, which creates divisions based on external factors such as identity, gender,

61. Schreiner, *1, 2 Peter, Jude*, 403–404.

62. N. Kingsley Okoro, "Ubuntu Ideality: The Foundation of African Compassionate and Humane Living," *Journal of Scientific Research and Reports* 8, no. 1 (2015): 1–9.

ethnicity, class, religion, and so on. We often define ourselves in opposition to others. We find this dichotomy in Jude. Jude makes a sharp contrast between the genuine believers and intruders by using the pronouns "you" (*hemeis*) and "these" (*hutoi*). The genuine believers are addressed as "you." Jude always speaks positively about them. They are referred to as the "called," "beloved," and "kept" (v. 1). They are the subject of Jude's exhortation (vv. 17–23). On the other hand, the intruders are usually identified as "these" (*houtoi*). The phrase occurrs in verses 8, 10, 12, 14, 16, and 19, and in each instance it is followed by a negative example or phrase. Jude describes them as outsiders who have "stolen in among you" (v. 4). The intruders are consistently the recipients of Jude's invectives.

Mbuvi notes that Jude's invectives, though reflective of the Greco-Roman rhetorical practices, should indeed be approached with caution, given how such language has been used to perpetuate or reinforce existing hierarchies and stereotypes, as is the reality of Africa. He notes that "the violence meted on the African peoples via slavery and colonialism was partly driven by the western caricature and stereotyping of the African person as 'uncivilized,' 'unreligious' and even less that human."[63] The colonial powers did not just use negative labels on Africans, they also deployed the "us" and "them" mentality to create divisions and a culture of distrust among different ethnic groups. In this way, they sowed seeds of animosity and competition, contributing to the divisions and conflicts that persist to this day. In several African countries, such as Nigeria, Rwanda, and Sudan, this negative dichotomy has sparked violent conflicts rooted in ethnic or religious identities.

As we note the potential negative consequence of Jude's invectives, it is important to pay attention to Reese's illuminating observation regarding Jude's rhetoric. According to Reese, "the relationship between the Beloved and the Others in Jude should not be read solely as an 'us against them' polemic. . . . While these boundaries between the Beloved and the Others appear, at a glance, to be impermeable, they are more fluid than first appearances would make them."[64] Despite Jude's invectives, there exists a subtler theme of calling for the salvation of the intruders rather than their complete condemnation or destruction. The Epistle of Jude does not endorse violence and should not be used to advocate violence toward or the oppression of others. For the African reader, it is important to bear in mind that the essence of our Christian identity is rooted in love and unity. The message of unity calls for a shared commitment to the values of love, reconciliation, and acceptance. Embracing this call as Africans requires us to move beyond ethnic or cultural affiliations. It invites us to recognize our shared humanity and our common identity as children of God.

Salvation

The noun salvation (*sōtēria*), from the Greek word *sōzō*, means to save, deliver, protect, or to make whole. Jude touches on a number of substantial issues in Christian soteriological discourse. First, there is a Trinitarian dimension to Jude's soteriology: God is called "our savior"

63. Mbuvi, *Jude and 2 Peter*, 66.

64. Reese, *2 Peter & Jude*, 85–86.

(v. 25). Jesus also is portrayed as a savior "The Lord saved a people out of Egypt" (v. 5).[65] It is through the mercy of Jesus Christ that the believers' eternal life is secured (v. 21). Jude also recognizes the vital role of the Holy Spirit in building and sustaining the final perseverance of believers (vv. 19–20). Second, Jude's soteriology is participatory: While believers' final perseverance is anchored on God's sovereign election, love, and preservation (v. 1, 24–25), human responsibility is never negated or denied. There is still the necessity for the believers to prove themselves, to contend for the faith (v. 3), and to practice Christian ethics (vv. 20–23) in order to appear blameless before God at the eschaton (v. 25). This participatory soteriology is best exemplified in the Exodus narrative where the people whom the Lord saved from Egypt were later destroyed because of their unbelief, since they failed to live in a way that resonated with their salvation.

Another issue to address in Jude's soteriology is: What are human beings saved from in Jude's perspective? The answer to this question is found in Jude's allusion to the Exodus event (v. 5), when God dramatically liberated the Israelites from their slavery in Egypt (Exod 6–14). In this narrative, salvation is conceived as a saving from a physical place of suffering and oppression. It is not an abstract theological speculation, as it seems to be portrayed in many Western soteriological discourses. This Exodus-informed understanding of salvation resonates with Christian Africans. Although Africans have a holistic understanding of salvation that embraces both the physical and spiritual, in many instances, it is the physical, this-worldly salvation that is emphasized. This is captured in *Agyenkwa*, the Akan concept of a savior.[66] Henry J. Mugabe also confirms this understanding of salvation among the Shona (Zimbabwe). According to him, salvation in Shona religion is "concerned about protection, restoration, preservation, survival and the continuance of human, societal, and environmental life in this world."[67] This understanding of salvation contrasts with the Western other-worldly, spiritualized, personal, and futuristic view of salvation.[68] Such an understanding of salvation has been used to justify passive acceptance of unnecessary suffering in this world. By recognizing salvation as encompassing the material, social, and spiritual dimensions, we can adopt a broader understanding of the Christian faith that values both present living conditions and future expectations with regard to the ultimate salvation of our souls.

Ancestors/Living Dead in Jude and Africa

At the core of an African cosmology is a holistic understanding of life that integrates the spiritual, physical, and social dimensions. Africans view the cosmos as a harmonious whole where the divine and the human are not seen as wholly separate. They embrace a cosmological

65. Some manuscripts have different reading of v. 5. Some have "*Jesus* delivered his people out of Egypt" in place of "Lord." Some scholars think that "Jesus," which is the more difficult reading, may be the original, thereby reflecting the tradition in 1 Cor 10:4, where Paul identifies Christ as the "rock" that followed the Israelites in the desert.

66. Mercy A. Oduyoye, *Hearing and Knowing: Theological Reflections on Christianity in Africa* (Wipf & Stock, 2009), 98.

67. Henry J. Mugabe, "Salvation from an African Perspective," *Indian Journal of Theology* 36, no. 1 (1994): 32.

68. John S. Mbiti, *Bible and Theology in African Christianity* (Oxford University Press, 1986), 158–159.

outlook in which the visible and invisible worlds interpenetrate. Chinua Achebe captures this reality in his novel *Things Fall Apart* as follows: "The land of the living was not far removed from the domain of the ancestors. There was coming and going between them, especially at festivals and also when an old man died, because an old man was very close to the ancestors."[69] What this means is that for Africans, death is not seen as a complete obliteration of life since there is always a vestige of life that remains.

Africans believe that their dead ones are still alive, and continue to exert great influence in the affairs of the living through their guidance, protection, and intercession. The deceased are believed to exert either positive or negative influence in African communities, and in many of them both the ancestors (individuals who have passed on but continue to influence the lives of their descendants) and the living dead (the recently deceased individuals who are honored and remembered) are seen as integral to the spiritual well-being of the community.[70] Their influence is perceived not only in the rituals and traditions that commemorate them, but also in the lived experiences of the community.

We find a somewhat similar worldview in the Epistle of Jude, where the author invites the collective memory of the living dead through his references to the wicked dead people whose stories are captured in Israel's foundational narratives (cf. vv. 5–7, 11), as well as the positive words of the apostles who were the foundation pillars of the early church (v. 17).[71] In his study of the impact of the living dead on Jude's community, Stephan Joubert explores the positive and negative influences of the dead on Jude's community, arguing that through Jude's recollection of the premortem deeds of the wicked dead (cf. vv. 5–7; 11), they are kept alive within Jude's community. According to him, the unsettling influence of the dead is manifested in the activities of the intruders within the community who belong to the same species as they do. In similar fashion, references to the premortem deeds of the righteous dead also serve to keep them alive, particularly when the readers imitate their godly deeds, which are also recorded in Israel's official narratives.[72]

First, for the African reader, the relationship between ancestors/living dead and their living ones can be deployed to shed light on important aspects of the Christian faith. In Christology, as noted above, some African scholars have explored a deeper understanding of Jesus Christ through the lens of ancestor.[73] For instance, Charles Nyamiti has used the ancestor category to speak of God the Father as ancestor, Christ as brother-ancestor, and the

69. Chinua Achebe, *Things Fall Apart* (Heinemann, 1958), 97.

70. John S. Mbiti, *African Religion and Philosophy* (Anchor Books, 1970), 32.

71. Note that while Jude acknowledges the influence of the dead in the actions of the intruders, it does not explicitly affirm the idea that the dead actively guide, protect, or intercede for the living, as it is believed in African Traditional Religions. In the context of Christian belief, the views on the intercession of the dead, particularly regarding saints or ancestors, tend to be derived from other texts and traditions outside the Epistle of Jude. For this view see 2 Mac 15:11–16; Heb 12:1; Rev 5:8.

72. Stephan J. Joubert, "When the Dead Are Alive! The Influence of the Living Dead in the Letter of Jude," *HTS Teologiese Studies/Theological Studies* 58, no. 2 (2002): 590.

73. Kwame Bediako, *Christianity in Africa: The Renewal of a Non-Western Religion* (Edinburgh University Press, 1995); Bénézet Bujo, *African Theology in Its Social Context*, trans. John O'Donohue (Wipf & Stock, 2006).

"communion of saints" as ancestors.[74] The unbreakable relationship between the ancestors and their living ones can be used to explain the intimate and inseparable relationship between Christ and the African believers. We can be guaranteed that Jesus as our brother-ancestor is constantly mediating for us before God.

Second, ancestor veneration (and in some contexts, worship) can shed light on the cult of saints in Christianity. Some Africans believe that their ancestors are in communion with them. They honor and venerate them because of their closeness to God. The ancestors in turn play a mediatory role between God and their living ones. This practice finds a parallel in the Christian *communio sanctorum*. The communion between the living and dead is an important article of faith among Roman Catholics. Catholics believe that the members of the body of Christ who are alive and those who are dead share a bond of communion. Hence, they venerate and seek the intercession of the saints in heaven, and also pray for the souls in purgatory.

Third, the roles ancestors play can help us in understanding certain scriptural passages, such as the concept of the "cloud of witnesses" in Hebrews 12:1, which resonates deeply within the framework of African ancestors. In Hebrews 12:1 the author accentuates the fact that Christians are surrounded by "a great cloud of witness," that is, the heroes of faith who have made it all the way to the finishing line and as such have paved the way for all Christians to walk with hope in their journey of faith. For the African reader, this passage serves as a profound reminder of the collective spiritual witnesses (our exemplary ancestors in the faith) that surround contemporary African believers. By reflecting on the virtuous lives of those who have gone before, Christians are inspired to persevere in their own spiritual journeys. Finally, behind the practice of commemorating the dead in some Christian traditions lies the hope in the resurrection of which Jesus's own resurrection has become the prototype of our own resurrection. Christ's resurrection over the powers of evil and death is the sign of hope for the African culture that naturally looks beyond death.

The Function of Collective Memory in Jude and Among Africans

The theme of remembrance is a prevalent motif not only in the Epistle of Jude but throughout the Bible as a whole. Memory is critically important for any social group because of its function in the construction of a collective identity.[75] Collective memory refers to the memory that a group shares in common which influences and shapes their social identity. It is the memory that remains embedded in a group long after the eyewitnesses to historical events have died. The memory becomes part of the group's shared identity which is stored in the narratives that

74. See Charles Nyamiti, *African Tradition and the Christian God* (Gaba, 1977); Charles Nyamiti, "African Christologies Today," in *Jesus in African Christianity*, ed. J. N. K. Mugambi and Laurenti Magesa (Initiatives Publishers, 1989), 17–39; Charles Nyamiti, "Uganda Martyrs: Ancestors of All Mankind," *African Christian Studies* 2, no. 1 (1986): 37–60.

75. Jeffrey K. Olick, "Products, Processes, and Practices: A Non-Reificatory Approach to Collective Memory," *Biblical Theology Bulletin* 36, no. 1 (2006): 5–6.

the group recounts.[76] The concept of collective memory plays a fundamental role in Jude's theology. The main body of Jude began in verse 5 with the call "to remember" and closes in verse 17 with the same word, thereby forming an *inclusio*.

Jude frequently appeals to the community's collective memory by directing his audience to their common Scriptures, which serve as a lens through which they must view and interpret their present circumstance, namely the infiltration by godless people within the community. Jude does not reveal much about the real identity of the intruders; however, he selects six narratives of villains from Jewish collective memory (the wilderness generation, the fallen angels, Sodom and Gomorrah, Cain, Balaam, and Korah) as illustrating the true character of these intruders. For Jude, just as these villains function as models of social reality, but not as models to emulate, so do the intruders.[77] Jude also appeals to the positive characters within the community's collective memory. In verse 17, the readers are instructed to "remember" the predictions of the apostles of our Lord Jesus Christ. Here the collective memory that Jude evokes is the words of the apostles who are the authentic and authoritative interpreters of the gospel. The apostolic prediction to be remembered concerns the end time when ungodly people will infiltrate the community.

Africa as a continent is characterized by a millenia of diverse and complex history that forms the collective memory of the people. The memories of our ancient kingdoms and civilizations, our people's rich oral and wisdom traditions, spiritual heritage, vibrant and dynamic cultures, and so on, form an important part of our collective memory. Also embedded within the collective memory of Africans are the violent experiences of colonization, the horrific transatlantic slave trade, myriad civil wars and conflicts, poverty, diseases, and so on. But the collective memory also includes the stories of struggles and resilience of many brave Africans who fought against colonial rule. Nelson Mandela, Kwame Nkrumah, Nnamdi Azikiwe, Funmilayo Ransome-Kuti, and Jomo Kenyatta are remembered for their roles in the Pan-African movement and their advocacy for justice, equality, and freedom. Movements like the African National Congress (ANC) in South Africa encapsulate the spirit of resistance and the quest for freedom, forming a crucial part of the historical narrative that informs African postcolonial identities.

Conclusion

When one of the early Christian communities was on the verge of relaxing the Christian bonds of morality, due to the infiltration by ungodly persons who promoted antinomian attitudes and immoral behaviors, Jude penned a brief but powerful letter, urging believers to contend for the faith by resisting the ungodly ideologies, wrong theology, and unethical behaviors of the intruders. Contending for the faith entails living the principles of the Christian

76. Ruth Anne Reese, "Remember 'Jesus Saved a People Out of Egypt,'" in *Muted Voices of the New Testament Readings in the Catholic Epistles and Hebrews*, ed. Katherine M. Hockey, Madison N. Pierce, and Francis Watson, LNTS 565 (T&T Clark, 2017), 88.

77. Nienhuis and Wall, "The Catholic Epistle of Jude," 233.

faith. The message of Jude is relevant not only for the early church but also for the church in modern times, including the church in Africa, where she continues to encounter issues of false doctrines, moral relativism, and external pressures that threaten the integrity of the Christian faith. African readers can draw insights from many aspects of Jude's theology, such as his Trinitarian theology, soteriology, judgment and mercy, and grace as they navigate their journey of faith.

Further Reading

Adeyemo, Tokunboh. "Jude." In *Africa Bible Commentary: A One-Volume Commentary Written by 70 African Scholars*, edited by Tokunboh Adeyemo. WordAlive Publishers; Zondervan, 2006.

Asale, Bruk Ayele. *1 Enoch as Christian Scripture: A Study in the Reception and Appropriation of 1 Enoch in Jude and the Ethiopian Orthodox Tewahedo Canon*. Pickwick, 2020.

Bauckham, Richard. *Jude, 2 Peter*. WBC 50. Word, 1983.

Brosend, William F. *James and Jude*. NCBC. Cambridge University Press, 2004.

Frey, Jörg. *The Letter of Jude and the Second Letter of Peter: A Theological Commentary*. Translated by Kathleen Ess. Baylor University Press, 2018.

Jones, Stanly. "The Letter of Jude." In *An Asian Introduction to the New Testament*, edited by Johnson Thomaskutty. Fortress Press, 2022.

Mbiti, John S. *African Religions and Philosophy*. Heinemann, 1970.

Mbiti, John S. *Concepts of God in Africa*. SPCK, 1970.

Mbiti, John S. *Introduction to African Religion*. Heinemann, 1975.

Mbuvi, Andrew M. *Jude and 2 Peter*. New Covenant Commentary Series. Wipf & Stock, 2015.

Nyamiti, Charles. "African Christologies Today." In *Jesus in African Christianity*, edited by J. N. K. Mugambi and Laurenti Magesa. Initiatives Publishers, 1989.

Nyamiti, Charles. *Christ as Our Ancestor: Christology from an African Perspective*. Mambo, 1984.

Nyamiti, Charles. "Uganda Martyrs: Ancestors of All Mankind." *African Christian Studies* 2, no. 1 (1986): 37–60.

Park, Rohun. "The Letter of Jude." In *A Postcolonial Commentary on the New Testament Writings*, edited by Fernando F. Segovia and R. S. Sugirtharajah. T&T Clark, 2009.

Reese, Ruth Anne. *2 Peter & Jude*. THNT. Eerdmans, 2007.

CHAPTER TWENTY-FOUR

The Book of Revelation

Cornelia van Deventer
South African Theological Seminary
South Africa

Introduction

In June 2023, the following message was making the rounds on social media in South Africa:

> I have read Revelation. I do understand quite plainly that I do not wish to spend eternity in hell. Keep in mind. The rapture comes before the antichrist. I have been reading the Bible, in many different forms and it really does always come down to this.

The post goes on to identify microchips, a cashless society, martial law, and total government dependency and control as signifying signs of the beast and his mark, describing 2020 (i.e., the COVID-19 pandemic) as a turning point that set the world in gear for the new world order. This is followed by an elaboration on the "Rapture" that will cause many to disappear. This is not the first time a chain message like this has reached me on social media. In the month of June, I saw many acquaintances posting it. Several jarring elements need to be pointed out. First, from the content of the post, it is resoundingly clear that those sharing it have *not* read Revelation in its entirety. When one uses words like "the antichrist" and "Rapture," that do not appear in the book—even once—believing the first sentence becomes difficult. What the post does get right is the call to repentance and gospel proclamation. However, reposting a chain message is a far cry from the self-denying ethos that John's visions call their hearers to. Rather, such interpretations mystify the book of Revelation and estrange us from its core message.

Michael Gorman speaks to this:

> How one reads, teaches, and preaches Revelation can have a powerful impact on one's own—and other people's—emotional, spiritual, and even physical and economic well-being. Therefore, interpreting the book of Revelation is a serious and sacred responsibility, not to be entered into lightly. Furthermore . . . it must be clearly stated that some readings are not only inferior to others, they are in fact unchristian and unhealthy.[1]

1. Michael Gorman, *Reading Revelation Responsibly: Uncivil Worship and Witness. Following the Lamb into the New Creation* (Cascade, 2011), 12, italics in original.

In this chapter, we look at Revelation's background and core message, considering its relevance to readers and hearers in Africa. After discussing introductory matters, we go on to read Africa through apocalyptic eyes, noting points of convergence between biblical and African realities, while simultaneously demonstrating how the text challenges postures and sins on the African continent.

Introductory Matters

Authorship

There is an abounding lack of consensus about Revelation's authorship. The author simply identifies himself as John (1:1, 4, 9; 22:8). What is clear is that the churches in Asia Minor knew him, which is why he did not need to add any additional identifiers to his name. Uncertainty about Revelation's author is nothing new. Some, like Papias and Dionysus of Alexandria believed that there were two Johns—the beloved disciple (John, son of Zebedee) and the elder—and that the latter penned Revelation.[2] Church fathers like Irenaeus,[3] Justin Martyr,[4] Tertullian, Clement of Alexandria, and Origen[5] believed that the book was written by the apostle John, the son of Zebedee, known as the beloved disciple. Others, like Eusebius, are unclear.[6]

The primary argument offered against apostolic authorship is the so-called stylistic and theological dissimilarities between Revelation and the Johannine Gospel. This argument deserves some critical engagement. Not only was Revelation written later than the Fourth Gospel, but its genre differs vastly from the Gospel and the letters. John is recounting a visionary experience, which dictates the content, language, and style of his writing. Rather, those who challenge apostolic authorship ought to explain the many striking similarities between the Gospel and Revelation. For documents that do not share a purpose, style, genre, and even audience, communal themes abound. These include, among others,[7] the imagery of water,[8] life/living,[9] the shared Ἐγώ εἰμι (I am) statements,[10] and the emphasis on witness.[11]

2. Eusebius, *Hist. eccl.* 3.39.

3. Irenaeus, *Haer.* 3.1.2.

4. Justin Martyr, *Dial.* 81.4.

5. Eusebius, *Hist. eccl.* 6.25; See Grant R. Osborne, *Revelation: Verse by Verse*, ONTC (Lexham Press, 2016), 17.

6. See Charles B. Puskas, *Hebrews, the General Letters, and Revelation: An Introduction* (Cascade, 2016), Perlego ed.

7. For more similarities between the two, see Luke Timothy Johnson, *The Writings of the New Testament*, rev. ed. (Fortress Press, 1999), 580–581.

8. John 1:26, 31, 33; 2:6, 7, 9; 3:5; 4:7, 10–11, 13–15, 28; 5:7; 7:38; 13:5; 19:34; Rev 1:15; 7:17; 8:10–11; 11:6; 12:15; 14:2, 7; 16:4–5, 12; 17:1, 15; 19:6; 21:6; 22:1, 17.

9. John 1:4; 3:15–16, 36; 4:10–11, 14, 36; 5:24, 26, 29, 39–40; 6:27, 33, 35, 40, 47–48, 51, 53–54, 57–58; 6:63, 68; 7:38; 8:12; 10:10–11, 28; 11:25–26; 12:25, 50; 14:6; 17:2–3; 20:31; Rev 1:18; 2:8, 10; 3:1, 5; 4:9–10; 7:17; 10:6; 11:11; 13:8; 15:7; 17:8; 20:4–5, 12, 15; 21:6, 27; 22:1, 214, 17, 19.

10. John 6:48; 8:12; 10:11, 14; 15:1; Rev 1:8, 17, 18; 2:23; 21:6; 22:16.

11. John 1:7–8, 15, 19, 32, 34; 2:25; 3:11, 26, 28, 32–33; 4:39, 44; 5:31–39; 7:7; 8:13–14, 17–18; 10:25; 12:17; 13:21; 15:26–27; 18:37; 19:35; 21:25; Rev 1:2, 5, 9; 2:13; 3:14; 6:9; 11:3, 7, 10; 12:11, 17; 15:5; 17:6; 19:10; 20:4; 22:16, 18, 20.

Also, the matching of the purpose statement in Revelation 22:6–20 to that in John 20:30–31 and 1 John 5:12–13 is quite remarkable and could be indicative of a shared author.[12] While any authorship theory will come with unresolved tensions, the most compelling view is the traditional perspective, namely, that Revelation was written by the apostle John, the beloved disciple, who also authored the Gospel and the Johannine Letters.

Date, Audience, and Occasion

The book is believed to have been written during the reign of Emperor Domitian (81–96 CE),[13] who demanded to be worshipped (see Rev 13:4). While dating it back to Nero's reign in the mid-50s to late 60s is probable, it is unlikely, primarily because Nero's persecution of Christians was limited to Rome. Additionally, the historical situations of the seven churches seem to match the later date better. John identifies his audience as the seven churches in Asia (1:4). While the letters single out the churches in Ephesus, Smyrna, Pergamum, Thyatira, Sardis, Philadelphia, and Laodicea, there is good reason to believe that Revelation was meant to be circulated among all churches in Asia Minor. Nevertheless, the mention of seven churches located in seven historical places is crucial. Not only does it speak to a flesh-and-blood audience which demystifies the Apocalypse, but it reveals a pastoral function, even beyond Revelation 2 and 3.

The seven churches were situated in Asia Minor, under the Roman Empire.[14] Here, the imperial cult was firmly set since its establishment during the reign of Augustus,[15] and under the emperor Domitian, emperor worship through the imperial cult was a standard practice, with Domitian being called, "Lord and God."[16] Markets and other economic hubs were often housed in imperial sanctuaries where pagan worship occurred. Likewise, trade guilds, which enforced emperor worship, controlled the economic activities of a city. Faithful Christians thus struggled to trade and access goods, leaving them economically vulnerable and suffering for their allegiance to the one true God.[17] This would range from ostracism and economic exclusion to violent persecution and death. Some scholars hold that the churches in Asia Minor were not yet under persecution at the time of writing of Revelation and that, perhaps, a persecution was only to break out later should the

---

12. Onesimus Ngundu, "Revelation," in *Africa Bible Commentary: A One-Volume Commentary Written by 70 African Scholars*, ed. Tokunboh Adeyemo (WordAlive Publishers; Zondervan, 2006), 1570.

13. Mark Allan Powell, *Introducing the New Testament*, 2nd. ed. (Baker, 2018), 545; Bitrus A. Sarma, *Drums of Redemption: A New Testament Theology for Africa* (HippoBooks, 2023), 286. Dean Flemming, *Foretaste of the Future: Reading Revelation in Light of God's Mission* (InterVarsity Press, 2022), 27.

14. Powell, *Introducing the New Testament*, 546.

15. Sigve K. Tonstad, *Revelation*, Paideia (Baker Academic, 2019), 50; see pp. 45–50 for a discussion of the inception of the imperial cult.

16. Osborne, *Revelation*, 21.

17. Powell, *Introducing the New Testament*, 546; Puskas, *Hebrews, the General Letters, and Revelation*, chap. 6; Osborne, *Revelation*, 20.

Christians resist.[18] While there is little evidence for a widespread, emperor-sanctioned persecution of all Christians at the time of writing, the exile of John (1:9) and the martyrdom of Antipas (2:13) suggests that, at least, *some* form of persecution had already begun and was expected to increase (see, e.g., 2:10). This marks the worship of God as both a religious and political act.[19]

While it is important to paint a picture of the outside pressures, Revelation also addresses some internal issues among the churches in Asia Minor. Amid looming intensification of persecution, it makes sense that the book begins by addressing these internal issues first, as overcoming them would set the churches up to endure well.[20] Each letter contains an οἶδα ("I know") statement: to the churches in Ephesus, Thyatira, and Philadelphia, Jesus affirms a knowledge of (good) deeds (2:2; 2:19; 3:8); to the church in Smyrna, Jesus expresses knowledge of afflictions and poverty (2:9); to the church in Pergamum, Jesus demonstrates understanding of a difficult context ("where Satan's throne is") and of perseverance in the faith (2:13); to the churches in Sardis and Laodicea, Jesus demonstrates a knowledge of incomplete or sinful deeds (3:1; 3:15). The specific vices entertained by some of these churches and the inflictions suffered by others are not strange to African readers. Churches in Africa are familiar with afflictions and poverty (2:9, 8), persecution (2:13), hypocrisy (3:1), and false teachers who often lead others into idolatry, sexual immorality, and sin (Rev 2:6, 14–15, 20, 24).

There is also a timeless audience to keep in mind when reading Revelation. Like other New Testament writings, its meaning and application survives its historical audience. John identifies the beneficiaries of the Apocalypse as δοῦλοι ("servants") (1:1; 22:6)—a universal group of faithful believers who will one day serve God in the new Eden (22:3). Revelation's central message thus echoes across time and space and should take firm root on African soil. Bitrus Sarma summarizes the effect of Revelation on the contemporary church thus: that believers "may understand [God's] mind concerning the church, the problem of evil, and his final triumph over evil."[21]

Genre and Style

Revelation is essentially a mosaic of genres. Three major literary types emerge. The book begins with the noun, ἀποκάλυψις (1:1), meaning a revelation, disclosure, or unveiling. While John is not necessarily referring to a literary genre here, the content and style of the book aligns closely with a well-known Jewish and Christian genre, which was especially pertinent during the first century, known as apocalyptic writing.[22] Apocalyptic literature is found in the Bible in

18. See Puskas, *Hebrews, the General Letters, and Revelation*, chap. 6.

19. Flemming, *Foretaste of the Future*, 150; see also Allan Aubrey Boesak, *Comfort and Protest: The Apocalypse from a South African Perspective*, repr. ed. (Cascade, 2015).

20. Gordon Fee, *Revelation*, NCCS (Cascade, 2012), 20.

21. Sarma, *Drums of Redemption*, 287.

22. Gorman, *Reading Revelation Responsibly*, 14.

Daniel 7–12 and Mark 13, but also in extrabiblical writings like 1 Enoch, 4 Ezra, Apocalypse of Peter, and Shepherd of Hermas.[23] Other Bible books with apocalyptic features include Isaiah 24–27, Ezekiel 1, 40–48, and Zechariah 9–14.[24] Such writings typically include divine visions, dreams, or supernatural experiences, interpreted and explained by spiritual beings and conveyed to God's people by a chosen seer (see Rev 1:1–2).[25] These visions can be quite spectacular and include mythical or bizarre images and symbolic and cryptic language.[26] Apocalyptic literature often portrays a dualistic battle between good and evil that culminates in a cosmic climax where a decayed world, beyond human intervention, sees good triumph over evil.[27] Such literature is generally produced in times of oppression, distress, or crisis.[28]

The book is also called ἡ προφητεία ("a prophecy"; 1:3; 22:7, 10, 18–19), with John identified as a prophet (22:9; see 10:11). The fact that John heard directly from God,[29] produced writings that called for obedience (1:3; 22:7), used vivid imagery, symbolism, and metaphor, and described the immanence of judgment and deliverance, all remind the reader of the Old Testament prophets.[30] However, readers ought to beware of reducing John's Apocalypse to a mere predictive text. Rather, prophecy is the mediation of God's words of comfort or repentance to a people in a specific time and space.[31] Finally, we see in Revelation features of an ancient letter or epistle. It identifies the author and recipients (1:4), contains a doxology (1:5b–6), and begins and ends with a typical epistolary greeting of grace and peace (1:4–5; see 22:21). Revelation was most probably circulated between the churches and, as was the custom, read aloud in their meetings.

One of the keys to faithful interpretation is leaning into the genre of a text. For Revelation, a few considerations are key. Due to the strong narrative and dramatic[32] style, a devotion to imaginative engagement is key. Revelation seeks to engage the earthly imagination with heavenly realities that lift the gaze to that which is eternal yet unseen—a reversal of realities if you will.[33] It is also important to recognize Revelation's references to the Old Testament. Grant Osborne refers to John's Apocalypse as using "the entire Old Testament as its playground."[34]

---

23. Gorman, *Reading Revelation Responsibly*, 14.

24. Ngundu, "Revelation," 1569.

25. Fee, *Revelation*, 14; Gorman, *Reading Revelation Responsibly*, 14; Osborne, *Revelation*, 11; Johnson, *The Writings of the New Testament*, 535.

26. Puskas, *Hebrews, the General Letters, and Revelation*, chap. 6; Fee, *Revelation*, 14; Gorman, *Reading Revelation Responsibly*, 15.

27. Gorman, *Reading Revelation Responsibly*, 16; Ngundu, "Revelation," 1569; Sarma, *Drums of Redemption*, 287.

28. Sarma, *Drums of Redemption*, 287.

29. Powell, *Introducing the New Testament*, 534.

30. Puskas, *Hebrews, the General Letters, and Revelation*, chap. 6 notes, in particular, parallels to Amos 1:1–2; 1:2–2:8; 4:1–2; 5:1–3; 5:18–20; 6:1–7; 7:1–9; 8:1–3; Isa 3:9–12; 5:8–23; 6; 28:1; 30:1; Ezek 1:5–10; 2:8–33; 24:6–14; 26–27; Mic 2:1–4; Lam 1.

31. Gorman, *Reading Revelation Responsibly*, 23.

32. For a discussion of Revelation's dramatic outline, see Ngundu, "Revelation," 1570–1571.

33. See Osborne, *Revelation*, 11.

34. Osborne, *Revelation*, 24.

Readers ought to be willing to read backwards and not just forward. In the same vein, the reader should avoid looking for chronology. Visions in ancient apocalypses appeared rather "in a concurrent than consecutive manner"[35] and John's layout is arranged topically rather than chronologically.[36] The seven seals, trumpets, and bowls, for instance, dramatize an ever-increasing cycle of judgment and calamity, reminding the reader of intensifying waves in the ocean. Readers should therefore commit to spend an extended time in John's Apocalypse, reading the text many times until the bigger picture emerges. Finally, readers should try to suspend eschatological views when embarking on the journey with John. It is for this reason that this chapter will not engage the various eschatological approaches that readers typically bring to the text when reading Revelation.[37] While it is difficult to escape our taught views of the eschaton, we cannot reduce Revelation to a blueprint for the end of the world.

Outline

While there are as many suggested outlines for John's Apocalypse as there are commentators,[38] I suggest a simplified approach:

Prologue (1:1–3)
Greeting and doxology (1:4–8)
Historic preamble: Encounter with Jesus (1:9–20)
Letters to the churches (2:1–3:22)
The throne room (4:1–5:14)
The unfolding judgment (6:1–20:15)
The New Jerusalem and creation (21:1–22:5)
Epilogue (22:6–21)

The Apocalypse is bookmarked with a prologue (1:1–3) and epilogue (22:12–21). After the prologue, John writes a greeting and doxology (1:4–8), followed by an encounter with Jesus (1:9–20), which serves as a preamble to the letters and further visions. Chapters 2–3 mark the letters to the seven churches. This is followed by the vision of the throne room in chapters 4–5. Chapters 6–20 can be summarized as the circular unfolding of judgment, marked by an ever-increasing presence of evil and intensifying waves of God's wrath. The primary plotting points in the portrayal of wrath and judgment include three sets of seven (the seals [6:1–8:5], trumpets [8:6–11:19], and plagues/bowls [15:1–21]), the introduction of various evil antagonists and their condemnation (the Dragon/Satan [12:1–17; 20:7–10], two beasts [13:1–18; 19:11–21], and Babylon, the harlot [17:1–18; 18:1–24]), the first resurrection (20:1–6), and a

35. Powell, *Introducing the New Testament*, 537.

36. Puskas, *Hebrews, the General Letters, and Revelation*, chap. 6; Osborne, *Revelation*, 26.

37. For discussions of the various views, see Ngundu, "Revelation," 1583; Osborne, *Revelation*, 15; Powell, *Introducing the New Testament*, 537; Sarma, *Drums of Redemption*, 288.

38. For an insightful discussion of Revelation's structure by use of prominent literary devices, see Ernst R. Wendland, "The Hermeneutical Significance of Literary Structure in Revelation," *Neotestamentica* 48, no. 2 (2014): 447–476.

final judgment of the dead (20:11–15). Chapters 6–20 also contain five significant interjections of worship (7:1–7; 10:1–11:14; 14:1–20; 19:1–10; 20:1–6), which pulls the reader back to the heavenly reality portrayed in chapters 4 and 5 and anticipates the climax of worship in the new Jerusalem (21:1–22:5).[39]

Reading Africa with Apocalyptic Eyes

In his recent book *Foretaste of the Future*, Dean Flemming remarks: "Perhaps Majority World (non-Western) Christians can help those of us in the West learn to read Revelation more imaginatively—and more faithfully."[40] The following section demonstrates how an African perspective could facilitate a more faithful reading of Revelation through analogous worldviews, challenges, and situations to that of first-century Christians in Ephesus, Smyrna, Pergamum, Thyatira, Sardis, Philadelphia, and Laodicea. At the same time, a faithful reading of the biblical text will unveil various points of dissonance between a biblical worldview and African beliefs and praxis. Therefore, we shall also delve into Revelation as a comfort and challenge in the face of certain African realities, demonstrating how the text confronts sins on the African continent.

Creative Communication

Revelation was meant to be read out loud while the saints were gathered (1:3; see 22:17, 18). It was thus composed for an oral culture. In Africa, communication is predominantly oral, marked by characteristics like the use of memorable devices and formulas, simplicity, pithy phrases, repetition, relationality, and even combative language. Africans largely prefer concrete rather than abstract expressions, including the use of symbols, metaphors, and proverbs in communication.[41] John often uses ὡς[42] and ὅμοιος[43] ("like"/"similar to") to express what he sees, hears, and experiences in concrete language accessible to him and his readers. Tribulation is concretized in natural phenomena, with angels and beasts unleashing all kinds of ruin upon the earth. Christ's sacrificial death and subsequent exaltation is not explained as in the Philippian Christ Hymn (Phil 2:6–11), but embodied in the singular and memorable image of a slaughtered Lamb on the throne (Rev 5). Other images are used to evoke emotion. The picture of a harlot for Rome would have evoked strong negative emotions. Also, the use of historical figures of the Old Testament to characterize problematic figures working their way into the churches in Asia Minor (2:14, 20) effectively underlines their disfavor in God's eyes.

---

39. Flemming, *Foretaste of the Future*, 120.

40. Flemming, *Foretaste of the Future*, 19.

41. Ezekiel A. Ajibade, *Expository Preaching in Africa: Engaging Orality for Effective Proclamation* (HippoBooks, 2021), 75–82; Ngundu "Revelation," 1569; see Kobus de Smidt, "Hermeneutical Perspectives on the Spirit in the Book of Revelation," *Journal of Pentecostal Theology* 14 (1999): 32.

42. 1:10, 14–16; 2:18; 4:1, 6–7; 6:1, 6, 12–14; 8:8, 10; 9:2–3, 5, 7–9, 17; 10:1; 12:15; 13:2, 11; 14:2; 15:2; 16:3, 13; 18:21; 19:1, 6, 12; 21:2, 11, 21; 22:1.

43. 1:13, 15; 2:18; 4:3, 6–7; 9:7, 10, 19; 11:1; 13:2, 11; 14:14; 21:11, 18.

The book's poetic and dramatic genius also aids memorization, which is important in oral contexts. In the letter to the church in Sardis, Jesus remarks that the church has a reputation (ὄνομα; lit. "name") of being alive, yet they are dead (3:1). Later he acknowledges that there are a few people (ὀνόματα; lit. "names") who have not soiled their clothes (v. 4), and assures them that he will never blot out the overcomer's name (ὄνομα) from the book of life but will acknowledge their name (ὄνομα) before the Father and his angels (v. 5). This stunning play on ὄνομα, reflective of John's literary style of semantic density,[44] concretizes the message with metaphor and emphasizes the contrast between earthly and eternal reputation in a way that hearers can remember and easily retell. The African hearer is well positioned to metabolize such forms of communication and to move the interpretation of Revelation beyond mere decoding into the exploration of what its imagery was meant to *do*—both then and now.

Wonder-Filled Worship

Revelation is a liturgical gold mine, filled with expressions of extravagant, loud, and emotive worship. From waving palms of victory (7:9–10), to an ensemble of worshipers joining in as one (7:11–12), to worship that continues "day and night" (7:15), Revelation's expressions of worship are emotive and participatory. Worshippers express their adoration verbally and physically with acts like the casting of crowns, singing (4:11; 5:9, 13–14), offering sacrifices (5:8), falling on their faces (7:11; 11:16), and even shouting (19:1, 3, 6). The variety of worshipers is also key. Not only do we find the twenty-four elders, representing Israel and the twelve apostles (i.e., God's people), but we also find the four living creatures (representing all creation) worshiping God and the Lamb.[45] The music coming from heaven is dynamic. John compares the music and singing from the 144,000 to the sound of many waters and loud thunder (14:3; see 19:6). Revelation thus acknowledges that authentic God-honoring worship can be expressed in a myriad of ways and that the body is not removed from it. As a holistic and communal people, Africans are naturally inclined to expressions that are exuberant, emotive, and participatory.[46] However, due to the impact of Western missionary work, many African churches have inherited Western worship practices and have done away with African expressions of song and dance as these were historically associated with paganism.[47] African expressions of music

44. Semantic density refers to the literary phenomenon where an author activates more than one meaning or implication through a single use of a word or expression. A good example of this is double entendre, where a specific word holds two possible meanings—both of which affirm or strengthen the overall argument that the author is making.

45. Ngundu, "Revelation," 1581.

46. Wanderi Jessee, "Advocacy for Contextualization of Christian Worship in Africa," *African Musicology Online* 9, no. 2 (2019): 108.

47. Jessee, "Advocacy for Contextualization of Christian Worship," 114–116. While Jessee holds that "the gospel of Jesus Christ must remain pure in every culture but at the same time clothed with indigenous garments" (127), he glances over the fact that not all African expressions of music are religiously neutral and that uncritical continuation of all practices emanating from African Traditional Religion is dangerous. This chapter argues for the adoption of a style of music-making and adoration unto God with the provision that anything at odds with the biblical witness should be done away with.

are marked by, among other things, a variety of instruments, a preference for polyphony (the singing of two of more parts simultaneously) or polyrhythm (the simultaneous combination of two or more rhythms), percussion, variation and improvisation, and dance.[48] Revelation's portrayal of exuberant, full-body worship invites believers in Africa to embrace a worship of God that involves voice, body, rhythm, and community and affirms wonder-filled worship as biblical. Africans are thus invited to embrace a worship style that "clothes the gospel with native idioms, a presentation that is identifiable and associable."[49]

The worship seen (and heard) in Revelation is not just beautiful and expressive—the songs sung arm its hearers with a "counter-imagination"[50]—but also a lens which visually transports them from the current reality to the reality where God reigns and where all other powers are subject to the Enthroned One. Addressing God as Lord God Almighty (1:8; 4:8; 11:17; 15:3; 16:7, 14; 19:6, 15; 21:22) was a daring and politically loaded statement for the first recipients.[51] It explicitly affirmed God as a ruler superior to the emperor. The call remains for Africans to formulate worship songs that address God as the one deserving ultimate allegiance. Using contemporary affirmations, like God as the one who lifts curses, who rules over nature, and who protects his children, are ways to push back against the claims made by those who worship and venerate other deities. This brings us to a central theme in John's Apocalypse, namely, the sovereignty of God.

God's Sovereignty

One cannot speak of African cosmology without acknowledging the active and pervasive role that fear plays. Kelvin Onongha explains:

> This fear derives from the consciousness of a cosmos pregnant with spiritual agencies in which humans are pawns. . . . Because of the pain, misery, misfortune, and death that divinities, ancestors, enemies, and demons can cause, life for the African must be lived carefully so as not to antagonize any of these agencies.[52]

The above quote aptly demonstrates one of the pertinent struggles that Africans face when coming to faith in Christ. While most Westerners see salvation as pledging a new allegiance, for Africans, it is a change of allegiance from existing and powerful masters to a new Lord. Hence, many African salvation prayers contain a renunciation of other deities and powers. With this change in allegiance, the question around sufficiency remains pertinent. Is God able to sufficiently protect, provide, commune, control, and communicate? As Africans grapple

48. Jessee, "Advocacy for Contextualization of Christian Worship," 122–123.

49. Jessee, "Advocacy for Contextualization of Christian Worship," 119.

50. Flemming, *Foretaste of the Future*, 155.

51. For a discussion of the importance of song amid times of oppression, see Boesak, *Comfort and Protest*, 60–61.

52. Kelvin Onongha, "The African Worldview and Belief in the Demonic," *Journal of Adventist Mission Studies* 18, no. 1 (2023): 41.

with needs previously met by human agents, spirits, and ancestors, many wrestle with a heightened fear of the demonic—often exceeding the fear of God.[53]

Analogously, the churches in Ephesus found themselves in a spiritual cosmopolitan. Appeasing the right deities was believed to be essential for life, protection, and prosperity. In addition to the political and economic implications, believers also grappled with the spiritual effects of turning their backs on the deities formerly worshiped. In light of such an existential crisis, John's Apocalypse proffers a well-developed view of a sovereign God. The most prominent title used for God in Revelation is ὁ παντοκράτωρ ("the Almighty"; 1:8; 4:8; 11:17; 15:3; 16:7, 14; 19:6, 15; 21:22). The term signals a rule and reign over everything, denoting an all-powerful and omnipotent ruler.[54] It is always used with κύριος ὁ θεὸς (Lord God),[55] signaling God's rule and divinity.

John also refers to God as the One seated on the throne (4:2–3, 9–10; 5:1, 7, 13; 6:16; 7:10–11, 15; 19:4–5; 20:11–12; 21:5)[56]—a description even used by those under his judgment (6:16). Unlike the beast's throne, which is destroyed when the angel pours out his bowl on it (16:10), God's throne is everlasting and present in the redeemed and eternal garden (22:1, 3). God is thus portrayed as eternal and all-encompassing. In the throne room, John recalls hearing every creature singing eternal praise, glory, and power to the One on the throne and the Lamb. These creatures are in heaven, on the earth, under the earth, on the sea, and in the sea (5:13). This broad description of locations underlines the all-encompassing nature of the worshipers of God. Creatures in every imaginable location acknowledge and adore him.

Finally, God's eternity is underlined by descriptions like "he who is, and he who was, and he who is coming" (1:4) and God's self-description, τὸ ἄλφα καὶ τὸ ὦ ("the Alpha and Omega"; 1:8; 21:6; see also 22:13), the bookends of the Greek alphabet. Not only does the book of Revelation "bookend" the divine narrative with a return to the restored garden (22:1–5), but God himself serves as the bookends of history. He was the first and will be the last. There is but a limited time for evil to reign on the earth (11:18; 12:12). Even the binding and release of Satan affirm the sovereignty of God. He is bound for a thousand years—a number signifying completeness.[57] This heralds that the period of Satan's binding has been predetermined by God and is occurring under his sovereign control. Likewise, Satan's release in 20:7–8 is no accident, but occurs under the sovereignty of God, who ultimately casts Satan into the lake of burning sulfur (20:10). This attention to detail where times and periods are concerned points to God being in absolute control. Such a reality should serve both as a comfort and a warning to Africans. While fear of deities formerly worshiped or venerated might drive believers back into the arms of these powers or beings (or at least result in to syncretistic practices), the comfort is that their rule or influence is temporary. God's rule, however, is eternal and all-encompassing:

53. Onongha, "The African Worldview," 41.

54. BDAG, 755.

55. With the exception of 16:14 and 19:15 where κύριος (Lord) is left out.

56. Implied in 1:4; 3:21; 5:6, 11; 7:9, 17; 8:3; 12:5; 14:3; 16:7; 21:3; 22:1, 3.

57. Ngundu, "Revelation," 1600.

a comfort to Christians who are tempted to seek cover elsewhere and a stark warning that the spiritual covering of other beings and powers is a hollow reassurance.

The Supreme Son and Spirit

While it is not difficult for Africans to accept the ultimate rule of a sovereign creator, traditional worldviews often result in a fragmented Trinity, with the Son and Spirit being afforded lesser-than status. In contrast, the primacy of Christ, as well as the cooperation between Father, Son, and Spirit is emphasized through John's Apocalypse. Jesus's inclusion in the doxological formula in 1:4–5 marks him as part of the Godhead as he functions as sender of grace and peace alongside the Father and Spirit. In this initial introduction, Jesus is referred to as the faithful witness, the firstborn of the dead, and the ruler of the kings of the earth. The emphasis on his victory over death (see also 1:18; 2:8) and all earthly powers doubly secures the reader. Not only does it strengthen believers in the light of persecution and unjust earthly rule, but it secures them eternally, reminding them that spiritual powers and agents of death have been overcome by Jesus.

Revelation contains three prominent descriptions of Jesus: One like the Son of Man, the Lamb, and the conqueror on the white horse. The first is introduced in John's encounter with the Christ in 1:12–20. This description reminds the reader of the divine figure in human form encountered by the prophet Daniel (Dan 10:5–6). John sees Jesus dressed in a long robe with a golden sash (Rev 1:13), an image that points to wealth. Long robes were generally reserved for the elite and Jesus wears a golden sash rather than a belt. The latter was used to elevate the tunic for hard work, while the former signified high status.[58] The description of his hair as white as wool and snow (Rev 1:14) connects him to the Ancient of Days (Dan 7:9), again underscoring his divinity. His blazing eyes (v. 14) emphasize Jesus as all-seeing, while his feet like burnished, refined bronze emphasize purity and stability. Finally, his voice like the sound of many waters (v. 15) demonstrates that his word cannot be drowned out by the chaos that has been unleashed on the earth.[59] He holds seven stars in his right hand (v. 16), marking him as cosmic ruler, and a sharp, double-edged sword comes out of his mouth (v. 16). This sword characterizes Christ as one who wars and conquers through his testimony. Finally, when Jesus speaks, he describes himself as the first and last (v. 17) and the one who overcame death, and the one holding the keys of death and Hades (v. 18).

The second striking image is that of the Lamb. After John describes the scene in heaven and the exuberant worship of the Enthroned One (Rev 4), the Lamb enters as the only one worthy to open the scroll and break its seven seals (5:5–6). He is positioned at the center of the throne, carrying absolute power and authority represented by seven horns, and is described as all-seeing and wise with the Holy Spirit as his eyes. Upon taking the scroll from the Enthroned One, the worship of the Father is seamlessly transferred to the Lamb (5:8). By falling down

58. James L. Resseguie, "One Like a Son of Man (1:12–20)," in *The Revelation of John: A Narrative Commentary* (Baker, 2009), 74–82.

59. Resseguie, "One Like a Son of Man (1:12–20)."

before the Lamb and worshiping him, the living creatures and elders signal that he is none other than God. Finally, the angels also join in and worship him (5:11). The authority of the Lamb is even recognized on earth, with the nations fearing his wrath (6:16–17).

Ultimately, Jesus comes as the divine warrior on the white horse in 19:11–21. This image connects to the one in 1:12–20 in many ways, with changes that signal military triumph. He now has many diadems on his head and his robe is dipped in blood (v. 12). Again, the sword in his mouth is mentioned, but this time John specifies that it is used to strike down the nations, which he will rule with an iron rod (v. 15). He also comes to judge (vv. 11, 15). In ancient Rome, the victorious general would ride a white horse through the defeated area. Here, Jesus comes down from heaven on the horse *before* the battle. This, in a way, preempts his victory before the final battle. In anticipation of this victory, he bears the name, King of kings and Lord of lords (19:16). This signifies the ultimate culmination of his reign and echoes his exuberant introduction in the doxological formula (1:5).

These three images work together to paint the picture of a uniquely divine person, equal in authority to God. Jesus's absolute rule, his victory over death, and his judgments elevate him above all earthly and spiritual powers, including angels, demons, and ancestors. This comes as a challenge to those who hold that there is a seamless continuity between African Traditional Religion's acknowledgment of a supreme being and the Christian faith. Allegiance to the Son, who is supreme and an acknowledgment of his unique and sufficient sacrifice necessitates discontinuity with African Traditional Religion beliefs and practices. This drum was repeatedly beaten by Byang Kato, the father of evangelicalism in Africa, who argued that a continuity with African Traditional Religion undermined the supremacy and divinity of Jesus Christ.[60] In Revelation, Jesus shares the throne with the Father (3:21; 5:6; 7:17; 22:1, 3), both are called Alpha and Omega (1:8; 21:6; 22:13) and the beginning and the end (21:6; 22:13), both of them reign (1:5; 11:15; 22:5), receive prayers (5:8; 8:3–4) and worship (5:9–14; 7:10; 22:3), and, finally, both of them pour out judgment (2:5, 16; 6:16–17; 14:14, 17–20; 19:15).[61]

Revelation's high view of the Holy Spirit is also significant. While not particularly known for its emphasis on the Spirit, Revelation paints a remarkable portrait of a sufficient and supreme Spirit as a worthy member of the Trinity. Unlike other New Testament books, Revelation refers to the Holy Spirit as τὰ ἑπτὰ πνεύματα ("the Seven Spirits," sometimes translated as "the Seven-fold Spirit"; 1:12; 3:1; 4:5; 5:6). The number seven represents fullness, wholeness, and divine perfection. This numerical value illustrates the Spirit's sufficiency as an empowering agent for the church.[62] The Spirit is also included in the doxological formula in Rev 1:4, wedged between the Father and Son, marking him as a worthy member of the Godhead, a co-sender of the apostolic message to John, and perfectly united with the Father and Son. We

60. Aiah Dorkuh Foday-Khabenje, *Byang Karo: The Life and Legacy of Africa's Pioneer Evangelical Theologian* (Langham Monographs, 2023), 11.

61. See Flemming, *Foretaste of the Future*, 61, for a comprehensive list of similarities between the Father and the Lamb. I have mentioned a few discussed by Flemming.

62. See Sarma, *Drums of Redemption*, 290.

encounter a perfect duet between the Son and Spirit in the letters to the churches, signifying the cooperation in the Godhead. While Jesus is initially identified as the speaker, the message to each church ends with the formula, "Let anyone who has an ear listen to what the Spirit is saying to the churches" (2:7, 11, 17, 29; 3:6, 13, 22). Finally, as the Lamb stands at the center of the throne, the Spirit, who is described as his seven eyes (5:6), occupies the throne with him. John thus sees a reigning, sufficient, and all-seeing spirit. This implies that all our spiritual needs—including communication with the divine, protection, and empowerment for life and ministry—are met in the person of the Holy Spirit, which rules out the need to consult or engage any other spirit or medium.

Evil Exists

While Revelation fixes the gaze on the triune God, its portrayal of evil holds particular utility for Africans. African spirituality is holistic: What happens in the natural is necessarily linked to the supernatural. This applies to both good and evil. That is why, for many Africans, fear is more readily evoked by the unseen than by the seen.[63] This is bolstered by a high view of causation which implies that, for every evil event, there must be an evil power behind it. The powers behind illnesses, calamity, and death include curses, the evil eye, and the use of *juju* (witchcraft).[64] However, in African Traditional Religions, evil is defined pragmatically/functionaly rather than ontologically. This means that something is judged to be evil when it disrupts the cosmic order. Spirits can, therefore, be either good or evil, depending on one's standing with them. When they cause calamity, they are deemed evil.[65] John's portrayal of evil challenges such a pragmatic view, most prominently in his portrayal of Satan as an ontologically evil person. He is vividly portrayed as a dragon (12:3, 4, 7, 9, 13, 16; 13:1–2, 4, 11; 16:13; 20:2) and serpent (12:9, 14–15; 20:2), and his destructive role in the lives of the world (12:9; 20:8) and saints (2:10; 12:9b, 10, 17) is acknowledged.

Satan's work is accomplished by a selection of agents. In Revelation 13, John introduces two evil beasts. These beasts, especially the one from the sea, harken back to Daniel's four beasts (Dan 7:2–27). While it makes good sense to identify the first beast as representing a political empire (Rome, but also godless empires beyond it), and the second beast as a powerful earthly figure, their Satanic origins cannot be ignored. The first beast is given authority by the dragon, meaning that the corrupt and violent rulers and systems represented are appointed or tasked by Satan himself (13:2–3). The second beast (the land beast) is given authority by the first, again signifying an indirect commissioning by Satan. Even persecution is portrayed in Satanic language, with Jesus warning the saints in Smyrna that the devil will soon have some of them imprisoned (2:10).

---

63. Onongha, "The African Worldview," 38.

64. Onongha, "The African Worldview," 42.

65. Pius Mosima, "African Approaches to God, Death, and the Problem of Evil: Some Anthropological Lessons Towards an Intercultural Philosophy of Religion," *Filosofia Theoretica: Journal of African Philosophy, Culture and Religions* 11, no. 4 (2022): 162–164.

John's Apocalypse thus illuminates a world where evil is no abstract sentiment—it emanates from the person of Satan, who appoints and sends evil entities to harass the saints and deceive the world. In light of the oft pragmatic evaluation of good and evil among Africans, Revelation's portrayal of Satan and his minions as ontologically evil and opposed to God is striking. It leaves no room for solidarity with the devil and his agents, even if breaking allegiance with them seemingly threatens cosmic peace. In light of this, God's eternal victory is important. The temporality and final demise of Satan and his agents is sharply contrasted to the eternal victory of the Enthroned One and the Lamb. Whilst not describing the battle at Armageddon in detail, John recounts the end where the beast and the false prophet are cast into the fiery lake of burning sulfur (19:20). Finally, the biblical narrative comes full circle with Satan, the ancient serpent and instigator of rebellion against God in Genesis 3, being thrown into the abyss, bound for the time that God has intended (20:1–3), and then being cast into the lake of burning sulfur for eternal torment (20:10). In comparison to the short-lived rule of some of the antagonists (e.g., the first beast's rule of forty-two in 13:5, with his throne being destroyed in 16:10), God's reign in the City of God is eternal (22:5). This marks the finality of the battle between good and evil, which is not a fight between two equals but God's victory over evil.[66]

Finally, one of the most prominent themes in Revelation is that of overcoming (Rev 2:7, 11, 17, 26; 3:5, 12, 21; 21:7; 5:5; 12:11; 15:2; 17:14; 21:7). To a first-century audience, *νικάω* ("I overcome") denoted military triumph. This is fortified by the language of war or battle employed in John's Apocalypse. In military language, Christ defeats evil through a victory won on the cross[67]—a strategy vastly different from that employed by earthly rulers. The church participates in this war, not through violence, but through faithful witness, the blood of the Lamb, and a self-sacrificial devotion (12:11).[68] God's holy warriors "follow the Lamb wherever he goes" (14:4). Part of the journey of the Lamb is the cross.[69] Osborne reminds us that this implies that the "great end-time victory over the powers of evil is not Armageddon but the cross."[70] Revelation thus acknowledges the unseen and the reality of evil, but emphasizes that fear need not lead to spiritual compromise. Through allegiance to the slain and reigning Lamb, Christian Africans have secured for themselves an eternal, spiritual victory. However, such a victory does not guarantee a life free from pressure and persecution.

Pressure and Persecution

According to the 2024 Open Doors World Watch List,[71] the persecution of Christians has seen a dramatic increase worldwide, notably in Africa. Twenty of the top fifty countries for

66. See Osborne, *Revelation*, 31.

67. Osborne, *Revelation*, 34.

68. Flemming, *Foretaste of the Future*, 53.

69. Flemming, *Foretaste of the Future*, 70.

70. Osborne, *Revelation*, 32.

71. "World Watch List 2024," Open Doors, accessed April 29, 2024, https://www.opendoors.org.za/christian-persecution/world-watch-list-2024.

persecution of Christians are on the African continent. While there is not sufficient proof of a widespread, state-sanctioned persecution of Christians in late first-century Ephesus, Smyrna, Pergamum, Thyatira, Sardis, Philadelphia, and Laodicea, John's audience certainly tasted persecution and were acutely aware of more to come. John introduces himself as a συγκοινωνός ("partner, co-sharer") in θλῖψις ("oppression, affliction, tribulation"), βασιλεία ("kingdom"), and ὑπομονή ("patient endurance") in Jesus (1:9). The relationship between author and audience thus hinges on a paradox of internal and inflicted suffering *and* the reign of God, signifying that for John and his hearers, these go hand in hand. Similarly, the word of God and the testimony of Jesus is both that which John boldly proclaims and that which causes his imprisonment on Patmos (1:9), the slaughtering of the martyrs (6:9), and the beheading of the faithful (20:4). Clearly, faithful witnessing most definitely leads to suffering and persecution, as was predicted by Jesus (Matt 5:1–12; 10:16–23, 34–36; Mark 10:29–30; Luke 6:26; 23:28–31), and as is the reality for millions of Christians in Africa.

So, what encouragement does the book of Revelation offer to Christian Africans and others who are persecuted for their faith? John's visions affirm that God sees such suffering and that there will be a determined time for relief. In 6:9–10, the martyrs cry out for justice and are heard, but the vengeance of their blood is delayed until their number is completed (6:11). Martyrs are again mentioned in 13:15 as those who refused to worship the beast, in 18:24 as those who were killed on the earth, and in 20:4 as those beheaded. John does not theologize about their suffering.[72] The consolation is that God knows, is sovereign, and will avenge their blood at the determined time. Additionally, the image of the slain Lamb, called the Lion of the tribe of Judah, with the seven horns in Revelation 5, demonstrates the paradox of one who has overcome by martyrdom through his atoning death. Osborne thus argues that Christ's victory is duplicated in his followers "in their own suffering and death as witness to Christ."[73]

Not only is persecution on the rise, but many Africans today suffer under grave corruption and misappropriations of power. A quick glance at the tenth Global Corruption Barometer Africa (2019) reveals the severity of the situation across thirty-five African countries. The study found that more than 25 percent of participants paid a bribe in order to access basic public services like education and health care in the preceding year. The prevalence of corruption especially impacts the economically vulnerable.[74] Topping the list for the most corrupt are the police and government officials—those who should be prioritizing justice and protection for their citizens.[75] What Revelation does is to lift the veil on corrupt systems of power and to expose them for what they truly are. In a sober evaluation, John acknowledges Satan and his agents' power and influence on the earth. The dragon, representing Satan, is introduced as having seven crowned heads and ten horns (12:3), signifying authority and rule. Likewise,

72. Ngundu, "Revelation," 1584.

73. Osborne, *Revelation*, 34.

74. Coralie Pring and Jon Vrushi, *Global Corruption Barometer Africa 2019: Citizens' Views and Experiences of Corruption* (Transparency International; Afrobarometer, 2019), 3, https://images.transparencycdn.org/images/2019_GCB_Africa3.pdf.

75. Pring and Vrushi, *Global Corruption Barometer Africa*, 4.

the first beast has seven heads and ten crowned horns (13:1), likely emphasizing military power.[76] He receives a throne and great authority over all people from the dragon (13:2, 7). He is followed by the inhabitants of the earth (13:3) and even worshipped (13:4, 8), with his military powers affirmed by all the peoples. The beast's reign involves the conquering of God's holy people (13:7). The second beast exercises the authority of the first (13:11) and is given great economic control, so much so that those who do not receive the mark of the beast cannot buy or sell (13:17–18). He also kills those who refuse to worship the image of the first beast, signaling political and military power (13:15). Powerful as they are, John's visions emphasize the temporality of their rule (e.g., 13:5) and their ultimate destruction (20:10).

Another apt example is the portrayal of Babylon, the harlot. To the ancient audience, this woman probably represented Rome: powerful and rich.[77] Her power, authority, and great wealth is acknowledged. She is called great and sits on many waters (17:1), representing her influence over peoples, masses, nations, and tongues (17:15). She wears purple, signifying rule, and is adorned with gold, precious stones, and pearls (17:4). Intoxicated by the blood of the martyrs (17:6), she rules over the kings of the earth (17:18) and corrupts the earth (19:2). As with the dragon and the two beasts, John paints a sober picture of her power, authority, and influence. She is not portrayed as weak or insignificant. However, in a lifting of the veil, she is described as a drunken harlot (17:1, 5, 15–16; 19:2) and the temporary nature of her reign is amplified by the imminent judgment that awaits her (14:8; 16:19; 17:1, 15–16; 18:10, 16, 18–19, 21). Her fall will be swift (18:10, 19) and final (18:21). So also with the ten evil kings who are given authority for one hour (17:12), with a seventh king reigning for "a little while" (17:10).

For those who endure oppression and persecution, Revelation reveals heaven's perspective, providing the downtrodden with "the language and literature of resistance."[78] When Babylon falls, the kings of the earth (18:9–10), the merchants (18:11–17a), and the sea captains (18:17b–20) all mourn for her. These weep as they are brought down (18:9–10, 15, 17–19). Yet, heaven erupts into choruses of praise (19:1–5). God's people then follow, exclaiming that the Lord God Almighty reigns (19:6). Whether it be violent persecution as in Eritrea and northern Nigeria, legacies of dictatorship as in Mali and Niger, oppression of certain people groups like we saw under South Africa's apartheid regime, or corruption like that currently plaguing Somalia and South Sudan, Revelation reminds us that God does not side with oppressive powers and that heaven will have the final say. Without glorifying or idolizing suffering, John's Apocalypse is a word of encouragement to persecuted and oppressed Christians, but it is also more than that. It speaks both to the crushed and confident, the poor and the proud, the persecuted and powerful. Jesus encourages the churches to remain faithful witnesses amid suffering, persecution, *and* temptation (2:1–3:22).[79] One of these temptations is the allure of prosperity.

76. Osborne, *Revelation*, 221.

77. Sarma, *Drums of Redemption*, 289.

78. Gorman, *Reading Revelation Responsibly*, 38.

79. Sarma, *Drums of Redemption*, 290.

Problematizing the Pursuit of Prosperity

In a context that can be described as predominantly occupied with the present, Africans often gravitate toward views of salvation that translate to prosperity, safety, and health in this life.[80] Revelation's upside-down reality speaks loudly into the area of prosperity and its pursuit. As faithful believers in first-century Asia Minor found themselves on the margins of society, it was important for God to lift the veil on the systems of power and wealth and reveal to the churches in Ephesus where they truly stand with him.

Jesus quotes the Laodicean church boasting that they are rich and need nothing (3:17). When one considers the fronting of the objects in the Greek text, a translation that captures the boastfulness of the congregation would be, "*rich* I am . . . *nothing* I need." Jesus's response launches with the emphatic σὺ ("*you* are wretched and pitiable and poor and blind and naked"),[81] emphasizing the contrast between how they have perceived their state and how it truly is. The flipside of the coin is offered to the church in Smyrna as an encouragement. Jesus affirms that he knows of their afflictions and their poverty, but immediately adds, ἀλλὰ πλούσιος εἶ ("but *rich* you are"; 2:9).[82] The fronting of the adjective πλούσιος ("rich") emphasizes the contrast between how they are perceived in a material sense and how they are eternally perceived by God. Such an emphatic reversal of conditions should be at the forefront of the minds of Africans as we navigate our emphasis on wealth.

Wealth and prosperity are not signs of God's blessing, nor is poverty a sign of sin or God's curse, as proponents of the prosperity gospel tend to teach. The detestable characters in Revelation are overwhelmingly adorned in wealthy garb. The harlot described in chapter 17 is clothed in purple and scarlet and adorned with gold, precious stones, and pearls (v. 4). Ironically, the golden cup in her hand is filled with detestable things and the uncleanness of her immorality. This imagery harkens back to Ezekiel's condemnation of Tyre (Ezek 28:1–19), a wealthy nation that grew in prosperity by trading with other nations. Clearly, the wealth of the woman was not a result of the blessing of God; it was wealth generated by the power of the beast, mainly through exploitation.[83] The prophet foretells how her prosperity will be turned into destruction (vv. 18–19).[84] Likewise when Babylon the great falls, the city is judged because of her adulteries, excessive luxuries, and boasts (18:3, 7, 9), and God's people are told to come out of her (v. 4). This image reaches beyond the political. For a continent with some of the poorest church members, Africa boasts with a of the wealthiest church leaders.[85] The prosperity gospel ironically flourishes in the poorest areas on our continent.[86] In these contexts, wealthy church leaders exploit the hope of a more prosperous future and encourage church

80. See Onongha, "The African Worldview," 38.

81. My translation.

82. My translation, emphasis mine.

83. Boesak, *Comfort and Protest*, 110.

84. Ngundu, "Revelation," 1596.

85. Thinandavha D. Mashau and Mookgo S. Kgatle, "Prosperity Gospel and the Culture of Greed in Post-Colonial Africa: Constructing an Alternative African Christian Theology of Ubuntu," *Verbum et Ecclesia* 40, no. 1 (2019): 3.

86. Mashau and Kgatle, "Prosperity Gospel and the Culture of Greed," 3.

members to give sacrificially while lining their own pockets with the offerings. The image of the harlot enriching herself through the exploitation of others is apt and should serve as a warning to those who exploit God's people for gain.

However, God's judgments are not limited to the rich. John describes both rich and poor, slave and free, crying out for the mountains to befall them (6:15–17). The temptation to receive the mark of the beast is directed at both small and great, with John again specifying rich, poor, free, and slave (13:16). Finally, judgment befalls both μεγάλοι ("great/significant") and μικροί ("small/insignificant") (11:18, 19:18, 20:12), with the powerful (kings, military leaders, the strong, horses and their riders) being mentioned first in 19:18. Moreover, the rich are not condemned *because* of their wealth. They are condemned because they have exploited others and have boasted in their wealth (18:14, 17). The nations are described as fallen due to Babylon's wine of *immoral* passion, the kings of the earth as those who *committed adultery* with her, and the merchants as those enriched by the *power of her sensuality* (18:3). In essence, Babylon's wealth is correlated to her sins (18:5–7). One therefore ought to be careful of formulating an anti-wealth and anti-power theology from Revelation. The new Jerusalem is described in all her splendor and majesty (21:18–21) and the kings of the earth are seen bringing their glory into her (21:24–26).[87] Revelation thus reminds us that all valuable goods belong to God.

Intriguing Idolatry

With a worldview that acknowledges the reality of the spiritual world, Africans are prone to seeking power in their religious endeavors. Whether for protection or for the sake of ambitions—primarily ones related to money and position—the pressures to consult with spiritual forces are ongoing.[88] Tradition and culture also play a role. Many Africans are expected to participate in ancestor worship/veneration and other pagan rituals by the head of their household, and opting out of such practices can thwart cultural and familial belonging.[89] Analogously, fear, desperation, and cultural expectations were driving forces in the first century, strengthening the allure of idolatry. Emperor worship had infiltrated the culture, essentially representing "a grassroots movement."[90] Participation in the emperor cult not only secured one politically, socially, and economically, but it was also believed to facilitate peace with various gods. It was thus important "to maintain the world order."[91] This was amplified by the competition between cities to demonstrate superiority over one another in emperor worship and devotion to Rome. All social and public gatherings were regarded as opportunities to honor pagan deities and the Roman emperor. Christians opting out of such practices were branded as unpatriotic and disloyal to the empire. No doubt such pressure infiltrated

87. Cf. Rev 17:4, where the people of God are told to "come out of" Babylon.

88. Onongha, "The African Worldview," 39.

89. Ngundu, "Revelation," 1577.

90. Flemming, *Foretaste of the Future*, 28.

91. Flemming, *Foretaste of the Future*, 154.

the church, with the temptation of allegiance bolstered by the need for social acceptance and belonging in wider society.

In Revelation 14:6–7 John witnesses an angel flying in midheaven and proclaiming an eternal gospel to the inhabitants of the earth. The message proclaimed to each nation, tribe, tongue, and people is, "Fear God and give him glory, for the hour of his judgment has come; and worship him who made heaven and earth, the sea and the springs of water" (14:7). The gospel proclaimed here is marked by three imperatives: φοβήθητε ("fear"), δότε [δόξαν] ("give [glory]"), and προσκυνήσατε ("worship"). These actions signify repentance and allegiance. The question of whom to fear, whom to glorify, and whom to worship resounds through Revelation, with hearers constantly having to choose between God or the enemy.

For Africans, who often resort to powerful people (e.g., divine healers, witches, shamans, diviners) or beings for help,[92] this denial of neutrality is significant. There are no neutral beings in the book of Revelation, nor are there neutral people. Unbelievers are those who actively *worship* the beast (see Rev 5:9–14; 13:4, 12–15; 14:9, 11; 20:4). To emphasize this, various counterfeits function in contrast to God and his agents. Jesus is honored for being the resurrected one (1:5, 18); likewise, the beast out of the sea is healed from his mortal wound, causing the world to marvel and follow him (13:3) and worship the dragon (13:4); both Jesus and the beast have their names inscribed on their followers (13:16–14:1), both have horns (5:6; 13:1), and are given authority over nations, tribes, languages, and rulers (see 1:5; 7:9; 13:7; 17:12). The second beast also has horns like a lamb (13:11) and performs great signs that lead the world astray (13:13; so also the false prophet in 19:20). What Revelation reminds its hearers is that all spiritual and powerful practices either emanate from God or from the Beast. Onongha points to pragmatism as a central feature of African identity. Whether it is going to a witch doctor or consulting demonic spirits, when a miracle has occurred, the consensus is that it must be good.[93] Revelation warns against such views, unmasking Satan and his evil agents at work in powerful and alluring ways.

Additionally, John's interactions with angels underscore the importance of reserving worship for God alone. Twice, John falls at the feet of an angel to worship and is rebuked for it (19:10; 22:9). In both cases the angel calls himself a σύνδουλος (fellow servant) and, in a command that fronts the Name of God for emphasis, he urges John, τῷ θεῷ προσκύνησον ("*God* [you must] worship"). This is noteworthy since angels are given incredible authority in John's Apocalypse (see 18:1). They control, summon, or affect creation (often in God's judgment) (7:1–2; 8:5–8, 10, 12; 9:1, 13–14; 16:2–5, 8, 10, 12; 18:21; 19:17), take life (9:15), fight against the dragon and his angels (12:7), proclaim the gospel and God's judgments (14:6–17), summon the reaping of the righteous (14:15–16) and the condemned (14:18), reap the unrighteous (14:19–20), and one holds the key to the abyss (20:1). These are powerful and privileged beings; yet, they are not given the privilege of being deified or worshiped. Likewise, idolatry is never an option for Christian Africans—neither for protection, provision, nor cultural participation.

92. Onongha, "The African Worldview," 37.

93. Onongha, "The African Worldview," 39–40.

Diversity as Divine

Many African countries have a complicated ethnic history. Whether it be wounds inflicted by colonization, ethnic war, and tribalism, or dehumanizing policies like that of apartheid in South Africa, the scars of ethnic strife are glaringly visible—even on the body of Christ. The church has also not been innocent in the affliction of racial and ethnic hurts. In South Africa, the segregation of people by race was a Dutch Reformed Church policy before it became a political policy, and the same church was instrumental in defending the apartheid regime—even theologically.[94] In sharp contrast to the aforementioned ills, John employs a fourfold description of people as coming from every tribe (φυλή), language (γλῶσσα), people group (λαός), and nation (ἔθνος). A combination of these fourfold characteristics is used to describe the faithful (5:9; 7:9), as well as the recipients of the gospel (14:6).[95] The Lamb is proclaimed as worthy by the four living creatures and twenty-four elders because he was slain and has purchased for God saints "from every tribe and language and people and nation" (5:9). This fourfold formula emphasizes the all-encompassing power of the gospel and hints at the fulfillment of the Abrahamic promise of God blessing all nations (Gen 12:3b). The song continues, "you have made them to be a kingdom and priests serving our God, and they will reign on earth" (Rev 5:10). Here, the language harkens back to Exodus 19:6, where, through Moses, God assures Israel that they will be his treasured possession, chosen to be separate. In a powerful and radical expansion, people from every tribe, language, person group, and nation are now included in this call to be set apart.

A similar expansion from homogeneity to diversity is seen in Revelation 7. John recounts the sealing of the 144,000—twelve thousand from each tribe of Israel. Flemming argues that the great multitude described in Revelation 7:9–17 is the same group as the sealed 144,000 in 7:1–8. The 144,000 represents the afflicted church—the restored Israel—receiving the divine seal in the face of suffering and tribulation, while the great multitude is the victorious church "after"—the heavenly church.[96] In this way, the great multitude again demonstrates the fulfillment of the Abrahamic promise. The ethnic veil is thus torn, as God's people are revealed to be profoundly diverse, yet holy (separate) as a collective. Finally, before the condemnation of Babylon is pronounced (14:8), John hears the eternal gospel proclaimed to this fourfold group (14:6), undergirding that God pursues across ethnic lines. This is further affirmed by the reference to God's benevolence to τὰ ἔθνη ("the nations") (15:3–4; 21:24–26; 22:2). Diversity also exceeds the ethnic. After the blowing of the seventh trumpet, the twenty-four elders worship God, declaring a time for God to reward the holy ones who fear his name (11:18). This group is fleshed out as both μικροί ("small") and μεγάλοι ("great"). Likewise, after the demise of Babylon, God's servants are called to praise him (19:5), with the voice from the throne

94. Boesak, *Comfort and Protest*, 104–105.

95. It is unclear whether the reference in 10:11, which uses βασιλεῖς used instead of φυλή refers to recipients of the gospel or judgment.

96. Dean Flemming, "Following the Lamb Wherever He Goes: Missional Ecclesiology in Revelation 7 and 14:1–5," in *Cruciform Scripture: Cross, Participation, and Mission*, ed. Christopher J. Skinner, Nijay K. Gupta, Andy Johnson, and Drew J. Strait (Eerdmans, 2021), 442.

specifying that both small and great should do so. Revelation thus paints a portrait of God's glory and Christ's salvific acts being fulfilled among a set-apart people who look and sound nothing alike. With its myriad of people groups, languages, and tribes, the church in Africa ought to take her seat at the table of the wedding feast and invite other faithful believers to do so without prejudice or condition.

However, just as diversity is represented in the heavenlies, so the fourfold description of humanity is also used to refer to those under the rule of Satan and his evil agents. They are the ones who celebrate the death of God's two witnesses (11:9–10),[97] and are ruled by the beast out of the sea (13:7) and the harlot (17:15; see 14:8; 18:3, 23). This demonstrates that God shows no favoritism—neither in gospel proclamation nor in judgment. On a continent where liberation theology and postcolonial lenses are on the rise, the church ought to keep a preference for the poor in tension with the reality that both powerful and powerless will have to give an account. While liberation theology does much to capture God's heart for the oppressed and his disdain for injustice, this view could create the impression that God's favor rests solely on the oppressed by virtue of them being oppressed. We cannot ignore the judgment of both powerful and marginalized.

Conclusion

John's historical audience was no monolith. The fact that the same document was read aloud in churches ranging from the faithful, to the sleeping, to the near-dead speaks of the efficacy and broad rhetorical weight of John's Revelation. The throne scene, drama of divine judgment, and ultimate renewal of heaven and earth is as fit for a compromising and corrupt church as it is for a faithful yet persecuted one. This simple fact underlines the gift that Revelation is to Africa—a continent housing a collection of contexts, tongues, ethnicities, challenges, sins, temptations, and opportunities. John's Revelation speaks to each of these. It is important to note that Revelation's central message is double-edged. It is good news to some and bad news to others. This fact is wonderfully illustrated by John eating the scroll in Revelation 10:9–10. First it tastes sweet in his mouth, but later it becomes bitter in his stomach. The message of Revelation mimics this bitter-sweet phenomenon in that it brings victory and hope to the downtrodden and faithful, yet it promises judgment and doom to those who rebel against the Enthroned One and the Lamb. There is also the reality that even the sweet message of victory is coated in the bitter promise of suffering with the call to endure. Only the faithful will taste the ultimate reward.

Further Reading

Boesak, Allan Aubrey. *Comfort and Protest*. Reprint. Wipf & Stock, 2015.
DeSilva, David. *Discovering Revelation*. Eerdmans, 2021.

97. We do, however, see the potential repentance of this diverse audience implied in 11:13; see Dean Flemming, "Divine Judgement and the *Missio Dei* in the Book of Revelation," in *Listening Again to the Text: New Testament Studies in Honor of George Lyons*, ed. Richard P. Thompson (Claremont Press, 2020), 175.

Fee, Gordon D. *Revelation*. NCCS. Cascade, 2011.
Flemming, Dean. *Foretaste of the Future: Reading Revelation in Light of God's Mission*. InterVarsity Press, 2022.
Gorman, Michael J. *Reading Revelation Responsibly: Uncivil Worship and Witness: Following the Lamb into the New Creation*. Cascade, 2011.
Longman, Tremper. *Revelation Through Old Testament Eyes*. Kregel Academic, 2022.
McKnight, Scot, and Cody Matchett. *Revelation for the Rest of Us*. Zondervan, 2023.
Mwombeki, Fidon R. "The Book of Revelation in Africa." *Word & World* 15, no. 2 (1995): 145–150.
Ngundu, Onesimus. "Revelation." In *Africa Bible Commentary: A One-Volume Commentary Written by 70 African Scholars*, edited by Tokunboh Adeyemo. WordAlive Publishers; Zondervan, 2006.
Okoye, James Chukwuma. *From Every People and Nation: The Book of Revelation in Intercultural Perspective*, edited by David Rhoads. Fortress Press, 2005.
Osborne, Grant R. *Revelation: Verse by Verse*. ONTC. Lexham Press, 2016.
Puskas, Charles B. *Hebrews, the General Letters, and Revelation: An Introduction*. Cascade, 2016.
Resseguie, James L. *The Revelation of John: A Narrative Commentary*. Baker, 2009.
Sarma, Bitrus. *Drums of Redemption: A New Testament Theology for Africa*. HippoBooks, 2023.
Tonstad, Sigve K. *Revelation*. Paideia. Baker, 2019.
Wright, N. T. *Revelation for Everyone*. 2nd ed. Westminster John Knox, 2004.

INDEX